Ethics for Today and Tomorrow

The Jones and Bartlett Series in Philosophy

Robert Ginsberg, General Editor

Ethics for Today and Tomorrow

Joram Graf Haber

Bergen Community College

Jones and Bartlett Publishers

Sudbury, Massachusetts

Boston   London   Singapore

Editorial, Sales, and Customer Service Offices
Jones and Bartlett Publishers
40 Tall Pine Drive
Sudbury, MA 01776
1-508-443-5000   info@jbpub.com
1-800-832-0034   http://www.jbpub.com

Jones and Bartlett Publishers International
Barb House, Barb Mews
London W67PA
UK

Library of Congress Cataloging-in-Publication Data

Haber, Joram Graf.
    Ethics for today and tomorrow / Joram Graf
  Haber.
      p.   cm.
    Includes bibliographical references and index.
    ISBN 0–7637–0226–9
    1. Applied ethics. 2. Professional ethics. I. Title.
  BJ1031.H25   1997
  170—dc20   96–27644
                                    CIP

Acquisitions Editors: Arthur C. Bartlett and Nancy E. Bartlett
Manufacturing Manager: Dana L. Cerrito
Design: Publishers' Design and Production Services, Inc.
Editorial Production Service: Publishers' Design and Production Services, Inc.
Cover Design: Marshall Henrichs
Typesetting: Publishers' Design and Production Services, Inc.
Printing and Binding: Hamilton Printing Company
Cover Printing: John P. Pow Company

Printed in the United States of America

01 00 99 98 97   10 9 8 7 6 5 4 3 2 1

To Nathan Haber (1961–1993).
My brother and friend.

Contents

Preface

Ethics for Today and Tomorrow combines the virtues of a textbook, anthology, workbook, and monograph, all under a single cover. The book's nineteen chapters introduce students to a plethora of contemporary ethical issues and at the same time expose them to the ideas of contemporary philosophers (and sometimes the thoughts of the book's author). The book achieves its objectives by asking students to not simply read the text and articles passively, but to participate in a dialogue with its constituents by answering the questions for discussion that precede and follow each chapter. While the book begins with a discussion of ethical theory setting the tone for the issues that follow, the topics are arranged in no particular order allowing instructors maximum flexibility.

Ideally, the book will be used in conjunction with the video series, *Ethics in the 90s* (available through Jones and Bartlett Publishers) which, despite the title, is not limited to ethical issues that become extinguished or settled by the turn of the century. *The book can, however, stand on its own and has been distinctly written to be used with or without the videos.* In using the book with the video series, students can actively engage in dialogue by "meeting" the individuals whose contributions appear in the book. This is an invaluable pedagogical tool as the current generation of students learn best with visual assistance. Thus, in addition to reading what Tom Regan has to say about animal rights or Stephen Nathanson about the death penalty, students can view and listen to these thinkers as well. The inclusion of a student discussion on each video makes for an even friendlier learning modality.

Instructors wishing to use the text with the accompanying video series should note that within each chapter is a boxed-off entry providing students with a synopsis of the video. Instructors not wishing to use the videos may ignore these summaries without loss of textual continuity.

Most if not all of the questions for discussion presume no familiarity with the video material.

Ethics for Today and Tomorrow includes discussion of most of the familiar issues that occur in most textbooks on applied ethics such as: capital punishment, animal rights, environmental ethics, war, terrorism, and racism. The book also includes issues that do not commonly occur such as: the homeless, date rape, anti-Semitism, and physician-assisted suicide. The book also addresses issues in professional ethics (e.g., legal ethics), and discusses some neglected though no less important issues such as moral education, and ethics and literature. Theoretical issues are also discussed such as the relationship between ethics and religion, feminist ethics, and the usual discussion of utilitarianism, deontology, and so forth.

For the most part, the individuals appearing on the video series *Ethics in the 90s* contributed to the book *Ethics for Today and Tomorrow*. Often, such contributions consist of essays written exclusively for this volume (e.g., Stephen Nathanson's article on capital punishment). Sometimes contributors answered a set of interrogatories (e.g., Hilary Putnams' entry.) Where it was not feasible to include contributions by the guests on the video series, articles were solicited from notable authorities (e.g., Patricia Mann on date rape, David Goldberg on racism, W. Miller Brown on sports ethics, etc.)

Finally, a decidedly useful pedagogical tool are the questions for discussion that follow each chapter. These provocative questions are designed to be removed from the book to be submitted pursuant to an in-class or take-home assignment and can also be used for examination purposes. In this way, the book comes equipped with a built-in test bank.

Acknowledgments

So many people were involved in the production of this book and its companion video series and I want to extend my gratitude to all of them. For asking me to put together the video that would become *Ethics in the 90s,* I want to think Jack Dirr of Bergen Community College's media center. Officially, Jack directed and co-produced the series, but he also oversaw the operation from start to finish. Without Jack's having originally thought of me in connection with the project, neither the series nor the textbook would have come to fruition. I thank him, then, for thinking of me initially, for his confidence in my ability to handle the project, for his patience in managing the many scheduling snafus, and for his patient responses to the plethora of questions I hurled his way.

Thanks also are due all those people involved in the production of that series, particularly Howard Dreispan, whose frantic camera work kept everyone on their feet, and Sheila Grieves, whose calm demeanor was an antidote to Howard's restless instruction. Thanks also go to Amelia Duggan on whose television series, *On Campus,* I began my video career. It was on Amelia's television show that I had the opportunity to discuss philosophy with such notables as John Searle, Stephen Stich, and Margaret Walker. I thank Amelia for inviting me to appear on these shows and for lending a sympathetic ear to philosophical issues. I also thank Richele Sacharis who seemed always to be available for technical support.

For taking an interest in seeing the series meet with a professional distributor, I extend a heartfelt thank you to Tom Magnell (Drew University). It was Tom who convinced me that the video medium was no less intellectually respectable than the written medium and that reaching people and influencing them is what philosophy done well is about. This same philosophy also introduced me to Bob Ginsberg, the series editor at Jones and Bartlett. Bob's enthusiasm was always welcome. He is also a great and dedicated editor from whom I learned so much about writing even if we did not always see eye to eye. I also thank Art and Nancy Bartlett with whom it was simply a pleasure to work.

When the video series was first produced and, later, when the text was being written, I greatly benefited from many of my students. Of particular help was Joanne Grand, who helped me with such dreadful details like handling travel arrangements for my guests. Michelle Roberts and Jennifer Weinberger are also to be thanked for proofreading some early chapters as is my long time friend Joni Edelman who helped with some valuable "detective work" in tracking down people for some needed permissions. Kathy Morley is also to be acknowledged for her thankless work with permissions.

When I first arranged to transfer the rights to the video series from Bergen Community College to Jones and Bartlett Publishers, I was faced with so much red tape that I nearly aborted the project. I thank my friend and colleague, Tirzah Schutzengel, for her help in this area. But for Tirzah's assistance, there would be neither a text called *Ethics for Today and Tomorrow* nor a video series called *Ethics in the 90s*.

I acknowledge the enthusiastic response of those reviewers who gave the text their ringing endorsement: Chalmers C. Clark (College of Staten Island), Mark Halfon (Nassau Community College); Laurence Mordekhai Thomas (Syracuse University); and Richard Hull (State University of New York at Buffalo). Even though I did not wisely follow all their astute recommendations, their comments were perceptive, welcome, and helpful. I also acknowledge the textbooks I've used to teach ethics over the years that have implicitly helped me to teach and write philosophy. Mappes and Zembaty's *Social Ethics* (McGraw Hill) and Victor Grassian's *Moral Reasoning* (Prentice-Hall) stand out among these latter. The *Encyclopedia of Ethics* also proved particularly useful as did Lisa Newton's *Ethics in America* (Prentice-Hall). Finally, my colleague at Bergen, John Patierno, must also be thanked for helping to educate me on sociological theories of crime.

Writing philosophy requires a lucrative profession and much leisure time. Professional philosophy provides neither. With that in mind, I thank my wife, Lina, whose lucrative profession provided me with the leisure time needed to write this book. I also thank Lina for picking my spirits up whenever they threatened to fall. Lina's father, Vladimir G. Levit, also helped in so many of the intangible ways that could easily destroy a philosopher's initiative, and my former housekeeper and current friend, Irene Kozlova, always seemed to keep the house in control when things threatened to become chaotic.

On a more somber note, writing a book marks an epoch in one's life and *Ethics for Today and Tomorrow* marked one in mine. From the time the project was first conceived to the time the project was completed, I was blessed with the birth of Naomi Alexandra and Rebecca Anne about whom, even if it is only partly true, I like to think I always have time for. But I also lost my friend and brother, Nathan, to whom this book is dedicated. Nathan was passionately interested in sports and would have particularly enjoyed the discussion of the chapter about sports ethics just as he enjoyed my interview with sportscaster Howie Rose. He also would have enjoyed so many of the other topical issues discussed throughout the book. To Nathan, then, I dedicate this work: he would have liked this book.

Ethics for Today and Tomorrow

Chapter 1

Introduction: Ethical Theory and Social Issues

Passages for Reflection

"Grub first, then ethics."
—*Bertolt Brecht*

"If people are friends, they have no need for justice."
—*Aristotle*

"Act only on that maxim by which you can at the same time will that it should become a universal law."
—*Immanuel Kant*

"By the principle of utility is meant that principle which approves or disapproves of every action whatsoever, according to the tendency which it appears to have to augment or diminish the happiness of the party whose interest is in question."
—*Jeremy Bentham*

"Ethical judgments . . . have no objective validity whatsoever."
—*A. J. Ayer*

"A philosophy is characterized more by the formulation of its problems than by the solution of them."
—*Suzanne K. Langer*

"A (moral) philosopher is not a parish priest or Universal Aunt or Citizens' Advice Bureau."
—*P. H. Nowell-Smith*

Opening Questions

1. What makes an action right or wrong?
2. Is it ever right to lie? To kill? To steal?
3. What are the most pressing contemporary ethical issues?

Is it morally wrong to kill animals for food? Is it permissible for a physician to help patients kill themselves? What is the status of the death penalty? These are some of the questions that confront us in the 1990s and are likely to confront us in the twenty-first century. Philosophers interested in these questions often analyze them within the context of theories that are designed to explain what makes actions right or wrong. Thus, you will find it useful to examine some of the more prominent theories that philosophers have proposed to explain moral conduct.

One powerful theory of moral philosophers is *utilitarianism*. This theory says that the rightness or wrongness of an action is wholly determined by the amount of happiness that results therefrom. As for the obvious question, "Whose happiness?", the utilitarian answers: "the greatest happiness for the greatest number of people" (the "Greatest Happiness Principle"). An action is right, according to utilitarianism, if it makes more people happy (or less people unhappy) than any other action that is open to the agent at the time of acting.

The key to understanding utilitarianism is to note that the theory is *consequentialist*. This means that the rightness of an action is determined exclusively by the consequences that result from the action. In the utilitarian's case, the relevant consequences are the amount of pleasure and pain (read: happiness or misery) an action produces. Recognizing that all actions result in both pleasure and pain, utilitarians employ the cost-benefit analysis of economics. If the benefits of an action, that is, its pleasure, outweigh its costs, that is, its pain, then the action is cost-effective and therefore right. No other factor is to be weighed in determining whether an action is right or wrong, and no action is right or wrong in and of itself. From the utilitarian point of view, all actions are morally neutral and receive their value as a result of their consequences.

In support of their theory, utilitarians invite us to consider cases they are convinced we will analyze along utilitarian lines. Suppose, for example, that you are a doctor in a hospital emergency room when six accident victims are brought in, one of whom is much worse off than the others. You could save this one person if you devote all your time and resources to him or her but the remaining five would die. Alternatively, you can save the five but at the expense of the one.[1] You are not to imag-

---

[1] The example is from Gilbert Harman, *The Nature of Morality* (New York: Oxford University Press, 1977), p. 3.

ine that any one of these people is of significance to anyone other than their immediate family or that you have any other options, such as asking a neighboring hospital for medical assistance. What should you do? If you say that you should save the five and let the one die because, all things being equal, five alive and one dead is better than one alive and five dead, then you are reasoning along utilitarian lines. You are, that is, implicitly subscribing to the "Greatest Happiness Principle."

Utilitarians cite other cases, famous in the literature, in support of their theory. Imagine that you are on a lifeboat with room for one more person, while two people are overboard who will otherwise drown. One of these is a research scientist on the verge of discovering a cure for cancer, while the other is a person of no special significance to anyone but his or her friends and family. Suppose further that the scientist is not likely to have left any notes behind. Whom should you save? If you choose to save the scientist since the needs of the many outweigh the needs of the few, then you are arguing again along utilitarian lines.

Suppose, to add a twist to the preceding case, the nonscientist is someone near and dear to you. How would this affect your decision? Presumably, many of you would save the one who is near and dear. But is this right? Knowing that we are prone to assigning greater weight to the interests of our loved ones than to the interests of strangers, when insisting that we maximize happiness, utilitarians point out that "each person is to count as one" (the "Equality of Interests Principle"). Furthermore, in determining how our actions will impact on all those affected, utilitarians insist that they be evaluated by an impartial observer. As utilitarians see it, assigning greater weight to the interests of some is one way of explaining how we sometimes do wrong. To see this, suppose that my wife is a student in my class and deserves an "A" for the course, but my dean has imposed a quota on this grade. Suppose further that another student is equally deserving of an "A" so I must choose between the students. If I choose my wife because she's my wife, then I would be guilty of assigning greater weight to one than I would to the other. This would violate the principle that each person's interests count as much as another's. An impartial observer would presumably recommend that I flip a coin, draw straws, or use some other procedure for deciding.

Utilitarians point out other cases to bolster their view. One case has it that you are the driver of a runaway rollercoaster and you meet up with a fork in the track. To the left, playing on the tracks, is one child, while to the right are five children. You can only turn one way. Which way should you turn? Here, again, utilitarians point out the power of their theory. Assuming that a sensitive person will certainly turn left, utilitarians argue that ethics is about maximizing happiness (or minimizing suffering) or doing what is most cost-effective, given the choices that face us. As they see it, it is simply irrational not to prefer the lesser of two evils.

A more familiar case of utilitarian reasoning concerns that famous

Vulcan, Mr. Spock. In the film *The Wrath of Khan*, Spock employed utilitarian reasoning in sacrificing himself in order to save the imperiled crew of the starship *Enterprise*. Viewers familiar with that film will recall Spock's dying words: "The needs of the many outweigh the needs of the few." This should not surprise us, since Spock is depicted as a paradigm of rationality, and Gene Roddenberry, the creator of *Star Trek*, had acquaintance with philosophy.

While utilitarians agree that right actions are actions that are cost-effective, important differences arise among utilitarians. One difference is between *act-utilitarianism* and *rule-utilitarianism*. So far, we've been speaking about act-utilitarianism, which says that an act is right if it is more cost-effective than any other action available to the agent. Rule-utilitarianism, on the other hand, says that an action is right if it falls under a rule that is more cost-effective than any other rule. The difference between the theories is one of emphasis: act-utilitarians focus on the cost-effectiveness of actions, while rule-utilitarians focus on the cost-effectiveness of rules under which actions may fall.

An example will make this clearer. Suppose you are invited to a wedding where the bride, who is ugly, asks you to comment on her looks. Suppose further, to fill in the details, that the bride has a low sense of self-esteem and is likely to be so distressed if you tell her the truth that she'll cancel the wedding, to everyone's dismay. If you lie to her, however, the wedding will take place as planned. Finally, let us stipulate that you may not evade her question by cleverly commenting that "all brides are beautiful" or saying that she has never looked better. You must lie or tell the truth. What should you do?

The act-utilitarian would recommend that you lie to the ugly bride since lying in this case will yield greater happiness than telling the truth. The rule-utilitarian would recommend that you tell her the truth since telling the truth, *as a rule*, yields more happiness than lying. (Honesty is the best policy.) This example is taken from the Talmud where Hillel is presumably representing act-utilitarianism while Shammai is representing rule-utilitarianism or perhaps some other moral theory. I mean nothing sexist about the example and find it useful to illustrate the point assuming, on whatever theory of aesthetics you happen to favor, that some women and men happen to be less than beautiful. For Hillel, as for many of us, the act-utilitarian is closer to the truth than the rule-utilitarian, at least as far as this example is concerned. And maybe that is so. But before we draw that conclusion, let's take a closer look at the reasoning behind rule-utilitarianism.

Anyone who drives a car in a congested city knows that if you are at an intersection, and a selfish driver tries to beat a light but fails and gets caught in the middle, traffic will intensify and all drivers, including the selfish driver, will suffer as a result. This dog-eat-dog mentality may intermittently work for the occasional driver who is obnoxious but fortunate enough to take advantage of traffic laws. But as a rule, traffic will flow more fluidly if otherwise selfish drivers regularly obey the traffic laws. This line of reasoning attracts rule-utilitarians. They will argue that even though in one situation you may get to your destination faster if you ignore the law, you will, as a rule, get to your destination faster if you obey the law.

Another difference exists between utilitarians, although this one is more of historical interest. Jeremy Bentham (1748–1832), the father of utilitarianism, maintained that in determining how much happiness results from an action, we need calculate only the *quantity* of pleasure and pain that results. John Stuart Mill (1806–1873), on the other hand, insisted that we must also calculate the *quality* of pleasure.

To appreciate the difference between Bentham's and Mill's versions of utilitarianism, consider a person interested in maximizing pleasure from chocolate candy. Suppose the choice is between five pieces of a popular brand of chocolate candy and one Lake Champlain American Truffle, an award-winning gourmet brand of chocolate. Here are the ingredients of the popular candy:

> Peanuts; milk chocolate (milk chocolate contains sugar, cocoa butter chocolate; nonfat milk; milk fat; and soya lecithin, an emulsifier); sugar; dextrose; blend of vegetable oils (contains hydrogenated palm kernel and soybean oils); salt; milk; cocoa; soya lecithin; TBHQ and citric acid to preserve freshness.

Here are the ingredients of the gourmet truffle:

> Bittersweet and milk chocolate (sugar, cocoa butter, milk powder, chocolate liqueur, vanilla and/or vanillin, lecithin as an emulsifier), sweet butter, heavy cream, sugar, coffee, natural raspberry, orange and cherry pastes, almond paste, hazelnut paste, pecans, walnuts, malted milk, vanilla extract, cinnamon, dealcoholized (boiled) champagne, cointreau, armagnac and brandy.

On the wrapping of the popular candy is simply its brand name. On the wrapping of the gourmet truffle is this:

> The perfect truffle is sought after, debated, exalted. It is a titillation of tastes and textures enraptured not just with chocolate, but with mystery. Its heart is the ganache center, truly unpredictable until the moment of exuberant discovery.
>
> The perfect truffle is sensual, romantic, elegant. It is a poem, a ballad, a love-letter. Like them, its reality is fleeting but its memory is forever.
>
> However, it is the local cream and sweet butter—plus the distinctively American natural flavorings of the ganache—that make

Lake Champlain American Truffles a never-before truffle experience. The spectacular dessert. The ultimate treat.[2]

Presumably, Bentham would say that your pleasure is maximized by consuming five of the popular brand since that gives five times the chocolate satisfaction than merely one of the gourmet truffles. But Mill would presumably say that more is not always better if what we consume more of is inferior in quality. While this example illustrates his point, Mill's real concern was with giving "higher" pleasures their due even when present in less quantity than "lower" ones. Thus, Mill would insist that listening to opera singer Luciano Pavarotti yields more pleasure (qualitatively) than listening to rock singer Bruce Springsteen, even if you get more pleasure (quantitatively) listening to Springsteen than you get from Pavarotti. The same holds true when comparing your reading of novelist Gustave Flaubert with your reading of popular science fiction writer Stephen King. It is an elitist position, but not false for that reason alone.

Bentham canonized his view by declaring, "Quantities of pleasure being equal, pushpin is as good as poetry." By this, he meant that doing something ennobling like reading poetry is just as good as doing something trivial like playing pushpin, the eighteenth-century equivalent to Nintendo, if the pleasure you get out of these is equal. Not to be outdone, Mill canonized his view by declaring, "It is better to be a human being dissatisfied than a pig satisfied; better to be a Socrates dissatisfied than a fool satisfied." By this, Mill meant that higher and lower pleasures occur, and that less of the higher pleasures is more valuable than more of the lower pleasures. He held firm to this view fully aware that having discriminating taste makes pleasure harder to come by. (Having experienced a Lake Champlain American Truffle, it becomes increasingly difficult to find chocolate satisfaction.) And it is no coincidence that Mill used Socrates to illustrate his point, for Socrates was famous for saying, "The unexamined life is not worth living," as opposed to "Ignorance is bliss." For Socrates, frustration at not solving the mysteries of life is still preferable to "pig happiness." Incidentally, if you disagreed with Mill and insisted that more of lower pleasures was preferable to less of higher pleasures, Mill would insist that you are a fool. Only a fool, he would say, would think that Springsteen is a better singer than Pavarotti and Stephen King is a better writer than Gustave Flaubert.

But whatever your preferred version of utilitarianism, the point to be emphasized is that consequences alone determine right conduct and that no action is right or wrong in itself. That this is controversial can be seen by considering the following case which is a twist on the hospital emergency room case discussed earlier. Suppose, again, that you are a

---

[2]It would be cruel not to include the address of Lake Champlain Chocolates. It is located at 431 Pine Street, Burlington, Vermont 05401 USA.

doctor in a hospital emergency room when five accident victims are brought in. Each of these victims is in need of a vital organ without which he or she certainly will die. Having gone on rounds earlier that day, you know that a person in the hospital for routine tests is of the right blood and tissue compatibility with the five accident victims. Having seen *Coma*, it occurs to you that you could kill that patient, distribute his organs to the five accident victims, and thereby save their lives. You could also do nothing and let the accident victims die.[3] Assuming you have no other options, what should you do?

If you are like the rest of us, you will ignore the lone patient and let the five victims die. And you will do this presumably because killing the one patient is an act of murder and murder is an act that one must not do. But if that is so, then what has become of the utilitarian claim that the needs of the many outweigh the needs of the few? Did we not say that five alive and one dead is preferable to one alive and five dead?

At this point, we are tempted to give up the claim that consequences alone determine right conduct and insist that while consequences are relevant to determining right and wrong, how we get to the consequences is no less relevant. If you find this line of thought enticing, then you are attracted to *deontological* moral theories (from the Greek, *deon*, meaning "duty") which say that consequences alone do not determine right conduct but that actions themselves have moral significance. Alongside utilitarianism, deontological theories constitute another powerful tradition in ethics.

In the case just discussed, we see the tension that exists between utilitarians and deontologists. The deontologist says that murder is wrong even if it is cost-effective, while the utilitarian says that if murder is cost-effective, it cannot be wrong. Having presented a theory of right and wrong, the utilitarian has put the ball in the deontologist's court. It will not do to simply declare that what is implied by utilitarianism is intuitively unsound since intuitions vary and are unreliable. What is needed is a theory that is philosophically respectable. Before we examine such a theory, it will be instructive to examine more hypothetical cases.

Suppose a psychopath has planted bombs that are scheduled to go off and kill hundreds of people unless you kill a perceived enemy of his whom you know to be innocent of any wrongdoing. What should you do? For the utilitarian, the answer is obvious: you should kill the one person. If you find this answer attractive, then you are admitting, against the deontologist, that murder is permissible under certain conditions. But if that is so, shouldn't you revise your analysis of the second hospital emergency room case? Shouldn't you say that murder is wrong because it is often not cost-effective, but where it is cost-effective it is morally right? That is what the utilitarian says.

---

[3]Harman, *Nature of Morality*, p. 3.

Consider two other actions, theft and adultery, that we usually deem wrong but are not clearly so under the utilitarian's microscope. We say that theft is wrong, yet at the same time we think kindly of what Robin Hood did because he maximized happiness. Most Americans—if not Europeans—say that adultery is wrong, but consider the marriage which has deteriorated owing to the wife's disappointment with the husband's earning power but which could be improved if the husband were to make more money at his appointed job. Suppose the husband's employer, a woman, will see to it that he gets a significant raise if he sleeps with her on only one occasion. Finally, suppose the couple's children suffer on account of their parents' constant quarreling. The utilitarian would presumably recommend that the husband give in to his employer's behest and insist that it would be unreasonable to do otherwise.

Incidentally, I have found that many students who accept the utilitarian analysis of the psychopath and Robin Hood cases reject the utilitarian analysis of the adultery case. Might this be because utilitarianism does not give proper weight to fidelity in marriage? When a couple exchanges wedding vows, do they not vow to be faithful to each other for better or worse, that is, no matter what the consequences?

The upshot of our analysis of these cases is that from a utilitarian perspective no action is wrong if the action is cost-effective, which is a claim deontologists deny. Just how much relevance consequences have is a question over which deontologists differ. For some deontologists, consequences count but do not wholly determine right and wrong conduct; for others, such as Immanuel Kant (1724–1804), consequences have nothing to do with morality. We will discuss deontology by focusing on Kant's moral philosophy since Kant is the champion deontologist.

Your understanding of Kant will be facilitated if we examine the question he is asking in his ethical writings and analyze his answer in terms of that question. Kant is concerned with answering the question, "How is morality possible?" He is interested, that is, in learning how we are able to make distinctions between right and wrong, good and bad, ought and ought not, and so on. Kant was convinced that morality is possible, that is, that these terms have moral as well as nonmoral meaning. We speak, for example, of "good" versus "bad" coffee, a "right" way of going to Boston from New Jersey as opposed to a "wrong" way, how one "ought" to dress for the theater, and so on. Used these ways, *good, right,* and *ought* have nonmoral meaning. But they also have *moral* meaning such as when we speak of war as a "bad" thing, telling the truth as the "right" thing to do, and whether we "ought" to keep a promise we have made. Kant's ethical theory may be viewed as an answer to the question, "How can we make these distinctions in their peculiarly moral senses?"

Kant's question, like everything else Kant worked on, is not easy to understand. Let's examine the question by asking not "How is morality possible?", but the analogous question, "How is smiling possible?" Noting that we live in a world in which people smile, we know upon reflection that this is possible only because people have faces. If a world existed in which people did not have faces, then smiling in that world would not be possible. In this sense, smiles presuppose the existence of faces.

Kant is concerned not with smiles and what is presupposed by them, but with morality and what is presupposed by it. Beginning with the premise that morality is possible (that is, we make moral distinctions as well as nonmoral ones), Kant argues that this is possible only because we are sometimes inclined to do what we should not; that is, our inclinations sometimes conflict with our duties. If this were not the case, and we were never inclined to do what we should not, then, like animals, we would never have a notion of what we ought to do from a *moral point of view*. This is not to say that we would not arrive at a notion of "ought" at all, but only that the notion we would arrive at would be a nonmoral one.

To see this more clearly, consider what it means for Fido to understand that he ought not to urinate indoors. It would strain the imagination to suppose that Fido, when inclined to urinate indoors, does not do so on account of his recognizing a moral obligation to urinate outdoors. Fido's refusal to urinate indoors comes about as a result of successful behavior modification. If we train Fido well, we will redirect his inclinations so that the discomfort he experiences as a result of our punishing him will be greater than the discomfort experienced at waiting to relieve himself outdoors.

For Kant, human beings are unlike nonhuman animals in an important sense. While sometimes we may refrain from doing "wrong" because our inclinations have been redirected toward the good, it is possible for us, as it is not possible for animals, to refrain from doing wrong *knowing that it is wrong*. We can, that is, resist our inclinations because we have a duty to do otherwise. That we are aware of such a duty means that we are rational beings or beings that can act on principle. That we can act in the face of inclinations to do otherwise means also that we have free will, since we cannot have an obligation to do what is not within our power. For Kant, then, morality is possible because we have *free will* and *rationality*. This is what gives us our dignity and distinguishes us from the beasts of the field.

Inasmuch as we are free to resist our inclinations and act ethically when we act out of a sense of duty, how do we know what our duty is when we are inclined to act in a certain manner? Suppose, for example, I am inclined to murder my next door neighbor who makes a habit of trespassing upon my back yard, and I now want to know whether it is permissible to do so. Kant's answer to this question is what he calls the *categorical imperative*, of which he gives three forms.

The first form of the categorical imperative says, "Act only according to that maxim which you can at the same time will that it should become a universal law." Kant is saying that the maxim on which we should act must be one that is binding on all rational beings. Logically, we have three possibilities: the principles that say murder is always wrong, sometimes wrong, or never wrong. That it is, as a matter of principle, always permissible to commit murder when inclined is absurd inasmuch as such a maxim nullifies the very basis of morality, life itself. The same holds for the principle, "Sometimes it is permissible to commit murder," since "sometimes" is consistent with "always." To see that "some" is consistent with "all," suppose, at the beginning of the term, your professor tells you that *some* of you will pass the course. Your professor would not have spoken falsely if *all* of you had passed, but would have spoken falsely if *no one* had passed. Thus, "It is *never* permissible to murder" is the only viable option and is, utilitarianism notwithstanding, a principle most of us accept. But don't confound the principle that says, "It is never permissible to *murder*," with the principle that says, "It is never permissible to *kill*." No one except pacifists accepts the latter.

But it is one thing to say that "murder is always wrong"; it is another to say that "lying is always wrong." Yet the latter is the judgment Kant accepts in just those cases where we are tempted to lie. Suppose, for instance, I am inclined to lie to the ugly bride in the case discussed earlier. For most of us, the relevant principle is something akin to, "Sometimes it is permissible to lie." Kant would argue that the principle "Lying is sometimes permissible" nullifies the very institution of truth-telling every bit as much as the principle "It is always permissible to lie" since, as we've said, "sometimes" is consistent with "always." There is, then, only one moral principle on which it is rational to act: "It is never permissible to lie." Like the principle, "It is never permissible to murder," this is an imperative that is expressed categorically, that is, without exception. So convinced was Kant of this that he even recommended that we not lie to inquiring murderers seeking their victims whose whereabouts we know.[4] As Kant saw it, making exceptions to moral principles in favor of inclinations is precisely what happens when we engage in conduct that is morally wrong.

The second form of the categorical imperative says, "Act so as to treat all of humanity, whether in your own self or in that of another, always as an end and never as a means only." Succinctly put, this tells us not to use people in a way that fails to respect them. Someone who befriends you merely to gain favor in the eyes of someone you know is an example of someone who violates this principle. As Kant saw it, people are beings for whom things have value, as opposed to things or objects whose value is relative to others. This is what Kant means when he says

---

[4]See Kant's "On a Supposed Right to Lie from Altruistic Motives," in *Critique of Practical Reason,* edited by Lewis White Beck (Chicago, 1949). Reprinted in my *Absolutism and Its Consequentialist Critics* (Savage, Md.: Rowman and Littlefield, 1994).

that people must be viewed as ends in themselves. Treating someone only as a means to an end is treating that person solely as an object with a quantifiable and determinate price, not as a dignified rational and autonomous being. Any self-respecting person who has ever been used merely as an object understands this distinction. As self-respecting persons, we want to be respected in and of ourselves, not just as the means for some ulterior purpose. This idea is the impetus for the third form of the categorical imperative which insists that we regard all of humanity as members in a "kingdom of ends."

Supporters of Kantianism are fond of pointing out that utilitarianism cannot account for justice. To show this, they ask us to suppose that we are the sheriff in a provincial town where a murder has been committed. Falsely believing that the crime was committed by the local derelict, an unruly mob threatens to wreak havoc on the town if we do not immediately lynch the derelict. We, however, know that the derelict is innocent but the mob has no patience for our plea; either we lynch the derelict or the mob will riot, leading to certain loss of life and property.

From the utilitarian's perspective, the right thing to do is to lynch the derelict, but from the Kantian point of view, that would be unjust. It would be unjust because the derelict is being treated as a means for satisfying the mob's thirst for vengeance. (It is also wrong because killing the innocent cannot be willed to be a universal law.) A Kantian would sooner suffer the consequences of justice than engage in wrongful activity. ("Let justice be done though the heavens may fall.")

For Kant, using people only as means to ends shows a lack of respect not only where the user's ends are repugnant to us, but also where the user's ends are laudable. To see this, consider the physician who performs a routine exam on a patient just prior to the patient's taking a two-week vacation and discovers that the patient suffers from an end-stage terminal illness. Convinced that delaying treatment for two weeks will not affect the patient's condition and that no compelling reason exists why the patient should not enjoy herself in what little time she has left, the physician lies to the patient when asked if she should be concerned about anything. From a Kantian point of view, the physician disrespects the patient no less than the sheriff disrespects the derelict, even though the patient might not be as indignant as the derelict. I say "might not be as indignant" since we could imagine a patient who would find such paternalistic treatment an anathema. To underscore this point, imagine how indignant a student might be who deserved an "A" for a course but received a "C" because the professor dislikes her. The student would complain that she was being treated unfairly and should get the higher grade. However, if a student deserved a "C" for a course but received an "A" because the professor was fond of her, she would hardly complain although she should by parity of reasoning.

For Kant, then, acting on principle, rather than on inclination or out of concern for consequences, is what ethics is about. When Kant says, at the beginning of his *Grounding for the Metaphysics of Morals,* that "there is no possibility of thinking of anything at all in the world, or even out of it, which can be regarded as good without qualification, except a good will," he is stressing the importance of acting out of respect for the moral law. No moral worth exists, say, in not cheating on an exam for fear of getting caught; moral worth exists only when you refrain from cheating because cheating is wrong. Indeed, as Kant sees it, we have a duty not to cheat precisely because we are sometimes inclined to do so. But, given the fleeting nature of our passions and inclinations, we cannot ground an ethic on how we feel. I should respect my neighbor not because I like her, but because she has dignity. Were I to ground how I treat her on how I feel about her, then, if I did not like her, it would be permissible to treat her with disrespect. This is why Kant distinguished between the categorical imperative, which has the form "Do X!" (or "Don't do X!") with no ifs, ands, or buts, with what he calls the *hypothetical imperative,* which has the form "Do X if you want Y as a result." The implication is that if you don't want Y, it is not true that you ought to do X.

What the utilitarian sees, then, as an ethical imperative is what Kant sees as a hypothetical imperative that has nothing to do with ethics. Admitting that sometimes it is prudent to do what is cost-effective, Kant adamantly denies that cost-effectiveness has anything to do with ethics. So convinced was Kant that consequences are morally irrelevant that it would not be misleading to say that, as Kant saw it, if you wanted to invent a theory that was the very antithesis of ethics, what you would get is utilitarianism.

Having explained Kant's theory, I point out that some deontological theories are not Kantian, for example, the ethical theory of Sir William David Ross (see Bibliography). But the upshot of our analysis is that utilitarians believe only consequences—particularly pleasure and pain—are relevant to ethics, while deontological theories (such as Kant's) argue that such notions as motive, responsibility, principle, and duty are relevant as well. Utilitarianism and deontology have in common the idea that ethical judgments transcend particular locales, a claim denied by *ethical relativism,* yet another theory that has attracted attention though not to the degree of utilitarianism and Kantianism.

Ethical relativism is a theory that says that right and wrong conduct is a function of time and place. Under the terms of this theory, if an action is considered to be wrong at one time or place, then the action *is* wrong in that time or place. (When in Rome, do as Romans do.) In other words, ethics is relative to the culture and time in which you live. Unlike utilitarians and Kantians, ethical relativists deny the existence of a universal moral code.

Ethical relativists often cite *cultural relativism* as an argument for their theory. This sociological theory asserts that different cultures have different moral codes at different times. History and anthropology have documented that many cultures have accepted as moral such practices as human sacrifice, polygamy, slavery, and infanticide. If this is so, say the ethical relativists, then morality must vary from culture to culture. An action that is morally wrong in one place can be right in another.

The appeal of ethical relativism lies in our desire for tolerance, particularly at a time when we are disposed to celebrate cultural diversity. For this reason, the theory has enjoyed considerable popularity, although not always among moral philosophers. For the most part, moral philosophers insist that a necessary feature of moral conduct is its universalizability. They maintain that it is incoherent to claim that an action is permissible in one place but impermissible in another. If two cultures viewed the same action as both right and wrong, then we would not be speaking about the *morality* of that action. Most probably we would be talking about some nonmoral cultural norms such as what side of the road to drive on. In this view, an important difference exists between cultural practices that vary from society to society, and ethical practices that do not. In Europe, for instance, it may be inappropriate to switch your fork from your left hand to right after cutting food with a knife, while it is entirely appropriate to eat that way in the United States. This is because what hand you hold your fork in is a cultural matter that can vary from place to place. Compare this with murder, which, if it is wrong, is wrong at any time and in any place. Were this not the case, it would be morally imperialistic, say, to condemn the Nazis for killing Jews; it would be a case of one culture wrongly forcing its judgments on another.

Other ethical theories have found support among moral philosophers. *Social contract theory,* associated historically with Thomas Hobbes[5] and recently with John Rawls[6] and David Gauthier,[7] asserts that right and wrong conduct is defined by reference to a "social contract" made among people prior to their entrance into political society. *Natural law theory,* associated with Saint Thomas Aquinas, asserts that actions are right insofar as they conform to the laws of nature, and wrong otherwise. *Divine command theory,* discussed in Chapter 2, asserts that an action is right if God approves of it and wrong if God disapproves of it.

Before leaving our discussion of ethical theory and looking at why it is relevant to study it, we should point out that not all theorists discuss ethical issues in the context of theories explaining right and wrong conduct. Some philosophers, like Annette Baier, are antitheory. For Baier, the search for a theory with which to discuss moral issues assumes too narrow a focus in its preoccupation with rules and principles. Against

---

[5]Thomas Hobbes. *Leviathan,* edited by C. B. Macpherson (New York: Penguin Books, 1968).

[6]John Rawls. *A Theory of Justice* (Cambridge, Mass.: Harvard University Press, 1971).

[7]David Gauthier. *Morals by Agreement* (Oxford: Clarendon Press, 1986).

this, she proposes a focus built on the concept of trust combined with a focus on love.[8] In her writings on moral theory, Baier has pointed out some of the limitations of a rule-based or principle-based conception of ethics such as those we've been discussing. She sees them, for one thing, as sexist, inasmuch as men rather than women typically prefer to resolve their conflicts by appealing to rules and principles as opposed to love and compassion. For this reason, many feminists have endeavored to make love or care the operative concept in their moral theories (see Chapter 8). Baier thinks an ethic based on trust combines the merits of both of these approaches since it informs us whom to trust and why for the enforcement of rules, as well as whom to trust and why to care for and do the work of love.

Related to Baier's concerns are other philosophers who object to what they consider to be an obsession with rules and principles. For these philosophers, we should not be asking, "What ought I do?" with its emphasis on action-guiding rules and principles, so much as, "What kind of person should I be?" with an emphasis on traits that define good and bad character. Virtue-theorists, as they are sometimes called, point out that in addition to making judgments about right and wrong *actions,* we also make judgments about good and bad *people.* They claim that a person's character is at least as basic as any rule or principle, and that a concern with character has methodological advantages over a principle-based approach.

You can easily see what motivates virtue-theorists. Consider the following story that Richard Taylor tells in his *Good and Evil*:

> A boy, strolling over the country-side on his way from Sunday school, came across a large beetle lumbering over the ground. Fascinated by its size and beauty, he took a pin, and impaled it on a nearby tree. Several days later, the boy found himself again in the same place and curiosity led him again to the tree. There was the beetle, its legs still moving, although very slowly, against the empty air.[9]

As Taylor sees it, it is the boy's cruelty that stirs our moral sentiments rather than any principles of morality, for we can debate whether principles exist that prohibit such conduct. (Beetles hardly have rights and probably don't feel pain.) What gives this story its "stamp of moral evil" is the boy's delight in torturing the insect. The cruelty of the person—

---

[8]See Annette Baier, "What Do Women Want in a Moral Theory?" in *Moral Prejudices* (Cambridge, Mass.: Harvard University Press, February, 1994). Reprinted in Raziel Abelson and Marie-Louise Friquegnon, eds., *Ethics for Modern Life*, 5th ed. (New York: St. Martins Press, 1995), pp. 112–124. See also "Trust and Antitrust," *Ethics* 96:2 (Jan. 1986): 231–260. Reprinted in my *Doing and Being* (New York: Macmillan, 1993), pp. 346–373.

[9]Richard Taylor, *Good and Evil* (New York: Macmillan, 1970), p. 207. Reprinted in my *Doing and Being*, pp. 329–339.

not the wrongness of the act—fills us with disgust. For reasons such as this, some philosophers reject a rule-based approach and confront moral issues within the context of a theory that makes virtue and vice the points of departure.

Having pointed out that not all philosophers analyze issues within the context of moral theories, I return to our discussion of moral theory in order to show how theorizing can have implications for social issues. Note, before doing this, that most of the theories we have been discussing are normative theories as opposed to metaethical ones. "Normative ethics" refers to the branch of ethics that purports to explain what makes an action right and wrong. "Metaethics" refers to the branch of ethics that purports to explain the meaning of ethical sentences and the terms that occur within them. Unlike normative ethics, metaethics is not action-guiding; it does not recommend what we should do or should not do. Instead, it may be viewed as a branch of linguistic philosophy whose concern is the meaning of terms and sentences.

Returning to the topic of social issues, consider the question, discussed further in Chapter 3, of whether our treatment of animals is morally justified. Undeniably, people cause animals a great deal of pain. Take the treatment of veal calves in the established practice of factory farming. Veal calves are kept in unnatural conditions to provide people with a more marketable product. They are quartered in dark, narrow stalls, tethered with chains around their necks to limit their activity and make their flesh tender and pale, and fed a nutritionally deficient diet that promotes rapid weight gain. Is this treatment justified?

For the utilitarian, the answer is no. For the utilitarian, the relevant concepts are pleasure and pain: an action is right if it promotes pleasure and wrong if it promotes pain. But if this is so, then the ability to experience pleasure and pain makes an individual morally considerable. And since nonhuman animals have this ability, it follows that animals are entitled to moral respect. A Kantian, on the other hand, might be disposed to argue that animals are not entitled to respect inasmuch as they lack the ability to act on principle, although Kant himself argued that we should be kind to animals lest we be cruel to our fellow human beings.

Consider, as well, the issue of the death penalty, discussed further in Chapter 4. A utilitarian will argue that the death penalty is justified if it deters crime and unjustified if it does not; if it deters, it is cost-effective, but if it does not then it isn't. A Kantian, on the other hand, will argue that deterrence is beside the point. What is important is whether the criminal to be executed deserves such punishment.

We see, then, that theorizing about ethics is not just intrinsically interesting (which it is), but also serves as a tool for making intelligent decisions about ethical issues. Most of us have strong opinions on such social issues as abortion, capital punishment, euthanasia, and so forth. Few of us, however, are able to provide a sustained defense of the opinions we hold. The task of philosophical reflection is to unify these judgments into some consistent whole while at the same time trying to discern the underlying theory that accounts for them. Having ascertained the theory, we could then apply it to novel issues such as those created by advances in technology.

Finally, the goal of unifying our judgments and justifying them with theory sometimes yields surprising results. Specifically, we may find that what is implied by a theory constitutes grounds for rejecting that theory. So convinced might we be, for instance, that animals are beings worthy of respect that we might reject Kantianism on that account alone. Alternatively, we might accommodate our theory by modifying our views. So convinced might we be that utilitarianism is true, we might decide that eating meat is wrong even if we previously believed that eating meat was permissible.

Theorizing about ethics, then, is reminiscent of the Dutch boy plugging leaks in the dam: we solve one problem only to see another emerge. Nevertheless, theorizing benefits us by forcing us to think clearly and systematically about our moral beliefs. Many of us come to the study of ethics laden with beliefs that have never been scrutinized. Typically, these beliefs were formed by our cultural, religious, and parental heritages and accepted in childhood unconsciously and uncritically. Theorizing about ethics enables us to transcend the dogmatism that often characterizes such beliefs and to develop a morality that is rationally satisfying.

Joshua Halberstam teaches ethics at New York University. He is the author of *Everyday Ethics, Acing College,* and *Virtues and Values*. He has also written essays on such topics as fame, work, and news.

Video Presentation

Guest: Joshua Halberstam, Professor of Ethics, New York University

Student Panel: Linda Thompson, Diana De LaRosa, Marge Laver

Halberstam's book, *Acing College,* serves as an introduction to a discussion of the ethics of cheating on college exams. After noting that college students cheat more often than we would like to admit, he chides those who exhort students not to cheat because they can get into trouble by doing so. This, says Halberstam, gives students the wrong message. Students should not cheat not because of potential disciplinary problems; they should not cheat because cheating is wrong. He uses this example to illustrate how people are prone to misconstrue ethical issues, and he calls for more targeted and sophisticated discussion. We then turn to the very point of studying ethics and to whether studying it is profitable.

As Halberstam sees it, the point of studying ethics (and philosophy generally, for that matter) is to ask the right questions. Imagine, he says, a baseball fan who arrives at a game in the ninth inning and, after finding out that the game is scoreless, is relieved to know that he did not miss anything. Halberstam quickly points out that he *did* miss something—the game! The point of going to a baseball game is not so much to get the score as to participate in the process. Similarly, the student of philosophy wants to know the answers to his or her questions, but the process of asking questions is the essence of philosophy.

I then ask Halberstam if "doing ethics" makes you a better person, drawing attention to the tendency of moral philosophers to claim you don't have to be moral to be a moral philosopher. While not arguing for his position, Halberstam notes the peculiarity of doing moral philosophy and not being a better person as a result. Pointing out that twentieth-century moral philosophers have not always had the best of personal reputations, he recommends that we be concerned with wisdom as much as we are concerned with cleverness.

The conversation turns to Halberstam's interest in personal values as a method of addressing ethical issues. He predicts that ethics will head in this direction, since tackling global issues such as war and capital punishment doesn't hit home for many of us. In contrast, he thinks a satisfactory ethics will result if we concentrate on the nature of the good life and how we should live it. In response to my question of how defining the good life fits in with a culturally diverse and pluralistic world, he points out that it is only a problem if we emphasize the differences rather than the similarities in people. He agrees with Aristotle that people are more similar than different and points out that moral wisdom consists of our being able to distinguish cultural issues from ethical ones.

Having discussed the nature and value of ethics, I ask Halberstam whether ethics can be taught. After answering that people can be taught to think more clearly about ethical issues, he laments the fact that we too often ask the wrong people for advice on moral questions such as when we ask physicians whether fetuses have rights. He also laments how we as a society do not tolerate scholarly discourse even though the questions we raise contain complicated issues. Ethics, says Halberstam, is both easy and hard; it is easy in that it's easy to have an opinion on any question, but it's hard since we can never be sure we have the right answers.

I then ask Halberstam to predict the direction he thinks ethics will take in the 1990s and beyond, at which point we return to his view that ethics will emerge out of a concern with personal values. He provides some examples having to do with racism and friendship, and considers the implications of technological advancements that will force us to redefine our understanding of life, death, personhood, and parenthood.

After the break, Diana De LaRosa asks Halberstam for his views on abortion. Halberstam replies with the interesting observation that pro-choice people and right-to-lifers talk past each other. Pro-choice, he says, is a purely legal position, while right-to-life is a legal and moral position. Beyond this, he thinks we need to ask whether people should or should not have abortions and identifies himself as being "pro abortion." Marge Laver asks Halberstam to comment on issues of professional ethics such as professor-student relationships, and Linda Thompson asks Halberstam about ethical issues that are created by advances in biotechnology.

With an eye on issues we presently face and are likely to face in the years to come, Joshua Halberstam asks whether the moral theories we have inherited from antiquity are equipped to handle our increasingly novel moral quandaries. He considers two answers in this regard. "Moral traditionalists," he says, argue that the moral theories we have inherited are adequately equipped to handle whatever complex problems the philosophers of antiquity did not envision. For example, whereas in the past our right to privacy meant that others could not peer into our windows with impunity, today the right to privacy might mean not taking a picture of our home via satellite. The right to privacy, however, remains what it always was. "Moral transformationalists," on the other hand, argue that technology itself shapes our moral judgments and calls for a revolutionary approach to ethics. If, as some transformationalists argue, morality is a result of heredity and we have the ability to determine our heredity, then morality will be shaped by technology in a way that was never anticipated. Without expressly endorsing the traditionalist account, Halberstam concludes by emphasizing some of its merits.

Tomorrow's Ethics Yesterday

Joshua Halberstam

I'm surely not the only one who imagines mounds of snow when looking out of an airplane window to the billowed clouds below. It's prosaic, perhaps, but this is just the sort of experience that gets me to wonder again about appearances and interpretation, about whether what we see is what we get or whether perhaps we just don't get it at all.

These thoughts, in turn, direct me back to the copy of Aristotle's *Nichomechean Ethics* sitting on my lap. It's quite extraordinary really—not just the book's insights but that this man's ideas could reach across the millennia, all the way up to me here, flying at a speed of hundreds of miles an hour, thousands of feet in the air, looking *down* at clouds for goodness sake, and be so timely, so plausible, so useful.

This push and pull between continuity and change underlies all discussion of ethics of the future. We are treated to a constant barrage of marvelous scientific developments that pose novel and perplexing moral dilemmas. Some argue that we human beings need to wise up and take these developments seriously and that includes preparing ourselves to jettison whole planks of our traditional morality. The old categories of good and bad, they argue, just won't fly in the century to come. Others argue in almost exactly the other direction. Sure we have new issues to deal with, they acknowledge, but this is all the more reason to reinforce our time-tested ethics. We have strayed so far from our traditional moral moorings that we've entered moral freefall and are poorly equipped to deal with these emerging ethical challenges.

Before we decide between these outlooks, we need to dig down a bit deeper and examine the moral reasoning that drives each of these views. We need to see more clearly how innovation affects morality (and vice versa too).

NEW TECHNOLOGIES, NEW MORALITIES

Let's dub one view *moral traditionalism.* According to the proponents of this view, however much the parade of technological advancements changes our lives, these transformations do not—and should not—entail a corresponding change in our values. Technology poses new dilemmas, yes, but they are at root, variations on old themes—and so it has always been. In the nineteenth century the invention of the stethoscope, refrigeration, the reaper, the sewing machine, the elevator, the telephone, the skyscraper, the automobile, and the radio effected major overhauls in the way people went about their lives. The inventions of the twentieth century were even more sweeping and their impact on our lives even more dramatic. Nevertheless, our fundamental values remained the same throughout. We continue to have the same commitment to the virtues of honesty, respect, charity, and compassion and ARE outraged by the same sorts of evil. And this, says the traditionalist, will continue to be the case in the century ahead.

Consider, for example, the right to privacy. Human beings are herd animals, genetically and socially structured to live with other humans, but we also have a need, as individuals, to maintain a sphere of privacy. The sort of information that we cherish as our own personal business isn't fixed but varies from culture to culture. In our own society, for instance, people are especially sensitive about publicizing facts about their incomes and sex lives. In the old days, namely most of human history, you could invade people's privacy by peering into their windows, by gossiping with their next door neighbors, or by raiding their mail. These are primitive trespasses compared to the spying techniques accessible today. Now we can extract your credit rating from a desk computer, scan what you buy at the checkout counter, take a picture of your home from a satellite, test for your drug use, and even determine your genetic makeup. But your moral right to privacy, however that right is established, hasn't changed, says the traditionalist; it's just that now privacy is so much more difficult to secure.

So too, many of our social choices are really variations on old themes. For example, several hundred years ago societies debated the wisdom and justice of allotting funds for the exploration of distant continents instead of using the money for domestic needs; "Should moneys be channeled to explore the New World or used here in Spain?" Today we undertake the same deliberation when we consider whether to fund the space program. New terrain; same dilemma.

What is this "moral framework" that the traditionalist assumes endures despite these developments in our lives? That depends on one's favored moral theory—the traditionalist wants to be neutral about that decision. Your adherence to theological ethics, utilitarianism, Kantian morality, or most any moral theory should not be undermined, they say, by new "gadgets" no matter how startling or sophisticated. Nevertheless, we must be careful not to translate this viewpoint into one of rigidity, an unwillingness to recognize that technological changes do influence moral decisions. Traditionalists certainly want to acknowledge that technology has immediate consequences for what we are and are not obliged to do.

A venerable maxim in moral philosophy is "ought implies can." The idea is commonsensical: you can't be obligated to do what you cannot do. You and I might have an obligation to feed the starving child on our block or in distant Africa, but as individuals, you and I aren't obligated to feed *every* starving child in the world. That can't be our obligation because that isn't something you and I could possibly accomplish. Now, as philosophers have been quick to point out, this maxim, "ought implies can," needs qualification. Some argue that we do, indeed, have a standing moral obligation to feed any and all starving people, but because this is now physically impossible, we are excused for not doing so. Being excused is not the same as not being obligated; in fact, exculpation entails obligation; you can only be excused for not doing what you should have done. (Moral philosophers have a number of ways of categorizing these standing obligations, but that discussion would take us far afield.)

Technology expands the realm of what we can do. As we enlarge the "can" we enlarge the "ought." One hundred years ago, doctors might have spent a few fleeting moments over lunch in the cafeteria wondering about whether it would be morally permissible to impregnate women through artificial insemination . . . if only they could. Nowadays they can perform this procedure and so many other innovations in the field of reproduction. As a result, doctors and the rest of us as well have new obligations and prohibitions in the area of reproduction. Other advances in medicine have spawned so many more new possibilities and corresponding new moral imperatives. For example, years ago we didn't have an obligation to keep people in irreversible comas alive for years because we couldn't accomplish this goal even if we wanted to. Now that we can, we also have a major dilemma on our hands.

Technological developments have yet another, related, important, and less often noticed impact on the "ought implies can" principle. Suppose an astronaut friend of yours borrows your pen and while out for a walk in space drops the pen and watches it float off into the endless abyss of the universe. You insist that you want the pen back—it has much sentimental value to you because your grandmother gave it to you on her death bed. Well, too bad. You can scream and yell, beg and plead all you wish, but your friend *cannot* return it to you. But the "cannot" in moral judgments is often not a genuine physical impossibility but a moral judgment call. You promised to meet your sister for a cup of coffee this afternoon but came down with a fever of 103 degrees. Surely you can't be blamed for not showing up for your appointment; "I *couldn't* get out of bed, I was too sick" is a reasonable response. But if your next door neighbor is dying of a heart attack and asks you to drive him to the emergency room, that same fever is no longer a sufficient excuse for not helping—I *couldn't* get out of bed, I was too sick" won't wash. In both cases you were physically *able* to meet your commitments but your sick condition is a good excuse for not showing up to your rendezvous, but not a good excuse for your failure to save a life. The "can" in "ought implies can" often depends, therefore, on the strength of the "ought"—

that is, the moral consequences of your action or inaction determine, in part, what we expect someone to do or not do. In this way, too, technology has a major impact on our moral obligations. Each of us can now bring about a much broader range of changes in the world than formerly possible; a skilled doctor can save more lives and a sadistic terrorist can destroy more lives.

Traditionalism, accordingly, fully recognizes that our physical circumstances change and so do the dos and don'ts of our moral lives. But what endures, they insist, are the moral concepts that form the basis of this morality.

Moral transformationalists disagree. In their view, technology has a much more profound effect on our moral thinking than merely presenting novel versions of earlier dilemmas. They believe that we are in the process of transforming basic elements in our metaphysical and moral outlook.

Transformationalists remind us at the outset that so much of what we might initially consider as descriptive or empirical definitions are really legal and moral judgments. This is true even—and perhaps especially—with regard to such basic notions as life and death. The question "When does a person die?" sounds as if it is asking for some scientific or medical answer, but none can be forthcoming—we never do "see" death occur. What we see over time is the cessation of certain bodily functions which we *decide* to call death. Such definitions are stipulative, not discoveries; we could have different definitions of death, as in fact we did in the past. We might now say that we were mistaken when, as was the case a hundred years ago, we declared someone dead when his or her heart stopped. We now consider death to be a function of brain activity. But what kind of mistake did we make back then? In what way could we be mistaken now? After all, it seems at least in principle that we could arrive at a different moral about the moment of death even if we did not have any new empirical information. For the same reason, medical doctors cannot tell us whether a fetus is a "person." They can tell us what the fetus is doing, its physical state, its prognosis for the future, but the decision to deem a fetus a "person" is not purely a scientific description but a legal and moral determination.

Technology, say the advocates of this approach, is forcing us to redefine many critical terms in our moral scheme.

You can see this metamorphosis perhaps most dramatically in the area of biotechnology. This field is still in its infancy—embryonic stage might be an even more accurate description. Nevertheless, we already have learned a great deal about recombinant DNA and how to splice genes in order to create original life forms. What is the moral status of these lab-created entities? In the past, we confronted either natural life creatures or artificial "objects" (viruses are a borderline case), and our moral obligations to these entities depended on which status we attributed to them. Natural beings, we say, have a sacredness, a sanctity of life that robots don't. But do we also ascribe "sacredness" to the quasi-natural life forms we develop in the laboratory? Do these quasi-synthetic life forms also have the same right to life? Science fiction writers, along with engineers who work in the field of artificial intelligence, go further and posit such complicated machines that we must hesitate before refusing to allow these "beings" the moral rights of living things. The real world is catching up to these fantasies. These challenges, the transformationalists point out, are not a straightforward matter of applying old moral principles to new situations; they demand that we reconsider the very criteria by which we establish the basic constructs of our moral systems.

Furthermore, technology strikes at the heart of moral theories themselves. Here is another example from biotechnology. A number of moral philosophers are persuaded that human evolutionary history determines, in large measure, our ethical attitudes. We can, of course, combat our inherited motivations, but we do so with obvious strain. (Sociobiologists who favor this view have in mind here such things as our sexual morality and our inclinations toward aggression.) But now we are on the threshold of a radical change in our evolutionary history: we can partially control our own evolution. During the twentieth-century, we perfected the means by which we could have sex without reproduction. We now are learning how to have reproduction without sex. And in the next years we will develop the capacity to determine what we reproduce. Presumably, for the first time in the history of the universe, a species will no longer be at the whim of biology but will have a say in the design of its offspring. The moral ramifications of this capacity are astounding. Should we exercise this ability? What kind of children do we want? But even beyond the particular decisions, note the theoretical implications: if the evolutionary ethicists are right and our morality is the result of heredity, then in determining our heredity we are, in fact, making moral decisions about how we will make moral decisions.

Medical science is just one area where technology dictates a reconsideration of our moral concepts. Transformationalists see this happening in the emerging world of information technology as well. Recent discussions of ethics in cyberspace cluster around such ethical chestnuts as the justification for deception, accessibility of information, and advertising on a public media for personal gain. But the development of the Internet has also required us to rethink such moral standbys as the notion of personal identity. In cyberspace, your identity is not circumscribed by your body or behavior or memory but by your self-definition as posted on the information superhighway (gender-swapping, for example, is not uncommon on the Internet). The "real you" in this world is not necessarily the same as the real you in the world off the Net. Much follows: the moral concerns about privacy and deception and the like all turn on how we define identity in this realm. Similarly, computer technology necessitates a major reconsideration of such notions as intellectual property rights. Do you own your electronic text? This seemingly specific legal question is actually just the surface of a much deeper nest of conceptual issues about property, rights, and the notion of information, all of which are critical elements in a comprehensive moral theory. Cyberspace is also changing the way we think about community, another fundamental moral feature of our lives. Traditional communities were formed on the basis of shared geography—you formed a community with your neighbors. The space in cyberspace, however, is not based on propinquity. The communities in this domain are based, rather, on shared interests and their members can be thousands of miles apart. Here again, says the transformationalist, information technologies will cause a significant shift in our ethics.

The link between technology and moral reevaluation isn't always direct. More typically, many social links are at play. The moral issues relating to ecology are a case in point.

From the get-go, human beings have been busy seeking to control the forces of nature. During these past centuries we've become much more adept at achieving this aim. We have also become much more adept at messing up nature and the world we live in. The litany of these ill-advised incursions is well known: pollution, destruction of natural resources, overpopulation, depletion of the ozone layer, nuclear and toxic waste, and on and on. This unfortunate fallout of technology has engendered the reintroduction of a slough of moral issues that were relatively neglected years before. Vegetarianism and animal rights are two examples of moral topics that have received renewed attention and are now discussed under the rubric of the larger question of humanity's place on the planet. Technology for better in some cases and for worse in others has pushed us to ask again the big questions with a new urgency.

This debate between transformationalists and traditionalists doesn't appear in the Aristotle I'm reading on this plane ride. For Aristotle the challenge of ethics is, finally, about how to live the good life, how to make sense of our personal relationships and responsibilities. Technology, as the traditionalists say, may pose new dilemmas or even, as the transformationalists say, force us to redefine basic conceptual elements of our moral theories, but the question of how best to live your life stands apart from these concerns. It is about how we as humans understand our lives and that question still resonates through the millennia.

This is, finally, what makes the philosophical conversation so engaging. It endures because the same basic questions of wonder endure. Human beings are still trying to make sense of how to live their lives with or without the technological wizardry at their behest. Some of the best answers in the future will continue to come from the best thinkers of the past.

Hilary Putnam is Walter Beverly Pearson Professor of Modern Mathematics and Mathematical Logic at Harvard University. Among his many publications are *Philosophy of Logic, Reason, Truth, and History, Meaning and the Moral Sciences,* and the three-volume *Philosophical Papers* (comprising *Mathematics, Matter, and Method; Mind, Language, and Reality;* and *Realism and Reason*).

Photo by: Toby Bornstein

Video Presentation

Guest: Hilary Putnam, Walter Beverly Pearson Professor of Modern Mathematics and Mathematical Logic, Harvard University

Panel: Professors Tom Slaughter and Michael Redmond, Bergen Community College

I begin by asking Hilary Putnam what it was that prompted his recent interest in ethics after having made his reputation in such fields as the philosophy of mathematics, metaphysics, and the philosophy of science. He answers by recalling his days in graduate school when the trend in ethics was metaethical inquiry. The prevailing view, he says, was that ethical choices are no more than subjective expressions of taste. He questioned this view and wondered whether this interpretation of ethical judgment corresponded with the judgments that he made in his own life. His reading of Kamala Markandaya's *A Grain of Rice* convinced him that even if it should turn out that ethical judgments are subjective, we don't perceive them as subjective from the inside looking out.

Returning to my original question, I then ask Putnam if there is a thread that connects his interest in ethics with his interest in the disciplines where he had made his name, particularly the philosophy of science. He answers by pointing out how impressed he was with science in the 1950s when there were philosophers who believed that science could answer all questions of a philosophical nature. Taking his cue from John Dewey that philosophy cannot give us a "theory of everything," he became convinced that some questions, like those in ethics, are not scientific ones.

Putnam's reference to Kamala Markandaya's *A Grain of Rice* inspires Tom Slaughter to ask if he is antitheory in ethics the way people like Martha Nussbaum are. After denying that Nussbaum is as antitheory as Slaughter suggests, Putnam says that he is not antitheory in ethics and warns that doing away with moral theory could lead to an empty situation-ethics. He advises that we regard moral rules as "fire breaks": sometimes we need to cross them but we better pause before we do. As a follow-up to Slaughter's question, I ask Putnam if he's interested in virtue theory since virtue theories have emphasized the importance of the novel for moral philosophy. Putnam says that he is interested in virtue theory and adds that much work in virtue theory has been directed against the moral philosophy of John Rawls. Putnam, in contrast, does not see any incompatibility between Rawls's theory of justice and the claims made by virtue theorists.

Michael Redmond joins the conversation by asking Putnam to elaborate on his earlier claim that ethics seems objective from the inside looking out. Putnam responds by pointing out that there are really two questions at work here. The first concerns the way ethics appears from inside; the second concerns whether we should take its perceived objectivity seriously. With respect to the first question, people speak as though ethical judgments are objective, but the interesting question is whether they are. As Putnam sees it, no one has yet to produce a persuasive argument that they are not.

At this point, Slaughter asks whether Putnam sees ethics as being in conflict with science, to which Putnam answers that he does not and notes that science itself is driven by considerations of value. Changing subjects, I then ask Putnam to comment on how his pragmatism impacts on his ethical views. After discussing what pragmatism is, he says that what has attracted him to pragmatism is its emphasis on fallibilism and experimentalism. This, he says, is what he has learned from thinkers like William James whose reference to ideals and moral images speak to Putnam in a way that virtues and rules do not. Waxing sentimental, he speaks of his mother-in-law whose moral image ("all men are brothers") served as a profound picture which enabled her to work in the anti-Hitler underground. Such images, he suggests, may enable us to settle issues we otherwise could not, at least among good and decent people.

Following the break, I ask Putnam to talk about his book, *Renewing Philosophy*. He says that half of this book is devoted to debunking the myth that science can solve all our problems, while the other half is devoted to his philosophical heroes, John Dewey and Ludwig Wittgenstein. Wittgenstein is his hero on account of his intolerance against those who are intolerant against religion, and Dewey is his hero for his concern with what democracy is really about as opposed to what people say it is about. After discussing some of the differences between Dewey and Marx, we wind up the show with some further talk about pragmatism ("it is a middle ground between authoritarianism and relativism") as well as some discussion of religion and the meaning of life.

Interview with Hilary Putnam

Haber: Dewey once remarked that philosophy should be concerned with "the problems of men." What did Dewey mean by this phrase and what do you understand it to mean? (What *are* the "problems of men?") Do you agree with Dewey? What generally does pragmatism have to say about ethics?

Putnam: Dewey's conception (which I partly agree with) was that philosophy should concern itself with the resolution of social and cultural conflicts. In Dewey's view, we should not seek for a God's-Eye View of the problems of human beings; each age must work out its own conception of what those problems are, and of which ones are the most urgent. In our time, Dewey thought, one thing is common to *all* of the problems that we collectively face: in each and every case we are reluctant to bring intelligence to bear on the problem. Whether the problem be how to educate our children (and this was *the* problem with which Dewey most continuously occupied himself), or how to secure peace in the world, or what to do about depressions and unemployment, or crime, or whatever, we are quite willing to listen to "experts" (and even to quacks) who propose quick technological "fixes," but unwilling to think seriously about what the intelligent choice of *ends* might be. In part, this is because we have bought a philosophical view according to which means can be rationally discussed but ends cannot (a legacy of positivism). Dewey believed that there is such a thing as the rational discussion of ends, and that unless we bring about the preconditions for such a discussion—preconditions which include what he called "education for democracy," reduction of inequalities in wealth and power (inequalities which invariably result in the distortion and manipulation of supposedly democratic processes), and continuing education (again *education*!) in how to find and how to use information of all kinds—not only will our political lives be as violent and unpleasant as they have been in the past, but, because of the far greater power of our technology, we will be in danger of putting an end to human society itself.

I agree with these views of Dewey's. But I do not agree that philosophy should or can be exclusively concerned with social problems. Dewey's view is one-sided. Philosophy, from Socrates on, has only flourished when concern for one's society and concern for *theoria*, for understanding for its own sake, have been brought into a fruitful relationship. But—and here I make a concession to Dewey—how to do that is something that each time has to solve in its own way; there is no timeless prescription for good philosophy.

I will not try to say "what pragmatism generally has to say about ethics" because the great pragmatists—James and Peirce as much as Dewey—had very different things to teach us, and it would take a very long essay to even begin to do justice to all of that.

Since you have begun with pragmatism, I will in what follows address your questions from the perspective of pragmatism (where I agree with that perspective).

Haber: What have we learned (or still have to learn) from the important events of the twentieth century? What have we learned from the advances in technology?

Putnam: Dewey's worry (expressed long before the atomic age) that our technological advances are more of a danger than a blessing if not accompanied by advances in our political intelligence is a legitimate worry. Indeed, just *how* legitimate is the main thing we have to learn. The solution, however—as again Dewey said—is not to imagine that we can go back to a golden age that never existed, or that we can find the answer in some form of fundamentalism; trying to do that will only compound the problem.

Haber: What mistakes in ethics have we made in the twentieth century? How can we avoid these mistakes in the future?

Putnam: "Mistakes don't seem to me to be the problem. To be sure, there are times when we make ethical mistakes; for example, before the Civil Rights Movement, many people in all economic classes were unthinking racists; the realization that that was what they were was a salutary shock for some people of good will. It was, and continues to be, for some men, an even harder struggle to give up unthinking prejudices (in the literal sense of prejudgments) about "the place of women." But these "mistakes" are part of a larger pattern that it is not helpful to describe by an intellectual term like "mistake" (as though all people needed were a piece of information, or perhaps a philosophical demonstration). Quite simply, there is a very deep psychological tendency to divide the human world into "us" and "them"—to imagine a metaphysical gulf between two sorts of humans, the fully human (who are, of course, "us") and the only semihuman or degenerately human (who may be Jews in Hitler's Germany, welfare mothers in the United States, Bosnians in what was Yugoslavia, foreign workers in a European country, or Hindus or Muslims in India, or . . .). This is not an intellectual mistake but a way of comforting oneself in the face of finiteness and mortality by imagining one belongs to a very exclusive pseudo-species. This can never wholly be eradicated, but it is a mistake—and I use the word deliberately—to think that it must always have the same power in every place and at every time. The extent to which people grow up understanding that we are all brothers and sisters, that we are interdependent beings who need to help one another, depends on many factors, but one of the most important is the kind of education they receive. The fact that in the United States we now have two educational systems—a dysfunctional one for the poor and a slightly better one for the middle class—is a very bad sign. We do not take seriously the very elementary moral principle that we have a responsibility to future generations. And we had better start doing so, or the consequences will be beyond reckoning.

Haber: What relationship do you see between ethics and religion?

Putnam: Ethics and religion: this, too, is a topic too large to do justice to here, so I will content myself with a brief personal statement. I believe that ethics dries up unless accompanied by some form of spirituality. I say "some form" deliberately, because there are many forms, not all theistic, including some whose proponents might not want to regard as "religion." Haym Soloveitchik put it very well recently, writing:

> When we state that "honesty" is "good," we are also saying that, ultimately, this is what is best for man, what we call at times "true felicity," to distinguish it from mere "happiness." We believe that, were we to know all there is to know of the inner life of a Mafia don and that of an honest cobbler, we would see that honesty is, indeed, the best policy. The moral life makes claim to be the wise life, and the moral call, to most, is a summons to realism, to live one's life in accord with the deeper reality. A statement of value is, in this way, a statement of fact, a pronouncement about the true nature of things. Conversely, I believe that spirituality dries up and turns into a rigid fundamentalism (which I regard as the death of the spirit) when religion is immunized from ethical and philosophical criticism. In this sense, "religion" and ethics need one another.

Haber: Can we do ethics without metaphysics or epistemology?

Putnam: That depends on what you mean by "metaphysics" and what you mean by "epistemology." Epistemology, for example, is often thought to be generated by the question, "What is the nature of knowledge?"; but Wittgenstein (who I see as, in some ways, a better "pragmatist" than the pragmatists themselves) has taught us that the very assumption that knowledge has a "nature" is one that we have not succeeded in giving a sense. And it will not help to restate it in the formal mode of speech, as, say, "What is the analysis of the concept of knowledge?" or "What is the meaning of the word 'know'?" because the idea that the word *know* has a meaning that surrounds it, like an "aura" that accompanies it in all its contexts of use, determining how we *must* use it in those contexts, is an illusion.

On the other hand, the pragmatists did not think (and, on my reading, Wittgenstein did not think) that this means that we can say nothing at all about human knowledge, or, to use a word the pragmatists liked better than the word *knowledge,* about how to fruitfully conduct *inquiry.* There are some things we have *learned* about inquiry, even if they do not constitute a set of definite "canons" for the conduct of inquiry, or a metaphysical theory of the "nature" of inquiry. In my own writing[1] I have stressed four "theses" of pragmatism:

1. *Fallibilism.* We have learned from the history of human inquiry that there is no such thing as an absolute guarantee that any piece of putative knowledge will never require revision.

2. *Antiskepticism.* Skepticism is a posture that we drop whenever we engage in serious practice, and for pragmatists what we have to believe when we engage in serious practice is what counts. To be sure, doubt is sometimes *warranted*—doubt of particular beliefs, for particular specifiable reasons. But that is very different from so-called "philosophical" doubt. *Doubt requires a justification in context, just as much as belief.* I have repeatedly insisted that the possibility of being simultaneously fallibilistic and *anti*skeptical is perhaps the unique insight of American pragmatism.[2]

3. *Interpenetration.* Knowledge of facts and knowledge of values, knowledge of the interpretations of beliefs and knowledge of the truth of the content of beliefs, far from being dichotomous, separated by enormous metaphysical gaps (as is suggested by such familiar philosophical notions as the notion that something has to be *either* a "factual assertion" *or* a "value judgment," *either* a "scientific statement" *or* a "translation") shade into and presuppose one another.

4. *The democratization of inquiry.* We have learned from the process of inquiry itself that the intelligent pursuit of inquiry requires a certain "ethic"; in particular, we have learned that cooperation is necessary both for the formation of ideas and for their rational testing.

But—and this is crucial—cooperation must be of a certain kind in order to be effective. Where there is no opportunity to challenge accepted hypotheses by criticizing the evidence upon which their acceptance was based, or the application of the norms that govern the inquiry to that evidence, or by offering rival hypotheses, and where questions and suggestions are systematically ignored, then inquiry always suffers. When relations among inquirers become relations of hierarchy and dependence, or when inquirers instrumentalize one another, again inquiry suffers. Both for its full development and for its full application to human problems, we require the *democratization* of inquiry. In sum, pragmatism represents a *middle way* in epistemology, a middle way between the extremes of seeking a Utopian finality, an apodictic account of the "nature and limits of human knowledge," of the kind that traditional epistemology sought to provide, on the one hand, and of falling into a "postmodern" skepticism about the possibility of saying anything normative at all, on the other.

While there was a pragmatist consensus on the broad outlines of a sound epistemology, at least to the extent that the classical pragmatists would all have accepted my four "theses," there was no such consensus on metaphysics, and here I shall speak only for myself.

Metaphysics, like epistemology, traditionally had aspirations that today appear quite fantastic. I mean the aspiration to describe a reality standing behind our ordinary empirical judgments, or our mathematical judgments, or our ethical judgments—"standing behind" both in the sense of standing invisibly behind and in the sense of guaranteeing our ordinary ways of speaking and acting, in so far as they met with the metaphysician's approval. To this tradition belong Plato's Ideas, Aristotle's Essences, Descartes' Two Substances plus God, Leibnitz's Monads, Kant's Noumenal World, Hegel's World Spirit, Peirce's Thirds, and so on. On the other hand, the recoil away from this particular sort of fantasy all too often took the form of an extreme empiricism, represented by the equally fantastic idea that "there is nothing really there but experiences." (James himself succumbed to that one). Here, too, we need a middle way, but the nature of that middle way is more difficult to discern.

Today, philosophers who seek to avoid the errors of both transcendent metaphysics and traditional empiricism often succumb to *scientism*. The error, they say, was to suppose that there could be a "first philosophy" above and outside of science. *Science* does what metaphysics claimed to do: it limns "the ultimate nature of reality." Like the later Wittgenstein, I see this sort of scientism as not a middle way at all, but as just another form of the metaphysical illusion.

It is an illusion, not because there are some scientific questions that science cannot answer (although that is doubtless the case), but because many of our questions are not scientific at all. "What does 'a priori' mean?" is a factual question, but we do not answer it by appealing to the "results" of some "science." History deals with facts, but it is useless to ask if history is "scientific." Indeed, even the methodology of science itself is only in limited areas something there is or can be a science of. (Statistics is a science, but there is no science which determines what it is for a theory to be "simple" or "plausible"). Science itself is an activity that makes sense only against the background of nonscientific knowledge.

What all these illusions—the illusions of transcendent metaphysics, of empiricism, and of scientism—share is the idea that "reality" is the name of a single super-thing, and that, therefore, there ought to be a super-subject (called "metaphysics," or, perhaps, simply "science") that "describes" it. "Reality" is an always extendible concept, and there is no more surveying "reality" than there is surveying all of human existence in the world.

Once one has perceived the emptiness of the idea of metaphysics as a super-subject, there is still a danger to be overcome, however, and that is, once again, the danger of a recoil to an extreme position, this time to the position that philosophy is at an end (a position represented today in American philosophy by Richard Rorty). Once again, what we need is not a recoil to the extreme, but a middle way.

So far I have spoken only of what is erroneous in the great metaphysicians. But that is not the whole story; if it were, Rorty would be right. Each of the great metaphysicians also had profound insights—insights concerning almost every aspect of human life including scientific activity, valuation, art, and human motivation. Like literature and like art, philosophy recognizes nothing as an "improper subject." I have recently tried to show, for example, that there were insights in Kant's philosophy upon which Wittgenstein built in his own later philosophy.[3] Those insights, and the insights of the other great metaphysicians, do not, indeed, constitute a "theory" or a "science" any more than life constitutes the subject matter for a "theory" or a "science." But they constitute reflections of lasting value—often reflections of a reflexive kind, reflections upon reflections. What they give us is not scientific explanation but conceptual clarity—and not just clarity, but sensitivity. To quote Dewey once again, philosophy, at its best, is "criticism of criticism."

I may seem to have strayed far from the question, which was whether we can do ethics without metaphysics or epistemology, but that question has been constantly in my mind. We can certainly do ethics without the illusions of traditional metaphysics and traditional epistemology, but we cannot do ethics without reflective criticism; that is why we continue to read, and to be instructed by, Plato, Aristotle, Kant, and Mill, even though we do not accept their metaphysical systems.

Haber: In the middle of the twentieth century, moral philosophers were primarily concerned with the analysis of ethical statements and the meaning of the terms that were contained in these statements. Later on, philosophers turned away from this esoteric approach and directed their attention to substantive questions. Do you view this shift as a good one? Do you foresee a return to metaethics and, if so, how will it be different from the kind of ethical analysis that typified twentieth-century moral philosophy? What do you foresee to be the important ethical issues in the coming years?

Putnam: When ethical discussion has flourished, it has always crossed—and in fact blurred—the boundaries between "substantive questions" and "metaethics." The question as to the objectivity of ethical judgments is as much a substantive question—because moral skepticism, the belief that there are no objective moral standards, has real-world moral consequences—as a "meta" question. Pragmatism, in particular Jamesian and Deweyan pragmatism, taught that we need not choose either moral dogmatism (often identified with fundamentalism) or moral skepticism, that once again there is a third way. That third way cannot be stated in a nutshell, but it involves the idea that criticism, whether of norms or of values, does not need an absolute foundation; that criticism is always situated, but that the situatedness of criticism does not entail a radical relativism, although it does entail a certain pluralism. But here I must stop.

Endnotes

1. See, for example, my *Pragmatism* (London, UK, and Cambridge, US: Blackwell, 1995).
2. It is, however, an insight which the later Wittgenstein restated in his own way in *On Certainty*.
3. See Lecture II, in my *Pragmatism*.

Closing Questions

1. John, hating his wife and wanting her dead, puts poison in her coffee, thereby killing her. Bill, also hating his wife and wanting her dead, accidentally puts poison in her coffee, thinking it's milk. Bill, who is a chemist, has the antidote but does not give it to his wife and allows her to die. Discuss whether Bill's failure to act is as bad as John's action.

   _____

   _____

   _____

   _____

2. Suppose that you are in desperate need of employment and have been offered a high position in a laboratory that pursues research in chemical and biological warfare that is potentially very hazardous. Suppose that you have serious moral qualms about accepting this offer but know that if you refuse, another less scrupulous candidate will certainly accept it. What would a utilitarian recommend that you do? Do you agree? Why or why not?

   _____

   _____

   _____

   _____

3. Suppose that you and a friend have been shipwrecked on a deserted island and it is virtually certain that one of you will die before you are rescued owing to scarcity of food. Suppose your friend tells you that you may have all of the food if you promise to see to it that his son gets his share of the treasure that the two of you have uncovered. You make the promise, your friend dies, and you are subsequently rescued. Intending to keep your promise, you later learn that your friend's son is leading an inauspicious life: he is dealing drugs and shows little promise of reform. Afraid that he will squander away his father's fortune, you contemplate donating the money to your friend's favorite charity knowing that since your friend is dead, what he won't know won't hurt him. What should you do?

   _____

   _____

   _____

4. Suppose you are married and in dire financial straits when a debonair millionaire offers you a million dollars to spend a night with your spouse. Assuming your spouse consents, should you accept this offer? Why or why not?

_____

_____

_____

_____

5. It is undeniable that alcohol use in our society has bad consequences. Drunken drivers are responsible for nearly half of the nearly 50,000 traffic fatalities that occur each year; alcohol is implicated in over half of the nation's 30,000 homicides; alcohol use in pregnancy has been linked to birth defects; and alcohol abuse causes cirrhosis of the liver. Are these good reasons to return to Prohibition when alcohol consumption declined by as much as 50 percent?

_____

_____

_____

_____

6. It is becoming increasingly possible to predetermine the sex of our children through genetic testing. At the same time, when people who are asked what sex they would have if they had that choice, some 80 percent favor males over females. If sex determination were readily available, should people have the right to choose the sex of their child or should the state have a say in what choice they should make?

_____

_____

_____

_____

7. What moral value does giving to charity have if one gives to charity solely to get a tax deduction?

_____

_____

_____

_____

8. What is the relationship between the rightness of an action and the consequences that result from it? What role do intent and motive play?

_____

_____

_____

_____

9. Must one be moral to be a moral philosopher?

_____

_____

_____

_____

10. Do you agree with Kant that one ought to tell the truth to an "inquiring murderer"?

_____

_____

_____

_____

11. It has been said that it is better for all the guilty to go free than for one innocent person to be wrongly convicted. Between utilitarians and deontologists, who would support such a statement? Do you agree with this statement? Why or why not?

_____

_____

_____

_____

12. Kant insisted that it was wrong to use a person solely as a means to an end. This can be used to explain what is wrong about prostitution: the john uses the prostitute as a means solely to an end, and the prostitute uses the john (and herself) solely as a means to an end. But if this is so, what difference is there between the prostitute-John relationship and the employer-employee relationship?

_____

_____

_____

_____

13. Suppose there existed an "experience machine" (similar to the one used in the film _Total Recall_) that could provide you with whatever experiences you desired once you are on the machine. Suppose that the experiences were so genuine that it was impossible to know you were on the machine although you would, in fact, be in a chair with electrodes wired to your brain. Finally, suppose that once you choose to become attached to this machine, you cannot detach yourself without suffering permanent brain damage. Discuss the reasons for and against becoming attached to the machine.

_____

_____

_____

_____

14. In certain overpopulated countries, there are policies against having more than one child (particularly girls) and infanticide is sometimes encouraged. In the United States, of course, infanticide is murder. Is infanticide wrong here but permissible in these other countries? Is there more than one "correct" moral code?

_____

_____

_____

_____

15. Can good people sometimes do wrong? Can bad people sometimes do right? What is the relationship between being good and doing right? Between being bad and doing wrong? Finally, what must a "good" person do before you conclude that he or she is bad, and what must a "bad" person do before you conclude that he or she is good?

_____

_____

_____

_____

For Further Reading

Brandt, R. B. *Ethical Theory*. Englewood Cliffs, N.J.: Prentice-Hall, 1959.

Cahn, Steven M., and Joram G. Haber, eds. *Twentieth Century Ethical Theory*. Englewood Cliffs, N.J.: Prentice-Hall, 1995.

Foot, Philippa, ed. *Theories of Ethics*. New York: Oxford University Press, 1967.

Garrett, K. Richard. *Dialogues Concerning the Foundations of Ethics*. Savage, Md.: Roman & Littlefield, 1990.

Gilligan, Carol. *In a Different Voice*. Cambridge, Mass.: Harvard University Press, 1982.

Glover, Jonathan. *Utilitarianism and Its Critics*. New York: Macmillan, 1990.

Halberstam, Joshua. *Everyday Ethics: Inspired Solutions to Real-Life Dilemmas*. New York: Penguin, 1993.

Kant, Immanuel. *Grounding for the Metaphysics of Morals*. Translated by James W. Ellington. Indianapolis, Ind.: Hackett, 1981.

Kurtz, Paul. *In Defense of Secular Humanism*. New York: Prometheus, 1983.

Mill, John Stuart. *Utilitarianism*. Edited by George Sher. Indianapolis, Ind.: Hackett, 1979.

Rachels, James. *The Elements of Moral Philosophy*. New York: Random House, 1986.

Ross, W. D. *Kant's Ethical Theory*. Oxford: Clarendon Press, 1954.

————. *The Right and the Good*. Indianapolis, Ind.: Hackett, 1988.

Sabini, John, and Maury Silber. *Moralities of Everyday Life*. Oxford: Oxford University Press, 1982.

Singer, Peter. *Practical Ethics*. New York: Cambridge University Press, 1979.

Smart, J. J. C., and Bernard Williams. *Utilitarianism: For and Against*. New York: Cambridge University Press, 1973.

Taylor, Richard. *Virtue Ethics: An Introduction*. Interlaken, N.Y.: Linden Books, 1991.

Wright, Robert. *The Moral Animal: The New Science of Evolutionary Psychology*. New York: Pantheon Books, 1994.

Chapter 2

Ethics and Religion

Passages for Reflection

"If God does not exist, anything is permissible."
—*Fyodor Dostoyevsky*

"God is clever, but not dishonest."
—*Albert Einstein*

"God is no more just or moral than he is blue or square."
—*Voltaire*

"God is dead."
—*Friedrich Wilhelm Nietzsche*

Opening Questions

1. Is morality possible without religion?
2. Is Dostoyevsky right that if God does not exist, anything is permissible?
3. Is God All-Good?

In *The Brothers Karamazov,* Dostoyevsky says through one of his characters that if God does not exist, anything is permissible. The implications of this view are clear: either God exists, in which case we have reason for acting morally, or God does not exist and morality is a waste of time. Whether Dostoyevsky is correct or not, the view he suggests is intriguing. It invites us to ask whether morality is possible without religion, or whether right and wrong conduct are necessarily connected with what God allows and forbids. What connection exists between actions that are right and wrong and actions that God commands or forbids us to do? In raising this question, I am assuming the existence not only of God but of the God presupposed by the Judeo-Christian-Islamic tradition.

Some two thousand years before Dostoyevsky questioned the viability of morality in the absence of God, Plato asked whether morality is a result of God's revelation of values. The discussion of this question occurs primarily in the *Euthyphro,* although it also occurs in Book One of Plato's *Republic* as well. In the *Republic,* Plato has Socrates ask whether a person who had access to the Ring of Gyges (a ring that could make you invisible) would have any reason not to do what he or she wanted regardless of right and wrong. While Plato did not couch the question in terms of the connection between ethics and God's will (or the gods' wills in Plato's case), possessing the Ring of Gyges has affinities with God's nonexistence since possessing the ring, like God's nonexistence, means that it is possible to escape moral responsibility. In the *Euthyphro,* Plato specifically asks whether morality depends on religion.

The *Euthyphro* opens up with Socrates about to face a charge of impiety in the Athenian court, when he meets Euthyphro on the steps of the courthouse. He learns that Euthyphro is about to bring a charge of impiety against his own father for having allegedly murdered a servant—an act that implies much confidence about what is just and pious. After some initial sparring, Socrates elicits from Euthyphro a definition of piety as "that which is dear to the gods." Socrates then asks "whether the pious is dear to the gods because it is pious, or whether it is pious because it is dear to the gods."

In more familiar terms, what Socrates is asking is whether an act is right because God approves of it, or whether God approves of an act because it is right. Let us analyze this question by means of an example. Assuming that the Ten Commandments are indicative of God's will, we may say that God disapproves of adultery since it is explicitly written, "Thou shalt not commit adultery." Now adultery, in most views, is morally wrong. The question we are asking, then, is whether adultery is wrong because God said, "Thou shalt not commit adultery," or whether God said, "Thou shalt not commit adultery" because adultery is wrong.

Let us suppose that adultery is wrong because God said "Thou shalt not commit adultery." This means that what makes adultery wrong is the fact that God commanded us not to commit it. Conversely, if God said, "Thou shalt not commit adultery" because adultery is wrong, then God recognizes the wrongness of adultery and for that reason commands us not to do it. And since the question can be raised about actions other than adultery, such as theft and murder, the question comes down to whether God is authoring or endorsing our code of ethics. In the first case, God is *authoring* our code; in the second case, God is *endorsing* it.

Those who accept the first horn of the Euthyphro dilemma and believe that an action is wrong because God prohibits it commit themselves to *divine command theory*. This theory says that an action is right because and only because God commands us to do it and wrong if God commands us not to do it. This theory is popular with religious extremists who fear subjectivism and relativism in ethics. They claim that we can avoid the uncertainty and vicissitudes that characterize secular ethical systems by grounding ethics in religion. However, the theory is more popular with religious extremists than with moral philosophers, even those of a religious persuasion.

The most straightforward reason why many philosophers reject divine command theory is that right and wrong, good and bad, and so on cannot be translated into what God wants or does not want. And yet, under the terms of theory, such a translation is necessary since the theory says that "right" *means* "what God approves of" and "wrong" *means* "what God disapproves of." But since the meaning of moral terms is not fixed in this way on most theories of meaning, divine command theory is often rejected.

A more interesting reason why some reject divine command theory has to do with an untenable implication of the view. Suppose we were to accept the view that an act is right because and only because God approves of it and wrong because God disapproves of it. Suppose further that God were to revise his list of commandments (which God could do because he can do anything). Instead of commanding us not to commit murder, suppose God were to make murder permissible. Suppose, that is, God were to announce "Thou mayest commit murder" while nullifying the Sixth Commandment. According to divine command theory, it would follow that murder would be morally permissible since anything

God commands is right by definition. And neither will it do for a defender of the theory to argue that this could never come about because God is good, for that would imply that the proponent of the theory is not a proponent of the theory after all! Since many of us would sooner deny that anything God commands is right than accept that "right" means "God commands it," we have yet another reason to reject the theory.

The point could be made another more interesting, if more technical, way. Philosophers have traditionally distinguished between two kinds of statements: analytic and synthetic. An *analytic statement's* predicate is contained in its subject. For example, "The bachelor is an unmarried male" is an analytic statement since the predicate "is an unmarried male" is contained in the subject, "the bachelor." So, too, the statement "The President of the United States is a president" is an analytic statement since the predicate, "is a president," is contained in the subject, "the President of the United States." In a *synthetic statement*, in contrast, the predicate is *not* contained in its subject. For example, "The President is a Democrat" is a synthetic statement since the predicate "is a Democrat" is not contained in the subject, "The President," and so is the statement, "The Pope is Polish."

Analytic statements are known a priori, are necessarily true, and are devoid of content. To say that analytic statements are known a priori means that they are known without the aid of experience. Consider the statement "The bachelor is an unmarried male." We know that if Jones is a bachelor, Jones is an unmarried male without our ever having to meet him. To insist that we must meet Jones to see if he is unmarried is to reveal our ignorance of the term *bachelor*. To say that analytic statements are necessarily true is to say that the denial of these statements is contradictory. The statement "The bachelor is a married male" is a contradiction in terms. Finally, to say that analytic statements are devoid of content is to say that they do not tell us anything we do not already know if we understand the meaning of the terms. Upon being told that a bachelor is an unmarried male, we have not been told anything we don't already know if we know the meaning of the term *bachelor*. To these, we may add that all definitions are couched in terms of analytic statements (for example, "a square is a geometrical figure with four equal angles") although not all analytic statements are definitions (for example, "the coffee cup is a cup").

Synthetic statements have very different features: they are known a posteriori (as a result of experience), are contingently true (their denial is not contradictory), and are filled with content (they add to our stock of knowledge). Consider the statement "The Pope is Polish." We know he is Polish only upon learning that he is of Polish descent, that is, as a result of experience. His being Polish is also not necessarily true. Had he been of Italian descent, he would be Italian instead. (There is nothing contradictory about being Pope and Italian.) Finally, his being

Polish tells us something about him that we did not already know; the information adds to our stock of knowledge.

Having made these distinctions, let us examine the status of the statement put forward by the divine command theorist. What should we make of the statement "What is right is that of which God approves" (or "what is wrong is that of which God disapproves")? The answer is that it is an analytic one, since what is right is *defined* in terms of what God approves, and definitions, as we have seen, are always analytic. But if this is so, then it follows that the statement is known a priori, is necessarily true, and is devoid of content. Divine command theorists have little difficulty construing the statement to be necessarily true; most theorists would insist on that. What they would presumably object to is the statement's being known a priori for if that were so, what was the need for Revelation? And, for obvious reasons, they would find it hard to accept that the statement is devoid of content.

These reasons make accepting the second horn of the Euthyphro dilemma more palatable. This says that "what God approves of is right," which is best construed to be a synthetic statement. The virtue of accepting this horn of the dilemma is that it makes Revelation necessary, which the divine command theorist presumably relishes. It also makes the statement pregnant with content. The down side, from the divine command theorist's point of view, is that this construction implies that it is logically possible for God to approve of what is morally wrong. For just as the Pope's being Italian is logically possible though factually false, so, too, God's approving what is wrong is logically possible even if in fact he endorses what is right.

Divine command theorists, then, are stuck between a rock and a hard place. If they insist that God cannot command evil, then the relationship between morality and religion is necessary but empty of content. The relationship between morality and religion would then be analogous to the relationship between bachelors and unmarried males. On the other hand, if they insist that the relationship is meaningful, then the relationship is contingent and opens up the possibility that God could approve of evil. The situation, however, is not as hopeless as it seems. It could be shown that the relationship between ethics and religion suggested by the second horn of the *Euthyphro* dilemma is not only consistent with a fundamentalist account of ethics and religion, but is the view presupposed by Scripture itself.

That Scripture puts forward such a view can be seen if we ask ourselves what it is we find astounding about the story of Abraham and Isaac, a story that has piqued the interest of many a philosopher, most notably the Danish existentialist Søren Kierkegaard. Recall in Genesis, Chapter XXII, verses 1–13 that Abraham was asked to sacrifice his beloved son Isaac after having been promised that it was through Isaac that Abraham would give birth to a nation. Without so much as objecting to God's order, Abraham binds Isaac to an altar and proceeds to sacrifice him only for God to intervene and command Abraham to sacrifice a ram instead. Presumably, if the relationship between what is right and what God wants were a necessary one, then the story of Abraham and Isaac would not be astounding. Why, it could be asked, should we be shocked by God's order if what God orders is by definition right? That we are so shocked is evidence that Scripture itself rejects such a view.

But perhaps even better support for this view is gleaned from another story involving Abraham: that of Sodom and Gomorrah. Recall that God informed Abraham that God was going to destroy these two cities on account of the irredeemable wickedness that went on there. Upon learning of God's intentions, Abraham asks whether God intends to indiscriminately destroy the righteous as well. After a round of bargaining, God assures Abraham that he will not destroy the righteous with the wicked if Abraham can locate (which he could not) at least ten righteous people in the cities. The point of the story, from our perspective, is that God had apparently intended to do evil; he was to destroy the good with the bad. Only after Abraham challenged God's plan did God do otherwise. It seems, then, that Abraham implicitly rejected divine command theory in allowing that God could do evil, though in fact God did not. But if Abraham was not a divine command theorist and Abraham was a saint of Scripture, we have reason to assert that Scripture itself implicitly rejects a necessary relationship between morality and religion.

One interesting consequence of the position put forward is that it allows for a conception of faith that its competing position does not. Suppose we were to say that the relationship between religion and ethics is a necessary one. Then, having faith that God will never approve evil is not to have faith in any meaningful sense. To have faith in any meaningful sense presupposes the possibility that what you have faith in might turn out to be wrong. Consider, for instance, what it means to have faith that your best friend is innocent of a crime she has been accused of committing. In proclaiming your faith, you are admitting that she might have committed the crime although you believe that she did not. If, however, you were with your friend at the time she was accused of committing the crime, then you would *know* that she did not commit it. But knowing that she did not do it, it is odd to say that you had "faith" in her. Analogously, to have faith in God is to admit that God might ask us to do evil although we believe that he won't. If God could not do evil by definition, then however you characterize your attitude toward God, you cannot characterize it as faith.

Paradoxically, then, divine command theory is not as attractive to the religious fundamentalist as the fundamentalist might expect. At the same time, not subscribing to divine command theory is not tantamount to rejecting religion as altogether irrelevant for morality. Immanuel Kant, who emphatically denied that obeying God's commandments has moral worth as such, nonetheless argued that for the world to be just, doing our duty must ultimately coincide with our being happy. But since this does not always happen in this world, there must be a guarantor that the virtuous will receive their reward in some other world. For Kant, we need God to satisfy our demand for agreement between justice and happiness.

Peter Geach is a contemporary Catholic philosopher who, while explicitly denying that we need revelation in order to *know* right and wrong, nonetheless argues that we need revelation to *do* right and wrong. As Geach sees it, not only do we not need revelation in order to have a morality, it is logically impossible that our knowledge of right and wrong should depend on revelation. Consider the prohibition against lying. "Obviously," says Geach, "a revelation from a deity whose 'goodness' did not include any objection to lying would be worthless; and indeed, so far from getting our knowledge that lying is bad from revelation, we may use this knowledge to test alleged revelations."[1] At the same time, Geach insists that we need revelation in order to see that we must not do evil that good may come of it, such as when we must lie to prevent a murder. In other words, we need God's guarantee that a situation won't arise in which we are required to violate one moral norm in order to satisfy another. Were situations to arise in which we must violate one moral norm in order to satisfy another, then situations would arise in which it would be impossible to act ethically. You would do wrong no matter which way you turned. As Geach sees it, we need God to guarantee for us the possibility of always doing what is right by making sure that we are never placed in such precarious situations.

If, then, the relationship between what is right and what is approved by God is a contingent rather than a necessary one, we are left with the absence of a theory of morality. Unlike the divine command theorist who defines morality in terms of God's will, a rejection of this theory leaves us looking for another. But unlike Socrates who professed ignorance at knowing right and wrong, moral philosophers have advanced theories that are theoretically powerful if not ultimately compelling. Two of these theories, utilitarianism and deontology, are discussed in Chapter 1.

Whether you are a utilitarian, deontologist, or the proponent of any theory other than divine command theory, sooner or later, if you believe in God, you must face the question of how to evaluate God's actions which, being possibly evil, give the appearance of evil on many occasions. In other words, if you subscribe to a theory that makes morality independent of God's will, then it becomes possible for God to do wrong and you can ask whether this in fact is the case. Theologians refer to this sim-

---

[1] Peter Geach, "The Moral Law and the Law of God." In Peter Geach, *God and the Soul.* (London: Routledge and Kegan Paul, 1969). Reprinted in Steven M. Cahn and Joram G. Haber, eds., *Twentieth-Century Ethical Theory* (Englewood Cliffs, N.J.: Prentice Hall, 1995).

ply as "the problem of evil," and it constitutes one of the most intractable problems in philosophy.

In its simplest formulation, the problem of evil is the problem of reconciling the existence of evil with a God who is omniscient, omnipotent, omnipresent, and omnibenevolent. One way to reconcile these is to deny that God exists, or that God has the properties that we ascribe to him. As to denying the existence of God, the solution is logical but is worse than the problem. As to denying that God has the properties attributed to him, we might claim that evil exists but that God is: (1) unaware of it, (2) powerless to stop it, (3) not available to stop it, or (4) not concerned to stop it. However logical these solutions are, most people would sooner deny that God exists than admit that God lacks these defining characteristics.

Another approach is to deny that *evil* exists. This approach initially strikes us as absurd. Newspapers abound with so many reports of evils that it stretches the imagination to wonder just how anyone can deny that evil exists. Even revisionist historians who assert that the Nazis did not murder millions of Jews do so despite all evidence to the contrary. How, then, can you in good faith claim that contrary to appearances, there is no evil?

One way to do this is to insist that what we call evil is really *punishment;* it is deserved suffering. Just as we might conclude that the suffering of an imprisoned criminal is a case of evil if we did not understand the reasons for the criminal's punishment, so, too, we might conclude that what looks like undeserved suffering is evil since we are ignorant of the agent's moral history. The theologian Jonathan Edwards held this view. Edwards apparently thought that all humankind deserves to be punished, and those that are not are spared on account of God's mercy. Maintaining that morality is independent of God's will, Edwards says:

> They [people] deserve to be cast into hell; so that . . . justice never stands in the way, it makes no objection against God's using his power at any moment to destroy them. Yea, on the contrary, justice calls aloud for an infinite punishment of their sins.[2]

This position, a bit more palatable than the outright denial of evil, is still problematic. Plainly and simply, some people do not deserve to suffer in any respectable sense of "dessert." Children of the holocaust, for instance, who were tortured by the perverted misanthropes who were the Nazis, were the victims of evil if anyone is. And this holds true even if, as some have argued, their ancestors were deserving of punishment.

---

[2]Vergilius Ferm, ed., *Puritan Sage: Collected Writings of Jonathan Edwards* (New York, 1953), p. 366.

Think only of being punished for a sin your parents committed and the absurdity of this view becomes painfully obvious.

Still another "solution" to the problem of evil concerns justice in an afterlife. The argument is that while it is true that sometimes the righteous suffer and the wicked prosper, that is only true in this lifetime. In the afterlife, people will receive their just desserts. But this solution has its own set of problems. One concerns the claim that later rewards can compensate for present suffering. Suppose, for instance, you were offered eternal happiness on the condition that you underwent a limited amount of suffering. Suppose, say, that you were offered eternal happiness on the condition that your loved one were to be slowly tortured. (You may even suppose that your eternal happiness included seeing your loved one resurrected and happy.) Would you accept the offer? From one point of view, the offer is reasonable: you trade a finite amount of suffering for an *eternity* of happiness. From another point of view, there can be no compensating the concrete and tangible suffering that your loved one (and you) experienced during that moment of torture. As Shakespeare put it, what is done cannot be undone. It is also not clear how an eternity of happiness would not be tedious.

Another objection to this "solution" concerns the fairness of punishing a person even if you intend to reward that person later. Consider the biblical story of Job on whom God visited all kinds of evils so as to win a bet with the Devil. Even if God intended to compensate Job in the afterlife, we can still ask whether it was fair of God to torture Job simply to win a bet.

Yet another solution to the problem of evil, and perhaps the most plausible of all, is the "free-will" solution. The argument is that since we have free will, the evil in the world is our responsibility. It is no reflection on God's goodness, say, that Hitler killed six million Jews. It was Hitler's fault, not God's. But even against this solution, we can ask whether it is not unreasonable to trade free will for a lesser degree of suffering. Why not trade freedom for happiness?

Friends of the free-will solution will point out that trading free will for greater happiness means trading in what makes us special. It is unreasonable, they say, to make this trade since doing so would be tantamount to denying our humanity. As John Stuart Mill said, "Better to be a human being dissatisfied than a pig satisfied." While not denying the bite of this rebuttal, it is not clear that it would not make sense to trade some free will for a little more happiness (or at least greater wisdom). We could also ask why God gave us free will at all knowing the terrible misfortunes that would be caused by it.

But let us admit that the free-will solution is the most powerful of those we've considered. Let us say, with Mill, that it does not make sense to trade our free will and very humanity for a greater amount of happiness since doing so would rob of us of our very humanity. Still, the implications of this view are far from happy. To see this, suppose that I was witnessing Jones push Smith off a perilous cliff. Suppose that just as Jones is struggling with Smith, Smith notices me and cries out for help. Assume that I can easily ward off Jones's attack and rescue Smith from a certain death but do not do so since interfering would undermine Jones's free will and rob Jones of his humanity. Certainly, Smith would be unpersuaded by my reasoning. I could hardly say, to Smith's face: "I would really like to prevent this from happening but you see it is our free will that gives us our dignity and I must not undermine what is the crowning glory of human existence."

I have tried to show that life is hardly made simpler when we put God in the right and ourselves in the wrong, despite the attractiveness of that view. The Nobel Prize winning novelist, Elie Wiesel, has cautioned us against so simple an equation. In his provocative play, *The Trial of God*,[3] Wiesel suggests that too much vindication of God legitimizes evil. Through an intriguing plot in which God is put on trial for visiting evil upon the Jews of Shamgorod, Wiesel suggests that those who vindicate God legitimize evil. On the other hand, those who call God to account affirm his reality. The relationship between morality and religion is complex and difficult. Those who have said, with Marx, that religion is "an opium for the masses," have not thought deeply enough about the connection between the two institutions.

---

[3]Elie Wiesel, *The Trial of God*, translated by Marion Wiesel (New York: Random House, 1979).

Benjamin Blech is Professor of Talmud at Yeshiva University and spiritual leader of Young Israel, Oceanside, New York. He has served as Scholar-in-Residence in numerous congregations throughout the United States, Canada, and Asia, and has written articles for *Tradition, Jewish Week, Newsweek,* and *Newsday.* He is the author of *The Secrets of Hebrew Words.*

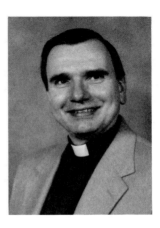

Robert O. Kriesat received his Doctor of Ministry degree from the Graduate Theological Foundation at the University of Notre Dame and currently serves as Pastor of Gloria Dei Lutheran Church in Chatham, New Jersey. In addition, he is the Ecumenical Officer of the New Jersey Synod of the Evangelical Lutheran Church in America as well as a representative of the Metro West Holocaust Remembrance Committee.

Video Presentation

Guests: Rabbi Benjamin Blech, Professor of Talmud, Yeshiva University
Reverend Robert O. Kriesat, Pastor, Gloria Dei Lutheran Church

Student Panel: Wolfe Lewis, Marc Gussen, Joanne Grand

We begin our discussion by considering Dostoyevsky's remark, "If God does not exist, then anything is permissible." Rabbi Blech remarks that this position is implicit in *Genesis* where Adam and Eve eat of the tree of knowledge. Drawing on the medieval Jewish philosopher Maimonides' interpretation of this event, Blech remarks that the significance of the story lies in Adam and Eve's forsaking divine knowledge of right and wrong, which is objective, for human knowledge of right and wrong, which is arbitrary. For Blech, the significance of the Fall lies in our imperfectly deciding for ourselves what is right and what is wrong. He says that once we rely on our fallible sense of reason, we invariably suffer dire consequences. ("Most people use reason the way a drunk uses a lamp post: for support and not illumination.") Reverend Kriesat, on the other hand, maintains that while we do not need revelation to know right and wrong, we certainly don't suffer from having it. He then turns the question around and asks why so many people are avowedly religious and at the same time unethical. In answer to this question, Blech maintains that those individuals who profess to be religious while doing unethical things are not as religious as they pretend to be. Kriesat agrees and reminds us that actions speak louder than words.

Changing the subject, I then ask Blech and Kriesat whether it makes sense to speak of a distinctly Jewish or Christian ethic inasmuch as many moral philosophers take the hallmark of ethics to be its universalizability. Kriesat's answer is that the concept of a Christian ethic *is* coherent, but gets refined and interpreted in the light of culture. Blech agrees while pointing out that Judaism and Christianity differ on how to interpret ethical imperatives. The discussion then turns to what Judaism and Christianity might say on whether it is permissible to lie to a Nazi soldier seeking a Jewish escapee whose whereabouts are known. After considering some possible answers, I ask whether the answer given by the respective religions has decidedly ethical rather than religious content, to which Blech remarks that Judaism does not distinguish between the two, while Kriesat comments that from a Christian perspective such a split is possible.

Blech's book, *Understanding Judaism,* is the next focus of discussion. Blech says that the gist of the book is Judaism's insistence that a person's relationship with another person has priority over a person's relationship with God. After some prompting as to what issues are discussed in the book, Blech mentions capital punishment and says that the Jewish position on the issue, contrary to popular opinion, is that it is *not* endorsed any more than a mother endorses killing her child when she says in anger, "I'll kill you if you do that." Kriesat, on the other hand, can identify no distinctly Christian position.

After the break, Marc Gussen asks Blech if he knows of any movement underway to add to the Talmud so as to allow it to speak to contemporary issues. Blech, an orthodox rabbi, predictably answers that the teachings in the Talmud implicitly contain answers to any dilemma not previously conceived of. Picking up on Kriesat's interest in the cultural interpretations of Christian norms, Wolfe Lewis asks Kriesat just how widespread this view of Christian ethics is. Kriesat responds that some people view Scripture as containing all answers to our ethical questions, while others view Scripture as providing a basis for such answers and leaving the rest up to interpretation. Finally, Joanne Grand asks Blech how Judaism responds to changing needs, and Wolfe asks Kriesat about his view of secular humanism.

In this excerpt from his book, Understanding Judaism, *Benjamin Blech seeks to show that Judaism has two kinds of religious requirements: those that are between God and people, such as the commandment to conduct a Seder on Passover, and those that are between people and people, such as the commandment to show kindness to strangers. Citing various anecdotes and authorities, Blech argues that where a conflict arises between the two kinds of precepts, Judaism insists that people-to-people commandments take precedence over God-to-people commandments.*

Who Comes First, Man or God?

Benjamin Blech

The following story comes from the Torah. It occurred immediately after Abraham circumcised himself, marking his covenant with the Creator as the very first Jew.

"And the Lord appeared to him [Abraham] in the groves of Mamre as he sat in the tent door in the heat of the day. And he [Abraham] lifted up his eyes and looked, and three men were standing directly towards him; and when he saw them, he ran to meet them from the tent door and bowed down to the earth. And he said [to their leader], 'My lord, if now I have found favor in your sight, please do not pass by your servant. Let a little water be fetched [so that you can] wash your feet, and you rest under the tree. And I will fetch a morsel of bread and you will eat to your heart's content; then you shall pass on, for this is the reason you passed by your servant'" (Genesis 18:1–5).

God had come to visit Abraham. According to our Sages, God was fulfilling the mitzvah of visiting the sick. It was three days after Abraham had undergone his circumcision, and he was in great pain. Yet he sat at the door of his tent in the heat of the day, hoping that he might be able to fulfill the mitzvah of hospitality to strangers (*Hakhnasat orḥim*).

Each one of our forefathers exhibited one unique and very special trait. The Mishnah in *Ethics of the Fathers* (1:2) tells us that "the world rests upon three basic principles: on Torah, on sacrifice, and on showing kindness to one's fellow man." Jacob, "the perfect man who lived in tents," would demonstrate the pinnacle that could be reached by the study of Torah. Isaac in the supreme moment of his life, bound to the altar on top of Mount Moriah, would demonstrate readiness for sacrificing his very life. Abraham always demonstrated the greatness of showing kindness to others.

Our Sages constantly stressed that the deeds of our ancestors are a sign for us, their descendants. We are to learn from them. And on the simplest level of all, the story we cited from the Torah portion of *Vayeira* (Genesis 18:1–5) is meant to show us that, even though Abraham did not know that the men he was approaching were angels (as far as he was con-

From Benjamin Blech, *Understanding Judaism: The Basics of Deed and Creed* (1991: pp. 51–66. Reprinted by permission of the publisher, Jason Aronson, Inc., Northvale, NJ, © 1991.

cerned, they could have been idol worshipers), he rushed to take care of them. It was his mitzvah, his mission.

But consider an additional aspect of the story. Abraham was not simply running to bring water to passing strangers. He was, after all, hosting a Guest. Abraham was in the middle of the most important meeting imaginable for any human being, an encounter with his Creator. That, too, is a mitzvah. "Standing before the Lord" entails the duty of prayer (hence the term "Amidah," which means "standing," refers to the Eighteen Benedictions recited in a standing position).

Abraham therefore was not merely fulfilling the mitzvah of hospitality. He was *leaving God to take care of Man*. He made a decision concerning priorities. God was in attendance, man was in need. Abraham was ready to overlook the former in order to deal with the demands of the latter. The Talmud in *Shabbat* (127a) derives an important conclusion from this biblical indicent. "It is a greater mitzvah to take in strangers than to receive the Divine Countenance" (*Gedolah hakhnasat orḥim mi-qabalat penei ha-Shekhinah*). What the Talmud contrasted was not simply one specific mitzvah against another. It was a confrontation between the two categories. Both God and Man beckoned. Abraham understood that when faced with a conflict between the two, he must choose Man rather than God.

It is the same conclusion that Hillel the Elder reached in the famous story of the heathen who came to convert and asked to be taught "the entire Torah on one foot." The renowned scholar Shamai chased the man away, but Hillel responded by rephrasing the famous verse "You shall love your neighbor as yourself" (Leviticus 19:18). What did the prospective convert mean when he asked to be taught the entire Torah "on one foot"? The standard interpretation is that he wanted a brief response. It has been suggested, however, that he was alluding to something else. The Torah also has two "feet." At the Seder, we sing: "Who knows two?" "I know two. Two are the tablets."

We have already identified these two foundations as commandments regulating the person–God relationship and those regulating the person–person relationship. "Teach me the entire Torah on one foot" may well be the very same question we posed regarding priorities within Judaism. If God is concerned with two dimensions, which one is more basic? Is God there for humanity or is humanity there for God? Shamai refused to entertain the question. It is enough for us to know that both areas exist, that both obligations are incumbent upon us. Hillel, however, would not dodge the challenge.

When Hillel reiterated the words "And you shall love your neighbor as yourself"—the words that would serve as the most fundamental principle in the Torah—he was saying that love of humanity is the "one foot" to choose over any other commandment of love in the Torah.

Hillel could just as easily have selected the verse recited twice daily immediately after the *Shema*, "And you shall love the Lord, your God, with all your heart, with all your soul and with all your might" (Deuteronomy 6:5). But he didn't. He chose the obligation to love our neighbor (Leviticus 19:18). We must recognize that the most significant dimension of this famous talmudic story is not just what was said, but what wasn't. If a choice must be made, then just as Abraham did, leave God and take care of a human being in need.

What rationale is there for this decision? Isn't God more important than anyone? Why is welcoming guests more important than receiving the presence of the Divine Countenance? Two answers suggest themselves readily. The first refers to need. A person may be hungry, starving, or even on the verge of death. These needs do not apply to God. Since human need is so much greater, God ordained that we leave Him for the moment to take care of another person.

That certainly must be the intent of the talmudic passage describing the *ḥasid shoteh*, a pious fool. Who is a pious fool? According to the Sages (*Sotah* 21b), it is one who, standing at the seashore, engrossed in prayer, refuses to heed the call for help of a drowning man because he is "in the middle of his service to God." To allow a human being to drown because you are busy telling God how much you care about Him and His world is the ultimate hypocrisy.

There is another, more concise and scientific reason for why our response to human need takes precedence over our response to God. Maimonides puts it well when he explains that every ethical act of goodness and kindness to another person is intrinsically a mitzvah. Every observance of religious ritual, being commanded by God, is also a mitzvah, a deed assuming its religious identity because God demanded it. The divine imperative invests it with sanctity. Likewise, every law governing person-to-person relations is also an expression of the will of God and consequently a divine imperative. The mitzvah towards others is thus doubly blessed. It comes from God and it achieves good for others. A commandment on the first tablet is a "plus one." It is good because God said so. But a law on the second tablet is a "plus two," because it relates to both our relationship to other people and our relationship to God.

This striking distinction has several other significant illustrations.

THE TWO GENERATIONS OF EVIL

At the beginning of human history we learn of two times when God was angry with the human species. In collective terms they represent the two occasions illustrating "original sin." In Jungian terms, our Sages long ago recognized them not simply as events but as archetypes; the first two rebellions in history serve as paradigms for the ways in which humankind can go against the will of the Creator.

The first rebellion was staged by the generation of the Deluge. "And the earth was corrupt before God, and the earth was filled with violence. And God saw the earth and behold it was corrupt for all flesh had corrupted its way upon the earth" (Genesis 6:11–12).

What is the "violence" (ḥamas) to which the Torah makes reference? The Talmud (Sanhedrin 108a) clarifies: "Their fate was not sealed except on account of theft." The Torah also states, "The earth was corrupt before God" to tell us that although they acknowledged God, they rejected the interpersonal ethics and laws that would later be known as the second tablet. The Midrash fills in countless details of what life was like in those days. They reveal a prevailing corruption and violence, in which no one cared about his or her neighbor.

A second, very different rebellion appears in chapter 11.

> And the whole earth was of one language and of one speech. And it came to pass as they journeyed east, that they found a plain in the land of Shinar and they dwelled there. And they said to one another, "Come let us make bricks and burn them thoroughly." And they had brick for stone, and slime for mortar. And they said, "Come let us build a city and a tower with its top in Heaven and let us make us a name, lest we be scattered abroad upon the face of the whole earth." [Genesis 11:1–4]

This was, according to the commentators, a critical moment in the history of the world. It was the turning point from the age of the farmer to the age of the builder, from the pastoral society to the era of science and "enlightenment."

Until the Tower of Babel, humans had only planted and sown, reaped and harvested. Farmers are dependent upon nature and, in their dependency, turn to God. Builders, however, seek to control nature. And in their sense of might they tend to overplay their own role and at times to believe that they are no longer dependent on God. "Come let us build a city and a tower with its top in Heaven" (Genesis 11:4). The Talmud adds (Sanhedrin 109a): "We will build a tower that reaches so high that we will be able to come to the very throne of the Almighty and topple him." The metaphor is profound. The scientist says if we build high enough, if we indicate our ultimate strength, if we reach the skies and soar to the very Heavens, then we, too, with Yuri Gagarin, the first Russian cosmonaut, can say with unbounded egoism, "There is no God, because I was in the Heavens and I did not see Him." "Let us make us a name" was the cry of the first technological wizards. "We will dethrone God." And so they built the Tower of Babel.

Two paradigms of evil. At Sinai they would each be addressed in a different manner. When God would bring law to the world, He would recall the dual capacity for sin. The first tablet would be directed to future generations that would try to duplicate the crime of the Tower of Babel builders. The second would address itself to the men and women of violence of all ages who long ago perished in the flood.

The archetypes of sin are meant not only to teach us of possibilities and potentials. The two stories, in their glaringly different conclusions, serve also to convey a lesson on the relative levels of sinfulness.

When His human creations became corrupt and violent, God wiped them off the face of the earth. The wicked were destroyed; only the righteous were allowed to survive. For had God allowed things to go on as they were, in a short time the wicked would have overwhelmed all the others and evil would have triumphed. Sins committed by one person against another were punished by death. It was the only way God could save His world.

The Tower of Babel had a radically different outcome. "Come let us go down and confound their language, that they may not understand one another's speech" (Genesis 11:7). Each one began to speak a different language. The age of technology ended with babbling; hence, the Tower of "Babel."

A threat to humanity is real. A threat against God is humorous. The first is dangerous and must be dealt with severely. The second is ludicrous and its proponents are simply "scattered abroad upon the face of the earth" (Genesis 11:9).

A "MET MIẒVAH"

There is a special category of the dead known as *met miẓvah*, a reference to a corpse that is not attended to properly. The peculiar expression relates to a law that is incumbent upon every Jew. Normally death places an obligation upon the closest relatives—spouse, parent, child, sibling—to bury and to mourn. They are called *onan* until burial and subsequently *avel*, mourner. No one else has any obligation to the deceased. But if a corpse is found in the field and there are no known relatives, then the Jewish people become the relatives of the deceased. Such a corpse is called a *met miẓvah*, for it is the duty of every single Jew to be involved with his or her burial.

The Talmud (*Berakhot* 19b) outlines a number of situations in which this law applies even for those whom we might assume would be exempt: a father on the way to circumcise his son or to slaughter his Paschal offering; a *Kohen* (priest) on the way to a sacrificial service; or even a *Kohen gadol* (High Priest) on the way to perform the services on Yom Kippur. If any of these individuals saw a *met miẓvah* in the field, he must interrupt his journey in order to bury the dead, even though this will make him spiritually unfit and unable to perform his mission. *Met miẓvah* comes first.

What happened to the halakhic ruling that a person engaged in the performance of one mitzvah is exempt from another? Why wasn't that applied here? Why didn't Abraham apply it when he was in the middle of his mitzvah of speaking to God?

Clearly, the man who was en route to redeem captives was told to ignore the holiday of Sukkot and continue on his way because the conflict pitted the laws governing human relations against those governing the human–divine relationship. In such a case, one proceeds with redeeming the captive and does not choose the sukkah. The exemption applies only if the conflicting laws are from the same category. But if one is in the midst of fulfilling a duty toward God—the sacrifice of a Paschal lamb in the Temple, etc.—and is confronted with the pressing need of another person, then of course one would have to be a "pious fool" to proceed with the service to God and ignore the pressing need of a human being who, unlike the Deity, is not self-sufficient.

MITZVOT WITHOUT BLESSINGS

Does a mitzvah have a blessing? Of course it does. Before we listen to the shofar, or sit in the sukkah, or put on phylacteries, we make a blessing acknowledging the divine source of the law and thanking God for giving us the opportunity to fulfill His will. Yet we know there are many mitzvot that do not have a blessing recited before them. We visit the sick, give charity, and invite strangers without making a blessing. Clearly there is something that these acts have in common that do not demand words of praise to God. Halakhah has made the following distinction: Only person-to-God mitzvot require a blessing. Person-to-person obligations do not. Why not? One beautiful explanation emerges in a moving story. A Sage was once approached by a poor man begging for food. Before responding, the Sage continued with his religious duties. The starving indigent was so far gone, however, that he died before help was offered. The rabbi spent a lifetime trying to atone for his sin. We learn from this that to take time to utter a blessing while another human being is in need is to commit the crime of the pious fool, who pays attention to God while ignoring those in desperate need. In not reciting a blessing before any kind and holy act in the arena of interpersonal duties, we dramatically state that we are so anxious to get to the deed, that God will forgive the renunciation of His praise.

THE DESTRUCTION OF THE TWO TEMPLES

Twice we reached great heights of spirituality. Two times in history we were able to build the Temple. Both times, on the very same date, the ninth of Av, these Temples were destroyed.

A Jew does not believe that the destruction of the Temples came about principally because of the Babylonians and the Romans. The month was Av—which means father, because our Father in Heaven was involved. The day was the ninth of Av because on that day, during their wanderings in the desert, the Jewish people sinned in the incident of the spies, when they cried and said, "We cannot go to Israel." Sin was responsible for the destruction of both Temples, because the spiritual symbol deserved to exist only so long as spiritual reality existed among the people.

But the specific crime of the Jews was different on each occasion: two Temples, two sins, two tablets, two archetypal sins going back to the story of the Generation of the Flood and the Tower of Babel.

The First Temple was destroyed because the Jews worshipped idols; humankind rejected God. The Second Temple was destroyed because of needless hatred between Jews (*sinat ḥinam*), a most horrible conclusion to the incident of Kamtza and Bar Kamtza. The Talmud relates that a man mistakenly invited his enemy to a lavish banquet and then humiliated him by ordering him to leave. The disgraced guest, angry that leading rabbis who observed the incident had not objected to his humiliation, exacted revenge by turning Caesar against the Jews, setting into motion the destruction of the Temple.

Jews do not deserve a Temple if they reject either tablet totally. But let us compare the severity of punishment in these two major events of our history. The First Temple lay in ruins for seventy years; God was ready to forgive and allow it to be rebuilt. The Second Temple, however, touched upon a far more fundamental area. Jews hating fellow Jews brought about a catastrophe whose effects have lasted from the year 70 C.E. to this very day.

Which is more severe? The length of punishment gives us the answer. God is prepared quickly to forgive transgressions against Himself. But the lack of unity and the lack of love among fellow Jews, the rejection of the commandment to love one's neighbor as one's self, is a far more serious matter.

YOM KIPPUR

This is precisely what the holiest day of the year has to teach us. Yom Kippur is a day of atonement and forgiveness. It has tremendous power to bring about rapprochement. We are after all human, and "there is not a righteous man upon earth who does only good and does not sin" (Ecclesiastes 7:20). God understands us and forgives us. But even Yom Kippur with its tremendous power can only achieve its end in one domain and not the other. As stated in the words of the last mishnah in tractate *Yoma*: "Sins between man and God, Yom Kippur atones for; sins between man and his fellow man, Yom Kippur does not atone for, until he appeases his friend." That is why the *The Code of Jewish Law* is so strict with regard to the preparations for this holy day; one may pray to God the entire day, fast, weep, and be contrite and yet still not have the day serve any meaningful purpose. If a person comes on this day to be at peace with God while still warring with parent, spouse, child, or friend, Yom Kippur becomes meaningless.

I will never forget the moment as a child when I was asked to be part of a most moving ceremony. I had just turned bar mitzvah and my father, a rabbi, asked me to come with him together with eight other people to the cemetery. There was a Jew in his congregation who had been at odds with another man. They had been friends who became enemies and then the "enemy" died. Yom Kippur was coming and the man could not face entering the holy day without ending his quarrel. Jewish law allows for a situation such as this, where one of the antagonists has passed away. *The Code of Jewish Law* (131:5) states: "If someone whom you wronged died, then you must bring ten people to his grave and declare: 'I have sinned against the God of Israel and against such and such a man.'" This is what we did. We went to the grave site and one Jew asked another for forgiveness. If he could not ask him in body, he would at least ask his soul. But a Yom Kippur without human reconciliation was recognized as a travesty.

THE HAFTARAH FOR THE HOLIEST DAY

The selection of the *haftarah* (a chapter from the Prophets, read after the portion from the Pentateuch) for Yom Kippur morning makes this vividly clear.

Why is a *haftarah* read every Sabbath and holiday? It goes back to a time when the Jewish people were not allowed by the law of the land to read the proper section from the Torah itself. Guards were stationed in the synagogue to ensure that the Torah would not be taken out of the Ark and that the Scriptural reading from the Five Books of Moses would not be recited.

Jews found an alternative, still in use, which is based both on the concept of maintaining tradition as well as the awareness that, in the Diaspora, similar decrees are always possible. A section was chosen from another portion of the Bible, comparable in content to the original required reading. In the case of the Sabbath, every *haftarah* contains a reference to what our Sages felt was the most important idea of that week's Torah portion. In the case of a holiday, the Sages selected a reading that captured its single most crucial idea.

The *haftarah* is therefore the most powerful "fixed sermon." When a rabbi is faced with the formidable task of selecting an idea for weekly discussion, it obviously varies from year to year. The Sages, however, had to choose one idea that would permanently serve to summarize the message of the particular day. Its importance can therefore not be underestimated.

And what did the Sages choose as the reading for Yom Kippur morning? It is one of the most moving sections in the Book of Isaiah (57:14–58:14), where the prophet addresses himself to the question Jews often asked with regard to God's apparent unresponsiveness. Why doesn't the Almighty pay attention to our fasting? If we are pious, why is there no proper Heavenly response? How to explain the punishment visited upon those who seem perfect in their fulfillment of the laws and responsibilities toward God?

Isaiah responds: (Chapter 58)

1. Cry aloud, spare not,
   Lift up they voice like a horn,
   And declare unto My people their transgression,
   And to the house of Jacob their sins.
2. Yet they seek Me daily,
   And delight to know My ways;

As a nation that did righteousness,
And forsook not the ordinance of
their God,
They ask of Me Righteous ordinances,
They delight to draw near unto God.

3. 'Wherefore have we fasted, and Thou
seest not?
Wherefore have we afflicted our soul,
and Thou takest no
knowledge?'—
Behold, in the day of your fast ye
pursue your business,
And exact all your labors.

4. Behold, ye fast for strife and
contention,
And to smite with the fist of
wickedness;
Ye fast not this day
So as to make your voice to be heard
on high.

5. Is such the fast that I have chosen?
The day for man to afflict his soul?
Is it to bow down his head as a
bulrush,
And to spread sackcloth and ashes
under him?
Wilt thou call this a fast,
And an acceptable day to the Lord?

6. Is not this the fast that I have chosen?
To loose the fetters of wickedness,
To undo the bands of the yoke,
And to let the oppressed go free,
And that ye break every yoke?

7. Is it not to deal thy bread to the
hungry,
And that thou bring the poor that are
cast out to thy house?
When thou seest the naked, that thou
cover him,

And that thou hide not thyself from
thine own flesh?

8. Then shall thy light break forth as the
morning,
And thy healing shall spring forth
speedily;
And thy righteousness shall go before
thee,
The glory of the Lord shall be thy
reward.

9. Then shalt thou call, and the Lord will
answer;
Thou shalt cry, and He will say: "Here
I am."
If thou take away from the midst of
thee the yoke,
The putting forth of the finger, and
speaking wickedness;

10. And if thou draw out thy soul to the
hungry,
And satisfy the afflicted soul;
Then shall thy light rise in darkness,
And thy gloom be as the noonday;

How can religious people not find favor in
the eyes of God? If they restrict their understanding of religion to the first tablet and ignore the second. What good is it to Me, asks
the Almighty, if you pile up a plethora of good
deeds towards Me, while at the same time you
strike with a Godless fist against another
human being?

Which are more important—commandments relating to people or those relating to
God? On Yom Kippur day, the day that only
has power to absolve us of our sins against
God but not against others, we read the *haftarah* in which the prophet clearly and powerfully proclaims the correct answer.

In this brief essay, Robert O. Kriesat takes up the question of whether there is a distinctly "Christian" ethic. Noting some of the difficulties that attend the delineation of what might be called the Christian conception of ethics, *Kriesat argues against such a conception and points out how adherents of the diverse religions of the world approach ethical issues always within the context of how they understand their respective traditions.*

The Possibility of a "Christian" Ethic

Robert O. Kriesat

Among theologians concerned about the relationship between morality and religion, it is often asked whether it is possible to have a "Jewish" or a "Christian" ethic. The question is a valid and good question; but it is one which defies a simplistic answer.

It has often been noted that there are Christians who act ethically, but there is no "Christian" ethic. This, it seems to me, is too simple an answer, especially when one looks over the many books and seminary courses titled "Christian Ethics."

In a recent essay in *Time* magazine (October 31, 1994), Barbara Ehrenreich seems to be taking the entire Judeo-Christian faith tradition to task for failing to live up to some common ethical standard. She notes, "As it approaches the estimable age of 2,000, the Judeo-Christian ethic seems to be going all soft and senile." She then concludes, "We're the post-Judeo-Christian generation, and the Christian Right is turning out to be nothing more than Christian Lite."[1] Such comments in a nonreligious publication suggest that the secular world perceives little difference between Jewish, Christian, or other ethical systems. Are views such as these valid?

In Rabbi Benjamin Blech's article, "Who Comes First, Man or God?," (pp. 51–57) the answer seems to be man. While the article draws upon Jewish faith and life, the end result is one with which few Christians would find fault. Is this then "Jewish ethics"? If Christians can subscribe to such ideas, do such ideas become Christian? I believe we'd have to say no.

The frustrating part of trying to delineate a "Christian position" is knowing there is not a single Christian position, but a number of them. Being either theologically liberal or conservative would greatly affect the position a denomination or an individual would take on a given issue. One must bear in mind that speaking of the Christian faith includes traditions such as Roman Catholic, Eastern Orthodox, mainline Protestant, and the more conservative Protestant churches; and this does not even take into account the various independent churches and religious movements, all of which claim to be Christian and to speak and act in a Christian way. Very often these positions and actions are in opposition to each other, in some cases even within the same denominational family.

In some seminaries, courses bear the name "Christian Ethics;" in others, similar courses bear the name "Biblical Ethics." The content often varies, with the former often attempting to move beyond the thought patterns of the biblical world, yet remaining faithful to it. Yet, even in Biblical Ethics courses, great differences arise over the interpretation of a given text and its relationship to action today.

To illustrate the complexity of the issue of determining *a* Christian ethic, I will look to my own denomination, the Evangelical Lutheran Church in America. This denomination of some 11 million members came into being in 1988 as the result of a merger of three smaller Lutheran bodies. This church is committed to providing social statements that provide guidance for its membership. However, social statements of the Evangelical Lutheran Church in American cannot "bind the individual conscience, or presume to provide definitive judgment on all the moral questions in dispute."[2]

This method of dealing with ethical decisions, while broadly based, does raise some problems. In the work being done on a statement of human sexuality, the following paragraph was communicated to the entire church regarding the process:

> Through this process, many have communicated what they want the social statement to say. A common insistence is that it clearly be grounded in the Scriptures and theology of the Church. Some expected the study itself to provide the definitive answers they seek, rather than to open up questions and invite the people of God to reflect and share their thinking and convictions about these matters. Some found such question-raising to compromise the authority of the Scripture, or to be manipulative or confusing. Others expressed appreciation that Lutherans continue to explore difficult ethical issues with openness, seeking new understandings in light of Scripture.[3]

Such a process of reaching consensus on various ethical and social issues takes many items into account before issuing a statement to the church community. In a study booklet leading up to a statement on the environment, the process was stated as follows:

ELCA deliberation pays attention to God's Word and God's world. It relies upon God's revelation, God's gift of reason, and the guidance of the Holy Spirit. It benefits from the experience, knowledge, and imagination of people who study the earth, live close to the land, or already feel the effects of environmental degradation.[4]

When the process is completed and seminary faculty, bishops, and congregations have studied and responded to the statement, it is sent to a national convention of the church to be voted upon. Only then does it become the position of the Evangelical Lutheran Church in America, though "not binding the individual conscience."

The church has provided statements on issues as varied as *Peace and Politics* (1984), *Aging and the Older Adult* (1968), *Capital Punishment* (1966), *Conscientious Objection* (1968), *Death and Dying* (1982), *Sex, Marriage, and the Family* (1970), *Abortion* (1984), and *World Community—Ethical Imperatives in an Age of Interdependence and Economic Justice* (1980).

These statements, plus many more, stated the official position of the church, but did not claim to be "the Christian" position on a given issue. It was only the position of one church engaged in a study of an ethical issue, meant to give guidance to its members. Thus, while informing the individual by providing background (both scriptural and cultural), it never settled the issue. In many cases, just the opposite occurred.

An example would be the recent release of the first draft of *The Church and Human Sexuality: A Lutheran Perspective* in 1993. This document was meant as a study document and dealt with issues relating to our sexual beings: teenagers and sex, marriage, responsible procreation and parenting, single adults, gay and lesbian persons, and other issues. The outcry from many parts of the church forced the Division for Church in Society to restudy and rewrite the entire document.

Complaints were voiced that the document was un-Christian, unbiblical, un-Lutheran, and not responsive to peoples' needs. This was most notable on the sections relating to gay and lesbian people and the call for a more loving response to issues related to homosexuality. A new document entitled *Human Sexuality: A Working Draft* was published in October 1994.

Thus, reviewing the history of social statements in my own denomination, we can begin to see how difficult it is to say that a given position is *the* Christian ethic. While church bodies such as the Roman Catholics can issue statements binding the consciences of its members, most other Christian churches cannot. I am not sure that I personally would want to share in that tradition, even though in some situations it might indeed be easier.

Can we thus answer a resounding no to the question of whether or not there can be a "Christian" ethic? I don't believe we can. None of us—Jew, Christian, Hindu, or a follower of Islam—comes to the study of ethics in a vacuum. As Rabbi Blech so ably shows in this book *Understanding Judaism,* we make our ethical decisions based on our faith, traditions, or lack thereof. While adherents of Christianity, Judaism, Unitarianism, and the Ethical Culture Society could stand together on many ethical issues facing humanity today, each would approach the issues differently and draw upon different illustrations to support their positions.

Even those positions arrived at from the understanding of divine revelation will not be the same. Our understanding of that revelation differs; and, therefore, in many cases the ethical positions arrived at also will differ. Therefore, it would be possible to say there is such a thing as a "Christian" ethic, but defining that ethic in a specific case may be almost impossible.

In dealing with issues such as abortion and homosexuality, it may be easier to bring together from Jewish, Catholic, and Protestant communities groups opposed to both issues than to have a group from the same religious tradition united in its views. This in itself is not bad, only a reality. It allows us to see and experience the growing cooperation among all of humanity in dealing with some of the most confusing ethical issues of our growing technological society. The future will demand of us the ability to draw on our traditions to make informed ethical decisions and the willingness to join hands with those of other traditions in making our society a truly ethical one for all peoples.

Therefore, I would answer the original question—"Is it possible to have a Jewish or a Christian ethic"—with a definite yes, and no. As with so many ethical issues, this answer is less than helpful, even though it may be honest. It would seem to me imperative for individuals to be fully immersed in their religious tradition before attempting to speak authoritatively for such. This is yet another way of saying that all our decisions ought to be well thought out and based on the available knowledge.

Endnotes

1. Barbara Ehrenreich, "Remember the Sermon on the Mount?" *Time*, October 31, 1994.
2. *Introduction—The Church and Human Sexuality: A Lutheran Perspective (First Draft)* (Chicago, Ill.: Evangelical Lutheran Church in America, October 1993).
3. Ibid.
4. *Introduction. Caring for Creation* (Chicago, Ill.: Division for Church in Society, Evangelical Lutheran Church in America, August 1991).

Closing Questions

1. Argue for or against the view that God is a utilitarian. Do the same for deontology.

   _____

   _____

   _____

2. It was suggested earlier in this chapter that the stories of Abraham and Isaac and Abraham and Sodom and Gomorrah provide evidence that Scripture does not support divine command theory. Can you think of other incidents from the Hebrew or Christian Bible or the Koran that lend support to this view?

   _____

   _____

   _____

3. In *Genesis*, Cain slew Abel and was held responsible for his action. What, if anything, does this say about the relationship between ethics and religion?

   _____

   _____

   _____

4. Distinguish between evil in nature and evil in humankind and discuss the problem of evil in the light of each.

   _____

   _____

   _____

5. Is the concept of a Jewish or Christian ethic coherent? Discuss this question in the light of the claim that the very essence of morality is its universalizability.

   _____

   _____

   _____

   _____

6. Kant argued that an action has moral worth only if the motive for performing it is respect for the moral law. Thus, Kant thought that we should not steal because stealing is wrong. How does this relate to not doing wrong because God commanded us not to?

_____

_____

_____

7. Think of some of the actions commanded or prohibited by your religion. Which of these, if any, would you classify as having moral content?

_____

_____

_____

8. What is the relationship between "sinning" and "doing what is morally wrong"? Are all sins morally wrong? If not, which ones are? Which ones are not?

_____

_____

_____

_____

9. Of the various solutions to the "problem of evil" discussed in the chapter, which do you favor and why? (If you do not favor any of them, what solution, if any, do you support?)

_____

_____

_____

_____

10. Comment on the Freudian claim that God is the "superego writ large."

_____

_____

_____

_____

For Further Reading

Aquinas, Saint Thomas. *Summa Theologica*, I–II. In *Basic Writings of Saint Thomas Aquinas*, vol. 2, edited by Anton C. Pegis. New York: Random House, 1945.

Augustine, Saint. *De civitate Dei (The City of God)*, pp. 413–426.

Flew, Anthony. *God and Philosophy*. London: Hutchinson, 1966.

Kant, Immanuel. *Religion within the Limits of Reason Alone*. Translated by Theodore M. Greene and Hoyt H. Hudson. New York: Harper & Row, 1960.

Kierkegaard, Søren. *Fear and Trembling*. Translated by Walter Lowrie. Garden City, N.Y.: Doubleday, 1954.

Nielsen, Kai. *Ethics Without God,* rev. ed. Buffalo: Prometheus Books, 1990.

Outka, Gene, and J. P. Reeder, eds. *Religion and Morality*. New York: Doubleday Anchor, 1973.

Plato. *Euthyphro*. In *Five Dialogues*. Translated by G. M. A. Grube. Indianapolis, Ind.: Hackett, 1981.

Quinn, Philip L. *Divine Commands and Moral Requirements*. Oxford: Clarendon Press, 1978.

Ramsey, I. T., ed. *Christian Ethics and Contemporary Philosophy*. London: S. C. M. Press, 1966.

Weiss, Raymond L., and Charles Butterworth, eds. *Ethical Writings of Maimonides*. New York: Dover, 1975.

Chapter 3

Animal Rights

Passages for Reflection

"Nothing can be more obvious than that all animals were
created solely and exclusively for the use of man."

—*Thomas Love Peacock*

"In studying the traits and dispositions of the so-called lower
animals, and contrasting them with man's, I find the result
humiliating to me . . . . Man is the only animal that blushes,
or needs to."

—*Mark Twain*

"It is difficult to picture the Creator conceiving of a program
of one creature (which he has made) using another living
creature for purposes of experimentation. There must be
other less cruel ways of obtaining knowledge."

—*Adlai Stevenson*

"Men sometimes speak as though the progress of science
must necessarily be a boon to mankind, but that, I fear, is one
of the comfortable nineteenth-century delusions which our
more disillusioned age must discard. . . . Moral progress has
consisted in the main of protest against cruel customs, and of
attempts to enlarge human sympathy."

—*Bertrand Russell*

Opening Questions

1. Are human beings more important than animals? Why?

2. Do animals have rights? If so, what rights do they have and what does this imply about how we should treat them?

3. What human needs, if any, are sufficiently important to warrant the infliction of pain and suffering on animals?

Are animals worthy of moral consideration, or are they strictly a resource to be used and abused? What rights, if any, do animals have and what obligations, if any, do these rights entail? These are just some of the questions we face if, as some people have urged, animals have rights that human beings are obligated to respect.

There is no denying that we use animals in many ways: we eat them, experiment on them, race them, fight them, hunt them for sport, and keep them as pets. We also test household products on them and make a variety of products from their uneaten carcasses. We hunt them for their tusks, their blubber, and their fur, and we kill them for candle wax, soap, oil, and perfume. But if animals have rights as their advocates contend, then such practices are wrong, and to the extent that we support those practices, we do so at our peril. It behooves us, then, to determine whether animals are morally considerable and whether we should withhold support from those institutions that use them as resources.

Let us begin by sharpening our inquiry. In asking whether animals are morally considerable, we are asking whether animals belong to the class of beings about whom it makes sense to apply moral terms, for example, *rights, obligations,* and *virtues.* In one sense, the answer is *no.* For one thing, animals are under no moral obligation to do or forbear from doing anything. Though I may be peeved with my dog for chewing the *Times,* or upset at my cat for clawing the sofa, it is absurd to say that the animals did what they *ought not to have done;* that they have violated a moral obligation. This is so even if my pets were trained to behave otherwise. For like infants, animals are not morally responsible for their behavior. To be responsible, it is necessary to understand what one's obligation is. This explains why human beings become more and more responsible as they mature—why we hold infants responsible for nothing, toddlers for getting into the Jello, and adolescents for not mowing the lawn or straightening up their rooms. In a word, the greater the cognitive development, the more accountable an agent is for its actions. For this reason, animals are not bound by moral obligations.

But if the concept of obligation is inappropriate for animals, the same cannot be said for the concept of a "right." Infants have rights but have no obligations, and the same may be said of the aged, the mentally retarded, and possibly fetuses. Thus, to ask whether animals are morally considerable is essentially to ask whether animals have rights. And while only beings who have both rights and obligations may be regarded as "fully" morally considerable, beings that have rights may still be regarded as "partially" considerable. The question comes down to whether animals have rights, in particular, the right to life but also, perhaps, the right to be free.

The question "What is a right?" has stirred much philosophical debate. For purposes of our discussion, we may say that whatever rights are, they entail (are correlative with) obligations; call this the "correlativity thesis of rights and obligations." According to this thesis, to say of a person that he or she has a right means that the rest of us are obligated to respect the person's right. This can be explained as follows. Consider what you mean when you say that your CD collection is yours or that you have a property right to it. This means that others are obligated not to use it without your permission. Or consider what having a right to liberty means. It means that others are obligated not to confine you or prevent you from speaking what is on your mind. Thus, to say of a person that she or he has a right means that the rest of us are obligated to respect that right. However, to say we are obligated to respect someone's rights does not mean that rights are absolute and inviolable. The bearer, say, of a right to privacy in the home has the right to exclude unwelcome guests, but not to manufacture child pornography. Similarly, the possessor of a right to liberty has the right to do whatever she chooses, but not to falsely yell "fire" in a public place. Rights end where other rights begin, and so whatever obligations we have toward the right holder, they are always qualified in a relevant way. Otherwise put, we are morally obligated to respect the rights of others provided the rights are exercised in legitimate ways leaving open the question of what is to count as "legitimate."

If, then, animals have the right to life, we have a moral obligation not to kill them. The obligation in question does not fall on other animals. A lion, for instance, is not obligated to refrain from killing a wildebeest, nor is a fox to refrain from killing a hedgehog. If animals have rights and rights are correlative with obligations, the obligations with which the rights are correlative fall on human beings. This follows from what has been said about human beings as fully considerable, whereas nonhuman animals are partially considerable.

This analysis of rights and obligations helps to resolve a dilemma that vegetarians must face if they own domestic pets. Vegetarians must sooner or later decide whether it is permissible to feed their pets store-bought products that invariably contain animal byproducts. Using the preceding analysis, the answer is yes, since even if people are obligated not to kill animals for food, animals are under no similar obligation. I reserve for later a discussion of the significance of the fact that some animals are carnivores while human beings are omnivores.

We can now identify three positions that philosophers have taken on the question of whether animals have rights that human beings are obligated to respect. The first position, sometimes referred to as the "no obligation view," holds that animals have no rights and so human beings may treat them as they wish with impunity. Supporters of this view are Plato, whom we find referring to animals as "lawless beasts," and the nineteenth-century Jesuit, W. D. Ritchie, who refers to animals as "of the order of sticks and stones." In this view, just as we may bend, twist, and otherwise mutilate sticks and stones at our pleasure, so may we mutilate cows, pigs, chickens, and other "lawless beasts."

The "no obligation view" has not found many adherents, owing, presumably, to its manifest callousness. A less abhorrent view, sometimes referred to as the "indirect obligation view," holds that while animals lack rights that doesn't mean we may treat them with impunity. Instead, we must treat them with respect because by disrespecting animals we disrespect one another, at least when animals are the property of people. Consider, in this light, the duty to respect another person's property. That we have such a duty is not explainable by any rights the property itself has; the duty we have is owed to its owner. Analogously, if we have a duty to treat animals with respect, we have it in virtue of the animal's relationship to our fellow human beings. Our duty not to be cruel to our neighbor's pet is, then, only indirectly owed to the pet, while it is directly owed to the pet's owner.

But what of stray or wild animals, that is, animals that have no owner? Here, friends of the indirect obligation view assume a connection between how we treat animals and how we treat people. This "causal thesis" says that how we treat animals is causally related to how we treat one another. The idea is that if we are cruel to animals, we will invariably be cruel to human beings, and, conversely, if we are kind to animals, we will be kind to one another. This explains why we should not be cruel to animals even if they are not the property of human beings. Kant and Aquinas hold this view. Kant says: "He who is cruel to animals becomes hard in his dealings with men," and "tender feelings toward dumb animals develop humane feelings toward mankind." Aquinas appeals to this view in an effort to explain how the Bible can at once exhort us to seek dominion over the beasts of the field while at the same time commanding us not to muzzle the ox or slay a bird with its young. This, at least, is Aquinas's understanding of the Christian position on animal rights. The Jewish philosopher Maimonides, on the other hand, maintains that while God cares for people as individuals, he cares for animals only as a species.[1]

---

[1] See Maimonides, *The Guide of the Perplexed,* translated by Chaim Rabin (Indianapolis: Hackett Publishing Co., 1995), pp. 166–168.

The causal thesis is plausible even if it is largely armchair psychology. Teenagers, for instance, who delight in seeing cats tortured are just those persons we would expect to become cruel adults. Similarly, a person who, as the saying goes, would not even hurt a flea is just the kind of person we would expect to be sensitive in her dealings with people. Yet we have reason to think that the thesis is false. Hunters, for example, are hardly the callous Nazis that the causal thesis would predict them to be, and some people, while kind to animals, are less than kind to their fellow human beings. We can imagine someone who is cruel to animals precisely so as not to be cruel to human beings. Think of beleaguered employees who vent their frustrations on their dogs so as not to take it out on their spouses or kids.

Regarding those who are cruel to people but kind to animals, imagine persons who are kind to animals because they find animals nonthreatening, while they are callous to people whom they find quite threatening. The villain in the early James Bond films comes to mind. Recall how he would lovingly stroke his Persian cat while plotting to destroy the civilized world. A film in which the causal thesis is given more serious consideration is Michael Cimino's *The Deerhunter* (1978).

We might also question whether how we treat some people is causally connected to how we treat others. Professional assassins, for example, are sometimes reputed to be tender and loving family members as were members of Hitler's notorious *SS*, the Nazis responsible for implementing Hitler's policy of genocide. On the other hand, we might question the assumption that professional assassins (and Nazis) are really the loving family members they are reputed to be. Recall, in this context, a famous scene from Francis Ford Coppola's *The Godfather* (1972) where Michael Corleone (Al Pacino) tells his wife (Diane Keaton) with the most believable face he could muster that he did not have his brother-in-law killed when in fact he did. Could someone who could so convincingly lie in such a manner (and kill a brother-in-law) really be considered a kind and loving husband? Analogously, we might question whether someone who is cruel to animals though kind to people is, when push comes to shove, really kind or whether he is, like Michael Corleone, a person on whom we should not turn our backs. In any event, the causal thesis is an empirical matter whose truth can be established only after controlled experiments by trained psychologists. Absent such tests, friends of the indirect view rest their case on speculative grounds.

Whatever the truth of the causal thesis, its implications are significant for the indirect view. Friends of the thesis hold that we should not be cruel to animals lest we be cruel to our fellow human beings. Animals themselves have no moral standing. This means, by implication, that should the thesis be false, we would have no reason to respect animals any more than we should respect sticks and stones. This "anthropocentric" implication leads some philosophers to reject the indirect obligation view and embrace the "direct obligation view." In this view, animals have rights that people are directly obligated to respect.

Two foundations exist for the direct obligation view: utilitarian and deontological. Utilitarianism has long recognized sentience, or the ability to experience pleasure and pain, as the morally relevant criterion for the possession of rights. Hence, we have every reason to include animals in the moral community since animals, or most of them, are sentient. While the question of which animals are sentient is finally one for biologists to decide, Peter Singer has suggested that crustaceans and lower forms of animals are not sentient. Technically speaking, then, the greatest happiness principle should be amended to read: "the greatest happiness for the greatest number of *sentient beings* with each sentient being counting as one." Indeed, Bentham anticipated this when he declared:

> The day may come when the rest of the animal creation may acquire those rights which could have been withholden from them but by the hand of tyranny. The French have already discovered that the blackness of the skin is no reason why a human being should be abandoned without redress to the caprice of a tormentor. It may one day come to be recognized that the number of the legs, the villosity of the skin, or the termination of the *os sacrum* are reasons equally insufficient for abandoning a sensitive being to the same fate. What else is it that should trace the insuperable line? Is it the faculty of reason, or perhaps the faculty of discourse? But a full-grown horse or dog is beyond comparison a more rational, as well as a more conversable animal, than an infant of a day or a week or even a month old. But suppose they were otherwise, what would it avail? The question is not, can they reason? nor can they talk? but can they suffer? (*Introduction to Principles of Morals and Legislation*, Ch. 17)

And Mill was ready to stake the entire principle of utility on the question of whether animals have rights.[2]

Among contemporary utilitarians, the Australian philosopher Peter Singer has most vociferously championed the rights of animals. In his celebrated book, *Animal Liberation,* Singer argues that the "equality of interests" principle should be understood to include the interests of animals. That is, we should, before we act, determine how our actions will affect all sentient beings and then choose the act that maximizes happiness. Failure to take into consideration all sentient beings leaves us open to the charge of *speciesism*—the practice of discriminating on the basis of species membership.

Singer is aware that speciesism sounds more like a parody of the animal rights movement than a serious philosophical doctrine. But he claims that it shares a logic similar to such pernicious "isms" as racism

---

[2]See John Stuart Mill, "Whewell on Moral Philosophy." In Mill's *Collected Works*, Vol. 10, pp. 185–187.

and sexism. The essence of racism is discrimination against members of a race, and the essence of sexism is discrimination against members of a sex. What racism and sexism have in common is that biological considerations are put forward as morally relevant, which, all things being equal, they are not. This is not to deny that biological considerations are never relevant. How tall you are is relevant to whether you are picked to play on your college basketball team; the short person who is left out cannot complain of unfair practices. But discriminating on the basis of color (or sex) is, more often than not, as arbitrary as, say, discriminating on the basis of eye color or hair color. So if biological considerations are morally irrelevant, then we should not discriminate on the basis of species. After all, our genetic makeup accounts for the color of our skin, for our sex, and for our species as well.

Some people will be impatient with this. They will say that a difference exists between genetic differences *inter* species and genetic differences *intra* species. However, a simple thought experiment will help fortify Singer's point. Imagine, if you will, an intergalactic space traveler (call him Galactus) who is as powerful to us as we are to animals. From time to time Galactus likes to snack on planetary life and he has landed on earth with the intention of devouring us. What claims, if any, would we have against such a menacing figure?

Unless you believe that might makes right, you will probably claim that we have rights that Galactus is obligated to respect notwithstanding our genetic differences. You would insist upon this even if, for one reason or another, we were unable to make it intelligible to him. (Perhaps our cries of help will sound no differently than the wails of cattle.) That infants are unable to defend their rights against adults does not mean that infants do not have rights. Similarly, in Singer's view, we would have rights against Galactus for no other reason than we are sentient creatures; our genetic differences would be simply irrelevant.

You may be tempted to argue that the situation is changed if Galactus needed human meat for survival rather than just as an intergalactic snack. We could no more expect Galactus to willingly die when he could survive and flourish only by consuming human flesh. So, too, you might argue, just as people need animal meat for survival, they have the right to feed upon nonhuman animals. This argument, however, will not do. It is false that people need the meat of animals to survive. Quite to the contrary, people can live well with no meat at all. Not only is avoiding animal flesh possible, it is, if we are to believe current scientific findings, highly desirable. We are told that consumption of red meat contributes to coronary heart disease and many forms of cancer. But even if we did need animal flesh to survive, we would be hard pressed to show why we need leather shoes, upholstery, handbags, and belts, not to mention why we must test household products on animals when less painful alternatives are readily available.

But the real point utilitarians want to make is that the benefits of exploiting animals do not outweigh the costs and for that reason alone it is unjustifiable. They point out, for instance, that giving up commercial animal farming would enable us to grow enough grain to feed people around the world several times over while at the same time eliminating needless suffering.[3] For the utilitarian, increasing happiness and decreasing suffering is what ethics is all about.

Suppose, however, that animal farming were not cost-effective. Suppose that the amount of pleasure we received from animal products exceeded the pain the animals went through to manufacture these products. Would the utilitarian at that point condone treating animals as a resource for human enjoyment? Presumably, the answer is yes. For even were we to give the interests of animals equal consideration in deciding what conduct is ethically permissible, nothing would be wrong with treating animals as a resource if the benefits of doing so outweighed the costs. But then, too, nothing would presumably be wrong with treating people as a resource if the benefits of doing so outweighed the costs. That, say its critics, is what is wrong with a position grounded in utilitarian ethics. For this reason, some thinkers have sought to ground the rights of animals in deontological considerations. Tom Regan is one such thinker and offers the most serious alternative to Singer.

Regan's point of departure is his insistence that animals have "inherent" rather than "instrumental" value. *Inherent value* means value in and of itself; *instrumental value* means value as a means to an end. Thus, happiness is often thought to have inherent value, while money is a classical example of an instrumental value. As Regan sees it, animals (and people for that matter) have inherent value; they are valuable in and of themselves and not merely for what they can provide. To put the matter in a Kantian way, animals are members of a kingdom of ends; they are to be treated as an end and never merely as a means to an end. But valuing animals only as a means to an end is precisely what utilitarians do even if utilitarians are animal rights activists. That this is so follows from the utilitarian claim that we should not use animals as a resource since it is not cost-effective to do so, implying that if things were otherwise, that is, if it were cost-effective to do so, we could use them with impunity.

The questions we must ask are: Why think animals have inherent value? Why not maintain that their value lies in their utility to human beings, that is, in their potential to serve as food and clothing? Regan's answer is that an animal's life matters to it. It matters to veal calves, for instance, that they are quartered in narrow stalls, tethered with chains around their necks, and fed a nutritionally deficient diet. This concern for its welfare, according to Regan, accounts for an animal's having in-

---

[3]See Peter Singer, *Animal Liberation* (New York: Avon Books, 1975), Ch. 4.

herent value. Animals have inherent value because they are beings for whom their lives have value.

But does an animal's welfare "matter" to it? If we think of what it means for something to matter, it becomes far from clear that an animal's welfare matters to it although it may matter to us. An animal's welfare would matter if it were able to make value judgments, but it is not so able. So it is questionable to say that an animal's welfare matters to it even if animals hide from their predators, protect their young, and migrate to different climates. Instead of maintaining that animals perform such actions for reasons owing to their concern for life, a better explanation is that animals are genetically programmed to behave in these ways. (Then again, the same may be true of human beings.)

But an even greater problem arises if we assume, with Regan, that animals have inherent value and have it in equal proportion to humans. If animals, like people, all have inherent value, then their relative value could not be compared. And that would mean that in trade-off situations, where, for example, we are forced to choose between saving the life of a person and the life of a goat, we would have no choice but to flip a coin. Would you flip a coin in that instance? If so, is Regan's response plausible?[4]

Serious problems, then, arise with grounding the rights of animals in either utilitarianism or the deontological considerations put forward by Regan. Perhaps, though, we do not need to resort to either theory to show that it is wrong to treat animals as a resource. Without committing to the view that right and wrong conduct is determined by consequences, and without committing to the view that what happens to animals matters to them, perhaps all we need to say is that animals suffer, and we should not inflict suffering for trivial purposes. Since treating animals that way is cruel, this may suffice to show why we should not mistreat them.

---

[4]For a fuller discussion of Regan's position, see my "The Utility of Intrinsic Value." In *Inherent and Instrumental Value,* edited by John Abbarno (The Netherlands and Atlanta: Rodopi Press, Forthcoming 1997).

Tom Regan is Professor of Philosophy at North Carolina State University. Specializing in ethics, he has written extensively on animal rights. He is the author of *The Case for Animal Rights* (1984) and editor, along with Peter Singer, of *Animal Rights and Human Obligations* (1976). He is also the founder of the "Culture and Animals Foundation" (Raleigh, N.C.) and is an award-winning videomaker.

Video Presentation

Guest: Tom Regan, Professor of Philosophy, North Carolina State University, and Founder of the "Culture and Animals Foundation"

Student Panel: Cathy Capasso, Jennifer Romeo, Michael Wright

Regan and I begin our discussion by establishing the fact that animals suffer before they reach us in the guise of food, and that they are treated cruelly in an effort to test the toxicity of common household products. Since a picture speaks a thousand words, a clip is shown from Regan's video, *We Are All Noah*, portraying some of the ways that animals suffer. Regan says that the goal of these and other videos he produces is to make "the invisible visible, the inaudible audible. To educate, educate, educate." We enter into a discussion of whether it is best to go easy on the viewers of such tapes. Regan maintains that he prefers to be honest but in small doses, fearful that too much exposure to animal suffering will alienate his viewers. I, on the other hand, question whether such reluctance is good policy, suggesting that we already have too many ways of disguising the way we mistreat animals. I mention the way we disguise our food, preferring to call such things as ground cow "hamburgers" and decorating them with condiments on bread. Citing Porphyry, Regan adds that whatever we may call it, what we are eating are decaying corpses.

Having established that animals suffer, we next question what should be done about it. Regan talks about how the battle to liberate animals is an ethical battle in addition to a political and ideological one. He decries that special interest groups such as the meat and fashion industries have portrayed animal activists as a group of crazies who are antihuman and antiscience.

We next turn to the philosophical arguments offered in defense of animal rights, whereupon Regan expounds his position. Playing devil's advocate, I offer some standard objections to Regan's position. I argue, for instance, that animals lack rights because they cannot reason. Regan's response is that the same holds true for children and the mentally retarded, yet no one denies that these people have rights. I also ask whether he sees any relevant differences between using animals for food, medical science, and cosmetics, to which he replies no. He then reminds viewers that moral evolution is a slow process and that we are only now realizing that we can do the things we are used to doing (brush our teeth, shampoo our hair, etc.) in a more peaceful way.

Following the break, Cathy Capasso asks Regan whether the scientific community has reliable alternatives to the animal models. Regan says yes and discusses what some of these alternatives are. Having viewed Regan's video, *Declaration of War on Vivisection*, Michael Wright is suspicious of Regan's methods. He asks Regan if it is the proper business of the moral philosopher to be a social activist. Commenting that academics too often sit in their ivory towers, Regan responds that the job of a moral philosopher is to be a whole human being, which sometimes entails being socially active. Finally, Jennifer Romeo asks what, practically, can be done to alleviate animal suffering. Regan answers that we can start by purchasing products that are cruelty free ("think globally and act locally"), but most of all, stop eating meat. Calling the fork a "weapon of violence," he reports the astonishing fact that in the United States alone, more than 10,000 animals are slaughtered per minute for purposes of human consumption.

In this essay, Regan asks whether the practice of animal farming is morally justified and whether we are morally obligated to become vegetarians. He begins his inquiry with a discussion of moral anthropocentrism, a view he attributes to Kant and others that asserts that only human interests should be considered when we decide how we should act. In this view, the interests of animals do not matter (or do not matter much). After demonstrating how utilitarians such as Peter Singer reject this view and are thus opposed to commercial animal farming, Regan nonetheless argues that we have a duty to become vegetarians, but it is not a duty that is grounded in considerations of utility. Among the reasons he gives is a problem he sees with utilitarianism itself; it makes the rightness of an action dependent on how others behave. Because of this, Regan is drawn to another line of argument that makes deontological considerations relevant to the duty to become vegetarians. Regan begins with the premise that having a right means that others have a duty to respect that right. Because persons, claims Regan, have moral rights, and some animals are persons, it follows that human beings have a duty to respect animal rights. The way this is done is by abolishing commercial animal farming and becoming vegetarians.

Ethical Vegetarianism and Commercial Animal Farming

Tom Regan

INTRODUCTION

Time was when a few words in passing usually were enough to exhaust the philosophical interest in the moral status of animals other than human beings. "Lawless beasts," writes Plato. "Of the order of sticks and stones," opines the nineteenth-century Jesuit W. D. Ritchie. True, there are notable exceptions, at least as far back as Pythagoras, who advocated vegetarianism on ethical grounds—Cicero, Epicurus, Herodotus, Horace, Ovid, Plutarch, Seneca, Virgil: hardly a group of "animal crazies"! By and large, however, a few words would do nicely, thank you, or, when one's corpus took on grave proportions, a few paragraphs or pages. Thus we find Kant, for example, by all accounts one of the most influential philosophers in the history of ideas, devoting almost two full pages to the question of our duties to animals, while St. Thomas Aquinas, easily the most important philosopher-theologian in the Catholic tradition, bequeaths perhaps ten pages to the topic at hand.

Times change. Today an even modest bibliography listing titles of the past decade's work on the moral status of animals would easily equal the length of Kant's and Aquinas' treatments combined, a quantitative symbol of the changes that have taken place, and continue to take place, in philosophy's attempts to rouse slumbering prejudices lodged in the anthropocentrism of western thought.

With relatively few speaking to the contrary (St. Francis always comes to mind in this context), theists and humanists, rowdy bedfellows in most quarters, have gotten along amicably when questions were raised about the moral center of the terrestrial universe: *Human* interests form the center of that universe. Let the theist look hopefully beyond the harsh edge of bodily death, let the humanist denounce, in Freud's terms, this "infantile view of the world," at least the two could agree that the moral universe revolves around us humans—our desires, our needs, our goals, our preferences, our love for one another. The intense dialectic now characterizing philosophy's assaults on the traditions of humanism and theism, assaults aimed not only at the traditional account of the moral status of animals but at the foundation of our moral dealings with the natural environment, with Nature generally—these assaults should not be viewed as local skirmishes between obscure academicians each bent on occupying a deserted fortress. At issue are the validity of alternative visions of the scheme of things and our place in it. The growing philosophical debate over our treatment of animals and the environment is both a symptom and a cause of a culture's attempt to come to critical terms with its past as it attempts to shape its future.

At present there are three major challenges being raised against moral anthropocentrism. The first is the one issued by *utilitarians;* the second, by proponents of *moral rights.* . . . This essay offers brief summaries of each position with special reference to how their advocates answer two questions: (a) Is vegetarianism required on ethical grounds? and (b) Judged ethically, what should we say, and what should we do, about commercial animal agriculture? To ask whether vegetarianism is required on ethical grounds is to ask whether there are reasons other than those that relate to one's own welfare (for example, other than those that relate to one's own health or financial well-being) that call for leading a vegetarian way of life. As for the expression "commercial animal agriculture," that should be taken to apply to the practice of raising animals to be sold for food. The ethics of other practices that involve killing animals (for example, hunting, the use of animals in science, "the family farm" where the animals raised are killed and eaten by the people who raise them, etc.) will not be considered, except in passing, not because the ethics of these practices should not demand our close attention but because space and time preclude our giving them this attention here. Time and space also preclude anything approaching "complete" assessments of the three views to be discussed. None can be proven right or wrong in a few swift strokes. Even so, it will be clear where my own sympathies lie.

TRADITIONAL MORAL ANTHROPOCENTRISM

Aquinas and Kant speak of the anthropocentric tradition. That tradition does not issue a blank check when it comes to the treatment of animals. Morally, we are enjoined to be kind to animals and, on the other side of the coin, not to be cruel to them. But we are not enjoined to be the one and prohibited from being the other because we owe such treatment to *animals themselves*—not, that is, because we have any duties *directly* to nonhumans; rather, it is because of *human* interests that we have these duties regarding animals. "So far as animals are concerned," writes Kant, "we have no direct duties. . . . Our duties to animals are merely indirect duties to mankind." In the case of cruelty, we are not to be cruel to animals because treating them cruelly will develop a habit of cruelty, and a habit of cruelty, once it has taken up lodging in our breast, will in time include human beings among its victims. "(H)e who is cruel to animals becomes hard also in his dealings with men." And *that* is why cruelty to animals is wrong. As for kindness, "(t)ender feelings towards dumb animals de-velop humane feelings toward mankind."[1] And *that* is why we have a duty to be kind to animals.

So reasons Kant. Aquinas, predictably, adds theistic considerations, but the main storyline is the same, as witness the following passage from his *Summa Contra Gentiles.*

Hereby is refuted the error of those who said it is sinful for a man to kill dumb animals: for by divine providence they are intended for man's use in the natural order. Hence it is no wrong for man to make use of them, either by killing, or in any other way whatever. . . . And if any passages of Holy Writ seem to forbid us to be cruel to dumb animals, for instance to kill a bird with its young: this is either to remove men's thoughts from being cruel to other men, and lest through being cruel to animals one becomes cruel to human beings: or because injury to an animal leads to the temporal hurt of man, either of the doer of the deed, or of another: or on account of some (religious) signification: thus the Apostle expounds the prohibition against muzzling the ox that treadeth the corn.[2]

To borrow a phrase from the twentieth-century English philosopher Sir W. D. Ross, our treatment of animals, both for Kant and Aquinas, is "a practice ground for moral virtue." The *moral game* is played between human players or, on the theistic view, human players plus God. The way we treat animals is a sort of moral warmup, character calisthenics, as it were, for the moral game in which animals themselves play no part.

THE UTILITARIAN CHALLENGE

The first fairly recent spark of revolt against moral anthropocentrism comes, as do other recent protests against institutionalized prejudice, from the pens of the nineteenth century utilitarians, most notably Jeremy Bentham and John Stuart Mill. These utilitarians—who count the balance of pleasure over pain for all sentient creatures as the yardstick of moral right and wrong, and who reject out of hand Descartes' famous teaching that animals are "nature's machines," lacking any trace of conscious awareness—recognize the direct moral significance of the pleasures and pains of animals. In an oft-quoted passage, Bentham enfranchises animals within the utilitarian moral community by declaring that "(t)he question is not, Can they talk?, or Can they reason?, but, Can they suffer?"[3] And Mill stakes the credibility of utilitarianism itself on its implications for the moral status and treatment of animals, writing that "(w)e (that is, those who subscribe to utilitarianism) are perfectly willing to stake the whole question on this one issue. Granted that any practice causes more pain to animals than it gives pleasure to man: is that practice moral or immoral? And if, exactly in proportion as human beings raise their heads out of the slough of selfishness, they do not with one voice answer 'immoral' let the morality of the principle of utility be forever condemned."[4] The duties we have regarding animals, then, are duties we have *directly to them*, not indirect duties to humanity. For utilitarians, animals are themselves involved in the moral game.

Viewed against this historical backdrop, the position of the contemporary Australian moral philosopher Peter Singer can be seen to be an extension of the attack on the tradition of moral anthropocentrism initiated by his utilitarian forebears. For though this sometimes goes unnoticed by friend and foe alike, Singer, whose book *Animal Liberation* is unquestionably the most influential work published in the 1970s on the topic of the ethics of our treatment of animals, *is* a utilitarian.[5] That view requires, he believes, observance of the equality of interests principle. This principle requires that, before we decide what to do, we consider the interests (that is, the preferences) of all those who are likely to be affected by what we do *and* weigh equal interests equally. We must not, that is, refuse to consider the interests of some of those who will be affected by what we do because, say, they are

Catholic, or female, or black. *Everyone's* interests must be considered. And we must not discount the importance of comparable interests because they are the interests of, say, a Catholic, woman, or black. Everyone's interests must be weighed *equitably*. Of course, to ignore or discount the importance of a woman's interests *because she is a woman* is the very paradigm of the moral prejudice we call sexism, just as to ignore or discount the importance of the interests of blacks (or Native Americans, Chicanos, etc.) are paradigmatic forms of racism. It remained for Singer to argue, which he does with great vigor, passion, and skill, that a similar moral prejudice lies at the heart of moral anthropocentrism, a prejudice that Singer, borrowing a term first coined by the English author and animal activist Richard Ryder, denominates *speciesism*.[6] Like Bentham and Mill before him, Singer, the utilitarian, *denies* that we are to treat animals well in the name of the betterment of humanity, *denies* that we are to do this because this will help us discharge our duties to our fellow humans, *denies* that acting dutifully toward animals is a moral warmup for the real moral game played between humans, or, as theists would add, between humans-and-humans-and-God. *We owe it to those animals who have interests to take their interests into account, just as we also owe it to them to count their interests equitably.* Our duties regarding animals are, in these respects, *direct* duties we have to them, not indirect duties to humanity. To think otherwise is to give sorry testimony to the prejudice of speciesism Singer is intent upon unmasking.

FARMING TODAY

Singer believes that the utilitarian case for ethical vegetarianism is strengthened when we inform ourselves of the changes taking place in commercial animal farming today. In increasing numbers, animals are being brought in off the land and raised indoors, in unnatural, crowded conditions—raised "intensively," to use the jargon of the animal industry, in structures that look for all the world like factories. Indeed, it is now common practice to refer to such commercial ventures as *factory farms*. The inhabitants of these "farms" are kept in cages, or stalls, or pens, or closely-confined in other ways, living out their abbreviated lives in a technologically created and sustained environment: automated feeding, automated watering, automated light cycles, automated waste removal, automated what-not. And the crowding: as many as nine hens in cages that measure eighteen by twenty-four inches; veal calves confined to twenty-two inch wide stalls; hogs similarly confined, sometimes in tiers of cages—two, three, four rows high. Could any impartial, morally sensitive person view what goes on in a factory farm with benign approval? Certainly many of the basic interests of the animals are simply ignored or undervalued, Singer claims, because they do not compute economically. Their interest in physical freedom or in associating with members of their own species, these interests routinely go by the board. And for what? So that we humans can dine on steaks and chops, drumsticks and roasts, food that is simply inessential for our own physical well-being. Add to this sorry tale of speciesism on today's farm the enormous waste that characterizes animal industry, waste to the tune of six or seven pounds of vegetable protein to produce a pond of animal protein in the case of beef cattle, for example, and add to the accumulated waste of nutritious food the chronic need for just such food throughout the countries of the Third World, whose populations characteristically are malnourished at best and literally starving to death at worst—add all these factors together and we have, Singer believes, the basis for the utilitarian's answers to our two questions. In response to the question, "Is vegetarianism required on ethical grounds?" the Singer-type utilitarian replies affirmatively. For it is not for self-interested reasons that Singer calls us to vegetarianism (though such reasons, including a concern for one's health, are not irrelevant). It is for ethical reasons that we are to take up a vegetarian way of life. And as for our second question, the one that asks what we should think and do about commercial animal farming, Singer's utilitarian argument prescribes, he thinks, that we should think ill of today's factory farms and act to bring about significant humane improvements by refusing to purchase their products. Ethically considered, we ought to become vegetarians.

THE CHALLENGE TO UTILITARIANISM

Singer, then, is the leading contemporary representative of the utilitarian critique of the anthropocentric heritage bequeathed to us by humanism and theism. How should we assess his critique? Our answer requires answering two related questions. First, How adequate is the general utilitarian position Singer advocates? Second, How adequate is Singer's application of this general position to the particular case of commercial animal agriculture and, allied with this, the case for ethical vegetarianism? A brief response to each question, beginning with the second, will have to suffice. Consider Singer's claim that each of us has a duty to become a vegetarian. How can this alleged duty be defended on *utilitarian* grounds? Well, on this view, we know, the act I *ought* to perform, the act I have a *duty* to do, is the one that will bring about the best consequences for all those affected by the outcome, which, for Singer, means the act that will bring about the optimal balance of preference satisfaction over preference frustration. But it is naive in the extreme to suppose that, were I individually henceforth to abstain from eating meat and assiduously lead a vegetarian existence, this will improve the lot of a single animal. Commercial animal farming simply does not work in this way. It does not, that is, fine-tune its production to such a high degree that it responds to the decisions of each individual consumer. So, no, the individual's abstention from meat will not make the slightest dent, will not effect the smallest change, in commercial animal agriculture. No one, therefore, Singer included, can ground *the individual's* ethical obligation to be vegetarian on the effects *the individual's* acts will have on the welfare of animals.

Similar remarks apply to the other presumed beneficiaries of the individual's conversion to vegetarianism. The starving, malnourished masses of the Third World will not receive the food they need if I would but stop eating animals. For it is, again, naive in the extreme to suppose that the dietary decisions and acts of any given *individual* will make the slightest difference to the quality of life for any inhabitant in the Third World. Even were it true, which it is not (and it is not true because commercial animal agriculture is not so fine-tuned in this respect either), that a given amount of protein-rich grain *would not be fed to animals* if I abstained from eating meat, it simply would not follow that this grain *would find its way to any needy human being*. To suppose otherwise is to credit one's individual acts and decisions with a kind of godlike omnipotence a robust sense of reality cannot tolerate. Thus, since the type of utilitarianism Singer advocates prescribes that we decide what our ethical duties are by asking what will be the consequences of our acts, and since there is no realistic reason to believe that the consequences of my abstaining from meat will make any difference whatever to the quality of life of commercially raised farm animals or the needy people of the Third World, the alleged duties to become a vegetarian and to oppose commercial animal agriculture lack the kind of backing a utilitarian like Singer requires.

Here one might attempt to defend Singer by arguing that it is the total or sum of the consequences of *many* people becoming vegetarians, not just the results of each individual's decisions, that will spare some animals the rigors of factory farms and save some humans from malnutrition or starvation. Two replies to this attempted defense may be briefly noted. First, this defense at most gives *a sketch of a possible* reply; it does not give a finished one. As a utilitarian, Singer must show that the consequences for everyone involved would be better if a number of people became vegetar-

ians than if they did not. But to show this, Singer must provide a thorough rundown of what the consequences would be, or would be in all probability, if we abstained from eating meat, *or* ate less of it, *or* ate none at all. And this is no easy task. Would the grains not fed to animals even be grown if the animal industry's requirements for them were reduced or eliminated? Would there be an economically viable market for corn, oats, and other grains if we became vegetarians? Would farmers have the necessary economic incentive to produce enough grain to feed the world's hungry human beings? Who knows? In particular, does Singer know? One looks in vain to find the necessary empirical backing for an answer here. Or consider: Suppose the grain is available. From a utilitarian point of view, would it be best (that is, would we be acting to produce the best consequences) if we made this grain available to the present generation of the world's malnourished? Or would it be better in the long run to refuse to aid these people at this point in time? After all, if we assist them now, will they not simply reproduce? And won't their additional numbers make the problem of famine for the next generation even more tragic? Who knows what the correct answers to these questions are? Who knows what is even "most likely" to be true? It is not unfair to a utilitarian such as Singer to mark the depths of our ignorance in these matters. And neither is it unfair to emphasize how our ignorance stands in the way of his attempt to ground the obligatoriness of vegetarianism on utilitarian considerations. If we simply do not know what the consequences of our becoming vegetarians would be, or are most likely to be, and if we simply do not know whether the consequences that would result would be, or are most likely to be, better than those that would obtain if we did not become vegetarians, then we simply lack any semblance of a utilitarian justification for the obligation to become vegetarians or for mounting a frontal assault on commercial animal agriculture. The decision to lead a vegetarian way of life and, by doing so, to lodge a moral complaint against commercial animal agriculture, viewed from the perspective of Singer's utilitarianism, must be diagnosed as at best symbolic gestures.

Aside from these matters, what can be said about the adequacy of utilitarianism in general? That is a question raised earlier to which we must now direct our attention. There is a vast literature critical of utilitarian theory, and it will obviously not be possible to survey it here. Here let us note just one difficulty. Utilitarianism, at least as understood by Singer, implies that whether *I* am doing what I ought to do is crucially dependent on what *other* people do. For example, although the consequences of *my* abstaining from eating meat are too modest to make any difference to how animals are raised or whether grains are made available to needy people, if enough *other* people join me in a vegetarian way of life we could collectively bring about changes in the number of animals raised, how they are raised, what use is made of grain, etc. The situation, in other words, is as follows: If enough people join me so that the consequences of what we do *collectively* make some impact, then what I do might be right, whereas if too few people join me, with the result that the consequences of what we do fail to make any difference to how animals are raised, etc., then I am *not* doing what is right.

To make the morality of an individual's acts depend on how others behave is a highly unsatisfactory consequence for any moral theory. When people refuse to support racist or sexist practices (for example, in employment or education), they do what is right, but their doing what is right does not depend on how many *other* people join them. The number of people who join them determines how many people do or support what is right, *not* what is right in the first place. Utilitarianism, because it makes *what is right* dependent in many cases on how many people act in a certain way, puts the moral cart before the horse. What we want is a theory that illuminates moral right and wrong independently of how many people act in this or that way. And that is precisely what utilitarianism, at least in the form advocated by Singer, fails to give us. For all its promise as

an attack on the anthropocentric traditions of humanism and theism, for all its insistence on the direct relevance of the interests of animals, and despite the radical sounding claims made by utilitarians in criticism of current practices on the farm and in the laboratory, utilitarianism proves to be more ethical shadow than substance. If we look beyond the rhetoric and examine the arguments, utilitarianism might not change these practices as much as it would fortify them.[7]

THE RIGHTS VIEW

An alternative to the utilitarian attack on anthropocentrism is what we shall call "the rights view."[8] Those who accept this view hold that (1) certain individuals have certain moral rights, (2) these individuals have these rights independently of considerations about the value of the consequences of treating them in one way or another, and (3) the duty the individual has to respect the rights of others does not depend on how many other people act in ways that respect these rights. The first point distinguishes proponents of the rights view from, among others, those utilitarians like Bentham and Singer who deny that individuals have moral rights; the second distinguishes advocates of the rights view from, among others, those utilitarians such as Mill who hold that individuals have moral rights if, and only if, the general welfare would be promoted by saying and acting as if they do; and the third point distinguishes those who champion the rights view from, among others, any advocate of utilitarianism who holds that my duty to act in certain ways depends on how many other people act in these ways. According to the rights view, certain individuals have moral rights, and my duty to act in ways that respect such an individual's (A's) rights is a duty I have directly to A, a duty I have to A that is not grounded in considerations about the value of consequences for all those affected by the outcome, and a duty I have to A whatever else others might do to A. *Those who advocate animal rights, understanding this idea after the fashion of the rights view, believe that some of those individuals who have moral rights, and thus some of those to whom we have duties of the type just described, are animals.*

GROUNDS FOR THE RIGHTS VIEW

To proclaim "the moral rights of Man" sounds good but is notoriously difficult to defend. Bentham, who writes more forcefully to support what he rejects than to establish what he accepts, dismisses rights other than legal rights as "nonsense upon stilts." So we will not settle the thorny question about human rights of an essay's reading or writing. And, it goes without saying, the moral rights of animals must remain even less established. Were Bentham in his grave (in fact he remains above ground, encased in glass in an anteroom in University College, London, where he is dutifully brought to dinner each year on the occasion of his birthday) he would most certainly roll over at the mere mention of *animal* rights! Still, something needs to be said about the rational grounds for the rights view.

An important (but not the only possible) argument in this regard takes the following form: Unless we recognize that certain individuals have moral rights, we will be left holding moral principles that sanction morally reprehensible conduct. Thus, in order to avoid holding principles that allow such conduct, we must recognize that certain individuals have moral rights. The following discussion of utilitarianism is an example of this general line of argument.

Utilitarians cut from the same cloth as Bentham would have us judge moral right and wrong by appeal to the consequences of what we do. Well, suppose aged Aunt Bertha's heirs could have a lot more pleasure than she is likely to have in her declining years if she were to die. But suppose that neither nature nor Aunt Bertha will cooperate: She simply refuses to die as expeditiously as, gauged by the interest of her heirs, is desirable. Why not speed up the tempo of her demise? The reply given by Bentham-type utilitarians shows how far they are willing to twist our moral intuitions to save their theory. If we were to kill Aunt Bertha, especially if we took care to do so painlessly, then, these utilitarians submit, we would do no

wrong to Aunt Bertha. However, if *other* people found out about what we did, they would quite naturally grow more anxious, more insecure about their own safety and mortality, and these mental states (anxiety, insecurity, and the like) are painful. Thus, so we are told, killing Aunt Bertha is wrong (if it is) because of the painful consequences for others!

Except for those already committed to a Bentham-style utilitarianism, few are likely to find this account satisfactory. Its shortcomings are all the more evident when we note that *if* others did not find out about our dastardly deed (and so were not made more anxious and insecure by their knowledge of what we did), and *if* we have a sufficiently undeveloped conscience not to be terribly troubled by what we did, and *if* we do not get caught, and *if* we have a jolly good time with Aunt Bertha's inheritance, a much better time, in fact, than we would have had if we had waited for nature to run its course, then Bentham-style utilitarianism implies that we did nothing wrong in killing Aunt Bertha and, indeed, acted as we morally ought to have acted. People who, in the face of this kind of objection, remain Bentham-type utilitarians, may hold a consistent position. But one pays a price for a "foolish consistency." The spectacle of people "defending their theory to the last" in spite of its grave implications must, to put it mildly, take one's moral breath away.

There are, of course, many ethical theories in addition to utilitarianism, and many versions of utilitarianism in addition to the one associated with Bentham. So even if the sketch of an argument against Bentham's utilitarianism proves successful, the rights view would not thereby "win" in its competition with other theories. But the foregoing does succeed in giving a representative sample of one argument deployed by those who accept the rights view: If you deny moral rights, as Bentham does, then the principles you put in their place, which, in Bentham's case, is the principle of utility, will sanction morally reprehensible conduct (for example, the murder of Aunt Bertha). If those who affirm and defend the rights view could show this given *any* initially plausible theory that denies moral rights, and if they could crystalize and defend the methodology on which this argument depends, then they would have a powerful reason for their position.

THE VALUE OF THE INDIVIDUAL

The rights view aspires to satisfy our intellect, not merely our appetite for rhetoric, and so it is obliged to provide a theoretical home for moral rights. Part, but by no means the whole, of this home is furnished by the rights views' theory of value. Unlike utilitarian theories (for example, value hedonism), the rights view recognizes *the value of individuals,* not just the value of their mental states (for example, their pleasures). Following custom, let us call these latter sorts of value "intrinsic values" and let us introduce the term "inherent value" for the type of value attributed to individuals. Then the notion of inherent value can be explained as follows. First, the inherent value of an individual who has such value is not the same as, is not reducible to, and is incommensurate with the intrinsic value of that individual's, or of any combination of individuals', mental states. The inherent value of an individual, in other words, is not equal to any sum of intrinsic values (for example, any sum of pleasures). Second, all individuals who have inherent value have it equally. Inherent value, that is, does not come in degrees; some who have it do not have it more or less than others. One either has it or one does not, and all who have it have it to the same extent. It is, one might say, a categorical concept. Third, the possession of inherent value by individuals does not depend on their utility relative to the interests of others, which, if it were true, would imply that some individuals have such value to a greater degree than do others, because some (for example, surgeons) have greater utility than do others (for example, bank thieves). Fourth, and relatedly, individuals cannot acquire or lose such value by anything they do. And fifth, and finally, the inherent value of individuals does not depend on what or how others think or feel about

them. The loved and admired are neither more nor less inherently valuable than the despised and forsaken.

Now, the rights view claims that any individual who has inherent value is due treatment that respects this value (has, that is, a *moral right* to such treatment), and though not everything can be said here about what such respect comes to, at least this much should be clear. We fail to treat individuals with the respect they are due whenever we assume that how we treat them can be defended *merely* by asking about the value of the mental states such treatment produces for those affected by the outcome. This must fail to show appropriate respect since it is tantamount to treating these individuals as if they lacked inherent value—as if, that is, we treat them as we ought whenever we can justify our treatment of them *merely* on the grounds that it promotes the interests other individuals have in obtaining preferred mental states (for example, pleasure). Since individuals who have inherent value have a kind of value that is not reducible to their utility relative to the interests of others, we are not to treat them merely as a means to bringing about the best consequences. We ought not, then, kill Aunt Bertha, given the rights view, even if doing so brought about "the best" consequences. That would be to treat her with a lack of appropriate respect, something she has a moral right to. To kill her for these reasons would be to violate her rights.

WHICH INDIVIDUALS HAVE INHERENT VALUE?

Even assuming the rights view could succeed in providing a coherent, rationally persuasive theoretical framework for "the rights of Man," further argument would be necessary to illuminate and justify the rights of animals. That argument, not surprisingly, will be long and tortuous. At least we can be certain of two things, however. First, it must include considerations about the criteria of right possession; and, second, it will have to include an explanation and defense of how animals meet these criteria. A few remarks about each of these two points will have to suffice.

Persons[9] are the possessors of moral rights, and though most human beings are persons, not all are. And some persons are not human beings. Persons are individuals who have a cluster of actual (not merely potential or former) abilities. These include awareness of their environment, desires and preferences, goals and purposes, feelings and emotions, beliefs and memories, a sense of the future and of their own identity. Most adult humans have these abilities and so are persons. But some (the irreversibly comatose, for example) lack them and so are not persons. Human fetuses and infants also are not persons, given this analysis, and so have no moral rights (which is not to say that we may therefore do anything to them that we have a mind to; there are moral constraints on what we may do in addition to those constraints that involve respect for the moral rights of others—but this is a long story. . . !).

As for nonhumans who are persons, the most famous candidate is God as conceived, for example, by Christians. When believers speak of "the blessed Trinity, three persons in one," they don't mean "three human beings in one." Extraterrestrials are another obvious candidate, at least as they crop up in standard science fiction. The extraterrestrials in Ray Bradbury's *Martian Chronicles*, for example, are persons, in the sense explained, but they assuredly are not human beings. But, of course, the most important candidates for our purposes are animals. And they are successful candidates if they perceive and remember, believe and desire, have feelings and emotions, and, in general, actually possess the other abilities mentioned earlier.

Those who affirm and defend the rights of animals believe that some animals actually possess these abilities. Of course, there are some who will deny this. All animals, they will say, lack all, or most, or at least some of the abilities that make an individual a person. In a fuller discussion of the rights view, these worries would receive the respectful airing they deserve. It must suffice here to say that the case for animal rights involves the two matters mentioned and explained—first, considerations about the criteria of right possession (or, alternatively, personhood), and, second, considerations that show that some animals satisfy these criteria. Those who would squelch the undertaking before it gets started by claiming that "it's *obvious* that animals cannot be persons!" offer no serious objection; instead, they give sorry expression to the very speciesist prejudice those who affirm and defend the rights of animals seek to overcome.

LINE DRAWING

To concede that some animals are persons and so have moral rights is not to settle the question, *Which* animals are persons? "Where do we draw the line?" it will be asked; indeed, it must be asked. The correct answer seems to be: We do not know with certainty. Perhaps there is no exact line to be drawn in this case, any more than there is an exact line to be drawn in other cases (for example, "Exactly how tall do you have to be to be tall?" "Exactly how old must you be before you are old?"). What we must ask is where in the animal kingdom we find individuals who are *most like* paradigmatic persons—that is, most like us, both behaviorally and physiologically. The greater the similarity in these respects, the stronger the case for believing that these animals have *a mental life similar to our own* (including memory and emotion, for example), a case that is strengthened given the major thrust of evolutionary theory. So, while it remains a matter of uncertainty *exactly* where we are to draw this line, it is implausible to deny that adult mammalian animals have the abilities in question (just as, analogously, it would be implausible to deny that eighty-eight-year-old Aunt Bertha is old because we don't know exactly how old someone must be before they are old). To get this far in the argument for animal rights is not to finish the story, but it is to give a rough outline of a major chapter in it.

THE INHERENT VALUE OF ANIMALS

Moral rights, as explained earlier, need a theoretical home, and the rights view provides this by its use of the notion of inherent value. Not surprisingly, therefore, the rights view affirms this value in the case of those animals who are persons; not to do so would be to slide back into the prejudice of speciesism. Moreover, because all who possess this value possess it equally, the rights view makes no distinction between the inherent value human persons possess as distinct from that possessed by those persons who are animals. And just as *our* inherent value, as persons, does not depend on our utility relative to the interests of others, or on how much we are liked or admired, or on anything we do or fail to do, the same must be true in the case of animals who, as persons, have the same inherent value we do.

To regard animals in the way advocated by the rights view makes a truly profound difference to our understanding of what, morally speaking, we may do to them, as well as how, morally speaking, we can defend what we do. Those animals who have inherent value have a moral right to respectful treatment, a right we fail to respect whenever we attempt to justify what we do to them by appeal to "the best consequences." What these animals are due, in other words, is the same respectful treatment we are. We must never treat them in this or that way merely because, we claim, doing so is necessary to bring about "the best consequences" for all affected by the outcome.

The rights view therefore calls for the total dissolution of commercial animal agriculture as we know it. Not merely "modern" intensive rearing methods must cease. For though the harm visited upon animals raised in these circumstances is real enough and is morally to be condemned, its removal would not eliminate the basic wrong its presence compounds. The *basic* wrong is that animals raised for commercial profit are viewed and treated in ways that fail to show respect for their moral right to respectful treatment. *They* are not (though of course they may be treated as if they are) "commodities," "economic units," "investments," "a renewable resource," etc. They are, like us, persons and so, like us, are owed treatment that accords with their right to be treated with respect, a respect we fail to show when we end their life before doing so can be defended on the grounds of mercy. Since animals are routinely killed on grounds other than mercy in the course of commercial animal agriculture, that human enterprise violates the rights of animals.

Unlike the utilitarian approach to ethical vegetarianism, the rights view basis does not require that we know what the consequences of our individual or collective abstention from meat will be. The moral imperatives to treat farm animals with respect and to refuse to support those who fail to do so do not rest on calculations about consequences. And unlike a Singer-type utilitarianism, the rights view does not imply that the individual's duty to become a vegetarian depends on how many other people join the ranks. *Each individual* has the duty to treat others with the respect they are due independently of how many others do so, and each has a similar duty to refrain in principle from supporting practices that fail to show proper respect. Of course, anyone who accepts the rights view must profoundly wish that others *will* act similarly, with the result that commercial animal agriculture, from vast agribusiness operations to the traditional family farm, will go the way of the slave trade—will, that is, cease to exist. But the *individual's* duty to cease to support those who violate the rights of animals does not depend on humanity in general doing so as well.

The rights view is, one might say, a "radical" position, calling, as it does, for the total abolition of a culturally accepted institution to wit, commercial animal farming. The way to "clean up" this institution is not by giving animals bigger cages, cleaner stalls, a place to roost, thus and so much hay, etc. When an institution is grounded in injustices, because it fails to respect the rights of those involved, there is no room for internal house cleaning. Morality will not be satisfied with anything less than its total abolition. And that, for the reasons given, is the rights view's verdict regarding commercial animal agriculture.

ENDNOTES

1. Immanual Kant, "Duties to Animals and Spirits," *Lectures on Ethics,* trans. Louis Infield (New York: Harper and Row, 1963), pp. 239–41. Collected in *Animal Rights and Human Obligations,* Tom Regan and Peter Singer, eds. (Englewood Cliffs, NJ: Prentice-Hall Inc., 1976), pp. 122–23.

2. St. Thomas Aquinas, *Summa Contra Gentiles,* literally translated by the English Dominican Fathers (Benzinger Books, 1928), Third Book, Part II, Chap. C XII. Collected in *Animal Rights and Human Obligations,* op. cit., pp. 58–59.

3. Jeremy Bentham, *The Principles of Morals and Legislation* (1789; many editions), Chapter XVII, Section 1. Collected in *Animal Rights and Human Obligations,* op. cit., pp. 129–30.

4. John Stuart Mill, "Whewell on Moral Philosophy," *Collected Works,* Vol. X, pp. 185–87. Collected in *Animal Rights and Human Obligations,* op. cit., pp. 131–32.

5. Peter Singer, *Animal Liberation* (New York: Avon Books, 1975). By far the best factual account of factory farming is J. Mason and Peter Singer, *Animal Factories* (New York: Collier Books, 1982).

6. Richard Ryder, "Experiments on Animals," in *Animals, Men and Morals,* ed. S. and R. Godlovitch and J. Harris (New York: Taplinger, 1972). Collected in *Animal Rights and Human Obligations,* op. cit., pp. 33–47.

7. These criticisms of utilitarianism are developed at greater length in my *Case for Animal Rights* (Berkeley: University of California Press. London: Routledge and Kegan Paul, 1983).

8. The rights view is developed at length in *The Case for Animal Rights,* ibid.

9. I use the familiar idea of "person" here because it is helpful. I do not use it in *The Case for Animal Rights.* I do not believe anything of substance turns on its use or nonuse.

Closing Questions

1. Evaluate the claim that eating animals is simply a matter of survival, no worse than a fox eating chicken or a bear eating fish.

   _____

   _____

   _____

   _____

   _____

   _____

2. Would we be justified in eliminating an entire species of animals (for example, the whale) if doing so meant saving the life of a single human being? Would we be justified in murdering a single human being if doing so meant saving an entire species of animals?

   _____

   _____

   _____

   _____

   _____

3. It has been said that our choice in food is a matter of personal preference much like our choice in sexual partners. Is this right? Consider the fact that while few of us have qualms about eating animals, most of us have qualms about fornicating with them. Is this rational? Why should fornicating with animals be repugnant while eating them is not?

   _____

   _____

   _____

   _____

   _____

4. Some philosophers distinguish between the wrongness of an act and the responsibility of an agent. They would maintain, for instance, that the kleptomaniac who steals a loaf of bread does something wrong but is not responsible for her action on account of her illness. With this in mind, which sounds more plausible: The view that: (1) animals can do wrong *but* they are not responsible for their actions, or (2) animals can do no wrong *because* they are not responsible for their actions?

_____

_____

_____

_____

_____

_____

5. Upon learning of the suffering animals are made to experience, people sometimes side with the animal rights movement while they continue to treat animals as a resource. Is this a consistent position? Answer the question in the light of what Michael Stocker has said about "moral schizophrenia": "Not to be moved by what one values bespeaks a malady of the spirit."

_____

_____

_____

_____

_____

_____

6. Is Tom Regan right that what happens to animals matters to them?

_____

_____

_____

_____

_____

_____

7. Beyond utilitarian and deontological considerations, can you think of any other reason for not mistreating animals? What are these and how well do they stand up to scrutiny?

_____

_____

_____

_____

_____

8. Is there a morally relevant difference between using animals for food and using them for clothing? For testing the toxicity of household products (say, laundry detergents)? For testing the toxicity of cosmetics? For medical experimentation?

_____

_____

_____

_____

_____

9. Suppose you were at the helm of a runaway train that encountered a fork in the track. To the left, a child is playing on the track, while to the right, a dog lies sleeping. Which way should you turn and why? If you turn to the right, how do you defend against the charge that you are speciesist? Suppose two dogs are on that side. Would that make a difference?

_____

_____

_____

_____

_____

10. Is speciesism as pernicious an evil as racism, sexism, and anti-semitism? What differences and similarities do you see among them?

_____

_____

_____

_____

For Further Reading

Clark, Stephen. *The Moral Status of Animals.* Oxford: Clarendon Press, 1977.

Dombrowski, Daniel A. *The Philosophy of Vegetarianism.* Amherst, Mass: University of Massachusetts Press, 1984.

Feinberg, Joel. "The Rights of Animals and Unborn Generations." In *Philosophy and Environmental Crisis,* edited by W. Blackstone. Athens, Ga.: University of Georgia Press, 1974, pp. 48–68.

Francis, Leslie Pickering, and Richard Norman. "Some Animals Are More Equal than Others." *Philosophy* 53 (October 1978): 507–527.

Frey, R. G. *Interests and Rights: The Case Against Animals.* Oxford: Clarendon Press, 1980.

Goldberg, Alan M., and John M. Frazier. "Alternatives to Animals in Toxicity Testing." *Scientific American* 261(2) (1989).

Leahy, Michael P. T. *Against Liberation: Putting Animals in Perspective.* New York: Routledge, 1991.

Loeb, Jerod M., et al. "Human vs. Animal Rights: In Defense of Animal Research." *Journal of the Medical Association* 262(19) (17 November 1989): 2716–2720.

McCloskey, H. J. "Moral Rights and Animals," *Inquiry* 22 (Spring-Summer 1979): 25–54.

Midgley, Mary. *Animals and Why They Matter.* Athens, Ga.: University of Georgia Press, 1983.

Pardes, Herbert, et al. "Physicians and the Animal Rights Movement." *The New England Journal of Medicine,* 234(23) (6 June 1991): 1640–1643.

Rollin, Bernard. *Animal Rights and Human Morality.* Buffalo, N.Y.: Prometheus, 1981.

Singer, Peter. *Animal Liberation.* New York: Avon Books, 1975.

Spiegel, Margaret. *The Dreaded Comparison: Human and Animal Slavery,* 2nd ed. New York: Mirror Books, 1988.

Chapter 4

Crime and Capital Punishment

Passages for Reflection

"No crime is rational."
—*Livy*

"Poverty is the mother of crime."
—*Magnus Aurelius Cassidorus*

"The source of every crime is some defect of the understanding; or some error in reasoning; or some sudden force of the passions."
—*Thomas Hobbes*

"To kill someone for committing murder is a punishment incomparably worse than the crime itself. Murder by legal sentence is immeasurably more terrible than murder by brigands."
—*Fyodor Dostoevski*

"The compensation for a death sentence is knowledge of the exact hour when one is to die. A great luxury, but one that is well earned."
—*Vladimir Nabokov*

"Men are not hanged for stealing horses, but that horses may not be stolen."
—*George Saville*

"Let us call [the death penalty] by the name which, for lack of any other nobility, will at least give the nobility of truth, and let us recognize it for what it essentially is: a revenge."
—*Albert Camus*

Opening Questions

1. What makes an act a crime?
2. What are the causes of crime?
3. Are there different kinds of crimes? How should you classify them?
4. Is the death penalty legalized murder?
5. Does capital punishment deter?
6. Do murderers deserve to die? Do rapists? Kidnappers? Hijackers?

In this chapter we will focus on three questions: (1) What makes an action a crime? (2) What are the causes of criminal behavior? (3) What action should we take toward those who commit crimes, specifically capital crimes?

What Makes an Action a Crime?

In asking "What makes an action a crime?", it is tempting to point to an action's wrongfulness since most crimes involve wrongful conduct. This answer, however, will not do since not all wrongful conduct is criminal. It is wrong, for instance, to break a promise, but promise-breaking is hardly a crime. Similarly, lying as a rule is wrong, but it is not a crime unless it is linked with forgery or perjury.

But if the wrongness of an act does not make it criminal, what does? We can answer this question if we consider that "crime" is a concept applicable only within civil society; it makes sense only within a system of laws. While there may be acts that are wrong outside of society—wrong, that is, in a "state of nature"—it makes no sense to speak of acts that are *crimes* outside of society. In this light, we can understand the defense of some Nazis at the Nuremburg trials that they did not commit any "crimes against humanity" since there were no such crimes to be committed. For this reason, we must look at how the legal system understands those acts for which we are criminally liable.

Blacks' Law Dictionary defines *crime* as "any act done in violation of those duties which an individual owes to the community, and for the breach of which the law has provided that the offender shall make satisfaction to the public." The key word here is *community*, since an offense to the community is the essence of crime. The theory is that some acts affect not only the victim of the crime but the very existence of the social order. Above and beyond the individual victim, the community is harmed by such conduct as murder, rape, burglary, and assault. Such actions are a threat to the very existence of society and incur society's moral condemnation.

Harming the community as opposed to the individual also explains the distinction between criminal and civil wrongs. Whereas criminal wrongs are acts that constitute injuries to society and for which *societal* rights and remedies exist, civil wrongs are acts that injure private citizens and for which *private* rights and remedies exist. Breach of contract, for instance, is a civil wrong since it normally involves only the particular parties to the action, and the same is true of such tortious conduct as negligence, slander, malpractice, and libel. On the other hand, homicide and embezzlement are crimes since they affect not only the victim of the crime but all of society. This explains why criminal charges are brought by the prosecutor or district attorney for the community in which the crime is committed, while private attorneys represent parties in a civil action. It also explains why it is sometimes possible to read off a lawsuit's subject matter from its title. *People of the State of New Jersey v. Smith* is most likely a criminal case, whereas *Jones v. Smith* is most likely a civil one.

Further differences exist between criminal and civil actions. One is that criminal defendants must be proved guilty "beyond a reasonable doubt," whereas civil defendants must be proved liable by a "preponderance of the evidence." The theory is that since criminal misconduct is more serious than civil misconduct and carries with it the potential loss of liberty, it requires more by way of a burden of proof. Note also the distinction between guilt and liability. By finding a defendant guilty of a crime, society expresses its moral condemnation; by finding a defendant liable of a civil wrong, the defendant's responsibility is acknowledged but without a message of moral condemnation.

To be sure, different types of crimes exist, and it may be misleading to speak as if it named an unequivocal concept. *Black's*, for instance, distinguishes between felonies and misdemeanors, crimes that are *mala in se* (wrong in themselves) and *mala prohibitum* (wrong by statute), infamous crimes versus noninfamous ones, major versus petty crimes, crimes that do and those that do not involve moral turpitude, and common law versus statutory crimes. Acts also can be cited that are criminal which arguably should not be, such as the possession of dangerous firearms. At the risk, then, of giving a false unity to the subject, we take crime to consist of actions that undermine the social order—acts that arouse the contempt of society and incur its moral condemnation.

Under the American system of jurisprudence, there are two components of criminal conduct: an *actus reus* component, which requires the commission of some overt act, and a *mens rea* component, which requires the intent to commit a crime. The *actus reus* requirement implies that the mere intent to commit a crime will not suffice to constitute a crime; activity must accompany the intent. The *mens rea* requirement means that conduct otherwise criminal will not be construed as such unless the agent intends for the conduct to occur. The two requirements together mean that for a person to commit a crime, he or she must commit a criminal action as well as intend for that action to occur.

The *actus reus* and *mens rea* requirements accord well with our beliefs about wrongful conduct and moral responsibility. Where, for instance, Albert injures Betty but does so by accident, we do not hold Albert morally responsible. And where Carla intends to harm David but does not act on her intention, we do not hold Carla responsible either. For someone to be responsible for misconduct, we generally require that the person engage in some distinct behavior and do so with malicious intent. In this way, we differ from some normative systems which would hold us responsible for having evil intentions even if we fail to act on them. Christianity, for example, would hold us responsible for adulterous intentions even if we do not act on them. And some normative systems hold their adherents responsible for acts of omission or the failure to act. Judaism, for example, does not distinguish between sins of commission and sins of omission, between a sinful action and a sinful nonaction.

What Are the Causes of Criminal Behavior?

Having examined the nature of crime, we turn to the question of why people commit crime, that is, why it is that some people conform to society's norms while others do not. References in ancient Greek writings indicate that speculation on this question was prevalent at that high point of Western civilization. In Plato's *Protagoras*, (352a–358d), we find Socrates wondering whether people could do evil knowing it to be so, and in the *Laws* we find Plato arguing that if a person did evil, it was only because the person mistakenly thought that he or she was doing good. Plato writes:

> No wrongdoer is so of deliberation. For no man will ever deliberately admit supreme evil, and least of all in his most precious possessions. But every man's most precious possession . . . is his soul; no man, then, we may be sure, will of set purpose receive the supreme evil into this most precious thing and live with it there all his life through. (731c)

Modern criminology is primarily concerned with understanding crime, the characteristics of criminals, and how the consequences of crime can be prevented and repaired. It is an interdisciplinary science, with scholars from sociology, political science, biology, economics, and psychology each viewing crime from their favored perspective.

Historically, up until the eighteenth century, most Europeans explained criminal behavior largely in religious terms. They saw crime as a product of the devil's handiwork, or as a result of humanity's fall from grace. As late as the nineteenth century, indictments in both Europe and the United States often began with the preamble, "[the criminal], not having the fear of God before his eyes but being moved and seduced by the instigation of the devil, did commit [a particular crime]." Not surprisingly, religious ideas also controlled criminal procedure; confessions, for example, were often extracted through torture.

Cesare Beccaria's *Essay on Crimes and Punishments* (1764) marked the first attempt to explain crime in secular terms, and his ideas caught on in both Europe and America. As Beccaria saw it, crime is a species of rational conduct. It is a result not of the devil's handiwork, but of a person's rational deliberation and free choice. Beccaria argued that fear of punishment keeps most people in check and thus the severity, certainty, and speed of criminal sanctions served as controlling factors. He believed that the criminal justice system must be organized to ensure that punishment deters crime, and he was concerned that there be a manifest link between the gravity of a crime and the severity of its punishment. His work was to later influence the utilitarian philosopher Jeremy Bentham.

By the middle of the nineteenth century, Beccaria's theories fell out of favor. Criminologists declared that Beccaria and his followers had been too concerned with the libertarian idea that human beings had free choice and that they were responsible for their actions. Beccaria's critics also argued that the classical approach did not pay adequate attention to the characteristics of the criminal over and above the crime. Influenced by Darwin, a new theory emerged that viewed crime as behavior stemming from social, biological, and psychological factors. According to this theory, free will and responsibility played little part in understanding and solving crime. The solution to crime was to be a positivistic one: to understand the causes of criminality and its treatment.

Today, in the Western world at least, there are three main positivistic schools of thought: the biological, the psychological, and the sociological. And while the psychological and sociological schools have dominated criminological thought in the United States, the biological school, which views crime as linked to such factors as extra chromosomes, has recently made a comeback in the work of Edward O. Wilson.

Many psychologists relegate criminal behavior to such factors as mental conflict, repressed desires, and misplaced aggression. According to such theories, crime is a form of substitute behavior that compensates for abnormal urges and desires. And while psychological theories have been widely criticized, they have played a major role in criminal justice policy. Correctional policies emphasizing rehabilitation have been largely based on the idea that personality determines behavior.

Sociological explanations of crime, while not denying that personality is formed in childhood and is a key determinant of later behavior, emphasize the social conditions that bear on the individual as causes of criminal behavior. As sociologists see it, the criminal's personality and behavior are largely molded by such social forces as race, age, gender, and income. Thus, we find "social structure theory" suggesting that crime is caused by the existence of a lower-class culture based on poverty and deprivation. "Social process theory" suggests that crime is normal behavior, with the difference between the criminal and the law-abiding citizen resting chiefly on the social influences that impel one toward or away from crime. "Social conflict theory" suggests that the criminal law and the criminal justice system are means of controlling the poor and destitute.

We should ask, then, "What causes crime?" before addressing the question of how or whether to punish it. If, as Beccaria thought, crime is the result of deliberation and choice, then criminals are responsible for their conduct and punishing them would be fully justified. On the other hand, if crime is the result of hereditary factors, then crime is beyond the criminal's control and so punishing criminals is unjust. If Socrates is right, then, notwithstanding whether or not we ought to punish criminals, we ought to make educating them an important concern.

To a good extent, then, our ability to discourse intelligently about punishment presupposes the findings of criminologists. How we view punishment will depend on our commitments in ethical theory. Utilitarians, for instance, are not particularly concerned with whether criminals are responsible for their actions or whether their actions are caused by social conditions. For the utilitarian, what counts in ethics are consequences. If our lives are made better as a result of punishing criminals, then the utilitarian would say that we would do well to punish them. Other theories yield different results, and it remains to be seen whether and to what extent they accord with the findings of modern criminology.

What Action Should We Take Toward Those Who Commit Capital Crimes?

Having surveyed some answers to the question "What causes crime?", we are in a position to examine what action we should take toward those who commit it. Let us do this by focusing not on the perpetrators of crime in general, but on the perpetrators of *capital* crime, the most magnified case. Should we execute them on the grounds of "an eye for an eye?" or should we imprison them for life since "two wrongs don't make a right?" Or is punishment itself the wrong approach since crime is an illness that ought to be treated?[1]

---

[1]That crime is an illness to be treated is suggested by Karl Menninger in *The Crime of Punishment* (New York: Viking, 1969). The suggestion is raised but dismissed in Stanley Kubrick's controversial film *A Clockwork Orange* (1971), based on the book by Anthony Burgess.

In asking what action we should take toward those who commit capital crimes, I've deliberately avoided any mention of the death penalty or capital punishment. This is because of an incongruity that results if we juxtapose *death* with *penalty* and *capital* with *punishment.* Consider the distinction between a punishment and a penalty. Unlike a penalty, a punishment has an expressive function; it carries with it a message of social condemnation. It is our way of saying to the criminal: "What you did was wrong, and you must never do that again." A penalty, on the other hand, may be viewed as a "licensing fee," that is, as the price to be paid for doing the prohibited action. No underlying message of moral disapproval is implied.[2]

To see this, consider a penalty like the fee you must pay for late registration. The message to students is not "You must not register late, and may you be damned if you do"; instead, it is that registering late is permissible but because of such factors as administrative inconvenience, it will cost students an additional fee. The difference between a penalty and a licensing fee is that a penalty, unlike a licensing fee, is paid for afterwards and not in advance. The benefits of registering late may well be worth the cost (and the diminished choice of courses) to spend an extra week vacationing in Fort Lauderdale. No insinuation is made that selecting that option is morally wrong.

An illustration from football helps explain this distinction. Suppose a cornerback has fallen a step or two behind a wide receiver who has an unobstructed path toward the goal line. Rather than let the receiver catch the ball for a certain touchdown, the defender would be wise to illegally interfere with the receiver's chance of catching the ball. In this way, the offensive team gets to keep the ball at the spot of the penalty, thereby allowing the defensive team to regroup and possibly prevent what would otherwise have been a certain score. The same is not true for the concept of punishment. To view a punishment as the cost one must pay for engaging in the prohibited action is to misunderstand the logic of punishment. This is not to deny that some infractions are better construed as punishments, for example, high-sticking (and drawing blood) in hockey. And some infractions, such as roughing in hockey, straddle both notions.

To a certain kind of person it may be worth a stay in prison to commit a certain crime. Suppose, for instance, a homeless person desperately wanted to harm another person and placed little value on liberty on account of his or her homelessness. Even in this situation, we cannot deny that committing the crime is something this person must not do. In this light, the great Biblical commentator Rashi interprets "an eye for an eye" (*ayin tachat ayin*) to mean that a criminal should pay *monetary dam-*

---

[2]This analysis is owed to Joel Feinberg, *Doing and Deserving: Essays in the Theory of Responsibility* (Princeton, N.J.: Princeton University Press, 1970), pp. 95–97.

ages for inflicting bodily harm. The question arises, if this is what the Bible meant, why didn't the Bible say so explicitly? Rashi's answer prevents confusing a penalty with a punishment in the way suggested by the homeless criminal. Punishments, in short, have a symbolic significance that is largely missing from penalties. Given the distinction, then, between a punishment and penalty, it is easy to see the incongruity that results from juxtaposing *death* with *penalty*. Even if paying with one's life is worth, say, killing one's enemy, the underlying message is that killing is wrong and we must not kill on threat of damnation! If you still have doubts about the distinction between a punishment and a penalty, consider the parent who imposes a curfew on his teenage child and threatens to "ground" that child if the curfew is violated. The teen will be sadly mistaken if she views the parent as negotiating a deal. Indeed, imagine the teen responding to the parent, "You've got a deal!" Most teens will, after this, get an even harsher sentence.

Juxtaposing *capital* with *punishment* presents a different problem. Although punishment by death was originally called "capital" because the criminal was decapitated, the connotation is that death is the worst of all punishments. But fates worse than death might well be imagined, and life imprisonment may be an example. Similarly, if there are punishments worse than death, then it is misleading to speak of death as if it were the "capital" crime. In the film *The Vanishing* (1993), directed by George Sluizer, the protagonist buries his victim alive in an effort to commit what in his deranged mind is the worst of all crimes. And Dante, in his *Inferno* (Canto 34), counts treachery as the most sinful act. Other crimes worse than murder might also be imagined. Given a choice between being raped and murdered, some people will prefer to be murdered, and some people will prefer to be murdered than to have a child of theirs kidnapped. To suggest, then, that death is a punishment particularly appropriate for the capital crime of murder can be misleading. We will, however, continue to speak colloquially, once these points are acknowledged.

Having unmasked some issues underlying our terms, we return to the question: What action should we take toward those who commit capital crimes? We will address this question via an analysis of the Supreme Court cases that speak to the issue. We will do this because the question of the death penalty is essentially a legal question. There can be no death penalty without the institution of punishment, and the institution of punishment is a legal one. We will also do this because the ethical issues emerge from a discussion of the punishment's constitutional dimensions.

The constitutional history of the death penalty begins with *Furman v. Georgia* (1972).[3] In this case, the Court considered whether a Georgia

---

[3]408 U.S. 238 (1972).

death penalty statute ran afoul of the Eighth and Fourteenth Amendments. The Eighth Amendment prohibits the infliction of "cruel and unusual punishment," while the Fourteenth Amendment prohibits a state from depriving a person of "life, liberty, and property without due process of law"[4] and from denying to any person "equal protection" under the law. While the Court could not agree on whether the statute in question violated the Eighth Amendment—Justices Marshall and Brennan thought the death penalty was "cruel and unusual" while Justices Douglas, White, and Stewart were silent on the issue—it did hold that the statute violated the Fourteenth Amendment "as then administered."

A statute can be unconstitutional in two ways: it can be unconstitutional *per se* (by its very nature) or it can be unconstitutional *as administered.* Consider, for instance, the Fourteenth Amendment's guarantee that people be free from legislative discrimination (the "equal protection" clause). A statute that would overtly discriminate against African Americans would violate the amendment "by its very nature." Such a statute would also have little chance of being enacted. What those wishing to discriminate often do is enact legislation that *has the effect of discriminating,* though from all appearances the statute looks innocent. Then, too, any statute that has the effect of discriminating against a suspect class violates the Fourteenth Amendment just the same. In one case,[5] the Court held unconstitutional the enforcement of a San Francisco ordinance banning the operation of hand laundries in wooden buildings. It was demonstrated that the vast majority of such laundries were owned and operated by Chinese residents of the city. On its face, the ordinance looked innocent; a city has the right to regulate business within its jurisdiction. Where, however, the effect of an ordinance is to discriminate against a class of people (the Chinese in this case) the Court will strike down that piece of legislation.

A recent case involved the so-called Boom Box law enacted in New York City by then mayor, Edward Koch. The law prohibited the playing of "boom boxes" on public transportation. Members of the African-American community argued that the law worked to discriminate against African Americans. However, where, as in this case, grounds for upholding legislation can be found that are independent of its discriminatory effects, the law will withstand a constitutional attack. In this case, the playing of boom boxes on public transportation constituted a public nuisance.

In *Furman*, the Court held that Georgia's death penalty statute had the effect of discriminating against African Americans, an unsurprising oc-

---

[4]Notice that the Fourteenth Amendment does not prohibit the State from taking life, liberty, or property; it prohibits the taking of these *without due process of law.*

[5]*Yick Wo v. Hopkins,* 118 U.S. 356 (1886).

currence given the time and place in which this case took place. Georgia is known as the "buckle of the death belt" by opponents of capital punishment. The Court noted that the statute in question gave judges and juries unlimited discretion in deciding to whom it would give the punishment of death and concluded that such punishments were disproportionately given to blacks. (Historically, black criminals have received more than their share of executions, especially from predominately white juries and where the victims of the crimes are white.) For this reason, the Court struck down Georgia's death penalty statute while at the same time stopping short of declaring that the death penalty is unconstitutional *per se.*

In the aftermath of *Furman,* several states devised death penalty statutes that would be free of *Furman* defects. Some states (for example, North Carolina) drafted legislation making the death penalty mandatory for certain crimes, while others (for example, Georgia) drafted statutes that provided guidance for judges and juries in deciding to whom they should assign the death penalty. Some four years later, the Court tested both of these strategies. In *Woodson v. North Carolina* (1977), the Court held that mandatory death penalty statutes are unconstitutional. In *Gregg v. Georgia,* the Court held that death penalty statutes are constitutional when they provide adequate safeguards against indiscriminate sentences.

At issue in *Gregg* was an amended statute that retained the death penalty for six categories of crime: murder, kidnapping, armed robbery, rape, treason, and aircraft hijacking. (The Court was later to hold that it is unconstitutional to impose the death penalty for the crime of rape).[6] It considered, however, only the constitutionality of imposing the punishment of death for the crime of murder, since it was for the crime of murder that Troy Gregg was sentenced to death. Upon reviewing the statute, the Court held that the amended statute was free of *Furman* defects. The revised statute did this by instructing the jury to focus on the crime as well as the criminal (the act as well as the agent).[7] With respect to the *crime,* the jury's attention was directed to such issues as whether the crime was committed in the course of another felony, whether it was committed for money, whether it was committed in a particularly heinous way, and so on. With respect to the *criminal,* the jury's attention was directed to such issues as whether the criminal had a record of prior convictions for capital offenses, whether the criminal cooperated with the police, and whether the criminal was a youth, emotionally disturbed, and the like. Given these criteria, the Court was satisfied that whatever jury discretion remained would be controlled by clear and objective guidelines.

---

[6]*Coker v. Georgia* (1977), 433 U.S. 584.

[7]See my *Doing and Being: Selected Readings in Moral Philosophy* (New York: Macmillan, 1993) which is written from the conviction that ethics is best understood when we attend to both the agent and the act.

The question remained, then, of deciding whether the death penalty was unconstitutional *per se;* that is, whether it ran afoul of the Eighth Amendment's "cruel and unusual punishment" clause. Led by Justices Stewart, Powell, and Stevens, the Court held that a punishment is "cruel and unusual" if it fails to accord with "evolving standards of decency." This means that a punishment is unconstitutional if it does not measure up to contemporary moral values. Since some thirty-five states enacted death penalty statutes in the wake of *Furman,* the Court was convinced that American society regarded the death penalty as an appropriate punishment.

But measuring up to contemporary moral values is hardly a definitive test of a punishment's appropriateness. Judging by this standard, castrating rapists measures up to contemporary moral values, at least if we are to take seriously some of the comments surrounding the Lorraine Bobbitt trial, where Ms. Bobbitt was tried for having castrated her abusive husband. Aware of this, the Court held that even if a punishment accords with contemporary values, it still must comport with "the dignity of man," the "basic concept underlying the Eight Amendment." The Court took this second stipulation to rule out "excessive" punishment identified as: (1) the unnecessary or wanton infliction of pain, or (2) punishment which is grossly out of proportion to the severity of the crime. With respect to (1), the Court held that the death penalty is not wanton and unnecessary; it serves the dual purposes of deterrence and retribution. With respect to (2), the Court held that for the crime of murder, death is not a disproportionate punishment.

Interestingly, Justice Marshall dissented on the grounds that the Georgia statute failed the majority's threshold criterion of "evolving standards of decency." While not denying society's endorsement of the death penalty, Marshall argued that "fully informed" Americans would consider the punishment morally abhorrent. Marshall's argument was that if people really understood what is entailed by an execution, were aware of what it involved, in detail and richly described, then they would not support capital punishment. Analogous arguments are sometimes used by defenders of animal rights and antiabortionists. Of course, just as a person fully informed of what an abortion entails (or the slaughtering of an animal) might still be prochoice (and anti-animal rights), a "fully informed" person might still be a retentionist.

Do Americans truly believe that the death penalty "accords with contemporary moral values"? If so, what are we to make of the fact that the executioner does not know whether or not he or she put the criminal to death? Where the electric chair is concerned, there are typically three switches thrown by three "executioners" with only one switch actually working. None of the "executioners" knows which of the three switches is the operative one. (Analogous cases exist with other forms of executions.)

Furthermore, if we truly believed that executions were just, executioners would be confident in making public their calling. But this is not the case. What parent proudly proclaims, "My son, the executioner"? In contrast, not even "hanging judges" are apologetic about their calling. But if executioners were truly agents of justice, the reluctance to go public cries out for explanation. Might this reluctance suggest an ambivalence on behalf of society toward capital punishment?

In claiming that the death penalty serves the purposes of deterrence and retribution, the Court resorted to both utilitarian and deontological justifications. For the utilitarian, the rightness of an action is determined on the basis of its cost-effectiveness. Therefore, capital punishment will be justified on these grounds if and only if the benefit of executing murderers outweighs the costs. The costs here are, obviously, the lives of the criminals who are executed, while the benefits are the victims of the would-be murderers. If, as the Court maintained, more lives are saved because of the death penalty than would otherwise be saved without it, then the death penalty is justified.

But does it deter? The majority in *Gregg* notwithstanding, no statistical evidence exists to support the claim that the death penalty serves as an effective deterrent. Appeals to deterrence usually derive from armchair psychology rather than from hard statistical data. The same armchair psychology suggests that the death penalty does not deter since criminals rarely believe that they will ever get caught. (And even if caught, they rarely believe they will be executed.) If the death penalty does deter, it may not deter the targeted group. Rather than deterring prospective offenders whose actions are sometimes impulsive or irrational, the death penalty may deter persons who, like you and I, are rational in our actions and assign appropriate costs to crimes. Perhaps the strongest argument against deterrence is that even if the death penalty did deter, we would never know it. Without adequate control groups, we would never know if it was the death penalty that deterred (as opposed to other factors) in those jurisdictions where the penalty was retained and where it was abolished.

But deterrence was only one argument the Court relied on to justify its support of capital punishment. It also used the deontological argument that murderers deserve to die (the argument for retribution). The claim is that justice demands that we execute murderers whether or not the punishment deters. Typically, supporters of this position develop their case by saying that when the moral order is upset by the occurrence of some offense, justice demands that we rectify the disorder by a punishment that is equal to the offense. This view is reflected in such remarks as: "Measure for measure," "Let the punishment fit the crime," and "An eye for an eye."

Among classical philosophers, Hegel and Kant are well-known retributivists. As Hegel saw it, the criminal has upset the balance of the moral order and this can be restored only by the criminal being made to suffer. The Kantian position is that the criminal, as a moral agent, is a responsible person who has freely chosen to commit a crime. We therefore treat criminals as such by holding them responsible for their criminal conduct. Not to hold them responsible is to treat them as we would an animal whose actions are driven by uncontrolled stimuli. (Why is it that when people do evil, they seek to cast off responsibility and place the blame on such external factors as environment, genes, childhood, etc., but when they do good, they are eager to accept responsibility and dismiss such factors?) For Kant, then, we show respect to criminals when, paradoxically, we punish them for their crimes, and we show respect for murderers by executing them. In my book *Forgiveness: A Philosophical Study* (Savage, Md.: Rowman and Littlefield, 1991), I borrow this idea to argue, in a related vein, that we show wrongdoers respect when we resent them for wronging us. Not to resent wrongdoers is to symbolically declare that they are not moral agents but rather victims of stimuli over which they have no control.

But is the retributivist argument valid? Do murderers deserve to die? In *An Eye for an Eye?*, Stephen Nathanson argues that the principle of *lex talionis* ("an eye for an eye") cannot do the work that retributivists think it can do. He shows this by offering two interpretations of the principle and then by demonstrating how neither interpretation yields acceptable results. In his first interpretation, the principle is to be understood as saying that whatever the criminal did to the victim, that very thing should be done to the criminal. Understood this way, the principle implies that we should kill the murderer, but it also implies that we should rape the rapist, hijack the hijacker, burn the arsonist, and kidnap the kidnapper. These, however, are absurd. And even if we were to accept these punishments for these crimes, how would we apply the principle to such crimes as practicing medicine without a license? The claim is that the principle cannot be understood literally.

An alternative interpretation that Nathanson offers is to understand the principle as requiring matching sets of crimes and punishments, with each crime and punishment arranged ordinally from most to least severe. For example, we would first list crimes from most to least severe, then punishments from most to least severe, and then cross-match punishments to crimes. The thinking here is that we would list murder and execution first on each list and so the cross-matching would yield execution for murder. However, Nathanson points out that this interpretation of *lex talionis* does not necessarily yield the death penalty. We could, for instance, rank life imprisonment as our most severe punishment.[8] And even if we were to rank execution as the appropriate punishment for murder, what punishment would we rank for mass-murder?

---

[8]Stephen Nathanson, *An Eye for an Eye?: The Immorality of Punishing by Death* (Savage, Md.: Rowman and Littlefield, 1987), pp. 75–77.

What conclusions, then, ought we to reach? Let's sharpen this question by putting aside such practical issues as are raised by prejudiced juries and mistaken identities and ask if a person who is in fact guilty (materially and formally) of committing a capital crime (say, murder) ought to be executed. We must tread cautiously owing to the sanctity of human life. For however we decide, whether we are to be retentionists or abolitionists, we carry with our convictions a trainload of responsibility.

Perhaps it is because we carry with us this trainload of responsibility that we can arrive at a satisfactory answer, such as that we should *not* support the death penalty because of the very sanctity that necessitates caution. More specifically, if the sanctity of human life is our premise, we can infer that a person who kills deserves nothing less than execution since any other punishment fails to show respect for a human life. Or we can conclude that a person who kills should *not* be so punished as a way of showing that very same respect. In other words, from the same premise we can reach incompatible conclusions. But if that is so, then should we be confident enough to support the death penalty?

Kenneth Gribetz was district attorney of Rockland County, New York, where he has lived since 1974. He is the author (along with H. Paul Jeffers) of *Murder Along the Way,* a book Alan Dershowitz has called a "must read for anyone concerned about the state of crime and justice in America today."

Video Presentation

Guest: Kenneth Gribetz, District Attorney, Rockland County, New York

Student Panel: Louis Giordano, Greg Wilson, Alan Nunez

In this video, organized around the theme of "Crime in the Suburbs," Gribetz discusses his prosecution of some of the most infamous criminals in recent memory. He begins by discussing the celebrated "Brinks Trial" which took place in the early 1980s and involved members of the notorious Weather Underground. The Weather Underground, known in the 1960s as the Students for a Democratic Society (SDS), was a terrorist organization dedicated to combating social injustices by establishing what was to be the "New Republic of Africa," a state that was to consist of five of the U.S. states. Gribetz tells of how members of this organization—including the FBI's "most wanted" criminal, Kathy Boudin—robbed a bank in a suburb of New York City and killed two police officers and a Brink's guard in an effort to "finance" their operation. He tells of the costs of the trial (the most expensive in New York State history), how the defendants endeavored to politicize the trial, and how the crime could have occurred anywhere in the United States.

He next tells of what I mistakenly refer to as the "Crispo Case," an ongoing case implicitly involving the celebrated art dealer, Andrew Crispo. This case involved Crispo's employee, Bernard LeGeros, who, in a cocaine-induced stupor, brutally murdered one Eigil Dag Vesti. Gribetz uses the opportunity to discuss this case to point out that narcotics is the number one cause of crime in America. In response to my asking him whether drug-related crime is not an inner-city problem, he points out that it is a problem that cuts across race, gender, religion, and class and is not confined to geographic locale. He points out that no group is immune from crime and uses the affluent Eigil Dag Vesti as proof of this. He concludes his discussion of this case by citing the startling statistic that some two million criminals occupy state and federal prisons, with 57,000 in New York State prisons alone (up from 19,000 ten years prior). He argues that we, as a nation, are not really addressing the narcotics problem despite our rhetoric to the contrary. In response to my question as to whether he is for or against the death penalty (New York being one of those states that had *not* retained it under former governor Mario Cuomo), Gribetz responds that he favors it under certain circumstances for reasons having to do with retribution rather than deterrence. He personally does not think it is a deterrent, and instead makes a plea for drug prevention as well as a greater police presence. Finally, minutes before the break, Gribetz discusses his prosecution of Cheryl Sohn, a young woman who conspired to kill her parents for reasons again having to do with narcotic usage.

When we return, Lou Giordano asks Gribetz about the ethics of plea-bargaining to which Gribetz responds that it is a necessary evil, given the amount of crime that is committed, and that his office refuses to accept pleas when violent crimes take place. Greg Wilson asks Gribetz whether crime in the more affluent suburbs differs from crime in the impoverished inner cities. Finally, Alan Nunez asks Gribetz to discuss whether prosecuting has left him jaded. The show concludes with my asking Gribetz whether there is any truth to the rumor that some of the crimes he had prosecuted might be made the subject of a Hollywood movie, to which he responds that ongoing negotiations involve Philip D'Antoni, the producer of the award-winning film *The French Connection*.

Postscript. Some time after this video was made, following an extensive investigation by federal prosecutors, Kenneth Gribetz pleaded guilty to tax evasion and misuse of public funds. He resigned from office May 3, 1995 and was disbarred in July, 1996.

In this brief excerpt from his book, Murder Along the Way, *Gribetz gives us his view on capital punishment and talks of how narcotics usage is at the core of America's crime problem. He also tells the story of twenty-two-year-old Cheryl Ickson, who became a victim of a drug-related crime Gribetz successfully prosecuted. The story illustrates what Gribetz believes is the kind of crime typical in America in the 1990s.*

The Scarlet Thread

Kenneth Gribetz

There's the scarlet thread of murder running through the colorless skein of life," says Sherlock Holmes to Dr. Watson in "A Study in Scarlet," "and our duty is to unravel it, and isolate it, and expose every inch of it."

In this book I've attempted to describe extraordinary cases of murder that occurred during my current tenure as district attorney of Rockland County and the extraordinary professionals on police forces, in the office of the medical examiner, in the forensic laboratories, in the Bureau of Criminal Identification, and attorneys and detectives on my own staff who unraveled, isolated, and exposed every inch of them. They are modern-day sleuths who brought to each of these homicides their cunning and deductive reasoning plus the scientific and technological wizardry that has become part of criminology since Arthur Conan Doyle dreamed up his brainy detective over a century ago.

Of course, murder cases are a small part of the work of the police and of the office of district attorney, but it is murder that fascinates and holds people spellbound. In fiction, drama, movies, television shows, newspapers, and magazines throughout the history of humanity, murder has been right up there alongside love on our list of favorite topics.

It's been said that the detective story is the normal recreation of the noble mind. And the best detective story is, of course, a tale of murder. We crave to know "who done it" and are delighted if we figure out the solution even before the detective gathers all the suspects into a room to, as Hercule Poirot puts it, "reveal all."

"Murder will out," warn Chaucer and Cer-

Reprinted with permission from Kenneth Gribetz. Publisher unknown.

vantes. "Other sins only speak," writes John Webster, "murder shrieks out." William Shakespeare makes much the same point: "Murder, though it have no tongue, will speak with most miraculous organ" (Hamlet). "Murder cannot be hid long" (The Merchant of Venice). In Hamlet, King Claudius promises his nephew, "The murderer will be found. He will be brought to suitable punishment."

What is the suitable penalty for murder?

Today in America there is disagreement. Even though the Supreme Court of the United States has declared that the death penalty is permissible, a battle rages over its propriety. The dispute is probably one waged more according to one's own individual belief in the morality or appropriateness of government taking a life than in the validity of the arguments proffered by each side to support its own position. Whether there is any empirical data to back up the notion that the death penalty deters or does not deter further crime is an academic discussion, for proponents of the death penalty are content in the belief, founded or otherwise, that a human being cannot help but be deterred by the prospect of forfeiting his own life. Opponents, on the other hand, can always point to cases of murders being committed within hours of an execution.

I have always favored the death penalty. (My co-author, Mr. Jeffers, does not, taking the view that a government should not take life except in time of war.) I believe the death penalty does deter—perhaps not everyone, but surely some. Therefore, if it is instrumental in saving just one innocent life, albeit at the cost of another, then in my judgment it is worthwhile. Moreover, while I do not advocate its institution for a wide variety of offenses, I do believe that it is appropriate punishment for certain crimes.

I have no reservation about society's forfeiting the life of an individual who, out of greed or some other self-indulgent motive, was callously willing to take the life of another. So, for example, in the murders of the Sohns by Belton Brims and James Sheffield, or Richard LaBarbera and Robert McCain, who repeatedly stabbed and assaulted Paula Bohovesky, or Samir Zada, who within a period of ten days took two lives, I believe death at the hands of the state to be an appropriate—indeed, I believe, the only just—punishment.

The death penalty is not and never has been a cure for all of society's problems or a guaranteed deterrent to murder because there will always be those who give no thought to the possible punishment for their crime, or who believe the potential benefits are worth the risk. The existence of these individuals is not a sufficient reason to abandon totally that punishment that is the only one that fits the crime.

Some who believe the death penalty does deter the crime of murder have advocated its use to stem the gravest problem confronting law enforcement and society as a whole—drugs—by imposing it on the kingpins of the trade in narcotics. Whether it would have an effect remains to be seen.

Clearly, the way in which the drug problem is being addressed is woefully inadequate and ineffective. Illicit drugs have entered the United States in a flood, notwithstanding the involvement of the military in the air and on the sea to interdict the flow. A more concerted effort by the federal government to curb the traffic across our borders is required, as is a continuous effort to persuade the drug-producing countries to do more to help stamp out the narcotics business. Toward that end, the United States must be willing to offer economic incentives to these countries to encourage their cooperation. If such incentives fail, then more drastic "disincentives" will have to be employed even at the risk of straining relations with the governments of those countries. The problem is just that grave.

The federal government must also provide greater financial assistance to localities where the impact of drugs is felt most acutely, channeled in a manner that recognizes and addresses the broad nature of the problem.

In Rockland County we have created a narcotics task force that is wholly funded by the state and the county because, unfortunately, the federal government does not provide money for local narcotics task forces. However, despite this, our task force operating under director James V. Stewart has been very successful in grappling with street-level and middle-echelon dealers, removing hundreds of these predators from the county.

Prosecution and incarceration is not the answer to drugs, however. To wipe out this scourge, we must eliminate the demand. Drug use must become unacceptable. That means a dramatic reversal of past practice when "recreational" use was deemed acceptable.

I am appalled at suggestions that criminality associated with drugs can be eliminated by making drugs and their usage legal. To do so would be to surrender. It would be an abject declaration of defeat. Worse, it would condemn future generations to the eternal bondage of drug addiction.

The drug problem and its accompanying crime can be dealt with if we make a full commitment to the goal of ridding ourselves of the pestilence of narcotics, beginning with a realization that it is not merely a problem of law enforcement but a threat to our way of life as real and eminent as any enemy army.

The plague of drugs has contributed massively to the rise in this country's crime rate and the incidence of murder in particular, with many innocent victims caught in crossfire between drug gangs or simply murdered for their money or their valuable possessions.

That's what appeared to be the case of Cheryl Ickson, a twenty-two-year-old Rockland County resident who became enmeshed in the trap of drug abuse and wound up a victim.

On August 23, 1987, Cheryl was overdue at her job as a desk clerk at her family's motel in Stony Point. Because this was not typical of their daughter, her frantic parents contacted Sergeant Joe Liszack of the Stony Point police. Ordinarily, under state law action is not taken on a missing-person report for twenty-four hours, but this time Chief Stephen Scurti and Lieutenant Frank Tinelli decided to go ahead and send a teletype message about her car to regional police departments.

Within hours came a reply from New York City police reporting that the auto had been stopped in the Bronx for a traffic violation and the driver released for later court appearance. Driving the car was a man who identified himself as Dewayne Eurie. With him were another black man, a black woman, and a white woman who identified herself as Cheryl Ickson and told the police she would be in trouble with her parents if they found out she had been in New York City.

Refusing to believe this, the Ickson family persisted in asserting that Cheryl could not have left home under the circumstances described. Given a description of the woman who'd identified herself as Cheryl, Mrs. Ickson declared "That's not my daughter." Shown a photograph of the man who called himself Dewayne Eurie, she recognized him as a resident of the motel who had used the name Dwayne Johnson.

Advised of these developments, the Stony Point police put out a warrant for Johnson charging him with unauthorized use of a motor vehicle and set out to locate him. Working the case now were Lieutenant Tinelli, Sergeant Liszack, and Detective Joseph Denise of the Stony Point police and DA Detective John Gould, with the Ickson family members deeply involved by providing information on Cheryl's acquaintances and friends, most of them located in Haverstraw.

Based on conversations with persons there, the focus of the investigation centered on 33 Main Street, where Dwayne Johnson was reported to have been seen, but the woman who rented the apartment at that address said she had not seen Johnson.

Doubting the story, the police checked all parts of the building and located Johnson and Lori Ann Mitchell hiding on the roof.

An attractive eighteen-year-old with styled blond hair, dressed in pink slacks and a white jacket and insisting she'd done nothing wrong, Mitchell was soon telling the detectives what had happened to Cheryl Ickson.

It was around six o'clock on the twenty-third that Dwayne Johnson telephoned Cheryl and asked her for a ride to the city. They set up a meeting at a Grand Union market in Stony Point. When Cheryl arrived, Johnson, John Robinson, Nora Mann, and she, Lori Mitchell, got into Cheryl's car.

Johnson asked, "Can I drive?"

"No," said Cheryl. Did Johnson have anything for her? she asked, meaning cocaine.

He did, Johnson said, directing Cheryl to drive them to a secluded road in Mount Ivy and turn the car around. When she did so, he said he would need her keys in order to break down the cocaine, which was in the rock-hard form known as crack. Cheryl handed him the keys and he passed them to John Robinson in the back seat.

At that point, Johnson pulled out a gun; not a real one, but one made of plastic, although the toy was realistic-looking enough as he pressed it against Cheryl's head.

Resisting, Cheryl was forced into the rear of the car, where she was tied up with shoelaces, robbed, slapped, and beaten unconscious.

At a desolate construction site near Alpine, New Jersey, John Robinson dragged Cheryl into a wooded area and returned a few minutes later saying, "I took care of the bitch."

Detective Denise asked Mitchell, "Can you show us where the body is?"

"I think so," she said, nodding.

Because I had known Martin and Eleanor Ickson for nearly twenty years and because their children and mine had attended the same schools, they had come to see me in my capacity as district attorney about the mysterious disappearance of their daughter, expressing fears that she was dead and asking me to do whatever I could in helping to find her. Now, early in the morning of August 26 I was with Lieutenant Tinelli, Detective Denise, and Sergeant Liszack of the Stony Point police, Sergeant Wayne Dunn and Officer Jerry Sullivan of the Haverstraw Police, and Lieutenant Jim Stewart and detectives John Gould and Steve Colantonio of my own staff in a convoy of police cars heading into Bergen County, New Jersey, in the hope that Mitchell could find the location where they'd left Cheryl's body.

Because of her uncertainty, we roamed the back roads of the area for some time until, at last, around 2:00 A.M. she spotted a large clearing which was being prepared for homes and expressed her belief that it was the place where Cheryl Ickson's body had been dumped.

With the predawn blackness pierced by flashlights and the beams of light cut by the crouching shadowy, silent, grim-faced figures of the searchers moving slowly into thick woods, the search scene took on aspects of a surrealistic horror film.

Then, an urgent voice pierced the stillness: "Over here!"

Beneath a thin blanket of branches and leaves lay Cheryl's body with the hands and ankles tied with shoelaces, the head face down but turned slightly, the bruised and lacerated skin blackened by exposure, the hair tangled and matted with blood, and the pulseless, cold, and clammy body acrawl with insects, flies, and maggots.

Because this apparent murder was in Bergen County, calls needed to be made on the radio to Rockland headquarters to alert them to notify the Bergen DA, the New Jersey police, and the medical examiner, a task in which I assisted after we had all withdrawn to our vehicles, leaving only Sergeant Dunn to stand guard at the shallow grave.

After a few minutes as we waited for the Bergen officials to arrive, Dunn pierced the air with a cry of alarm.

Instantly, those with guns drew them and raced into the woods, not knowing what they might find.

Possibilities flashed through my mind. Had John Robinson or someone else connected with the crime mysteriously appeared on the scene? Were there other accomplices who for some reason decided to return to the gravesite? Had Sergeant Dunn stumbled upon other bodies? Had he himself been assaulted?

A few minutes later as I waited anxiously in the car with Lori Ann Mitchell, Jim Stewart dashed from the woods to exclaim breathlessly, "Boss, you're not going to believe it! The girl is alive."

Incredibly, after more than sixty hours in the shallow ditch, the person we'd seen a few moments earlier encrusted with dirt and blood and swarming with bugs had startled Sergeant Dunn by stirring in the shallow ditch and with an unearthly moan begun pushing herself upright.

Grabbing the microphone of the patrol car's radio, I now called for an ambulance instead of the medical examiner.

Although Cheryl remained semi-comatose for weeks and hospitalized for months, in due course she recovered sufficiently to identify her kidnappers and to assist in their prosecution.

Because the crime had been committed in Bergen County, it was tried there with assistance from Rockland County authorities.

Lori Ann Mitchell and Nora Robinson pleaded guilty in return for reduced prison sentences and testimony against Dwayne Johnson. "You ought to be ashamed of yourself," scolded Bergen County Superior Court Judge Charles Digisi as he pronounced a sentence of fifteen years for Mitchell and twenty for Robinson. "Isn't it a shame that you not only destroyed the victim's life but your own?"

Johnson refused to plead and was convicted, receiving a sentence of thirty-five years for attempted murder.

John Robinson decided to avoid trial for attempted murder by agreeing to plead guilty to kidnapping, aggravated assault, and armed robbery, an arrangement about which Cheryl Ickson was consulted and to which she agreed. His sentence of thirty years in prison made him ineligible for parole after fifteen years.

"This was just a cold-blooded, depraved, and heinous crime without rhyme or reason. The cruelty inflicted on this victim was worse than death. You just decided to take this young lady and snuff out her life—it's as simple as that," said Bergen County Judge Alfred Schiaffo, with Cheryl present in the court.

"I'm very happy with the sentence," she told reporters. "He'll just sit there and rot."

She had been very lucky. The warmth of her shallow grave, no rain in those sixty hours when she had been left for dead in a ditch in which she might have drowned in a heavy rainfall, the refusal of her family to accept the easy explanation that she had left home on her own volition, and diligent investigation and dogged detective work had produced a rare occurrence in the annals of crime . . . and a unique ending for this book—a case of murder with a happy ending.

Stephen Nathanson is Professor of Philosophy at Northeastern University. He is the author of *An Eye for An Eye? The Immorality of Punishing by Death* (1987) and *Patriotism, Morality, and Peace* (1993).

Nathanson, an enemy of capital punishment, begins by discussing some of the reasons people give for retaining the institution. Basically, he says that capital punishment: (1) allows society to vent the anger it feels when a capital crime has been committed; (2) deters would-be criminals from committing similar crimes; and (3) satisfies our demand for justice.

Asked whether it in fact deters, Nathanson says no. As Nathanson sees it, common sense would dictate that since death is a terrible thing, no one will risk crimes upon threat of death. However, he points out that people risk death for all sorts of activities, for example, smoking and speeding, so we have no reason to believe that it will act as a deterrent of criminal activity. This occasions some talk over whether people "risk" death as opposed to "deny" death. He also points out that virtually no study supports the view that the death penalty deters. After some discussion over the question of just how rational criminals are and to what extent they are influenced by the threat of execution, Nathanson addresses problems with those studies designed to determine whether the death penalty deters. He discusses Thorstein Sellin's seminal study in this regard (see Bibliography) as well as Bowers and Pierce's claim that the death penalty correlates with an *increase* of capital crimes. We also consider whether abolition of capital punishment might have a taming effect on society.

I now play devil's advocate and ask Nathanson whether deterrence is not beside the point, suggesting instead that murderers deserve to die irrespective of any secondary gains. I ask, that is, whether the issue should not be one of "an eye for an eye." (Nathanson surmises that anyone discussing capital punishment will, within 45 seconds, bring up the phrase "an eye for an eye.") As the title of his book indicates, Nathanson argues against the principle. He claims, first, that we really don't subscribe to such a principle at all. Consider, he says, that if we really subscribed to "an eye for an eye," we would not distinguish between the criminal guilty of first-degree murder and the criminal guilty of manslaughter since in both of these cases, the victim lies dead. Because we do differentiate the way in which victims are killed, we are actually appealing to some other principle. Beyond this, Nathanson feels we can't ever be confident the law will pick out those criminals who deserve to die even if we subscribe to "an eye for an eye." He cites various reasons why this is so.

Following the break, Cathy Capasso asks Nathanson whether it is fair for taxpayers to maintain in prison those criminals who are guilty of capital crimes. After objecting to viewing the issue from a financial perspective, Nathanson points out that executions are quite expensive, contrary to popular belief. Wolfe Lewis asks Nathanson whether the death penalty is a racist institution. Nathanson's answer is that race, along with other irrelevant factors, influences the decision to administer the death penalty. He also points out that the highest probability of receiving the death penalty is where the criminal is black and the victim white. Finally, Rich Masio raises the question of who has ultimate authority in deciding whether the death penalty is justified.

In this essay, written expressly for this book, Nathanson is concerned with showing that we do not have the reasons needed to justify the imposition of the death penalty and because of that legislators ought to abolish it and people ought not to support it. But before analyzing the reasons given in support of the death penalty, Nathanson calls for renewed debate in light of what he perceives to be little public interest in the question given its widespread grass-roots support. To keep the debate open, Nathanson urges that the issue be framed in a way that does not close off debate and that people be open-minded in evaluating the arguments pro and con. He laments that so many people who support the death penalty do so without adequately considering viable alternatives.

Having made a plea for renewed debate, Nathanson goes on to discuss the reasons people typically support capital punishment: namely, anger at the criminal, protection of society, and the concern to do justice. Nathanson argues that none of these arguments is strong enough to support retaining the death penalty. He concludes by trying to unite retentionists and abolitionists, urging them to marshal their efforts into making society safer by concentrating on eliminating the causes of crime.

The Immorality of Punishing by Death

Stephen Nathanson

INTRODUCTION

While there are many points of disagreement between supporters and opponents of the death penalty, all respectable parties to the debate agree that killing a human being is a matter of the utmost moral seriousness and that we ought only to take human lives if we have the strongest, most compelling reasons for doing so. It follows from this belief that we have a duty to think about the reasons given in favor of capital punishment and to subject them to scrutiny and criticism. No responsible person will support the death penalty if the reasons given for it cannot stand up to examination.

What kinds of reasons are there for and against the death penalty? While many different arguments have been given, the most important ones involve the protection of human life and the achievement of justice.[1] Many people seem to think that if we value human life and if we want to do justice, then we will be led to support the death penalty. While I do not deny that there is a certain plausibility to this view, I think that more careful examination of this claim shows it to be mistaken.

My aim here is to show that the death penalty is neither an effective defense against violent crimes nor an effective means of doing justice. If I am correct, then we lack substantial enough reasons to engage in the practice of punishing by death. Since it is wrong to kill people unless we have the strongest, most compelling reasons for doing so, the death penalty is an immoral practice. It should not be imposed by the state or supported by individuals.

IS THE DEATH PENALTY CONTROVERSY OVER?

Before discussing the arguments for and against the death penalty, I'd like to make some comments on the process of discussing and debating the death penalty. The question of whether we ought to punish people for various crimes by killing them is one of the classic disputes. It was, for example, the first subject I ever debated as a high school freshman. In the past, we expected it to be debated and probably thought that the debate would never be settled.

One of my concerns at present is that the death penalty will cease to be a controversial, debatable issue. One reason for this is that public opinion polls have shown that there is very strong public support for the death penalty, and politicians who oppose the death penalty risk paying a heavy price for their opposition. These facts together threaten to produce a kind of intimidation factor, where opposition to the death penalty immediately brands one as a deviant who is "outside of the mainstream."

While many people lament "government by public opinion poll," and while I certainly don't think that polls should be the last word, they are important indicators of public support for policies, and in a democratic system this must be taken seriously. But if public opinion is to play a positive role, it is important that polls not be conducted in a crude way. Most polls simply ask people whether they support or oppose the death penalty, and answers show strong support. The problem is that those who are questioned are usually given no idea of what the alternatives to capital punishment are. Yet, in virtually all policy decisions, what it is rational or moral to support depends on what the alternatives are. Even strong opponents of the death penalty would probably support it if the alternative were a $10,000 cash prize for every person guilty of homicide.

The real question is whether people favor the death penalty or some other plausible alternative, like life in prison without parole and with prison earnings paid as restitution to families of murder victims. These questions have been asked in several recent polls, and the results show that support for the death penalty diminishes significantly when alternatives are presented. In Georgia, for example, support for the death penalty dropped from 75 to 43 percent when people were given the alternative of life imprisonment plus restitution. In Florida, another active death penalty state, support for the death penalty dropped from 84 to 24 percent when the alternative of life imprisonment plus restitution was offered. Polls in New York, California, and Nebraska produced similar results.[2]

So, one obstacle to continued discussion—intimidation by public opinion polls—rests on a distortion of people's actual attitudes. It is simply false to assume that since so many people have firmly made up their minds in favor of the death penalty that continued public debate is useless. It is also true, however, that unless death penalty opponents can frame the question properly, people will choose the death penalty because they will be unaware of alternative punishments that are sufficiently severe.

This is not the only obstacle to serious debate, however. Another is the way we describe the death penalty controversy and think about what determines a person's position on it. It is frequently said that the death penalty is a "gut issue." Likewise, some people say that they oppose the death penalty as a matter of principle, but they often don't say what the principle is. In both cases, we have conversation stoppers or diverters. If we are to have meaningful discussion of the death penalty, people on both sides need to work harder at saying why they think it is right or wrong.

Finally, when people feel strongly about issues, they often form negative opinions of those with whom they disagree, and they give up on trying to reach them or dissuade them. It is especially important that opponents of the death penalty not reach this conclusion because our view is currently a minority view. Even people who might support alternatives think of themselves as death penalty supporters because of the way the issues are posed. In this context, death penalty opponents need to work to understand why many humane and morally conscientious people support a policy that we believe to be morally abhorrent.

My own view is that while there are people in public life who exploit the death penalty for political purposes, most people support the death penalty for reasons that are quite admirable.[3] It is important for death penalty opponents to recognize this and to stress the areas in which we agree with death penalty supporters because these areas of agreement form the basis of the strongest arguments against the death penalty. Likewise, people who favor the death penalty should realize that those who oppose it also value innocent life and are not motivated by a perverse humanitarianism that would favor criminals over victims. Unfair stereotypes of those we oppose are inconsistent with both rational debate and the spirit of democratic debate.

WHY PEOPLE SUPPORT THE DEATH PENALTY

What are the roots, then, of widespread public support for the death penalty? Based on my own readings and discussions over many years, I would identify three main sources of support: anger at those who perpetrate terrible crimes, a desire to protect human life, and a desire to see that justice is done.

Anger

The anger that people feel in the face of terrible crimes is entirely appropriate and should not be disparaged.[4] Indeed, it would be a discredit to death penalty opponents if we did not react in a similar way, and we need to stand with others in expressing our horror about murders and other terrible crimes. Nonetheless, anger at those who take people's lives does not by itself justify punishing by death. Our whole system of law requires that we act according to principles and that punishments be inflicted in a systematic, uniform, and just manner. Our anger about particular crimes, however, varies for many reasons. We are horrified, for example, if an American hostage is killed in a foreign country, while most of us have weak feelings about the killing of people who are distant and strange. More generally, our degree of anger at or sense of the grievousness over particular murders may be a function of our identification with the victim or our lack of sympathy for the killer. While someone like Jean Harris may strike us as a nice woman who did one bad thing, other people who kill may be poorer, less attractive people, whose race, appearance, or social status make us see them as more threatening. So, feelings like anger, sympathy, and personal vulnerability are too variable to serve as reliable guides for judging the appropriateness of particular punishments.

Protecting People from Attack

A second motivator of death penalty support is the desire to protect people by preventing murders from occurring. It is widely believed that the death penalty provides the best deterrent against murder. People think that the more severe the punishment, the less likely it is that someone will risk incurring that punishment. Since death is a more severe punishment than long-term imprisonment, then death, they think, will deter more potential murderers and hence save more lives.

Again, we need to distinguish the motivation from the argument. The desire to prevent murders and to save the lives of potential victims is important and good. Indeed, protecting people from violence is widely regarded as the central, most important function of government. So, governments have a duty to protect our lives, and if the death penalty were an effective way to do this, that would

be a powerful (though not a conclusive) reason to favor it.[5]

In fact, however, there is no reason to believe that the death penalty is any more effective in preventing homicides than long-term imprisonment. Many factors—ranging from economic conditions to cultural traditions to availability of weapons—contribute to homicide rates. Virtually all countries in the world that we think of as friends and allies have lower homicide rates than we have in the United States, and none of them punishes those guilty of homicide by death. Their citizens are safer than we are, though they lack the death penalty. Even within the United States, states that have death penalty laws frequently have higher homicide rates. So, it is reasonable to doubt that enacting death penalty legislation is an effective means for preventing murders and thus protecting human life.

In one of the most famous studies of deterrence, Thorstein Sellin examined homicide rates in the various states of the United States for a thirty-five-year period from 1920 to 1955. When neighboring states with and without death penalty statutes were compared, there was no systematic relationship between the presence of the death penalty and homicide rates. In many cases, states without death penalties had lower rates than death penalty states. In many, the rates were about equal, while in others, they were higher. There is no discernible pattern linking the death penalty with increased safety for citizens. In Massachusetts, which did have a death penalty during the period covered by the study, the homicide rate was about equal to that of Rhode Island, which did not have a death penalty. Both Massachusetts and Rhode Island had lower homicide rates than Connecticut, which was a death penalty state.[6]

Faced with statistics, many people respond that it is just common sense that people will be less likely to kill if faced with the prospect of death. But this common-sense view overlooks many well-known facts about human behavior, the most significant one being that all of us risk death all of the time, sometimes for reasons that are relatively trivial. People who climb mountains, people who run for president, people who join the military, and people who smoke cigarettes or drive too fast in bad weather all run the risk of death. Yet, it fails to deter these various activities. It is not plausible to believe that a person with a strong desire to kill would be undeterred by the threat of long-term imprisonment but would be deterred by the threat of death.

Supporting the death penalty, then, is not an effective way to provide protection for innocent people. While the motivation behind the deterrence argument is admirable, there is no good reason to believe that the death penalty actually does a better job of deterring murder than other severe punishments. Indeed, at least some studies indicate that the death penalty may have what is called a "brutalizing" effect, stimulating some murders that would not otherwise have occurred. If this claim is true, then the death penalty actually makes us less secure from attack.[7]

Doing Justice

Finally, people who support the death penalty often do so because they want to see justice done, and they think this is achieved by punishing murderers by death. Here again, the motivation is laudable, but the death penalty fails to achieve what people desire.

When people are asked why justice requires the death penalty, they often cite the "eye for an eye" principle. According to this principle, we do justice by treating criminals in the same way they treated their victims. According to this view, the only just punishment for people who have killed is for them to be killed.

While people often express this view, our legal system reflects a different approach. Many kinds of homicide require punishments that are less severe than death, and only some of those who commit first-degree murder are sentenced to die. In practice, we do not hold to the "eye for an eye" principle, and this is a good thing, since it appears to require that we treat all who kill alike. In this view, people guilty of vehicular homicide would be executed along with those who murder with premeditation. If we do not favor the first of these options, then we do not really subscribe to the idea of doing to those who kill what they have done to their victims.[8]

More generally, the "eye for an eye" principle fails because it requires that we punish barbaric crimes barbarically. It would lead us to burn arsonists and rape rapists. In other cases, the "eye for an eye" principle doesn't tell us what to do at all. It provides no guidance, for example, in deciding what a just punishment is for airline highjacking or tax evasion. While proponents of the death penalty often cite the "eye for an eye" principle as if it were an important criterion of justice, reflection shows it to be radically defective as a principle of just punishment.

Second, the appeal to justice as a reason for the death penalty fails because of the possibility of convicting and executing innocent people. Surely, the worst injustice is to execute an innocent person, and by choosing the death penalty, we choose to run this risk even though it could be avoided by opting for long-term imprisonment. As dreadful as the latter punishment is, it at least allows for correction of errors and the release of people who have been wrongfully convicted.

Conviction of the innocent is not just a hypothetical possibility. The case of Randall Adams in Texas was widely publicized by the movie *The Thin Blue Line*, a documentary that provides many important lessons about the workings of the criminal justice system. In a more recent case, Walter McMillan was freed from his death row cell in Alabama after his innocence was proved. He was convicted and sentenced for a murder he did not commit, and his appeal was turned down four times by the Alabama Court of Criminal Appeals. Only on the fifth appeal did he succeed in proving his innocence.[9]

Such cases are far from unique. In the most thorough study of errors in capital cases, Hugo Bedau and Michael Radelet have established that between 1900 and 1980, at least 350 people in the United States were wrongfully convicted of crimes punishable by death. In twenty-three of these cases, those convicted were actually executed.[10]

Of course, no system is perfect, but the causes of error that Bedau and Radelet cite are particularly troublesome, since they call into question the fundamental justice and fairness of our criminal justice system. In forty-nine cases, convictions came as a result of coerced confessions, while in thirty-five cases, prosecutors suppressed evidence that established the innocence of the accused. In 117 cases, perjury was committed by prosecution witnesses. Moreover, in the cases where innocence was later established, the errors were generally discovered by people outside the legal system. In only thirty-seven cases were errors discovered by officials.

Conviction and execution of the innocent, then, are a genuine possibility and provide a powerful argument against the death penalty. This is an argument against the death penalty that anyone who is genuinely concerned with justice and the protection of innocent life must take seriously.

ARBITRARINESS AND UNFAIR DISCRIMINATION

There is another reason why the death penalty fails to do justice. In our system, the death penalty is supposed to be imposed only in those cases of the most terrible murders. In the 1972 case *Furman v. Georgia,* the Supreme Court struck down death penalty laws because it judged that they were imposed in an arbitrary and discriminatory way. While the Court reinstated the death penalty in the 1976 case of *Gregg v. Georgia,* many studies have shown that racial prejudice continues to play a strong role in determining whether a person is sentenced to prison or death for murder. The greatest chance of receiving a death penalty occurs in cases where a black person kills a white person, while the least chance is found in cases where whites kill blacks.

The following chart shows the distribution of death sentences for homicides committed in Ohio between 1974 and 1977. It shows that the highest probability of receiving a death sentence occurred in cases where blacks killed whites, while the lowest probability of a death sentence is in cases where whites killed blacks.

Racial Combination	Total	Death Sentences	Probability
Black kills white	173	44	.254
White kills white	803	37	.046
Black kills black	1,170	20	.017
White kills black	47	0	.000

These death sentences were handed down under new laws which were supposed to end the arbitrariness and discrimination that the Supreme Court had condemned as unconstitutional in *Furman.* Studies of other states reveal a similar continuation of the influence of racial factors on the sentencing process. There are many studies of this phenomenon, and it continues into our own day, calling into question the ability of our society to provide "equal justice under law" to all people.[11]

If death penalty supporters are genuinely concerned that justice be done, then they should see that the death penalty itself contributes to serious injustice, creating a system in which the race of victims and criminals is a major determinant of the severity of sentences for murder.[12]

CONCLUDING THOUGHTS

In this brief discussion, I've tried to show that the usual reasons offered in support of the death penalty are much weaker than they first appear.

In closing, I would like to make two additional points. First, I want to stress the fact that people who oppose and people who support the death penalty have more in common than is usually supposed. We share a common anger in response to the killing of innocent people. We share a desire that people be protected from violence, and we all want justice to be done. Contrary to what many people believe, these common values do not provide a solid basis for supporting the death penalty, for the death penalty provides neither protection from attack nor justice for those who are guilty. A system that punishes murder with long-term imprisonment provides severe punishments for the guilty and as much protection for the innocent as a punishment system can provide. Because the death penalty does nothing to promote either justice or the protection of human life, it remains a form of unjustified violence that is unworthy of our support.

Second, since both supporters and opponents of the death penalty claim to care about the defense of people against violent attack, both have to do a better job thinking about how we can combat violence in our society. Too often, death penalty opponents have been content to oppose the death penalty without offering something positive in its place. Likewise, however, even if the death penalty is legitimate, death penalty supporters must know by now that by itself the death penalty cannot significantly diminish the level of violence in our society. Other approaches to the prevention of violence are necessary.[13]

People on both sides of the issue need to join together to devise positive strategies that will actually make our society safer, less violent, and more respectful of human life. Suppose that we could only achieve this by radically altering the ways in which children are raised, the traditional ways in which we argue and disagree, the forms of entertainment we enjoy, or the patterns of income distribution in our society. Would we be willing to pay the price to achieve a safer society? Or are we content with symbolic actions that have no real impact on the level of violence and suffering that people currently endure?

ENDNOTES

1. I discuss these and other arguments in *An Eye for an Eye? The Immorality of Punishing by Death* (Lanham, Md.: Rowman & Littlefield, 1987).

2. For these data and discussion of the impact of public opinion on the Supreme Court, see William Bowers, "Capital Punishment and Contemporary Values: People's Misgivings and the Court's Misperceptions." *Law & Society Review* 27 (1993): 157–175.

3. On the political use of the death penalty, see Glenn Pierce and Michael Radelet, "The Role and Consequences of the Death Penalty in American Politics." *Review of Law & Social Change* XVIII (1990–91): 711–728.

4. For a defense of the death penalty that appeals to the value of anger as a reaction to violent acts, see Walter Berns, *For Capital Punishment* (New York: Basic Books, 1979); excerpts reprinted in Hugo Bedau, ed., *The Death Penalty in America,* 3rd ed. (New York: Oxford University Press, 1982).

5. For discussion of why the deterrence argument by itself is not conclusive, see my *An Eye for an Eye?* Ch. 10.

6. For selections from Sellin and other relevant data, see Hugo Bedau, ed., *The Death Penalty in America,* rev. ed. (Garden City, New York: Anchor Doubleday, 1967).

7. For evidence of the "brutalization effect," see William Bowers, *Legal Homicide* (Boston: Northeastern University Press, 1984).

8. For a fuller discussion of the "eye for an eye" principle and the complexities of retributive punishment, see my *An Eye for an Eye?*, Chs. 6 and 7.

9. On the circumstances of McMillan's conviction and eventual release, see Peter Applebome, "Black Man Freed After Years On Death Row in Alabama." *The New York Times*, March 3, 1993, pp. 1, B11.

10. H. Bedau and M. Radelet, "Miscarriages of Justice in Potentially Capital Cases." *Stanford Law Review* 40 (1987): 21–179. For detailed discussion of some of these cases of wrongful conviction see, H. Bedau, C. Putnam, and M. Radelet, *In Spite of Innocence* (Boston: Northeastern University Press, 1992). The authors now claim to know of over 400 cases of wrongful conviction for capital offenses.

11. The figures in this chart come from William Bowers and Glenn Pierce, "Racial Discrimination and Criminal Homicide under Post-*Furman* Statutes." In W. Bowers, *Legal Homicide* (Boston: Northeastern University Press, 1984), Ch. 7. For additional studies of the arbitrariness of death penalty sentencing, see Urusula Bentele, "The Death Penalty in Georgia: Still Arbitrary." *Washington University Law Quarterly* 62 (1985): 573–646; and Samuel Mauro and Robert Gross, *Death and Discrimination* (Boston: Northeastern University Press, 1989).

The arbitrariness issue is forcefully discussed from a legal perspective by Charles Black in

Capital Punishment: The Inevitability of Caprice and Mistake, 2nd ed. (New York: W.W. Norton, 1978).

The arbitrariness argument is criticized by Ernest van den Haag in "The Collapse of the Case Against Capital Punishment." *National Review,* March 31, 1978. I defend the argument in *An Eye for an Eye?,* Chs. 4 and 5.

12. Another source of injustice is the unequal quality of legal representation that accused criminals have access to. Poor persons who are defended by court-appointed lawyers often have only minimal, ineffective legal representation. For a brief overview of the problem, see Ronald Smothers, "Court-Appointed Defense Offers the Poor a Lawyer, But the Cost May be High." *The New York Times,* February 14, 1994, p. A12.

13. For a general discussion of the limits of the punitive approach to crime prevention, see Elliott Currie, *Confronting Crime* (New York: Pantheon Books, 1985), and David Rothman, "The Crime of Punishment," *New York Review of Books,* February 17, 1994, pp. 34–38.

Closing Questions

1. Discuss the view that while orthodox criminal law focuses punishment on overtly coercive and violent acts, often of the poor, no comparable criminal sanction exists for the more subtle white-collar crimes such as insider trading, price-fixing, pollution, and employer tolerance of occupational hazards.

   _____

   _____

   _____

   _____

   _____

   _____

2. Is the distinction between recreational drugs (which are typically illegal) and therapeutic drugs (which are typically legal) sharp enough to support the law that rules them? Consider the fact that recreational drugs relieve stress and to that extent are a form of therapy.

   _____

   _____

   _____

   _____

   _____

   _____

3. In your judgment, what actions are criminal but should not be, and what actions are not criminal but should be? Give reasons for your answer in the light of the question, "What makes an action a criminal one?"

   _____

   _____

   _____

   _____

   _____

4. The Supreme Court has recently ruled that states are not required to have an insanity defense. Is the lack of an insanity defense justifiable? Do you think that crimes which might otherwise warrant the death penalty would warrant some other form of treatment (a prison term or therapy) if the criminal was psychotic?

_____

_____

_____

_____

_____

_____

5. Given the requirement that criminal activity must consist of overt activity (the *actus reus* requirement), is it fair not to hold people responsible for crimes of omission?

_____

_____

_____

_____

_____

_____

6. Comment on Karl Menninger's claim that "society secretly *wants* crime, *needs* crime, and gains definite satisfactions from the present mishandling of it! We condemn crime; we punish offenders for it; but we need it. The crime and punishment ritual is part of our lives."

_____

_____

_____

_____

_____

_____

7. In the debate between those who want the death penalty retained and those who want it abolished, who has the burden of proof? Why?

_____

_____

_____

_____

_____

_____

_____

8. Is it reasonable to assume that the death penalty is a better deterrent than life imprisonment?

_____

_____

_____

_____

_____

_____

_____

9. Assume that the death penalty is justified. Is the method used morally relevant? In other words, does a morally relevant difference exist between executing a criminal by the electric chair as opposed to hanging? To lethal injection? To lethal gas? Does it matter if executions are private or public? On national television? Would it be right to applaud at public executions?

_____

_____

_____

_____

_____

_____

10. If the murderer deserves capital punishment, what punishment does the mass-murderer deserve?

_____

_____

_____

_____

_____

_____

11. Assume that capital punishment is justified. Is it morally permissible for a citizen to kill a convicted murderer on the way to be executed if we are certain that the criminal is guilty materially as well as formally (factually as well as legally)?

_____

_____

_____

_____

_____

_____

12. The Georgia statute under which Gregg was sentenced retained the death penalty not only for the crime of murder but also for "kidnapping for ransom or where the victim is harmed, armed robbery, rape, treason, and aircraft hijacking." Is the death penalty a disproportionate punishment for these crimes?

_____

_____

_____

_____

_____

_____

13. The Georgia statute under which Gregg was convicted directed the jury to the circumstances of the crime. Among the questions the jury was to consider was whether the crime was committed upon a peace officer or judicial officer as opposed to a civilian. In your judgment, is this morally relevant? What arguments can you think of that would justify administering the death penalty specifically for killing a peace (or judicial) officer? What factors argue against this position?

_____

_____

_____

_____

_____

_____

_____

14. Some have argued (for example, Stephen Nathanson) that we should eliminate the death penalty since the legal system fails to do a satisfactory job at picking out those who deserve to die. But if this is true of the death penalty, is it not also true of all forms of punishment? Discuss whether we should eliminate all punishment for this reason.

_____

_____

_____

_____

_____

_____

_____

_____

15. Evaluate the following claim: If we do not know whether the death penalty deters, we are faced with two uncertainties. If we impose it and achieve no deterrent effect, the life of a convicted murderer has been needlessly expended. (We have a net loss.) If we impose the death penalty and it does deter some future murderers, we've spared the lives of some future victims. (We have a net gain.) Given these uncertainties, we should retain the death penalty since it is more cost-effective than its alternative.

_____

_____

_____

_____

_____

For Further Reading

Beccaria, Cesare. *On Crimes and Punishments.* Trans. Henry Paolucci. Indianapolis: Bobbs-Merrill, 1963 [1764].

Bedau, Hugo Adam. "Capital Punishment." In Tom Regan, ed., *Matters of Life and Death,* 2nd ed. New York: Random House, 1986.

———, ed. *The Death Penalty in America,* 3rd ed. New York: Oxford University Press, 1982 [1964].

Berns, Walter. *For Capital Punishment: Crime and the Morality of the Death Penalty.* New York: Basic Books, 1979.

Cole, George F. *The American System of Criminal Justice,* 6th ed. Pacific Grove, Calif.: Brooks/Cole Publishing Company, 1992.

Feinberg, Joel. *The Moral Limits of the Criminal Law* (4 vols). New York: Oxford University Press, 1984–1988.

Gorr, Michael J., and Sterling Harwood. *Crime and Punishment.* Boston: Jones and Bartlett, 1995.

Gross, Hyman. *A Theory of Criminal Justice.* New York: Oxford University Press, 1979.

Husak, Douglas N. *Philosophy of Criminal Law.* Totowa, N.J.: Rowman and Littlefield, 1987.

Jacoby, Susan. *Wild Justice: The Evolution of Revenge.* New York: Harper & Row, 1983.

Kadish, Sanford H., ed. *Encyclopedia of Crime and Justice* (4 vols). New York: Free Press, 1983.

Kant, Immanuel. *The Metaphysical Elements of Justice,* trans. John Ladd. Indianapolis: Bobbs-Merrill, 1965 [1797].

Mill, John Stuart. "Speech in Favor of Capital Punishment." In *Philosophical Perspectives on Punishment,* edited by Gertrude Ezorsky. Albany: State University of New York Press, 1972.

Primoratz, Igor. *Justifying Legal Punishment.* Atlantic Highlands, N.J.: Humanities Press International, 1989.

Reid, Susan Titus. *Crime and Criminology,* 6th ed. Fort Worth, Texas: Holt, Rinehart and Winston, 1991.

Reiman, Jeffrey H. "Justice, Civilization, and the Death Penalty: Answering van den Haag." *Philosophy and Public Affairs* 14 (Spring 1985): 115–148.

———. *The Rich Get Richer and the Poor Get Prison: Ideology, Class, and Criminal Justice,* 3rd ed. New York: Macmillan, 1990.

Sellin, Thorstein. *The Punishment of Death.* Beverly Hills, Calif.: Sage, 1980.

Van den Haag, Ernest, and John P. Conrad. *The Death Penalty: A Debate.* New York: Plenum, 1983.

Chapter 5

War and Terrorism

Passages for Reflection

"Morality is contraband in war."
—*Mohandas K. Gandhi*

"An unjust peace is better than a just war."
—*Cicero*

"Terrorism is the poor man's Atom Bomb."
—*Unknown*

"Throwing a bomb is bad,
Dropping a bomb is good;
Terror, no need to add,
Depends on who's wearing the hood."
—*Roger Woddies*

Opening Questions

1. Do ethical principles apply in war?
2. Is it true, as the saying goes, that "all is fair in war"?
3. Can the military afford to be ethical?
4. What is terrorism?
5. Can terrorism be justified?

Putting *ethics* together with *war* and *terrorism* sounds more like a parody than a topic for serious discussion. From one point of view, war and terrorism are inherently unethical and it is senseless to speak as if ethical principles could apply to them. From another point of view, the absurdity of war and terrorism is precisely the reason that we need ethical principles to pertain to them; we need ethics here if we need ethics at all. We will begin, then, by examining the ethics of war and proceed to discuss the ethics of terrorism. Analysis of the ethics of terrorism profitably grows out of analysis of the ethics of war.

Writers on the ethics of war roughly fall into three major groups. At one extreme are the *realists* who hold that "all is fair in war" or, more precisely, that moral considerations are not relevant to sovereign states acting in the international society of nations. Thomas Hobbes defends this view in *Leviathan* where he argues that nations are always in a "state of nature" since no social contract or common authority enforces standards of right and wrong. From the realist's perspective, relations among nations are ultimately based on *power*. This being so, military conduct may be ineffective, misguided, or uniformed, but what it cannot be is immoral. The only considerations that have moral relevance are those relating to the welfare of the state. War is one among many means of settling disputes when no other alternatives seem promising.

At the other extreme are the *pacifists* who hold that war is wrong by its very nature because it necessarily involves the intentional killing of human beings. Pacifism comes in several varieties. In what might be called *absolute pacifism,* all war is wrong since the value of life is absolute and cannot be overridden by other considerations. In what might be called *limited* or *contextual* pacifism, the value of human life is affirmed while leaving open the question of whether it is wrong to kill another human being in a particular context.

In between realism and pacifism is the more moderate view which lists the conditions under which a nation may fight an ethical war. Advocates of the so-called *just-war doctrine* distinguish between the conditions under which a nation may go to war (*jus ad bellum*) and what a nation may do within a war (*jus in bello*). Since the just-war doctrine neither rules war in or out in its entirety but speaks to the circumstances in which war is permissible, it is the most interesting of the three positions and the one we will analyze in detail.

The Just-War Doctrine: When May a Nation Go to War?

In answer to the question, "When may a nation go to war?", just-war theorists give a variety of answers. We may identify no less than seven requirements that just-war theorists have appealed to without insisting that all seven be present. Let us say that nation A has the right to go to war against nation B provided some or all of the following requirements are met. Afterwards, we will examine each of these requirements more carefully.

1. *The Just Cause Requirement.* A is attacked by B, or is helping another nation C that has been attacked by B, or A or C are about to be attacked by B.
2. *The Legitimate Authority Requirement.* The individuals in A who declare war on B have legitimate authority to do so.
3. *The Good Intentions Requirement.* A's intentions in waging war are limited to repelling B's attack and establishing a just peace.
4. *The Reasonable Chance of Success Requirement.* A has a reasonable chance of successfully achieving the good it intends.
5. *The Proportionality of Just Cause to Means Requirement.* The good A can reasonably hope to achieve is commensurate with the evils that can reasonably be expected to result.
6. *The Last Resort Requirement.* A has exhausted all peaceful alternatives and fighting the war is the last resort.
7. *The Moral Means Requirement.* A does not use or anticipate using immoral means in waging war.

Let us explain these requirements with an eye on those wars that have occupied center stage of world affairs in recent years, particularly America's wars against North Vietnam and Iraq.

The Just-Cause Requirement

This requirement states that a nation may to go to war only if it has been attacked by another nation. As most of us see it (realists notwithstanding), a nation does not have a right to begin a war although it does have a right to repel an aggressor. We can understand this better by drawing an analogy between the just-cause requirement and the common law doctrine of self-defense.

The common-law doctrine of self-defense states that force can be used against a person to repel an act of aggression. To *initiate* an act of aggression is to commit a *battery*—an "unpermitted touching" which, depending on the amount of harm inflicted, can be a criminal offense resulting in punishment. To say that you may repel an attacker is not to say how much force may be used. Since the law generally holds us responsible for acting "reasonably," the rule of law in self-defense is that one may use only that amount of force that is needed to repel an attack. To use more than what is needed is to turn an act of self-defense into an act of aggression. Similarly, where the victim is someone other than ourselves, the law allows for third-party defense, the rule of law being that the third-party defender is allowed to use as much force as would be reasonable for the victim to use in self-defense.

At first glance, the law of self-defense strikes us as odd. We might think that any amount of force is justified to repel an unlawful attack. But consider the would-be purse-snatcher who is shot by his victim in self-defense. While by no means excusing the purse-snatcher, the victim of the attack is hardly innocent. In shooting her attacker, she is using excessive force and by doing so has herself become an attacker.

What counts as "reasonable force" is a question open to interpretation. In the celebrated case in New York City of Bernard Goetz, the defense claimed that Goetz was justified in shooting a group of menacing panhandlers in the subway who presumably had brandished a screwdriver at him. The prosecution argued that the shooting was excessive evidenced by Goetz's shooting the men in the back as they fled from him. While the law does not require that a would-be victim stop and calculate what would count as reasonable force, the law does hold us responsible for acting reasonably in that failure to do so may be a criminal offense. For this reason, an individual may kill in self-defense only if that individual's life is threatened by an attacker and the threat can be met by killing the attacker first. In Goetz's case, Goetz successfully argued that the menacing panhandlers posed a threat to his life and that he was justified in shooting them. He was, however, convicted of unlawfully possessing a handgun and found liable in subsequent civil suits.

Applying what has been said about common law principles to principles governing international affairs, we can say that a nation cannot initiate an attack; that it can in self-defense use force to repel an attack; and that it can come to the defense of another nation that has been attacked. Thus, the just-cause requirement mirrors the common-law principle of self-defense. As far as the amount of force a nation may use to defend itself or a third-party nation, what is true in common-law is true here although degree of force is analyzed elsewhere in the just-war doctrine. (See the principle of proportionality, p. 137.)

America's war against Japan is a clear example of a war that satisfied the just-cause requirement. Japan's bombing of Pearl Harbor in 1941 gave the United States an undisputed right to defend itself. The Gulf

War in 1991 likewise satisfied this requirement although the war against Iraq was a case of third-party defense rather than a case of self-defense. When Iraq invaded Kuwait, the allied forces came to Kuwait's defense. America's war in Vietnam raises difficulties. You could argue that America's war against North Vietnam satisfied the third-party defense requirement inasmuch as America came to the defense of South Vietnam. However, the rationale offered at the time was that America itself would fall prey to communist influences if South Vietnam fell to North Vietnam like so many dominoes falling on one another. (America's concern was with stopping the Soviet Union from spreading its sphere of influence around the world.) But if resorting to the "domino effect" was the sole rationale for claiming that America had been "attacked," then it is highly dubious whether the just-cause requirement was met. This should not surprise us, given the moral controversy that war has generated among American citizens.

Before turning to the remaining and less complicated requirements of the just-war doctrine, let us look at that clause in the just-cause requirement that allows one nation to attack another if that nation *is about to be attacked* by the other. What this means is that a nation may go to war if it has reason to believe that an attack is imminent. The rationale is not so much that the best defense is an offense, which may or may not be true, but that the one who starts a war is not always the one who throws the "first punch." Thus, in the Six-Day War between Israel and its Arab neighbors (1967), Israel landed the first blow but only after the Arab states had marshalled their forces in preparation for an imminent assault. Israel at that point launched a preemptive strike on the Egyptian air force and destroyed 80 percent of its jet fighters. Likewise, Athens' attack on Sparta may be viewed as a preemptive strike that satisfied this portion of the just-cause requirement, as the United States would have had it attacked the Soviet Union following the Cuban missile crisis in 1962. But note that some just-war theorists reject the legitimacy of preemptive strikes.

The Legitimate Authority Requirement

This requirement is concerned with those who lack authority to send citizens off to war. How can that be? In the United States, only the Congress can declare war. But the United States is a bad example. Consider a country such as Haiti which, during the early 1990s, was occupied by a military junta that had ousted its exiled civilian president, Jean-Bertrand Aristide. If the military had declared war, citizens of Haiti could persuasively have argued that the war would be unjust because their elected leader, who has the legitimate authority to declare war, was not the one who made the decision.

The Good Intentions Requirement

The rationale behind this requirement is to prevent a nation from waging war for questionable reasons. In the Gulf War, for instance, critics of the war were rumbling that the United States entered the war to safeguard its interest in crude oil rather than to assist Kuwait with its defense. Critics of the war cited the fact that, historically, other non-oil-rich countries have been attacked without the United States coming to their defense. The critics felt that U.S. intentions were not confined to repelling Iraq's attack and that the U.S. had no right to enter the war. Notwithstanding the invalidity of this argument (that because a country does not go to every nation's defense does not mean it can go to no nation's defense), the point of the requirement is clear: a nation's intent must be to drive out the attacking nation and establish a fair peace. Had the United States driven into Iraq to claim its oil following Iraq's ouster from Kuwait, then the United States would have been in violation of this requirement's second clause.

The Reasonable Hope of Success and the Proportionality of Just Cause to Means Requirements

The reasonable hope of success requirement speaks to the injustice of a nation's sending its citizens to certain or near-certain defeat. If a nation stands little chance of winning a war and its leaders wage war nevertheless, this is tantamount to the nation's sending its citizens to be slaughtered, which no nation has the right to do. Where defeat is certain and the loss of lives will be significant, alternatives to war must be considered. In a similar vein, the proportionality of just cause to means requirement insists that the good the war is designed to achieve be worth the cost of the war. To lose many lives for a modest good is neither cost-effective nor just, and the proportionality requirements speaks to this concern. Few would argue that the loss of American lives in World War II was not worth the cost, though many would argue that the benefits of fighting the Vietnam war were not worth the cost. This is not to deny that death might be preferable to the rule of imperialistic nations. In the 1960s, when the threat of Communism was perceived as real, many Americans rallied around the slogan, "Better dead than red."

The Last Resort Requirement

This requirement needs no elucidation. What must be said is only that a nation can never be sure when it has exhausted all peaceful alternatives. If the Gulf War violated any requirement of the just-war doctrine, this was the one. The world community imposed economic sanctions on Iraq following its invasion of Kuwait. Critics of the war argued that the Bush administration failed to give the sanctions enough of a chance, claiming that such sanctions would have inevitably led to Iraq's retreat. The Bush administration argued that the allies had exhausted all peaceful alternatives and were left with little choice.

The Moral Means Requirement

Under the terms of this requirement, a nation may neither *use or anticipate using* immoral means in waging war. Here, we have the obvious question of what constitutes "moral means," a question discussed under the topic of what a nation may do within a war. Conduct is immoral if it is excessive or fails to discriminate between combatants and noncombatants. As for the requirement that a nation must not *anticipate* using immoral means, we have the interesting question of how to evaluate a nation that does not anticipate using immoral means at the beginning of the war but anticipates or uses immoral means when the war is in bloom. Consider in this light America's use of the atomic bomb on the cities of Nagasaki and Hiroshima. That the United States didn't anticipate using the bomb is evidenced by the fact that the war began in 1941 and the bomb was invented some three years later. This raises the question of whether a war can begin as just but become unjust at a later date. For this reason, proponents of the just-war doctrine insist that wars be evaluated from beginning to end.

What May a Nation Do within a War?

Having discussed the conditions under which a nation has a right to go to war, we have to address what a nation may do within a war. *The principle of proportionality* states that the level of force employed must be commensurate with the good that the action is intended to achieve. *The principle of discrimination* states that force be used in a way that discriminates between combatants and noncombatants.

The principle of proportionality requires that the good of an action be commensurate with any bad consequences caused by that action. Suppose, for example, a battalion can accomplish an objective of marginal value, say, the taking of a bunker, but only by means that would lead to many civilian casualties. Under the terms of the principle of proportionality, such an objective would be impermissible. Or consider the allied policy of taking prisoner those German soldiers who surrendered after World War II. Had the allies adopted the policy of taking no prisoners alive, then the evils caused by this policy would have been disproportionate to the result achieved.

The principle of discrimination is usually understood as prohibiting the direct intentional killing of noncombatants. But controversy arises over the meaning of *intentional* and *noncombatants*. While some supporters of the principle of discrimination would not distinguish between intended and foreseen consequences, many just-war theorists interpret the prohibition against "intentionally" killing a noncombatant along the lines of the *doctrine of double effect*. Under the terms of this doctrine, an act that has both good and bad effects, both of which can be foreseen, is permissible provided:

1. The act itself is not impermissible.
2. The good but not the bad effect is intended.
3. The bad effect is not the means to the good effect.
4. The good effect is commensurate with the bad effect.

An example will illustrate this principle. In the Gulf War, Sadaam Hussein set up munitions factories in schools and hospitals so that bombing these targets could not be accomplished without civilian casualties. This was a brilliant if unethical strategy as he played on America's vulnerability to moral criticism following its war in Vietnam. Under the doctrine of double effect, it was permissible to bomb the munitions factory since: (1) bombing military targets is permissible in times of war; (2) the intention was to destroy the munitions factory notwithstanding the foreseeability of civilian casualties; (3) the deaths of the civilians were not the means to destroying the military target; and (4) the military target was strategically important relative to the innocent lives that were lost as a result.

In the Gulf War, the allied forces tried to comply with the doctrine of double effect. This is evidenced by their use of "smart bombs"—weapons designed to discriminate between combatants and noncombatants—as well as "surgical strikes"—maneuvers designed to respect that same distinction. (It was also evidenced by President Bush's carrying a statement of the just-war doctrine in his shirt pocket!) In contrast, America's involvement in Southeast Asia during the Vietnam War included many impermissible weapons such as napalm (a volatile firebomb) and agent orange (a carcinogenic defoliant), and included maneuvers that failed to discriminate between combatants and noncombatants. Other weaponry that would not be permissible under the doctrine of double effect includes saturation bombs of the kind used in World War II and biological and nuclear weapons.

The question remains, then, of deciding what is to count as a "combatant." In the Middle Ages, this distinction was easy to make. Combatants were the knights in armor carrying lances on horseback, and noncombatants included everyone else. Today, the distinction is more difficult to make if we leave aside members of the Red Cross. In Southeast Asia, the North Vietnamese employed such traditional noncombatants as women and children to perform military operations. This made ethical conduct virtually impossible for American soldiers who wished to respect the distinction.

In *Apocalypse Now,* Francis Ford Coppola poignantly depicts how difficult a problem this posed for some soldiers. Early in the film, in the infamous helicopter attack on a North Vietnamese village (to the forbidding tune of Wagner's "The Ride of the Valkyries"), a woman is seen running to an American helicopter about to take off following the raid. Apparently running for help, the woman is carrying a bomb in the guise of a hat and places it in the helicopter, destroying the aircraft and its crew. Later in the film, the crew is heading down the Do Lung River when they encounter what is apparently a civilian boat. Upon inspecting the boat for possible insurgents, they order everyone to leave, only to see one young woman reach for a package whereupon a soldier opens fire and kills her. We then learn that she was reaching for her puppy.

While not a comprehensive analysis, the best that might be said about the distinction between combatants and noncombatants is this: A combatant is anyone who bears a "family resemblance" to a soldier at the front (a paradigm case of a combatant), while a noncombatant is anyone who bears a "family resemblance" to an infant (a paradigm case of a noncombatant). The notion of family resemblance was introduced by the philosopher Ludwig Wittgenstein who maintained that some concepts, like the concept of a game, cannot be clearly delineated. We can, however, recognize resemblances that exist between a group or family of concepts the way we recognize a resemblance between members of a family. To use Wittgenstein's favorite example, even though no one game has features that all games have in common, we can nevertheless recognize all things that are games. So, even though no combatant has all features that all combatants have in common, a family resemblance might obtain between fighting soldiers and other combatants.

The question "What is a combatant?" figures prominently in discussions of terrorism as well as war if we take the targeting of noncombatants as a central feature of terrorist activity. Since terrorism is frequently objected to because noncombatants or "innocents" are attacked, it stands to reason that the targeting of noncombatants figures prominently in an attempt to define terrorism. Surprisingly, this is not always so.

What Is Terrorism?

Several definitions have been proposed as an answer to the question "What is terrorism?", each concentrating on various features of terrorist activity. Martin Hughes defines terrorism as "a war in which a secret army . . . spreads fear"[1]; he emphasizes the secrecy of terrorist activity as

---

[1]Martin Hughes, "Terrorism and National Security." *Philosophy* 57 (1982): 5–26.

well as its ability to cause widespread fear. Barrie Paskins and M. L. Dockrill define it as an "indiscriminate war of evasion"[2]; they emphasize the randomness of terrorist violence as well as its being an attack on the state. And Grant Wardlow emphasizes the effects of terrorism and the purposes for which violence is used when he defines terrorism as political violence "designed to create extreme anxiety and/or fear in a target group larger than the immediate victims with the purpose of coercing that group into acceding to the political demands of the perpetrators."[3]

In the most controversial of definitions, Carl Wellman defines terrorism as "the use or attempted use of terror as a means of coercion"[4] and remarks that while violence often enters the picture since it is an effective means of causing terror, "the ethics of terrorism is not a mere footnote to the ethics of violence because violence is not essential to terrorism. . . ."[5] As examples of "nonviolent terrorism," Wellman mentions cases of blackmail where the threat of exposure is used as a means of intimidation; a judge sentencing a convicted criminal to death in order to deter potential criminals; and the threat to flunk a student who fails to hand in a paper in a timely fashion. Of this last threat, Wellman says:

> I must confess I often engage in nonviolent terrorism myself, for I often threaten to flunk any student who hands in his paper after the due date. Anyone who doubts that my acts are genuine instances of terrorism is invited to observe the unwillingness of my students to hand in assigned papers on time in the absence of any such threat and the panic in my classroom when I issue my ultimatum.[6]

Not all definitions of terrorism do justice to the term. Nevertheless, defining terrorism continues to be a major concern for philosophers writing on the subject. The reason for this is clear: if, as the saying goes, one person's terrorist is another person's freedom fighter, then what counts as terrorism has moral implications. But rather than formally defining terrorism, let us take an unequivocal case of terrorism and see if we could provide a rough description. Such a description, while falling short of supplying the distinguishing features of terrorist activity, is useful in allowing us to examine moral evaluations of conduct exhibiting key features of terrorism. It also has the virtue of capturing what most people think terrorism is as the term is used in the modern world where terrorism has

---

[2]Barrie Paskins and M. L. Dockrill, *The Ethics of War* (London: Duckworth; Minneapolis: University of Minnesota Press, 1979).

[3]Grant Wardlow, *Political Terrorism* (Cambridge, New York: Cambridge University Press, 1982).

[4]Carl Wellman, "On Terrorism Itself." *The Journal of Value Inquiry* 13 (1979): 250.

[5]Ibid., p. 251.

[6]Ibid., p. 252.

assumed unprecedented proportions during the past three decades and for that reason alone lays claim to providing a paradigm of sorts.

While examples abound from which to choose, let us focus on a "terrorist" attack that took place in October 1994: the Hamas suicide bombing of a public bus in Tel Aviv, killing twenty-two Israelis and wounding about forty. (The attack on the World Trade Center works just as well.) No doubt some will oppose this choice. One opposition will come from Palestinian sympathizers who will argue that the Hamas are "freedom fighters" rather than terrorists and that singling them out is question-begging or ideological. Opposition will also likely come from those who maintain that the activities of other groups such as the Irish Republican Army are as paradigmatic as those of Hamas.

To those who maintain that the choice of Hamas is question-begging or ideological, we can respond by saying that Hamas's activities lay *some* claim to being "terrorist" no matter how we propose to analyze the term. We can even go so far as to say that it would be better to reject a definition that excluded Hamas's activities than accept one that leaves them out. And to those who maintain that any number of terrorist activities could have served as a starting point, I freely admit that Hamas's activities have no privileged status. Having said this, I stipulate that if the activities of so notorious a group as Hamas is not considered "terrorist," then no activity can be described as such.

Who then are the Hamas and what do they stand for? Born in 1987 out of the strife of the *intifada* (the Palestinian uprising in the West Bank and Gaza), Hamas is an Islamic resistance movement pledged to destroy Israel and create an Islamic state based on Koranic law. With more than thirty-five murders in Israel to its "credit" after the 1994 bombing of the Tel Aviv bus, Hamas's military wing, the Qassam Brigades, is intent on killing however many people it takes until Israel gives up its push for peace. Violence, say many of Hamas's supporters, is the only way left to kill off the peace. The very word *hamas* means "zeal" in Arabic and is also an acronym for *Harakat al-Muqawama al-Islamiya*—the Islamic Resistance Movement. In addition to frustrating Israel's push for peace with its Arab neighbors, Hamas would also like to see Israel renounce or embarrass Palestine Liberation Organization Chairman Yasser Arafat.

If we take Hamas's bombing of a civilian bus as a model case of terrorism, what we find is this: (1) a group of individuals (2) who intentionally inflict violence (3) against civilians (4) for the purpose of furthering political objectives. These features provide us with a description of terrorism that goes far to preserve many of the properties we take terrorism to possess: the etymological connection between terrorism and *terror*, the targeting of civilians as a means to achieve a goal, a political agenda, and a revolutionary (non-state-sponsored) organization. The description also has affinities with the definition proposed by Jan Schreiber in his book, *The Ultimate Weapon: Terrorists and World Order*. As

Schreiber sees it, terrorism is "a political act, ordinarily committed by an organized group, involving the death or the threat of death to non-combatants."[7] The main difference between Schreiber's analysis and the one proposed is that Schreiber's is vague as to what is meant by "involving" noncombatants, whereas the proposed analysis specifically lists noncombatants as the intended victims of terrorist activity. C. A. J. Coady, too, emphasizes "violence targeted upon noncombatants" in his perceptive analysis of terrorism.[8]

To be sure, we can think of activities that have come under the label of "terrorism" which would not fit the proposed description. The description does not countenance, for instance, guerrilla warfare, political assassination, violence against property, criminal executions, revolutions, insurrections, tyrannicide, and state-sponsored terror. What the description does countenance are activities that are intended to cause harm to noncombatants for purposes that are political in nature. An act fully characteristic of terrorism will normally have all of these features, and so the description has the virtue of capturing many of the more notorious "terrorist" activities in recent memory such as the Irish Republican Army's bombing of pubs, stores, and public transport, and the activities of fundamentalist Islamic organizations like Hamas. It also describes as terrorist the 1994 attempt of Islamic radicals to seize in Algiers a Paris-bound commuter jet with the intention of destroying it in mid-flight. That aborted attempt was led by Armed Islamic Group, a fundamentalist organization fighting to install Islamic rule in Algeria.

Putting forward criteria that "fully characterize" an act of terrorism does not mean that borderline cases do not exist. An interesting borderline case is the fictitious one given to us by Paul Auster in his novel *Leviathan*.[9] Here we meet Benjamin Sachs, a man bent on blowing up imitation Statues of Liberty that are scattered across the country. Nicknamed the Phantom of Liberty by the press, Sachs is intent on continuing the work of a man he had inadvertently killed, a man who was a member of a left-wing ecology group (Children of the Planet) committed to shutting down the operations of nuclear power plants, logging companies, and other "despoilers of the earth." And while Sach's motives are complex and obscure—he seems driven by his fate as much as he his driven by ideology—he is portrayed by the media in the novel as a terrorist.

Is Benjamin Sachs a terrorist? It is best to say no, while admitting that what he did bears resemblance to normal terrorist activities. He spread fear in those towns that had Statues of Liberty at least partly for political pur-

---

[7]Jan Schreiber, *The Ultimate Weapon: Terrorists and World Order* (New York: Morrow, 1978), p. 20.

[8]C. A. J. Coady, "The Morality of Terrorism." *Philosophy* 60 (1985): 47–69.

[9]Penguin Books, 1992.

poses. But he acted alone and not in concert with any group of individuals (although the man whose activities he took over was a member of such a group), and he took care to bomb property—not people—and then only in the early hours of the night when people were asleep. Had Sachs become a bona fide member of Children of the Planet and had he embarked on advancing its causes by destroying people rather than statues, his activities would have been characteristically terrorist.

But what if Sachs had joined Children of the Planet, sought to advance its causes, yet did not take care to prevent people from being harmed? In other words, what if Sachs did not intend to kill innocent people but foresaw that they would die as a result of the explosions? Sooner or later, a custodian would be found in a statue whose presence would be apparent to Sachs. Would this have been terrorism, properly called? It would be easy to say no, given our definition, were it not that this activity bears a striking resemblance to terrorism as it is often understood. We need to decide, then, whether our concept of terrorism is elastic enough to embrace *foreseen but unintended deaths* in a way that supporters of the doctrine of double effect embrace the foreseen but unintended deaths of noncombatants in war.

The question is difficult. At issue is not just what is terrorism but whether terrorism can be justified. Consider that terrorism, as we have construed it, is an act of violence intentionally inflicted on noncombatants. If we agree that it is wrong to intentionally kill noncombatants, then it makes no sense to speak of "justified terrorism." But if we acknowledge a species of terrorism that foresees though does not intend the deaths of innocent people, then "justified terrorism" is logically possible. It would be justified only on those occasions when the other criteria of the doctrine of double effect are satisfied. We would have to determine whether the act was permissible, whether the bad was the means to the good, and whether the bad was commensurate with the good. Only then could we decide whether a case of terrorism was justified. But the question is largely academic inasmuch as most modern-day terrorists are not in the habit of complying with the doctrine of double effect. Perhaps all we need to say is that activities of the Benjamin Sachs variety (suitably modified) are not fully characteristic of terrorism—at least not when measured against modern and notorious instances thereof.

Our analysis sees terrorism as wrong per se inasmuch as it essentially involves the intentional targeting of noncombatants, and this is something wrong to do. We are back to square one inasmuch as we never really fixed the definition of *combatant*. The Puerto Rico Christian pilgrims who were gunned down in the Tel Aviv airport were labeled "combatants" by terrorists simply because they had chosen to visit Israel! But even if we could clearly distinguish between combatants and noncombatants, some would defend terrorism by arguing that killing noncombatants is only wrong to do when it is not cost-effective. It is possible, that is, to agree that terrorism involves the intentional deaths of noncombatants while denying that that is something wrong to do. Kai Nielsen, for one, while not explicitly agreeing with our definition of terrorism, nonetheless argues that terrorism can be justified when it involves the intentional deaths of innocent people. Speaking from a tradition of utilitarianism, Nielsen argues that terrorist acts, like all acts, must ultimately be justified by their consequences. "If," says Nielsen, "revolutionary violence in the service of socialism were to lessen . . . suffering, degradation, and injustice more than would any other practically viable alternative, then it is justified, and if not, not."[10] For Nielsen as for any other utilitarian, the rightness of an action is wholly determined by the resulting consequences.

Out of respect for Nielsen, we should ask, then, whether terrorism works. Here, the evidence is equivocal. The Black September attack on Israeli athletes in Munich did precisely what it intended to do: make the world take notice of the Palestinians. At the same time, it increased Israel's resolve to fight against terrorism and roused the European governments into realizing the dangers they were facing. Other cases will spawn similar uncertainties. So until the evidence is in, it is hard to say whether terrorism works. But beyond its efficacy, we must see that the question of whether terrorism works is relevant only from a utilitarian point of view. For those with a deontological bent, the effectiveness of terrorism is beside the point.

---

[10]Kai Nielsen, "Violence and Terrorism: Its Uses and Abuses." In Burton M. Leiser, ed., *Values in Conflict: Life, Liberty and the Rule of Law* (New York: Macmillan, 1981), p. 449.

David E. Johnson is Professor of Philosophy at the United States Naval Academy, Annapolis, Maryland. He is currently writing a book about the Tailhook incident.

Video Presentation

Guest: David E. Johnson, Professor of Philosophy, United States Naval Academy

Student Panel: Mark Esposito, Tara Turnbull, Lynn Talamini

I begin the discussion by identifying a continuum of views that a person might have on the question of whether we can speak of an ethics of war. I mention in this context the views of pacifism, just war, and realism. Johnson agrees that this continuum exists and, after likening political leaders to parents, he mentions how both parents and politicians place constraints on what children/soldiers may rightfully do. He thus rejects realism and sketches an outline of the just-war doctrine, noting that while he subscribes to the doctrine, he does so on such a strict interpretation that little difference can be seen between his own view and pacifism.

After discussing the relationship between pacifism and the common-law principle of self-defense, I ask Johnson to elaborate on the just-war doctrine, which he does while giving a history of the doctrine. We then briefly touch upon a host of issues, including the distinction between combatants and noncombatants, the ethics of morale bombing, the ethics of preemptive attacks, and gays in the military.

Regarding the combatant/noncombatant distinction, I ask Johnson how a nation ought to respond when an enemy nation, like Iraq in the Gulf War, uses its civilians as a shield, giving its enemies the unhappy choice of killing civilians or fighting an ineffective war. His answer is that the onus of killing civilians in such a situation is with the nation that engages in such conduct, Iraq in this example. The task of the allies during Operation Desert Storm was to do all that was within their power, given the requirements of just-war principles.

Regarding the ethics of morale bombing, that is, the ethics of bombing civilians in an effort to weaken their resolve, Johnson cites the ineffectiveness of such a policy as evidenced by Hitler's bombing of London and the allied bombing of Dresden in World War II. Johnson also points out how curious Churchill's decision was to proceed with the morale bombing of Dresden, knowing full well, following Hitler's attack on London, that it works to *increase* a country's resolve to fight a war.

Finally, regarding gays in the military, Johnson notes how present attitudes mirror those held toward blacks in the military in the not too distant past. He remarks that so long as homosexuals do not engage in predatory behavior against heterosexuals, a person's sexual orientation should not be an issue.

Following the break, Mark Esposito asks Johnson about the ethics of abandoning MIAs, those American soldiers who have not been accounted for or who are "missing in action." He suggests that the Nixon administration pulled U.S. forces out of Southeast Asia with no apparent regard for U.S. MIAs. Tara Turnbull wants to know to what extent sexual discrimination exists in the armed forces, and Lynn Talamini asks Johnson to comment on the anomaly that gays are an asset in war even though they are discriminated against during peacetime. Taking a cue from Turnbull, the show ends with a discussion of Tailhook, a scandal occurring when, at a conference for the Naval Academy, some male officers sexually assaulted some female officers.

In this essay, David E. Johnson raises provocative questions about "military ethics." He begins by noting that while the military is in the profession of arms, the issues that concern it differ from other professions inasmuch as its task is the unique one of fighting and being prepared to die for a way of life. This understood, he examines some questions of military ethics against the backdrop of Republic *where Plato suggests that every nation must sooner or later engage in warfare to either keep what it has or procure what it wants. This suggests the questions, "When is it permissible to wage a war?" and "What may a nation do within a war?" After discussing these questions within the context of the just-war tradition, Johnson asks such questions as whether technology has rendered the just-war tradition obsolete; whether the nation the military serves is itself ethical; whether some practices in the military, such as not allowing homosexuals to serve, are ethical; and whether warfare is the necessity that Plato and we believe it to be.*

Can the Military Afford to Be Ethical?

David E. Johnson

What relationship can there be between philosophy and the military (the profession of arms)? Philosophy is in the business of critically examining our behavior, the beliefs that lead to that behavior, the arguments offered to justify those beliefs, and the concepts in terms of which the beliefs and justifications are stated. The military, on the other hand, is in the business of accomplishing missions and not tolerating insubordination that might compromise those missions. The two come together in the debate about whether or not the military must both conceive of those missions and carry them out in an ethical manner. The reason that it is important to apply ethics to the profession of arms, just like it is with regard to the medical profession, is that the military deals with life-and-death issues. More specifically, the military is in the business of taking human life. This distinguishes it from the medical profession which claims to be in the business of preserving human life.

In the United States, the major goals for the military are established by the civilian government. In very general terms, we can say that the military's task is to be prepared to fight, to kill, and to die in order to defend a way of life. An underlying assumption, not to be discussed here, is that this way of life is something worth fighting, killing, and dying for. If we look at this point through a "consequentialist" lens, it becomes the claim that both the way of life (the end) and the way of defending it (the means) are moral. The allowable means of defending our way of life are defined by laws. In the United States, the Constitution, statutes, and treaty obligations define much of this way of life. Our military leaders take an oath to defend and uphold the Constitution of the United States.

Within the context of the Constitution and in addition to the major moral issue of the taking of human life, there are other aspects of the conduct of military life that can be assessed ethically. For instance:

- Procurement
- Fraternization
- Sexual harassment
- Sexual preference
- Pollution from ships, planes, and bases
- The environmental impact of weapons testing
- The nature and role of technology (for example, is nuclear warfare a form of just war?)
- Racial discrimination
- The best methods of leadership/management (that is, respecting the dignity of each member of the armed forces)
- The best allocation of finite resources
- The most equitable way to downsize after the end of the cold war
- Accountability for budgets
- Truthful reporting, for example, body counts in Vietnam and performance reports in general

These issues are ones that the military shares with other professions in society.

In order to engage in "military ethics," we need to recognize that the military is a unique profession with some unique ethical concerns. To provide a context, I want to reflect on a story in the first book of Plato's *Republic*. This dialogue constitutes an inquiry into the nature of justice in the individual and in the state. Issues of peace and war are closely related to those of justice. This story leads to questions of the origin of the military and of justice in the area of warfare.

The story is a myth of the formation of societies. How and why do people live in cities and states? According to the story, people get into cities because they think it is *better* for them. The first kind of city that they construct is one that deals only with the necessities of life. Such a city is portrayed as small and at peace. As needs grow, the city grows. Plato says that cities keep an eye out against poverty *or* war.[1] The implication of that disjunction is very important. The crucial shift in the nature of the city is from a city providing necessities to a city providing luxuries. In some translations, this is put in terms of people in the city wanting *relishes*.[2] With this shift, the city changes from *healthy* to *feverish*.[3] In order to procure these luxuries, the city must grow and must eventually engage in warfare (to gain what it wants or to keep what it has). According to the story, we have just discovered the origin of war. It lies "in those things whose presence in cities *most of all* produces evils both private and public."[4] The morality of the military can now be seen in the context of what the society wants the military to do. In the twentieth century, increasing emphasis has been placed on defense being the primary (or only) function of the military of any nation. However, it should be obvious that if every military organization functioned only for defense of its own country, there would be no wars. The rhetoric of defense is often distorted so that wars of aggression and acquisition are justified as defensive wars.

Plato's view, which is also a modern notion, is that society benefits from a division of labor. That way, the most qualified persons are performing each task for the city. When this conception is applied to the military, the conclusion is that war is an art. An art benefits most by specialization. One consequence of this view is that the military requires its own education, particularly moral or character education.

In order to facilitate the work of the warriors (guardians), Plato urges the following beliefs on the citizens: that the work of the warriors (1) is more important, (2) requires more leisure time, (3) requires more art and diligence, (4) requires a nature fit for the pursuit.[5]

For the purposes of this volume, it is important to realize that professional military ethics is a branch of the philosophic discipline, ethics. Conclusions reached in ethics remain conclusions in military ethics. For instance, if lying is wrong in general, it is wrong in the military.

The purpose of the military is to wage war. And one point of warfare (perhaps the main one) is in some sense to win (to succeed in defending the country). Two major ethical issues associated with the profession of arms are: (1) when is it permissible to wage war and (2) how is a nation to go about waging war? The Christian-derived just-war doctrine undertakes to provide criteria by which to resolve both these issues.

In the context of the Constitution of the United States, the decision of when to wage war is a concern of the civilian leadership. In recent conflicts involving the U.S. military, a major concern of the civilian leadership has been to follow the tenets of the just-war theory (or at least to give the appearance of following those tenets). This concern has taken the nation's leadership to the incredible length of naming the invasion of Panama "Operation Just Cause."

Just-war theory lies on a continuum between pacifism at one end and holy war on the other end. There are several positions of pacifism along the continuum.[6] For this discussion, we will focus on antiwar pacifism and ignore the others. So, from left to right, the continuum consists of antiwar pacifism, just war, and holy war.

The characteristics distinguishing these three can be stated as follows. Antiwar pacifism argues that humans have a duty to refrain from engaging in warfare. Holy war theory argues that humans have a duty *to* engage in warfare. Just-war theory claims that there may be occasions on which participation in warfare can be justified. Note well that with this third position the burden on proof is on those who would justify warfare.

All three positions (with their variations) share the view that warfare can be morally evaluated. The opposite view—that while conflict within a nation can be morally assessed and regulated, conflict between nations cannot—is often called *realism*.[7] These distinctions provide a context within which to understand one of the most important criteria in just-war doctrine: the concept of proportionality.

Just-war theory consists of two major divisions: justification of whether or not to go to war at all (*jus ad bellum*) and criteria for how to conduct a war once it has begun (*jus in bello*). The concept of proportionality occurs in both divisions of the theory.

In addition to proportionality, *jus ad bellum* rules include competent authority, right intention, just cause, and just peace. The rule of proportionality is variously stated. Douglas Lackey puts it this way: "The rule of proportionality states that a war cannot be just unless the evil that can reasonably be expected to ensue from the war is less than the evil that can reasonably be expected to ensue if the war is not fought."[8]

How is this rule to be interpreted? Answering this question confronts us with the incommensurability of goods or values among themselves (and the incommensurability of evils among themselves). Can we say that the loss of X number of lives (of all combatants or even just those on our side) is a greater evil than the loss of certain rights or freedoms? Without that issue, this rule seems to imply "that a war is just only if there will be more death, suffering, and so forth if the war is not fought than if the war is fought."[9] In this view, the rule would censure most wars and just-war theory would be difficult to distinguish from antiwar pacifism.

The rule of proportionality in the *jus in bello* part of the just-war doctrine holds that the harm committed in fighting the war must be proportionate to the value of the objective.[10] If the *jus ad bellum* rule governs political decisions, this *jus in bello* rule governs military strategy. For example, using this section of the rule of proportionality, the American Roman Catholic Bishops issued a pastoral letter in 1983 stating that the use of nuclear weapons violated the rule of proportionality. In other words, military personnel conducting warfare by means of nuclear weapons would be engaged in an unjust form of warfare.

How does this rule mesh with the other rules in just-war theory?

The criteria in the just-war doctrine (*jus ad bellum*) are that:

1. Going to war be the last resort.
2. War be declared by a (the) legitimate authority.
3. Those declaring war operate with the right intention and a just cause. They should not be motivated by revenge or aggression, but by charity and/or defense.
4. There be a chance of success; futile resistance cannot be justified.
5. Waging war have a goal of peace, a situation that is preferable to the one that would prevail if the war was not fought.

Has technology rendered the entire just-war tradition obsolete? This is a very important question in light of the rule of discrimination, which states that military operations be directed against military targets, not against noncombatants. Both modern weapons of mass destruction and techniques of conducting warfare (most notably guerrilla warfare) have made it very difficult to maintain a distinction between combatants and noncombatants. The issue of how to wage war most concerns the military. The two central just-war criteria here are proportionality and discrimination.

Before civilians and the military can learn about the ethical conduct of war in these two senses, we first need to unlearn certain negative attitudes toward ethics that have existed in the military. Once this is accomplished, we can proceed to develop an ethical military. The story from Plato recounted intimates that the need for and nature of the military grow out of the larger society. In other words, the military reflects and is shaped by civilian values. Thus, the military needs to examine critically what those values are (i.e., what is it being asked to fight for). If the ends for which the soldiers are being asked to fight, kill, and die are not moral, that is, there is no just cause, then the morality of the means (i.e., how they are waging war) will not make what they are doing right.

So, in order for the military to be ethical, the nation the military serves must also be ethical. This issue has at least two aspects. First, the nation must be ethical in what it asks the military to do. Second, the ethics of the military must square up with the ethics of the larger society. What does this mean for our topic? If the country wants the military to do something unethical, being ethical would include refusing to do that. Can the military afford to be ethical in this sense?

Let me use the case of Third World development to illustrate the nature and importance of this question. What if one major function of our military is to enforce the inequitable distribution of resources that currently exists in the world? What are the relationships between First World militarism and regional conflicts in the Third World in the post-World War II period? A quotation from George Kenan in 1948 when he was head of the State Department Policy Planning Staff sets the tone and tells most of the story.

We have about 50 percent of the world's wealth but only 6.3 percent of its population. . . . In this situation, we cannot fail to be the object of envy and resentment. Our real task in the coming period is to devise a pattern of relationships which will permit us to maintain this position of disparity without positive detriment to our national security. To do so we will have to dispense with all sentimentality and daydreaming: and our attention will have to be concentrated everywhere on our immediate national objectives. We need not deceive ourselves that we can afford today the luxury of altruism and world benefaction. . . . [W]e should cease to talk about vague and—for the Far East—unreal objectives such as human rights, the raising of living standards, and democratization. The day is not far off when we are going to have to deal in straight power concepts. The less we are then hampered by idealistic slogans, the better.

As far as I can see there are only three options in the distribution of the world's resources. One, we can maintain the status quo. The consequence will necessitate participating in regional conflicts like those we are in now. Second, standards in the Third World can be raised to equal those in the First World. In this option, the resources of the planet will be exhausted in a short time unless we are able to find a "technological fix" that will enable all of us on planet earth to meet our needs. Third, we can reduce the standard of living in the First World in order to distribute more resources to the Third World. Since we are looking at the issues of justice underlying war and peace, the major issue here is how to assess social (or distributive) justice.

Because there are understandable pressures to rectify the present situations where people suffer because consumers in the rich nations receive more than their fair share, military force is brought in to keep the lid on. The claim is that our affluent life-styles require us to defend our resources making it difficult to achieve a peaceful world until we achieve a just world. Is the military astute enough to recognize that being asked to dominate the Third World is a request to do something immoral? If so, can or will the military refuse to carry out those orders from its civilian superiors? To summarize: The inequitable distribution of resources promotes conflict and violence (Plato). Policies like Kenan's that underwrite the inequitable distribution of resources are not a just cause. Thus, they do not fall under the heading of just war. So, members of the military need to consider their duty not to participate in military operations that perpetuate policies like Kenan's.

Ethical evaluation of the military comes under the heading of how people relate to each other. In these relationships, certain facets of our existence stand out: for example, race, sex, sexual preference, nationality, and so on. The profession of arms stands at one end of a continuum of approaches to conflict resolution. According to Carol Gilligan, men and women tend to focus on different bases for morality and conflict resolution.[11] Not surprisingly, the military has traditionally fallen into the male pattern. The military discriminates in various ways, some legitimate and some illegitimate. Legitimate ways have to do with height, weight, physical skills (as tested by completing an obstacle course), willingness to obey, and so on. However, it has discriminated and continues to discriminate in illegitimate ways, for instance, in terms of race, sex, and sexual preference. Racial discrimination continued until the end of World War II, when President Truman ordered the military services integrated. In the mid-1990s, discrimination against women is beginning to topple as women enter more and more combat positions. Traditionally, the path to promotion to the highest ranks led through leadership in combat positions. Denying women access to these positions has limited their possibilities for promotion to the ranks of general and admiral.

A current issue, which will date this essay for readers in the twenty-first century, is the "morality" of allowing open homosexuals to serve in the armed forces. Today, there are many people on active military duty who feel that homosexuality is an immoral lifestyle and that in some sense it is immoral to allow homosexuals to serve in the military. However, given our Constitution, if Congress passes and the president signs a law stating that people who are open about being homosexual can serve in the military, then such service will be legal. Under those circumstances, a member of the armed forces who feels that his personal morality would be compromised by serving alongside homosexuals has no other moral option than to resign his commission and go into another line of work.

The previous issues have been discussed from a perspective within a society that accepts the military and warfare as a necessary evil. Now our focus turns to the question, "Is war necessary, or merely evil?"

To being this discussion, consider the charge often leveled against pacifism: it won't work. Generally, this charge means that pacifism will not promote peace or enhance security and national defense. In other words, pacifism will lead to defeat and subjugation rather than victory and national pride. Robert Holmes, in the General Introduction to *Non-Violence in Theory and Practice,* suggests that we must ask this question in two senses. We must ask it about pacifism as a tactic and about pacifism as a way of life.[12] As a tactic, pacifism has seldom been tried. Gandhi is credited with liberating India from British colonialism using the techniques of pacifism. Very seldom has history recorded one nation using pacifism as a tactic in international relations. The same would be true of pacifism as a way of life. Generally, groups within a nation, such as the Quakers and Mennonites in the United States, adopt pacifism as a way of life. But this does not extend to the policies of the nation as a whole or to international relations.

But to ask whether pacifism (repudiating war but not necessarily all violence) works is to inquire whether it works better than warfare. Thus, it is important to ask, "Does war (or the military solution) work?" What does this question mean? Will war promote peace? Will war enhance (improve) the prosperity of the nation? Will war promote national interests? We generally ask this question about warfare as a tactic in situations in which both sides are employing warfare. In these situations, it is important to note that violence only works half the time. For every nation that is victorious (in either aggression or defense) there is a nation that is not victorious (successful). "In all such cases, violence fails precisely as often as it succeeds."[13] Are there cases in which violence is employed by only one side? Historically, there are few, if any, cases. Logically, it seems improbable since nations employ violence because their enemies are employing violence. "So while it certainly *may* happen that violence is used successfully at the international level without an offsetting failure, such successes are not particularly common; and victory in war does not represent such success."[14]

We have to ask further, even if violence succeeds, at what cost? This question brings up an important philosophical distinction, between means and ends. Gandhi argued against this distinction, referring to means as ends in process. The paradox of trying to use means that preclude reaching your end was made evident in antiwar demonstrations in the United States in the 1960s and 1970s in the slogan "Fighting for peace is like f-----g for chastity." "Revolutions, even when they overcome violent resistance, often end up breeding the same sorts of abuses their promoters hoped to eliminate, just as wars set the stage for new wars."[15]

So far this argument has looked at warfare as such. The negative claims about warfare not working can also be applied to preparing for warfare. What are the consequences for a nation in spending part of its time, initiative, economic resources, human resources, and so on in preparing for war? In the modern world, this question needs to be discussed at both the conventional and nuclear levels of weaponry. The advance of weapons technology in the nuclear age has cast the discussion of preparations for warfare in the form of "deterrence" issues. That is, to what extent will one's massive preparations for warfare with nuclear weapons *deter* a potential aggressor from striking first? This raises the question of whether attack by that aggressor nation is the worst consequence among the possible options facing our nation. What are some of the other consequences of arming for nuclear war? On the moral side, you could be seen as preparing to do something immoral. In 1983, the American Catholic Bishops published a pastoral letter applying the just-war tradition to nuclear warfare. The letter concluded that nuclear warfare is a violation of the just-war standards.[16] On the pragmatic side, the consequences need to be addressed by asking what could be done otherwise with the resources devoted to nuclear stockpiling. That is, how many resources are being diverted from education, health care, housing, safety, domestic research and development, and so on? It could be argued that the collapse of the Soviet Union occurred largely because of its attempt to

match the United States in warfare expenditures. As of this writing, the consequences for the United States' economy are not fully apparent. There are also consequences in terms of the international climate within which nations operate. Consistent arming by one or more nations tends to develop a mood of distrust and fear among other nations. Further, the citizens of the arming nation(s) would conceivably be changed into bitter and brutal people in relation to people and nations regarded as the enemy. So it becomes apparent that not only warfare itself but also the preparation for warfare has consequences that may be quite different from what we desire for ourselves: prosperity and caring people and communities.

If this consequentialist lens reveals such bad results, it is necessary to ask what is it about *us* that makes warfare and its preparations seem so good? The question goes to the heart of military education and propaganda. Members of the armed forces and citizens of the country agree to sacrifice their lives, their prosperity, and the lives of their loved ones, even though the preceding arguments indicate that warfare does not work. Is there some sort of massive self-deception going on? Or, are we like *addicts* who are so hooked on the military fix that we cannot liberate ourselves? Our understanding of human nature, of the behavior of organizations, of the workability of violence, and the importance we place on ourselves and our own nation are all factors in this preoccupation with violence as the best (or at least very necessary) way of conducting our lives on the international level.[17]

What about the arguments on the other side? What would the consequences be of not going to war? Mal Wakin would say that a valuable way of life would probably be lost. Bertrand Russell speculated that the consequences would be much better than for going to war and not the horrors that opponents of pacifism imagine. Douglas Lackey argues that the consequences probably would not have been much different than those that resulted *from* going to war. One result would be that the nation would not commit aggression. If every nation did not go to war, then warfare would be over. In terms of defense, the concern is that one's country would be overrun and oppressed by an aggressor nation. One response to this concern has been the development of the concept of civilian or citizen or social national defense. In this view, the entire citizenry would be trained in techniques of nonviolent resistance and noncooperation. Thus, the costs of anyone coming in would make the effort futile. Sure, the attacked nation would lose some lives. But remember that there would in all likelihood be much greater loss of life in warfare.

ENDNOTES

1. *The Republic of Plato*, translated by Allan Bloom. New York: Basic Books, 1968, 372c.
2. Ibid., 372c.
3. Ibid., 372e.
4. Ibid., 373e.
5. Ibid., 374d, e.
6. Duane Cady. *From Warism to Pacifism: A Moral Continuum*. Philadelphia: Temple University Press, 1989.
7. Douglas P. Lackey. *The Ethics of War and Peace*. Englewood Cliffs, N.J.: Prentice Hall, 1989, p. 1.
8. Ibid., p. 40.
9. Ibid., p. 40.
10. Ibid., p. 59.
11. Carol Gilligan. *In a Different Voice*. Cambridge, Mass.: Harvard University Press, 1982.
12. Robert Holmes, *Non-Violence in Theory and Practice*. Belmont, Calif.: Wadsworth, 1990, p. 3. In what follows in this essay, I am adapting some of Holmes queries and arguments about violence in general to warfare in particular.
13. Ibid., p. 4.
14. Ibid., p. 4.
15. Ibid., p. 5.
16. National Conference of Catholic Bishops, *The Challenge of Peace: God's Promise and Our Response; A Pastoral Letter on War and Peace*. Washington, D.C.: U.S. Catholic Conference, May 3, 1983.
17. It seems that we do this to our own detriment, since international cooperation is preferable to international violence.

Theo Solomon is Professor of Sociology at Bergen Community College and past Director of the Institute of Law and Social Process.

Video Presentation

Guest: Theo Solomon, Professor of Sociology, Bergen Community College

Student Panel: Patrick McMahon, Ursula Selbach, Juanita Sanchez

We begin our discussion by addressing the question of whether terrorism can be justified. Alluding to the Boston Tea Party and how "we" thought we were justified from our perspective while "they" (Great Britain) did not from theirs, Solomon points out that we should refrain from discussing terrorism as if it were a monolith since terrorism means different things to different people. Different organizations exist with diverse interests united only by a felt need for justice and a mechanism for obtaining it.

After a digression in which he names Barabbas as the first known terrorist, Solomon discusses a model for distinguishing legitimate and illegitimate terrorism inspired by Max Weber's three rules of social deviancy. In deciding if terrorism is legitimate, Solomon says that we need to decide (1) whether the activities in question conform to international law as specified, particularly, by the Geneva Convention; (2) whether the group that commits the activities in question is legitimate; that is, whether the group has a geographical territory, the assent of the people it represents, is in a position of authority, and so on; and (3) whether the aims of the organization are clear and negotiable. If all three conditions are met, then, as Solomon sees it, the terrorist organization and the activities it represents are legitimate. As an example of a legitimate terrorist organization, he mentions the Basques whose goal is independence from France and Spain and whose operations have never resulted in civilian casualties. As an example of illegitimate terrorism, Solomon mentions the Baader-Meinhof gang whose unrealistic goal is nothing less than world communism. In the light of these criteria, Solomon argues that legitimate terrorists are entitled to their day in court, while illegitimate terrorists may be dealt whatever measures the international community desires.

Just prior to the break, after comparing the activities of the Weather Underground in the United States with those of the Basques, we discuss the targeting of civilians, which I suggest is the essence of terrorism. A definition of terrorism that does not include the targeting of civilians—as Solomon's conception of "legitimate" terrorism does not—is too innocuous to be of interest since it fails to account for what is terrifying about terrorism. Solomon sticks to his position, using the Basques again as his model of legitimate terrorists. He points out how of the Basques' 480 terrorist events since 1947, not one civilian has been hurt, whereas the Palestine Liberation Organization (prior to their agreement with Israel) was only questionably legitimate inasmuch as its chairman, Yasser Arafat, did not clearly have the consensus of the people he claimed to represent.

Following the break, Patrick McMahon asks Solomon how we can distinguish between being inconvenienced and being treated unjustly for purposes of identifying legitimate terrorism. Ursula Selbach asks Solomon about Basque activities that apparently are aimed at government installations of nonbelligerent powers. Juanita Sanchez asks Solomon about state-sponsored terrorism. The discussion concludes with brief remarks about the relationship between means and ends.

In this essay, Theo Solomon, a sociologist, attempts to provide a value-free definition that would allow us to distinguish between "legitimate" and "illegitimate" varieties of terrorism. Not content with defining terrorism simply for academic purposes, Solomon's goal is to lay bare terrorism's features with an eye on framing policy decisions that would flow therefrom.

Terrorism: Legitimate and Illegitimate

Theo Solomon

There is a fast-growing body of literature relating to the general subject of terrorism. Authors have tried to differentiate among national, international, and transnational terrorism for both research and operational purposes. The perspective of these authors, however dissimilar, must be characterized as structure-functional, which is, by definition, conservative in nature. That is, from the point of view of a "legitimate" regime, any terrorist act is considered dysfunctional to the system, outside the purview of national and/or international law.

> First, terrorism is an attack against democracy. Terrorism is totalitarianism, a denial of basic human rights. And I agree that this is fundamental. (Alexander, 1981, p. 12)

> We may concede to the revolutionaries that the state—any state—can indeed be violent and often is. And yet, if the state engages in violence, its people can, at least, try to restrain it in ways short of violence, such as by mass-scale passive resistance. (Parry, 1976, p. 12)

> The transnational terrorist sees order as oppression and stability as tyranny disguised and is apparently beyond reconciliation through accommodation or control through the power of conventional force. (Bell, 1975, p. 5)

Adherents of the structure-functional model include both Western industrial powers and those military governments and dictatorships whose application of this principle is self-defensive, because it provides an aura of political legitimacy necessary to be in the good company of Western democracies.

A viewpoint closer to the conflict perspective may be characterized by those nations of the Middle East that consider competing interests as negotiable to obtain the "best-bargain" and do not perceive terrorist acts to be clearly and negatively defined as the structure-functionalists do. These governments provide a gamut of services to terrorists that range from the passive (neglecting to prosecute) to the active (financial and tactical support). There are currently at least three sovereign nations (Syria, Iran, and Libya) in this group who publicly admit active support for terrorist activity, with little consequence from the international legal community.

Some Marxist Eastern bloc nations might have condoned terrorist activity on the grounds that terrorist groups are in reality fighters for liberation against the oppressors, and therefore any tactic may be employed as legitimate in this ceaseless struggle. This position is greatly strengthened by the knowledge that there have not been any transnational terrorist activities counter to the Eastern bloc nations within their borders.

None of these theoretical positions provides fertile ground for the development of a "value-free" definition regarding terror or terrorism. A question may arise as to the need to have a value-free definition in the first place. Most of the definitions promoted by the authors cited describe the general phenomenon and provide a mechanism to recognize and identify a terrorist act. These definitions are certainly for research or census purposes, since most terrorist acts are identified as such by the group that claims responsibility. Definitions of terrorism are mostly for the sake of the press who at times confuse terrorist and criminal acts, leading to a romanticization of terrorist groups. A new definition is needed so that we may better understand terrorism.

Rarely has a phenomenon been discussed by governments and the press from every perspective with as much depth of understanding of names, dates, places, reasons, counter-reasons, and methods. The international legal and law enforcement community understands the phenomenon well. Do the definitions lead us through the spectrum from causes of terrorism to its counter-strategies?

> I do not see any technology on the horizon that would allow us to cope with the situation. On aircraft hijackings for example, there is talk about a gas that could be used, but such gases have side effects. . . . [T]he only way to deal with terrorism is to try to prevent it. We also need experienced people who know how to handle hostage negotiations and to resolve them peacefully. . . . The United States now has much improved ability to assault, if that becomes necessary, in a terrorist situation, but I do not see any magic solution on the horizon through technology. (Perez, 1981, p. 13)

An appeal for a "value-free" definition may provide the stage upon which we may view and segregate the legitimate claims of populations who are suffering unjustly from the illegitimate assertions of criminals who wish to glorify their cowardly acts.

RATIONALE FOR DEFINITIONS

To determine legitimate versus illegitimate terror may be to determine the ultimate policy decisions that arise from such definitions. That is, where there is a claim of "full legitimacy" an appeal may be made to a world body or official third party to open negotiations that may in some degree reduce an otherwise impassible conflict. Where a definition of illegitimacy is clear, Draconian methods may be adopted that would possess a moral force that cannot be provided by unilateral decisions by the ter-

rorized government. Where the illegitimacy of the terror is clear, the terrorists may be persuaded to adopt definitionally "legitimate" terrorist tactics to be considered worthy of ameliorative attention.

In this manner, definitions of terrorism need not be academically sterile and removed from reality, as currently, nor self-serving, as when there is a need to defend the actions of a sovereign state, no matter how unjust or immoral.

THE DIMENSIONS OF THE DEFINITION

It would seem that there are diverse dimensions to the initiations of terror. Those that seem the most fruitful to pursue are:

1. The terrorist act.
2. The terrorist group carrying out that act.
3. The cause for which the act is being carried out.

L. C. Green (1980) informs us:

> Political assassination directed at alleged tyrants will be considered terrorism only by those who sympathize with the policy and establishment represented by that tyrant; for others it may well amount to a higher act of patriotism.

Similarly, we have become accustomed to acts that would normally and formerly have been described as terrorist, such as the destruction of villages inhabited by sympathizers of either government or the rebels; the government claims such activities are "legitimate" since they are part of wars of national liberation (from the rebels), while the sympathizers of the rebel "liberationists" describe such acts by the government as genocidal.

Here we see one of the problems as terror and terrorism emerge as a de facto policy in many nations today. As illustrated by the preceding quote, Green posits that terrorism is in the eye of the beholder. Within the definition of terrorism, then, is it possible to entertain the notion of "legitimate terror" and "illegitimate terror"? If there can be an agreement that the basic definition of terrorism may contain within its parameters the notion of "legitimacy" under a prescribed set of circumstances, then a claim of value-free interpretation may be possible.

Let us examine some of the modern definitions of terrorism in the light of the legitimacy of the acts described. One of the earliest attempts to define and categorize acts of terrorism was made under the auspices of the League of Nations by the 1937 Convention for the Prevention and Punishment of Terrorism. The purpose of the Convention was to label acts of terrorism as crimes against humanity which no state should condone, on the grounds that such acts are political in nature, directed only against a particular tyranny. Many states sympathetic to decolonization movements were unwilling to support such a document; a small minority of the nations in attendance (24) signed it, and it never came into force.

The Convention attempted to define terrorism and to categorize its inclusive acts as "all criminal acts directed against a state and intended and calculated to create a state of terror in the minds of particular persons, or a group of persons or the general public." In the category of terrorism are included all acts or attempts that cause death or bodily harm to the heads of state or government, their spouses, and other public figures; that cause damage to public property; that endanger the lives of the public; and that deal with arms and ammunition for the commission of any of these offenses in any state.

This definition has determined that terrorism is criminal when persons or property are harmed in specified ways. This extends our definition of criminal acts, but not necessarily our definition of terrorism, except in the political or propagandistic sphere. The term *terrorism* has become, in our age, a pejorative term; to successfully attach the label "terrorist" to one's opponent is to persuade others, of an international or domestic audience, to adopt one's moral and political position. Therefore, definitions of terrorism are introduced by the various countries to define their opponents and exclude their allies.

In order to avoid the problem of a political definition of terrorism, Jenkins (1984) has defined only the quality of the act, not the identity of the perpetrator, nor the nature of the cause. He posits:

1. Terrorism has political objectives.
2. It is usually carried on by an organized group.
3. There is an element of premeditation in it.
4. It is usually directed against civilians.
5. It is usually carried out in a way to achieve maximum publicity.
6. It is unlike other forms of crime.
7. The perpetrators of terrorist crimes usually claim credit, at least as an organization, not as individuals, for the act.
8. The act is intended to produce psychological effects beyond the immediate physical effects of the violence itself; terrorism is intended to terrorize.

This definition, although imperfect, is more objective than the political one in that it removes us from the problem of defining a terrorist *group* and allows us to define a terrorist *act* with only a few areas of debate.

> It is not an act of terrorism to kill a soldier in combat; but for a guerrilla force to engage in combat with an army, and in combat, to kill a soldier, is it an act of terrorism? Or let's say in the course of an insurgency, to assassinate a general who is living at home? That is kind of a grey area. It certainly is an act of terrorism to toss a bomb in a cafe. This definition reduces the grey area about ten percent. I don't know if we can get more perfect than that. (Jenkins, 1984)

According to Jenkins, the assassination of a general living at home is a "grey area." It is suggested that Jenkins' definition does *not* contain this element in the framework of a terrorist act: that is, item 4: "it is usually directed against civilians." It is necessary, therefore, to define the belligerents within a conflict. As has been observed over the years, the term *civilian* is not so clear-cut as it once was. Nor is the concept of an army, which has changed from meaning uniformed combatants to sporadic or ill-equipped guerrillas, to a continually "civilian-dressed" military, and finally to an army that includes people formerly defined as noncombatants (the aged, youth, women). Guerrillas and their warfare became accepted as a de facto opposition army once it was understood that such an "army of liberation," if less equipped that the incumbents, could *only* fare well using a nontraditional set of strategies. The acceptance of guerrilla warfare was partially due to the militaristic stance and ordinance used, as well as the method of collective engagement, however haphazard, reminiscent of a regular army unit. One may, in fact, view Jenkins' definition to consider that acts in a guerrilla-type war and terrorist acts are more alike than not. However, rarely are guerrilla acts considered terroristic.

LEGITIMATE TERRORIST ACTS

If acts normally committed by guerrillas during the course of an armed conflict are not considered terroristic (even when directed toward civilian populations), does Jenkins' item 2 (that terrorism is usually carried on by an organized group) help delineate an "acceptable" size or organization for it to be considered a guerrilla group? Parry (1976, p. 18 ff) inadvertently provides a partial answer:

Regarding themselves as the possessors of the only possible remedy to the evils of the Establishment, terrorists assert the "legality" of their actions and the "illegality" of the State to which they are opposed. They solemnly claim sovereign rights for their organizations as they flaunt sovereignty's trappings and mannerisms.

Many call themselves "the Army." The Irish Republican Army set the precedent in taking such a name. Various Latin American guerrilla groups were among the first to use the term "People's Army" and the "People's Armed Forces." North American terrorists, such as the Black Liberation Army and the Symbionese, followed the practice of military pomp. The word "Peoples" is incorporated into their organizational names to demonstrate the alleged source of their sovereign power.

Parry does not differentiate between groups such as the IRA and the various Latin American guerrilla movements and others like the Black Liberation or the Symbionese Armies, nor does he discuss the "alleged sources of the sovereign power" of the People's Red Army of Mao, the Viet Cong, or any of the successful People's Armies that currently attempt to repel other insurgent People's Armies.

A legitimate terrorist act strikes at any individual, group, or property associated with an active belligerent in an announced conflict. That is, the definition is a purely military one in which only a small number of people may be considered "legitimate" targets. Terrorist acts are considered legitimate when they are performed within the national boundaries of the belligerents. An act of terrorism may also be seen as legitimate transnationally when committed by an organization banned from occupation of contested territory it has no possibility of gaining unilaterally. A legitimate transnational act would be one considered upon a combatant nation (or its property) with due regard for the civilians of that nation.

Within this framework, then, a "legitimate" terrorist organization may use all the devices open to traditional military organizations as well as traditional guerrilla warfare fighters, within a doctrine of "limited arbitrariness." The end product of psychological terror, as well as all the other "benefits" described by Jenkins, would still result.

IDENTIFYING A TERRORIST GROUP

Once an individual or group has been labeled as "terrorist," every criminal activity in which it engages tends to be popularly characterized as "terroristic." Even such acts as extortion, kidnapping for ransom, and bank robbery are generally labeled as terrorism when staged by a group previously branded as terrorists (Hoffman, 1983).

There is a fine line between criminal banditry and social banditry. Present day Provo bank robberies in Ireland and England have virtually obscured that distinction. It is now widely believed by both sides that the ideological conflict for control of Northern Ireland is being used in many instances to mask simple crime (Friedlander, 1981).

In Germany, the Baader-Meinhof group, although initially espousing ideological goals (worldwide communization), quickly deteriorated into a criminal gang that came to enjoy a high lifestyle—luxury cars, flashy clothes, and expensive weapons—and committed many more crimes to support their acquired tastes. The Symbionese Liberation Army is another example of a criminal gang whose character was altered and its image enhanced when it was portrayed by the mass media as a genuine revolutionary movement.

> What is most disturbing about this case is the fact that the media have given a small group of criminal misfits a Robin Hood image and transformed it into an internationally known movement possessing power and posing an insurmountable problem for authorities. (Alexander, 1979 p. 161)

Another band that continued to masquerade as a terrorist organization—fully supported by the cooperative efforts of the mass media—was the Black Liberation Army. Its members were responsible for a number of police assassinations and ambushes, one of the first taking place in New York City in 1973.

> The Black Liberation Army consisted of these violent outcasts of the urban jungle, driven to hatred of the system, and outraged at their own limited prospects. Having absorbed the contemporary political language of revolution, they claimed that the system had destroyed them, that the prisons, not the prisoners, were at fault. For these murderous, frustrated Blacks, the Black Liberation Army was not so much a revolutionary conspiracy, as an acceptable self-rationale for violent revenge against authority. (Bell, 1975, p. 8)

> Such rebels reveal the categorization and the hazy boundary dividing the committed revolutionary from the violent eccentric. (Bell, 1975, p. 19)

Bell does not assist us in determining the boundaries of the committed revolutionary. We are able to read into the previous statement that the violent eccentric is an illegitimate member of a group, whereas a committed revolutionary is legitimate.

The point has been made by several writers that American colonialists would have been considered terrorist by contemporary definitions:

> If the term had been invented, the ragtag group of dissidents who engaged in violence against established authority would have been labelled terrorists. They called themselves revolutionaries. We call them patriots. (Ridemour, 1976, p. 18)

Were the actions of Samuel Adams and the Sons of Liberty against the British in Boston justified? Were the members of the French resistance in World War II justified in their use of violence against the Nazis? Very few would argue that these rebels weren't vindicated. The protagonists were patriots fighting for liberty against the tyrants. Yet terrorists also refer to themselves as revolutionaries or liberationists. At what point do terrorists become certified revolutionaries in the eyes of the world? When the terrorism has been successful enough to secure power; in other words, when their terrorism works.

Hoffman's research into a universal definition of terrorism begins with the caveat that "terrorists, under any name or from any political position, were not considered to be part of the legitimate political process by the researcher" (Hoffman, 1983, p. 22). With this stated bias, he defines terrorism solely from the point of view of the holders of power, whether their authority was obtained by legitimate or illegitimate means. This definition cannot be objective, as there is only one "correct" or moral position: that of the de facto government. This support of authority is rather interesting in light of some of the quotes that head various chapters in his book: "Tyrannicide, that is, the killing of a tyrant, is not only lawful, but also laudable" (John Milton), or, "The tree of liberty must be refreshed from time to time with the blood of patriots and tyrants. It is its natural manure" (Thomas Jefferson). At what point, if any, are there legitimate heroes and when are there legitimate terrorists?

LEGITIMATE TERRORISTS

Third World countries of Asia, Africa, and the Middle East have accepted opposition violence as an expression of "self-determination." Force used by oppressed peoples to fight what is, to them, tyranny, colonialism, and imperialism, is completely justified. Arab states, for example, have provided the Palestinian guerrillas with financial, diplomatic, and military assistance; trained Palestinians in guerrilla warfare methods; permitted their territories to be used as bases for attack and their embassies abroad to function as recruiting offices for volunteers to aid Palestinian groups; and maintained close liaisons with them, offering their members freedom of movement and places of refuge (Alexander, 1976).

Similarly, socialist states have been supporting insurgent and revolutionary activities in cases where the struggle followed a strict party line and was tightly centralized. Granting a certain clandestine support of selected terrorist groups (by third world states as well as by the former Soviet Bloc countries), what is the motivating rationale for such support? Most terrorist groups share the same general political goals; negatively expressed, their goals are to destroy a government, alter a policy or law, oust a foreign power or economically dominant class, attack imperialism/colonialism/Zion-

ism, and so on (Russell, Banker, and Miller, 1979). Again, the authors do not differentiate between terrorist groups and ideologies or goals. Some of the political goals seem laudable, and many are probably necessary in many countries in the world today. Why, then, do authors frame these ambitions in negative terms? Is it because there is the shadow of revolution behind these motives? Is revolution only within the enemy camp? Even this is doubtful. The authors do not differentiate between *rebellion* and *revolution*, nor is there a differentiation between full insurrection and a legitimate demand for redress, such as an alteration of a policy or law.

Terrorist activity is usually precipitated after more legitimate avenues of redress fail. In our rush to condemn all terrorists and terrorism, we must allow for the legitimate mechanisms for the improvement of human rights as well.

Under general international law, these qualities define a legitimate terrorist group:

1. Is organized with one spokesman responsible for the actions of the group.
2. Represents a population.
3. Has some claim to territoriality (i.e., to occupy a part of the disputed territory).
4. Has existed as a group over time.

This schema attempts to identify a recognizable national entity under international law, and includes:

1. A government.
2. A population.
3. A territory.
4. Stability.

In addition to these considerations, dimensions of cause or motivation and goal achievability must be reviewed and defined. A legitimate terrorist group must:

1. Have a cause that is clearly identifiable.
2. Have attempted, as a political unit, within the sovereignty, to ameliorate the grievance through means prescribed by the constitution of the country.
3. Represent a disadvantaged population.
4. Have a goal or goals that are achievable, among "reasonable men."

It is clear that this schema identifies groups such as the Baader-Meinhof and general Marxist revolutionaries (whose goal is the destruction of the capitalist system) as illegitimate, because such groups are unrepresentative of a willing subject population, have unachievable goals, espouse a cause of doubtful validity, and so on. The final scheme of permutations may then be visualized as follows:

Type	Act	Group	Cause
1	L	L	L
2	L	L	I
3	L	I	I
4	I	I	I
5	I	I	L
6	I	L	L
7	I	L	I
8	L	I	L

Key: L = legitimate; I = illegitimate.

Type 1 represents an organization that deserves media attention to focus on the cause rather than the act. Further, in providing a mechanism for conflict resolution, the forum itself may provide an understanding to the nonparticipants as to the seriousness of the cause. Simply stated, the forum could determine whether the terrorist group was willing to participate in actual conflict resolution, or if the group existed only as a mechanism to maintain constant world disorder.

Type 4, the polar opposite of Type 1, may clearly be identified as a threat to world order, thereby meriting Draconian strategies espoused by third-party consensus-pact nations. These strategies have a philosophical history provided by Locke, Mill, and Kant. Locke's notion of forfeiture explains that, although one's right to life and other rights are inalienable, they may be forfeited whenever that person violates another persons' rights; in such a case, the criminal act committed is one "that deserve death" (Bedau, 1980).

Mill (1868) stated:

Just as it is to think that to take a life of a man who has taken that of another is to show want of regard for human life,
we show on the contrary, most emphatically, our regard for it, by the adaption of a rule that he who violates that right in another forfeits it for himself.

Kant's requirements for this type of forfeiture include:

1. That the actor had no excuse of justification for the act.
2. By virtue of an "inner viciousness," one has rationally willed to kill another who is entirely innocent and undeserving of harm.

It is also interesting to note that Beccaria (1977), who considered that the punishment of death is not authorized by any rights, considered the death penalty necessary in the case of treason, or where established order was threatened. Draconian strategies may therefore include appropriate use of convicted members of terrorist gangs as hostages for deterrence of future acts or as reprisals for current acts. Wherever terrorists are, if they haven't attempted legitimacy over time, their territory should then be treated as a war zone.

The schema as envisioned would also indicate to certain terrorist organizations that operations may be redirected in such a way as to legitimize a currently defined illegitimate activity, and thereby bring the organization into a legitimate negotiating position. This tradeoff is a Benthamite concept that requires, if not a moral calculus, at least acknowledgment that there are escalating options of illegitimacy, and that it may be as sound to select a lesser crime than a greater one.

The Weberian "ideal type" for the Type 1 terrorist is the ethnic terrorist model of Brittany, a distinctive geographical and cultural region in northwestern France. The Breton language, akin to Welsh, Manx, and Gaelic, is spoken by about half-million people, although many more claim a Breton identity by virtue of speaking a dialect of French called Gallo, or by having a Breton surname. Brittany shares cultural links with other Celtic regions, such as England and Scotland. Until 1532, Brittany was autonomous; it became part of France in that year by a treaty whose terms guaranteed Breton autonomy. In 1790, the Breton assembly was unilaterally abolished, and Brittany officially, and reluctantly, became an integral part of the French state. Breton political activity during the nineteenth century was virtually dormant. In the twentieth century, various nationalistic parties began to evolve. It was, however, only in the 1970s that the Breton Separatist movement spawned a serious terrorist problem.

> Although there were isolated terrorist incidents before 1976, it was in that year that the campaign of violence really began. Most of the incidents have been confined to Brittany itself, and the targets have almost invariably been ones symbolizing French authority in the region. Thus legal, military, transport and administrative buildup have been very much in the front line. There has been meticulous policy of minimizing the threat to life and limb, and the occasional injuries have been clearly accidental. (Moxon-Browne, 1983, p. 9)

Moxon-Browne also indicates that after the Mouvement pour l'Organisation de la Bretagne (MOB) sought autonomy for Brittany within the French state by peaceful means and failed, the armed struggle passed on to another nationalistic group, the FLB-ARB, which had been outlawed previously, in 1974. The ARB faction represents a more militant Marxist-oriented wing of the movement, but both factions are committed to violent methods. It is interesting to note that in detailing the outcome of a trial of these Marxist-oriented violent groups, Moxon-Browne tells us:

> Eighteen of the accused were jailed for periods ranging from two to fifteen years, and six were acquitted. These sentences were generally regarded as lenient and they undoubtedly took into account the fact that *the FLB-ARB in the course of over 300 bombings since 1966 had success-*

fully avoided killing a single person. (1983, p. 10, emphasis added)

The terms *militant, Marxist,* and *violent* lose some of their sting in light of the end product described above. Other ethnic terrorist situations, such as the PLO, the IRA, or South African blacks, would lend themselves to "Type 1" terrorist considerations with adherence to legitimacy in the terrorist act category. In each cause, there is a historically viable and negotiable goal.

EXCLUSIONS FROM LEGITIMACY

It is obvious that there are certain biases to the framework presented, which excludes criminal groups attempting to portray themselves as patriots. Also excluded are groups such as the Baader-Meinhof gang primarily because of the illegitimacy of the "cause" category, which requires the goal to be achievable. Worldwide destruction of the colonial/capitalist/imperialist society is too general to be a realistically achievable goal. However, where that goal is focused on a particular country and fulfills the other requirements of legitimacy, revolutionary movements may be considered as legitimate rebellious movements and are entitled to the same international forum.

What is being suggested here is a method of defining terrorism in a manner that would marshall world opinion, as well as action by consensus-sovereign nations, in regard to terrorist activity. This schema may be the basis for a system of conflict resolution that could appeal to the largest segment of terrorists active today: ethnopolitical groups. It would also identify, in a more rational fashion, the fanatic and illegitimate fringes of terrorism for differential treatment, and therefore gain public support for more drastic forms of treatment toward these groups. Definitions for definitions' sake cannot affect the course of terrorism. The nonconsensual status quo has not only cost innocent lives and affected property, but now threatens to have disastrous economic impact (especially on tourism) in many nations simply based on the verbal threats of fanatical charismatic leaders. Three and a half billion people have potentially changed their lifestyles because of the activity of, at a conservative estimate, fewer than a thousand terrorists. Some have even placed the number as low as *two hundred*.

REFERENCES

Alexander, J. *Terrorism: What Should Be Our Response?* Washington and London: American Enterprise Institute for Public Policy Research, 1981.

———. *Terrorism and the Media*. Alexander, Carlton & Wilkinson (Eds). p. 161.

Beccaria, C. *On Crimes and Punishment*, 6th ed., translated by Paolucci. Indianapolis: Bobbs-Merrill, 1977, p. 11.

Bedau, H. A. "Capital Punishment." In Tom Regan, Ed., *Matters of Life and Death*. Philadelphia: Temple University Press, 1980.

Bell, J. B. *Transnational Terror*. Washington DC: American Enterprise Institute for Public Policy Research, 1975, p. 5.

Friedlander, R. A. *Terrorism: Documents of International and Local Control* 3. New York: Oceana Publications, 1981, p. 6.

Green, L. C. *The Tehran Embassy Incident and International Law*. Toronto: Canadian Institute of International Affairs, 1980.

Hoffman, R. P. *Terrorism: A Universal Definition*. Doctoral thesis, Claremont Graduate School, 1984, p. 24.

Jenkins, B. M. *Combatting Terrorism Becomes a War*. Santa Monica, Calif.: Rand Corp., 1984.

Moxon-Browne, E. *Terrorism in France*. London: Institute for the Study of Conflict, 1983, p. 8.

Parry, A. *Terrorism: From Robespierre to Arafat*. New York: Vanguard Press, 1976, p. 12.

Perez, F. *Terrorism: What Should Be Our Response?* Washington and London: American Enterprise Institute for Public Policy Research, 1981, p. 13.

Ridemour, R. "Who Are the Terrorists and What Do They Want?" *Skeptic* 11 (January/February, 1976), p. 18.

Russell, A., Banker, L. B. and Miller, R. In Y. Alexander, D. Carlton, and Wilkinson, P., Eds., *Terrorism: Theory and Practice*. Boulder, Colorado: Westview Press, 1979.

Closing Questions

1. Critically discuss the doctrine of double effect.

   _____

   _____

   _____

   _____

   _____

2. Is double effect a doctrine that would find advocates among deontologists? Utilitarians? Why or why not?

   _____

   _____

   _____

   _____

   _____

3. Was the atomic bombing of Hiroshima and Nagasaki justified under the terms of the just-war doctrine? What conditions of the just-war doctrine did it arguably violate? Why?

   _____

   _____

   _____

   _____

   _____

4. Discuss whether it is reasonable to expect nations and soldiers to conduct wartime activities in accordance with the just-war doctrine.

   _____

   _____

   _____

   _____

   _____

5. What criteria should be used for distinguishing combatants from noncombatants? If soldiers on the front are clearly combatants, what of civilians who work in munitions factories? What of the farmers whose food feeds the soldiers? What of the civilians who support the war but take no active measures in the name of such support?

_____

_____

_____

_____

_____

_____

6. What criteria should be used for distinguishing between moral and immoral weaponry? List as many kinds of weapons you can think of and evaluate them in the light of your criteria.

_____

_____

_____

_____

_____

_____

7. List as many wars as you can think of and evaluate them in the light of the just-war doctrine.

_____

_____

_____

_____

_____

8. According to the "Just Cause Requirement" of the just-war doctrine, a nation may attack another if it has reason to believe the other will attack it first. What problems do you see with this requirement? In your opinion, was Israel justified in launching its preemptive strike against the Arab nations during the Six-Day War? Was it justified in launching a preemptive strike on Iraq's nuclear facilities in 1981?

_____

_____

_____

_____

_____

9. Utilitarian reasoning on the ethics of war involves assessments of the potential good and bad consequences of alternative policies. For the utilitarian, the morally best policy is cost-effective, that is, one that on balance will produce the best consequences when the interests of everyone affected are calculated. Compare and contrast the utilitarian position with: (a) pacifism, (b) realism, and (c) the just-war doctrine.

_____

_____

_____

_____

_____

_____

10. Is it ever morally acceptable to kill innocent civilians?

_____

_____

_____

_____

_____

11. Suppose an aggressor nation refuses to abide by the principles of discrimination and proportionality. Is the victim nation free of any obligation to abide by these principles? Must the victim nation abide by moral principles if doing so means certain defeat?

_____

_____

_____

_____

_____

12. Should homosexual men and women be allowed in the military?

_____

_____

_____

_____

_____

13. Would you count as a combatant a soldier who was drafted and entered the war reluctantly? Would you count as a combatant a civilian who enthusiastically supported the war effort?

_____

_____

_____

_____

_____

14. Discuss the claim that one person's terrorist is another person's freedom fighter; that revolutionaries are terrorists successful enough to secure power.

_____

_____

_____

_____

_____

15. Some animal rights activists have been accused of bombing laboratories engaged in animal experimentation. Is this a case of terrorism?

_____

_____

_____

_____

16. According to the United Kingdom's Prevention of Terrorism Act, "Terrorism means the use of violence for political ends, and includes any use of violence for the purpose of putting the public or any section of the community in fear." Is this definition sound or problematic?

_____

_____

_____

_____

_____

17. Were the founders of the United States terrorists or freedom fighters?

_____

_____

_____

_____

_____

18. Technically speaking, are the paramilitarists who bombed the federal building in Oklahoma City in 1995 terrorists?

_____

_____

_____

_____

_____

19. What assumptions must a pacifist make and how do they relate to the question of terrorism?

_____

_____

_____

_____

_____

20. Terrorists are often criticized for their willingness to kill noncombatants for some allegedly higher good. But do terrorist activities significantly differ from those of governments that send their military forces into battle knowing that many of them will never return? Discuss this question in the light of the U.S. attempt in April 1980 to rescue American hostages being held at the American Embassy in Tehran, Iran.

_____

_____

_____

_____

_____

For Further Reading

Anscombe, G. E. M. "War and Murder." In Walter Stein, ed., *Nuclear Weapons: A Catholic Response*. (London and New York). Reprinted in Joram Graf Haber, ed., *Absolutism and Its Consequentialist Critics*. Lanham, Md.: Rowman & Littlefield, 1994.

Cady, Duane. *From Warism to Pacifism: A Moral Continuum*. Philadelphia: Temple University Press, 1989.

Christopher, Paul. *The Ethics of War and Peace: An Introduction to Legal and Moral Issues*. Englewood Cliffs, N.J.: Prentice Hall, 1994.

Clausewitz, Karl von. *On War*. Princeton, N.J.: Princeton University Press, 1976 [1833].

Coady, C. A. J. "The Morality of Terrorism." *Philosophy* 60 (1985): 47–70.

Edel, Abraham. "Notes on Terrorism." In Abraham Edel, *Exploring Fact and Value* (Transaction Book, 1980).

Homes, Robert L. *On War and Morality*. Princeton, N.J.: Princeton University Press, 1989.

Hughes, Martin. "Terrorism and National Security." *Philosophy* 57 (1982): 5–26.

Johnson, David E. "Terror Tactics: A Conceptual Analysis." In *Moral Obligation and the Military*. Washington, D.C.: National Defense University Press Publications, 1988.

Johnson, James. *Can Modern War Be Just?* New Haven: Yale University Press, 1984.

Kennan, George. *American Diplomacy, 1900–1950*. Chicago: University of Chicago Press, 1951.

Lackey, Douglas P. *Moral Principles and Nuclear Deterrence*. Totowa, N.J.: Rowman and Allenheld, 1984.

Nielsen, Kai. "Violence and Terrorism: Its Uses and Abuses." In Burton Leiser, ed., *Values in Conflict: Life, Liberty and the Rule of Law*. New York: Macmillan, 1981.

Primoratz, Igor. "What is Terrorism?" *Journal of Applied Philosophy* 7 (1990): 129–137.

Teichman, Jenny. "How to Define Terrorism." *Philosophy* 64 (1989): 505–517.

———. *Pacifism and the Just War*. Oxford: Basil Blackwell, 1986.

Chapter 6

Physician-Assisted Suicide and Living Wills

Passages for Reflection

"There is but one truly serious philosophical problem, and
that is suicide."

—*Albert Camus*

"Suicide is not abominable because God prohibits it; God
prohibits it because it is abominable."

—*Immanuel Kant*

"The worst death for anyone is to lose the center of his being,
the thing he really is. Retirement is the filthiest word in the
language. Whether by chance, or by fate, to retire from what
you do—and what you do makes you what you are—is to
back up into the grave."

—*Ernest Hemingway*

"Suicide sometimes proceeds from cowardice, but not always;
for cowardice sometimes prevents it; since as many live
because they are afraid to die, as die because they are afraid
to live."

—*Charles Caleb Colton*

Nor dread nor hope attend
A dying animal.
A man awaits his end,
Dreading and hoping all.

—*W. B. Yeats*

Opening Questions

1. What is suicide?
2. Is suicide rational? Is it ethical?
3. Do people have a right to die?
4. Is Dr. Jack Kevorkian a saint or sinner?
5. What is a living will? Should you have one?

Dr. Jack Kevorkian has made headlines by helping terminally ill patients commit suicide by means of his infamous "suicide machine." Nicknamed "Dr. Death," Kevorkian has argued that patients have the right to commit suicide, and this implies that it is permissible for physicians to assist them. In this chapter, we will ask whether people have the right to commit suicide and, if so, whether physicians should partake in the process. We will also examine the pros and cons of executing a "living will"—the document that extends a person's right to receive or refuse medical treatment into a possible future period of incompetency.

It is customary to distinguish between suicide, which is the intentional taking of one's own life, and euthanasia, which is the intentional killing of another out of mercy. But when a physician helps another person to commit suicide, as Dr. Kevorkian does, little distinguishes the two activities. For this reason, a discussion of physician-assisted suicide will inevitably involve a discussion of euthanasia. We will proceed, then, by discussing the ethics of suicide as it has been traditionally understood and then examine the ethics of euthanasia with an eye on determining what differences arise between killing yourself and having someone else assist you to do it.

Let us begin by asking, not whether it is permissible to take your life, but the related question of whether it is rational to do so. From one perspective, it is rational to take your life. If you are terminally ill, suffering, and have no reasonable chance of recovery, we can plausibly say that your decision to terminate your life is rational. You may simply decide that the costs of living do not outweigh its benefits. The philosopher Richard Brandt is a defender of this utilitarian view. He argues that suicide involves "a choice between future world-courses." Given the empirical information available at the time, and taking into account a person's present desires as well as future ones, Brandt believes that the decision to commit suicide is rational, provided it is reasonably clear that one's future world-course is not preferable to eliminating one's present misery.[1]

---

[1] See Richard Brandt, "The Morality and Rationality of Suicide." In S. Perlin et al. *A Handbook for the Study of Suicide.* (Cambridge: Oxford University Press, 1975). Reprinted in John

Others argue that the decision to commit suicide is irrational. Immanuel Kant argued that it is self-contradictory to will our self-destruction.[2] Many psychiatrists believe that suicide inevitably stems from depression, and that someone who is depressed is incapable of assigning proper weights to costs and benefits.[3] Against Brandt, Philip Devine has argued that it is not rational to kill ourselves inasmuch as we lack knowledge about the "world-courses" available to us as a result of our death. In order to make a rational choice between life and death, we require considerable knowledge about both. But since death is unknowable, the decision to kill ourselves can never be rational.[4]

An interesting argument against the rationality of suicide is suggested by Ernest Becker in his provocative book, *The Denial of Death.* Becker's contention is that the fear of death is the motivating force behind all human endeavors: "The idea of death, the fear of it, haunts the human animal like nothing else; it is a mainspring of human activity—activity designed largely to avoid the fatality of death, to overcome it by denying in some way that it is the final destiny of man."[5] If this thesis is true, it raises the possibility that under no circumstances can one make a rational decision about one's death, but that one is always *in extremis* about one's ultimate destiny. While it is an intriguing idea, Becker's thesis suffers from the criticism that any evidence running counter to his thesis should be discounted on account of denial. This makes the thesis sound more like an article of faith than an empirical truth.

Whether suicide is *rational* or not is a question that is arguably different from whether it is *permissible*. I say "arguably," because in some views, a person has the right to make irrational decisions provided such decisions do not adversely affect others. John Stuart Mill championed this libertarian view when, in an oft-quoted passage, he declared:

> The sole end for which mankind are warranted, individually or collectively, in interfering with the liberty of action of any of their num-

---

Donnelly, ed., *Suicide: Right or Wrong?* (Buffalo: Prometheus Books, 1990). Others who have argued that suicide is rational include Seneca ("On the Proper Time to Slip the Cable," *Epistulae Morales,* Vol. 2, R. M. Gummere, trans. (Cambridge, Mass.: Harvard University Press, 1920) and Glenn Graber ("The Rationality of Suicide," in Samuel E. Wallace and Albin Eser, eds., *Suicide and Euthanasia: The Rights of Personhood* (Memphis: The University of Tennessee Press, 1981).

[2]Immanuel Kant, *Lectures in Ethics,* translated by Louis Infield (New York: Harper & Row, 1963), pp. 147–157.

[3]But see Thomas Szasz, "The Ethics of Suicide." *The Antioch Review* 31 (Spring 1971): 7–17.

[4]Philip Devine, *The Ethics of Homicide* (Ithaca, N.Y.: Cornell University Press, 1978), pp. 138–143.

[5]Ernest Becker, *The Denial of Death* (New York: The Free Press, 1973), p. ix. For what it's worth, I count this book among the two most profound books I've ever read. Stephen Jay Gould's *Wonderful Life* (New York: W. W. Norton & Co., 1989) is the other.

ber is self-protection. That the only purpose for which power can be rightfully exercised over any member of a civilized community, against his will, is to prevent harm to others. His own good, either physical or moral, is not a sufficient warrant. He cannot rightfully be compelled to do or forbear because it will be better for him to do so, because it will make him happier, because, in the opinion of others, to do so would be wise or even right. These are good reasons for remonstrating with him, or reasoning with him, or persuading him, or entreating him, but not for compelling him or visiting him with evil in case he do otherwise.[6]

However, in an important but often overlooked paragraph, Mill adds that what he says is meant to apply "only to human beings in the maturity of their faculties. Those who are . . . in a state to require being taken care of by others must be protected against their own actions as well as against external injury."[7] Others who have held more consistent libertarian views include Thomas Szasz, Seneca, and Joseph Fletcher, and these are to be contrasted with views, such as Kant's, that no action that is irrational can have moral worth.

Turning, then, to the ethics of suicide, we note that the question has been the object of philosophical debate going back to the earliest roots of Greek philosophy. In Plato's *Phaedo*, for example, we find Socrates arguing that suicide is wrong even though the true philosopher desires death. Socrates' contention was that the true philosopher desires death since it is at death that the mind is freed from the body, enabling it to philosophize without interference from the body. That being so, the obvious question (put to Socrates by Cebes) is, "Why then should philosophers not hasten their death?" Socrates answers with might be called the "divine ownership theory" which says that our life is not ours, but is on loan from God (or the gods, in Socrates' case). Just as a person may not tamper with property that is on loan from another without the owner's permission, so a person may not tamper with his or her life without divine permission. Latter-day adherents of divine ownership theory include St. Thomas Aquinas, who argued that suicide is a breach of God's sovereignty over us,[8] and Kant, for whom "God is our owner."[9]

Not everyone subscribes to divine ownership theory if only because not everyone believes in God. And since God's existence is at least as con-

---

[6]John Stuart Mill, *On Liberty* (Indianapolis, Ind.: Hackett Publishing Co., 1978 [1859]), p. 9.

[7]*Ibid.*

[8]St. Thomas Aquinas, "Whether It Is Lawful to Kill Oneself?" *Summa Theologica*, Vol. 2 (New York: Benziger Brothers, Inc.; London: Burns & Oaks, Ltd., 1925), Part 2, Question 64, A5.

[9]See Kant, *supra*, note 2.

troversial as suicide, those who think suicide is permissible can contend that no argument has been given to persuade them otherwise. Furthermore, as David Hume has argued, suicide may even be permissible if you *do* believe in God. As Hume saw it, if it is permissible to usurp God's will by interfering with the laws of nature as we surely do when we cure diseases, then, by parody of reasoning, it is permissible to usurp God's will by committing suicide. Hume also contends (with a bit of sarcasm) that the commission of suicide might even be viewed as the expression of gratitude to God for the good enjoyed throughout our life and for the ability to escape current misery.[10]

Other arguments for suicide's permissibility include the Epicurean one that death is not the terrifying object we take it to be. To the Epicurean, death was nothing more than the end of life and an end that should be hastened when a person desires. The Epicurean viewed life as something to be lived so long as it is enjoyed. When the hope for happiness diminished, the door to death was open. In similar fashion, utilitarians such as Brandt contend that suicide is permissible under just those circumstances when it is cost-effective. For utilitarians, the cost-effectiveness of an action makes it ethical.

All of this discussion presupposes that we are clear on what suicide is, while at the beginning of the chapter we observed that the concept of suicide is obscure, especially when it involves the assistance of another. For this reason, we must explore what suicide is.

We are tempted to define *suicide* simply as the termination of a person's own life. A moment's reflection will prove this inadequate. Consider the oft-discussed case of Captain Oates who fell ill and found himself physically unable to continue on with a party of explorers in the Antarctic. The explorers were struggling to find their way out of a blizzard. Captain Oates, determined not to further endanger his colleagues by hindering their progress but unable to convince them to leave him to die, walked off to meet his death in the blizzard.

Did Oates commit suicide? By the definition proposed, he did, since he took his own life. However, even the staunchest critics of suicide would hesitate to call this a suicide if only because Captain Oates's conduct, far from unethical, was courageous and heroic. This leads us to amend our definition to include the *intentional* termination of a person's own life. Defined this way, Captain Oates did *not* commit suicide since his intention in turning back was to save his colleagues. This is true even though he knew that his death would be a consequence of his facing the blizzard.[11] The distinction between what we intend and

---

[10]David Hume, "On Suicide." In *The Philosophical Works of David Hume* (London: Adam and Charles Black, 1826).

[11]For more on the doctrine, see "Double Effect," *Encyclopedia of Ethics*, Lawrence and Charlotte Becker, eds. (New York: Garland Publishers, 1992).

what we foresee is part of the doctrine of double effect, discussed on page 138.

Not everyone would agree with this proffered definition. Emile Durkheim, whose work on suicide is a classic in sociology, defined suicide as "death resulting directly or indirectly from a positive or negative act of the victim himself, which he knows will produce this result."[12] By Durkheim's definition, Oates committed suicide as did Socrates and Jesus.[13]

R. G. Frey has challenged the widely held view that suicide must be *self-inflicted*. He maintains that cases of suicide can be imagined where people want to die and purposely place themselves in perilous situations leading to their deaths. Frey, who is superb at conjuring up colorful cases, cites the case of an actor who puts real bullets in a gun that he knows will be fired at him in a play. Frey's contention is that this counts as a suicide despite the fact that the actor's death is not self-inflicted.[14]

Frey's case is a good lead-in to our discussion of physician-assisted suicide. Suppose the actors in Frey's play wanted to kill the suicide victim. Would we have a case of murder as well as suicide? Arguably, the answer would turn on whether the actors intended the death of their victim. If the person firing the gun knew it was loaded, then, notwithstanding the wishes of the victim, we would ostensibly have a murder as well as a suicide. This is true from a legal perspective since neither good motive nor consent is a defense to murder. So from a purely legal point of view, third-party suicide is indistinguishable from murder. The law might not follow morality in cases such as Frey's.

Historically, third-party suicide has been viewed as a species of murder although rarely would a state prosecute a person who killed someone who was terminally ill, suffering, and had no reasonable chance of recovery. If the authorities saw fit to prosecute at all, they would typically allow the defendant to plead down to a lesser offense since convictions for first-degree murder were hard to come by. What this has led to is a discrepancy between the law as it is written and the law as it is applied, a discrepancy owing to the law's regarding third-party suicide as *active euthanasia* which, unlike *passive euthanasia*, has historically been viewed as a species of murder and, as such, a criminal act.

Although the distinction between active and passive euthanasia is problematic, *active euthanasia* is ordinarily defined as mercy killing where the agent of death is an individual. By contrast, *passive euthanasia* is ordinarily defined as mercy killing where the cause of death is the disease that is responsible for the person's terminal condition. Thus, administering a lethal dose of morphine to a terminally ill patient is considered

---

[12]Emile Durkheim, *Suicide: A Study in Sociology* (New York: Free Press, 1951).

[13]R. G. Frey has argued that Socrates indeed committed suicide. See Frey, "Did Socrates Commit Suicide?" *Philosophy* 53 (1978): 106–108.

[14]R. G. Frey, "Suicide and Self-Inflicted Death." *Philosophy* 56 (1981): 193–202.

active euthanasia, while ceasing to employ a respirator is a case of passive euthanasia. An additional distinction often employed is between voluntary and nonvoluntary euthanasia, where voluntary euthanasia refers to mercy killing with the consent of the terminally ill person, while nonvoluntary euthanasia refers to mercy killing without (not against!) the consent of the person. Nonvoluntary euthanasia typically involves cases where the patient is in an irreversibly comatose condition and consent cannot be obtained (although the consent of others such as parents or relatives can be obtained). Active or passive euthanasia can be either voluntary or nonvoluntary.

If a standard view on the morality of euthanasia exists, it is that passive voluntary euthanasia (for example, withholding life support at a patient's request) is the least problematic of the varieties of euthanasia, whereas active euthanasia is the most problematic, especially where it is nonvoluntary but also when it is voluntary. This, in fact, is the official position of the American Medical Association. What accounts for this position is the intuition many of us have concerning the value of "killing" versus "letting die." Many of us are of the persuasion that killing, which is what takes place in active euthanasia, is morally worse than letting die, which is what takes place in passive euthanasia. This is because, again, when a killing occurs, the cause of death is the agent, whereas in a case of letting die, the cause of death is the patient's underlying disease.

But can the standard view withstand scrutiny? In an oft-discussed paper, James Rachels has argued against the view that a morally relevant distinction between active and passive euthanasia can be defended.[15] From his perspective, active euthanasia is in many cases more humane than passive euthanasia. Take the case where a patient has an incurable disease, is in terrible pain which cannot be alleviated, and is certain to die within a few days. The standard view says that while withholding treatment is permissible since the patient is going to die soon anyway, administering a lethal injection is not. As Rachels sees it, once the decision not to prolong agony has been made, active euthanasia is preferable to passive euthanasia inasmuch as it is more humane. Others, while not denying Rachels's position, insist on an important difference between dying at the hands of nature and dying at the hands of a person. From their point of view, morality forbids us to kill regardless of whether our motives are good or the victim consents.

But whatever we conclude about the relative merits of active and passive euthanasia, it is not clear that physician-assisted suicide is either of them. It has affinities with active euthanasia inasmuch as the physician is in some sense responsible for the patient's death, and it has affini-

---

[15]James Rachels, "Active and Passive Euthanasia." *New England Journal of Medicine* 292(2) (January 9, 1975): 78–80. This article is reprinted in a host of anthologies.

ties with suicide inasmuch as death is brought about at the patient's hands. It may also differ in an important sense from assisted suicide at the hands of a nonphysician; a difference may be found, that is, between *physicians* assisting patients to die and lay people doing the same. The challenge then is to determine whether we can distinguish among killing, letting die, and cases whereby a person provides the means for enabling another to die. In this light, the task is to decide whether physician-assisted suicide is more like active euthanasia or suicide as usually understood, or whether it is something new and unique. The task is also to ask whether these distinctions are morally relevant.

Jack Kevorkian, M.D., has taken care to distinguish between euthanasia and physician-assisted suicide. "On the one hand (euthanasia), the physician is obligated to be the direct agent of killing and, on the other hand, is merely the indirect agent abetting the killers—the patients themselves—and consequently less vulnerable to moral censure."[16] As Kevorkian conceives of it, patients wishing to die would be provided with a "suicide machine" that could be operated by pushing a lever with one finger to inject a lethal dose of potassium chloride through an intravenous needle. Alternatively, patients could be provided with a mask through which they may breathe carbon monoxide. By such means, patients otherwise unable to kill themselves could carry out their suicidal wish. Unlike euthanasia, patients would be the agents of their own death.

Kevorkian also strongly advocates physicians being the ones to assist patients with carrying out their desires. He goes so far as to propose that we form a subspeciality, *obitiatry*—from the ancient roots for "treatment" (Greek) and "death" (Latin). "Obitiatrists" would be the new specialists and would specialize in *medicide,* Kevorkian's term for "medically assisted suicide." As Kevorkian sees it, there is a grave danger in leaving the dilemma of assisting suicide to family members. For one thing, such a practice could lead to abuse caused by familial disputes and economic factors. For another, mistakes could be made based on inaccurate medical information. Kevorkian cites the tragic case of a Californian woman who was mistakenly diagnosed as having a brain tumor. Her son gave her a gun that she used to kill herself.

To help curb mistakes and abuses, Kevorkian proposes that a panel of five obitiatrists be required to participate, actively or in a consulting capacity, in each proposed death. Three of the five would serve in an advisory capacity to determine whether death is justifiable, with at least one of the three being a psychiatrist. For the death to take place, all three advisory obitiatrists would have to agree. Furthermore, the patient would have to review all evaluations on an ongoing basis. If the patient shows any ambivalence, the entire procedure would be stopped and the patient could no longer or ever again be a candidate for medicide.

---

[16]*Psychiatric News,* 27(6) (March 20, 1992): 8.

Physician-assisted suicide has not found support in the medical community. Among the arguments against it is the claim that patients could wind up being pressured to kill themselves on account of such considerations as the cost of health care. People also argue that doctors could recommend suicide for the wrong reasons such as unconscious biases against minorities, people with AIDS, or even a misdiagnosis of a terminal illness. And people argue that patients usually follow doctors' recommendations, so that if doctors were to suggest an easy death, seriously ill or poorly educated patients might not feel strong enough to make their own reasoned decision. Underlying this argument is the fear of shifting too much power into the hands of physicians.

Opponents of physician-assisted suicide also point out that people prone to consider suicide might view it as an acceptable option before exhausting all treatment possibilities. In other words, they worry about the consequences of making it too easy to not think of ways to help people live.

A further argument against physician-assisted suicide is the impact a field like obitiatry might have on the perception of physicians as health-care providers. The perception we have of physicians as professionals committed to promoting life and health would be significantly altered if they were to engage in practices associated with inducing death. Since perception is reality for a large part of the patient population, our confidence in physicians might be drastically reduced, with adverse consequences for medicine generally.

Other people argue against legalizing physician-assisted suicide on the grounds that it erodes the value of human life. Recalling the horrors of the Nazi holocaust which allowed involuntary euthanasia, the concern now is that by legalizing physician-assisted suicide, we may slide down the slippery slope and eventually legalize involuntary euthanasia. Some critics take this concern seriously, based on their analysis of what has occurred in The Netherlands where physician-assisted suicide is legal. In The Netherlands, where what Kevorkian terms medicide and euthanasia occur routinely, the distinction between euthanasia and physician-assisted suicide is not made. Instead, physicians perform euthanasia, defined as "the intentional termination of life by someone other than the person concerned at his or her request." No suicide machines have been developed to separate physicians from what Kevorkian sees as the ethical line dividing medicide from euthanasia.

Beyond the problems that attend physician-assisted suicide in cases where patients are suffering from terminal illnesses, cases exist where patients suffer from painful and incapacitating illnesses that are not terminal, such as crippling arthritis, emphysema, degenerative neurologic diseases, and stroke. Kevorkian endorses medicide for such patients as well, although for depression and other psychiatric illnesses, he draws a line while suggesting that at some point these, too, might be considered.

Inasmuch as the right to refuse medical treatment is a fundamental precept of Anglo-American law incidental to the right to self-determination, it may be that any objections to physician-assisted suicide can ultimately be overcome. Furthermore, if physician-assisted suicide is implied by the right to self-determination, then we have no reason to restrict it to terminal illnesses. The right to self-determination implies that people have their reasons for doing what they want. This means that people, while healthy and competent, have the right to specify the medical procedures they would like administered at such time as they would enter into a state where they would be unable to make such decisions. *Living wills* or *advance directives* exist for just this purpose as does the health care proxy, a document authorizing an agent to act on behalf of an incompetent patient. Both have been in use in the United States for several years.

In 1979, in order to investigate the ethics of research as well as a wide range of bioethical issues, Congress established the President's Commission for the Study of Ethical Problems in Medicine and Biomedical and Behavioral Research. The Commission was chaired by Morris Abram, with Alexander M. Capron as its executive director, and consisted of eleven persons from medicine, nursing, the behavioral sciences, law, and ethics. The charge to the Commission was to investigate such issues as the nature of death, decisions to forego life-sustaining treatment, genetic engineering screening and counseling, equitable access to health care, and informed voluntary consent. Among its findings, the Commission concluded that the ideal of informed voluntary consent to health care is an ethical ideal that has substantial foundations in the law. This doctrine provides that each individual has the right to decide what shall be done to his or her body—the right to control, that is, any decision affecting medical treatment for better or for worse. The Commission found that this right applies directly to competent adults and indirectly through proxy decision making to those who lack decision-making capacity. This being so, the Commission supported the legal mechanism by which competent adults may give advance directives for the acceptance or refusal of medical treatment in the event they should become incapacitated for decision-making. The living will allows for direct control, and the durable power of attorney allows for the identification of surrogate decision makers. In 1983, when the Commission published its report, only thirteen states had enacted "Natural Death Acts" giving legal status to the living will, but by the end of 1985, thirty-five states had such laws in effect. Today, most states have living will laws in effect.

While an uncontroversial document, the living will has had its share of critics. For example, some people have urged that we have a God-authored duty to live that supersedes any right to die.[17] (See preceding

---

[17]See my "Living Wills and Directives to Provide Maximum Care: The Scope of Autonomy," *Chest* 90 (Sept. 1986): 3. (Reprinted in the American Philosophical Association *Newsletter on Philosophy and Medicine*, Spring 1992).

"divine ownership" argument.) This argument, however, holds force only for those adhering to a religious point of view. A more serious objection is that by executing a living will, we lock ourselves into a course of treatment which, if not periodically revised, may not express our intentions at such time when we become incompetent. This objection, while serious, is mitigated by the fact that living wills are often accompanied by health care proxies that empower another person to speak on a patient's behalf. This same consideration applies to the objection that living wills invariably involve reference to such vague terms as "extraordinary treatment" and "heroic measures." While such terms change in meaning as medical technology advances, a health-care proxy could give content to the terms based on familiarity with the patient's intentions.

In addition to preserving a patient's autonomy, a major advantage of having a living will is financial. It has been estimated that as much as a third of the nation's medical costs stem from care given in the final year of life. Medical experts say that extremely high costs can be incurred when trying to keep someone alive against high odds, costs that can be avoided if an advanced directive exists against employing expensive means to keep a person alive. In 1993, when President Clinton was lobbying for his health-care program, he urged families to consider living wills as a means of controlling spiraling medical costs. Some very good reasons, then, exist for having living wills and the trend is in that direction. At the time of this writing, forty-five states plus the District of Columbia have passed some form of living will/health-care proxy legislation.

Jay Kantor is a bioethicist and Professor of Psychiatry at New York University School of Medicine. He is the author of *Medical Ethics for Physicians in Training* and editor of the forthcoming *Encyclopedia of Biomedical Ethics*.

Video Presentation

Guest: Jay Kantor, bioethicist and Professor of Psychiatry, New York University School of Medicine; author of *Medical Ethics for Physicians-in-Training* (Plenum, 1989), and editor of *Encyclopedia of Biomedical Ethics* (forthcoming)

Student Panel: Maria Alarcon, Yahav Shoost, Cathy Sylvester

I begin by asking Kantor to discuss the role of a bioethicist. He answers the question by putting the role into a historical context. He explains that while the relationship between physician and patient has traditionally been a personal and paternalistic one, this has changed of late due to such factors as increased specialization and the role of third-party health-care providers. Seeking to understand what this relationship is in the light of prevailing medical practice, scholars have examined the ethical principles underlying the doctor-patient relationship. This in turn has led to the creation of a field of expertise in the ethical issues that arise in medical science. In addition to their scholarly activities, experts in this field now train medical students and residents to look at the ethical issues underlying medical cases, to make recommendations regarding medical protocol, to develop policy on such issues as "Do Not Resuscitate Orders," and to serve as teachers and advisors on hospital medical ethics committees.

Having established the role of the bioethicist, I ask Kantor to identify the issues surrounding physician-assisted suicide. What he says, in essence, is that with the sophisticated technology that has been developed recently, patients who previously would certainly have died are being kept alive to a point that they might be better off dead or helped to die. When I ask him if he approves of helping patients to die, he hesitantly says that he does, provided the patient is abundantly clear as to what the diagnosis and prognosis are and what the implications are for the patient's decision.

Having discussed physician-assisted suicide generally, I then ask Kantor to comment on Kevorkian's proposals, including that obitiatry be a legitimate subspecialty of medicine. Noting that Kevorkian's proposal is permissible in principle, Kantor is quick to point out that it is dangerous in fact owing to the possibility that a patient might be influenced to commit suicide for the wrong reasons such as the desire to contain medical costs. For this reason, Kantor cautions us to go slow and to construct many safeguards before we introduce obitiatry as a subspecialty of medicine. When I wonder whether we have the wisdom to proceed with this practice, Kantor remarks that society has already come to terms with the view that sometimes a patient is better off dead than alive and declares that he has more faith than I in our ability to carefully legislate physician-assisted suicide.

I next ask Kantor to comment on Kevorkian's claim that a physician's morals should not enter into the doctor-patient relationship, that a physician is a provider of health care, and that a patient is a consumer of health care. Citing the Nuremberg trials of the Nazi doctors, Kantor's response is that a physician is not simply a provider of services and that a physician's morals are always relevant.

Just before the break, I ask Kantor if people have the right to commit suicide and, if so, whether physicians have the obligation to provide the means to do it. Recognizing how hard this question is, Kantor contends that such a right exists but reiterates the view that physicians need never violate their moral convictions to do what they believe is unethical. After discussing his book, *Medical Ethics for Physicians in Training*, we discuss the trend in the United States toward physician-assisted suicide legislation and the referenda that have been proposed in various jurisdictions.

Following the break, Maria Alarcon asks Kantor about surrogate decision making where the patient is an infant. Kantor responds by saying that he is generally skeptical of surrogate decision making. Cathy Sylvester, a fourth-year nursing student, asks Kantor whether it is possible to reconcile the goals of medicine with the principles underlying assisted suicide and euthanasia. Kantor responds that the goals of medicine have changed over the years. No longer is the patient's goal to simply stay alive, and no longer is medicine's goal merely to keep patients alive. Yahav Shoost asks Kantor about some of the conflicts that may arise between patients and their families when they differ on proposed courses of treatment. Kantor reminds us that in cases of conflict, the patient's right to self-determination is controlling.

In this essay, written expressly for this book, Jay Kantor endeavors to distinguish physician-assisted suicide from the related but distinct concept of active euthanasia. Having made this distinction, and having distinguished both from the concept of "the right to refuse life-sustaining treatment," Kantor delineates the arguments for and against suicide generally and moves specifically to physician-assisted suicide. Kantor considers some of the objections to physician-assisted suicide, such as that patients might be lured into committing suicide when other options are available and that it is likely to be implemented inequitably among members of society. Without exactly endorsing the practice, Kantor provides some answers to these objections. He concludes by asking whether physicians should ever be required to assist a suicidal patient, and he briefly addresses physician-assisted suicide in the context of non-terminally-ill patients.

Physician-Assisted Suicide

Jay E. Kantor, Ph.D.

The successes of modern medical technology in prolonging the lives of many seriously ill and terminally ill patients who, in the past, would have died earlier in the course of their diseases have called into question the accepted notion that medicine ought to prolong life as long as possible. It has been said that, in some cases, medicine is really inappropriately prolonging dying rather prolonging life.

Open debate in "respectable" circles about the termination of life is quite new. Only a few years ago, now respectable groups such as The Society for the Right to Die[1] were looked upon as fringe groups. Open talk about allowing patients to die was practically forbidden in hospitals and within the health-care community, although such decisions were sometimes made on an ad hoc basis by staff alone, or staff in consultation with the patient's family. These decisions were made on an informal basis by providers, using what they might refer to as "good clinical judgment." There was no consistency in approaches to such cases; informal policy might vary from hospital to hospital, from ward to ward. There were no rules of "good clinical judgment" to guide physicians in terminating care. Presumably, such judgment was supposed to come from long experience as a clinician working with dying patients. Certainly there was no consistency about whether there was a need to include the patient, if he or she still had the capacity to make decisions, or the family, in the making of such decisions. Thus, for example, decisions to forego care were sometimes made for a patient who still had decisional capacity by his or her providers alone without his or her consent, or by the providers in informal consultation with family members out of the hearing of the patient.

Society finally reached a point where it was felt that open debate and consensus was necessary. The President's Commission for the Study of Ethical Problems in Medicine and Biomedical and Behavioral Research, put together to study and make recommendations on various issues, covered the issue in part in one volume, *Deciding to Forgo Life-Sustaining Treatment*.[2] That discussion has remained influential in current debates about the issues.

Public debate began to emerge about morally permissible and morally advisable ways of treating dying patients. Unfortunately, sometimes the debate has been clouded because a number of very different sorts of proposals and concepts were thrown into the hopper and sometimes treated as if they were factually and morally equivalent. These concepts include (just to name a few): "Voluntary Active Euthanasia," "Involuntary Active Euthanasia," "Voluntary Passive Euthanasia," "Involuntary Passive Euthanasia," and "Physician-Assisted Suicide."

With that in mind, it is best of preface this discussion with some clarification of a few of these crucial concepts.

There is sometimes some confusion in peoples' minds about the very meaning of the phrase *physician-assisted suicide*. Often the concept is confused with the related, but distinct, concept of *active euthanasia* performed by physicians. Both, in turn, are sometimes confused with the concept of "the right of refusal of life-sustaining treatment."

THE RIGHT TO REFUSE TREATMENT

In our time, there has been a growing acceptance that adult persons who have the mental capacity to make decisions about their medical care have the right to refuse almost any medical treatment offered to them.[3] That is true even if the likely consequences of refusal are that they will die of their illness or of complications of their illness. So, for example, a patient with advanced and incurable lung cancer who develops pneumonia may refuse the antibiotics necessary to treat that pneumonia. He will likely die, and the true cause of his death will be attributed to his disease state, not to the fact that he refused treatment for the pneumonia that was a complication of that disease. Even putting aside the law's recognition of the patient's right to refuse to consent to treatment, many in society are willing to believe that it would be appropriate for such a patient with a terminal illness to choose to forego aggressive and often very invasive, uncomfortable attempts to prolong his life, and opt instead to allow the disease to kill him more quickly.

ACTIVE EUTHANASIA AND PHYSICIAN-ASSISTED SUICIDE

However, in both active euthanasia and physician-assisted suicide, the direct cause of the patient's death will neither be the patient's disease or complications arising because of the disease, nor the patient's refusal to accept treatment for his disease, but will be the introduction of some outside process, such as an overdose of drugs, which could very well cause the death of any person, healthy or ill. While the right to refuse life-sustaining treatment has been well-established in law, and the right of the terminally ill to allow death to replace medical technology has been well-established in both law and public consensus, the right to receive another's help in directly causing one's own death has not.

ACTIVE EUTHANASIA PERFORMED BY PHYSICIANS

In cases of active euthanasia performed by a physician, the physician actually performs a physical act on the patient that is intended to be the immediate and direct cause of the patient's death. An example might be that of a physician knowingly injecting a terminally ill patient with a lethal dose of pain-alleviating drugs. Active euthanasia is always intended for the sake of the patient—to provide him or her with a "good" (painless, dignified, or quick) death. Such direct acts of killing are termed *active euthanasia* whether they are voluntary (performed with the consent of the patient), involuntary (performed against the expressed wishes of the patient), or nonvoluntary (performed on a patient who does not have the capacity to make a decision). No forms of active euthanasia are presently legal in this country, and none are condoned by any medical professional societies' codes of ethics.[4] Active euthanasia is legally considered a form of homicide.

PHYSICIAN-ASSISTED SUICIDE

In physician-assisted suicide, the physician does not perform the act of killing the patient,[5] but instead provides the patient with the means or instructions that will enable him or her to perform an action (or combination of actions) that will cause his or her own death. In theory, at least, it is then up to the patient to decide if and when he or she will follow through, and up to him or her to perform the action that will cause his or her death.

Presumably, none of the above would fit into the category of active euthanasia or killing by the physician. The physician in each case has more or less provided the *means* for suicide, but in each case (assuming there are no friends or relatives involved), the action that actually kills the patient must be performed by the patient himself or herself, with or without the physician present.

No professional medical society condones physician-assisted suicide. However, while it is illegal for any person, physician or not, to assist in another person's suicide in most states, laws in some states are somewhat ambiguous about the legality of the practice. In general, courts are reluctant to prosecute in cases in which it was clear that the patient was suffering and that there was no apparent ulterior motive on the part of the person who assisted in the suicide. That reluctance to prosecute is probably a reflection of society's ambiguous feelings about these cases.

Society is currently debating the ethics of both active euthanasia and physician-assisted suicide primarily in the context of what choices should be available for terminally ill patients. However, it is important to note that the debate's context also often includes discussion of the choices that should be available for patients who have chronic, incurable, debilitating illnesses, who do not meet current definitions of having a "terminal condition."[6] We shall reserve discussion of this very difficult issue until later.

When speaking of physician-assisted suicide, the means or information provided to the patient may include a very wide range of options. The physician may provide the patient with an apparatus that will enable the patient to inject himself or herself with a lethal drug. (Presumably, the physician will also provide the patient with the lethal drug.) The physician may provide the patient with a lethal quantity of sleeping pills, along with an explanation of how many pills the patient would need to take to cause death. The physician may provide information about "primitive" ways to suffocate oneself with carbon monoxide exhaust from a car engine or gas stove, or with a plastic bag tied over the head.

THE DEBATE

Suicide[7]

While some might characterize an ill patient's removal or refusal of a life-sustaining measure as "suicide," the consensus is that the ensuing death, because it is caused by the disease, is not definable as a "suicide." Thus, for example, a patient with respiratory failure due to lung cancer who has an oxygen tube removed and suffocates, has died of the cancer, not of the tube being removed. "Suicide" requires a direct action taken by a person who has the intention to kill himself or herself by that action. It is the action itself that must be the direct cause of death.

In the past there have been a number of secular arguments against suicide, and at present there are a number of religious arguments against the taking of one's own life. Some secular arguments derived from early monarchal claims that persons were the property of the state and therefore could not dispose of their own lives as they wished. Another secular argument, presented by Plato,[8] claimed that because the state had nurtured, educated, and protected a person during youth and during periods of vulnerability, the person has incurred a debt to the state and owes it to the state to stay around and repay his or her debt. Still another claim is that we have an inborn instinct to stay alive; to go counter to that instinct would be irrational, or a "crime against nature."[9] With the development of the liberal democratic modern state, with its emphasis on individual rights, these secular arguments have withered away. Now, for example, very few, if any, of the individual United States have laws against suicide. Certainly, other important factors in the change of attitude toward suicide were the developments in medical technology. There was a growing awareness that modern medicine sometimes can prolong life in which there is little or no consciousness, or, perhaps, consciousness with much pain, and no possible outcome other than continued deterioration followed by death. With this was a realization that to want to commit suicide under such conditions could be conceived of as a rational desire, rather than simply symptomatic of a mental illness that was clouding the person's reasoning powers.

On the other hand, many of the religious arguments against suicide are still forwarded by religions. The basis for most of these arguments is a claim that we were put here by God and are, so to speak, the property of God. Therefore, only God has the right to decide when our lives should come to an end.

Rational Suicide in the Context of Modern Medicine

We shall speak here of suicide in the most direct meaning of the term, that is, the intentional taking of one's own life by performing actions which one believed would cause one's death.

Those who argue for permissible suicide claim that there are persons with illnesses that have progressed so far that even the sudden, unexpected development of a new cure for the disease would be of no help to them. They would claim that often medical technology could be said to be prolonging such persons' deaths rather than prolonging their lives. They argue further that since patients are allowed to refuse life-sustaining measures or have them withdrawn, knowing full well that the consequences of the withholding or withdrawal will be death, then why not allow those patients a quick death without suffering. For, while it is true that the pain and suffering of many terminal illnesses can be relieved with analgesic medication, there are cases in which medication will not help or will leave the patient in a semiconscious state. Sometimes, the doses large enough to relieve pain are likely large enough to cause the death of the patient. In some cases, the dying process may take weeks even after life-sustaining measures are withdrawn.

If the patient has expressed a well-thought-through intention to end his or her own life, it would (it is argued) be wrong to intercede and either prevent him or her from following through with his or her intentions, or try to save him or her if he or she is found during a suicide attempt. In these cases, it seems easier to build a case for suicide. It seems less easy to build a strong case when the person is not suffering from a terminal illness, but is suffering from a chronic but not life-threatening condition and does not wish to continue living or adjusting to the condition. Examples might be accomplished career athletes or dancers who suffer untreatable severe spinal injuries, and who would prefer to die rather than be forced to start another career.

Putting these cases aside for the moment, the proponents of permitted suicide may argue that some patients, at least, have a right to be helped to end their lives. They may argue that in instances in which it is known or foreseeable that the amount of pain medication needed to alleviate pain will, as an "unintended side effect," predictably kill the patient, the distinction between the impermissible "primary intention" to cause death and the permissible "unintended side effect" of causing death is really meaningless and empty.

The Physician

At last, we are able to consider the place of the physician in physician-assisted suicide.

One might argue that if suicide is legal, why don't these patients just sign out of the hospital, go home, and kill themselves? Why are they asking for the help of a physician? There are a number of possible reasons. Clearly, in some cases, patients do not have the physical ability to end their own lives with some semblance of dignity. They may be bed-ridden and unable to tend to their basic bodily needs. In other instances, the patient may not know how to commit suicide in the least painful, surest, most dignified way. They may be afraid that they will make mistakes and end up alive, but in even worse condition than before. Such patients may wish for the help or advice of a physician who, presumably, has the expertise to know what actions or doses of drugs will surely prove fatal. If these patients intend to use a lethal dose of drugs, they may require a prescription from a physician in order to get those drugs. Other patients may want final professional reassurance that there is no cure for their disease. Some patients, perhaps bed-ridden and unable to manipulate utensils or needles, may not want to involve family members or home health-care staff, for both legal and emotional reasons. More controversial, the patient may desire that the physician, being made aware of the patient's intentions, will be available to assure that the patient was successful.

If continued medical treatment would be futile, then isn't it consistent with the physician's obligation to work in the "best interests" of his or her patient, to help the patient end his or her life?

While suicide itself is not illegal, assisting someone else to commit suicide is against the law in most, if not all, states. That is true whether the person assisting is a layperson or a health-care provider such as a physician. Moreover, the Hippocratic Oath esteemed by physicians for centuries, contains the phrase that "I [the physician] will neither give a deadly drug to anybody if asked for it, nor will

I make a suggestion to this effect." Thus there are legal and professional precedents mitigating against the practice. But, of course, just because there exists a law or directive in a code of ethics, doesn't mean that the law or directive is morally justifiable and ought not to be changed.

On a broader level, there are those who would argue that provision of at least the means for a quick death may be an appropriate option to be made available to individuals who are terminally ill and who do not want to face a dying process unnecessarily prolonged by modern medicine. They would argue that, as already mentioned, there are cases in which pain cannot be controlled, even with large doses of analgesics or, if controllable, will leave the patient in a prolonged stupor prior to finally dying of his or her illness. They would argue that physician-assisted suicide could be considered consistent with the concept of humane, dignified, appropriate, and even good medical care of the dying. Moreover, as a legalized option, it would allow the patient control in deciding when he or she is ready to die. Sometimes, it would also allow the patient to choose the surroundings in which he or she would prefer to die. At present, sometimes the patient is left with the limited options of either dying in the institution or leaving the hospital against medical advice and dying without the support measures that might be needed for an easier, more dignified death.

ARGUMENTS AGAINST PHYSICIAN-ASSISTED SUICIDE

In the case of the terminally ill, one argument is that often the terminally ill are "lured" toward suicide because other options are denied to them or are difficult to obtain. For example, it is argued that many terminally ill patients suffer needless pain because their treating physicians are reluctant to prescribe sufficient pain medication and, even if they do, nursing staff are often unwilling to administer the prescribed doses. There appear to be a number of reasons for that. A pain medication may very well depress the patient's respiratory functions and, in some cases, the amount of medication needed to contain pain will have the secondary effect of shortening or even ending the patient's life. Health-care providers may have moral objections to that side effect, or they may fear legal repercussions.[10] Added to that is some indication that patients themselves are reluctant to ask for sufficient pain medication. We are living in a time when society has very negative feelings toward the use of narcotics. Those negative attitudes, originally directed against the recreational use of narcotics and possible subsequent addiction, appear to have spilled over to the medical situation in which they are totally inappropriate. (There have been reports that some health-care providers are afraid that they may induce an addiction in a patient who has but a few days to live!)

Others argue[11] that society limits the availability of other options for the terminally ill patient, such as hospice care. Hospice care is intended for dying patients. The thought is to attend to the patient's emotional and physical needs (including pain management) without providing aggressive attempts to keep the patient alive (though hospice patients always have the choice to change their minds and enter an aggressive care setting). Hospice care may be provided in free-standing units (a separate building or wing of a hospital, for example) or may be provided to the patient in his or her own home. It is argued that if more hospice options were available, there would be less clamor for physician-assisted suicide.

It is also argued that patients who lack a support system of friends and family may "choose" suicide simply because they have no close persons to provide emotional support. The claim here is that if these patients had a support system of family, friends, and perhaps professional aid, such as social workers seen on a regular basis, they might be more willing to "hang on."[12]

Perhaps a more telling argument against physician-assisted suicide is that it is likely that its availability and implementation will be inequitable among members of society. Many who favor legalization of the practice believe that a close relationship between physician and patient is a prerequisite for the practice. By that is meant that the physician has known the patient well enough and over a long period to be somewhat assured that the patient's wishes for suicide are firm and well thought through. However, in the context of the way health care is presently delivered, it is rare that such a physician-patient relationship exists. Less-affluent patients may not have a physician who knows them well. In the course of their medical histories and in the course of a hospital stay, they are likely to have only short-term contact with a number of physicians.

The counterargument is that, at present, a patient with an advance directive specifying that all life-sustaining treatment be withdrawn, can enter a hospital where he or she is unknown to staff and those wishes, under ordinary conditions, must be honored by health-care providers who are strangers to the patient. Therefore, it is argued, if we are willing to accept the inflexibility and validity of a document that, in essence, will quicken the dying of a patient, why should we require that the patient have a special relationship with a physician when physician-assisted suicide is at stake?

SHOULD PHYSICIANS BE FORCED TO ASSIST IN A PATIENT'S SUICIDE?

This is a more difficult question than it first may appear to be. Usually, hospital policies that have some tinge of moral controversy to them contain a proviso that a health-care provider who feels strong moral convictions against the practice may refuse to take part in the practice as along as he or she transfers care of the patient to another provider who will honor the right. While some might argue that suicide in certain cases is part of appropriate treatment, and thus a physician who refused to acquiesce could be accused of abandoning a patient, it is doubtful that any possible policy allowing assisted suicide will omit the "conscience clause." Whether there will be sufficient numbers of physicians willing to assist in suicide if the practice becomes legal is an unanswerable question at this time.

THE NON-TERMINALLY-ILL PATIENT AND ASSISTED SUICIDE

As we have mentioned, many are willing to accept assisted suicide and even active euthanasia for patients who are terminally ill and who have had the mental capacity and opportunity to try or consider all other alternatives. There is likely far less agreement that assisted suicide (or active euthanasia, of course) be allowed, or at least encouraged in any way, as an option for persons who suffer from debilitating chronic illnesses that are not considered to be "terminal illnesses" under the current definition of the term.

When such patients are dependent on medical technology to stay alive (respirators, for example), the courts have been consistent in allowing them to have such measures withdrawn so that they may die. Those who argue that often there really is little or no distinction between withdrawing life-sustaining measures and actively killing[13] might also argue that a law that permits physician-assisted suicide should be broad enough to encompass a right to assisted suicide without terminal illness as a precondition.

There are instances in which a chronically ill patient's request for assisted suicide might seem reasonable, for example, a quadriplegic with severe loss of speech capacities, along with inabilities such as the capacity to take food and water by mouth. However, there are other cases of chronically ill patients who desire assisted suicide that are not as "clear cut." These would be people with lesser disabilities where it may seem reasonable to expect that, given help to do so, they could rebuild their lives in meaningful ways, rather than choosing death. Such patients, when physically capable, do have the option of choosing to commit suicide without the help of a physician. However, when such patients lack the physical capacity to perform suicide without aid, one wonders whether they should have the right to demand that a physician intercede to help them.

These difficulties with physician-assisted suicide in regard to non-terminally-ill patients might be reason to restrict any initial legisla-tion legalizing physician-assisted suicide to patients who are terminally ill.

ENDNOTES

1. Now called "Choice in Dying."
2. The President's Commission for the Study of Ethical Problems in Medicine and Biomedical and Behavioral Research. *Deciding to Forgo Life-Sustaining Treatment.* Washington, D.C.: U.S. Government Printing Office, 1983.
3. Of course, problems may arise if the patient wants to be cured but rejects a measure that is believed to be medically necessary in order to effect a cure. For example, it is questionable that there would be an obligation to continue treating a patient with an infection who requests treatment for the illness, but rejects all the tests necessary to determine the nature of his or her infection.
4. However, it is rare that, in cases in which the patient was quite ill or quite near death, that the law has prosecuted or, at least, demanded heavy sentences for those who have performed active euthanasia without malice. These cases often involve active euthanasia performed by a close family member.
5. However, the physician may be morally compelled to stay in attendance to make sure that the patient was successful in his or her attempt. This raises another set of moral issues discussed in the body of this text.
6. *Terminal condition* has begun to be defined in rather broad ways. For example, in the past it might have been strictly defined as an "illness or injury from which there is no recovery, and which reasonably can be expected to cause death within one year" (New York State Task Force on Life and the Law, *Do Not Resuscitate Orders: The Proposed Legislation and Report of the New York State Task Force on Life and the Law,* 1986). A more typical present definition might read: "A chronic condition which is incurable by any foreseeable medical developments, and is expected to cause death in the patient." Thus, for example, a patient with Alzheimer's disease, which causes deterioration of the central nervous system and eventual death, may be diagnosed with the disease at a time when the symptoms are not debilitating. Such a patient may not suffer intolerable symptoms for at least a few years and may not die for some period after that. Nevertheless, under most present de-

finitions, the patient, even at the onset of the disease, would be characterized as "terminally ill" (c.f. New Jersey Commission on Legal and Ethical Problems in the Delivery of Health Care, *The New Jersey Advance Directives for Health Care Act,* 1992, p. 3). Some hospice programs still retain a "death within six months" criterion.

7. For a fuller discussion, see M. Pabst Battin, *Ethical Issues in Suicide* (Englewood Cliffs, N.J.: Prentice Hall, 1982).

8. Plato, *Crito* 49E–53A.

9. However, some argue that it is effectively suicide, or at least immoral, to refuse simple ("ordinary") life-sustaining measures such as food and water. That is argued to be true even if food and water must be given through tubes. This is the present position of the Roman Catholic Church and some denominations of Orthodox Judaism.

10. As we have said, that fear is unfounded as long as the primary intent of administering the medication was to alleviate suffering.

11. The New York State Task Force on Life and the Law, *When Death Is Sought—Assisted Suicide and Euthanasia in the Medical Context* (New York: Author, 1994).

12. Virginia Beyer, Evan DeRenzo, Edward Matricardi, "Rational Suicide or Involuntary Commitment of a Patient Who Is Terminally Ill." *Journal of Clinical Ethics* 4(4): 327–329.

13. Dan W. Brock. *Life and Death: Philosophical Essays in Biomedical Ethics* (New York: Cambridge University Press, 1993).

This excerpt from the President's Commission for the Study of Ethical Problems in Medicine and Biomedical and Behavioral Research discusses the legal mechanisms by which competent adult persons may give advance directives for the acceptance or refusal of medical treatment in the event that they should enter a future period of incompetency. The living will allows for direct control, and the durable power of attorney allows for the identification of surrogate decision makers. See Figure A following the Commission's report for an example of a living will (courtesy of Choice in Dying, Inc.) and Figure B for an example of a document designed to comply with New York's Health Care Proxy law (also courtesy of Choice in Dying, Inc.).

Advance Directives

President's Commission for the Study of Ethical Problems in Medicine and Biomedical Behavioral Research

ADVANCE DIRECTIVES

An "advance directive" lets people anticipate that they may be unable to participate in future decisions about their own health care—an "instruction directive" specifies the types of care a person wants (or does not want) to receive; a "proxy directive" specifies the surrogate a person wants to make such decisions if the person is ever unable to do so[1]; and the two forms may be combined. Honoring such a directive shows respect for self-determination in that it fulfills two of the three values that underlie self-determination. First, following a directive, particularly one that gives specific instructions about types of acceptable and unacceptable interventions, fulfills the instrumental role of self-determination by promoting the patient's subjective, individual evaluation of well-being. Second, honoring the directive shows respect for the patient as a person.

An advance directive does not, however, provide self-determination in the sense of active moral agency by the patient on his or her own behalf. The discussion between patient and health care professional leading up to a directive would involve active participation and shared decision-making, but at the point of actual decision the patient is incapable of participating. Consequently, although self-determination is involved when a patient establishes a way to project his or her wishes into a time of anticipated incapacity, it is a sense of self-determination lacking in one important attribute: active, contemporaneous personal choice. Hence a decision not to follow an advance directive may sometimes be justified even when it would not be acceptable to disregard a competent patient's contemporaneous choice. Such a decision would most often rest on a finding that the patient did not adequately envision and consider the particular situation within which the actual medical decision must be made.

Advance directives are not confined to decisions to forego life-sustaining treatment but may be drafted for use in any health care situation in which people anticipate they will lack capacity to make decisions for themselves. However, the best-known type of directive—formulated pursuant to a "natural death" act—does deal with decisions to forego life-sustaining treatment. Beginning with the passage in 1976 of the California Natural Death Act, 14 states and the District of Columbia have enacted statutory authorization for the formulation of advance directives to forego life-sustaining treatment. . . .[2] In addition, 42 states have enacted "durable power of attorney" statutes; though developed in the context

of law concerning property, these statutes may be used to provide a legal authority for an advance directive. . . .

Despite a number of unresolved issues about how advance directives should be drafted, given legal effect, and used in clinical practice, the Commission recommends that advance directives should expressly be endowed with legal effect under state law. For such documents to assist decisionmaking, however, people must be encouraged to develop them for their individual use, and health care professionals should be encouraged to respect and abide by advance directives whenever reasonably possible, even without specific legislative authority.

Existing Alternative Documents

Several forms of advance directives are currently used. "Living wills" were initially developed as documents without any binding legal effects; they are ordinarily instruction directives. The intent behind the original "natural death" act was simply to give legal recognition to living wills drafted according to certain established requirements. They are primarily instruction directives, although their terms are poorly enough defined that the physician and surrogate who will carry them out will have to make substantial interpretations. "Durable power of attorney" statutes are primarily proxy directives, although by limiting or describing the circumstances in which they are to operate they also contain elements of instruction directives. Furthermore, durable powers of attorney may incorporate extensive personal instructions.

Living Wills People's concerns about the loss of ability to direct care at the end of their lives have led a number of commentators as well as religious, educational, and professional groups to promulgate documents, usually referred to as living wills,[3] by which individuals can indicate their preference not to be given "heroic" or "extraordinary" treatments. There have been many versions proposed, varying widely in their specificity. Some explicitly detailed directives have been drafted by physicians—outlining a litany of treatments to be foregone or disabilities they would not wish to suffer in their final days.[4] The model living wills proposed by educational groups have somewhat more general language[5]; they typically mention "life-sustaining procedures which would serve only to artificially prolong the dying process." One New York group has distributed millions of living wills.[6] The columnist who writes "Dear Abby" reports receiving tens of thousands of requests for copies each time she deals with the subject.[7] Despite their popularity, their legal force and effect is uncertain.[8] The absence of explicit statutory authorization in most jurisdictions raises a number of important issues that patients and their lawyers or other advisors should keep in mind when drafting living wills.

First, it is uncertain whether health care personnel are required to carry out the terms of a living will; conversely, those who, in good faith, act in accordance with living wills are not assured immunity from civil or criminal prosecution. No penalties are provided for the destruction, concealment, forgery or other misuse of living wills, which leaves them somewhat vulnerable to abuse. The question of whether a refusal of life-sustaining therapy constitutes suicide is unresolved, as are the insurance implications of a patient's having died as a result of a physician's withholding treatment pursuant to a living will.

Yet even in states that have not enacted legislation to recognize and implement advance directives, living wills may still have some legal effect.[9] For example, should a practitioner be threatened with civil liability or criminal prosecution for having acted in accord with such a document, it should at least serve as evidence of a patient's wishes and assessment of benefit when he or she was competent.[10] Indeed, no practitioner has been successfully subjected to civil liability or criminal prosecution for having followed the provisions in a living will, nor do there appear to be any cases brought for having acted against one.[11]

Natural Death Acts   To overcome the uncertain legal status of living wills,[12] 13 states and the District of Columbia have followed the lead set by California in 1976 and enacted statutes that formally establish the requirements for a "directive to physicians."[13] The California statute was labeled a "natural death" act and this term is now used generically to refer to other state statutes. Although well-intended, these acts raise a great many new problems without solving many of the old ones.

No natural death act yet deals with all the issues raised when living wills are used without specific statutory sanction. For instance, the acts differ considerably in their treatment of penalties for failing to act in accord with a properly executed directive or to transfer the patient to a physician who will follow the directive.[14] In some jurisdictions, the statutes consider these failures to be unprofessional conduct and therefore grounds for professional discipline, including the suspension of a license to practice medicine.[15] Other statutes fail to address the issue; presumably, however, existing remedies such as injunctions or suits for breach of contract or for battery are available to patients or their heirs,[16] although there do not appear to be any instances of such penalties being sought.

Some of the statutes attempt to provide patients with adequate opportunity to reconsider their decision by imposing a waiting period between the time when a patient decides that further treatment is unwanted and the time when the directive becomes effective. Under the California statute, for example, a directive is binding only if it is signed by a "qualified patient," technically defined as someone who has been diagnosed as having a "terminal condition." This is defined as an incurable condition that means death is "imminent" regardless of the "life-sustaining procedures" used.[17] A patient must wait 14 days after being told of the diagnosis before he or she can sign a directive, which would require a miraculous cure, a misdiagnosis, or a very loose interpretation of the word "imminent" in order for the directive to be of any use to a patient. The statute requires that when a directive is signed, the patient must be fully competent and not overwhelmed by disease or by the effects of treatment, but a study of California physicians one year after the new law was enacted found that only about half the patients diagnosed as terminally ill even remain conscious for 14 days.[18] There is an inherent tension between ensuring that dying patients have a means of expressing their wishes about treatment termination before they are overcome by incompetence and ensuring that people do not make binding choices about treatment on the basis of hypothetical rather than real facts about their illness and dying process. If a waiting period is deemed necessary to resolve this tension the time should be defined in a way that does not substantially undercut the objective of encouraging advance directives by people who are at risk of becoming incapacitated.

Although the California statute was inspired in part by the situation of Karen Quinlan, whose father had to pursue judicial relief for a year in order to authorize the removal of her respirator, it would not apply in a case like hers.

> The only patients covered by this statute are those who are on the edge of death *despite the doctors' efforts*. The very people for whom the greatest concern is expressed about a prolonged and undignified dying process are unaffected by the statute because their deaths are not imminent.[19]

The class of persons thus defined by many of the statutes,[20] if it indeed contains any members, at most constitutes a small percentage of those incapacitated individuals for whom decisions about life-sustaining treatment must be made. Although some statutes have not explicitly adopted the requirement that treatments may be withheld or withdrawn only if death is imminent whether or not they are used, this requirement is still found in one of the most recently passed natural death acts.[21] Such a limitation greatly reduces an act's potential.

Some of the patients for whom decisions to forego life-sustaining treatment need to be made are residents of nursing homes rather than hospitals. Concerned that they might be under undue pressure to sign a directive, the California legislature provided additional safeguards for the voluntariness of their directives by requiring that a patient advocate or ombudsman serve as a witness.[22] The Commission believes that health care providers should make reasonable efforts to involve disinterested parties, not only as witnesses to the signing of a directive under a natural death act, but also as counselors to patients who request such a directive to ensure that they are acting as voluntarily and competently as possible. Yet statutory requirements of this sort may have the effect of precluding use of advance directives by long-term care residents, even though some residents of these facilities might be as capable as any other persons of using the procedure in a free and knowing fashion.

Paradoxically, natural death acts may restrict patients' ability to have their wishes about life-sustaining treatment respected. If health care providers view these as the exclusive means for making and implementing a decision to forego treatment and, worse, if they believe that such a decision cannot be made by a surrogate on behalf of another but only in accordance with an advance directive properly executed by a patient, some dying patients may be subject to treatment that is neither desired nor beneficial. In fact, although 6.5% of the physicians surveyed in California reported that during the first year after passage of the act there they withheld or withdrew procedures they previously would have administered, 10% of the physicians reported that they provided treatment they formerly would have withheld.[23]

In addition, there is the danger that people will infer that a patient who has not executed a directive in accordance with the natural death act does not desire life-sustaining treatment to be ended under any circumstances.[24] Yet the person may fail to sign a directive because of ignorance of its existence, inattention to its significance, uncertainty about how to execute one, or failure to foresee the kind of medical circumstances that in fact develop.[25] Unfortunately, even the explicit disclaimer contained in many of these laws—that the act is not intended to impair or supersede any preexisting common-law legal rights or responsibilities that patients and practitioners may have with respect to the withholding or withdrawing of life-sustaining procedures—does not in itself correct this difficulty.

First, the declarations about the right of competent patients to refuse "life-sustaining procedures" take on a rather pale appearance since such procedures are defined by the statutes as those that cannot stop an imminent death. (In other words, competent patients may refuse futile treatments.) Second, it is hard to place great reliance on preexisting common law rights, since had the common law established such rights there would have been no real need for the statutes. Thus, if health care providers are to treat patients appropriately in states that have adopted natural death acts, they will need the encouragement of their attorneys—backed by sensible judicial interpretation of the statutes—to read the acts as authorizing a new, additional means for patients to exercise "informed consent" regarding life-saving treatment, but not as a means that limits decisionmaking of patients who have not executed binding directives pursuant to the act.

The greatest value of the natural death acts is the impetus they provide for discussions between patients and practitioners about decision to forego life-sustaining treatment.[26] This education effect might be obtained, however, without making the documents binding by statute and without enforcement and punishment provisions.

Durable Power of Attorney Statutes   Of the existing natural death acts, only Delaware's explicitly provides for the appointment of an agent for medical decisionmaking if the patient becomes incapacitated.[27] In view of the Commission's conclusion that both instruction and proxy directives are important for medical decisionmaking that respects patients' wishes, this deficiency in the other statutes constitutes a serious shortcoming. Proxy directives allow patients to control decisionmaking in a far broader range of cases than the instruction directives authorized by most existing natural death acts.

Nonetheless, authority to appoint a proxy to act after a person becomes incompetent does exist in the 42 states that have laws authorizing durable powers of attorney. A "power of attorney" is a document by which one person (the "principal") confers upon another person (the "agent") the legally recognized authority to perform certain acts on the principal's behalf. For instance, a person who moves to a new city and who leaves behind an automobile for someone else to sell can execute a power of attorney to permit an agent to complete the necessary legal documents in connection with the sale. In this case the power of attorney is a limited one; it gives the agent authority to perform only a specific act—the transfer of title to a particular piece of property. Powers of attorney may also be general, conferring authority on the agent to act on behalf of the principal in all matters. Such actions by agents are as legally binding on principals as if the latter had performed the acts themselves.

A power of attorney—general or limited—may be employed in making decisions not only about property but about personal matters as well, and in this role powers of attorney might be used to delegate authority to others to make health care decisions. A power of attorney, therefore, can be an advance proxy directive. Using it, a person can nominate another to make health care decisions if he or she becomes unable to make those decisions.

One barrier to this use of a power of attorney, however, is that the usual power of attorney becomes inoperative at precisely the point it is needed; a common-law power of attorney automatically terminates when the principal becomes incapacitated.[28] To circumvent this barrier, many states have enacted statutes creating a power of attorney that is "durable"—which means that an agent's authority to act continues after his or her principal is incapacitated. As a result, durable power of attorney acts offer a simple, flexible, and powerful device for making health care decisions on behalf of incapacitated patients.[29]

Although not expressly enacted for the problems of incompetent patients' health care decisionmaking, the language of these statutes can accommodate the appointment of a surrogate for that purpose and nothing in the statutes explicitly precludes such a use.[30] The flexibility of the statutes allows directives to be drafted that are sensitive both to the different needs of patients in appointing proxy decisionmakers and to the range of situations in which decisions may have to be made.

The Commission therefore encourages the use of existing durable power of attorney statutes to facilitate decisionmaking for incapacitated persons, but it also recognizes the possibility for abuse inherent in the statutes. These statutes do not have rigorous procedures because they were enacted primarily to avoid the expense of full guardianship or conservatorship proceedings when dealing with small property interests.[31] Adapting them to the context of health care may require that greater procedural safeguards be provided: precisely which safeguards are needed might best be determined after more experience has been acquired. Existing durable power of attorney statutes need to be studied, therefore, as they are applied to decisionmaking for incapacitated patients facing health care decisions.

Proposed Statutes

Various concerned groups have proposed statutes that might improve upon natural death acts, by being more generally applicable and authorizing proxy designation, as well as upon durable power of attorney statutes, by providing protections and procedures appropriate to health care decisionmaking.

The Society for the Right to Die has proposed a "Medical Treatment Decision Act," which is similar to the existing natural death acts.[32] The proposal shares the narrowness of application of most such acts and makes no explicit provision for designating a proxy for medical decisionmaking.

The National Conference of Commissioners on Uniform State Laws has drafted a "Model Health Care Consent Act."[33] Despite its comprehensive title, this act does not have consent as a central concern; more correctly it is a "substitute authority to decide" act. It provides for the appointment of a health care representative to make decisions should a patient be incompetent. Although its intent to provide for proxy directives is laudable, the proposal does not resolve certain central issues. In particular, it does not specify which standard should guide a health care representative (best interests or substituted judgment). The act is also imprecise in the determination of capacity to consent. Procedures governing revocation of the appointment of a health care representative and redelegation of authority are uncertain and liable to abuse.

A national educational group called Concern for Dying has had its Legal Advisory Committee draft a "Uniform Right to Refuse Treatment Act."[34] The Act enunciates competent adults' right to refuse treatment and provides a mechanism by which competent people can both state how they wish to be treated in the event of incompetence and name another person to enforce those wishes. In terms of its treatment of such central issues as the capacity to consent and standard by which a proxy decisionmaker is to act, the Uniform Right to Refuse Treatment Act is carefully crafted and in conformity with the Commission's conclusions. Greater opportunity for review of determinations of incompetency and of proxy's decisions may be needed, however, to protect patients' self-determination and welfare.

Another proposed statute was developed by a committee of concerned citizens in Michigan. First submitted to the state legislature in 1979, their bill would have established the authority of a competent person to designate a proxy specifically for health care decisionmaking.[35] Although Michigan had a durable power of attorney statute, it was not used for health care, perhaps because many people did not know of its availability and it seemed to require a lawyer's drafting services. The proposed proxy decisionmaking bill is simple and direct, yet includes significant procedural safeguards.

General Considerations in Formulating Legislation

The Commission believes that advance directives are, in general, useful as a means of appropriate decisionmaking about life-sustaining treatment for incapacitated patients. The education of the general public and of health care professionals should be a concern to legislators, as the statutes are ineffective if unknown or misunderstood. Many of the natural death and durable power of attorney statutes are less helpful than they might be. In the drafting or the amending of legislation to authorize advance directives, a number of issues need attention.[36]

Requisites for a Valid Directive Some way should be established to verify that the person writing a directive was legally competent to do so at the time. A statute might require evidence that the person has the capacity to understand the choice embodied in the directive when it is executed. The statute should clearly state whether the witnesses that are required attest to the principal's capacity or merely ensure that signatures are not fraudulent. Since such witnesses are likely to be laypeople, the standard of decisionmaking capacity they apply will rest on common sense, not psychological expertise. Furthermore, the standard they are asked to attest to may be as low as that used in wills, unless specified differently.

The principal and the prospective proxy should recognize the seriousness of the step being taken, but this will be difficult to guarantee by statute. One way to increase the likelihood that due regard is given to the subject matter would be to provide that before a directive is executed, the principal (and proxy, where one is involved) must have had a discussion with a health care professional about a directive's potential consequences, in light of the principal's values and goals. This would also help ensure that any instructions reflect a process of active self-determination on the part of the patient.

Legal Effect of Directives A statute should ensure that people acting pursuant to a valid directive are not subject to civil or criminal liability for any action that would be acceptable if performed on the valid consent of a competent patient. Since directives—particularly those including instructions—may contain unavoidable ambiguities, some recognition of the need for interpretation will be needed to provide adequate reassurance for health care professionals and proxies. Some of the existing statutes speak of protection for actions taken in "good faith,"[37] which provides sensible protection. Some standard of reasonable interpretation of the directive may need to be imposed, however, on an attending physician's reading of the document, lest "good faith" offer too wide a scope for discretion. Such a standard might best be developed in case law and scholarly commentary rather than in the statute itself.

The wisdom or necessity of penalties for noncompliance (fines, for example, or suspension or revocation of professional licenses[38]) depends upon the problem a statute is attempting to remedy. If health care professionals are unwilling to share responsibility with patients and, in particular, tend to overtreat patients whose physical or mental condition leaves them unable to resist, then—unless they are made legally binding—advance directives are unlikely to protect patients who want to limit their treatment. On the other hand, if health care professionals are simply unsure of what patients want, or if they are willing to share decisionmaking responsibility but are apprehensive about their legal liability if they follow the instructions of a person whose decisionmaking capacity is in doubt, then the threat of penalties would be unnecessary and potentially counterproductive by fostering an adversarial relationship between patient and provider. The evidence available at present does not clearly support substantial penalties.[39]

Proxy's Characteristics and Authority Several special questions arise in the context of health care concerning who may act as a proxy and what the proxy may do. A proxy should have the decisionmaking capacity needed for a particular health care situation. The criteria for determining presence of adequate capacity in a proxy are the same as for patients themselves.

Statutes might limit who may serve as proxy so as to avoid the appointment of anyone likely to act upon interests that are adverse to a patient's. In some natural death statutes, the criteria for witnesses explicitly exclude anyone financially involved (as debtor, creditor, or heir) with the patient.[40] If a similar restriction were applied to proxies, this might eliminate virtually everyone who cares about the patient, however. Special restrictions on who may be a proxy may be warranted for patients in long-term care and psychiatric institutions, though the appropriate form of such conditions is uncertain.

In certain circumstances a proxy may be temporarily or permanently unable or unwilling to serve as a substitute decisionmaker. When that occurs, alternate proxies could be limited to people who were named by the principal in an original or amended directive; or, alternately, a proxy could be allowed to delegate his or her authority to another person of the proxy's choosing.[41] This issue might be affected by whether either the original or a substitute proxy was a close relative of the patient, as opposed to a stranger.

Since the proxy stands in the shoes of the patient and is expected to engage in a comparable decisionmaking process, logically the proxy should have access to the patient's medical record. Yet it may sometimes be advisable to allow the proxy's access to be limited to the information needed for the health care decision at hand, in order to respect the patient's privacy.

Any directive issued by a competent person, and especially an instruction directive, can use the Commission's preferred standard for surrogate decisionmaking—substituted judgment. The interpretation of such a directive should ordinarily lie with the surrogate decisionmaker, particularly in the case of a proxy designated by the patient. Provision may have to be made for an administrative mechanism to decide situations in which a health care professional challenges a proxy's decision on the ground that it is based on neither a reasonable interpretation of the patient's instructions nor on the patient's best interests.

Administrative Aspects Several procedural concerns probably need to be addressed in any statute for advance health care directives. A statute needs to specify how a directive becomes effective. Some of the natural death acts, as already mentioned, require that a directive be executed after the patient has been informed of a diagnosis, so that the person's instructions are arrived at in the context of the actual, rather than the hypothetical, choices to be made. Some statutes also provide that the directive be renewed every few years so that the signatory can reconsider the instructions or designation in light of changed circumstances or opinions.

The trigger for a valid directive becoming operative also needs to be specified. A statute may leave that question to the document itself, to be specified by the person executing the directive, or it may provide that a particular event or condition brings the document into play. In either case, the triggering event will require both a standard for action and a specification of who will determine that the standard is met. For example, a directive may become operative when a physician makes a particular prognosis ("terminal illness") or determines that a patient lacks decisional capacity regarding a particular health care choice.

Provision must be made for the process and standard by which a document can be revoked. The value of self-determination suggests that as long as the principal remains competent, he or she should unquestionably have the power to revoke a directive. But what about an incompetent (incapacitated) person? The natural death acts have uniformly provided that *any* revocation by a principal negates a directive. In the context of foregoing life-sustaining treatment, that result may be sensible, since it would generally seem wrong to cease such treatment based upon a proxy's orders when a patient, no matter how confused, asks that treatment be continued.[42] In other circumstances, however, allowing revocations by an incompetent patient could seriously disrupt a course of treatment authorized by a proxy. When the proxy intends to override the principal's contemporaneous instructions because the incompetent principal is contradicting earlier competent instructions and/or acting contrary to his or her best interests, the question of whether to follow the proxy or the principal may have to be resolved by an independent review.

In general, when disputes arise about such things as the choice made by a proxy or an attempted revocation by an apparently incapacitated principal, a review process will be an important safeguard for the patient's interests. In some circumstances the review mechanism need only judge whether the decisionmaking process was adequate. In other circumstances it may be advisable to review the health care decision itself and the application of the appropriate decisionmaking standard. In the absence of a special provision in the statute, questions of this sort should lead to intrainstitutional review and, as needed, to judicial proceedings.

Conclusions

The Commission commends the use of advance directives. Health care professionals should be familiar with their state's legal mechanisms for implementing advance directives on life-sustaining treatment and encourage patients to use these resources. In particular, practitioners can alert patients to the existence of durable power of attorney devices (in states where they exist) and urge them to discuss their desires about treatment with a proxy decisionmaker. In states without applicable legislation, practitioners can still inform their patients of the value of making their wishes known, whether through a living will or more individual instructions regarding the use of life-sustaining procedures under various circumstances.

Institutions concerned with patient and practitioner education have an important role to play in encouraging patients to become familiar with and use advance directives, and in familiarizing practitioners with the ethical and practical desirability of their patients using these mechanisms. Finally, legislators should be encouraged to draft flexible and clear statutes that give appropriate legal authority to those who write and rely upon advance directives. Such legislation needs to balance the provisions aimed at restricting likely abuses and those intended to allow flexibility and individuality for patients and proxies.

From the President's Commission for the Study of Ethical Problems in Medicine and Biomedical and Behavioral Research, *Deciding to Forego Life-Sustaining Treatment* (Washington, D.C.: U.S. Government Printing Office, 1983), pp. 136–53.

ENDNOTES

1. This Report uses "proxy" to mean a surrogate whose appointment rests on the designation of the patient while competent.
2. One of these states, Virginia, has a statute awaiting the Governor's signature as of March 17, 1983. *See also* Michael Garland, *Politics, Legislation and Natural Death*, 6 HASTINGS CTR. REP. 5 (Oct. 1976); Richard A. McCormick and André Hellegers, *Legislation and the Living Will*, 136 AMERICA 210 (1977); Barry Keene, *The Natural Death Act: A Well-Baby Check-up on Its First Birthday*, 315 ANNALS N.Y. ACAD. SCI. 376 (1978).
3. *Questions and Answers About the Living Wills* (pamphlet), CONCERN FOR DYING, New York, (n.d.).
4. Walter Modell, *A "Will" to Live* (Sounding Board), 290 NEW ENG. J. MED. 907 (1974); *Last Rights* (Letters), 295 NEW ENG. J. MED. 1139 (1976); *See also* Sissela Bok, *Personal Directions for Care at the End of Life*, 295 NEW ENG. J. MED. 367 (1976).
5. Among the groups that have promulgated living wills are the Society for the Right to Die, the Euthanasia Education Council, the American Protestant Hospital Association, the American Catholic Hospital Association, and the American Public Health Association.
6. *See note 3 supra.*
7. Letter from Abigail van Buren to Joanne Lynn (Sept. 10, 1981). Ann Landers reports similar

public enthusiasm. Letter from Ann Landers to Joanne Lynn (Sept. 16, 1981).

8. For a discussion of the legal effects of living wills, *see* Luis Kutner, *Due Process of Euthanasia: The Living Will, A Proposal,* 44 Ind. L. J. 539, 552 (1969); Michael T. Sullivan, *The Dying Person— His Plight and His Right,* 8 NEW ENG. L. REV. 197, 215 (1973); Comment, *Antidysthanasia Contracts: A Proposal for Legalizing Death With Dignity,* 5 PAC. L.J. 738, 739–40 (1974); Note, *The "Living Will": The Right to Death With Dignity?,* 26 CASE W. RES. L. REV. 485, 509–526 (1976); Note, *Informed Consent and the Dying Patient,* 83 YALE L.J. 1632, 1663–64 (1974); Note, *The Right to Die,* 10 CAL. W.L. REV. 613, 625 (1974).

9. *See* Note, *Living Wills—Need for Legal Recognition,* 78 W. VA. L. REV. 370 (1976); *See also, In re* Storar, 52 N.Y.2d 363, 420 N.E.2d 64 (1981) (on reliance on oral advance directives with burden of proof being clear and convincing evidence).

10. *See* Kutner, *supra* note 84; Note, *The "Living Will": The Right to Death with Dignity?, supra* note 84; David J. Sharpe and Robert F. Hargest, *Lifesaving Treatment for Unwilling Patients,* 36 FORDHAM L. REV. 695, 702 (1968).

11. A UPI study, reported in *The Right to Die,* 12 TRIAL (Jan. 1976), stated that no living will had been tested in the courts. None since has come to the Commission's attention.

12. *See* Note, *Living Wills—Need for Legal Recognition,* 78 W. VA. L. REV. 370, 377 (1976); Note, *The "Living Will": The Right to Death With Dignity?,* . . .

13. *See* note 2 *supra.*

14. Like most provisions of the statutes, the requirement that the physician who refuses to comply must effectuate a transfer to another physician has not been tested. Such a transfer might at times be very difficult and a "good faith" effort might be the appropriate standard rather than the actual transfer.

15. The California statute stipulates that a physician's failure to effectuate a binding, though not a merely advisory, directive, or to transfer the patient to another physician who will effectuate the directive of the qualified patient, shall constitute unprofessional conduct. . . . The Texas statute weakens this penalty by stipulating that such a failure *may* constitute unprofessional conduct. . . . The statutes of Kansas and the District of Columbia, which do not contain the binding/advisory distinction, provide that the failure to properly transfer a patient when the physician cannot comply with a valid advance directive shall constitute unprofessional conduct. . . . The statutes of the remaining states make no explicit provision for penalties for physicians who do not comply with valid advance directives or transfer patients to physicians who will effectuate the directives. . . .

16. *See* Michigan House Bill No. 4492 (March 26, 1981), . . . which provides for the appointment of an agent for medical decisionmaking and presents an approach to physician penalties that is worth considering. Section 12(2) states:

A physician or other health care professional acting under the direction of a physician who fails to observe a refusal of medical treatment or a request for continued medical treatment by an agent shall be legally liable in the same manner and degree as would have been the case if the appointor had been capable of making the decision and had refused or requested the treatment in his or her own right under similar circumstances.

See also Bruce L. Miller, *Michigan Medical Treatment Decision Act,* in Cynthia B. Wong and Judith P. Swazey, DILEMMAS OF DYING: POLICIES AND PROCEDURES FOR DECISIONS NOT TO TREAT, G. K. Hall Med. Pub., Boston (1981) at 161.

17. Cal. Health & Safety Code §§ 7187(e), 7191(b) (Deering Supp. 1982), . . .

18. Note, *The California Natural Death Act: An Empirical Study of Physicians' Practices,* 31 STAN. L. REV. 913, 928 (1979). Only two of the statutes passed since California's have followed that state's lead on these provisions. Although they differ in details, both Oregon and Texas treat only those directives executed after the patient has been informed that he or she has a terminal illness as "conclusively presumptive" of the patient's desires regarding the withholding or withdrawal of life-sustaining procedures.

19. A. M. Capron, *The Development of Law on Human Death,* 315 ANNALS N. Y. ACAD. SCI. 45, 55, (1978).

20. *See* state statutes for Alabama, California, Delaware, the District of Columbia, Idaho, Kansas, New Mexico, Oregon, Texas, Vermont, and Washington.

21. Del. Code Ann. tit. 16, § 2501(e) (1982).

22. The California statute, . . . refers to a patient advocate or ombudsman "as may be designated

by the State Department of Aging for this purpose pursuant to any other applicable provision of law." A companion statute providing for such a service was not approved by the legislature, however, precluding residents of California nursing homes effectively from making valid directives. . . .

23. *Note, supra* note 18, . . .
24. McCormick and Hellegers, *supra* note 47. McCormick has since withdrawn his opposition to "living will" legislation, despite continuing concern with overtreatment of those who have not signed.

> Our experience of recent rulings by the . . . Courts on the need for legislative direction on these questions, and the fact that an overwhelming number of physicians, attorneys and legislation continue to believe an individual's statement has no legitimacy without a statutory enactment, force us to revise our previous opposition to this legislation.

John J. Paris and Richard A. McCormick, *Living-Will Legislation, Reconsidered*, 145 AMERICA 86, 86–87 (1981).
25. Leon R. Kass, *Ethical Dilemmas in the Care of the Ill: II. What is the Patient's Good?*, 244 J.A.M.A. 1946, 1948 (1980).
26. A California Medical Association study of the effects of the California Natural Death Act, conducted one year after it went into effect, emphasized that "the Act has been a positive force in encouraging patients and their families to discuss the subject of terminal illness." Murray Klutch, *Survey Result After One Year's Experience With the National Death Act*, 128 WEST. J. MED. 329, 330 (1978).
27. Del. Code Ann. tit. 16. § 2502(b) (1982). In the 1981 legislative session in Michigan, House Bill No. 4492 contained provisions designed to authorize the appointment of an agent for medical decisionmaking. . . .
28. *See* RESTATEMENT (SECOND) OF AGENCY, American Law Institute Publishers, St. Paul, Minn. (1957) § 122.
29. Virtually all the durable power of attorney statutes enacted in approximately 40 states have been modeled on three acts: (1) Virginia Code Sections 11-91. to .2 (1950), (2) Model Special Power of Attorney for Small Property Interests Act (Uniform Law Commissioners, 1964), and (3) Uniform Probate Code Section 5-501 to 502 (1969). In 1979, the National Conference of Commissioners on Uniform State Law promulgated a Uniform Durable Power of Attorney Act, which has been enacted in four states as of February 1983. . . .

The provisions of the Uniform Durable Power of Attorney Act are typical. Its basic provisions provide for the appointment of an attorney whose authority continues notwithstanding the principal's subsequent disability or incapacity (Sections 1 and 2). Other provisions protect those who engage in transactions with an attorney in fact (a proxy) by ensuring that, in the absence of the proxy knowing of the principal's death and provided the proxy acts in good faith, the authority to act is not revoked by the principal's death (Sections 4 and 5).
30. Four states—California, Kansas, Massachusetts, and Wisconsin—have adopted the Uniform Durable Power of Attorney Act, which creates a strong presumption for conservator of person but does not establish that power. . . .
31. National Conference of Commissioners of Uniform State Laws, HANDBOOK AND PROCEEDINGS OF THE ANNUAL CONFERENCE MEETING 1964 (1964) at 273–74.
32. Yale Law School Legislative Services Project, *Medical Treatment Decision Act*, SOCIETY FOR THE RIGHT TO DIE, New York (1981). . . .
33. *Model Health Care Consent Act* (draft), National Conference of Commissioners on Uniform State Laws, Chicago (1982). . . .
34. *Uniform Right to Refuse Treatment Act* (draft), Concern for Dying, New York (May 1982). . . .
35. Michigan House Bill 4492 (March 26, 1981), . . . *see also* Arnold S. Relman, *Michigan's Sensible "Living Will*," 300 NEW ENG. J. MED. 1270 (1979).
36. These considerations were developed at greater length in MAKING HEALTH CARE DECISIONS, at 155–66.
37. Statutes of Ala., Del., Ks., N.M., Ore., Wash.; *Medical Treatment Decision Act; . . . Uniform Right to Refuse Treatment Act. . . .*
38. *See* state statutes for California, the District of Columbia, Kansas, Oregon, and Texas. . . .
39. There are no cases know to the Commission of penalties being imposed under any of the natural death acts that provide for them.
40. *See, e.g.,* the statute for California. . . .
41. For example, the *Model Health Care Consent Act* . . . provides for a limited delegation of power by some individuals, authorized to con-

sent to health care for another. The only proxies who may delegate their decisional authority are family members. Nonfamily health care representatives, who may be appointed according to the terms of the Act, are not authorized to delegate their decisional authority. All delegations must be in writing, and unless the writing so specifies, no further delegation of decisional authority is permitted. Any delegated authority terminates six months after the effective date of the writing.

42. An exception might be the patient who knows that foregoing a treatment is likely to bring about a period of incompetence prior to death, during which the patient might ask for the treatment. If such a patient wants to bind all parties concerned—health care professionals, family, and patient—in a promise to act in accord with the preferences expressed by the patient while competent, such a request might be honored. *See* Gail Povar, *Case #11,* in James F. Childress, WHO SHOULD DECIDE? PATERNALISM AND HEALTH CARE, Oxford Univ. Press, New York (1982) at 224–25.

Figure A: New York Living Will

INSTRUCTIONS

This Living Will has been prepared to conform to the law of the State of New York, as set forth in the case In re Westchester County Medical Center, 72 N.Y.2d 517 (1988). In that case the Court established the need for "clear and convincing" evidence of a patient's wishes and stated that the "ideal situation is one in which the patient's wishes were expressed in some form of writing, perhaps a 'living will.'"

PRINT YOUR NAME

I, _____, being of sound mind, make this statement as a directive to be followed if I become permanently unable to participate in decisions regarding my medical care. These instructions reflect my firm and settled commitment to decline medical treatment under the circumstances indicated below:

I direct my attending physician to withhold or withdraw treatment that merely prolongs my dying, if I should be in an incurable or irreversible mental or physical condition with no reasonable expectation of recovery.

These instructions apply if I am (a) in a terminal condition; (b) permanently unconscious; or (c) if I am minimally conscious but have irreversible brain damage and will never regain the ability to make decisions and express my wishes.

I direct that my treatment be limited to measures to keep me comfortable and to relieve pain, including any pain that might occur by withholding or withdrawing treatment.

While I understand that I am not legally required to be specific about future treatments if I am in the condition(s) described above I feel especially strongly about the following forms of treatment:

CROSS OUT ANY STATEMENTS WITH WHICH YOU DO NOT AGREE

     I do not want cardiac resuscitation.
     I do not want mechanical respiration.
     I do not want artificial nutrition and hydration.
     I do not want antibiotics.

However, I do want maximum pain relief, even if it may hasten my death.

Other directions:

These directions express my legal right to refuse treatment, under the law of New York. I intend my instructions to be carried out, unless I have rescinded them in a new writing or by clearly indicating that I have changed my mind.

Signed _____ Date _____

Address _____

I declare that the person who signed this document is personally known to me and appears to be of sound mind and acting of his or her own free will. He or she signed (or asked another to sign for him or her) this document in my presence.

**YOUR
WITNESSES
MUST SIGN
AND PRINT
THEIR
ADDRESSES**

Witness 1 _____

Address _____

Witness 2 _____

Address _____

Courtesy of Choice in Dying, Inc., 200 Varick Street, New York, NY 10014. ©1993.

Figure B: New York Health Care Proxy

INSTRUCTIONS

PRINT YOUR NAME

(1) I, _____, hereby appoint:

(name)

PRINT NAME, HOME ADDRESS AND TELEPHONE NUMBER OF YOUR PROXY

_____

(name, home address and telephone number of proxy)

_____

as my health care agent to make any and all health care decisions for me, except to the extent that I state otherwise.

This Health Care Proxy shall take effect in the event I become unable to make my own health care decisions.

ADD PERSONAL INSTRUCTIONS (IF ANY)

(2) Optional instructions: I direct my proxy to make health care decisions in accord with my wishes and limitations as stated below, or as he or she otherwise knows.

(Unless your agent knows your wishes about artificial nutrition and hydration [feeding tubes], your agent will not be allowed to make decisions about artificial nutrition and hydration.)

(3) Name of substitute or fill-in proxy if the person I appoint above is unable, unwilling or unavailable to act as my health care agent.

_____

(name, home address and telephone number of alternate proxy)

_____

(4) Unless I revoke it, this proxy shall remain in effect indefinitely, or until the date or condition I have stated below. This proxy shall expire (specific date or conditions, if desired):_____

_____

(5) Signature _____ Date _____

Address _____

Statement by Witnesses (must be 18 or older)

I declare that the person who signed this document is personally known to me and appears to be of sound mind and acting of his or her own free will. He or she signed (or asked another to sign for him or her) this document in my presence. I am not the person appointed as proxy by this document.

Witness 1 _____

Address _____

Witness 2 _____

Address _____

Courtesy of Choice in Dying, Inc., 200 Varick Street, New York, NY 10014. ©1993.

Michael Nevins, M.D., is co-director of medical education and chairperson of the bioethics committee at Pascack Valley Hospital in New Jersey. He is also a trustee of the New Jersey Citizens Committee on Bioethics.

Carol Pagano (also known as Carol Porter) is an emergency room nurse at Englewood Hospital, New Jersey, and a member of the New Jersey Citizens Committee on Bioethics.

Video Presentation

Guests: Michael Nevins, M.D., co-director of medical education and chairperson of the bioethics committee, Pascack Valley Hospital; trustee of the New Jersey Citizens Committee on Bioethics

Carol Pagano (also known as Carol Porter), M.P.A., R.N., Englewood Hospital, New Jersey

Student Panel: Phyllis Van Velkinburg, Vincent Cisternino, Carol Coppola

I begin by inquiring what The Citizens' Committee on Bioethics, Inc., is about. It is a New Jersey-based grass-roots organization founded in 1984 to investigate bioethical issues including but not limited to living wills. I ask my guests to explain what a living will is and learn from Dr. Nevins that the term *living will* conjures up different ideas in different people.

Nevins says that what he refers to as a living will includes a document in which people indicate what medical treatment they want when they become incompetent to articulate their desires. It also includes a person appointed as proxy to indicate what the patient wants when the patient has expressly indicated his or her desires, or what the patient would want based on the patient's personal philosophy. Both the document and the proxy are subsumed under the term *advance directive*.

Having clarified our terms, I ask my guests what would happen if a conflict arose between the proxy and the patient in a case where the proxy may not be faithfully expressing the patient's desires, or where a conflict exists between the patient and his or her family. Pagano thinks such circumstances are more theoretical than real and points out how a great deal of communication takes place that usually results in agreement among the relevant parties. Nevins agrees and adds that people have the misconception that advance directives serve as an end point of what the patient's wishes are, whereas it is a means for beginning a discussion regarding treatment options and patient desires. I press my point about possible conflicts of interest at which point Nevins says that if no resolution occurs, then the case gets referred to an ethics committee and possibly to a court of law. However, he insists that the virtue of an advance directive is that, with proper communication between doctor and patient, patients can control their treatment options with little interference from outside agencies.

I then read pertinent passages from a New Jersey document developed by the state's Bioethics Commission. Nevins points out that included in what I read is the crucial point that advance directives specify not only what treatment people don't want, such as, for example, artificial respiration, but they also specify what treatment people might want. Nevins's comment brings to mind a debate I had entered into when I served as a bioethicist at a New York hospital. Referring to living wills specifically, my colleague argued against that document since, as he saw it, the document locked the patient into a course of treatment that might not be desired at the time the patient became incompetent, and also because the language of such a document is inherently vague, given the rapidly changing world of medical technology. To this, both Pagano and Nevins reiterate that an advance directive is a living document that is intended to encourage rather than stifle dialogue. Just prior to the break, Pagano speaks of her experiences with advance directives in an emergency room setting and Nevins cites statistics on how many people have advance directives.

Following the break, Vincent Cisternino, who is an emergency medical technician, shares with Pagano problems he faces in treating patients on an emergency basis, advance directives notwithstanding. Phyllis Van Velkinburg wants to know whether advance directives ever override a physician's duty to treat in cases of conflict. And Carol Coppola inquires about the role of the nurse in determining the patient's desires. The show concludes with a discussion of why people often think advance directives are a good idea yet stop short of executing one.

In this brief column, Michael Nevins, M.D., identifies several trends of the Patient Self-Determination Act (PSDA) fifteen months after its implementation in the State of New Jersey.

Implementation of the PSDA: How Are We Doing?

MICHAEL A. NEVINS, M.D., F.A.C.P.

Fifteen months after implementation of the Patient Self-Determination Act (PSDA), several trends are worth noting:

- At my community hospital, which serves a relatively affluent suburb, 15% of newly admitted patients already have Advance Directives. Of the rest, 33% want more information and only a few complete directives during their hospital stay.
- New Jersey's statute obliges physicians to independently determine whether or not their patient has an Advance Directive. However, very few physicians are aware of this new requirement and most learn of it when they are told that their discharged patient's chart is incomplete for lack of documentation. We can hope that by "backward learning" physicians will learn to inquire about Advance Directives before or during hospitalization rather than afterwards.
- In my own internal-medicine practice, I introduced the same routine inquiry of all patients that the PSDA requires for hospitals. Of the first 100 patients, 16 had Advance Directives. Eleven more said they would get to it soon but nine months later only two had. 45 acknowl-

edged that although it was a good idea, they had never gotten around to doing it. (Procrastination was also a major stumbling block in a study reported by Sachs, *et al.,* at an outpatient inner-city geriatric clinic. *JAGS:* 40: 269–273, 1992).

I surveyed the attitudes of New Jersey physicians who attended a geriatrics review course on March 19, 1992, and turned up some interesting responses. A questionnaire was completed by 50 physicians (30 male, 20 female, average age 39), all of whom said either that 50% or more of their patients were elderly or that 10% or more were in nursing homes. *Only 30% had Advance Directives themselves!* If physicians are not sufficiently impressed with the value of Advance Directives, it is unlikely that they'll be effective educators of their patients.

- Three months after the onset of PSDA, 30% felt that the new law was having a substantial effect upon their practice and 70% characterized the effect as being positive. Thirty-two percent said that they frequently ask their office or clinic outpatients about Advance Directives (60% occasionally) and 20% frequently distribute forms and/or advice (34% occasionally).

- Fifty-four percent are often called upon to make decisions to withhold or withdraw life support and 74% believe that they generally know their patients wishes about how they would want terminal care to be conducted.
- Ten percent generally make DNR decisions unilaterally without consulting either the patient or family.
- For a patient in a persistent vegetative state whose prior wishes are unknown, 18% would perform CPR and 34% would maintain a feeding tube. Eighty percent would comply with a family's request not to insert a feeding tube, 96% if it was clear from an Advance Directive that this would be the patient's own wish.
- Eighty percent agreed that a physician should do what in his or her judgment would benefit the patient (a reformulation of the Hippocratic Oath).
- Ten percent felt that life itself is of such fundamental value that all methods of treatment should always be provided to sustain it.
- Eighty-eight percent believed that quality of life is the most important consideration in deciding on a form of treatment.
- Eighty percent thought that cost to society should be an important consideration to a physician who is contemplating treatment that will not provide any meaningful benefit to the patient.
- Despite court rulings to the contrary, 80% found decisions to withdraw life-support to be more troubling than decisions not to start treatment.
- For a terminally ill nursing-home patient who develops an acute life-threatening complication, 86% would order only such treatment that could be provided at the nursing home. Of the seven who would transfer such a patient to a hospital for more aggressive care, only two actually cared for nursing-home patients.
- Thirty-two percent had experienced an ethics committee review of one of their cases. Eleven of these 16 thought that the decision-making process was enhanced by the review.
- Thirty-nine percent said that they would indirectly help a terminally-ill patient to die if asked by the patient. Forty percent believed that New Jersey should have a law that legalizes physician-assisted death under controlled circumstances, such as the Dutch approach.

The validity of any generalizations derived from such a questionnaire, particularly with such a small sampling, is limited. Nonetheless, it is instructive to evaluate the attitudes of those physicians who are most likely to be involved in clinical decision-making which concerns foregoing of life-sustaining treatment. Such data should be particularly helpful in designing future medical education programs on this subject.

The following case studies are based on cases in which Carol Pagano, R.N. (also known as Carol Porter) has been involved. Following each case is a set of questions Porter invites us to consider.

Three Cases Involving Patients with Bioethical Dilemmas

Carol Pagano, R.N.

CASE 1

Theme: Health Care Choices in Terminal Illness

Mrs. Claire Ross is a 29-year-old married female, and mother of two children, Richard 2½, and Kevin, 5 years old. Claire was diagnosed two years ago with Adenocarcenoma of the left breast with metastasis to the auxiliary lymph nodes. Currently, in spite of chemotherapy and radiation therapy, Claire has metastasis to the chest wall and lung. Her oncologist estimates her life expectancy to be less than 6 months.

Claire is aware of her diagnosis and has vowed to herself to make the most of her remaining time with her family. She has an excellent relationship with her husband and is a devoted mother to her children. She has taken great strides to involve Richard and Kevin in her care and to gradually prepare them for her death.

Claire is also working closely with her husband and sister to make her wishes known regarding how she would have raised Richard and Kevin. Claire hopes that they will integrate some of her parenting wishes into Richard and Kevin's lives.

While at home, Claire began to experience periumbilical pain which, within a few hours, localized to right lower quadrant abdominal pain. She went to her local hospital emergency department and was examined by her family physician and a general surgeon. She was found to have a 101 degree temperature, nausea with vomiting, and increasing right lower quadrant abdominal pain. Claire was diagnosed with acute appendicitis and in need of emergency surgery. Without surgical intervention, her condition would probably result in a ruptured appendix, peritonitis, sepsis, and subsequent death.

Claire has an advance directive that documents her health-care wishes once diagnosed with an irreversible, terminal illness that may cause her to experience severe and progressive physical/or mental deterioration. She has outlined that life-sustaining measures may be withheld or discontinued.

Dr. Farley, the general surgeon, discussed Claire's treatment options with her, including the appendectomy surgery and possible complications. Claire, although terminally ill with breast cancer, decided to consent to emergency surgery due to the acute nature of the appendicitis and the potential for resuming her lifestyle and continuing her job of preparing her family for her ultimate death.

Claire signed her surgical consent and had her advance directive included in the medical record. She also requested that a DNR order (Do Not Resuscitate) be entered in her medical record.

Claire was brought to the operating room holding area where she met with the anesthesiologist, Dr. Brown. Dr. Brown was concerned that Claire's terminal condition, her advance directive, her current request for a DNR order, and yet her consent for emergency surgery/anesthesia were somewhat inconsistent and in need of clarification.

Claire told Dr. Brown that she wanted emergency treatment for her appendicitis, but did not want cardiac resuscitation in the event that she were to have a cardiac emergency during this hospitalization.

Dr. Brown explained that the anesthetization involves administration of medication that causes a deliberate depression of vital systems followed by the active resuscitation by the anesthesiologist. The differentiation between anesthesia administration and resuscitation is difficult.

Claire verbalized her understanding of Dr. Brown's dilemma and agreed to rescind her advance directive and DNR during the surgical procedure.

Claire was then brought into the operating room.

Discussion:

1. Does the patient's "biography"—who he or she is in the family/community/society—have bearing on treatment decisions?
2. Would you consider the value society places on the work that the terminally ill patient has left to do prior to death (such as preparing children) in treatment decisions?
3. If Claire chose not to have the appendectomy, which may result in her subsequent death, yet required hospitalization due to her severe acute condition, would you be comfortable providing comfort measures only?
4. When there is inconsistency in the patient's advance directive (such as Claire, who is terminally ill, having chosen to have lifesaving measures withheld or discontinued yet consenting to a lifesaving surgical procedure), what discussion/documentation needs to take place? With whom?
5. Considering that anesthesia administration and management are closely related to active resuscitation, what would have happened if Claire wanted her advance directive and DNR maintained during anesthesia?
6. In an environment of limited health-care access and resources, is Claire's case futile (keeping her life expectancy and underlying terminal illness in mind)?

CASE 2

Theme: Patient Confidentiality

Tom Sands is a 38-year-old male who is married and the father of two children. Tom scheduled an appointment with his physician, Dr. Shefter, due to his complaints of a sore throat and tongue for several days.

On examination, Tom was found to have white patches on his tongue and pharynx which appeared to be caused by a fungus. Tom denied taking antibiotics or inhaling steroids for asthma, both of which can sometimes cause a similar presentation. Dr. Shefter began considering the possibility of Tom being part of a high-risk behavior group for HIV.

Tom was questioned by Dr. Shefter as to his sexual preference or any history of promiscuity, use of intravenous drugs, or past blood transfusions. Tom told Dr. Shefter that he was heterosexual and had never used intravenous drugs or had a blood transfusion. Tom denied having behaved promiscuously.

Tom had a smear and culture done which proved to be fungal in origin. Tom was treated with oral anti fungal medication. On follow up two weeks later his throat was found to be clear.

Over the next several months, Tom experienced repeated upper respiratory infections. Tom went to Dr. Shefter with a low-grade fever, cough, and shortness of breath. Dr. Shefter examined Tom and found nothing remarkable; however, x-ray revealed possible PCP (pneumocystis carini) which was later verified. Dr. Shefter again questioned Tom regarding his sexual preference, promiscuity, drug use, or blood transfusion history.

Tom told Dr. Shefter that he has had homosexual relations for the past five years with multiple partners. Tom also stated that during this same time period he has had occasional sexual relations with his wife. Tom relayed the fact that his wife is unaware of his homosexuality. Tom submitted to HIV testing which proved to be positive. He pleaded with Dr. Shefter to refrain from telling his wife of his homosexuality.

Dr. Shefter discussed with Tom the importance of informing his wife of his HIV status. Tom continued to refuse to speak with his wife regarding his HIV status. Dr. Shefter told Tom that if he continued to refuse to allow his wife to be informed of his HIV status that he should arrange for further follow-up care with another physician. Dr. Shefter explained to Tom that he would continue treating Tom until the transfer of care took place and gave Tom several referrals.

Tom decided not to inform his wife of his HIV status.

Discussion:

1. Does Tom have an ethical obligation to be truthful with his physician regarding his homosexuality?
2. What is the morality of his refusal to inform his wife and children of his HIV status while continuing to have a sexual relationship with his wife?
3. What is Tom's obligation in notifying his homosexual partners of his HIV status?
4. What is the physician's ethical/legal obligation to notify Tom's wife? Tom's homosexual partners?
5. Does the physician have a right to refuse to continue to treat a patient with whom he is in ethical conflict?
6. Does the mode of transmission of HIV (blood transfusion versus IV drug abuse versus homosexual relations) ever affect the way a patient is viewed by the health-care team? If so, why?

CASE 3

Theme: Advance Directives, Legal Implications

Samantha Jones, a 42-year-old female, was brought to the emergency department via ambulance accompanied by paramedics.

Samantha had a history of depression and was now presenting as a possible attempted suicide by hanging. She was unresponsive with a narrow area of redness and swelling around her neck.

Samantha was brought immediately into the emergency department treatment room and was evaluated by an emergency medicine physician, Dr. Sodel. Treatment was initiated.

Mr. Jones arrived right behind the ambulance, visibly upset but able to give information about his wife and her bout with

depression. Mr. Jones informed Dr. Sodel that Samantha would not want any heroic measures done to save her life. He went on to state that Samantha was very unhappy with her life and had often told him that she wished for death.

Mr. Jones then took several pieces of paper out of his pocket and handed them to the physician. After briefly scanning the documents Dr. Sodel realized that she had in her hands what appeared to be Samantha's advance directive. The document listed Mr. Jones as Samantha's health-care representative to make all health-care decisions for her. Samantha further outlined that she did not want her life to be prolonged by further life-sustaining measures and, if these measures had been initiated, they then should be discontinued. Dr. Sodel checked for signatures, dates, and witnesses. Everything appeared to be in order.

Mr. Jones emphasized to Dr. Sodel that his wife had been in such emotional agony that she had pleaded with him to make sure he would carry out her wishes if she were unable to make her own choices.

While Dr. Sodel spoke with Mr. Jones, Samantha was having lab tests, portable x-rays, a cardiogram, and other diagnostic tests.

Samantha showed signs of cerebral anoxia (lack of oxygen to the brain); she was intubated and placed on a ventilator. She remained comatose and in extremely critical condition.

Dr. Sodel reevaluated Samantha, ordered further testing, and spoke with Mr. Jones. Dr. Sodel explained that she was in receipt of Samantha's advance directive but felt that she needed to treat Samantha's emergent condition. Mr. Jones became anxious, reminding Dr. Sodel of Samantha's advance directive. Dr. Sodel tried to explain her actions to Mr. Jones who did not agree with her treatment plan at all. Mr. Jones's focus on his wife's advance directive and anxious behavior drew concern from the emergency department nursing and medical staff.

The local police were soon in the emergency department to complete their report on

Samantha's attempted suicide. The staff alerted the police to Mr. Jones's concerns and behavior prior to their interviewing him.

Samantha continued to be treated while further details were obtained about the events leading up to her arrival at the emergency department. Dr. Sodel had chosen not to honor Samantha's advance directive until she had time for careful review and verification that it was truly Samantha's document.

Dr. Sodel had made the right decision, as it was later discovered that the angle of the reddened areas on Samantha's neck was not consistent with a hanging but rather an attempted strangulation with a cord by her husband.

Further investigation proved that the ad-vance directive Mr. Jones presented was not signed by Samantha but by Mr. Jones.

Discussion:

1. Should advance directives be honored by all health-care members?
2. Why are emergency staff exempt from honoring advance directives unless there is time for careful review?
3. Are there cases where emergency staff should honor advance directives? Give examples.
4. What kind of policies need to be in place to safeguard patient rights in regard to implementing advance directives?

Closing Questions

1. A poll conducted by Prodigy (December 1994) asked subscribers whether they supported a Detroit jury's decision to find Jack Kevorkian not guilty of violating Michigan's ban on assisted suicide. Kevorkian was charged with helping thirty-year-old Thomas Hyde commit suicide. Hyde was suffering from Lou Gehrig's disease, a nerve disorder that left him barely able to walk, talk, or feed himself. Of the 33,591 people surveyed, 76 percent agreed with the verdict, 21 percent disagreed, and 2 percent were undecided. How would you respond?

_____

_____

_____

2. Is suicide heroic? Is it cowardly? In the early 1990s, the philosopher Michael Bayles committed suicide. Thomas Steinbuch, a member of the American Philosophical Association, wrote a letter to that organization glorifying Professor Bayles's killing himself rather than submitting to psychotherapy. Comment on the following letter which was written in response to Steinbuch's letter:

To the Editor:

Not knowing the particulars surrounding Michael Bayles's suicide, Thomas Steinbuch's aggrandizement of his death (*Proceedings and Addresses,* Vol. 65, No. 1, Sept. 1991) is nonetheless unfortunate. It bespeaks a skewed conception of mental illness and the therapeutic modalities that are available to treat it.

Contrary to what Mr. Steinbuch believes, suicide is seldom a heroic choice by which one affirms one's individual autonomy. Rather, it is typically an act that is the product of mental illness and which usually originates from a chemical imbalance. Left untreated, depression—*like any other illness*—works to impair the functioning of a healthy and normal individual. Consequently, the effect of treatment (therapy, medication) is not to leave patients "half-persons" whose self of moral action is lost, but to *restore* autonomy and *affirm* moral agency.

No doubt it is a tragedy that Michael Bayles ended his life. But it is also tragic that an educated person such as Mr. Steinbuch can have a vision of mental illness and psychiatry that flies in the face of scientific evidence. It is tragic because views like his serve to foster dysfunctioning and to glorify suicide that could result therefrom. It is also tragic since it might inhibit those who would otherwise seek treatment. In our opinion, Mr. Steinbuch's view is at best false, and at worst dangerous.

Joram Graf Haber, J.D., Ph.D.
Asst. Prof. of Philosophy
Bergen Community College

Jack Nass, M.D., Director
Dept. of Psychiatry
Hempstead General Hospital

Lina Levit Haber, M.D.
Dept. of Psychiatry
Franklin General Hospital

Bernard H. Baumrin, J.D., Ph.D.
Prof. of Philosophy
Graduate School CUNY; Lehman
    College
Mt. Sinai School of Medicine

_____

_____

_____

_____

3. What does the following fable from Aesop tell you about the rationality of suicide?

It was a bitter cold day in the wintertime, and an old man was gathering branches in the forest to make a fire at home. The branches were covered with ice, many of them were frozen and had to be pulled apart, and his discomfort was intense. Finally the poor old fellow became so thoroughly wrought that he called loudly upon death to come. To his surprise, Death came at once and asked what he wanted. Very hastily the old man replied, "Oh, nothing; nothing except to help me carry this bundle of sticks home so that I may make a fire."

_____

_____

_____

_____

4. Did Socrates commit suicide? Did Jesus?

_____

_____

_____

5. Physicians have been charged with opposing physician-assisted suicide owing to their sense of failure and helplessness in the face of death. Assess this claim.

_____

_____

_____

_____

6. If a patient has the right to physician-assisted suicide, do physicians have a duty to assist the patient? Would physicians be derelict in their duties if they refused?

_____

_____

_____

_____

7. Comment on the claim that if I give you permission to destroy my property, you may do so with impunity, but if I give you permission to destroy me or a part of me, you may not do so. What might this say about whether our bodies belong to ourselves?

_____

_____

_____

_____

8. The Hippocratic Oath, which is taken by most graduating medical school students, admonishes physicians to "Do no harm." Discuss whether physician-assisted suicide violates this admonition.

_____

_____

_____

_____

9. Is the withdrawing of life support from a terminally ill patient a case of active or passive euthanasia?

_____

_____

_____

_____

10. Virginia Held has challenged the view that a relevant distinction exists between killing and letting die. As she sees it, the distinction is

"bourgeois" inasmuch as it is a distinction that would be made by "haves" as opposed to "have nots." Otherwise put, only those who would worry about losing their lives would say that killing is worse than letting die, whereas those who would worry about not getting what they need to live would say that letting die is at least as bad as killing. If this is so, then the distinction between killing and letting die is slanted in favor of those who have versus those who do not, making it tainted and not the conceptually neutral distinction its supporters believe it to be. Assess this argument.

_____

_____

_____

_____

11. To what extent would a deontologist support the distinction between killing and letting die? A utilitarian?

_____

_____

_____

_____

12. Using the guidelines provided by the New York Living Will and New York Health Care Proxy, make out your own living will. Discuss any problems you experience in filling out these documents.

_____

_____

_____

_____

13. Read the *Case Studies Involving Patients with Bioethical Dilemmas* provided by Carol Pagano on pp. 213–216 and discuss the questions raised by Pagano in connection with each.

_____

_____

_____

_____

For Further Reading

Battin, Margaret Pabst. *Ethical Issues in Suicide*. Englewood Cliffs, N.J.: Prentice Hall, 1982.

Camus, Albert. *The Myth of Sisyphus*. Translated by Justin O'Brien. New York: Vintage, 1955.

Donnely, John, ed. *Suicide: Right or Wrong?* Buffalo: Prometheus Books, 1990.

Downing, A. B., and Barbara Smoker. *Voluntary Euthanasia*. Atlantic Highlands, N.J.: Humanities Press International, 1986.

Durkheim, Emile. *Suicide: A Study in Sociology*. Translated by J. A. Spaulding and G. Simpson. New York: Free Press, 1951.

Haber, Joram Graf. "In *re* Storar: Euthanasia for Incompetent Patients, A Proposed Model." *Pace Law Review* 3,2 (Winter 1983). Reprinted in Anthony Serafini, ed., *Ethics and Social Concern*. New York: Paragon House, 1989.

———. "Living Wills and Directives to Provide Maximum Care: The Scope of Autonomy." *Chest* 90, 3 (September 1986).

———. "Should Physicians Assist the Reaper?" *Cambridge Journal of Healthcare Ethics* 4,1 (Winter 1996).

Horan, Dennis J., and David Mall, eds. *Death, Dying and Euthanasia*. Frederick, Md.: University Publications of America, 1980.

Kant, Immanuel. *Lectures on Ethics*. Translated by Louis Infield. New York: Harper & Row, 1963, pp. 147–154.

Novack, David. *Suicide and Morality: The Theories of Plato, Aquinas, and Kant and Their Relevance for Suicidology*. New York: Scholars Studies, 1975.

Oates, Joyce Carol. "The Art of Suicide." In *The Reevaluation of Existing Values and the Search for Absolute Values. Proceedings of the Seventh International Conference on the Unity of the Sciences*. New York: International Cultural Foundation Press, 1978, pp. 183–190.

Rachels, James. "Active and Passive Euthanasia." *New England Journal of Medicine* 292, 2 (January 9, 1975), pp. 78–80.

Styron, William. *Darkness Visible*. New York: Random House, 1990.

Chapter 7

Legal Ethics

Passages for Reflection

"An advocate, in the discharge of his duty, knows but one person in all the world, and that person is his client. To save that client by all means and expedients, and at all hazards and costs to other persons."

—*Lord Henry Brougham*

"It is not the lawyer's responsibility to believe or not to believe—the lawyer is a technician."

—*Roy Cohen*

"A lawyer with his briefcase can steal more than a thousand men with guns."

—*Mario Puzzo*

"An honest man is not responsible for the vices or stupidity of his calling."

—*Montaigne*

Opening Questions

1. Why do lawyers have a bad reputation? Is it deserved?
2. What are the virtues of a good lawyer?
3. Are lawyers subject to ethical standards different than those that apply to nonlawyers?

Since 1969, when the American Bar Association enacted its *Model Code of Professional Responsibility*, there has been a great deal of interest in legal ethics. Much of this interest has come from lawyers and philosophers. From the legal side, the interest is obvious. The ABA's *Code* often has the force of law, with sanctions for noncompliance. It both inhibits what lawyers may do and protects them when what they do is not prohibited by the *Code*. From the philosophical side, the very phrase "legal ethics" suggests that the duties and responsibilities of lawyers are different from those of everyday life. And that suggestion is philosophically interesting inasmuch as the requirements of morality are often thought to extend to all persons regardless of their profession. Imagine someone insisting that philosophers have one set of moral requirements, engineers another, nurses still another, and so forth.

Much of the work in legal ethics has centered around the question of whether lawyers, in performing actions otherwise criticizable, can escape such criticism by appealing to their role in the legal system. Such actions include "greymailing" (threatening to run up costly legal bills), defending criminals believed to be guilty, making truthful opposing witnesses look like liars, and defeating just claims on technicalities. Typically, the question has turned on whether the legal system of which lawyers are members is itself a justified system. Depending on the answer to this question are the answers to several other questions, such as to what extent a lawyer must respect a client's confidences. In this chapter, we will lay out some general features of the legal system, examine the way in which the system is designed to function, and address the problem of the lawyer's "role morality" within the context of that system.

In the United States, an adversary system of justice is used for settling disputes in accordance with rules designed to ensure a fair resolution. In broad outline, the system works as follows: When two parties have a legal dispute, they bring their dispute to a court of law; the side initiating the action (suing) is the called the *plaintiff*, and the side defending the action (being sued) is called the *defendant*. Represented by their respective attorneys, the plaintiff and defendant present their competing versions of what occurred to an impartial arbitrator, usually a judge and jury. The judge's job is to ensure that the attorneys comply with procedural rules of justice as well as to resolve any questions of law. The jury's job is to decide questions of fact, that is, to decide which version of the facts has the greater plausibility.

The theory behind the system is that if the attorneys for both the plaintiff and the defendant present their cases in the light most favorable to their clients—if they defend their clients' interests competently and zealously—then, given the procedural rules designed to assure fair play, the right side will win for the right reason (truth will out and justice will be served). Otherwise put, if both attorneys do their jobs (defend their clients' interests), the judge does his or her job (ensures that the rules of procedure are complied with), and the jury does its job (impartially decides questions of fact), then the jury's decision will reflect what really transpired between the parties.

In some ways, the adversary system is like a professional boxing match where two boxers fight before three judges and a referee. In theory, the better boxer of the two will win, assuming the boxers are well trained and put forward their best effort. If, however, the better boxer fails to train well or puts forward a meager effort, the inferior boxer will win. Think, then, of the attorneys as the boxers, the judge as the referee, and the jury as the panel of judges. If one of the attorneys does not put forth his or her best effort, the attorney might lose even though truth and justice are on the attorney's side. The point is that the adversary system is both *adversarial* and a *system;* it works best when the parties play their assigned roles, that is, work as adversaries before a judge and jury. The system will not work if the attorney for the defendant, say, fails to zealously defend her client, believing, for instance, that the defendant is in the wrong. If the defendant is in the wrong, it is the *jury's* job to make that determination.

An example will underscore the point. Suppose a defendant, Jones, is on trial, charged with having burglarized a house in his neighborhood. Suppose further that he has in fact committed the burglary. In theory, Jones will be found guilty since, being in fact guilty, the defendant's attorney has the weaker case and the jury will detect its weaknesses. As many a lawyer will happily tell you, the jury's job is to decide guilt or innocence while the lawyer's job is to defend the client. That means, first and foremost, making sure the client's constitutional rights are not violated. Our belief that the side with the truth will win allows an attorney to defend a client believed to be guilty.

Not all attorneys are equally competent and equally zealous. Neither are all judges and juries fair and impartial. But if that is so, then the system may work in theory though not in practice. This means that an attorney who, say, defeats a just claim on a technicality cannot put forth the excuse that she is just doing her job and that if others did theirs, her client would lose and justice would be served. She could only say this if, in fact, all attorneys were equally competent and zealous and all judges and juries were equally fair.

But without appealing to the lawyer's role in the adversary system, that is, without appealing to the "adversary system excuse," no apparent justification exists for doing what appears to be unethical. The lawyer, in this context, appears no different from the professional assassin who also claims that he is doing his job. Without this excuse, what the lawyer does *is* unethical, at least in the absence of a reason to the contrary.

The question we must ask, then, is whether a reason to the contrary exists. In an oft-discussed paper, "The Lawyer as Friend,"[1] Charles Fried offers an answer. Beginning with the premise that friends are permitted to do things for each other that they are not permitted to do for others, Fried argues that the lawyer-client relationship is based on friendship, thereby permitting the lawyer to do things for the client (for example, help the client defeat a just claim) that the lawyer would not be otherwise permitted to do.

Fried sees the lawyer-client relationship as a special kind of friendship, a "one-way limited friendship," in which the lawyer helps the client secure legal rights. Just as friends may do for each other what they might not do for others, so, too, Fried believes that lawyers may do for clients what might be questionable in the absence of that relationship.

Fried's position has been widely criticized, often on the grounds that the analogy between friendship and the lawyer-client relationship fails. One reason it fails is because friendship is essentially a relationship between equals, whereas the lawyer-client relationship is based on status.[2] Others have argued that the emotional component so important to friendship is lacking in the lawyer-client relationship.[3] Still others have pointed out that the concept of a "one-way friendship" is incoherent since friendship by its nature is bilateral.[4] One critic has noted that lawyers accept clients for a fee, not out of a concern for their client's well-being, so in trying to characterize the lawyer-client relationship, what Fried has done is describe *prostitution*![5]

The most perceptive criticism of Fried concerns his assumption regarding what people may do in the name of friendship. Fried is assum-

---

[1]"The Lawyer as Friend: The Moral Foundations of the Lawyer-Client Relation." *Yale Law Journal* 85 (1976): 1060.

[2]Michael Bayles, *Professional Ethics*. Belmont, Calif.: Wadsworth, 1981, p. 65.

[3]Dauer and Leff, "Correspondence—The Lawyer as Friend." *Yale Law Journal* 86 (1977): 573.

[4]See my (with Bernard H. Baumrin) "The Moral Obligations of Lawyers." *The Canadian Journal of Law and Jurisprudence* 1, 1 (Jan. 1988): 108.

[5]W. Simon, "The Ideology of Advocacy: Procedural Justice and Professional Ethics." *Wisconsin Law Review* 29 (1978): 30.

ing that friends are permitted to behave in ways that would be impermissible in the absence of friendship. That even in the name of friendship, people can, say, help others to defeat justice is by no means clear. If that is so, then even if the lawyer-client relationship is one of friendship, the analogy does not answer the charge that a lawyer's questionable conduct is morally permissible.

Fried is sensitive to criticisms of his position and tries to ward off objections by distinguishing between "personal" and "institutional" wrongs. It is one thing, he argues, to humiliate a witness or lie to a judge and quite another to assert the statute of limitations or lack of a written memorandum to defeat a just claim. Actions of the first sort are wrongs perpetrated by the lawyer for which he or she is personally accountable. Actions of the second sort are wrong (if they are wrong) only because the legal system permits them. This being so, the system, and not the lawyer, bears the burden of moral accountability.[6]

To bolster his argument, Fried draws an analogy to a soldier in wartime. If the soldier is a citizen of a just state, it is not up to him to question the propriety of the war he is fighting. But he is personally bound not to fire dum-dum bullets or to inflict injury on innocent civilians, for these actions are personal rather than institutional wrongs. If a wrong is institutional, Fried contends that it should be corrected on an institutional level. Consequently, it is one thing to do for friends (clients) what the institution of friendship (law) permits; it is another thing to question the institution itself.

Fried's argument hinges on the moral propriety of the institution in question. We would not be permitted an "institutional excuse" if the institution in question were morally wrong. If a soldier, for instance, were to kill an enemy soldier in an unjust war, he would not be protected from blame on account of his role as soldier. He could not claim that he was just doing his job. Furthermore, a soldier's duty is to question whether the war he is fighting is just. So even if the lawyer is absolved from any personal wrongdoing in doing what the role of lawyering permits, we must still ask whether the institution of lawyering affords the lawyer the excuse she needs.

In his article, "The Professionalism and Accountability of Lawyers," Murray Schwartz calls attention to what he calls "The Principle of Non-accountability," according to which "when acting as an advocate for a client . . . a lawyer is neither legally, professionally, nor morally accountable for the means used or the ends achieved."[7] By and large, this is the accepted position of most lawyers. However, after introducing this principle, Schwartz raises the following points:

---

[6]See Fried, *supra* note 1, pp. 1,082–1,087.

[7]M. Schwartz, "The Professionalism and Accountability of Lawyers." *California Law Review* 66 (1978): 669.

It might be argued that the law cannot convert an immoral act into a moral one, by simple fiat. Or, more fundamentally, the lawyer's nonaccountability might be illusory if it depends upon the morality of the adversary system and if that system is immoral. . . . If either [of these challenges] were to prove persuasive, the justification for the application of the Principle of Nonaccountability to moral accountability would disappear.[8]

In his article "The Adversary System Excuse," David Luban agrees with Schwartz that the lawyer's nonaccountability depends on the adversary system, but Luban is concerned to show that the adversary system is insufficient grounds for nonaccountability. According to Luban, two types of justification are typically offered in defense of the adversary system: (1) the utilitarian claim that the adversary system is the best system we have for arriving at truth and protecting rights and (2) the deontological claim that the adversary system is the best system for upholding human dignity in the dispute-resolution context.[9]

For several reasons, Luban rejects each of these claims. He argues that the superiority of the adversary system in the search for truth has never been demonstrated, and that the system does not obviously uphold dignity better than alternative systems. His conclusion, however, is not that the adversary system is wholly unjustified; it is unjustified in the sense that it fails to promote what Luban calls a "positive moral good." But Luban also thinks the costs of replacing the system outweigh the benefits. The system, he says, does an adequate job of settling disputes, some system of adjudication is necessary, and the system is steeped in American tradition. The question, however, is whether this "pragmatic justification" is reason enough to provide the lawyer with an institutional excuse. As Luban sees it, the answer is no, at least with regard to civil actions. For while committing an immoral act to further a positive moral good might be permissible, committing an immoral act is impermissible because: (1) the system under which one operates is adequate; (2) this is the way we have always done things around here; or (3) the cost of replacing the system outweighs the benefits.

While a person's position on the adversary system often determines his or her position on the lawyer's role obligations, there is no necessary connection between the two. A person can, for instance, defend the adversary system yet criticize the practices it licenses. We see this, for instance, in the debate over the extent to which the adversary system should license lawyer-client confidentiality. Monroe Freedman and Alan Donagan, for instance, defend the adversary system on what

---

[8]Ibid., p. 674.

[9]David Luban, "The Adversary System Excuse." In D. Luban, *The Good Lawyer* (Totowa, N.J.: Rowman & Allenheld, 1983).

are essentially the same grounds, but differ on the issue of lawyer-client confidentiality.

Freedman's position on confidentiality is well known and has been defended in several publications. He takes a strong "protectionist" stance arguing for maximum protection of client confidences except in cases where protecting a confidence would manifestly result in serious harm to a third party. In such cases, Freedman thinks disclosure should be "required," although in other cases (to obey court rules, to defend the lawyer against charges) disclosure should be "permitted," and in still other cases (to prevent financial ruin to third parties, to rectify a fraud on the court, and to collect a fee), disclosure should be "forbidden."

Freedman bases his position on the values incorporated in the adversary system. His contention is that the lawyer must establish a relationship of trust and confidence with the client, and that only in such a relationship can the lawyer learn all the relevant facts, determine which are helpful and which are not, and give the client adequate representation. Such a relationship also furthers two important purposes: it enhances individual autonomy by enabling clients to learn their legal rights, and it enables lawyers to counsel clients to rectify past wrongs and to forego future ones. If, Freedman argues, confidentiality were to be eroded beyond what he suggests, the trust and confidence so essential to the lawyer-client relationship would be effectively undermined. This, in turn, would undercut the right to counsel that is guaranteed by the Sixth Amendment.

Alan Donagan has defended the adversary system on deontological grounds, that is, on grounds similar to those to which Freedman appeals. Donagan has argued that the moral nature of the obligation to present the client's best case derives from respect for client dignity. This, he believes, is what makes the adversary system justified in the first place. According to Donagan, "this justification demands that lawyers be willing to suspend their own beliefs about the merits of their clients' aims or the truth of what they attest to, provided that the morality of their aims be rationally defensible and that what they attest to be possibly true."[10] But if the client's aims and version of the facts are neither rationally defensible nor possibly true then, according to Donagan, disclosure would not violate the client's dignity, nor would the adversary system justify keeping such information confidential. As Donagan sees it, respecting human dignity means, in part, keeping confidential information that has been received in confidence. But it is not part of respecting human dignity to keep in confidence information that a person has no right to keep secret in the first place, such as contemplated crimes and intentions to deceive the court.

---

[10]Alan Donagan, "Justifying Legal Practice in the Adversary System." in D. Luban, 1983, p. 133.

But if the limits of confidentiality are ordinary moral limits, what about the attorney-client relationship that leads one to think otherwise? In raising this question, Donagan considers two answers. The first concerns the Fifth Amendment's right against self-incrimination. Freedman has argued that if a lawyer is permitted to be a conduit to the court of incriminating information that a client has a right to withhold, the client would forfeit her Fifth Amendment right. But if the client must withhold confidences in order to guard against self-incrimination, the client would lose her Sixth Amendment right to effective counsel. As Freedman observes (citing Justice John Marshall Harlan), it is "intolerable that one constitutional right should have to be surrendered in order to assert another."[11] Donagan's rejoinder is that the right against self-incrimination is a legal one and one that society is perhaps morally obligated to grant, but it is not necessarily a moral right.

The second answer that Donagan considers for extending the duty of confidentiality centers around Freedman's argument that if (1) the dignity of clients is not respected if lawyers cannot ascertain all the facts of the case and (2) clients cannot be expected to reveal all relevant information, it follows that (3) the dignity of clients will not be respected if lawyers may disclose even incriminating information.

While not denying the validity of Freedman's argument, Donagan contends that (1) is false since a client's dignity is not violated if a lawyer exposes his intention to lie to commit a crime. It is true that the client may be disadvantaged, but that is different from having one's dignity violated. Donagan also argues that (2) is false since a competent lawyer should be able to flesh out whatever facts a client withholds in the belief that they are irrelevant. Finally, as for the client who is in fact guilty, Donagan reiterates his claim that the client's dignity would not be violated on account of the client's guilt.

In the final analysis, it might be said that the lawyer is largely an extension of the client in an unfamiliar technical domain. To the extent that this is true, the lawyer's burden is to do for the client what the client would do if he or she knew how, for example, to write a will, record a lien, file for divorce, evict a tenant, or prepare and argue a motion. It would be false, in this view, to say that in such circumstances the lawyer's morality is substitutable for the morality of the client. The lawyer's morality would be irrelevant, at least insofar as the system under which the lawyer operates does a credible job at such commendable tasks as finding truth and protecting rights. Since, when all is said and done, the adversary system is reasonably proficient at achieving these goals, we can confidently say that it is a good system and the practices it licenses are at least apparently justified. Thus, if the maker of a will, say, wants to enlist a lawyer to help him cut off his heirs, the lawyer's moral qualms are out of place.

---

[11]Monroe Freedman, "An Important Issue." *The National Law Journal* 8, 8 (1985): 13 at 24.

Monroe Freedman is the Howard Lichtenstein Distinguished Professor of Legal Ethics at Hofstra University. His first book, *Lawyers' Ethics in an Adversary System* (1975), received the American Bar Association's Gavel Award Certificate of merit. His most recent book, *Understanding Lawyer's Ethics,* was published in 1990.

Video Presentation

Guest: Monroe Freedman, Howard Lichtenstein Distinguished Professor of Legal Ethics, Hofstra University School of Law

Student Panel: Mary Stuart, Ceasar Zuniga, Patricia Rodriguez

In the tradition of lawyers, I begin by posing to Freedman a hypothetical case and asking him to respond. The case I present is a thinly disguised version of the "Lake Pleasant Bodies Case." In that case, lawyers Frank Belge and Frank Armani were told by their client, Robert Garrow, of two murders he had committed. Subsequently, they found and photographed the bodies but kept secret the information for half a year despite the fact that the father of one of the victims, knowing that Armani was representing an accused murderer, personally pleaded with him to tell him if he knew anything about his daughter. The attorneys later provided the prosecutor with the information as part of a plea bargain for their client. I solicit Freedman's reaction to the case in the light of the morally questionable conduct of Belge and Armani. Freedman's reaction is that what the attorneys did in this case was entirely proper, given the role that attorneys play in the adversary system. He also points out that Garrow was accused of having committed other crimes, and that, as part of the plea bargain agreement, the prosecutor was helped to solve these other crimes.

  As Freedman sees it, the lawyer's conduct is, and should be, determined by his or her role in the adversary system. To that end, Freedman spends much time discussing the system, indicating how it procures truth and justice and how it pays heed to the Bill of Rights. In answer to my question of whether truth gets short-changed by the system, given its emphasis on rights, Freedman argues that the system does an excellent job at arriving at truth even though it regards justice as paramount. I then ask whether truth may sometimes take a back door to justice, to which Freedman wittily responds yes, noting that if it's truth we want, the best way to secure it is to rub pepper in a witness's eyes.

After discussing the workings of the adversary system, I return to my hypothetical case with a twist. I ask Freedman how he would respond to a client's confidentially telling him not that he has already committed a murder, but that he will do so in the future. Freedman responds that the ethical rules that govern lawyers' conduct permit—but do not require—divulging confidential information in such circumstances, and that he agrees with this. At the same time, he points out that many future crimes are actually ongoing ones involving past criminal conduct, and so we must be careful in deciding what is to count as a "future" crime.

After discussing some other features of the adversary system, Freedman provides a brief history of the *Code of Professional Responsibility* which governs what lawyers may and may not do, after which I ask Freedman whether it is possible to be both a good person and good lawyer. I suggest that this may not be possible since the qualities that make for a good lawyer (as in "I need a good lawyer") are just those that are inimical to being a good person. Freedman thinks it *is* possible to be both a good person and a good lawyer, cautioning us that if lawyers have moral qualms about defending a particular client or cause, they are always free to reject that case. However, once a lawyer agrees to accept the case, he or she is duty-bound to zealously protect the client's interests as the client understands them.

After the break, Mary Stuart asks Freedman about any movement that might exist that is analogous to socialized medicine given the rising costs of legal services. Freedman says some movements are under way, though he doesn't see increased legal costs as presenting a problem that is not presented in any other profession. As Freedman sees it, the problems in this area pertain to capitalism generally and not to the legal profession specifically. Ceasar Zuniga asks Freedman about what Zuniga perceives to be overzealous lawyers defending spurious claims out of greed. Becoming increasingly impatient with this attack on his profession, Freedman responds by complaining about those who, like Zuniga, know of such matters and fail to do anything about them. Finally, Patricia Rodriguez asks whether lawyers' salaries are in line with those of other professionals and if they are deservedly so.

In this selection, taken from his book, Understanding Lawyer's Ethics, *Monroe Freedman explains how the adversary system of justice works and defends the system against those who see rival systems as being superior. As Freedman sees it, the adversary system functions primarily to protect individual rights and preserve human dignity by requiring lawyers to function as neutral partisans on behalf of their clients. Freedman defends the system against the European "inquisitorial system" in which the judge, not the attorneys, conducts an inquiry into the facts and the law and develops a judgment largely on his or her own initiative. Against defenders of the inquisitorial system such as Marvin Frankel, Freedman contends that the American system protects rights and procures truth at least as well as its European counterpart. He shows how it does this in both civil and criminal contexts.*

The Adversary System

Monroe Freedman

In its simplest terms, an adversary system is one in which disputes are resolved by having the parties present their conflicting views of fact and law before an impartial and relatively passive judge and/or jury, who decides which side wins what. In the United States, however, the phrase "adversary system" is synonymous with the American system for the administration of justice, as that system has been incorporated into the Constitution and elaborated by the Supreme Court for two centuries. Thus, the adversary system represents far more than a simple model for resolving disputes. Rather, it consists of a core of basic rights that recognize and protect the dignity of the individual in a free society.

From Monroe Freedman, *Understanding Lawyers' Ethics*, Pp. 13–42. © 1990, Matthew Bender & Co., New York, NY.

The rights that comprise the adversary system include personal autonomy, the effective assistance of counsel, equal protection of the laws, trial by jury, the rights to call and to confront witnesses, and the right to require the government to prove guilt beyond a reasonable doubt and without the use of compelled self-incrimination. These rights, and others, are also included in the broad and fundamental concept that no person may be deprived of life, liberty, or property without due process of law—a concept which itself has been substantially equated with the adversary system.[1]

An essential function of the adversary system, therefore, is to maintain a free society in which individual rights are central.[2] In that sense the right to counsel is "the most pervasive" of rights, because it affects the client's ability to assert all other rights.[3] As Professor Geoffrey Hazard has written, the adversary system "stands with freedom of speech and the right of assembly as a pillar of our constitutional system."[4] It follows that the professional responsibilities of the lawyer within such a system must be determined, in major part, by the same civil libertarian values that are embodied in the Constitution.[5]

CRITICISMS OF THE ADVERSARY SYSTEM

In recent years, attacks upon the adversary system have been unprecedented in their breadth and intensity, and at times have been "scathing [and] venomous."[6] For example, at a conference of twenty-five of the country's "professional elite"[7] (most of them lawyers and judges) the adversary system was "thoroughly savaged."[8] Efforts by the conferees to produce an acceptable alternative to the adversary system ended unsuccessfully on a "note of resignation."[9]

It is not coincidental that these attacks on the adversary system have taken place in the context of critical analyses of lawyers' ethics. Critics concerned with the negative aspects of zealous, client-centered advocacy have recognized that the reforms they believe necessary in lawyer's ethics can come about only through a radical restructuring of the adversary system itself.

For example, former Federal Judge Marvin Frankel has proposed significant restrictions on confidentiality that would subordinate clients' interests to those of non-clients.[10] Mr. Frankel acknowledges that his proposals are "radical"[11] and that they would effect an "appreciable revolution" in procedure, in lawyer-client relations, and in the lawyer's self-image.[12] Significantly, although he professes "a profound devotion to a soundly adversary mode of reaching informed decisions,"[13] Mr. Frankel concedes that his reforms will be impossible "until or unless the adversary ethic comes to be changed or subordinated."[14] Indeed, an entire chapter of his book is titled "Modifying the Lawyer's Adversary Ideal,"[15] and another chapter closes with a hope for "wiser, more effective ideas for breaking the adversary mold...."[16] Thus, the adversary system has become a battleground on which fundamental issues of lawyers' ethics are being fought out.

THE ADVERSARY SYSTEM AND INDIVIDUAL DIGNITY

It is not surprising to find a sharp contrast in the role of a criminal defense lawyer in a totalitarian society. As expressed by law professors at the University of Havana, "the first job of a revolutionary lawyer is not to argue that his client is innocent, but rather to determine if his client is guilty and, if so, to seek the sanction which will best rehabilitate him."[17] Similarly, a Bulgarian attorney began his defense in a treason trial by noting that "[i]n a Socialist state there is no division of duty between the judge, prosecutor, and defense counsel.... The defense must assist the prosecution to find the objective truth in a case."[18] In that case, the defense attorney ridiculed his client's defense, and the client was convicted and executed. (Sometime later the verdict was found to have been erroneous, and the defendant was "rehabilitated.")

A Chinese lawyer, Ma Rongjie, has described the role of counsel in similar terms.[19] Lawyers are "servants of the state."[20] The function of the defense lawyer in criminal cases is, at most, to plead mitigating circumstances on behalf of clients whose guilt is largely predetermined.[21] Mr. Ma represented Jiang Qing, widow of Mao Tse Tung, in the trial of the "Gang of Four." Jiang Qing had requested a lawyer who would assert her innocence, but such a request was impossible to honor, Mr. Ma said. On the contrary, in representing "the criminals" (as Mr. Ma referred to his clients) he and the other defense lawyers conducted no investigations of their own, objected to no prosecution questions, cross-examined no prosecution witnesses, and called no witnesses themselves. Nor did the defense attorneys even meet with their clients. "There was no need to talk to them," Mr. Ma explained. "The police and the prosecutors worked on the case a very long time, and the evidence they found which wasn't true they threw away."[22]

Commenting on a similar legal system in the Soviet Union, Alexander Solzhenitsyn has written sardonically:[23]

> On the threshold of the classless society, we were at last capable of realizing the conflictless trial—a reflection of the absence of inner conflict in our social structure—in which not only the judge and the prosecutor but also the defense lawyers and the defendants themselves would strive collectively to achieve their common purpose.

Under the American adversary system, a trial is not "conflictless," because the lawyer is not the agent or servant of the state. Rather, the lawyer is the client's "champion against a hostile world"[24]—the client's zealous advocate against the government itself. Unlike Mr. Ma, therefore, the American defense lawyer has an obligation to conduct a prompt investigation of the case.[25] All sources of relevant information must be explored, particularly the client.[26] Rather than accepting the government's decision to preserve or destroy evidence, the defense lawyer has a duty to seek out information in the possession of the police and prosecutor.[27] Defense counsel has those duties, moreover, even though the defendant has admitted guilt to the lawyer and has expressed a desire to plead guilty.[28] As explained by the ABA *Standards for Criminal Justice*, the client may be mistaken about legal culpability or may be able to avoid conviction by persuading the court that inculpatory evidence should be suppressed; also, such an investigation could prove useful in showing mitigating circumstances.[29]

Such rules, reflecting a respect for the rights even of the guilty individual, are a significant expression of the political philosophy that underlies the American system of justice. As Professor Zupancic has observed, "In societies which believe that the individual is the ultimate repository of existential values, his status vis-a-vis the majority will remain uncontested even when he is accused of crime. He will not be an object of purposes and policies, but *an equal partner in a legal dispute . . . .*"[30]

THE ADVERSARY SYSTEM AND INDIVIDUAL RIGHTS

There is also an important systemic purpose served by assuring that even guilty people have rights. Jethro K. Lieberman has made the point by putting forth, and then explaining, a paradox:[31]

> The singular strength of the adversary system is measured by a central fact that is usually deplored: The overwhelming majority of those accused in American courts are guilty. Why is this a strength? Because its opposite, visible in many totalitarian nations within the Chinese and Russian orbits, is this: Without an adversary system, a considerable number of defendants are prosecuted, though palpably innocent. . . . In short, the strength of the adversary system is not so much that it permits the innocent to defend themselves meaningfully, but that in the main it prevents them from having to do so.

Lieberman concludes that "[o]nly because defense lawyers are independent of the state and the ruling political parties and are permitted, even encouraged, to defend fiercely and partisanly do we ensure that the state will be loathe to indict those whom it knows to be innocent." This benefit, however, is largely invisible. "We rarely see who is not indicted, we never see those whom a prosecutor, or even a governor or president might like to prosecute but cannot."[32]

There is another systemic reason for the zealous representation that characterizes the adversary system. Our purpose as a society is not only to respect the humanity of the guilty defendant and to protect the innocent from the possibility of an unjust conviction. Precious as those objectives are, we also seek through the adversary system "to preserve the integrity of society itself . . . [by] keeping sound and wholesome the procedure by which society visits its condemnation on an erring member."[33] Professor Lawrence H. Tribe has added that "procedure can serve a vital role as . . . a reminder to the community of the principles it holds important."[34] He goes on to explain:

> The presumption of innocence, the rights to counsel and confrontation, the privilege against self-incrimination, and a variety of other trial rights, matter not only as devices for achieving or avoiding certain kinds of trial outcomes, but also as affirmations of respect for the accused as a human being—affirmations that remind him and the public about the sort of society we want to become and, indeed, about the sort of society we are.

These rights to which Professor Tribe refers are essential components of the adversary system as it has evolved in American constitutional law.

THE ADVERSARY SYSTEM IN CIVIL LITIGATION

The adversary system has also been instrumental, principally in civil litigation, in mitigating the grievances of several minorities, women, consumers, tenants, citizens concerned with health and safety in our environment, and others. As one who celebrates these advances in individual rights and liberties (and those in criminal justice too), I view with concern and some suspicion the calls for basic changes in adversarial zeal. Of course, it is preferable to negotiate a satisfactory resolution of a dispute. Experience teaches, however, that those in power do not ordinarily choose to negotiate unless there is a credible threat of successful litigation.

In a report to his Board of Overseers in 1983, Harvard President Derek Bok decried "the familiar tilt in the law curriculum toward preparing students for legal combat," and called instead for law schools to train their students "for the gentler arts of reconciliation and

accommodation."[35] These are themes long associated with retired Chief Justice Warren Burger.[36]

In response to such critics, Professor Owen Fiss has observed that they see adjudication in essentially private terms. Viewing the purpose of civil lawsuits to be the resolution of discrete private disputes, they find the amount of litigation we encounter to be evidence of "the needlessly combative and quarrelsome character of Americans."[37] Fiss, on the other hand, sees adjudication in more public terms. That is, civil litigation is "an institutional arrangement for using state power to bring a recalcitrant reality closer to our chosen ideals."[38] Thus, we turn to courts not because of some quirk in our personalities, but because we need to, and we train our students in the tougher arts not because we take a special pleasure in combat, but to equip them to secure all that the law promises.[39] Fiss concludes:[40]

> To conceive of the civil lawsuit in public terms as America does might be unique. I am willing to assume that no other country . . . has a case like *Brown v. Board of Education*, in which the judicial power is used to eradicate the caste structure. I am willing to assume that no other country conceives of law and uses law in quite the way we do. But this should be a source of pride rather than shame. What is unique is not the problem, that we live short of our ideals, but that we alone seem willing to do something about it. Adjudication American-style is not a reflection of our combativeness but rather a tribute to our inventiveness and perhaps even more to our commitment.

Comparing "adjudication American-style" with that in England, Ralph Temple has observed[41] that there are no lawsuits in Britain challenging the legality of an oppressive law, no injunctions against illegal government actions, and no class actions to protect civil liberties. British law "has yet to discover the principle flowing from *Marbury v. Madison* . . . , that a healthy legal system requires that the courts have the power to declare unlawful those acts of the majority, through its legislature or its executive, which are abusive."[42] Mr. Temple notes that there is no greater animosity between Irish Protestants and Catholics than there was between Southern Whites and Blacks. Nevertheless, the bitterness has been deeper and the violence greater in Ireland because the British legal system is "incapable of producing social revolution and justice through its legal system—incapable of producing a *Brown v. Board of Education*, a *Baker v. Carr*, or a *United States v. Richard Nixon*."[43] That is, through our constitutional adversary system, "[t]ime and again the heat of our social struggles has been effectively transmuted into courtroom battles, and our society is the stronger for it."[44]

As indicated by their citation of *Brown v. Board of Education* and other cases of national import, Professor Fiss and Mr. Temple are directing their attention principally to civil litigation in which the outcome of the particular case is an expression of public policy that extends beyond the interests of the immediate parties. The point they make is of broader significance, however, and is not limited to the overtly "political" case or even to the leading case that establishes the new rule.

For example, a case might hold for the first time that a tenant has a right, apart from the express terms of her lease, to safe and habitable premises, or that a consumer can avoid an unconscionable sales-financing agreement, or that an employee under a contract terminable at will can sue for wrongful discharge, or that an insurance company can be held liable in punitive damages for arbitrarily withholding benefits due under a policy. Such a case, establishing new rights and deterrents against harmful conduct through civil litigation, is also "a tribute to our inventiveness," using "state power to bring a recalcitrant reality closer to our chosen ideals." If the leading case is to have meaning, however, it will come to fruition in the series of every-day cases that follow and apply it, cases that will truly make the ideal into reality.

In that sense, even ordinary personal injury litigation is an expression, procedurally and substantively, of important public policies. Through the adversary system we provide a social process through which a person with a grievance against another can petition the government for redress in a peaceable fashion. Echoing Professor Fiss and Mr. Temple, therefore, the Supreme Court has noted that "[o]ver the course of centuries, our society has settled upon civil litigation as a means for redressing grievances, resolving disputes, and vindicating rights."[45] The Court added: "That our citizens have access to their civil courts is not an evil to be regretted; rather, it is an attribute of our system of justice in which we ought to take pride."[46]

THE JURY AS AN ASPECT OF THE ADVERSARY SYSTEM

Another constitutional element of our adversary system is the jury. In criminal cases the right to trial by jury is guaranteed by Article III, section 2, of the Constitution and by the Sixth Amendment; in civil cases at law, trial by jury is required by the Seventh Amendment. State constitutions have similar provisions.

The jury serves in criminal cases to prevent oppression by the government.[47] Justice Lewis F. Powell, Jr. (neither a radical nor a cynic) has observed:[48]

> Judges are employees of the state. They are usually dependent upon it for their livelihood. And the use of economic pressure to express displeasure with decisions unfavorable to those in power is not novel. Congress' exclusion of the Justices of the Supreme Court from the general pay increase for other federal judges [in 1965] is an unfortunate example . . . .

Justice Powell went on to note, by contrast, that reprisals against jurors for verdicts disagreeable to those in power are less likely because they would involve far greater political risks.[49] As the Supreme Court has held, therefore, the jury provides "an inestimable safe-guard against the . . . compliant, biased, or eccentric judge."[50]

Trial by jury is particularly important in criminal litigation but, like other aspects of the adversary system, its value in civil trials is considerable. One of our most respected federal trial judges, William G. Young, has commented that:[51]

> Without juries, the pursuit of justice becomes increasingly archaic, with elite professionals talking to others, equally elite, in jargon the elegance of which is in direct proportion to its unreality. Juries are the great leveling and democratizing element in the law. They give it its authority and generalized acceptance in ways the imposing buildings and sonorous openings cannot hope to match.

Further, as Chief Justice Rehnquist has reiterated, jurors' "very inexperience is an asset because it secures a fresh perception of each trial, avoiding the stereotypes said to infect the judicial eye."[52] Dean Paul Carrington adds the pungent comment that juries are "a remedy for judicial megalomania, the occupational hazard of judging."[53]

Beyond those purposes, the American jury system is "our most vital day-to-day expression of direct democracy," in which "citizens are themselves the government."[54] Another effect of the jury, therefore, is to "limit . . . the power of legislatures who eventually must countenance the nonenforceability of [criminal] laws which citizens are unwilling to enforce."[55] Similarly, jurors can bring the moral sense of the community to bear in civil cases in finding for plaintiffs or defendants and in assessing damages.

THE SEARCH FOR AN ALTERNATIVE SYSTEM

In both civil and criminal cases, therefore, the adversary system of justice comprises a constitutional system that includes the right to retained counsel, trial by jury, and other processes that are constitutionally due to one who seeks to redress a grievance through litigation. It is not surprising, therefore, that those who urge fundamental changes in the adversary system typically ignore the constitutional impediments to their proposals.

In one of the most important critiques of the adversary system, for example, Marvin Frankel acknowledges that the system is "cherished as an ideal of constitutional proportions" in part because "it embodies the fundamental right to be heard."[56] He recognizes too that his proposals for change run counter to constitutional interests in "privacy, personal dignity, security, autonomy, and other cherished values."[57] His book, however, includes barely a paragraph describing in positive terms the right to counsel,[58] refers only in passing to the privilege against self-incrimination,[59] and makes scant if any reference to privacy, personal dignity, autonomy, and other fundamental rights that gain vitality from the adversary system. Although the thesis of his book is that the adversary system too often sacrifices truth to "other values that are inferior, or even illusory,"[60] Mr. Frankel does not identify which of our "cherished rights" are in fact inferior or illusory, nor does he suggest how those rights are to be subordinated without doing violence to the Constitution.

Those who would either replace or radically reform the adversary system must ultimately sustain the burden of showing how their proposals can be reconciled with constitutional rights. Even before that point is reached, however, they must demonstrate, in their own utilitarian terms, that the adversary system is inferior to the proposed alternatives. To the contrary, however, the available evidence suggests that the adversary system is the method of dispute resolution that is most effective in determining truth, that gives the parties the greatest sense of having received justice, and that is most successful in fulfilling other social goals as well.

One system of justice that recently received serious although brief consideration is the way in which trials are conducted under autocratic regimes like the Soviet Union and China, where lawyers are "servants of the state." For example, at the conference of "members of the country's professional elite" referred to earlier,[61] the discussants considered whether the United States should adopt "the system of adjudication used in the countries that describe themselves as socialist," including the Soviet Union.[62] Specifically, the advocate would not be chosen by and owe primary allegiance to a party to the litigation; rather, each lawyer would be a member of the court's staff, responsible to the court for investigating and presenting an "assigned" side of the case.[63] This proposed abandonment of the traditional ideal of the right to counsel was not limited to civil cases; indeed, it was being contemplated principally for criminal cases.[64] The discussants concluded, however, that despite the "perversions" of client-centered advocacy, "the detachment of advocate from client might beget worse."[65] It was on that "note of resignation" that the discussion of alternatives to the adversary system "died out."[66]

More sophisticated (and more persevering) critics have turned to the inquisitorial systems of continental European democracies for an alternative to the adversary system.[67] The central characteristic of the inquisitorial model is the active role of the judge, who is given the principal responsibility for searching out the relevant facts. In an adversary system the evidence is presented in dialectical form by opposing lawyers; in an inquisitorial system the evidence is developed in a predominantly unilateral fashion by the judge, and the lawyers' role is minimal.[68]

One contention of those who favor the inquisitorial model is that the adversary system limits the factfinder to two sources of data or to one of two rival factual conclusions.[69] Frequently, of course, there is no need for more than two submissions, for example, if the sole issue is whether one car or the other ran the red light, or whether the defendant was the man who had the gun. In such a case, it is ordinarily appropriate for the factfinder to rely upon two sets of conflicting data, which may come, of course, from numerous sources.

Where there truly are more than two sides of a case, however, the adversary system provides a variety of devices for presenting them. Such procedures include joinder of plaintiffs and defendants, impleader, interpleader, intervention, class actions with more than one class representative and with subclasses, and amicus presentations. To take a relatively simple illustration, a single adversary proceeding may involve the following diverse submissions of fact: (a) D1 was negligent in driving; (b) D2 was negligent in repairing the brakes; (c) D3 manufactured a car with a faulty brake-system design; (d) D4 supplied the car manufacturer with brakes that had a latent defect; (e) P was actually the only party at fault; and (f) P was contributorily negligent.

EFFECTIVENESS IN THE SEARCH FOR TRUTH

Those who favor the inquisitorial model also contend that it produces a larger body of relevant information for the decisionmaker than does an adversarial system. For example, Professor Peter Brett argues that the inquisitorial system is preferable because the judge is not limited to the material that the opposing parties choose to present. Rather, the judge "may if he wishes" actively search out and incorporate in his decision materials that neither party wishes to present.[70] All other considerations, Professor Brett asserts, "pale into insignificance beside this one."[71] Unfortunately, however, just as the inquisitorial system "allows the fact-finder free rein to follow all trails,"[72] it also allows the fact-finder to ignore all trails but the one that initially appears to be the most promising. It does so, moreover, without the corrective benefit of investigation and presentation of evidence by active adversaries.

This concern was expressed in a prominent thesis that was put forth by Professor Lon L. Fuller and adopted by a Joint Conference of the American Bar Association and the Association of American Law Schools.[73]

What generally occurs in practice is that at some early point a familiar pattern will seem to emerge from the evidence; an accustomed label is waiting for the case and without awaiting further proofs, this label is promptly assigned to it. It is a mistake to suppose that this premature cataloguing must necessarily result from impatience, prejudice or mental sloth. Often it proceeds from a very understandable desire to bring the hearing into some order and coherence, for without some tentative theory of the case there is no standard of relevance by which testimony may be measured. But what starts as a preliminary diagnosis makes a strong imprint on the mind, while all that runs counter to it is received with diverted attention.

An adversary presentation seems the only effective means for combating this natural human tendency to judge too swiftly in terms of the familiar that which is not yet fully known.

As suggested by its adoption by the Joint Conference, Professor Fuller's thesis is undoubtedly shared by the overwhelming majority of American lawyers and judges, on the basis of both intuition and experience in decision-making processes.

The validity of the Fuller thesis can be considered in both theoretical and practical contexts. If the inquisitorial judge is to pursue the truth of a particular matter, where does she start? The "most sophisticated modern view" in Europe recognizes an inescapable "circularity" in the inquisitorial judge's role: "You cannot decide which facts matter unless you have already selected, at least tentatively, applicable decisional standards. But most of the time you cannot properly understand these legal standards without relating them to the factual situation of the case."[74] In addition, "[i]t stands to reason that there can be no meaningful interrogation [of witnesses by the judge] unless the examiner has at least some conception of the case and at least some knowledge about the role of the witnesses in it."[75]

The solution in Europe to the inquisitorial judge's "circularity" problem is the investigative file, or dossier. The dossier is prepared by the police, who, in theory, act under the close supervision of a skilled and impartial judge or examining magistrate. "The practice, however, is in striking contrast to [this] myth."[76] The examining magistrate's investigative and supervisory role is minimal. The dossier—on which the trial judge relies to decide what facts and law are relevant to the case—is little more than a file compiled by the police.[77] "The plain fact is that examining magistrates are no more likely than comparable American officials to leave their offices, conduct prompt interrogations of witnesses or of accused persons, or engage in searches or surveillance. For such tasks, they rely almost entirely upon the police."[78] The trial judge, in turn, tends to rely heavily upon the police-developed dossier.[79]

The prosecutorial bias that inevitably results from this process is confirmed by the personal experience of Bostjan M. Zupancic. Professor Zupancic clerked for several investigating magistrates in the Circuit Court of Ljubljana, Yugoslavia. "One cannot start from the presumption of innocence" under an inquisitorial system, he writes.[80]

In purely practical terms, if one opens a file in which there is only a police report and the prosecutor's subsequent request for investigation and develops one's thought processes from this departing point—one cannot but be partial. A clear hypothesis is established as to somebody's guilt, and the investigating magistrate's job is to verify it. But just as a scientist cannot start from the premise that his hypothesis is wrong, so the investigating magistrate cannot start from the premise that the defendant is innocent.

Professor Zupancic found that, as a result, prosecutorial bias on the part of the inquisitorial judge is not a matter of probability; it is a certainty.[81]

Meanwhile, the prosecutor plays a distinctly secondary role to the police and the judge, and defense counsel is "particularly inactive."[82] "Rarely does [the defense attorney] conduct his own investigation in preparing for trial. Even if his client should suggest someone who he thinks will offer testimony favorable to the defense, he often passes the name on to the prosecutor or judge without even troubling first to interview the witness himself."[83] Very likely, European defense lawyers do not conduct the kind of thorough interview of a potential witness that is professionally required in the United States, because they could be charged with a criminal offense or with professional impropriety for obstructing justice if they did so.[84]

Only in the rare case in which the defense lawyer assumes an active—that is, an adversarial—role, is there an exception to the typical situation in which the inquisitorial judge follows the course plotted out by the police.[85] In those few cases, "genuine probing trials" do take place.[86] The European experience itself seems to confirm, therefore, that adversarial presentation by partisan advocates is more effective in developing relevant material than is unilateral investigation by a judge.

Our constitutional adversary system is based in part on the premise that the adversary system is more effective in the search for truth. As the Supreme Court has reiterated in an opinion by Justice Powell:[87]

> The dual aim of our criminal justice system is "that guilt shall not escape or innocence suffer," . . . . To this end, we have placed our confidence in the adversary system, entrusting to it the primary responsibility for developing relevant facts on which a determination of guilt or innocence can be made.

In the criminal process there are special rules, particularly the exclusionary rules, that recognize values that take precedence over truth. The adversary system should be even more effective in determining truth in the civil process, therefore, where such values are not ordinarily applicable. A study of civil litigation in Germany conducted by Professor Benjamin Kaplan (later a Justice in the Supreme Judicial Court of Massachusetts) found the judge-dominated search for facts in German civil practice to be "neither broad nor vigorous,"

and "lamentably imprecise."[88] Professor Kaplan concluded that the adversary system in this country does succeed in presenting a greater amount of relevant evidence before the court than does the inquisitorial system.[89]

There is support for that conclusion in experiments conducted by members of the departments of psychology and law at the University of North Carolina.[90] One study[91] tested the thesis, which I had put forward, that the most effective means of determining truth is to place upon a skilled advocate for each side the responsibility of investigating and presenting the facts from a partisan perspective.[92] Although that proposition is related to the Fuller thesis, its focus is different. Professor Fuller was concerned with the factfinder and with her mental processes in developing a working hypothesis and then unconsciously becoming committed to it prematurely. The second thesis focuses on the adversaries and on their incentive to search out and to present persuasively all material that is useful to each side, thereby providing the factfinder with all parts of the whole.

The study produced conclusions that tend to confirm both the Fuller thesis, regarding the judge's psychological risk of premature commitment to a theory, and the second thesis, regarding the adversaries' incentive to investigate diligently. First, as soon as they become confident of their assessment of the case, inquisitorial fact investigators tend to stop their search, even though all the available evidence is not yet in.[93] Second, with one exception of major importance, even adversary investigators have a similar but lesser tendency to judge prematurely.[94]

Third (the crucial exception), when adversary fact investigators find the initial evidence to be unfavorable to their clients, they are significantly more diligent than are inquisitorial investigators in seeking out additional evidence.[95] The researchers conclude, therefore, that the adversary system "does instigate significantly more thorough investigation by advocates initially confronted with plainly unfavorable evidence."[96] That is, in those situations of "great social and humanitarian concern" the adversary system maximizes the likelihood that all relevant facts will be ferreted out and placed before the ultimate factfinder.[97]

Another finding, which surprised the researchers, is that the opponent of an adversarial lawyer transmits more facts that are unfavorable to her own client. Apparently, awareness that one has an adversarial counterpart is a significant inducement to candor.[98]

I do not mean to suggest that these studies prove that the adversary system is preferable as a means to determine truth. Such experimental efforts to replicate real life and to quantify it statistically are surely limited in their usefulness. On the other hand, the research that has been done provides no justification whatsoever for preferring the inquisitorial search for truth or for undertaking radical changes in our adversary system.

INDIVIDUALIZED DECISIONMAKING VERSUS BUREAUCRACY

There is more to the adversarial-inquisitorial dispute, however, than efficacy in the search for truth. There is also an underlying difference in basic attitudes towards official power and individual rights. The conservative political philosopher, Ernst van den Haag, once described the genius of American democracy, in which official power is subject to checks and balances, as "institutionalized mutual mistrust." It has been observed similarly that "a cornerstone of our adversary system . . . is distrust of bureaucratic and rigidly controlled decisionmaking."[99] That is, the adversary system reflects not only respect for the individual, but also a lesser respect for bureaucratic authority.

A tennis anecdote helps to illustrate the point. In the 1937 Wimbledon Tournament, Don Budge won a decisive break point in his semifinals match because an official called his opponent's ball out when, as Budge knew, it was in. Budge therefore gave back the point by making an obvious error in returning the next serve. After Budge had won the match, he was approached by Baron Gottfried von Cramm, the German star whom he was to play in the finals. To Budge's surprise, von Cramm criticized Budge for having engaged in unsportsmanlike conduct. It is preferable, von Cramm explained, for a player to suffer an injustice than for an official to be embarrassed by exposure of the erroneous call that caused the injustice.[100] As that anecdote suggests, there are political, social, and humanist values that are expressed in the American preference for a system in which there is relatively greater regard for the individual litigant and less for the bureaucratic decisionmaker.

One of the ways in which our constitutionalized adversary system controls the bureaucratic tendencies of a professional judiciary is through trial by jury.[101] As discussed earlier, the jury system serves several crucial functions—preventing governmental oppression, countering compliant, biased, or eccentric judges, leveling and democratizing the law, bringing a fresh perspective to familiar fact patterns, and governing by direct democracy. Achievement of those goals requires an independent jury that could not exist under the judicial control that is characteristic of an inquisitorial judge.[102] The judge would investigate the facts; the judge would select the witnesses; the judge would conduct virtually all of the examination of witnesses; and, then, the judge would instruct the jury. In short, the trial would most closely resemble the presentation of evidence by a prosecutor to a grand jury. Although the grand jury was conceived as a safeguard against government abuse, it has become so dominated by the prosecutor that there are frequent suggestions that it be abolished as useless. In an inquisitorial system, we could expect a similar fate for the petit jury.

Professor Damaska provides another perspective on the greater tolerance in continental Europe for bureaucratic justice. He has found in Anglo-American law a striving for "the just result" in the light of the particular circumstances of the individual case.[103] He contrasts this traditionally strong attachment to "individualized justice" with the relatively greater concern of continental decisionmakers for "uniformity and predictability: they are much more ready than the common-law adjudicator to neglect the details of the case in order to organize the world of fluid social reality into a system."[104] For anyone trained in the American constitutional system, there is something chilling about a bureaucratic determination to organize the world of fluid social reality into a uniform and predictable system, without regard to the particular cases of individuals.

THE SENSE OF HAVING BEEN TREATED FAIRLY

The concept of individualized justice connotes two related but distinct ideas. First, there is individualized justice in the sense of respect for the individual in the light of his or her particular circumstances. Second, there is the idea of individual autonomy—that each of us should have the greatest possible involvement in, if not control over, those decisions that affect our lives in significant ways. With regard to the latter, the empirical studies that have been done suggest, again, a preference for the adversary system over the inquisitorial.

In one such study,[105] the experimenters sought to use the insight of John Rawls[106] that individuals who are ignorant of their own status of relative advantage or disadvantage will choose ideal principles of justice. Subjects in one experimental group were told the details of a dispute, which strongly favored one party, but they were not told which side they would ultimately have to assume. Thus, the subjects were kept behind a Rawlsian "veil of ignorance" regarding their tactical interest in the procedure that might be used to resolve the dispute. Subjects in another experimental group were told about the same dispute but were informed at the outset which side they would be on. The subjects of the study were thus in three groups—those who were ignorant of what their status would be, those who knew that they would have the advantageous position, and those who knew that they would be in the disadvantageous position.

Members of each group were next presented with various models of hearing procedures, ranging from inquisitorial to adversarial, with mixed procedures in between; that is, the procedural models were designed to provide dispute resolution choices ranging from maximum decisionmaker control to maximum party control. The subjects were then asked to express their preferences among the procedural models.

"One of the clearest findings in our data," the researchers concluded, "is that the adversary procedure is judged by all of our subjects—both those in front of and behind the veil of ignorance—to be the most preferable and the fairest mode of dispute resolution."[107] More significantly, those subjects who were seeking the fairest procedural model in ignorance of what their own status would be were the most strongly in favor of the adversary system.[108]

Similar results were obtained in further studies conducted in the United States and Germany.[109] One conclusion of the experiment in Germany is that the results in the United States were not significantly affected by cultural bias.[110] Most important, when the ultimate decisional power is in a third party, "participants in both Hamburg and Chapel Hill prefer to use an adversary procedure," in which their control over the presentation of the case is highest.[111]

Researchers also have conducted studies to determine whether a litigant's acceptance of the fairness of the actual decision is affected by the litigation system used. Their conclusion is that "the perception of the fairness of an adversary procedure carries over to create a more favorable reaction to the verdict for persons who directly participate in the decision-making process."[112] This is true "regardless of the outcome."[113] Therefore, "the attorney should see himself as the agency through which the client exercises salutary control over the process. In this client-centered role, the attorney best functions as an officer of the court in the sense of serving the wider public interest."[114]

THE PROBLEM OF SOCIO-ECONOMIC UNFAIRNESS

There is, nevertheless, a troubling question, about the fairness of a client-centered adversary system in which the wealth of the contending parties—and, therefore, the quality of the representation—may be seriously out of balance. "How much justice can you afford?" the lawyer in a New Yorker cartoon pointedly asked a client.

One response is that unequal justice is one of the costs of the American economic system. How much food, housing, clothing, education, or other basic needs can one afford? Sadly, equal justice may be far down on the list for a major portion of our citizens. The criticism is not of an adversary system but of a capitalist one.

Yet an expressed purpose of the Constitution is to "establish Justice,"[115] the judiciary is one of the three branches of our constitutional structure, and due process of law and equal protection under the law are explicitly guaranteed to all persons.[116] If another system of justice were likely to reduce significantly the unfairness caused by an imbalance in litigation resources, without introducing comparable unfairness, one would have to embrace it.

There is no persuasive evidence, however, that the inquisitorial system does that job. Certainly the proponents of that system have never shown the extent of unequal advocacy or its practical effect on results in the adversary system. At least in personal injury cases, the contingent fee is a great equalizer of legal resources between rich and poor, as Bhopal has demonstrated.[117] Legal clinics and prepaid legal plans also mitigate the problem. Moreover, if we are sufficiently concerned about unequal advocacy to revolutionize our system of justice, a more sensible course would be a genuine effort to equalize advocacy through a vastly expanded system of government-supported legal aid.[118]

In any event, it is doubtful that we would be better off with a system of inquisitorial judges instead of zealous advocates. As long as we maintain a capitalist society (or something approximating one) the judges will come predominantly from the upper socio-economic classes. The judges will also be interested in advancing their careers. One need not be a Marxist to expect class, political, and other bias to play a significant part in inquisitorial judging. Even in the face of superior resources, therefore, representation by a member of the bar before a jury of one's peers seems a safer choice.

CONCLUSION

The adversary system, like any human effort to cope with important and complex issues, is sometimes flawed in execution. It is both understandable and appropriate, therefore, that it be subjected to criticism and reform. The case for radically restructuring it, however, has not been made. On the contrary, based upon reason, intuition, experience, and some experimental studies, there are good grounds to believe that the adversary system is superior to other modes of determining truth when fact are in dispute between contesting parties.

Even if it were not the best method for determining the truth, however, the adversary system is an expression of some of our most precious rights. In a negative sense, it serves as a limitation on bureaucratic control. In a positive sense, it serves as a safeguard of personal autonomy and respect for each person's particular circumstances. The adversary system thereby gives both form and substance to the humanitarian ideal of the dignity of the individual. The central concern of a system of professional ethics, therefore, should be to strengthen the role of the lawyer in enhancing individual human dignity within the adversary system of justice.

ENDNOTES

1. G. Hazard, Ethics in the Practice of Law 122 (1978).
2. *Code of Professional Responsibility,* Preamble:

   The continued existence of a free and democratic society depends upon recognition of the concept that justice is based upon the rule of law grounded in respect for the dignity of the individual and his capacity through reason for enlightened self-government. Law so grounded makes justice possible, for only through such law does the dignity of the individual attain respect and protection. Without it, individual rights become subject to unrestrained power, respect for law is destroyed, and rational self-government is impossible.

3. Schaefer, *Federalism and State Criminal Procedure,* 70 Harv. L. Rev. 1, 8 (1957).
4. G. Hazard, Ethics in the Practice of Law 123 (1978).
5. *Model Code of Professional Responsibility,* EC 7–1:

   The professional responsibility of a lawyer derives from his membership in a profession which has the duty of assisting members of the public to secure and protect available legal rights and benefits.

   Model Rules of Professional Conduct, Preamble:

   As an advocate, a lawyer zealously asserts the client's position under the rules of the adversary system.

6. Lieberman, Book Review, 27 N.Y.L. Sch. L. Rev. 695 (1981).
7. Foreword by J.N. Green, Jr., to G. Hazard, *supra* note 1, at ix.
8. G. Hazard, *supra* note 1, at 123.
9. *Id.* at 126.
10. M. Frankel., Partisan Justice (1980).
11. *Id.* at 83.
12. *Id.*
13. *Id.* at 9.
14. *Id.* at 18.
15. *Id.,* ch. 6.
16. *Id.* at 100.
17. J. Kaplan, Criminal Justice 264–265 (1973); Berman, *The Cuban Popular Trials,* 60 Colum. L. Rev. 1317, 1341 (1969).
18. *Id.* at 264–265.
19. N.Y. Times, Jan. 6, 1982, at B5, col. 1.
20. The phrases used in the United States to convey a similar notion is "officers of the court" or "officers of the legal system." *See, e.g., Model Rules of Professional Conduct,* Preamble.
21. N.Y. Times, Jan. 6, 1982, at B5, col. 1.
22. *Id.*

23. A. Solzhenitsyn, Gulag Archipelago, 374 (Harper & Row, 1974), quoted in Temple, *In Defense of the Adversary System,* ABA Litigation, vol. 2, no. 2, 43, 44 (Winter, 1976).
24. *See* ABA, *Standards Relating to the Defense Function* 145–146 (Approved Draft, 1971).
25. *ABA Standards for Criminal Justice* 4–4.1 (1979).
26. *Id.,* 4–3.2, 4–4.1.
27. *Id.,* 4–4.1.
28. *Id.,* 4–4.1.
29. *Id.,* Commentary to Standard 4–4.1.
30. Zupancic, *Truth and Impartially in Criminal Process,* 7 J. Contemp. L. 39, 133 (1982) (emphasis added).
31. Lieberman, Book Review, 27 N.Y.L. Sch. L. Rev. 695 (1981).
32. Lieberman, 27 N.Y.L. Sch. L. Rev. at 695.
33. Fuller, "The Adversary System," in Talks on American Law, 35 (H. Berman ed., 1960). In more down-to-earth language, John Condon, a Buffalo criminal defense lawyer, once commented that he is "an expert in quality control."
34. Tribe, *Trial by Mathematical Precision and Ritual in the Legal Process,* 84 Harv. L. Rev. 1329, 1391–1392 (1971).
35. *See* Fiss, *Against Settlement,* 93 Yale L.J. 1073 (1984), *citing* Bok, *A Flawed System,* Harv. Mag. 45 (May–June, 1983), *reprinted,* N.Y. St. B.J. 8 (Oct., 1983), N.Y. St. B.J. 31 (Nov., 1983); *excerpted,* 33 J. Legal Educ. 579 (1983).
36. *Id., citing* Burger, *Isn't There a Better Way?,* 68 A.B.A. J. 274 (1982); Burger, *Agenda for 2000 A.D.—A Need for Systemic Anticipation,* 70 F.R.D. 83, 93–96 (1976).
37. *Id.* at 1089–1090.
38. *Id.*
39. *Id.*
40. *Id.*
41. Temple, *In Defense of the Adversary System,* ABA Litigation, vol. 2, no. 2, 43, 47 (Winter, 1976).
42. *Id.*
43. *Id.*
44. *Id.*
45. *Zauderer v. Office of Disciplinary Counsel,* 471 U.S. 626, 105 S.Ct. 2265, 2278 (1985).
46. *Id.*
47. *Duncan v. Louisiana,* 391 U.S. 145, 155 (1968).
48. Powell, *Jury Trial of Crimes,* 23 Wash. & Lee L. Rev. 1, 9–10 (1966).
49. *Id.* at 10. *See U.S. Judge Retracts Criticism of a Juror,* N.Y. Times, Feb. 10, 1987, at cols. 1–3. The judge publicly apologized for criticizing the sole juror who had held out for acquittal after a two-

week trial, thereby causing a mistrial. On its editorial page, the Times denounced the criticism of the juror as an "outrage." N.Y. Times, Feb. 12, 1987, at A30, col. 3.

50. *Duncan v. Louisiana*, 391 U.S. at 156.

51. W. Young, Trying the High Visibility Case, text at note 26 (1984).

52. *Parklane Hosiery Co., Inc. v. Shore*, 439 U.S. 322, 355 (1979) (Rehnquist, J., dissenting), *quoting* H. Kalven & H. Zeisel, The American Jury (1966).

53. Carrington, *Trial by Jury*, Duke L. Mag. 13 (vol. 5, no. 1, 1987).

54. W. Young, *supra* note 86, text at note 20.

55. Carrington, *supra* note 88; P. Devlin, Trial by Jury 160 (1956).

56. M. Frankel, Partisan Justice 12.

57. *Id.*

58. *Id.* at 5–6.

59. *Id.* at 76.

60. *Id.* at 12.

61. G. Hazard, *supra* note 1.

62. *Id.* at 125–126.

63. *Id.*

64. *Id.*

65. *Id.* at 126.

66. *Id.*

67. *See, e.g.,* J. Langbein, Comparative Criminal Procedure: Germany (1977); L. Weinreb, Denial of Justice: Criminal Process in the United States (1977).

68. *See* Damaska, *Presentation of Evidence and Factfinding Precision*, 123 U. Pa. L. Rev. 1083, 1087–1090 (1975).

69. Brett, *Legal Decisionmaking and Bias: A Critique of an Experiment*, 45 U. Colo. L. Rev. 1, 23 (1973).

70. *Id.* at 9.

71. *Id.* at 22.

72. *Id.*

73. Fuller, *The Adversary System*, in Talks on American Law 34 (H. Berman ed., 1971); *Joint Conference on Professional Responsibility, Report*, 44 A.B.A. J. 1159 (1958).

74. Damaska, 123 U. Pa. L. Rev. at 1087.

75. *Id.* at 1089.

76. Goldstein & Marcus, *The Myth of Judicial Supervision in Three 'Inquisitorial' Systems: France, Italy, and Germany*, 87 Yale L.J. 240, 248 (1977); *See also* Weigand, *Continental Cures for American Ailments*, in Crime and Justice, vol. 2, 381 (Morris & Tonry eds., 1980); Tomlinson, *Nonadversarial Justice: The French Experience*, 42 Md. L. Rev. 131 (1983).

77. Goldstein & Marcus, 87 Yale L.J. at 247–250, 259.

78. *Id.* at 250.

79. *Id.* at 166.

80. B. Zupancic, Criminal Law: The Conflict and the Rules 54, note 45.

81. *Id. See also id.* at 54–63.

82. *Id.* at 265.

83. *Id.*

84. Damaska, 123 U. Pa. L. Rev. at 1088–1089 and note 12.

85. Goldstein & Marcus, 87 Yale L.J. at 265–266.

86. *Id.* at 265.

87. *United States v. Nobles*, 422 U.S. 225, 230, 95 S.Ct. 2160, 2166 (1975), *quoting Berger v. United States*, 295 U.S. 78, 88 (1935), and *citing United States v. Nixon*, 418 U.S. 683, 709 (1974); *Williams v. Florida*, 399 U.S. 78, 82 (1970); *Elkins v. United States*, 364 U.S. 206, 234 (1960) (Frankfurter, J., dissenting).

88. Kaplan, *Civil Procedure—Reflections on the Comparison of Systems*, 9 Buffalo L. Rev. 409, 420–421 (1960).

89. *Id.*

90. The first of those studies purports to validate the Fuller thesis. Thibault, Walker, & Lind, *Adversary Bias in Legal Decisionmaking*, 86 Harv. L. Rev. 386 (1972). The researchers conclude: "The adversary mode apparently counteracts judge or juror bias in favor of a given outcome and thus indeed seems to combat, in Fuller's words, a 'tendency to judge too swiftly in terms of the familiar that which is not yet fully known.'" *Id.*, at 401. However, the methodology of that study has been subjected to devastating criticism. *See* Damaska, *Presentation of Evidence and Factfinding Precision*, 123 U. Pa. L. Rev. 1083 (1975); Brett, *Legal Decisionmaking and Bias: A Critique of an Experiment*, 45 U. Colo. L. Rev. 1 (1973). Although those criticisms destroy the usefulness of the study, they do not, of course, invalidate the Fuller thesis. Also, the subsequent studies, which are discussed below, have avoided the methodological criticisms of the first study.

91. Lind, Thibault, & Walker, *Discovery and Presentation of Evidence in Adversary and Nonadversary Proceedings*, 71 Mich. L. Rev. 1129 (1973).

92. The proposition was taken from Freedman, *Professional Responsibilities of the Civil Practitioner*, in Education in the Professional Responsibilities of the Lawyer 151, 152 (D. Weckstein ed., 1970).

93. Lind, Thibault, & Walker, 71 Mich. L. Rev. at 1141.

94. *Id.* at 1141–1143.
95. *Id.*
96. *Id.* at 1143.
97. *Id.*
98. *Id.* at 1136.
99. Saltzburg, *The Unnecessarily Expanding Role of the American Trial Judge,* 64 Va. L. Rev. 1, 19 (1978).
100. Bodo, *Whatever Happened to Sportsmanship?* Eastern Rev. 29 (Oct., 1983).
101. W. Young, *Trying the High Visibility Case,* text at notes 18–26; Saltzburg, 64 Va. L. Rev. at 19.
102. In fact, the "episodic" nature of investigation and presenting evidence in Germany makes a jury a practical impossibility. Kaplan, 9 Buffalo L. Rev. at 418–419.
103. Damaska, *Presentation of Evidence and Factfinding Precision,* 123 U. Pa. L. Rev. 1083, 1103–1104 (1975).
104. *Id.* at 1104.
105. Thibault, Walker, LaTour, & Houlden, *Procedural Justice as Fairness,* 26 Stan. L. Rev. 1271 (1974).
106. J. Rawls, A Theory of Justice (1971).
107. Thibault, Walker, LaTour & Houlden, 26 Stan. L. Rev. at 1287–1288.
108. *Id.* at 1288–1289.
109. LaTour, Houlden, Walker, & Thibault, *Procedure: Transnational Perspectives and Preferences,* 86 Yale L.J. 258 (1976).
110. Assuming that there is a culturally determined bias in the United States in favor of an adversary system, that would be a reason to retain that system. Also, Professor Hazard has suggested another perspective on the cultural aspects of procedural models. In our political culture, he notes, "the interrogative system of trial could well turn out to resemble congressional hearings." G. Hazard, Ethics in the Practice of Law 128.
111. LaTour, Houlden, Walker, & Thibault, 86 Yale L.J. at 282.
112. Walker, Lind, & Thibault, *The Relation Between Procedural and Distributive Justice,* 65 Va. L. Rev. 1401, 1416 (1979).
113. *Id.* at 1417.
114. *Id.*
115. *U.S. Constitution,* Preamble.
116. *U.S. Constitution,* Am. 5 and 14.
117. *See* ch. 11, *infra.*
118. M. Frankel, Partisan Justice, ch. 9.

Closing Questions

1. Can someone be both a good person and a good lawyer? Why might you think otherwise? Compare and contrast the qualities that constitute an effective lawyer with the qualities that constitute an ethical person.

_____

_____

_____

_____

2. The adversary system presupposes that the lawyers for both the plaintiff and defendant are equally competent and equally zealous. To what extent is this true?

_____

_____

_____

3. Given that poor and middle-income people do not have sufficient access to the legal system, should lawyers be morally obligated to provide free legal services?

_____

_____

_____

4. Given that we are a litigious society, is widespread recourse to the legal system good or bad for society?

_____

_____

_____

5. If the lawyer-client confidentiality privilege were eroded, wouldn't clients resist consulting lawyers, thereby undermining effective counsel?

_____

_____

_____

6. Analyze the view that lawyers are primarily extensions of their clients and that a lawyer's moral qualms about the client's legal if unethical conduct is out of place.

_____

_____

_____

7. Should lawyers police themselves? If not, who should?

_____

_____

8. Should the adversary system be replaced, say, by the inquisitorial system? If it should not be replaced, should it be revised? What revisions would you make?

_____

_____

_____

9. Suppose the legal system prohibited lawyers from defending clients believed to be guilty. What would be the implications of this?

_____

_____

_____

10. Official codes of ethics insist that lawyers uphold the integrity of the legal system. At the same time, lawyers typically argue for any construction of a rule that favors their clients. To what extent does such behavior undermine the values central to the rule of law?

_____

_____

_____

11. To what extent did *California v. O. J. Simpson* serve or blemish the adversary system of justice?

_____

_____

_____

For Further Reading

Bayles, Michael. *Professional Ethics*, 2nd ed. Belmont, Calif.: Wadsworth, 1988.

Davis, Michael, and Frederick A. Elliston, eds. *Ethics and the Legal Profession*. Buffalo, N.Y.: Prometheus, 1986.

Freedman, Monroe. *Lawyers' Ethics in an Adversary System*. Indianapolis, Ind.: Bobbs-Merrill, 1975.

Fried, Charles. "The Lawyer as Friend: The Moral Foundations of the Lawyer-Client Relationship." *Yale Law Journal* 85 (1976): 1060–1089.

Haber, Joram Graf, and Bernard H. Baumrin. "The Moral Obligations of Lawyers." *The Canadian Journal of Law and Jurisprudence* 1, 1 (January 1988).

Hazard, Geoffrey C. *Ethics in the Practice of Law*. New Haven: Yale University Press, 1978.

Kipnis, Kenneth. *Legal Ethics*. Englewood Cliffs, N.J.: Prentice Hall, 1986.

Luban, David, ed. *The Good Lawyer: Lawyers' Roles and Lawyers' Ethics*. Totowa, N.J.: Rowman & Allenheld, 1983.

———. *Lawyers and Justice: An Ethical Study*. Princeton, N.J.: Princeton University Press, 1988.

Wasserstrom, Richard. "Lawyers as Professional: Some Moral Issues." *Human Rights* 5 (1975): 1–24.

Wolfram, Charles. *Modern Legal Ethics*. St. Paul, Minn.: West, 1986.

Chapter 8

Feminist Ethics

Passages for Reflection

"Feminism is doomed to failure because it is based on an attempt to repeal and restructure human nature."

—*Phyllis Schlafly*

"The extension of women's rights is the basic principle of all social progress."

—*Charles Fourier*

"Much male fear of feminism is the fear that, in becoming whole human beings, women will cease to mother men, to provide the breast, the lullaby, the continuous attention associated by the infant with the mother. Much male fear of feminism is infantilism—the longing to remain the mother's son, to possess a woman who exists purely for him."

—*Adrienne Rich*

Opening Questions

1. What is feminism? Do you consider yourself a feminist?
2. List as many deep-seated and more subtle causes of women's oppression as you can. How might society go about eliminating them?
3. What is the difference between sex and gender?

"Feminist ethics," says Alison Jaggar, "far from being a rigid orthodoxy, instead is a ferment of ideas and controversy, many of them echoing and deepening debates in nonfeminist ethics."[1] This sentiment is echoed by Claudia Card who, in her book *Feminist Ethics,* speaks of the subject not as a monolith but as a family of approaches to ethics in general.[2] To understand, then, what feminist ethics is about, let us attend to the "ferment of ideas" and "family of approaches" which Jaggar and Card say characterize the field. Particularly helpful is Jaggar's analysis of feminist ethics as discussed in her article, "Feminist Ethics: Some Issues for the Nineties."

Jaggar and Card both understand feminist ethics as part and parcel of ethics generally, conceived as a discipline concerned with answering questions about the right and the good. Hence, it is a mistake to see feminist ethics as marginal relative to the theories of Kant, Mill, and other ethical theorists. Instead, feminist ethics is construed in the tradition of ethical inquiry beginning with Plato, continuing through Kant and Mill, up to and including present-day theorists.

But if feminist ethics—or the cluster of approaches that goes by that name—is part and parcel of ethics generally, what is decidedly feminist about it? While no consensus answers this question, it is safe to say that feminist ethics is driven by an explicit commitment to correcting the male biases of traditional ethics, biases that manifest themselves in a spectrum of ways ranging from disregarding women's moral experiences to downright subordination of women. Beyond this, feminist ethics is committed to the idea that women's moral experiences count no less than the experiences of men and that to ignore such experiences is philosophically perilous.

But why think that traditional ethics is biased against women or, as some feminists suggest, outright misogynous (antiwomen)? That the moral theories of Aristotle, Kant, Hobbes, or Mill are biased is not obvi-

---

[1] Alison M. Jaggar, "Feminist Ethics: Some Issues for the Nineties." *Journal of Social Philosophy* 20, 1–2 (Spring/Fall 1989). Reprinted in James E. White, ed., *Contemporary Moral Problems,* 4th ed. (St. Paul, Minn.: West, 1991), p. 68.

[2] Claudia Card, ed. *Feminist Ethics* (Lawrence: University of Kansas, 1991), p. 6.

ous even if they are authored by male philosophers, most of whom were unmarried.

Let us consider the charge of misogyny. E. Victoria Spellman has pointed out that what philosophers have historically had to say about women typically has been nasty, brutish, and ugly.[3] Plato is Spellman's favorite target. Having distinguished between the soul and the body and having argued that the soul alone knows the Good, Plato argues that women cannot know the Good because they are driven by the demands of the body. Comparing women to children, slaves, and brutes, Plato cites women as the worst possible model for ethical guidance. Like Socrates' wife, Xanthippe, who wailed just as he tried to contemplate his death (*Phaedo* 60b), Plato viewed women as reckless in matters that pertain to the soul or the "higher" faculty of man (yes, "man!"). And while Spellman counts Aristotle, Hume, and Nietzsche among the philosophers who have had contempt for women, she identifies Plato as being misogynous in a decidedly systemic way.

Other putative examples of misogynous philosophers include John Locke who, in his *Second Treatise,* maintained that in a state of nature only men can own and bequeath property;[4] Rousseau, who excluded women from the Social Contract;[5] and Kant, who insisted that women can only be citizens in a passive or secondary sense.[6]

Examples of philosophers who have been biased if not misogynist abound in subtle and intricate ways. One such way is suggested by the very body/soul distinction that Plato employs, although Descartes is typically made to shoulder the blame. In his *Meditations on First Philosophy,* Descartes argued that his existence as a *res cogitans* (soul or mind) can be known even when his existence as a body can be doubted. This proved to Descartes that he, speaking for knowing subjects in general, is essentially a mind incidentally housed in a body. Furthermore, he discovered this by use of his intellect at a time when he distrusted his more physical side.

The feminist charge against Descartes is that his philosophy lends itself to a world view that is inimical to issues of gender. For instance, the mind/body dichotomy is itself something that a man would typically

---

[3]E. Victoria Spellman, "Woman as Body." In G. Lee Bowie, Meredith W. Michaels, and Robert C. Solomon, eds., *Twenty Questions: An Introduction to Philosophy,* 2nd ed. (New York: Harcourt Brace Jovanovich, 1988).

[4]John Locke, *Two Treatises of Government, with Filmer's Patriarcha* (New York: Hafner Press, 1947), p. 134. (*Second Treatise,* sec. 26).

[5]Margaret Canovan, "Rousseau's Two Concepts of Citizenship." In Ellen Kennedy and Susan Mendus, eds., *Women in Western Political Philosophy* (New York: St. Martin's Press, 1987), pp. 78–105.

[6]Susan Mendus, "Kant: An Honest but Narrow-Minded Bourgeois?" In E. Kennedy and S. Mendus, eds., *Women in Western Political Philosophy,* pp. 21–43.

experience. Feminists argue that women are not as alienated from their bodies as men often are and do not experience the mind/body dichotomy so vital to Descartes's (and Plato's) philosophy. At right angles to this is the claim that reason itself is a tool of male domination. Since Descartes viewed the purest form of reason as dissociated from the emotional life, feminists argue that his philosophy subordinates women once it assumes that women are more emotional than men. The traditional view that regards reason but not emotions as morally significant is itself thought to be driven by a male bias (see Chapter 15). Thus, the rational beings, contractarians, and impartial observers that moral theorists have historically adored are all targets of feminist attacks.

Finally, feminists argue that the individualistic or "atomistic" strain running through Descartes is indicative of a male bias. Nancy Chodorow and Carol Gilligan both have argued that the way males are reared in patriarchal cultures encourages them to define their identify in terms of separation and distinctness, while the very same cultural patterns lead women to identify themselves in terms of attachments and relations.[7]

Some feminists have charged that the theories of other philosophers are tacitly biased; others have accused the theories of being biased in what they omit rather than in what they include. Annette Baier, for one, has charged that too often moral philosophers operate as if moral agents are mature, rational adults able to judge one another's actions and to exert some control over their own degree of vulnerability, paving the way for a contractarian conception of ethics. If, argues Baier, we took cognizance of relationships of *inequality* such as the relationships women have historically had vis-a-vis men, then contract theory would look less appealing and other conceptions would likely emerge, such as Baier's own concept which is based on trust.[8]

Here, then, is one of the approaches that forms the cluster of approaches that is feminist ethics: the laying bare of biases that have blighted ethics as it has historically been practiced. A good deal of feminist ethics consists of exposing biases in just this way. Other feminist ethicists try to respond to this bias working within the framework other feminists reject. Simone de Beauvoir is a case in point. She has argued that women's emancipation will come when woman, like man, is freed from her association with the life of the emotions construed as a less important aspect of human existence. Other feminists approach ethics in a way that corrects for the perceived lack of appreciation for women's

---

[7]Nancy Chodorow, *The Reproduction of Mothering* (Berkeley, Calif.: University of California Press, 1978), and Carol Gilligan, *In a Different Voice* (Cambridge: Harvard University Press, 1982).

[8]See Annette Baier, "Trust and Antitrust." *Ethics* 96, 2 (January 1986): 231–260, and "What Do Women Want in a Moral Theory?" *Nous* (March 1984): 53–63.

moral experiences, an approach that is characterized by the attempt to give women's moral experiences their proper due. The pioneering work of Carol Gilligan best exemplifies this approach, although the work of Virginia Held illustrates it too.

In her 1982 book, *In a Different Voice: Psychological Theory and Women's Development,* Harvard psychologist Gilligan tried to empirically show that the moral development of women is significantly different from that of men. Claiming that females tend to fear separation or abandonment, whereas males tend to fear closeness and attachment, Gilligan found that females tend to construe moral dilemmas as conflicts of responsibilities rather than of rights and duties, and they seek to resolve such dilemmas in ways that repair and sustain relationships. Additionally, Gilligan found that females are less likely than males to make moral decisions by applying abstract rules and principles. Instead, she claimed that females are prone to act on feelings of love for particular individuals. The conclusion she draws from these findings is that men tend to adhere to a morality of principle whose primary values are justice and equality, whereas women tend to adhere to a morality of care whose primary values are inclusion and protection from harm. For this reason, studies of moral development based exclusively on a morality of justice (for example, Lawrence Kohlberg's work) fail to provide an appropriate standard for measuring female development.[9]

Virginia Held has argued that traditional moral theory has ignored the experience of women, particularly their experiences of birthing and mothering. Contractarianism and Kantianism in particular, she says, have too often regarded moral agents as rational contractors interested in reconciling their selfish needs with the needs of other rational contractors. This, says Held, ignores women's experiences, since reconciling a person's interest with the needs of others is only one setting in which moral reasoning takes place. Mothering is another, and a fundamental one at that. In deciding how to reconcile the needs of a child with, say, the needs of adults, few mothers would employ a contractual model. Few mothers, either, would decide such issues in terms of the principle of utility or categorical imperative. The extent to which moral issues are typically framed in terms of reconciling our interests via abstract principles convinces Held that moral theory traditionally ignores the experiences of women. To rectify this, Held calls for a shift away from rational contractors and toward such concrete relationships as obtain between family and friends, at least in contexts other than economic ones.[10]

---

[9]See p. 470 for a discussion of Gilligan's theory in the context of moral development theories.

[10]Virginia Held, "Feminism and Moral Theory." In Eva Feder and Diana T. Meyers, eds., *Women and Moral Theory* (Savage, Md.: Rowman and Littlefield, 1987).

Against theorists like Held, some feminists employ the model of *homo economicus* to generate feminist conclusions. Operating within traditional schema, they seek to determine the worth of the unpaid housewife and mother and explore what their economic rights should be. To Held, however, we show more respect for women's moral experiences when we extend to the wider society some of the feminist values, such as concern, care, and nurturing, rather than applying economic models to what has historically been regarded as female affairs. "Why," she asks rhetorically, "should not organizations for work, whether for service or production, be places where members care about one another, and why should they not try to provide satisfying work and produce useful products, in ways that will reflect concern for the human development and freedom of all members?"[11]

So far, from what has been discussed, we can glean six distinct concerns of feminist ethics:

1. The critique of Western philosophy (ethics in particular).
2. The exposing of misogyny and stereotypes in writings of historical philosophers.
3. The bringing of women's moral experiences to bear on moral philosophy.
4. The examination of ethical concepts in the light of women's experiences.
5. The examination of conventional theories for focal points of feminist issues.
6. The critical examination of feminist philosophers by other feminist philosophers.

To this list we can add:

7. The discussion of issues not usually discussed by women.
8. The reclamation of ideas of moral theorists who have come to the defense of women against sexist practices.[12] Regarding item 7, we can cite feminists like Bat-Ami Bar On whose essay, "Why Terrorism Is Morally Problematic,"[13] is unusual in its treatment of a topic usually reserved for men. Regarding item 8, we can cite feminists whose reclamation projects have included Mary Wollstonecraft's *A Vindication of the Rights of Woman* (1792), John Stuart Mill's *The Subjection of Women* (1860), and Frederick Engels's *The Origin of the Family, Private Property, and the State* (1884).

---

[11]Virginia Held, *Rights and Goods: Justifying Social Action* (Chicago: The Free Press, 1984), p. 180.

[12]Claudia Card, *Feminist Ethics* (Lawrence: University of Kansas Press, 1991), p. 16.

[13]Bat-Ami Bar On, "Why Terrorism Is Morally Problematic." In Claudia Card, *Feminist Ethics*, pp. 107–125.

This list is not exhaustive. We can also add:

9. A concern with topics that have not enjoyed prior attention from moral philosophers, such as Annette Baier's work on "trust"[14] and Lynn McFall's work on "bitterness."[15]

And keeping in mind Baier's work on David Hume, we can add:

10. A concern with identifying theorists who do not appear to be androcentric (male centered).

Finally, for the sake of completeness we can add a catch-all concern:

11. An examination of issues of particular concern to women such as rape (discussed in Chapter 9), preferential hiring (discussed in Chapter 12), abortion, sex roles, lesbianism, surrogate motherhood, pornography, and marriage.

This last concern is one that some people identify as synonymous with feminist ethics, and so it is worth discussing the concerns that attach to some of these issues.

Let us begin with sex roles. *Sex roles* are the patterns of behavior which the sexes are socialized into adopting. Boys, for example, are typically rewarded for developing "masculine" characteristics, while girls are rewarded for developing "feminine" characteristics. Note that the masculine/feminine distinction is not identical to the male/female distinction. What makes someone a male or a female is the person's biological makeup, while what makes someone masculine or feminine are sociological expectations. Just as boys can be feminine if they exhibit traits typically construed as feminine, such as compassion, so girls can be masculine if they exhibit traits typically construed as masculine, such as bravery. Technically speaking, this is what distinguishes sex from gender. Individuals who show a mixture of the two types of traits are called *androgynous* from the Latin *andros* and *gyne* meaning "man" and "woman," respectively.

Beyond the question of whether sex differences are biologically based as opposed to being taught, feminist ethicists are interested in analyzing the extent to which sex-role stereotyping is ethical. To be sure, sex-role stereotyping limits the freedom to develop the interests of one's choosing and often dictates assignments in the work place. It also prescribes special interests for the sexes that undermine opportunities for communication and understanding. Women, we are told, are sup-

---

[14]Annette Baier, "Trust and Antitrust." *Ethics* 96, 2 (January 1986): 231–260.

[15]Lynn McFall, "What's Wrong with Bitterness?" In Claudia Card, *Feminist Ethics*, pp. 146–160.

posed to be interested in cooking and shopping, while men are supposed to be interested in sports and cars. To correct for such stereotyping, some feminists are concerned with developing alternative models that are morally superior.

Concern with sex roles is closely connected with concern for marriage and the family. Troubled that women are traditionally expected to be homemakers and mothers, while men are expected to be breadwinners and fathers, many feminists have turned to reexamining the institution of marriage, asking such questions as whether marriage is necessarily exploitive, whether it must be heterosexual and exclusive, and how it is related to the family.

By far the most impassioned issue of concern to feminists is that of abortion. While reproductive freedom is of concern to both sexes, we cannot deny that women have always shouldered most of the burdens. In addition to the physical inconvenience of pregnancy and childbirth, women have had the onus of rearing children and have suffered the consequences of unwanted pregnancies. Because of such matters, the issues of reproductive freedom are of special concern to feminist ethicists.

Concerning abortion, the battle lines have typically been drawn around conservative and liberal views. The conservative view is that abortion is wrong because the fetus is a person at the moment of conception, and to take the life of an innocent person is murder. Liberal views are more diverse. In some views, the fetus is not a person but a part of the mother and so within the mother's province to do with as she pleases. Other views regard the fetus as a person but construe the mother's right to do with her body as she pleases to outweigh whatever rights the fetus is said to possess. Thus, the battle lines are often drawn around the question of whether the fetus is a person and what rights it possesses—a line which has itself been attacked by feminists as misguided since few women considering having an abortion ask themselves which rights trump which.

I would be remiss if I did not add to the list of ethical issues the feminist concern with language and the ways it subordinates women. Although sexist language was more of an issue in the 1960s and 1970s than it is today, feminists have historically been anxious to show that the distinction between sexist language and nonsexist language is important, since the way we talk reflects the way we think, and the way we think reflects the way we act. If, say, the term *man* is used to refer to people generally, then the term *woman* is implicitly assigned an inferior status. For this reason, the terms *man*, *he*, and the like are now often reserved for the male of the species.

Without claiming to offer a complete list of concerns that goes by the name of feminist ethics, we have identified some eleven concerns characteristic of the enterprise. I conclude with Alison Jaggar's analysis of feminist ethics as discussed in her article, "Feminist Ethics: Some Issues for the Nineties" (1990). Out of a consideration of concerns like the ones just discussed, Jaggar maps out what she believes are the relevant contemporary issues feminists must address.

First, says Jaggar, feminist ethics must address the question of sexual equality. For example, it must ask whether a sex-blind system of justice is preferable to one that affords women special protection. Despite its attractiveness, a sex-blind system is fraught with difficulties as evinced by "no fault" divorce settlements that divide property equally between husband and wife, leaving wives in worse economic situations than their husbands. So, too, the benefits of special legal protection may be outweighed by its costs. Mandating disability leave for women on account of pregnancy or childbirth may encourage the perception that women are less reliable than men.

A second issue Jaggar thinks feminist ethics must address is the way to characterize and evaluate the concept of impartiality. In the Western tradition, impartiality has been historically regarded as a preeminent value, but its preeminence has been challenged as disregardful of our particular identities, as a preference for "masculine" impartialism as opposed to "feminine" particularism. Nell Noddings, for one, has been vociferous in critiquing impartiality, arguing that we are psychologically only able to care for particular others and that concern with an overall good (such as the happiness of the many) is a chimera. Other feminist philosophers have argued that impartiality can be consistent with feminist concerns. For Jaggar, a pressing concern of feminist ethics is to find a satisfactory analysis among the competing options.

Closely related to the first two issues is that of subjectivity. Noting how feminists have criticized the Cartesian model of the moral self as being disembodied, separate, autonomous, and rational, Jaggar says that feminist ethics must develop ways of thinking about moral subjects that are sensitive to their concrete particularity without ignoring claims about equality and impartiality. This, in turn, will involve rethinking the concept of autonomy, a fourth issue of pressing concern. Skeptical of the claim that the moral self is a disconnected independent self that is the ultimate authority in matters of morality, Jaggar maintains that feminist ethics must find ways of conceptualizing moral agency that are compatible with the recognition that moral development is gradual, not fixed, and is constructed by gender under historical conditions.

Noting the feminist challenge to moral theory understood as an impartial system of rationally justified by universal principles, Jaggar believes that feminist ethics must devise an alternative understanding without falling into the trap of an unwelcome relativism. This, she says, is an easy trap to fall into once it is assumed that women's moral experiences differ from those of men.

However feminists respond to the challenges that lie ahead, Jaggar insists that feminist ethics must meet minimum conditions for it to be adequate as a decidedly *feminist* theory. First, it must offer a guide to action that subverts rather than reinforces the subordination of women that exists in the historical present. It must, in other words, be sensitive to women's struggle for equality in a world in which they are subordinated. Second, it must be equipped to handle moral issues in the private as well as public domain. Historically, moral theory has tended to ignore the private domain of moral conduct, focusing instead largely on contractual relationships and issues of justice. An adequate feminist theory will provide guidance on issues of intimate relationships such as affection and sexuality. Finally, an adequate feminist ethics must take the moral experiences of women seriously though never uncritically.

Diana T. Meyers is Professor of Philosophy at the University of Connecticut (Storrs). She is the author or editor of many books and articles on feminist ethics.

Video Presentation

Guest: Diana T. Meyers, Professor of Philosophy, University of Connecticut (Storrs)

Student Panel: Gary Louizides, Michelle Harknett, Wanda Tarapata

I begin by asking Meyers to explain what feminist ethics is, which she does by way of explaining what *feminism* is. Noting that feminism is not a monolith, she identifies two themes common to any doctrine that goes by that name. The first is the conviction that sexism is pervasive and that male dominance institutionalizes sexist attitudes. The second is the felt need to articulate a theory to accommodate the aims of feminism by eliminating these attitudes. Driving both of these themes, says Meyers, are the experiences endemic to women, negative as well as positive. On the negative side are the problems women historically have had getting equal pay for equal work, avoiding sexual harassment in the work place, getting access to reproductive technologies, and so on. On the positive side are female experiences with friendship and child care.

At this point, I ask Meyers how feminist ethics differs from more traditional ethics. Her answer concerns the notion of moral agency. Unlike the traditional concept of the self which is conceived as atomistic, ahistorical, and disconnected from other selves, the feminist perceives the self to be essentially social, connected with others, and embedded in history. Furthermore, unlike the more traditional self which is guided by reason in search of impartial principles universally binding on all moral agents, the feminist self is emotional though never in an unreflective way. When I ask Meyers to clarify this point, she says that feminists see the reflective process in terms of the best way to maintain relationships consistent with the agent's own sense of integrity.

Talk of integrity leads to talk of autonomy and Meyers' work on that subject. What, I ask her, are the paradoxes connected with autonomy to which she refers in her writings? She begins by distinguishing two concepts of autonomy. *Moral autonomy,* says Meyers, as feminists use the term, refers not to matters of abstract reasoning, but to discussion and dialogue as ways of communicating with others. Its form is contextual and its purpose is to maintain relationships. *Personal autonomy,* on the other hand, refers to the need to be true to one's self in the pursuit of one's values and goals. What Meyers means by the paradox of autonomy is the question of how to be personally autonomous in the face of the expectations that women have been socialized to possess.

Finally, citing a discussion I once had with Margaret Urban Walker, I ask Meyers to comment on the bad name feminism has received in lay circles. After pointing out that anything she has to say is pure speculation, Meyers cites the media's highlighting the negative aspects of feminism when the movement began in the late 1960s and early 1970s. The media, she said, portrayed feminists as being radical left-wingers who are antimen and antiheterosexuality.

Following the break, Gary Louizides asks Meyers for hints in combatting male insecurity which Gary believes leads to male resistance to feminist ideas. Michelle Harknett expresses concerns about children who get lost in the "battle of the sexes." And, just before the show ends, Wanda Tarapata tries to draw Meyers into a controversial discussion about quota systems and preferential hiring policies.

According to many feminists, feminine socialization assists in subjugating women by instilling in them traits that undermine their personal autonomy or right to decide how they should live their lives. At the same time, some feminists celebrate a decidedly feminine style of moral agency that pays heed to women's autonomy. Focusing on the issues raised by these competing views of feminine socialization, Diana T. Meyers elaborates a conception of autonomy that is responsive to each of these ideas.

Personal Autonomy and the Paradox of Feminine Socialization

Diana T. Meyers

People are personally autonomous when their conduct is morally permissible and is not dictated by any technical rule, and when they are doing what they, as individuals, want to do. On this account, autonomous personal decisions might seem reducible to straightforward questions of maximizing desire satisfaction, but Freud and Marx have shown how opaque the divide between perceived desire and actual desire commonly is. Their insight exposes the inadequacy of understanding personal autonomy as nothing more than doing what one wants without undue interference from others, and it highlights the need for an account of the difference between doing what one wants and doing what one *really* wants. The autonomous self is not identical with the apparent self; it is an authentic or "true" self. Autonomous conduct expresses the true self.

Since modern social science numbers socialization among the prime threats to personal autonomy, a good way to get one's bearings in regard to this topic is to examine the effects of a socialization process that is widely believed antithetical to autonomy. Traditional feminine socialization—the set of practices which instills in girls the gentle virtues of femininity along with homespun feminine goals—is one such process.[1] According to many feminist scholars, feminine socialization is crucial to the persistence of women's subjection. Yet, against the claim

Diana Myers, "Personal Autonomy and Paradox of Feminine Socialization". *Journal of Philosophy*, LXXIV, 11 (November, 1987), 619–628. © 1987 The Journal of Philosophy, Inc., NY, NY.

I would like to thank Kathryn Jackson for her helpful comments and the American Council of Learned Societies for the support of an ACLS/Ford Fellowship.

that feminine socialization suppresses personal autonomy, some feminist thinkers have celebrated what they regard as distinctively feminine styles of agency. I shall begin by focusing on the issues these diametric views of feminine socialization raise, and I propose to ask what sort of account of personal autonomy would be adequate to both of these views. Though I am taking feminist theory as my point of departure, I believe that the conception of personal autonomy implicit in this literature has general application, and that it is a more satisfactory one than we have heretofore had.

I. THE PROBLEM OF PERSONAL AUTONOMY IN FEMINIST THEORY

Much recent feminist theory has adopted the attractive, but somewhat paradoxical position that women have traditionally occupied oppressive, subordinate social positions, but that traditional women and their work should be respected as such. Feminists have not always subscribed to the latter thesis, however. In *The Second Sex*, Simone de Beauvoir[2] repeatedly declares that, as a result of their exclusion from public life and their socialization for domesticity, women in their present condition are "mutilated." Their work consists of deadly maintenance routines, and their creative potential is stunted. Whereas men are capable of transcendence, women are trapped in immanence—a state of passivity and objectification. Thus, de Beauvoir concentrates on explaining how women, who are capable of being men's equals, are systematically rendered inferior to men.

Though few feminists today would concur with de Beauvoir's virulent condemnation of women as mutilated beings, the basic line of argument which de Beauvoir developed remains in currency as an explanation of why women's status remains subordinate to men's despite the fact that women have had full political and economic rights for over two decades. It could be argued, of course, that prejudice against women lingers and that this era of legal equality is brief in comparison with the time needed to prepare for and establish careers. There is evidence, however, that women pursuing careers outside the home often suffer from conflicts regarding their sexual identity which never afflict men.[3] Discrimination cannot explain such ambivalence. To account for this phenomenon, some feminists have argued that differential childhood socialization continues to funnel girls into the psychology of dependency and altruistic devotion to others which is traditionally associated with femininity. If this is true, it is no surprise that women would resist acting aggressively and self-interestedly and would therefore be less successful in public vocations than their male peers. On this view, women have been crippled by a mind set instilled in them when they were children.

Still, the conclusion that women have been made inferior to men is by no means a palatable one. Not only does it strip countless homemakers of any dignity whatsoever, but also it fails to take account of the sensitivity and imagination that childcare requires. To redress this unbalanced view of women, many contemporary feminists have valorized the traditional feminine role. Hence, a second argument now in circulation points out that their domestic role has uniquely situated women to develop practices which focus on the particular needs of individuals and which maintain lasting relationships among people. Whereas men's capacities for calculated maneuvering and for achieving their goals are highly developed, women's capacities for intimate interaction and for resolving differences among people are highly developed. Since both types of capability are vital to social life, the ways in which women and men approach decision making must be regarded as equal, albeit different.

Although the argument deprecating women's autonomy is in tension with the argument celebrating it, they both ring true. Thus, it seems to me advisable to embrace both lines of argument. There is ample social-psychological evidence to the effect that women are less able to exert control over their lives than men, but the claim that feminine socialization altogether excludes most women from the class of autonomous agents is both morally repugnant and factually unsubstantiated. What is needed is an account of personal autonomy which comprehends the experiences of traditional women but which also acknowledges the liabilities that curtail these individuals' autonomy.

II. PERSONAL AUTONOMY AND THE TRADITIONAL WOMAN'S LIFE

Together, the two arguments I have sketched yield a composite portrait of traditional women as attentive to others' welfare, adept at orchestrating harmony within groups, and dependent on others for approval and direction. This is not particularly promising material on which to base an account of personal autonomy. Since autonomous people are self-governing, the self must be a pivotal element in any conception of personal autonomy. But, in this portrait of the traditional woman, the self is conspicuously absent. Furthermore, no account of personal autonomy could be complete without an explanation of how autonomous individuals govern their lives. But this portrait of the traditional woman depicts an individual more deferential to others than assertive of her own concerns.

To salvage whatever personal autonomy the traditional woman may have, an account of personal autonomy must accommodate three features of the traditional woman's position: (1) strongly directive prior socialization; (2) deep emotional ties to other people; (3) a home-centered, rather than a work-centered, orientation. Now, the initial response to this list might be to object that these are the very conditions that prevent traditional women from attaining personal autonomy. To forestall this objection, I shall sketch some reasons for countenancing these constraints on personal autonomy. My contention will be that our normal attribution of some degree of personal autonomy to most men obliges us to allow that these features of the traditional woman's life do not necessarily rule out personal autonomy.

Taking the third point first, it is puzzling why, from the standpoint of personal autonomy, life in the public sphere should be privileged over life in the private sphere. To be autonomous, people must conduct their lives in accordance with the dispositions of their authentic selves. Since individuals differ, it is unlikely that one sort of environment would give every self maximal opportunity to flourish. Indeed, the public sphere is itself a highly variegated setting that compasses diverse occupations befitting different individuals. Thus, it seems appropriate to view the home as yet another arena in which the true self might find expression.

Still, it might be countered that, since homemaking is unsalaried labor, the homemaker is economically dependent on her husband, and this dependency prevents the traditional woman from acting on her views when this would antagonize her husband. However desirable economic self-sufficiency may be from the standpoint of personal autonomy, all employees are dependent on their bosses. Since they are sometimes forced to choose between their convictions and their jobs, working for pay does not guarantee independence. Moreover, some benefactors intrude so little in their dependents' lives that these beneficiaries' autonomy is in no way compromised. Although the homemaker's reliance on her husband's income could undermine her autonomy, she may be no more constrained—indeed, she may be less constrained—than many paid employees. Since economic dependency usually leaves considerable latitude for personal choice, requiring freedom from economic encumbrances as precondition of personal autonomy would be too restrictive. Still, in assessing any given individual's autonomy, it is important to ascertain the impact of economic necessity on that person's choices.

At this point, it might be urged that the second of the conditions I mentioned—that is, deep emotional ties to other people—compounds the traditional woman's dependency on her husband in a way that beleaguers few wage-earning employees. Not only does economic self-interest militate against the traditional woman's opposing her husband, but also her love for him keeps her subservient.

Although it may be an added disadvantage to love the person upon whom one's livelihood depends, it is a mistake to think that the commitments involved in profound affection are peculiar to the traditional woman's attachments. Excluding love from the autonomous life would imply the exclusion of a whole range of life plans which an autonomous person could reasonably take up. Success in many of the more stimulating, prestigious, and well-paid careers involves identification with a set of standards and objectives ordained by the profession, not by each of its individual practitioners. Similarly, political advocacy or dedication to other sorts of causes is often passionate and often involves relinquishing some of one's prerogatives in the service of one's convictions. Certainly, people can become so absorbed in their careers or in social movements that they cease to be capable of discerning a mismatch between their activities and their selves. But, since it is hard to believe that shallow commitments are the only ones which can give expression to anyone's authentic self, it is necessary to discover how an equilibrium can be maintained between the integrity of the self and the people and projects the self embraces.

Returning to the problem presented by the traditional woman, it is a truism that her loving attachment to her family can supplant her self. Yet, it is not clear that her affection altogether eclipses her self, and it would be a severely impoverished conception of the authentic self which denied that love could be an expression of it. On the assumption that few people are so unfortunate as to love no one and to be unloved, either personal autonomy is reserved for those whose lives are emotionally empty, or personal autonomy is possible in the context of ongoing love. Although the commitments and interdependencies implicit in love complicate the problem of autonomy, it seems better to contend with these complexities than to trivialize autonomy.

Finally, if anything can, strongly directive socialization seems to controvert personal autonomy. Since the traditional woman has been assiduously groomed for the feminine role from the moment she was first wrapped in a pink blanket, her fulfilling her duties as housewife and mother seems a paradigmatic case of someone's doing what others want and expect one to do, regardless of one's own desires. In contrast, men seem blessed with options: they may choose from an array of careers, and bachelorhood does not carry the connotations of rejection and loneliness which stigmatize spinsterhood. Nevertheless, masculine socialization is powerfully directive. Little boys are taunted for "sissyish" behavior, and, through identification with their fathers or other male models, they are firmly guided into the role of paterfamilias. For men as well as women, then, personal autonomy, if it is ever attained, must be attained within a context of choice tempered by childhood socialization.

I do not mean to suggest that the traditional woman is somehow an ideal exemplar of personal autonomy. Quite the contrary, her autonomy is seriously threatened in a number of ways. I do want to insist, however, that the standard doubts about her credentials as an autonomous agent can be cogently lodged against most men, and that these doubts do not warrant the conclusion that the traditional woman altogether lacks autonomy.

III. THREE FORMS OF AUTONOMY

To leave room for personal autonomy despite pervasive childhood role preparation coupled with compelling incentives to accede to social norms, it must be possible for people to act autonomously in isolated situations, and to adopt some projects and policies autonomously without having control over the basic direction of their lives. In other words, it must be possible for a life to contain pockets of autonomy and threads of autonomy which do not add up to an autonomous life. In defense of this conception, I shall argue that viewing personal autonomy as an all-or-nothing phenomenon is misguided in several respects. Specifically, I shall urge that the scope of programmatic autonomy compasses narrow as well as global issues, that episodic autonomy is intelligible with programmatic autonomy, and that a measure of personal autonomy can be gained through partial insight into one's authentic self.

Programmatically autonomous people pose and answer the question: "How do I want to live my life?" But this question cannot be addressed unless it is broken down into subsidiary questions, such as: "What line of work do I want to get into?" "Do I want to have children?" "Do I care more about material gain or spiritual values?" and the like. A person is programmatically autonomous when that person is carrying out a life plan that embodies that person's answers to this family of questions.

Still, it is evident that questions about the overall course of one's life can be pegged at different levels of generality. With respect to procreation, for example, one can ask questions as broad as whether one wants to have any children at all, or as narrow as which contraceptive method to use. Moreover, autonomy at the highest level of generality is not necessary for autonomy at lower levels. Indeed, since less is at stake, people may find it easier to discern what they really want in regard to narrower matters. Although people who query themselves regarding the most general aspects of their life plans are plainly more autonomous than people who by and large conform to social expectations and only attend to themselves regarding the minutiae of their lives, the latter may display narrowly programmatic autonomy.

A person is episodically autonomous when, in a particular situation, that person asks "What do I really want to do now?" and acts on the answer. Here, the individual is not formulating a long-term plan or setting a policy to be applied in other circumstances; the question is confined to a single action. Autonomy is enhanced to the extent that the convictions and attitudes entering into the decision have been previously examined and endorsed. Yet, people can gain a measure of autonomy by addressing situation-specific questions that occasion introspective reflection. For they get to know themselves better, and they give greater expression to their own beliefs and desires than someone who mindlessly apes convention or caves in to others' wishes.

The traditional woman's personal autonomy is suspect, because she has been induced into the feminine role willy-nilly. But traditional women cannot always rely upon popular formulas or feminine norms to handle the predicaments they confront. Thus, a traditional woman who summons the courage to demand that her child's teacher show respect for values that she cherishes may be acting in an episodically autonomous fashion. This is not to imply that individuals who never ask themselves whether the general life plans they are pursuing are the ones they really want to pursue are nonetheless fully autonomous, but it is to affirm that such people may have more personal autonomy than one might suppose if one never examined the details of their lives.

We have seen that the autonomy of a life is a matter of degree inasmuch as distinct undertakings can be autonomous, though the overarching life plans that subsume them are not autonomous. It is equally important to recognize that the autonomy of any particular decision is also a matter of degree. Consider the case mentioned above of the mother protesting a teacher's contempt for the mother's values in her child's school. To be fully autonomous, the mother's action must not only be the most sincere and effective expression of her concern, but also it must articulate values that she has independently accepted. Yet, someone could fall short of this ideal and still evidence some degree of personal autonomy.

Suppose that the mother is a Christian fundamentalist who is angered by the teacher's glib dismissal of creationism, and suppose further that she is a fundamentalist preacher's poorly educated daughter who has never been exposed to less benighted theological doctrines and who has never questioned her faith. Plainly, her conduct is heteronomous to the extent that it voices beliefs that she regards as immune to criticism. Yet, insofar as she succeeds in conveying the outrage that she genuinely feels in a manner that enables the teacher to fathom and to respect the intensity of her conviction, she is exercising control over her life. In this limited manner, she is acting autonomously. Thus, partial access to and expression of the self must not be overlooked as a form that autonomy can take.

Autonomy can be compromised in a number of ways. Although lack of critical rationality in considering one's traits, convictions, and plans subverts personal autonomy, lack of sensitivity to one's feelings, lack of inventiveness in conceiving plans and actions, and lack of determination to carry out one's decisions undermine personal autonomy, too. Accordingly, personal autonomy must be gauged along a number of dimensions, and fragmentary autonomy can sometimes be descried in lives that are, in many important respects, heteronomous.

IV. A COMPETENCY APPROACH TO PERSONAL AUTONOMY

If we accept that there are at least three lesser forms of autonomy, it is necessary to ask what conception of autonomy would account for them. Various theories of autonomy come to mind. One possibility would be that, when a person achieves episodic, narrowly programmatic, or partial access autonomy, she in some measure defies her prior socialization. A second possibility would be that this person occasionally gives some degree of expression to those of her qualities which are innate. A third possibility would be that this individual sometimes decides more or less definitely to identify with her effective desires. None of these proposals is devoid of appeal. I would urge, however, that, whatever account of the autonomous self one adopts, it will be necessary to introduce a repertory of skills to explain how this self finds an outlet.

Since one must exercise control over one's life to be autonomous, autonomy is something that a person accomplishes, not something that happens to a person. If insanity enabled one to overcome one's socialization, to project one's innate qualities, or to identify with one's desires, one would not thereby become autonomous. Only if one expresses one's authentic self by exercising assorted introspective, imaginative, reasoning, and volitional skills would we agree that the resulting conduct was autonomous.

Consider how people might achieve programmatic autonomy in the broadest sense—that is, how people could autonomously direct the overall course of their lives. Roughly, this sort of autonomy requires that people vividly envisage different life plans and seriously entertain them. Attuned to the feelings evinced by their alternatives, they must interpret these feelings correctly, and evaluate them critically. In light of relevant factual information, they must assess the practicality of these options. Likewise, they must judge the merits of sundry proposals in terms of their other values. Moreover, autonomous people must recognize and act on signs of discontent with previous decisions. They must be prepared to acknowledge inner change and must be willing to modify their plans in response to such change. Finally, comprehensive programmatic autonomy requires that people be ready to resist the unwarranted demands of other individuals along with conformist societal pressures, and that they be resolved to carry out their own plans. In sum, to the extent that individuals survey their options guided by their self-scrutinized feelings, values, goals, and the like, and then marshall the determination to follow their own counsel, they live autonomously.

Personal autonomy, then, can only be achieved through the exercise of a repertory of coordinated skills, which constitutes autonomy competency. People are prevented from extending their autonomy to global programmatic decisions when they lack proficiency in one or more of these skills or when these skills are ill-coordinated. These deficiencies can explain the traditional woman's limitation to sporadic and gradated forms of autonomy—narrowly programmatic autonomy, episodic autonomy, and partial access autonomy. Not only does traditional feminine socialization propel women into the low status role of housewife and mother, but also it curtails the development of autonomy competency.[4] Thus, the efficacy of this early childhood experience is redoubled.

This view of autonomy and feminine socialization enables us to see how both of the feminist positions with which I began can be correct. The traditional woman achieves a measure of personal autonomy, for she does not altogether lack autonomy competency. But, because the traditional woman's autonomy competency is underdeveloped, she cannot resolve the conflict between her internalized image of womanliness and her career aspirations. In addition, this view of autonomy and feminine socialization explains why feminists are justifiably suspicious of the professed fulfillment of many traditional women. Since traditional women do not use autonomy skills adeptly, there is no reason to believe that they are doing what they really want to do. Conversely, however, if an adult who has been raised to assume the tasks of housekeeping and parenting embraces this role, feminists would have no grounds for complaint provided that the individual is skilled in autonomy competency. Since, in principle, the traditional feminine role could be the object of autonomous choice, feminists cannot presume to exclude it as a candidate life plan. Yet, insofar as feminine socialization impedes the development and the exercise of autonomy competency, feminists must seek to overhaul these socialization practices.

ENDNOTES

1. I am confining my discussion to prevalent practices within the dominant cultures in Western industrialized nations.

2. (New York: Bantam, 1961), pp. 274, 295, 306, 451, and 642.

3. Matina Horner has argued that talented women whose prospects are excellent fear success and avoid success because they regard achievement as masculine and therefore associate success with loss of femininity. For helpful reviews of this research, see Lenore J. Weitzman, "Sex-role Socialization: A Focus on Women," in *Women: A Feminist Perspective*, Jo Freeman, ed. (Palo Alto, CA: Mayfield, 1984), pp. 202–204; and Janet Shibley Hyde, *Half the Human Experience: The Psychology of Women* (Lexington, Mass.: D.C. Heath, 1985), pp. 204–206.

4. See part 3 of my *Self, Society, and Personal Choice* (New York: Columbia, forthcoming).

Closing Questions

1. Some feminists have claimed that reason is a tool for male dominance. To what extent is this true?

   _____

   _____

   _____

2. Is the feminist contention correct that the historical emphasis on obligations and rights, as opposed to care, love, and trust, is due to the fact that most philosophers have historically been males? Is an emphasis on rights and obligations typically masculine?

   _____

   _____

   _____

3. How would a deontologist or utilitarian respond to the feminist claim that traditional moral theory betrays a male bias?

   _____

   _____

   _____

4. Does feminist ethics ignore the moral experiences of men? If so, is this a criticism of it?

   _____

   _____

   _____

5. Why might some thinkers reject the idea of a feminist ethic?

   _____

   _____

   _____

6. Immanuel Kant had argued that "ought implies can," that is, that moral obligations make sense only if we have the ability to carry them out. What are the implications of this view for an ethic that takes love and care as preeminent values?

   _____

7. Discuss the claim that pornography is inherently degrading to women.

_____

_____

_____

8. Make a list of some of the ways language betrays a sexist bias and discuss the relationship between how we talk and how we think. Can you think of a criterion for distinguishing between language that is sexist and language that is nonsexist? What connection is there between eliminating sexist language and doing away with unfair practices against women?

_____

_____

_____

9. Adrienne Rich has argued that heterosexuality is a political institution that serves to disempower women. Assess this thesis.

_____

_____

_____

10. Inasmuch as men cannot become pregnant or give birth, to what extent are men competent to comment on such issues as abortion and surrogate motherhood?

_____

_____

_____

11. Discuss some of the ways traditional ethical theories can address feminist concerns such as abortion, sexual discrimination, and equal opportunity. Can such responses adequately address feminist concerns?

_____

_____

_____

For Further Reading

Baier, Annette. "What Do Women Want in a Moral Theory?" *Nous* (March 1984): 53–63.

Blum, Lawrence. "Gilligan and Kohlberg: Implications for Moral Theory." *Ethics* 98 (1988): 472–491.

Calhoun, Cheshire. "Justice, Care, Gender Bias." *Journal of Philosophy* 85 (1988): 451–463.

Card, Claudia. *Feminist Ethics.* Lawrence: University of Kansas Press, 1991.

De Beauvoir, Simone. *The Second Sex.* New York: Bantam, 1961.

Haber, Joran G. and Mark Halfon, eds. *The Realm of the Spirit: Essays in Honor of Virginia Held.* Savage, Md.: Rowman and Littlefield, (forthcoming).

Haber, Joram G. "Putting the Care Into Healthcare." *Mount Sinai, Journal of Medicine* (forthcoming, 1997).

Held, Virginia. *Feminist Morality: Transforming Culture, Society, and Politics.* Chicago: University of Chicago Press, 1993.

———, ed. *Justice and Care: Essential Readings in Feminist Ethics.* Boulder, Col.: Westview Press, 1995.

Jaggar, Alison M. "Feminist Ethics: Some Issues for the Nineties." *Journal of Social Philosophy* 20 (1990): 91–107.

Kittay, Eva, and Diana T. Meyers, eds. *Women and Moral Theory.* Savage, Md.: Rowman and Littlefield, 1987.

Klein, Ellen R. *Feminism Under Fire.* Amherst, N.Y.: Prometheus, 1996.

Schott, Robin May. *Cognition and Eros: A Critique of the Kantian Paradigm.* Boston: Beacon Press, 1988.

Vetterling-Braggin, Mary, Frederick Elliston, and Jane English, eds. *Feminism and Philosophy.* Savage, Md.: Rowman and Littlefield, 1977.

Chapter 9

Sex, Date Rape, and Videotape

Passages for Reflection

"All is fair in love."
—*Unknown*

"The only unnatural sex act is that which you cannot perform."
—*Alfred Kinsey*

"The hurting of women is . . . basic to the sexual pleasure of men."
—*Andrea Dworkin*

"End the silence, no more violence! Take back the night! Hey, hey, ho, ho, Date rape has got to go."
—*Students at William Paterson College*

Opening Questions

1. Do ethical principles exist especially for sex?
2. What is date rape and how does it differ from stranger rape?
3. What sexual practices can you think of (if any) that are unethical?

In matters of sex, morality is said to play a role that it does not play in other matters of human concern. Roger Scruton, for one, writes that "it is in the experience of sexual desire that we are most vividly conscious of the distinction between virtuous and vicious impulses."[1] If this is so, then it can be argued that special moral principles exist that uniquely apply to this discrete part of life, that there is a distinct ethic for sexual conduct. On the other hand, we might suppose that the desire for sex is little different than the desire for nourishment and that the role of morality in sexual affairs is no different than the role of morality in culinary affairs. Just as no distinct ethic governing culinary needs exists, so too, no distinct ethic governing sexual needs exists.

We can frame the issue another way. Suppose that Alice prefers to eat her fettuccine alfredo with peanut butter and sardines and her ice cream topped with onions. Whatever else we might think of her gastronomic habits—that they are coarse, vulgar, or repulsive—they should not be thought of as unethical or wrong. Might this not likewise be true of our sexual habits? Suppose Bob prefers animals to human beings, or (worse yet?) dead people to live ones. Might Bob's preference for bestiality or necrophilia not be akin to Alice's preference for ice cream and onions? Might we not say that just as most of us prefer our ice cream with sprinkles or hot fudge, so, too, most of us prefer our sexual partners to be live human beings? Why then think that our sexual preferences play a unique role in human affairs requiring distinct ethical principles?

One reason to think this is because in sexual intercourse, two people unite themselves as intimately and as totally as is physically possible. Far from being a simple union of two organs, sexual intercourse is an intimate union of two selves that speaks to the deepest mysteries of human existence. It is a union in which the parties become distinctly aware of their personhood and physical embodiment. For this reason alone, sexual desire and its satisfaction ought not to be treated as analogous to hunger and its satisfaction.

Another reason for thinking that sex is unique is its unparalleled ability to undermine our reason and dominate our will. In the service of the libido, people may objectify others, manipulate them, and treat them

---

[1]Roger Scruton, *Sexual Desire: A Moral Philosophy of the Erotic* (New York: The Free Press, 1986), p. 377.

as instruments for use and abuse. In sex, more than in any other activity, our ability to act rationally is put to the test.

Finally, there is the issue of sex's potential consequences: the creation of another human being together with its effects on its parents and on the society of which it becomes a part. Not only can sex result in the creation of a person for whom the parents are responsible, which alone might argue for a special set of principles, but sex is alone in its propensity to provoke powerful emotions (for example, hatred and jealousy) that are difficult to control. If we add to this the fact that sex can result in the transmission of diseases such as AIDS and syphilis, we have the sketch of an argument for why it is unique.

To see why sex might *not* be unique and why there might *not* be ethical principles peculiar to it, consider the practice of adultery and the reason why many people presume it to be wrong. Let us define *adultery* as "having sex with one to whom one is not married, if at least one of the parties is married." This way, if Jack is married to Jill, then Jack commits adultery if he has sex with Jane (or Jill has sex with Jim). But suppose we learn that Jill has given Jack permission to have sex with Jane. Has Jack committed adultery? Clearly, he has. Jack has had sex with one to whom he is not married. What is less clear is that Jack has done something that is morally wrong. What wrong, after all, has Jack done if he has sex with Jane with Jill's permission? Presumably, none at all.

We might ask, at this point, why Jack and Jill bothered to get married if their marriage contained such a clause. (A student of mine once referred to such a marriage as "a marriage made in Sears.") But that is a different question from whether Jack did anything wrong. For all we know Jill has given Jack a "moral holiday" once a year upon learning that many spouses cheat at some point in their marriages and many marriages end in divorce. The moral holiday is an effort to stem the tide.

To this, we might reply that the open marriages of the late 1960s and early 1970s are generally thought to have failed. But even raising this question flies in the face of the answer we have already given about fidelity and divorce. Furthermore, what does it mean to say that the open marriages of the 1960s "failed"? Surely we do not want to say that a marriage has failed if and only if it ends in divorce, which is how most open marriages ended. For then we would call a marriage "failed" if a married couple lived happily for, say, twenty-nine years but left for greener pastures in the thirtieth year. Conversely, we would call a marriage "successful" if the couple never got divorced even if they endured hell together.

We could respond in other ways, as well. We could say, a la Bertrand Russell, that marriage is an institution that is ideal for rearing children but less than ideal for sexual gratification.[2] Or we can say, per-

---

[2]Bertrand Russell, "Our Sexual Ethics." In B. Russell, *Why I Am Not A Christian and Other Essays on Religion and Related Subjects* (New York: Simon & Schuster, 1957), pp. 168–178.

haps even more controversially, that a relationship that contains a moral holiday is not a marriage; that the very concept of marriage contains a commitment to fidelity. If that is the case, then Jack (or Jill) in our example does not commit adultery! But all of these responses are beside the point. Even if we can accuse Jack and Jill of doing something imprudent, something stupid and unwise, that is not the same thing as doing something *wrong*. Presumably, the wrongness of adultery comes about only when deception is involved. But if that is so, then the deception of adultery is merely a case of deception in general which is something we should generally try to avoid.[3] But then, what looked like a case of a sexual act being wrong as a sexual act turns out to be a case simply of an act being wrong as a wrongful act. In other words, against those who insist that an ethic peculiar to sex exists, it turns out for this case, at least, that nothing of the kind exists at all.

Still another way of arguing against a distinctly sexual ethic is as follows. Suppose you were asked to choose between your significant other (s.o.) having a single casual sexual encounter and your s.o. having an ongoing Platonic liaison where he or she discussed intimate things about life (perhaps even your sexual life) but did not physically touch this other person. While many of us would no doubt prefer that our s.o. have the ongoing Platonic liaison, enough of us would prefer the one-time encounter to give us reason to pause. Presumably, the reason for such a choice is that the ongoing liaison betrays more of the trust that is characteristic of good marriages than the one-time sexual encounter. But if that is so, then it is not the act of sex itself that is problematic; it's what the act of sex implies within a relationship based on fidelity. As Shirley MacLaine has said, sex is hardly ever just about sex. Otherwise put, when one objects to one's s.o. having sex with someone else, what is objected to is not the sex per se but the absence of the loyalty and faithfulness that is the foundation of a good relationship. And if that is so, then faithfulness and loyalty are doing the work they ordinarily do whenever they are put to the test, pointing once more to an ethic that is not uniquely applicable to sex.

Another reason why many of us would prefer the one-time encounter to the ongoing liaison is that ongoing liaisons can easily turn into overtly sexual relationships. In this light, consider the Biblical injunction against "coveting your neighbor's wife" over and above the prohibition against committing adultery. Might it be because coveting is so difficult to control that the Bible forbids the one as much as the other?

The medieval philosopher Abelard wondered how the Bible could ask us to refrain from coveting inasmuch as coveting—unlike adultery—

---

[3]This analysis is suggested by Richard Wasserstrom, "Is Adultery Immoral?" In R. Wasserstrom, ed., *Today's Moral Problems*, 3rd ed. (New York: Macmillan, 1985), pp. 208–219.

is not in our control. His answer was that the prohibition against coveting was a prohibition against "consenting to evil impulses." That Abelard was concerned with such questions is understandable enough. He was castrated by the father of his student Heloise with whom he had been having a romantic affair.

But let us put aside the question of monogamy and fidelity and return to our discussion of bestiality and necrophilia. Despite what Alfred Kinsey says at the beginning of this chapter, the feeling persists that we can intelligibly speak of some sex acts as inherently wrong and that the reason for this has to do with what is natural and unnatural in sexual activity. Many of us regard bestiality and necrophilia as wrong because they are "unnatural," whereas heterosexual sex between living human beings is "natural." The challenge this presents is to define what counts as "natural sex." In doing so, we must be careful not to cast our net either too broadly or too narrowly. If we define *natural sex* too narrowly, say, as human heterosexual sex for the purposes of procreation, then not only does bestiality come out as unnatural, which is the way most of us want it to come out, but so too does sex purely for pleasure, which is not the way most of us want it to come out. It would also exclude as "unnatural" such acts as masturbation and oral sex which, presumably, are not "unnatural." Conversely, if we defined *natural sex* too broadly, say, as sex for purposes of gratifying our desires, then masturbation and oral sex come out natural which is what we want, but so do bestiality and necrophilia, which we do not want. (So does having sex with a shoe for that matter.) We have not yet touched on homosexuality. The gay community would surely have something to say about including heterosexual activity in a model of "natural sex," and some lesbian feminists have gone so far as to argue that regarding heterosexual sex as "natural" betrays a political ideology that serves to perpetuate male dominance over women.[4]

Philosophers interested in providing a model for natural sex have traditionally appealed to "natural law theory." Simply put, this theory says that what is natural is permissible and what is unnatural is impermissible. The theory has been attractive to the Catholic Church because God is the author of nature, and so our acting according to nature is acting in accordance with God's will. Conversely, violating the laws of nature is tantamount to usurping God's will. It implicitly says to God: "You did a good job, but we can do better." But you do not have to be a theist to subscribe to natural law theory. You could believe that violating laws of nature invariably has adverse effects on the world.

Much of the Catholic Church's position on sexual matters can be explained along natural-law lines. Witness its position on birth control. The

---

[4]Adrienne Rich, "Compulsory Heterosexuality and the Lesbian Experiences." *Signs* 5 (1980): 631–660.

Church is opposed to all kinds of birth control save for the rhythm method which is a natural method for controlling birth. The Church is opposed to the condom, the IUD (intrauterine device), and the pill since each of these work to interfere with nature. Incidentally, different methods of birth control present different moral problems. The condom and the pill work to prevent conception from taking place, whereas the IUD and the RU 486 morning-after pill work to destroy a fertilized ovum. If, as the Church and some others believe, life begins at conception, then the IUD and the RU 486 pill are morally tantamount to murder! Other practices the Church opposes include abortion, since mothers would naturally carry the fetus to term; homosexuality, since male and female genitalia are naturally designed for each other; masturbation, oral sex, and nonmarital sex. Regarding these last three activities, some people have a tendency to see them as "natural" irrespective of their desirability. The Church, however, insists on their unnaturalness because it views all forms of nonmarital sex for purposes other than procreation as unnatural and immoral.

This last point about the "unnaturalness" of sex that is not for the purpose of procreation signals a problem with natural law theory.[5] For one thing, it is not consistent. If natural law theory argues against abortion, masturbation, homosexuality, and certain forms of birth control all because they violate the laws of nature, it should presumably argue against getting a haircut and getting a manicure since these violate nature every bit as much. That advocates of natural law theory never argue to this conclusion leads one to suspect that natural theory is doing whatever work its adherents want it to do. Small wonder that natural law has been compared to a harlot who will do anything for a price.

A more serious problem with natural law theory concerns the meaning of the term *natural.* When a proponent of the theory says that bestiality is "unnatural" or that homosexuality "violates the laws of nature," what this means is far from clear. In one sense of the term, "laws of nature" are purely descriptive; they represent regularities of nature. The law of gravity is a law in this sense. But this cannot be the sense in which bestiality is "unnatural," for if that were the case, then homosexuality (or bestiality) would be impossible just as violating the law of gravity is. And even if it were possible to violate the laws of nature in this sense, nothing of ethical importance would follow from it. What ethical implications could be drawn from a violation of the law of gravity?

Sometimes when the natural law theorist argues against a practice's being "unnatural," the theorist means unnatural in the sense of "artificial." Birth control other than the rhythm method is thought to be un-

---

[5]For an extensive discussion of natural law theory, see S. Prakash Sinha, *What Is Law?* (New York: Paragon House, 1989), Ch. 3.

natural in this sense. The problem with this construction is not only that we lack a clear distinction between the natural and the artificial, but that even if there was a clear distinction, it would not do the work the natural law theorist wants it to do.

That we lack a clear distinction is apparent once we focus on what we mean by natural as opposed to artificial. You may be tempted to say that *natural* means something like "without human intervention," whereas *artificial* means "with human intervention." In this sense, the rhythm method is natural whereas the IUD is artificial. The problem with this is that we can easily make the case for the "naturalness" of the condom if we maintain that reason is natural and that the condom is a product of reason. And if we objected that this is an illegitimate use of the term *natural,* we would only have to be reminded that it is because of reason that humans have been able to survive. Surely it will not do to insist that human beings naturally would dwell in caves instead of condominiums, go naked instead of wear clothes, and walk across continents instead of travel by plane. For a being that is a rational animal whose very existence depends on its ability to use its rational faculties, it is only "natural" to live in condominiums, wear Dockers, and fly United. Beyond this, the natural/artificial distinction is a useless one as soon as we realize that what is "natural" is not always preferable to what is "artificial." For a woman burdened by a large family with a modest source of income, use of the "artificial" but highly effective IUD is in many ways preferable to the less reliable rhythm method.

But this objection does not touch the heart of the matter. No natural law theorist worth her salt maintains that bestiality is unnatural in the sense that it is artificial. Instead, when the natural law theorist claims that bestiality is unnatural, she means something like "putting an organ to a use that is contrary to its principal purpose." The underlying claim behind this argument is that every organ has a natural function to perform, one for which it is particularly suited. Just as the principal purpose of teeth is to grind food, so the principal purpose of genitalia is to reproduce. Thus, bestiality is unnatural in the sense that having sex with an animal involves putting your genitals to a use that is contrary to their principal purpose. The same goes for necrophilia, homosexuality, masturbation, and fetishism.

The problem with this line of attack is that it is far from clear that it makes sense to speak of an organ's principal purpose, one for which it is particularly suited. The ear, we say, is well suited for hearing just as the eye is for seeing. But the ear is well suited for holding up eyeglasses just as the eye is well suited for flirting. Without assuming what we are trying to prove, why insist that ears and eyes are particularly suited for hearing and seeing, respectively? And why insist that male and female genitalia are particularly suited for reproduction any more than for pleasure? If our genitals are well suited for gratification of pleasure every bit as much as for reproduction—a point feminists, particularly, have insisted upon—then we have no reason to believe that using our genitals for pleasure is unnatural. We have, then, no sense of the term *natural* in which such practices as we have been discussing are unnatural in the sense envisioned by natural law theorists. The one possible exception is if *unnatural* is construed to mean "selected out for survival." In this interpretation, heterosexual intercourse is natural (and bestiality and homosexuality are not) since human male and female genitalia are "made" for each other in the sense of nature's having selected them out for reproduction. This would explain why the penis seems well suited for the vagina and not the rectum or any other part of our anatomy. On the other hand, to the extent that sex is for pleasure, male and female genitalia do not appear to be made for each other. Vaginal penetration is wonderful for the achievement of male orgasm, but is less satisfactory when it comes to the achievement of female orgasm.

Interestingly, no less a philosopher than Aristotle believed that each organ has a purpose for which it is uniquely suited. He argued that just as each organ has a distinct purpose, one for which it is particularly well suited, so, too, does *homo sapiens* have a unique purpose since what is true of the parts must be true of the whole (*Nicomachean Ethics* 1097b). In addition to mistakenly thinking that each organ has a unique function, Aristotle is committing the fallacy of composition which occurs when you argue fallaciously that what is true of the parts is true of the whole.

Having failed to locate a sexual ethic in natural law theory, many people maintain that any kind of sex is permissible between two consenting adults. We subscribe to this idea in theory even if we are more conservative in practice. But what is behind our theoretical belief that anything is permissible between two consenting adults?

Several possible answers can be found. One is provided by John Stuart Mill who, in his *On Liberty,* argues that no one has the right to interfere with a person's liberty of action for reasons having to do with that person's own well-being. As Mill saw it, people should be free to experiment with alternative lifestyles in the interest of maximizing the happiness of society, provided no one else is harmed in the process. By our ruling out some lifestyles as bad simply because they are unconventional, Mill was convinced that we would shut ourselves off from finding happiness like the scientist who, in the pursuit of truth, shuts himself off from truth by refusing to look for it in the "wrong" places. Provided no one gets hurts in the process, Mill fervently argued that people should experiment with whatever unconventional lifestyles they think might contribute to the betterment of society. Because of this conviction, Mill would have been put to the test when, in the 1960s and 1970s, couples experimented with open marriages just as today they experiment with lesbian "marriages." Read Robert H. Rimmer's novel *The Harrad Experiment*[6] for a fictional account of Mill's ideas in the sexual arena.

Another consideration behind the idea that anything is permissible between two consenting adults can be found in the second formulation of Kant's categorical imperative. Here, Kant tells us: "Act so as to treat all of humanity, whether in your own self or in that of others, always as an end and never as a means only to an end." Kant is telling us not to use people *solely* as a means to an end. In treating people solely as a means to an end, we are conveying the message that other people have only instrumental rather than any inherent value—that their value lies solely in what they can do for us rather than for who they are. It is, finally, to treat as an object what should be regarded with dignity and respect.

One way to disrespect human beings is to treat them as if they are only objects to be used and abused. The rapist, for one, treats women this way. The rapist conveys to his victim that she does not have value beyond her usefulness to him, that she is only a means to his end. (I use "she" on purpose since I am not sure that women can rape men any more than I am sure that blacks can be racists. Just as in some views blacks cannot be racists since being racist entails empowerment, so, too, women might be incapable of rape since they have historically been powerless. I am not denying that women cannot coerce men into having sex or that men can rape men.) Conversely, were a woman to give a man her consent and he to give her his consent, then each would be treating the other as ends who are dignified and worthy of respect. They would do this by conveying the idea that each is a subject and not just an object of experience. Thus, so long as two people mutually consent to having sex, then, notwithstanding what it is they are consenting to, each treats the other in a dignified way and the categorical imperative is honored.

Or is it? Rather than saying that the categorical imperative explains why anything is permissible between two consenting adults, we might say that two people who mutually consent to sex use each other (in addition to themselves) and thereby *violate* the categorical imperative. Consider what is wrong with prostitution—if anything is wrong with it—in light of Kant's principle. In treating herself as a commodity, the prostitute treats herself merely as a means to an end just as the john treats the prostitute merely as a means to an end and the prostitute treats the john merely as a means to an end. How, we may ask, does this relationship differ from a relationship where two people mutually agree to having casual sex? (How, we might ask, does it differ from an ordinary employer-employee relationship where the employer uses the employee merely as a means to an end just as the employee uses the employer merely as a means to an end?) How does this relationship differ from the one por-

---

[6]Rimmer, Robert H. *The Harrad Experiment* (New York: Bantam, 1966).

trayed in the then scandalous 1972 Bernardo Berttolucci film, *The Last Tango in Paris,* where the characters played by Marlon Brando and Maria Schneider agree to have sex for sex's sake and agree not to so much as inquire about each other's names? The film asks whether such a relationship is possible as well as ethical. Might we not say that in all of these relationships the parties use themselves and each other exclusively as means to ends and never respect each other as ends, thereby running afoul of the categorical imperative?

Without commenting on the merits of Marlon Brando-Maria Schneider-type relationships, it is undeniable that people use each other exclusively for sexual gratification, and we want to distinguish the Brando-Schneider relationship from these others. The way to do so is suggested by Kant's use of the word *only* when he admonishes us against using people *only* as a means to an end. I use my wife as a means to an end when I use her to gratify my sexual desires. But as I do not value her only insofar as she gratifies me sexually, I do not value her *only* as a means to an end. Marlon Brando, on the other hand, presumably does not value Maria Schneider beyond her ability to gratify him sexually— at least not at the beginning of the film—just as the john does not value the prostitute beyond what she can do for him and the rapist does not value his victim beyond what she can do for him. Analyzed this way, we can safely distinguish between using people in a context of love and respect and using them in these other contexts. The problem with this is that we now have the conventional view that sees sex as permissible only in a context of love and respect. I call this a "problem" only because we have now swayed from the view that anything is permissible between consenting adults.

Whatever your position is on what is permissible sex, sex is impermissible when your consent to sex is flagrantly ignored. This, again, is what is wrong with rape. An interesting scenario is where it is not clear whether one consents to having sex such as in so-called "date rape" or "acquaintance rape."

Date rape, in its most interesting form and the form in which it is most opposed to "stranger rape," typically takes place when a woman gives off mixed signals as to whether she wants to have sex with a man she knows and has reason to trust or when the man reasonably misinterprets the signals she gives. In this form, it typically occurs following a date where the man and woman, playing the games that men and women often play, act amorously toward each other (often with the help of alcohol), with the man believing that the woman desires intercourse despite her protestations to the contrary. Where the woman does not give off mixed signals, "date rape" does not mark a distinct kind of rape. Compare date rape, then, to stranger rape, where a woman is typically confronted in some secluded place (a dark alley, a rooftop) and is forced to have sex at the threat of physical harm.

An important similarity does occur between date rape and stranger rape. In both cases, the woman is forced to have sex against her will. This is what makes each wrong as cases of rape; being forced to have sex against their will, rape victims are treated exclusively as instruments of use and are made to suffer harm. The question is whether differences arise between the cases and whether the differences are more important than the similarities.

Those who assert that no relevant difference arises between date rape and stranger rape point to the fact that at the point during a date when the woman refuses the man's advances and the man ignores the refusal, there is no relevant distinction between the two kinds of rape. While the circumstances leading up to the rapes differ in the respective cases, it is just at that point in both cases that the man ignores the woman's right of refusal and asserts his dominance over her. That she didn't know the rapist in the one case but knows the rapist in the other is hardly relevant to whether rape has occurred.

Those who assert that a difference between date rape and stranger rape does exist point out that it is not always clear what a woman's intentions are even when she refuses a man's sexual advances. Pointing out how the meaning of a sentence is always relative to the context in which it is uttered, the purpose for which it is uttered, and the intentions of the speaker whose utterance is at issue, some people argue that even when a woman says "no," it may not be clear that she means "no" especially from the vantage point of the listener. How it is said (is it said emphatically or coyly? Loudly or softly?), when it is said (is it said in the heat of sexual passion or when the man initiates his advances?), and where it is said (is it said in the bedroom or in the foyer?) all play a role in determining the meaning of the sentence. In this view, sentences lack meaning in the absence of a relevant context. To say that "no means no" in all instances does not do justice to the nuances implicit in interpersonal communication, particularly between the sexes.

Another difference we might point to concerns the motives behind date rape and stranger rape. Where stranger rape is concerned, the motive is to cause violence to the woman. This is the thought behind the oft-repeated comment that rape is a crime of violence, not a crime of sex. On the other hand, the date rapist's motive is not so much to do violence as it is to have sex. Otherwise put, if the stranger rapist were unable to rape his victim, if he were impotent for instance, he would presumably be satisfied to beat the woman or do violence to her in some nonsexual way. The date rapist, on the other hand, would not be so assuaged; what the date rapist wants is sex, and his crime lies in his inability to keep his libido under control.

While this analysis has much to recommend it, it raises problems. If we take classical psychoanalysis at its word, then a distinction between sex and aggression as implied by the preceding analysis is not really clear. In this theory, we are not motivated by sex in some domains and by aggression in others; sex and aggression form a mixed bag with most human activities being driven by both.

But despite the implications of psychoanalysis, a distinction between date and stranger rape is apparent and the difference in motives explains it. While not denying that date rape is bad, perhaps no less bad than stranger rape, we could say that the agent in date rape is less culpable than the agent in stranger rape. Desiring to inflict violence on a woman, the stranger rapist forcibly has sex with her and is culpable for intending to do violence and acting on that intent. The date rapist, on the other hand, desires to have sex with a woman and, unsure whether the woman gives her consent, acts with reckless disregard of what her intent truly is. In this respect, the difference between the culpability of each is analogous to the difference in culpability between someone who is guilty of premeditated murder and someone else who is guilty of manslaughter or, more precisely, a "crime of passion." This analysis in no way detracts from those cases of date rape where the woman's intent is manifestly clear. But then, in such a case, why mark a special case of rape? Maybe it is to argue that date rape is *worse* than stranger rape inasmuch as date rape implies a breach of trust that is not implied by stranger rape.

Beyond the question of how to distinguish date rape from stranger rape is the more fundamental question of the extent to which women should be responsible for their sexual behavior. Some feminists insist that the backlash against all forms of sexual harassment is valid and necessary given the past history of male dominance. These feminists maintain that even though, admittedly, the list of what hurts women seems to grow no slower than the list of opportunities that help them, this is justifiable until such time as women have become completely empowered. But consider such feminists as Katie Rophie who, in her book *The Morning After: Sex, Fear, and Feminism on Campus,*[7] argues that hysteria over date rape on college campuses reduces women to passive vessels with no responsibility for what happens and thus undermines their hard-fought gains.

---

[7]Katie Rophie, *The Morning After: Sex, Fear, and Feminism on Campus* (New York: Bantam Books, 1994).

Alberta Montano-DeFabio is an internationally renowned date rape consultant who frequently lectures on date rape and related topics.

Video Presentation

Guest: Alberta Montano-DeFabio, Date Rape Consultant

Student Panel: Diana De La Rosa, Chung Yi, Melissa Moore

I begin with a botched attempt at telling a joke that is designed to illustrate the difficulty of communication between the sexes:

"When a woman says no, she means maybe. When a woman says maybe, she means yes. When a woman says yes, . . . well, what kind of woman says yes?"

Montano-DeFabio graciously points out how the confusion I had in telling the joke is rooted in the failure of men and women to fully understand the changing contours of sexual relationships. Until such time as roles are made clear, she says, men must be made to understand that a woman's decision not to have sexual relations has to be unequivocally respected.

After reading a newspaper report quoting Montano-DeFabio, I turn the conversation to a discussion of the differences between date rape and stranger rape. Considerable confusion exists in this regard as we try to situate incest within this scheme. Montano-DeFabio points out that like incest but unlike stranger rape, date rape involves a betrayal of trust. The main difference between date rape and stranger rape lies in the circumstances leading up to each. In the case of stranger rape, we are referring to the proverbial stranger wielding a knife in a dark alley whom the woman has no reason to trust, whereas in date rape, we are referring to the woman who has been raped by a man she has reason to trust, such as someone she met at a party. At this point, I suggest that this difference is relevant since what motivates the stranger rapist is violence, while what motivates the date rapist is sex. Montano-DeFabio disagrees and retorts: "If you hit someone over the head with a frying pan, you don't call it cooking."

Continuing with our effort to clarify the distinction between the types of rapes, Montano-DeFabio cites a seminal study by Mary Koss which reported that of 7,000 college students interviewed, one out of eight women felt that they had at one time been forced to have sex, whereas only one of twelve men reported having forcibly tried to have sex with a woman. After pointing out that men also are raped, although such rapes are infrequently reported, Montano-DeFabio's solution to the study's disparity is to better educate men on the rights of women.

We next discuss the case where three members of the New York Mets allegedly raped a woman in Florida after which the woman made the bed, kissed the players good night, and dated yet a fourth member. The allegations of rape came several months later after the woman had evidently discussed the incident with friends and counselors. Without commenting on this case, Montano-DeFabio points out how late reporting of a rape is common on account of the initial trauma and loss of power that is a consequence of rape. She also acknowledges that allegations of rape can be abused. Just prior to the break, we discuss Harvard Law School Professor Alan Dershowitz's call for the establishment of a new category of rape—criminally negligent rape. Montano-DeFabio is somewhat sympathetic to this category inasmuch as she sees the teenager who commits a date rape as more reformable than the typical stranger rapist.

Following the break, Diana De La Rosa asks Montano-DeFabio to comment on the situation where a woman consents to having sex, regrets her decision the following day, and later says she was date raped. Chung Yi asks whether a typical date rapist profile can be depicted. And Melissa Moore asks how we are to teach women that they have the right of refusal. The show concludes with some discussion as to whether different views about date rape cut across gender lines.

In this article, written exclusively for this book, Patricia Mann, Hofstra University, analyzes the concept of date rape, shows the interplay of historical and contemporary forces that define it, and discusses what she feels are appropriate ways of responding to it. Along the way, Mann discusses the infamous Mike Tyson and William Kennedy Smith affairs as well as the famous stairway scene between Rhett Butler and Scarlett O'Hara in the film version of Margaret Mitchell's Gone with the Wind. *She also analyzes Antioch College's controversial "Sexual Offense Prevention and Survivor's Advocacy Program" which mandates that explicit consent be obtained prior to engaging in sexual relations. Patricia Mann is author of* Micro-Politics: Agency in a Postfeminist Era *(Minneapolis: University of Minnesota Press, 1994).*

Date Rape: Sexual Politics in a Postfeminist Era

Patricia Mann

Gender is everybody's problem in the 1990s. It is in the back pages and often on the front pages of newspapers on a daily basis, and it is a pervasive media presence from "Court TV" to talk shows and sit-coms. These are not stories about feminists, for the most part. Rather, we read about waitresses at Wendy's, legal secretaries at Baker and McKenzie (the largest law firm in the nation), and women in all branches of the military charging their employers with sexual harassment. We hear of female agents filing charges of sexual discrimination against the FBI. Newly aware of the frequency of domestic abuse, we are yet shocked as Lorena Bobbitt narrates the abusiveness that led up to her own resort to violence and fearful as we hear Nicole Simpson's sister recounting O.J.'s abusiveness. As Mike Tyson leaves prison in March 1995, we remember that the famous boxer has spent the last three years in jail after being convicted of date rape in 1992.

Every semester, at some point, I say to my philosophy students: "Most of you are not feminists, but all of you have gender problems." Hearing this, my students nod in ready assent, suddenly interested in what philosophy can offer them to deal with this troublesome aspect of everyday life. Gender problems, daily conflicts and misunderstandings between women and men, are at an all-time high in our postfeminist era.[1] The new roles of women and men in both workplace and home have ruptured traditional family relationships. Unleashing creative new energies of women and men alike, the new roles also alter traditional power relationships, creating tensions and actual injustices that can only be fully resolved through changes in the institutional arrangements of our public and private lives.

The phenomenon of "date rape," alternatively referred to as "acquaintance rape," is an exemplary problem of our postfeminist era. Comprehensible in the context of the changing roles and relationships of women and men today, date rape is not a problem particularly associated with feminists, but instead with mainstream women and men who are finding that they need to renegotiate all the old relationships today, even sexual ones. While it raises issues of sexual agency and entitlement relevant within the personal lives of all sexually active adults, it is a problem of particular relevance to high school and college-age students who are first experimenting with their sexuality and attempting to define their sense of sexual identity and agency. One might suppose that concerns with gender roles and power in the bedroom might receive the dreaded label of political correctness and be dismissed as trivial in a day of AIDs and neo-conservatism. On the contrary, the mortally high stakes of sex today intensify the concerns of young women, as well as young men, to have their personal desires heeded within intimate relationships.[2] In this article, I will analyze the category of date rape, showing the interplay of historical and contemporary forces defining it and suggesting appropriate ways of responding to this problem.

DATE RAPE: IDENTIFYING THE SITUATION

In the paradigmatic date rape situation, a woman accuses a man of subjecting her to sexual intercourse against her will, but within the context of a personal or intimate interaction that had been mutually agreed upon. According to the woman, she indicated at some point in the interaction that she did not want to engage in intercourse and the man, ignoring her wishes, coercively or violently insisted on having intercourse. By contrast, according to the man, the woman either consented to everything or he had no reason to think that she did not consent. The woman feels that she has been violated, and the man feels that he has acted quite normally and is being pilloried by a vindictive woman who does not like sex.

What is going on here? How is it that a woman and a man have such different perceptions of what has occurred? Is this a problem properly characterized as one of miscommunication? If so, is it properly addressed by encouraging greater verbal interaction during sex? When the student body of Antioch College decided that linguistic clarity was the answer and wrote a sexual offense policy specifying the necessity of verbal consent before proceeding to a higher level of sexual engagement, a nationwide public furor ensued. Many people were incensed by the idea of mandating conversation in the midst of what they deemed a natural and necessarily spontaneous interaction.[3] While I will show that date rape is much more than a failure of communication, I will also argue that the most effective program for dealing with the problem may be to encourage specific sorts of verbal interaction during sex.

Consider first the sorts of situations in which women today are asserting that date rape has occurred and the social and moral ambiguities they raise. A high proportion of date rape accusations involve college students, and fraternity members are those most likely to be charged with acts of rape. According to Patricia Martin and Robert Hummer, "fraternities create a sociocultural context in which the use of coercion in sexual relations with women is normative."[4] Martin and Hummer explain that the group ethos of fraternities encourages men to engage in a competitive game wherein they consciously utilize alcohol as a weapon against women's sexual reluctance, having no qualms about obtaining sex from women who are semiconscious or even unconscious from the effects of alcohol. While a woman who has been plied with alcohol prior to sex may now use this as grounds for claiming she has been raped, it is also the case that a woman "who drinks too much" may be viewed as "causing her own rape."[5] Martin and Hummer pessimistically conclude that "unless fraternities change in fundamental ways, little improvement can be expected."[6]

Consider next the case of Desiree Washington and Mike Tyson. Eighteen-year-old Desiree Washington met Mike Tyson while she was participating in the Miss Black America beauty pageant in Indianapolis in July 1991. Having taken her phone number, Tyson called Washington from his limousine at 2 a.m. on July 19, inviting her to come down from her hotel room and join him in driving around to some of the celebrity-filled parties going on that night as part of the Indiana Black Expo, a cultural festival of which the beauty pageant was a part. After she joined him, Tyson made an excuse to go up to his hotel room before going on to the parties, and once there, Washington says, he attacked and raped her. Tyson was convicted and served three years for rape.

By contrast, consider the case of Patricia Bowman and William Kennedy Smith, a nephew of Senator Ted Kennedy. Bowman and Smith met at Au Bar, a trendy local hangout in Palm Beach, Florida, on Easter weekend of 1991. After agreeing to drive him home to the Kennedy compound when the bar closed, Bowman accepted Smith's invitation to tour the house and take a walk on the beach in front of the Kennedy home. Bowman says she was tackled and raped by Smith after she had declined his invitation to go for a swim and climbed the stairs from the beach and begun walking back to her car. Smith was acquitted.

Finally, consider the case of Rhett Butler and Scarlett O'Hara in *Gone with the Wind*. Rhett and Scarlett are married, but they have quarreled, and Scarlett has announced her desire to have no further children, threatening to lock her door every night, to which Rhett has replied, "If I wanted you, no lock would keep me out." In the fateful scene, after drinking and quarreling further, Rhett suddenly takes her in his arms and carries her up the stairs, Scarlett protesting. When Rhett passionately kisses her on the landing, however, Scarlett finds herself responding in kind and intercourse follows.

These four situations differ immensely in terms of the quality of the interaction prior to intercourse and in terms of the race, class, age, and marital status of the participants.[7] Yet in each case, it can and has been argued that sexual intercourse was a product of coercion rather than mutual consensus, and was, therefore, wrongfully achieved. Others vehemently deny that such incidents represent a phenomenon of date rape, asserting that the women had either consented or acted in such a manner as to make them fully responsible for the final act of intercourse. Perhaps most surprising is the fact that two feminist philosophers have clashed vitriolically over their interpretations of the famous scene in *Gone with the Wind*. Marilyn Friedmann maintains that insofar as Scarlett O'Hara has previously indicated her desire not to have sex with Rhett and is portrayed as being violently handled and physically dominated by Rhett in this scene, it constitutes a form of rape, even if she ultimately acquiesces to sex. Christina Hoff Sommers expresses contempt for this interpretation, arguing that it demonstrates the degree to which some feminists are out of touch with the feelings of actual women. She cites a survey that finds that the majority of women consider this scene "erotically exciting" and "emotionally stirring."[8] Intensely opposing views were similarly expressed and left unresolved in the context of the Washington-Tyson, and Bowman-Kennedy trials; there would seem to be a deep vein of confusion over what exactly the problem of date rape is all about.

EXAMINING THE GENDERED DIMENSIONS OF SEXUAL AGENCY

We can best analyze the phenomenon of date rape by examining traditional concepts of sexual agency and recent transformations in these conceptions. More precisely, we want to investigate what we suspect to be the gender-specific and historically variable meanings of

our sexual actions and interactions. In fact, there is little to be learned from modern philosophers about the qualitative issues of agency I am raising.[9] The mind/body dualism of Descartes and the materialist and mechanistic predispositions of modern science have encouraged doubts about the very existence of human agency and freedom. Modern philosophers have engaged in extended metaphysical debates about the relationship between the mind and the body, leaving analysis of the qualitative and social dimesions of our actions to thinkers who have particular applications in mind. While economists, psychologists, and neurophysiologists have interpretations of the meaning of our actions corresponding with concerns specific to their disciplines, I have found the analysis of individual agency employed in everyday life to better encompass the social complexity and breadth of our social actions, and it is this analysis that I rely on as a basis for deriving conceptual insights into our sexual agency.[10]

For instance, when people are attempting to decide on a career, perhaps choosing medicine and philosophy, we may begin by asking them about their interests and desires, whether they want to work with people, with ideas, or with their hands. We then go on to ask them about their responsibilities. Do they, for example, have familial time constraints or economic obligations that would make it difficult for them to spend the long hours and years training as a doctor, regardless of intense desires to devote themselves to medicine? We also ask about the sort of social recognition and monetary rewards they are looking for from a career. Medical doctors receive very good money as well as more intangible forms of social recognition—so much so that individuals who experience very little desire to work with sick bodies may nevertheless choose a career in medicine. By contrast, we who become philosophers tend to be motivated almost entirely by a desire to philosophize.

In order to fully understand the meaning of someone's activities, we need to consider *three* dimensions of their agency: their desires, their responsibilities, and their expectations of recognition and reward. For different people, one or another dimension will count more than the others. In fact, until very recently most women would have explained their actions primarily in terms of their obligations toward others. As a society, we understood the significance of women's actions almost solely in terms of their responsibilities as mothers and as helpmates to men, restricting female possibilities for recognition and reward to those attainable through familial relationships. We looked at a boy child and wondered, what will he become? By contrast, we looked fondly at a girl child and confidently predicted she would make a very good mother someday. (We find a similar emphasis on duties and obligations and lack of concern for the agent's desires in the case of various subordinate categories of men: servants, factory workers, and the like.)

Historically, there was a gender-specific distribution of the dimensions of agency, and in many situations men and women exhibited complementary dimensions of agency. In sexual relationships, for example, we attributed sexual desire and passion to men, while holding women responsible for placing the appropriate limitations on sexual interactions. While boys developed their individual plans for how they wanted to earn a living and achieve social recognition, they also learned that this was a world in which male sexual desire was encouraged in many different ways. As teenagers, they learned they would be positively recognized for "wanting it," "getting it," "making it," or "doing it" with any available female body; to manifest a lack of sexual desire or aggressiveness was to invite the contempt of one's peers.

Insofar as male sexual desire was presumed intense and unremitting, the responsibility for regulating sexual interactions was left up to women. As wives, women had the obligation of being totally available and responsive to the sexual desires of their husbands. Just as dutifully, they made themselves physically unavailable to other men who might experience uncontrollable sexual urges in their presence. Women who were raped were typically blamed for bringing it on themselves—insofar as it was a woman's responsibility not to provide the physical occasion for male sexual desire to satisfy itself inappropriately.

Freud famously theorized sexual agency in terms of male desire and then, turning his attention to women, he asked what women wanted. Finding no comparable form of desire, he dismissively labeled women a "dark continent." Of course, he simply asked the wrong question, overlooking the very different quality of women's sexual agency. As soon as we apply our three-dimensional model for understanding the actions of individuals within social relationships, we see the sexual agency of women outlined very clearly against the background of male desire. Men were recognized for the boldness and intensity of their desires, while women were recognized and rewarded for their dutiful accommodation to male projects and purposes. Women's sense of responsibility and obligation as mothers, wives, and daughters was what made it possible for men to be unrestrained in their desires. Girls were not encouraged to have individualized desires, whether of a career sort or of a sexual sort. Indeed, while there were always women who did dare to risk having independent sexual desires, they were vulnerable to community disgrace, expulsion, or even death upon being found out.

Let us now evaluate our four cases of posited date rape in terms of this traditional perspective, to provide a historical frame of reference for later comparisons. Consider the first three cases: (1) College girls are sexually accosted in the context of drinking at fraternity parties; (2) Desiree Washington was accosted after accompanying Mike Tyson to his hotel room alone at 2 a.m.; (3) Patricia Bowman was sexually attacked after walking and engaging in acts of kissing on the beach late at night with William Kennedy Smith. In all these cases, a traditional perspective on sexual relationships would hold the women responsible for sexual misconduct, for making themselves physically vulnerable to the raging male sexual instincts of someone not their husband. The woman's body was defiled and her honor tarnished insofar as this incidence of extra-marital sexual intercourse became known; the harm to her reputation was considered just recompense for her wrongful behavior.

In the case of Rhett Butler and Scarlett O'Hara, the relevant difference is that they were married. As a married woman, Scarlett had a responsibility to submit to her husband's desires. Indeed, viewers would consider Scarlett lucky to have such a handsome and romantic husband, lucky to have a husband whose passion could actually evoke a responding passion.

According to the traditional understanding of male and female sexual agency, male sexual coerciveness and female lack of desire are unremarkable features of sexual interactions. It is the marital status of the sex partners that is the distinguishing feature of a sexual incident. Married sex accords with the agency of both parties, while in the case of unmarried sex, a man's reputation for masculinity is enhanced at the same time that a woman's reputation for purity and femininity is sullied.

CONTEMPORARY SEXUAL POLITICS: WHAT'S CHANGED AND WHAT HASN'T?

In the last twenty-five years, as large numbers of women have entered the public workplace, our notions of female agency have changed considerably. It is now apparent that women have the capacity to become materially desiring economic selves, with hopes and expectations for recognition and reward quite similar to those of men. With women's new economic autonomy and the availability of contraception, our understanding of women's familial and reproductive agency has also been transformed. No longer are women conceived of as organic maternal beings, participating in a natural and inevitable cycle of marriage and reproduction. We now expect women to consciously decide when and if to become married, as well as pregnant, in accordance with their individual desires.

Given such dramatic changes in the economic and familial status of women over the past twenty-five years, is it any wonder that women today are demanding new respect for their sexual agency as well?[11] Women want to be recognized as desiring beings and to have their desires, whatever they may be, taken seriously. Because of the complementary dynamic within sexual interactions, however, sexual politics cannot be solely about women's new-found desires. Women's desires will only be satisfied insofar as individual men learn to be responsive to them, and insofar as society comes to recognize and respect women as sexually active beings. Women are really demanding a gendered redistribution of the three basic dimensions of sexual agency.

In date rape cases, women are asserting the relevance of a woman's particular desires *within* any personal encounter. They are declaring the responsibility of a man to recognize the presence or absence of a woman's sexual desires, and his responsibility to act upon his own sexual desires only when he is quite certain of the presence of affirmative female desires. In the first place, women are asserting that a personal encounter should not turn into a sexual encounter unless both parties actively desire this to happen. And in the second place, women are claiming their right to refuse to proceed from other forms of sexual intimacy to intercourse. Women are now insisting that personal and sexual encounters be shaped and determined at each moment by the desires of both partners. Each person must understand the desires of his or her partner as a necessary component of any interaction in which he or she hopes to satisfy his or her own desires. This is a new sexual ethos of mutual respect, and it provides the basis for what I will label norms of "sexual civility." Standards of sexual civility, like standards of political civility, create the normative basis for individuals to assert rights against other individuals, defining the terms according to which one individual claims to have been morally or politically wronged by another.[12]

Consider once again our cases of posited date rape. These cases will serve to illustrate how our perceptions of intimate encounters between women and men are changing, as well as the confusions and problems involved in this process of change. In the cases of both Desiree Washington and Patricia Bowman, we can well imagine Washington or Bowman as reasonable contemporary women saying "no" as Mike Tyson seeks to transform a personal encounter into a sexual one, or as William Kennedy Smith seeks to progress from one form of sexual intimacy to a higher level. According to standards of sexual civility, Tyson and Smith were obligated to recognize and act in accordance with the negative sexual desires of Washington and Bowman. Insofar as one of the most basic requirements of sexual civility involves the right of either party to refuse to proceed further with the interaction, we can appreciate Washington's and Bowman's anger at not having their desires respected.

It is very interesting that accusations of date rape are being made by women like Patricia Bowman and Desiree Washington who are no more devotees of recent feminist theory than the men they accuse. They rather seem to have been affected by a general cultural ambiance in which new lip service, at least, is paid to the equal rights of women in all walks of life. These "untutored" charges of date rape reflect how egregiously traditional sexual practices ignore the rights of women and how obvious, in some sense, the new norms of sexual civility are.

Not necessarily so obvious to men, however. Nuanced relationships of sexual civility conflict with the normatively aggressive role of male desire in traditional sexual relationships. For example, both Tyson and Smith claim to have acted in accordance with the women's apparent desires for intercourse. Since Washington and Bowman both claim to have loudly protested against intercourse, it is tempting to dismiss Tyson and Smith's statements as disingenuous. Yet we should not overlook the potential for miscommunication in these situations. Until very recently, women were taught that it was ladylike to say "no" even when one wanted intercourse, and men have been taught accordingly to discount women's negative verbal protestations. Women who say "no" today are thus set up to be misread as actually consenting.[13]

In addition to such literal problems of communication, however, the disagreement over whether women have actually consented to intercourse is also a function of confusion and uncertainties created by changing notions of sexual entitlement. According to standards twenty-five years ago, a woman who allowed herself to be alone with a man late at night was a likely seductress, and any complicit sexual behavior at all was enough to indicate full sexual consent. We tend to allow women a greater degree of sexual discretion today, but it is not clear how much we allow them. Assuming we agree that traditional notions of male sexual entitlement were oppressive and unfair to women, we are yet likely to disagree about the actual points at which it is reasonable or unreasonable for one person to call a stop to a sexual interaction. We are also likely to be uncertain about the ways in which such consent and refusal might be communicated, whether verbally or by physical gestures alone.

For example, suppose we agree that the mere physical presence of a woman in a man's room or on a man's private beach, even late at night, does not necessarily indicate her consent to sexual intercourse. If we reject the standard of mere physical presence, the question then becomes one of determining what words or physical gestures should count as consent in such a situation. Is consent implied when a woman kisses a man, or when she lies down next to a man on his beach while kissing and embracing him? Is consent implied when a woman removes some of her clothing or even all of it, in such a situation? Woman are questioning the traditional patriarchal assumption that sexual interactions necessarily progress toward and culminate in male penetration of a woman in intercourse. Insofar as kissing and erotic touching have a different sexual and physical quality than intercourse, women argue that their desire for kissing and embracing may be unaccompanied by a desire for intercourse. Yet insofar as men have been taught a unitary notion of sexual desire as culminating in ejaculation through intercourse, they are unlikely to listen or perhaps even to hear female requests to stop short of intercourse.[14]

Women who charge date rape are denying the legitimacy of this traditional notion of male sexual entitlement and demanding the right to say "yes" and to say "no" at discrete junctures prior to and within any sexual encounter. They may well speak for vast numbers of contemporary women who would like to have their desires within sexual interactions listened to on a more regular basis. Respect for female desires will imply female initiation of sexual interactions, as well as trajectories of sexual interaction which may or may not end with intercourse. Sexual civility would seem to require that we find a way to highlight the increasingly divergent sexual expectations and desires of men and women so that these differences can be resolved constructively and fairly.

Our third exemplary case, fraternity house date rape, raises additional issues having to do with the quality of sexual consent. Insofar as fraternity men engage in sex after women have become unconscious from alcohol consumption, their acts can be readily condemned as failing the most basic standards of sexual civility and consent. The more interesting situation exists when a certain amount of alcohol smoothes the path of a successful seduction. How should we judge those cases in which a woman gives consent under the influence of alcohol or any other substance and the next day regrets having given consent? On the one hand, it is not unreasonable to think that there may be morally illegitimate ways of securing another person's consent to proceed within sexual relationships. Within economic relationships, by analogy, one is prohibited from using various forms of deceit in order to get another party to sign a contract. And within logic, there is a whole category of persuasive techniques called *fallacies* that are deemed illegitimate ways of convincing someone to accept a particular conclusion. One shows a lack of respect for the other person by relying on fallacious forms of reasoning in order to convince him or her of a particular conclusion,

and once the fallacy has been exposed, the conclusion is invalidated.

On the other hand, if we continue to value notions of sexual seduction, we will want to proceed very cautiously in any effort to distinguish between legitimate and illegitimate sexual consent. Recognizing that seduction frequently relied upon patriarchal power differentials, we also know that traditionally women seduced men. Distinguishing between (good) seductive and (bad) manipulative sexual behavior may prove to be very difficult.

Our fourth case of posited date rape, the famous stairway scene between Rhett Butler and Scarlett O'Hara, raises the issue of sexual civility within marriage. Insofar as women no longer have the obligation of accommodating all male sexual desires within marriage, the possibility (even likelihood) for wrongfully coercive or violent male sexuality exists within marriage. The question is whether this scene from *Gone with the Wind* provides an instance of it. In fact, I think not. Rhett Butler has been portrayed as a handsome and romantic husband with whom Scarlett O'Hara has fallen passionately in love and married. Moreover, the viewer is sympathetic to Rhett's anger and frustration insofar as Scarlett is portrayed as emotionally unfaithful to him in her love and desire for Ashley Wilkes. Despite their bitter wrangling, a viewer is quite likely to project onto the scene her hopes for a rekindling of their previous love and passion. Through such a viewer's eyes, we can thus construe a "reasonable" woman as saying "yes" as Rhett carries a struggling Scarlett up the stairs.

While this scene does not provide a persuasive illustration of wrongfully coercive male sexual behavior within marriage, there can be little doubt that such behavior exists.[15] Indeed, marriage remains the normative site of heterosexual activity, and traditional conceptions of sexual agency may be more difficult to dislodge here than elsewhere. It may be easier to recognize the need for conscious forms of civility and respect within casual sexual relationships than within marital relationships, in which "love" is supposed to supplant such formal principles of interpersonal regard. Thus, we will want to articulate methods of reconstructing sexual relationships that address notions of male and female sexuality regardless of their location within or outside marriage.

BRINGING ABOUT SEXUAL CIVILITY: JURIDICAL STRATEGIES

This is a paper about date rape, more precisely about the phenomena of coercive sexuality we currently identify with this term. In fact, I have attempted to explain date rape phenomena as part of a broader canvas of gendered conflicts and confusions resulting from changing conceptions of women's and men's sexual agency. While there are obvious historical and ideological reasons why this issue has been framed in terms of "rape," there are compelling grounds for discarding the terminology of rape and rethinking the discourse of gendered sexual agency in a thorough-going fashion.

Rape is a historically embedded concept that gains its meaning from traditional features of male and female sexual agency that women are today protesting. In the Anglo-American tradition, rape has primarily been understood as a crime against a man's property. The seriousness of the crime of rape reflected the seriousness with which men took their right to exclusive sexual possession of daughters and wives. As a result of the patriarchal focus of rape laws, only certain forms of sexual assault or coercion were (until recently) illegal. As Deborah Rhode explains, "One form of abuse—intercourse achieved through physical force against a chaste woman by a stranger—has been treated as the archetypal antisocial crime. By contrast, coercive sex that has departed from this paradigm frequently has been denied or discounted."[16] By means of the legal category of date rape, women are currently attempting to broaden the juridical perception of actionable sexual forms of assault or coercion.[17] The problem with such a strategy, as I see it, is that the rape paradigm is geared to enforce certain sorts of patriarchal relationships, and proves an ob-stacle to rethinking gendered patterns of sexual initiative and desire.

The rape paradigm is an unwieldy anachronism that misrepresents the quality of women's anger and expectations when sexual coercion or assault occurs within the context of a personal relationship. In the first place, there can be no affirmative conception of a woman's own sexual desires within the standard rape narrative. Rape laws seek to reward chaste female victims who have been socially devalued by the experience of rape. Yet those who complain of sexual coercion and assault today are frequently sexually experienced women who feel morally and politically wronged, but not socially devalued by particular forms of sexual experience. Moreover, I am troubled by evidence that the date rape framework encourages teenagers and other sexually inexperienced women who report incidents of sexual coercion or assault to feel degraded and devalued in an all-too-traditional fashion.[18]

In the second place, rape laws misrepresent the character of the sexual situation women are attempting to reform. Rape laws exist to punish abnormal forms of sexual behavior perpetrated by "criminals"—not simply men who do not respect women's desires. Yet women are bringing charges of date rape against men they have chosen to have intimate contact with. Does it make narrative sense to think that such a man suddenly becomes a criminal, or reveals himself to have been a monstrous individual all along when he coercively proceeds to intercourse? Does he change from being a person a woman wants to share intimate moments with to being a criminal assaulting her when he becomes obnoxiously forward with his penis? The sorts of coercive and assaultive sexual behavior women are presently demanding an end to are all too normal in our society, and the men who commit coercive or even assaultive sexual acts within the context of intimate relationships are rarely perceived as criminals, even by the women they have mistreated.

The struggles of women to have their sexual desires recognized and respected by men are a very basic component of heterosexual life today, as are the various phenomena of male resistance to any diminishment of their patriarchal sexual perquisites. It is in the interests of women to normalize the critique of coercive and assaultive male sexual behavior, precisely in order to make the critique more inclusive and relevant to everyday issues of sexual initiative and choice.

What alternatives do women have to filing criminal charges of date rape in response to violent, coercive sexual incidents? In the legal realm, women can choose to file a civil lawsuit, accusing a man of an "intentional tort," instead of pressing criminal charges of rape. According to the common law, an intentional tort occurs whenever one person commits assault, battery, or false imprisonment or intentionally inflicts emotional distress upon another person.[19] Not only is the standard of proof much easier to meet in a civil lawsuit, but the legal framework of tort better accords with women's contemporary social status, as well as their particular goal in bringing a legal action.[20] In claiming that a man has committed an intentional sexual tort against them, women enter the legal system as wronged, but formally equal, citizens rather than as female victims of rape. Rather than submitting herself to the criminal justice system, a woman maintains important procedural elements of control when pursuing a civil lawsuit, deciding if the case will go to trial, as well as when it will be settled.

Women today turn to the law not as passive victims but in the dual capacity of injured citizens and micropolitical agents seeking social recognition and vindication of the sexual injustices that a particular man has committed.[21] Women want redress for specific harms done to their individual psyches. A woman might claim that her sense of sexual confidence, or more generally, her sense of personal autonomy was damaged by this encounter. She might claim to suffer from lasting psychological effects, nightmares, or fears of sexual intimacy with other men as a result of sexual coercion at the hands of a particular man. Such women reasonably seek the sorts of monetary damages individuals obtain in a variety of circumstances in which they feel injured by the behavior of another person.[22]

Yet women are also concerned with the micropolitical goals of education and deterrence. They need a chance to go back over the patriarchal sexual game plan so that they may point out exactly where a man has stepped out of bounds according to the new rules of civility. Only thus can they hope to ensure that a man who has mistreated them does not go on to treat other women similarly.[23] Indeed, substantive analysis of the harm of sexual coercion is more likely to occur in a tort proceeding than in a criminal trial. As Catharine MacKinnon points out, "The examination of tort shows that the law is quite accustomed to treating cloudy issues of motive and intent, the meaning of ambiguous acts, the effect of words on liability for acts, and the role of excessive sensitivity in determining liability and damages, all in a sexual context. These issues have arisen before. They have not been thought so subtle as to preclude a judicial resolution once a real injury was perceived to exist."[24] If our micropolitical goal is to rethink the sexual practices of normal men and women, renegotiating sexual transactions so as to embody notions of equality and respect for the sexual desires of each party, then civil lawsuits would seem to offer a better source of juridical support for this project than criminal lawsuits.[25]

While it might seem that neither date rape trials nor civil lawsuits have very much to do with most of our private sexual lives, symbolic legal and political controversies have proven very important in the process of changing norms of gendered behavior. The Hill-Thomas judiciary hearings provide only the most dramatic example of how a political incident can generate public discussion—in this case of sexual harassment—that both changes the level of societal awareness and creates a new site of social and legal contestation within everyday life. If it was a truism of 1970s feminism that the personal is political, it was a lesson of the 1980s that paradigmatically personal issues of reproduction or sexuality must receive public acknowledgment and generate public controversy before individual women can hope to make much headway in renegotiating these issues in their private lives. The ultra-personal and private quality of sexual relationships is entirely consistent with a need for public representation and dialogue as a foundation upon which individual women and men can rethink their sense of sexual agency and rework their sexual practices to better correspond with their current understandings of themselves and their relationships.

INTERPERSONAL STRATEGIES FOR SEXUAL CIVILITY

There are actually two very differently motivated groups of people interested in transforming our everyday patterns of sexual interaction. On the one hand, there are the feminists who deal with sexuality as yet another site of moral and political problems between men and women in a postfeminist era. While sexual coercion and assault are unremarkable features of patriarchal sexuality, feminists argue that a (Kantian) duty of reciprocal respect now provides the standard for male as well as female sexual civility. This paper was written from the perspective of this feminist orientation toward sexual practices.

On the other hand, there are the sex therapists who are concerned with enhancing our capacity for sexual pleasure and satisfaction. Treating sexuality as a complicated set of physical and psychological techniques through which we are capable of interacting with others, sex counselors offer us the hope of dramatically improving our sex lives by means of changing various aspects of our sexual behavior.

What seems clear is that neither perspective is fully adequate to the situation we face in this postfeminist moment. Many women readily identify with the moral and political analysis of feminists, insofar as it speaks to their growing sense of social and sexual entitlement and their corresponding impatience with men who fail to respond sympathetically to their efforts to articulate their own sexual desires. The husbands and sexual partners of these women are

likely to respond to the moral and political analysis of sexual relationships defensively; the new expectations and demands of their female partners may seem unfair and certainly confusing in the context of their previous sexual experiences and practices. The feminist moral and political critique of patriarchal forms of sexuality says very little about how to reconstruct sexual relationships in an egalitarian form.

Sex therapists, on the other hand, talk very explicitly about how to change sexual practices in order to enhance the pleasure of both partners within a sexual relationship. They focus on physical and psychological techniques by which both men and women can improve their own level of sexual satisfaction as well as that of their partners. Increasingly conscious of the differential qualities of female and male expectations and desires, they address the need for each partner in a heterosexual relationship to be concerned with these differences and suggest methods for exploring them as well as responding to them. Linking concern for one's partner with ideal sexual performance, men are persuaded to become more communicative and responsive to their partner's feelings and needs in the context of improving their sexual performance. Insofar as sex therapy encourages women to articulate and express their desires and teaches men to respond to these new female desires, it goes a good part of the way toward creating a dynamic of sexual civility.

But the discourse of sex therapy does not typically address issues of power and the asymmetrical notions of sexual entitlement that patriarchy teaches women and men. In fact, in acknowledging typical male and female sexual differences and teaching partners how to respond to each other in terms of these differences, sex therapy may reinforce stereotypically asymmetrical forms of male and female sexual agency. Thus women will feel empowered to express certain sorts of desires and not others; men will feel obligated to respond to certain needs and expectations of women, but not to others. Women may learn to accept certain desires and expectations on the part of men that they might have entered therapy wanting to criticize. For sex therapy, a good relationship will be achieved if there is good will and good communication between the partners. In some cases, a therapeutic program may encourage couples to create an egalitarian sexual relationship in which the partners fully realize all dimensions of the sexual agency and the norms of sexual civility are fully satisfied. In many cases, however, couples will learn the importance of becoming more responsive to the preexisting desires and expectations of their partners and may well become more satisfied with some variation on patriarchal sexual practices.

A postfeminist sexual counselor must appeal to the self-interest of both men and women, as sex therapists do in promising to improve a couple's sex life. However, they must also recognize the structural features of patriarchal power within typical sexual relationships and be committed to helping individuals reconfigure their notions of sexual agency in order to make a dynamic of sexual civility possible.

In this context, consider Antioch College's "Sexual Offense Prevention and Survivor's Advocacy Program," first proposed in the fall of 1990 in response to several sexual assaults and the agitation of women's groups for a serious college response to the problem. The sexual offense policy was a product of Antioch's unusual system of community governance whereby students, faculty, and administrators gather together weekly to resolve campus issues of significance. Although there are critics, the prevailing sentiment on campus at Antioch is supportive of the codification of standards of sexual behavior resulting from this democratic process.[26]

The Antioch policy stipulates the necessary consensual basis for all sexual contact. It specifies the meaning of *consent* in the following directives:

1. *Consent* shall be defined as the act of willingly and verbally agreeing to engage in specific sexual contact or conduct.
2. If sexual contact and/or conduct is not mutually and simultaneously initiated, then the person who initiates sexual contact/conduct is responsible for getting the verbal consent of the other individual(s) involved.
3. Obtaining consent is an ongoing process in any sexual interaction. Verbal consent should be obtained with each new level of physical and/or sexual contact/conduct in any given interaction, regardless of who initiates it. Asking "Do you want to have sex with me?" is not enough. The request for consent must be specific to each act.
4. The person with whom sexual contact/conduct is initiated is responsible to express verbally and/or physically her/his willingness or lack of willingness when reasonably possible.
5. If someone has initially consented but then stops consenting during a sexual interaction, she/he should communicate withdrawal verbally and/or through physical resistance. The other individual(s) must stop immediately.
6. To knowingly take advantage of someone who is under the influence of alcohol, drugs, and/or prescribed medication is not acceptable behavior in the Antioch community.[27]

It is all very well to talk about respecting the desires of one's partner in an abstract setting such as the therapist's office. The question is how one puts such a goal into practice. Given current confusions and conflicts about even our own sexual desires at any point in time, the idea of introducing verbal dialogue as a means of discovering the content of one's partner's desires seems quite reasonable. But how precisely are we to insert our words within a passion-filled sexual encounter? The norms of spontaneity and physical passion would seem to preclude verbal discussion as intrusive and unnecessary.

In requiring verbal consent for each new sexual initiative, the Antioch code has hit upon an ingenious way of unsettling the traditionally unspeakable dynamics of passionate sexual interaction, where grunts, groans, and gasps usually prevail. By requiring the verbal consent of the party not initiating the sexual act, the code forces the passive person to announce his or her conscious presence and to identify himself or herself as a particular sexual agent within the interaction. Just as a student must speak in class in order to develop a class identity, to speak in a sexual context surely involves creating an identity for oneself. Even the affirmative words of a woman appreciatively consenting to a particular sexual move will disrupt traditional patterns of wordless male initiation and female response. The woman's affirmative verbal response transforms the meaning of the physical interaction from one of asymmetrical sexual agency to one of dialectically expressed desire.

In mandating frequent verbal interaction between sexual partners, the Antioch code creates a communicative paradigm for sexual relationships, opening up discursive and psychic space for individual women and men to fluidly and passionately renegotiate the terms of the sexual relationship. Antioch students now emphasize "the importance of talking about sex," reporting that it "makes women more straightforward about what they want and men less preemptory in how they behave."[28] It is not difficult to imagine the appeal of such a policy on any college campus, where a large proportion of students are uncertain about their sexuality and concerned with finding how best to express themselves both inside and outside of sexual relationships.

The public response to the Antioch sexual offense policy was intensely negative, perhaps because of a fixation on its punitive features. While Antioch students see it as a helpful set of guidelines for sexual civility, it is easy to imagine those who are more settled in patterns of nonverbal sexual interaction reacting with fear at the thought of being required to learn new modes of communicative sexuality.[29] Indeed, if times were very different, we might have imagined Hillary Clinton supporting a sexual verbalization code as a part of a "politics of meaning," perhaps inserting the guidelines within a new single-payer health

coverage plan.[30] The fact is, of course, that this is not a time of progressive governmental visions and none of us is likely to find ourselves subject to guidelines for sexual civility in any imaginable future. Yet the popularity of books, videos, and all sources of advice about how to improve our sex lives indicates that a great many of us want to change aspects of our sexual relationships.[31] The Antioch sexual policy is valuable as a paradigm for communicative sexuality precisely insofar as it explicitly mandates verbal consent at every act of sexual initiation by one partner, thereby creating the behavioral structure for a "dialectic of desire" in which both partners necessarily take part.[32] If we can imagine the effects of a sexual code requiring verbal request and consent at the initiation of every sexual act, then we can surely reflect on the possible value of more dialogue, more points of verbally articulated desire and verbally articulated consent, and refusal or counterproposal within our own everyday sexual interactions.

ENDNOTES

1. See Patricia S. Mann, *Micro-Politics: Agency in a Postfeminist Era* (Minneapolis: University of Minnesota Press, 1994), for my (feminist) explanation for why we should think of this as a postfeminist era. In brief, I think we need to dramatically signal how much has changed in the thirty years since the beginning of second-wave feminism. The feminist movement has declined as a discrete cultural presence at the same time as gender-related conflicts and issues have gained a central place in our culture. We need to cast off our previous feminist identity as radical troublemakers, asserting a new identity as sophisticated and wise troubleshooters. We have a gendered analysis that will enable people to make sense of lives thrown into confusion by changing roles and relationships. We also have constructive moral and political suggestions for how to respond to the multiple, complex familial and workplace problems associated with the ongoing changes in gender roles.

2. In a recent discussion of the Hofstra University Philosophy Club (March 8, 1995), several male students maintained that we should also use

the term to refer to coercive forms of female sexual behavior, experienced by men as violations of their personal sense of respect.

3. Jane Gross, "Combatting Rape on Campus in a Class on Sexual Consent." *The New York Times,* September 25, 1993.

4. Patricia Martin and Robert A. Hummer, "Fraternities and Rape on Campus." *Gender and Society* (December 1989): 457–473.

5. Julie K. Ehrhart and Bernice R. Sandler, "Campus Gang Rape: Party Games?" Washington, D.C.: Association of American Colleges, 1985.

6. Martin and Hummer forestall easy solutions involving the banning of alcohol at fraternity parties, referring to evidence that shows that this "results in heavy drinking before coming to a party and an increase in drunkenness among those who attend"—potentially aggravating the problems for women.

7. *Gone with the Wind* is, of course, a film and a novel, rather than a real incident, as the other examples are. One aspect of postmodernism I agree with, however, is its tendency to blur the boundaries between narratives with real and fictional discursive status, at least in particular instances. See Patricia S. Mann, "On the Postfeminist Frontier." *Socialist Review* (Fall 1994), for a discussion of the contrasting virtues of real and fictional narratives for doing social theory.

8. See "Word for Word/A Scholarly Debate: Rhett and Scarlett: Rough Sex or Rape? Feminists Give a Damn," a pastiched presentation of an extended dialogue between Christina Hoff Sommers and Marilyn Friedman, *The New York Times*, Week in Review (Section 4), February 19, 1995.

9. This is not to say that philosophers have not recently broached the subject of sexual relationships. A flurry of articles evaluating sexual desire, sexual perversions, and so on appeared in the 1970s in response to the so-called "sexual revolution" and the feminist movement. See in particular Alan Soble's *Philosophy of Sex: Contemporary Readings* (Totowa, N.J.: Littlefield, Adams, 1980), a collection of articles from the *Journal of Philosophy, Philosophy and Public Affairs,* and *Ethics,* etc. See also Robert Baker and Frederick Elliston, eds., *Philosophy and Sex* (Buffalo: Prometheus Books, 1984).

Many of these accounts of sexuality build upon or react against the seminal existential analysis of modern sexuality by Jean-Paul Sartre, in Part III of *Being and Nothingness*, trans. Hazel Barnes (New York: Washington Square Press, 1966). While Sartre does gives a gendered account of sexual agency, he is not interested in a historical or even a normative analysis of the gendered feature of sexual agency. The analytic philosophers reject Sartre's normative vision of all agency as a project of transcendence and focus on alternative models of sexual relationships: as fulfilling goals of reproduction, love, pleasure, communication, and so on, the gendered quality of sexual *agency* dropping out of the picture.

10. Janice Moulton also emphasizes the "social nature of sexual behavior" and argues that sexual behavior should be evaluated by the social and moral standards of other social behavior. See Moulton's "Sexual Behavior: Another Position," *The Journal of Philosophy* 73, 16 (September, 1976); reprinted in Alan Soble, ed., *Philosophy of Sex* (Totowa, N.J.: Littlefield, Adams, 1980), pp. 116–117.

11. See Patricia S. Mann, *Micro-Politics: Agency in a Postfeminist Era,* where I analyze this transformation as a process of "social enfranchisement."

12. As Alan Goldman has pointed out, it should be intuitively obvious that a Kantian moral framework, calling for reciprocity within human relationships, may readily be extended to govern sexual activities, as well. See Goldman's "Plain Sex," *Philosophy and Public Affairs* 6, 3 (Spring 1977); reprinted in Alan Soble, ed., *Philosophy of Sex* (Totowa, N.J.: Littlefield, Adams, 1980), p. 132.

13. Deborah Rhode reports that "law review commentators throughout the 1950s and 1960s asserted that it was customary for a woman who desired intercourse to say 'no, no, no' while meaning 'yes, yes, yes'. Since it was always difficult in rape cases to determine whether the female really meant 'no', she should be required to convey her resistance by more than mere verbal protest, or such infantile behavior as crying."!! See Rhode's *Gender and Justice* (Cambridge: Harvard University Press, 1989), p. 247.

14. See Susan Brownmiller, *Against Our Will: Men, Women and Rape* (New York: Bantam, 1976); Rosemarie Tong, *Women, Sex, and the Law* (Totowa, N.J.: Rowman and Allanheld, 1984).

15. Deborah Rhode reports that between 10 and 15 percent of married women experience forcible sex with their husbands, and many suffer severe physical or psychological injuries as a conse-

quence. . . . Indeed, marital rape victims report more long-term injuries than women raped by strangers. See *Gender and Justice*, p. 250.

16. Deborah Rhode, *Gender and Justice*, p. 245.

17. Susan Estrich's *Real Rape* (Cambridge: Harvard University Press, 1987) is a powerful plea for such a broadening of rape laws.

18. See Robin Warshaw, *I Never Called It Rape* (New York: HarperCollins, 1988) for numerous case histories of young women's experiences of sexual assault.

19. As Catharine MacKinnon explains, "Sexual touching that women do not want has historically been considered tortious under a variety of doctrines, usually battery, assault, or, if exclusively emotional damage is done, as the intentional infliction of emotional distress. A battery is a harmful or offensive contact which is intentionally caused. While contact must be intentional, hostile intent, or intent to cause all the damages that resulted from the contact, is not necessary. . . . Battery, the actual touching, is often combined with assault, the fear of such a touching. The tort of assault consists of placing a person in fear of an immediate harmful or offensive contact. It is a 'touching of the mind, if not of the body.'" See MacKinnon's *Sexual Harassment of Working Women* (New Haven: Yale University Press, 1979), p. 165.

20. As Burt Neuborne, a professor at New York University Law School, said in commenting upon the Bowman-Smith case, the standard of proof "beyond a reasonable doubt" demanded for a criminal conviction makes an acquittal in date rape cases almost a foregone conclusion. (Private conversation with Neuborne, January 1991). By contrast, in a civil lawsuit the standard of proof is much lower, requiring a tort victim to demonstrate either by a "preponderance of the evidence" or with "clear and convincing evidence" that a wrong has been committed. In addition, as Eileen N. Wagner reports, "a criminal charge of rape usually requires proof of genital penetration, while the tort of battery requires only proof of 'offensive touching.'" Eileen F. Wagner, "Campus Victims of Date Rape Should Consider Civil Lawsuits as Alternatives to Criminal Charges or Colleges' Procedures." *The Chronicle of Higher Education*, August 7, 1991. See also Ann Russo, "An Unhealthy Climate for Women," in *Women's Review of Books* (February 1992), for a further discussion of some of the pros and cons of a civil suit.

21. See Chapter 5 of *Micro-Politics: Agency in a Post-feminist Era*, for my analysis of micropolitical agency.

22. I am aware that many people will be offended by the idea that women should seek monetary damages as the appropriate recompense for sexual assault. Such a procedure violates deeply felt beliefs about the spiritual and psychic significance of sexual encounters, particularly for women. The very idea of vindicating an act of sexual dishonor with monetary damages horrifies many women, for whom any exchange of money in relation to sex evokes images of prostitution rather than wrongful male sexual behavior. But such perceptions need to change; and if civil suits become common, they will change.

   Insofar as women seek juridical support for their efforts to reconfigure gendered sexual relationships, they need to develop a strategic sense of what often seems like a very personal struggle, in this case, accepting the political significance of an award of monetary damages in civil suits charging men with sexual assault.

23. Desiree Washington said that she was persuaded to take Mike Tyson to court when her parents asked her whether she could live with herself if Tyson attacked another woman. "I thought about it, and the answer was 'No'," she said. E. R. Shipp, "Tyson's Accuser Tells Jury of Assault." *The New York Times*, January 31, 1992.

24. Catharine MacKinnon, *Sexual Harassment of Working Women*, pp. 170–171. MacKinnon has strong arguments for why sexual harassment is a social injury involving workplace power relationships, which should be juridically treated as a form of sexual discrimination rather than as either a crime or a tort. But one of the distinctive features of coercive sexual behavior is precisely its privatized quality and the lack of any institutional context in which to embed the intimate interaction. MacKinnon is critical of the previous moralistic quality of sexual tort doctrines and discerningly points out that a corrective "ordinary woman" standard would need to be developed if contemporary women were to resort to sexual tort claims.

25. In a civil lawsuit, of course, the person who has been harmed sues the person who has committed the offense in order to recover monetary damages for the injuries he or she has incurred. To many people, however, the idea that a woman who has been the victim of date rape

could accept monetary damages as appropriate recompense for such an offense profanes deeply held notions of sexuality. It seems to violate traditional assumptions about the spiritual and psychic significance of sexual encounters for a woman to respond to an instance of sexual assault or coercion with such an impersonal, even crass sense of material redress. The very idea of vindicating an act of sexual dishonor with monetary damages horrifies many women. Yet I think that such a response reflects the coy and constrained way women have been taught to value their sexuality rather than the actual implications of a civil lawsuit. Like it or not, in our society money is the primary vehicle for representing value and also for revaluing resources and relationships when these are publicly contested. In nonsexual contexts, it is well understood that in suing for monetary damages one may be suing to vindicate personal or professional honor or to punish and deter actions of various immoral sorts.

Monetary damages are a primary token of fungible power relations within noncriminal legal discourses. Insofar as women seek juridical support for their efforts to reconfigure gendered sexual relationships, they may need to develop a strategic sense of what often seems like a very personal struggle and accept the political significance of an award of monetary damages in civil suits charging men with sexual assault.

26. See Jane Gross, "Combating Rape on Campus in a Class on Sexual Consent." *The New York Times*, September 25, 1993.

27. The Antioch College Sexual Offense Policy, p. 4. Document available through The Office of University Relations, Antioch University, Yellow Springs, Ohio 45387.

28. Ibid.

29. Clearly, for those who assume a standard Freudian image of the sexual scenario as solely a function of male sexual desire, the Antioch code can be understood as introducing infinite possibilities for a woman to say "no" to the normal progress of events. As one Antioch freshman reputedly wailed, "I'll never even get to kiss anyone." It thus appears to a Freudian as a cruel and repressive policy that will not even make women happy, insofar as they expect men to masterfully overcome their female fears about sex.

30. The notion of a "politics of meaning" originates with the social thinker Michael Lerner, whose views Hillary Clinton has briefly sought to incorporate into her visions of contemporary government.

31. Consider the books of John Gray: exploring differences in men's and women's language and sexual desires, the success of his two books appears an exemplary case of the sexual advice phenomenon. His first book, *Men Are From Mars, Women Are From Venus* (New York: HarperCollins, 1992) has sold over three million hardcover copies since publication, and remains No. 1 on the Advice, How-to and Miscellaneous lists of *The New York Times* (as of April 16, 1995). His second book, *Mars and Venus in the Bedroom* (New York: HarperCollins, 1995) sold 500,000 copies in its first two weeks in the bookstores.

32. See Lois Pineau, "Date Rape: A Feminist Analysis." *Law and Philosophy* 8 (1989), pp. 217–243. Pineau advocates "communicative sexuality as a norm for sexual encounters" in a legal context, explaining communication in terms of a "dialectics of desire."

Closing Questions

1. Why might the phrase "loose morals" refer specifically to loose morals in matters of sex? Might this not support Roger Scruton's claim that in matters of sex we are most aware of virtue and vice? If not, of what view is it evidence?

   _____

   _____

   _____

   _____

2. Which is more problematic? (1) your significant other (s.o.) having a meaningless one-time affair or (2) your s.o. having an ongoing Platonic relationship with a member of the opposite sex?

   _____

   _____

   _____

   _____

3. Is Christianity correct that one can commit "adultery in one's heart"? Consider in this context the remark of former President Jimmy Carter who, in an interview with *Playboy,* admitted that he had "lusted after women in his heart" and thereby committed adultery. (Query: Why did we not hold this against Jimmy Carter or alleged adulterer Bill Clinton, but held it against former presidential candidate Gary Hart?)

   _____

   _____

   _____

   _____

4. Is a person who copulates with a nonhuman animal sick, eccentric, or immoral? What are the implications of each?

   _____

   _____

   _____

   _____

5. Many heterosexual people view male homosexual sex as unnatural inasmuch as the male homosexual puts his genitals to a use for which they were not intended. The same people have no qualms about anal sex between consenting heterosexual adults. Is this consistent?

_____

_____

_____

_____

_____

6. Is sex something a person has as opposed to something a person does? What are the implications of referring to sex as something a person "has?"

_____

_____

_____

_____

7. Argue for or against prostitution.

_____

_____

_____

_____

8. What is wrong with having sex with children?

_____

_____

_____

9. In *Logic and Sexual Morality* (Baltimore: Penguin Books, 1965), John Wilson suggests that no morally relevant difference can be found between sex and other human activities. He says that the question "Will you have sex with me?" is no different from the question "Will you play tennis with me?" Is sex an activity that stands alone among all other human activities?

_____

_____

_____

_____

10. It has been said that blacks cannot be racists since they have traditionally not been politically enfranchised and only the politically enfranchised can be racists (which is not to deny that blacks can be
prejudiced against whites). Along the same line of thought, might
it be that women cannot be rapists (while not denying that women
can sexually attack men)?

_____

_____

_____

_____

11. Compare and contrast date rape with stranger rape. What are the
differences and how should you compare them morally?

_____

_____

_____

_____

12. Maintaining that date rape often occurs over a failure of communication, students at Antioch College instituted a sexual offense
policy specifying the necessity of verbal consent just prior to sexual
involvement. Do you support such a policy?

_____

_____

_____

_____

For Further Reading

Baker, Robert, and Frederick Elliston, eds. *Philosophy and Sex*, 2nd ed. Buffalo, N.Y.: Prometheus Books, 1984.

Bar On, Bat-Ami. "Violence Against Women: Philosophical Literature Overview and Biography." *American Philosophical Association Newsletter on Feminism and Philosophy* 88, 1 (1988): 8–13.

Bellioti, Raymond. *Good Sex: Perspectives on Sexual Ethics.* Lawrence: University of Kansas Press, 1993.

Curley, E. M. "Excusing Rape." *Philosophy and Public Affairs* 5 (1976): 325–360.

Foa, Pamela. "What's Wrong with Rape?" In M. Vetterling-Braggin, F. Elliston, and J. English, eds., *Feminism and Philosophy* (pp. 347–359). Totowa, N.J.: Littlefield, Adams, 1977.

Held, Virginia. "Coercion and Coercive Offers." In J. Roland Pennock and John W. Chapman, eds. *Coercion: Nomos* 14. Chicago: Aldine-Atherton, 1972.

Leiser, Burton. "Homosexuality and the 'Unnaturalness' Argument." In Burton Leiser, *Liberty, Justice, and Morals*, 3rd ed. New York: Macmillan, 1986.

Paglia, Camille. "Date Rape: Another Perspective." *Spin* 7, 6–7 (1991).

Pineau, Lois. "Date Rape: A Feminist Analysis." *Law and Philosophy* 8 (1989): 217–243.

Soble, Alan, ed. *The Philosophy of Sex.* Savage, Md.: Rowman & Littlefield, 1991.

Wasserstrom, Richard. "Is Adultery Immoral?" In Richard Wasserstrom, ed., *Today's Moral Problems.* New York: Macmillan, 1975, pp. 240–252.

Chapter 10

Ethics and Sports

Passages for Reflection

"It's not whether you win or lose, it's how you play
the game."

—*Unknown*

"Serious sport has nothing to do with fair play. It is bound up
with hatred, jealousy, boastfulness, disregard of all rules and
sadistic pleasure in witnessing violence: in other words it is
war minus the shooting."

—*George Orwell*

"Winning is not the most important thing; it's the
only thing."

—*Attributed to Vince Lombardi*

"Where have you gone Joe DiMaggio?, a nation turns its
lonely eyes to you."

—*Simon and Garfunkel*

Opening Questions

1. Should sports be accorded the importance assigned to it in North America?
2. Do athletes and sports fans put too much emphasis on winning and competition?
3. Do sports contain too much violence?

Sports play a significant role in the lives of people throughout the world. In America alone, 96.3 percent of the population plays, watches, or reads articles about sports or identifies with teams or players, and nearly 70 percent follow sports every day with 42 percent participating on a daily basis.[1] In most daily newspapers, the sports section is one of the two largest sections devoted to a single subject (business being the other), and some 135 million people watch the Super Bowl in a given year.

But despite the role that sports play in North America and other cultures, they have not attracted philosophical interest. With a few exceptions, there is a dearth of literature in "the philosophy of sport," and few philosophers pay it serious attention. This is curious inasmuch as philosophers usually heed the activities and phenomena that are central to a culture. Witness, in this regard, the philosophy of science, religion, art, and law—all established species of philosophy. It behooves us then, to ask why philosophy has ignored sports and investigate whether it might not profit by focusing on them.

We can only speculate on why philosophy has ignored sports, despite their pervasive appeal, while concentrating on science, religion, art, and law. History, unfortunately, will be of little help. Despite their evident enjoyment of athletics, the ancient Greeks do not provide reasons that explain this neglect. At most, we find occasional remarks by philosophers treating sport as an example of some larger point or as a metaphor for a greater concern. We don't find Plato, for example, writing a treatise on sports even though some of his dialogues, for example, *Lysis and Charmides,* take place in a gymnasium where people are trained as well as educated. In the *Republic* (411e, ff), we find Plato's Socrates emphasizing the importance of gymnastic training for a sound moral education and in the *Laws* (803c, ff), the Athenian Stranger praises sport as the pinnacle of human activity. Aristotle, at most, employs athletes only as examples for points he wishes to make.

---

[1] See the Miller Lite Report on American Attitudes toward sports as reported by George Vecsey, "A Nation of Sports Fans." *The New York Times* (March 16, 1983), p. B11.

Later in history—in the nineteenth and twentieth centuries—we find such thinkers as Nietzsche, Martin Heidegger, and Michel Foucault using sport as a metaphor for a larger point, although they use the term to refer more to the spontaneous play of children than to the rule-governed play of athletes.[2] Jean-Paul Sartre uses a description of skiing to clarify his distinction between "being," "doing," and "having,"[3] and Ludwig Wittgenstein uses the notion of "game" if not "sport" in order to explain how language operates.[4] But we rarely find philosophers analyzing sports for their own sake the way they have analyzed other institutions.

The best guess why philosophers have ignored sports as a philosophical topic is that philosophy has historically been perceived as elitist whereas sports have historically been perceived as vulgar. Even today, the stereotypical philosopher is perceived to be someone perched in an ivory tower contemplating the meaning of life, while the stereotypical sports fan is perceived as a beer-guzzling, blue-collar jock. Add to this that athletes have never been renowned for their academic achievements and what results is a practical contradiction.

In my graduate school days at Columbia University, I recall trying to hide the fact that I was an avid sports fan for fear that my love for sports would be perceived as inconsistent with my love for philosophy. How surprised and happy I was to learn that the professor I most admired, Sidney Morgenbesser, was an avid baseball fan. Not far from the portrait of John Dewey was a photograph of Sidney on first base at the annual faculty-student softball game. Then again, he was smoking a pipe.

The following comment by Isocrates is typical of the contempt aristocrats have traditionally had for athletes:

> Although in natural gifts and in strength of body he [Alcibiades] was inferior to none, he disdained gymnastic contests, for he knew some of the athletes were of low birth, inhabitants of petty states and of mean education, but turned to the breeding of race horses, which is possible only for the most blest by Fortune and not to be pursued by one of low estate.[5]

The implication of this passage is that sports is beneath the cultivated and genteel aristocrat for whom philosophy and such disciplines alone are

---

[2]See Chapter 5 of Drew Hyland's *The Question of Play* (Lanham, Md.: University Press of America, 1984).

[3]Jean-Paul Sartre, *Being and Nothingness*, translated by Hazel Barnes (New York: Philosophical Library, 1956), p. 580 ff.

[4]Ludwig Wittgenstein, *Philosophical Investigations*, translated by G. E. M. Anscombe (New York: Macmillan, 1953), Part I.

[5]*Isocrates*, Vol. 3, translated by LaRue Van Hook, Loeb Classical Library (Cambridge, Mass., 1961), in "Concerning the Team of Horses," pp. 194–195.

worthy. Obviously, Isocrates never saw the likes of Michael Jordan or Wayne Gretsky whose performances are poetry in motion.

But whether or not the perceived vulgarity of sports turns out to be the reason for its neglect by the philosophical community, it remains to be seen whether sport can serve as a topic of philosophical interest. Certainly, sports raise a host of interesting ethical issues: at the collegiate level, sports are afflicted with recruiting scandals involving submission of falsified transcripts, under-the-table payments, and cheating on entrance examinations; at the professional level, the athletes that once served as role models are spoiled and overpaid, often arrested for narcotics use, and are frequently racist and sexist. Focusing on sports, then, can provide us with a fertile field for ethical inquiry. To cite one example, they can give us a forum for which we can ask whether drug tests violate a right to privacy. Beyond this, if there is truth to the saying that sports are a microcosm of society, then the values present in sports may well reflect the values of society.[6] Because of its more circumscribed nature, sports can offer us a focused look at such problems that afflict us on a larger scale, how they've been perpetuated, and how they might be overcome.

Presumably, sports that emphasize such values as teamwork, industriousness, courage, and self-discipline tell us something about the values of the society in which these sports take place. So, too, do sports that emphasize winning at all costs, willingness to hurt others in pursuit of victory, lying, and cheating. For this reason, it would be reasonable to expect that the teams and athletes we admire most shed light on the values of our society. Before he was banished from baseball on account of his association with illegal gambling, we admired baseball star Pete Rose for his work effort in spite of his less than extraordinary athletic ability. We admire Jack Nicklaus for his integrity on the golf course and tennis star Billy Jean King for her grit and determination. At the same time, we look disdainfully at former Oakland Raider cornerback Jack Tatum who tried to injure opponent players and succeeded in paralyzing Patriots pass receiver Daryl Stingley. We also abhor figure skater Tonya Harding for having orchestrated the attack on Nancy Kerrigan just prior to the 1994 Olympics; the shooting death of Andres Escobar in Columbia's 1994 World Cup loss to the United States; track star Ben Johnson's use of anabolic steroids; and Brian Hunter's malicious attempt to injure Pierre Turgeon of the New York Islanders during the 1993 Stanley Cup Playoffs. The list goes on. What is important, here, is to recognize that the values in sports reflect the values of the society of which they are a part. For this reason, an examination of sports promises to be valuable for ethics.

---

[6]Robert Simon, for one, argues against the view that sports reflect the values of society. See *Fair Play: Sports, Values, and Society* (Boulder, Col.: Westview Press, 1991) Chap. 8.

Small wonder, then, that Albert Camus once remarked that it was in sports that he learned all that he ever really knew about ethics.[7]

Assuming, then, that sports serve as a microcosm of the society of which they are a part, and that sports reflect the values therein, it comes as no surprise that the most pressing issue in the world of sports is whether professional athletes deserve the million-dollar salaries they have come to expect. In what is largely a laissez-faire capitalistic society, questions of economics naturally occupy center stage in the world of contemporary professional sports.

Professional sports in the 1990s has been distinguished by the unprecedented player strikes in professional baseball and hockey. The 1994 baseball season marked the first time in the history of professional sports that a championship game—the World Series—was interrupted by a work stoppage, and the 1994–95 hockey season was in jeopardy of being canceled before it started were it not for frenzied eleventh-hour negotiating. As purists who lament the situation note, not even World War II was able to accomplish what player and management greed had achieved: an unprecedented strike that lasted more than eight months. Without taking sides with the players or management, let us ask whether professional athletes deserve the enormous salaries that they have come to earn or whether the owners are justified in asking to impose a salary cap.

It is no secret that top professional sports stars receive far more in salary than professors, scientists, nurses, and even the president of the United States. The average salary of a professional baseball player in America is $1.2 million. How do we decide whether professional athletes are entitled to salaries that are largely disproportionate to the salaries of others? Is superior athletic ability sufficient to entitle them to greater rewards than others? One answer to this question is provided by Harvard philosopher Robert Nozick whose *Anarchy, State, and Utopia* is a contemporary classic on the topic of distributive justice and whose famous "Wilt Chamberlain" example cries out for inclusion in this discussion.

According to Nozick, people are entitled to all the things they have acquired without resorting to force, theft, and fraud. This is true even if some people have acquired substantially more than others. Imagine, says Nozick, that society has already been set up in such a way that the goods therein are distributed according to some preferred pattern of justice, say, the principle of equality (to each person equally.) Suppose further that a talented athlete, such as former basketball great Wilt Chamberlain (substitute Shaquille O'Neill, if you wish), sets up a series of games where, according to a contract he has negotiated (fairly), he is to get $.25 out of every $1.00 paid for admissions. Suppose that a mil-

---

[7]Albert Camus, "The Wager of Our Generation." In *Resistance, Rebellion, and Death,* translated by Justin O'Brien (New York: Vintage Books, 1960), p. 242.

lion people pay $1.00 each to see Wilt play and, as a result, Wilt ends up $25,000 richer, with each spectator ending up $1.00 poorer. Obviously, the pattern of justice is shattered. Instead of each person in society possessing an equal amount of money, some have more than others. Should something be done about this? Should we insist that Wilt return his wealth so that our pattern of justice can be realized? Nozick thinks not.

> The general point illustrated by the . . . example . . . is that no . . . distributional patterned principle of justice can be continually realized without continuous interference with people's lives. . . . To maintain a pattern one must either continually interfere to stop people from transferring resources as they wish to, or continually (or periodically) interfere to take from some persons resources that others . . . wish to transfer to them.[8]

For Nozick, then, people are entitled to the possessions they acquire provided they come upon them fairly. To deprive an individual of what he or she rightfully earns is an unjust deprivation of liberty. And this is true even if some, like Wilt Chamberlain, earn significantly more than others. Generalizing from this case, Nozick's position is that if professional athletes obtain salaries that are obscene by conventional standards, we should not be troubled provided they earn them fairly. And this is true even if individuals exist who barely earn enough money to feed and clothe themselves. What should trouble us, as Nozick sees it, is if the Wilt Chamberlains of the world are coerced through taxation into providing for those who cannot provide for themselves.

John Rawls's *A Theory of Justice* (to which Nozick's view is a response) provides an alternative view. Rawls is concerned with deriving principles of justice from a hypothetical consideration of the moral principles that self-interested and rational people would choose to regulate the practices of their society. Realizing that self-interested people seeking to maximize their own interests would never agree on any specific principles, Rawls insists that choice of such principles be made under a "veil of ignorance" in which the people are ignorant of their particular mental and physical attributes, tastes, values, and social status. He argues that behind such a veil, rational and self-interested people would agree that:

1. Each person is to have an equal right to the most extensive basic liberty compatible with a similar liberty for others.
2. Social and economic inequalities are to be arranged so that they are both (a) reasonably expected to be to everyone's advantage, and (b) attached to positions and offices open to all.[9]

---

[8]Robert Nozick, *Anarchy, State, and Utopia* (New York: Basic Books, 1974), p. 238.

[9]John Rawls, *A Theory of Justice* (Cambridge, Mass.: Harvard University Press, 1971), p. 60.

What Rawls is saying can be explained as follows. Suppose we were concerned with establishing a society in accordance with fair and just principles. One way to do this is to stipulate that everyone receive equal amounts of power, wealth, and other resources. Those who already are in a position of power and wealth will no doubt object to this since they would have much to lose, just as those who are impoverished or marginalized have much to gain. Because of such biases, Rawls insists that we formulate our principles ignorant of the place we will occupy in our society. He also insists—and this is vital for our analysis—that we formulate our principles of justice ignorant of the talents and abilities (including athletic ones) that are indicators of our ability to flourish.

Rawls writes: "It seems to be one of the fixed points of our considered judgments that no one deserves his place in the distribution of native endowments, any more than one deserves one's initial starting place in society."[10] By this, Rawls is saying that we do not "deserve" the talents we are born with or the environment we are born into since our talents and skills are not of our making. That Nolan Ryan had the good fortune of being able to throw a baseball faster and more accurately than I can hardly serves as the basis for claiming that he deserves more money. For this reason, Rawls insists that in the "original position," we operate from behind a veil of ignorance where we are denied knowledge of our talents, skills, and social status, as well as any other of our abilities to flourish. This will ensure that the principles we settle on will be fair and impartial.

Given the conditions that attach to the original position, Rawls contends that we will be conservative and that we will secure for ourselves the highest minimum payoff. But he also thinks we would realize that such a society would not be greatly efficient and that we could increase efficiency by rewarding people for their talents and skills. According to the second principle of justice, such unequal rewards would be justified if they were to everyone's advantage and then under conditions of equal opportunity. (Rawls says elsewhere that the principle would be satisfied provided the "worst-off" members of society benefited.) In our hypothetical society, it would not be unjust, say, if physicians were allowed to earn greater salaries than nonphysicians (provided that everyone has an equal opportunity to become a physician), since it is to everyone's advantage that there be physicians. For Rawls, then, justice is finally "an agreement to regard the distribution of natural talents as a common asset and to share in the benefits and burdens of this distribution whatever it turns out to be. Those who have been favored by nature, whoever they are, may gain from their good fortune only on terms that improve the situation of those who have lost out."[11]

---

[10]Ibid., p. 104.

[11]Ibid., p. 101.

It follows that, for Rawls, professional athletes deserve their inequitable salaries only on the condition that the institutions and practices that generate such inequalities (including professional sports itself) operate for the benefit of the disadvantaged and there is equal opportunity to become a professional athlete. So whether the salaries of professional athletes are deserved is, like the salaries of anyone, a question to be decided against the backdrop of our social institutions.

We are left to ask, "Who is right, Nozick or Rawls?" The question is a large one, but we can make a few remarks. Critics of Nozick will point out that there is something heartless about professional athletes earning exorbitant salaries while there are individuals who fail to live minimally decent lives through no fault of their own. As Peter Singer has pointed out, "If it is within our power to prevent something bad from happening, without thereby sacrificing anything of comparable moral importance, we ought, morally, to do it."[12] Certainly, the Wilt Chamberlains of the world (and the Derrick Colemans, Steffi Grafs, Mark Messiers, and Barry Bonds) could well afford to prevent people from starving without running the risk of starving themselves and because of that should do their share to alleviate hunger and starvation. On the other hand, adherents of Nozick's position will argue that implementing a policy such as Singer's would require an interference with liberty no less evil than the evil it is designed to eliminate.

Critics of Rawls will argue that on the premise that natural talent is an undeserved asset to be shared by members of his society, we might as well infer that those with natural talents be handicapped to make up for their natural abilities.[13] This way, we could ensure equality and fairness. Other critics of Rawls argue that if natural talent is an undeserved asset, then so is the possession of bodily organs. Just as it is absurd to require individuals to keep their healthy organs only if doing so favors the least advantaged members of society, it is absurd to require athletes to regard their talents and abilities as common assets.

Beyond the important question for social justice, "Who is right, Nozick or Rawls?", I have tried to show that sports reflects the values of the broader culture, in this case, its preoccupation with the acquisition of wealth. Some may object that issues of wealth are outside the purview of sports and only incidentally related to sports per se. Those who would make this objection should be reminded that we have been speaking of sports insofar as they have been *professionalized.* This makes contemporary sports as much a business as it is a game. The more complicated answer comes from Marxists who see sports as reflecting the worst of

---

[12]Peter Singer, "Famine, Affluence, and Morality." *Philosophy and Public Affairs* 1, 3 (Spring 1972).

[13]See John Wilson, *Equality* (New York: Harcourt, Brace and World, 1966), pp. 73–74.

capitalistic society: the alienation supposedly endemic to capitalistic competition; the self-degradation in the name of "beating" an opponent; the mindless obedience to authority; the willingness to hurt others; and so on. Some Marxists have gone so far as to claim that sports would vanish in a universalistic communist society.[14]

Noneconomic issues also pervade sports and reflect the values of the larger society. Racism, for instance, is a problem in professional sports no less than in society at large. When blacks were segregated from whites in the greater American society, they were segregated in sports as well. When segregation became outlawed in the larger society, the same was true in professional sports. And just as the end of segregation did not mean the end of racism in society, it did not mean this in sports either. In addition to a dearth of blacks in coaching and management positions, sports had has its fill of racial incidents. Witness, in this regard, the Jimmy the Greek and Al Campanis incidents. Jimmy "the Greek" Snyder and Al Campanis were influential sports figures guilty of making racist remarks.

There are other ethical issues in sports which we have not even touched: questions concerning competition itself; sports-specific issues such as the ethics of boxing; and questions of interest for virtue theory such as whether athletes should serve as role models. Given what we have supposed to be the relationship between sports and society, an analysis of such issues promises to be interesting and enlightening. It also promises to be practically valuable to the extent that sports teach and endorse the values they recommend.

---

[14]See Jean-Marie Brohm, *Sport: A Prison of Measured Time* (London: Ink Links Press, 1978), p. 52.

Howie Rose is a professional sportscaster, and television announcer for the New York Mets and for the New York Islanders.

Kathleen Pignatelli is Professor of Physical Education at Bergen Community College and coach of its women's softball team. She received her Master's degree in education from the University of Illinois.

Video Presentation

Guests: Howie Rose, Television Announcer for the New York Mets and for the New York Islanders (Sports Channel, New York)

Kathleen Pignatelli, Professor of Physical Education, Bergen Community College

Student Panel: Deborah Schader, Farris Rabah, Andrew Leight

This video differs from others inasmuch as it is one hour long instead of the usual half hour, includes footage from an earlier interview with Howie Rose at WFAN studio in New York City, and includes the participation of the student panel throughout the discussion. We begin with a general discussion of the nature of ethics, after which I ask Coach Pignatelli what she thinks the major ethical issues are in sports. After briefly discussing the saying, "It's not whether you win or lose, it's how you play the game," I ask Howie Rose (via tape) to comment on a remark cited by *Newsday* reporter Steve Jacobson (who himself was quoting a sports psychologist) that "whereas for athletes, the real world takes place within the foul lines, it takes place outside the foul lines for the rest of us." Rose agrees with this observation and remarks how athletes are coddled from birth, giving them unrealistic expectations of their value to society. He points out how colleges sometimes provide money, cars, and women in order to keep their male athletes happy, and that this plays a significant role in the formation and corruption of the athlete's character. I then discuss with Pignatelli and the student panel the extent to which we are guilty of corrupting the athlete.

Having agreed that we do deify our athletes, I ask Rose whether the media oversteps its bounds in scrutinizing the private lives of our athletes. Howie's answer is that the private lives of professional athletes are no business of the fan and are therefore beyond the purview of the media's concerns. Pignatelli disagrees, maintaining that, as public figures, professional athletes should be held to a higher standard of conduct, whereas Andrew Leight thinks that what an athlete does on the field is all that matters. After suggesting that the distinction between public and private may not make much sense, Pignatelli reiterates her position, drawing an analogy between professional athletes and teachers: just as we want to know whether our children's teachers are engaged in unsavory behavior outside of class, we want to know if our athletes are doing the same thing since they inevitably serve as role models for our youth. This occasions a larger discussion of whether athletes should serve as role models.

The discussion turns to the question of whether professional athletes deserve the exorbitant salaries that they have come to command. Maintaining that this is a purely economic issue, Howie Rose insists that what a team pays its players is its own business so long as the team stays solvent. I suggest, to the contrary, that the issue transcends economics inasmuch as desert might finally be measured by contribution to society. Waxing nostalgic, we compare today's players with those of a time gone by.

The next issue we consider is racism in sports. Rose thinks that racism exists but that it is no more prevalent in sports than elsewhere. Deborah Schader agrees and suggests that if we are more attuned to racism in sports it is only because we are more aware of what goes on in sports than of what goes on in boardrooms of major corporations. Pignatelli suggests that sports can go a long way toward alleviating racism as they often require cooperation in the service of success that forces teammates to view one another as people. She mentions the film *Brian's Song* to illustrate this.

Our discussion of racism leads, finally, to a discussion of sexism which occasions further discussion about Mike Tyson's criminal conviction for rape and the allegations of sexual harassment against members of the New York Mets in the early 1990s. Against the backdrop of the Mets case,

I ask Rose to comment on whether male athletes use their status to take advantage of women, or whether women use the threat of sexual harassment to take advantage of male athletes. Without explicitly answering my question, he relates a personal incident involving himself, former New York Mets star Keith Hernandez, and a cluster of "groupies" who were a nuisance to both him and Hernandez. Deborah and Andrew concur with Rose and insist that male athletes are exploited by female groupies at least as much as female groupies are exploited by male athletes. The show concludes with conversation about women in the men's locker room (including the time some members of the New England Patriots made obscene gestures at reporter Lisa Olsen) and whether the need exists for greater female participation in sports.

In this article, written expressly for this book, noted sports ethics authority W. M. Brown critiques several of the arguments often made to resolve the controversy over the use of performance drugs in sports. After carefully distinguishing recreational drugs, such as cocaine, from performance drugs, such as anabolic steroids, Brown maintains that much of the controversy over drug use in sports centers on the public's failure to distinguish between athletes using recreational drugs outside of sports as opposed to their using performance drugs within sports. Having made that distinction, Brown considers the arguments for and against the use of performance drugs in sports. While not antagonistic to their use, he argues for a more critical examination of their use relative to how we understand what it means to flourish in sports.

As American as Gatorade and Apple Pie: Performance Drugs and Sports

W. M. Brown

As long as people have played at sports they have tried to develop their skills and capacities with all the means at their disposal.[1] In recent years, public discussion of such efforts has focused on the use of performance-enhancing drugs, in part because we are caught up in a quagmire of issues relating to illegal drug use, and in part because we are perplexed by ethical and practical issues relating to developments in biotechnology. Our sports have changed and our attitudes toward them and the athletes who perform in them are undergoing similar changes. By and large, the controversies over professionalism and race in sport are over, those over sex and gender are passing, but the controversy over performance drugs is unresolved.

This paper is a critique of a number of arguments that are frequently made to resolve that controversy by showing why performance drugs should be forbidden to all athletes participating in organized sports such as amateur and professional leagues and international competitions like the Olympic Games. The arguments have moral as well as practical aspects, focusing as they do on athletes' rights and principles of liberty or of avoiding harm. Surprisingly, perhaps, one of the most curious aspects of the controversy is what people mean when they argue about drugs in sports.

One reason for this is that much of the notoriety of drug use in sports is related to athletes' use of recreational drugs: cocaine, alcohol, and tobacco, for example. Few of these drugs are thought by anyone to enhance athletic performance. Indeed, aside from the illegality of some of them, they are deplored because they diminish one's skills and produce aberrant behavior on and off the playing fields. Another reason is that many of the substances used to enhance athletic performance are not usually thought of as drugs at all, for example an athlete's own blood, or hormones, or widely used food products like caffeine or sugar. And finally, there is puzzlement over the availability of synthetically produced substances that naturally occur in the human body such as testosterone, human growth hormone, and erythropoietin which have widespread therapeutic uses and even uses for otherwise healthy individuals coping with the processes of aging.[2]

But having mentioned a few, I will not catalogue the list of substances that are used to enhance athletic performance or seek to define them.[3] The issues I will discuss cut across such lists and concern more general views about fairness, health, consensus, autonomy, and the nature of sports as they are brought to bear on the practice of enhancing athletic performance. Nor will the arguments I will consider hinge on the effectiveness of such substances. No one really knows whether many of these products are effective at all or in what ways or with what risks. Virtually no serious major studies of their use by athletes have been made, and most of our evidence is speculative and anecdotal, extrapolated from very different contexts or reported by journalists. So I will assume that some performance drugs are effective and some are not, that some are risky and some are safe, and proceed to explore what conclusions we can reach about their use by athletes.

1. FAIRNESS

Perhaps the most frequently cited issue concerning drugs and sports is that of fairness. The claim is that taking "performance drugs" is a form of cheating, that it is therefore fundamentally unfair. After all, if some athletes are using something that gives them a decisive advantage, it is argued, it is unfair to the basic premise of competition in sports (whether competition against present opponents or competition for records). Competition in sports (as opposed to competition in love and war) assumes some basic similarities among all participants so that contests are close and, therefore, both bring out the best in the competitors and are exciting to watch. Such a situation also, it is claimed (rightly, it seems to me), makes it more likely that the contest will be won in the margin where various factors come into play that are dear to our traditions: effort, will, determination, fortitude, and courage, among others.

And it is true: when an athlete breaks the rules, such as those banning the use of performance drugs, that is clearly a form of cheating, and its practice introduces an aspect of unfairness into the sport. But in an important way this argument misses the point. The ethical issue we are addressing is precisely that of the value of such rules, of the wisdom or justification of prohibiting the use of performance drugs. It therefore begs the question to stress that such drugs are forbidden and so it is wrong to use them.

There is a version of this argument that

seems to acknowledge this point, but goes on to claim that when some athletes use drugs and others do not (for whatever reason other than that they are banned), an inequality is introduced that renders competition unfair, not because of any cheating, but because of the discrepancy in performance that drug use may introduce. The short answer to this argument is that there are always likely to be differences among athletes (even if they are clones) and that these differences are (to mention a particular sport) what makes for horse racing. Without them, sports competition would surely hold little interest for us. Competition would resemble the predicament of Buridan's ass with unresolveable stalemates or contests won by random chance.

A more persuasive version of this argument is to note that in highly competitive sports where there are many pressures from family, coaches, teammates, managers, and owners, there can be no free choice to use performance drugs. At best it is a subtle form of coercion, a "forced choice," that produces for some athletes an unhappy dilemma: don't compete or take drugs.[4] We can acknowledge the crucial premise that individual autonomy is a central value. (Indeed, it is one I will employ frequently.) The additional factual premise that no one can be expected to withstand such pressures is more problematic. For one thing, it is clear that although many athletes now use performance drugs, many do not, and the latter are among the finest and most successful athletes now performing. But for another, every innovation or change in training, techniques, and equipment places similar pressure on athletes to adopt the changes or lose a competitive edge (assuming also that the changes are really effective in enhancing performance). The charge of coercion hinges on the prior assumption that the choice to use performance drugs is deeply objectionable and therefore many people would not want to use them. Of course, if their use is illegal or harmful, many athletes will be reluctant to use them. So athletes who choose not to use drugs are at an unfair advantage only if there is a good reason not to use them. And that, of

course, is just the issue at stake. But these reasons need to be assessed. Someone might complain that he can be a boxer only if competitors are allowed to punch the head, and since that is very dangerous, he is unfairly forced to choose between boxing and getting his head punched (and punching others in the head) or not competing at all. The wise choice may be to switch to swimming, but the choice is not in any interesting sense coerced.

The argument can be changed, however, to make a different point, and this refinement involves noting that sports are often segregated into classes by such things as age, sex, and weight. In this form, the argument deserves a separate consideration, and I return to it in section 6.

In the discussion to follow, various additional arguments concerning the use of performance drugs are examined to assess their cogency and persuasiveness.

2. HEALTH

Performance drugs are dangerous, so this argument goes, and banning their use is a way of protecting athletes from their own ill-conceived acts. The danger lies in the injuries that the use of performance drugs may cause. Recently, this case has been made most vociferously in regard to anabolic steroids, the drug of choice for athletes seeking to increase muscle mass useful for various sports ranging from football to track to gymnastics. But many other drugs are also available, including beta-blockers, growth hormones, and food ingredients such as caffeine; presumably the argument can be made in regard to them as well.

There are, however, two issues that need to be separated in this regard. One is an empirical issue concerning the actual harms likely to be caused by performance drug use. The other is the ethical issue of paternalism, the justification of restricting the actions of others ostensibly for their own good. A byproduct of this argument is what appears to be a remarkable case of hypocrisy.

As for the first issue, there is some evidence that the use of some performance drugs carries risks of injury to the users. But the evidence is remarkably sparse and, of course, differs for different drugs. Much of it is anecdotal—the lore of boxing and weight-lifting aficionados, the stuff of locker room banter. Such research-based evidence as is available is often inconclusive. Some studies suggest that steroids are effective in enhancing performance; others claim that is no significant enhancing effect.[5] Athletes tend to discount the extreme claims of risk of injury because their own experience has not confirmed them; and much of the research evidence has been based not on studies of efforts to enhance athletic performance but rather on cases of medical therapy and extrapolation to nonmedical circumstances. What this suggests is that the factual claims concerning performance drugs remain significantly unsubstantiated both in regard to drug risks and in regard to performance enhancement.[6] The sensible thing to do would surely be to find out who is right by encouraging careful and competent research into both kinds of claims.[7]

But this would not be the end of it. It seems likely that some substances or procedures would be relatively dangerous and others relatively risk-free; some would be relatively effective, others ineffective. In this case, it could be argued that dangerous ones especially should be carefully used, if effective, to eliminate or minimize their side effects, but that all performance drugs should be studied and the results be widely and publicly available to athletes and their coaches and physicians.[8] The goal should be to eliminate or reduce the likelihood of harm to athletes, as it is for other risks in sport.

A brief comment is in order about relative risk. In many sports, the activities of the sports themselves are far more dangerous than the use of any of the performance drugs that have even a bare chance of being effective. Deaths and injuries due to the use of performance drugs are rare.[9] Scarcely more than a dozen deaths are noted by some authorities, and most of these can be attributed not to performance drugs, but to recreational drugs like cocaine and alcohol used off the playing fields

and unconnected to competitive efforts.[10] But deaths and serious injuries due to the sports themselves number in the hundreds in sports like football, boxing, mountain climbing, hockey, cycling, and skiing.[11] Where the sports themselves are far more dangerous than anything risked by using performance drugs, one can only wonder at the hypocrisy that prompts the extraordinary tirades directed at the latter but seldom at the former. The most vociferous criticism of performance drugs seems far more closely linked to our national hysteria about illicit drugs in general than to the health of our athletes.[12]

Still, if we assume that there are dangers in using performance drugs, and clearly there are some even if their use is monitored by knowledgeable physicians, should we prohibit them on the grounds that athletes cannot be expected to make rational choices about their use and hence are at risk of excessive injury to their health? I have argued elsewhere that child athletes should be prohibited on paternalistic grounds from using such drugs.[13] But the issue is not so clear with adult athletes. Unlike airline pilots or subway train drivers, for example, athletes who use performance drugs pose no obvious dangers to others. Nor are the drugs in question related to diminished performance, but rather to enhanced and improved performance. So concerns about athletes' health are paternalistic in the strong sense of being directed not toward preventing harm to others, but to the drug users themselves. There often seems to be a discrepancy between concerns about athletes' health and safety in general and concerns about risks of using performance drugs. In any case, one could equally well argue that making their use safer while preserving the autonomy and freedom of choice of the athletes is a far preferable approach. If there are effective performance-enhancing drugs (and there seem to be some), and if they are or could be relatively safe to use (and some are), then the health argument, as I have called it, seems ineffective as a general argument against their use.

One final note. Hormonal supplements for healthy adults are not a new item in the pharmacopoeia. More recently men and women are being given sex hormones and growth hormone supplements to offset the effects of aging, apparently with favorable results.[14] Women have taken estrogen for years to offset the effects of menopause. The World Health Organization is currently administering steroids as a male contraceptive in doses greater than those said to have been used by Ben Johnson when he was disqualified after his victory at the Seoul Olympics.[15] It is hard to argue in light of such practices that the use of performance drugs, even the most risky kinds, including steroids, should have no place in the training or performance of athletes.

3. NATURALNESS AND NORMALITY

The argument shifts at this point, therefore, to the claim that performance drugs are unnatural additives to the athlete's training or performance regimen. Even if their careful use is relatively harmless, the argument goes, they are objectionable because they are artificial and unnatural additives to sporting activities. There are two versions of this argument. One is that it is the drugs that are unnatural; the other is that it is the athletes who use them who are unnatural or abnormal.

The first version is the less plausible. The reason is that many of the drugs used to enhance performance are as natural as testosterone, caffeine, or an athlete's own blood.[16] True, some drugs are the product of manufacturing processes or are administered using medical technologies. But, of course, so are many of our foods, vitamins, and medicines, all routine parts of the athlete's regimen. If by *natural* one means not artificially synthesized or processed, or known to occur in nature independent of human intervention, few of the nutritional and medical resources available to athletes today would be allowed. Performance drugs, therefore, cannot be identified or forbidden under this rubric without taking many things we find indispensable down the drain with them.

The claim for abnormality may be a bit stronger. After all, to the extent that perfor-

mance drugs work effectively at all, they are designed to render their users superior in ability and rates of success beyond what we would expect otherwise. And this, the argument concludes, renders them abnormal. Of course, this is in one sense true. If normality is defined in terms of statistical frequencies, then highly effective athletes are abnormal by definition. Such people are already abnormal if compared with the rest of us; their reflexes, coordination, neuromuscular development, and fitness levels already place them far to the right on the bell-shaped curves showing the range of human capacities and performance. Performance drugs are scarcely needed to place them among the abnormal, that is, the statistically rare individuals who can run a mile under 3:50, accomplish a gymnastic routine, slam dunk a basketball, or climb Mt. Everest without canisters of extra oxygen. Looked at another way, however, athletes are probably the most natural components of their sports; their efforts reveal to all of us various ranges of human abilities as currently manifested under the very artificial and unnatural constraints of our present-day sports and their assortment of bats, balls, rules, shoes, training techniques, and ideologies.

Surely, however, those who make this argument know this. Perhaps they are using the word *abnormal* in its other sense of connoting what is bad or undesirable, and since they can't quite articulate what is so bad about performance drugs, they rely on the claim of abnormality or unnaturalness to carry the weight of their condemnation. Here again, then, we need to move on to other arguments that may make the case more substantively and effectively, or at least make clearer what it is about the use of performance drugs that seems to some critics so deplorable.

4. ROLE MODELS

Athletes, especially professional athletes, are among the most widely publicized figures in Western societies and often in other countries as well. The reasons for this are many, but some are fairly obvious. Athletes are young, extraordinarily gifted in their physical abilities, and display the grace and power, and sometimes wealth, that many others may wish to share. For this reason they are often featured in commercial and nationalistic promotions as well. Given this prominence, sports figures easily become "role models" for others who seek to emulate their careers and behavior. This argument capitalizes on the social prominence of some athletes to claim that the use of performance drugs by them will be copied by others, especially young people, to their great detriment.[17]

I have some sympathy for this claim. There is some evidence for harmful use by adolescent male body builders of steroids especially. And it may be that publicized cases of professional athletes and others using such drugs effectively has encouraged this behavior. But there has also recently been a strong critical reaction to the status of athletes as role models. By far the most notorious cases of athlete drug use have been concerned with recreational drugs: alcohol, cocaine, and marijuana, not performance drugs. Further criticism has come from those who note that the vast majority of professional athletes do not live lives of grandeur and opulence, but rather ones characterized by brief and somewhat tawdry careers plagued by injury and the bleak prospects in our society of the uneducated and untrained. The attractiveness of athletes as role models is accordingly due more to media and commercial exploitation than to the inherent qualities of the athletes themselves. In reality they show roughly the same limitations in their conduct as do the rest of us and the promotion of them as living exemplary lives is, as Jonathan Schonsheck notes, a central hypocrisy of our times.[18] Moreover, in other areas where people serve as role models, we do not seek to institute policies that collectively control their conduct. And in the case of athletes themselves, we do not attempt to forbid other forms of conduct that might be objectionable to some: other forms of drug use (alcohol, caffeine, nicotine), divorce, gambling, self-promotion, and greed (though all of these at one time or the other have been the object of censure or prohibition). Consistency at least requires that we question the singling out of one form of behavior from others without good reason.

The issues here are so intermixed, juxtaposing as they do attitudes toward drugs in general with our ambivalent views of sports as a focus of national self-esteem, that it may be impossible to sort them out. Still, it seems reasonable to argue that the promotion of other people than sports figures as role models for the young, and a more sensible attitude toward the understanding and use of performance drugs, would accomplish much of what those who deplore their use seek in this regard. Perhaps, too, we need a reevaluation of our national policies toward recreational drugs and the associated costs in enforcement, punishment, crime, and disease.[19]

5. THE NATURE OF SPORT

Some claim that there are central characteristics of sports that mitigate against the use of performance drugs. I want to consider one such claim, formulated by Alasdair MacIntyre, and developed by others.[20] The claim is that sports are practices, coherent forms of organized social activity that create certain goods and values intrinsic to them and which are attained by performing in accordance with the standards of excellence integral to the practices.[21] This characterization of practices gives rise to a distinction between those goods that are internal to the practices and those that are external to it. Internal goods arise out of the exercise of skills developed to fulfill the defining goals of the activities; external goods are rewards typically offered by institutions that support the practices but also tend to exploit them for reasons of their own that are unconnected with the practices' own immediate activities. Thus a well-thrown pitch, a stolen base, and a perfect bunt are exercises of skill within the practice of baseball and offer their own rewards. The fame, salaries, and trophies that are also rewarded are external to the game and provided by institutions not directly involved in the practice itself.

There is much to be said for this conception of sports. It highlights some of the features of a favorite view of them: the virtuous and innocent player motivated by the love of the game; the power and skill of the practitioner, a thing of beauty and grace; the corrupt and venal exploiters of youth and innocence for worldly gain. But it divides motives and satisfactions too neatly, borrowing the metaphor of inside and outside to suggest that practices are like the bodies of the players themselves, inwardly pure and driven by their own dynamics, confronted by external forces of corruption and greed. The idea is that performance drugs, like an invading microorganism, infiltrate from the outside to foul the internal workings of sports, the athletes themselves, distorting their skills, depriving them of the internal goods of the sports, and motivating them toward the external rewards of larger social institutions. The argument then goes something like this. Performance drugs are not relevant to the internal goods of sports which derive from "achieving those standards of excellence" characteristic of the practice. Their use tends rather to be driven by external goals of winning and victory and the fame or riches attendant on them.

But this argument is unpersuasive for several reasons. The first is that the basic distinction between internal and external goods, though serviceable for some purposes, blurs at crucial places. For example, there are clearly satisfactions to be gained from the exercise of the skills one develops in sport. Such skills are largely specific to given sports: taking a turn on a 400m track and other tactical skills in a foot race, for example, are not easily carried over to golf or basketball. This is due by and large to the arbitrary character of sports, their curious separateness from the skills of the workplace and home. Nevertheless, such skills are sometimes carried over to other sports. And in sports where many diverse skills are called for—in the biathlon, triathlon, and decathlon—for example, skills developed in one sport are transferable to others. No matter that the combination often limits performance to less than that of the specialist; the satisfaction of each skill's development, not just in their combination, is still present. But now such skills and their attendant satisfactions must be both internal and external to specific sports, and if transferable to practices other than the sports themselves—as are the skills, many argue, of teamwork, cooperativeness, and planning—are doubly external.[22]

Or take the good of winning. Winning it is said is an external good of sports and as such would seem to cut across various sports.[23] But winning in one sport is surely not the same as winning in another, and winning at one level of competition is surely different from winning at another. Indeed winning surely emerges as the final, overall configuration of the game itself, internal to the dynamics of the play, its culmination, not an externally imposed determination by those external to the activity. Even in those rare cases where controversial results lead to reviews by others, they are decided by the internal constraints of the sport, not by external institutional needs. And the rewards of winning may be internal or external. True, fortune is usually introduced from outside sports these days, but fame and admiration run deep within the sports themselves and are not just the province of institutional or social renown.

Health and fitness would seem to be external goods imposed on sports, as we have seen in our earlier discussion of the effects of performance drugs. But both are elusive. Fitness is to sports as intelligence is to tests: both seem specific to the ways in which they are measured, by essentially arbitrary cultural norms. Just as there seems no clear way to measure a general intelligence or IQ, so there seems no way to measure general fitness beyond capabilities developed in specific sports or other activities. (Questions like, "Are musicians smarter than lawyers?" give place to "Are basketball players more fit than swimmers?") Health is a notoriously slippery concept. Indeed, it is an uneasy companion of sports like boxing, mountain climbing, football, and many others, which carry with them inherent risks of injury that may be reduced but not eliminated: those risks are integral to the sports themselves and help define the excitement and challenge that are among their internal goods.

So little is to be gained for our purposes from the distinction between internal and external goods. And this is brought out by the second reason, that performance drugs are intended to enhance performance, as measured by the sports' own activities and standards, their own internal goods. Schneider and Butcher have argued that such enhancement is tantamount to changing the skills required by a sport and thus "changes the sport."[24] But this claim is implausible. Training at high altitude greatly enhances the oxygen transport capacity of long-distance runners, but few would argue that it changes the skills required to run a marathon or changes the sport itself. The jump shot, a basketball skill first performed in the late 1940s, changed the sport only in the sense that it added excitement and challenge to the game. Indeed, Schneider and Butcher emphasize this point themselves.[25] And to the extent that performance drugs could enhance performance, they would contribute to the exercise of skills at a higher level where the challenges and satisfactions might be all the greater.

Surely this is the reason why athletes have always tried to better their opponents, to find ways to excel, in spite of the fact that no one doubts that their secrets to success will soon be out. No one would seek to ignore a new training technique, equipment modification, or diet on the grounds that since one's opponents will soon catch on, the discovery will just escalate the competition, soon making it harder than ever to win. To this extent, sports recapitulate life and reflect a constant striving to win and enjoy, to compete and share in the competition of the game. In this sense, performance drugs may be as relevant to sports and their internal goods as any other way of enhancing one's performance.

6. DIFFERENCE

I combine here a number of points that challenge the general trend of my comments to other objections. They involve differences among athletes that may suggest grounds for acknowledging the differences performance drugs may make. One way to isolate the objections to performance drugs is to note that they apply to the participants in sports rather than to the constitutive rules of the sports themselves. Like proscriptions of earlier generations against some people participating in sports because of their race, sex, social status, or religion, forbidding the participation of those who use drugs may seem like a similar kind of discrimination since in using drugs, one is not breaking the rules of the sports themselves but rather challenging limits on who may play in them. The Negro baseball leagues followed the same rules as the white leagues, their players just weren't allowed to play on the same teams, or in the same competitions. How is the case different for drugs?[26]

There are a number of cases, however, where competition is decided on the basis of the players rather than on the rules of the game. Participation is often based, for example, on sex. Women were officially allowed to run in the Boston Marathon only in 1972, after several women, beginning in 1966, unofficially broke the sex barrier. Even so, when women began running the marathon in the Olympic Games in 1984 it was in a separate women's race. And similar divisions into men's and women's events are familiar in other sports. In other cases, such as boxing, wrestling, and crew, participation is also based on weight. (Body-building competitions are now organized into new "natural" or drug-free and traditional, "open" events, the latter widely assumed to feature contestants who use steroids.) In amateur sports such as running, tennis, swimming, and golf, participants are often classified by age as well as sex.

What are we to make of these differences among people as a basis for classifying sports? To some extent they no doubt reflect long social traditions and prejudices. Barriers to involvement in sports by girls and women whether as overt prohibitions, as social practices based on rigid sex roles, or as subtle social pressures have long been part of our society and others. But such practices also reflect inherently different developmental patterns of males and females, and these, when combined with the characteristics of sports developed largely for men, produce on the average striking differences in the athletic capabilities of men and women. Still, since the overlap of such traits is large, it would be easy to match some groups of women with similarly skilled groups of men to have sports with combined and roughly equally matched male and female participants. In fact, this often happens in informal sports in schools and elsewhere when (mostly) male exclusiveness is overcome and efforts are not directed primarily at competitive excellence. Why isn't this done more often?

One reason is that sports are one of the most effective ways our society has of reinforcing and maintaining gender identities just as they were once used to reinforce racial and socioeconomic or class identities. After all, biologically it is not always easy to distinguish male and female: these are not two platonic categories unblurred in their essential difference.[27] Genetic testing notwithstanding, who is to count as a male or female is finally a determination of social as well as biological intent. (Even age, with its inexorable chronological exactitude, must be reinforced by social constraints to become an effective determinant of participation in sports.) So the differences we are concerned with, though largely "natural," biologically or statistically, are also partly social constructs.

Adopting William James's remark that a difference to be a difference must make a difference, we can nevertheless look to some pragmatic indications of where our line-drawing can reasonably be made. As it turned out, race and social class make very little difference to the outcome of participation in sports, although the residue of the old arguments still simmers in fatuous claims about the inherent abilities of black athletes who now predominate in some sports, and social class and wealth remain entrance qualifications in yachting and polo. Age more clearly takes its toll on the skills and achievements of all ath-

letes. Cutting across as it does all other categories, it can be left to exact its own inevitable classifications. But within limits, it doesn't matter. Most sports make no concessions to age save to even the competitive zest for those who find themselves past their prime. If older athletes do better than their younger competitors, they get their double victory.

Perhaps, however, sex does make a difference, in general. This is not a comment on gender equity issues in our schools and universities, but one on how, minus as best we can tell our social reinforcement of differences, things fall out for men and women in sports. At the levels of high-performance athletics, for intercollegiate and professional sports, men and women will perform on average so differently that it is often reasonable to organize sports by sex. The case is not nearly so clear for sports in elementary schools and for amateur adult sports. The dividing line at puberty makes high school athletics the place where separating participation by sex begins to make sense. If so, then for sports as they are now configured, the differences between men and women will produce corresponding differences in athletic performances and offer a rationale for preserving the competitive balance achieved when participants are organized by sex. Surely this is the rationale of weight classes in boxing, wrestling, and crew, although the absence of such classes in other sports where size and strength make a substantial contribution shows the degree of arbitrariness in such decisions.

But a similar case cannot be made, I think, for performance drugs. By and large, where such drugs work at all, and the evidence here is inconclusive, the results are usually relatively minor. Depending as they do on the initial characteristics of the athletes and their training, performance drugs may sometimes marginally enhance the performance of the athletes.[28] But to the same extent so, too, may a new training technique, different food, or better equipment. A striking exception may be the androgenic effect of anabolic steroids on female athletes. If we ignore for the moment the dangers of such drugs for women (and men), and if we assume that they do promote significant changes in muscle development and corresponding weight and strength, then my argument in the preceding paragraph is undercut and organizing sports by sex would lose some of its rationale (though perhaps for other reasons not all). If women were to close the gap between male and female developmental norms, there would be less justification for separating men and women in sports.[29]

My response here depends on an empirical claim, namely that the likely effects of performance drugs are slight. But suppose that the appropriate use of such drugs could result in substantial improvements in competitive performance. If this were the case, then wouldn't there be a reasonable basis for organizing sports for those who do and those who do not use performance drugs, the same basis adduced to justify classifying athletes by weight, for example? My inclination here is still to argue against such a division. The separation of sports based on drug use is poorly supported by an analogy to the cases of sex and weight classes where the performance ranges are inherently greater. A stronger analogy, that I will discuss further in section 7, is to new developments in training or equipment, or improvement in talent through selection from larger pools of potential athletes. Because of these changes, performances over the years have changed remarkably in virtually all sports, but this has not prompted new classification of athletes. It is worth noting, too, that the issue in this case would be not the banning of performance drugs altogether, but the relegating of those who do use them to separate categories.

But I must return specifically to the case of androgenic anabolic steroids for female athletes. I have argued that most performance drugs have marginal benefits for athletic performance, but this may not be the case for female athletes who use steroids. More importantly, however, are the effects of these drugs on the secondary sexual characteristics of those who use them. (This is true for men as well, but to a much lesser extent.) For women these effects are masculinizing, and hence directly affect their sexual or gender identities. I have already noted that sports tend to reinforce society's stereotypical gender classifications, and the use of steroids by female athletes may make these classifications increasingly problematic. (Indeed, early objections to the participation of women in sports were often based on gender stereotyping, including claims that sports would endanger women's reproductive organs, were unsuited to their inherent feminine natures, or would result in unseemly masculine women. Today, few people give credence to these claims.) There is the further concern that the use of steroids may have long-lasting or permanent androgenic effects, especially on women who use them in high doses and over long periods of time. Of course, athletes who perform at high levels of achievement for long periods of time face many long-term, even permanent, changes in their bodies whether from injury, stress, or training. Sports are even touted by some as being valuable for producing such changes: boys can become men, ninety pound weaklings may be transformed into strong, assertive, and confident citizens capable of leading and enjoying the goods of life. If there is truth to these claims, then sports already touch deeply on central features of personal identity.

Still, sexual or gender characteristics strike us as so central to human identity as to require separate consideration. If the use of steroids threatens such a core identity—physically, psychologically, and culturally—then their use may finally be too detrimental to sanction. But once again, the problem may not be as intractable as it appears at first. There is already a wide range of characteristics among females (as there is among males). Some are small and frail, others large and muscular; some have few masculine traits, some have many. The same is of course true of men. It is in the average that men and women diverge in significant ways, but the overlap is large and significant. And, as I have already mentioned, dividing us into male and female classes is not as easy as it might seem. Genetics, for example, is an important but not always decisive measure. Steroids, like the sports themselves, will therefore affect different women (and men) in different ways, depending on use and on the initial characteristics of the users. Sexual and gender identity concerns will also figure in different ways for different people, never arising for some and requiring careful choices for others.

Because, in our society and others, sports reflect the general cultural interests and values of men, female athletes are more likely to seek to emulate the performance capabilities of men than men are to seek those of women. (There are exceptions. The rare male transsexual, such as Renee Richards, or the female impersonator, such as Herman Ratjen in the 1936 Olympics, may seek to enter women's sports. Ironically, in these cases success has not been notable. Ratjen was beaten in his event, the high jump, by three female competitors.)[30] But this is already the case in sports today. Steroids may therefore have no more of an effect on women's sports than they do on men's. The growing athletic achievements of women, performance drugs aside, have already begun to put pressure on sports and the sex barrier to participation, just as women have increasingly put pressure on other male institutions, such as military academies and traditionally male professions, to allow women full participation. Resistance is strong, and we do not yet know whether the fuller participation of women will change women or change men and their institutions. The same questions with few answers also confront our sports.[31]

So, perhaps the efforts to ban performance drugs, especially steroids, in sports derive in part from a desire to preserve the predominant character of our sports as reflecting social norms of sexual and gender stereotyping. These norms are not likely to change soon or easily. But two directions of change might be possible. One would be to let classifications be blurred, opening participation to everyone based on qualifications to play safely and successfully. Perhaps women would dominate in long-distance swimming and running and in gymnastics and rhythmics, while men would

continue to dominate in other sports. But a secondary effect might be to change the sports themselves, reducing the violence and brutality of some and introducing new sports requiring mixed skills that rarely develop together in men or women. The other change would be to allow classifications throughout sports to proliferate, recognizing a wider variety of human types, emphasizing relatively stable characteristics like height, age, and sex, where shifting among the categories would be minimal, but perhaps also allowing for other classes, like weight, gender identity, or handicaps which may shift and change for individuals.

7. SLIPPERY SLOPES

I want to continue the arguments of the last section by pushing them a bit harder. Another way, I think, of expressing worries that some have about performance drugs is by seeing their claims as slippery slope arguments.[32] I have considerable sympathy for such arguments because they force us to consider longer-range consequences of proposals and to factor in both the past history of human folly and the broad outlines of human behavior as telling evidence for prospects of the future. I have touched on this kind of argument by noting that we might imagine that performance drugs were highly significant factors in athletic achievements rather than marginal or sometimes even negative ones as they now in fact seem to be. In such imaginary circumstances, it is probable that our sports would change. Certainly high-performance sports or professional sports might well come to seem far different for us as spectators from the everyday variety of sports that most of us participate in as amateurs. But in many ways, this is already true. Few of us play basketball or tennis or swim in ways that even our fantasies can liken to professional or even collegiate athletics. So such changes are not necessarily ones we need deplore. The range of abilities and achievements in sports is already enormous and provides niches for us all to enjoy our various skills and interests.

Furthermore, performances in sports have changed in astonishing ways over the last century independently of what we now think of as performance drugs. Training methods, diet, equipment, and above all the selection of the most gifted potential athletes from larger pools have all contributed to these changes that are, I suspect, far greater than any we might expect by the use of performance drugs even in the distant future. In 1900, for example, the record in the marathon was scarcely under three hours; in 1995 the record time was 2:06.50. In the mile run, the record at the turn of the century was 4:12.75; today it is 3:44.39.[33] And no one can watch old films of football or basketball games and suppose that today's players are of the same caliber. Contrast these changes with Ben Johnson's margin of victory in the 1988 Olympics, one of the best known cases of documented drug use. Johnson ran in 9.79, winning by .13 second to Carl Lewis's second place 9.92, a wide margin for the 100-meter dash, bettering Johnson's world record of 9.83 the summer before. Both records have been denied by world track authorities. In 1995, the world record was considered to be Leroy Burrell's 9.85 (of 1994), only .06 second off Johnson's best time. Assuming no one else used performance drugs in this event, a dubious assumption, Johnson's best is likely to be beaten without drug use in the near future.

But if performance drugs are allowed, what's next? Aren't there further ways in which athletic performance could be enhanced? And are we to tolerate these, too, in the name of personal choice and autonomy on the part of athletes? For example, some years ago someone invented a mechanical device for moving one's legs fast enough to enable one to run at record-breaking speed.[34] We need only recall the fictional "bionic man" of television to imagine more sophisticated aids to physical activity. Such cases seem to challenge our very conception of athletic endeavor. As Robert Simon noted, "If all we are interested in is better and better performance, we could design robots" to do it for us.[35] But, of course, what we are interested in is human performance, our own and that of those we watch as spectators, though we can easily imagine interest in android or robot performance, too, just as we acknowledge our interest in competition among other animals in dog and horse racing, for example. But the issue here is the limits of human performance, even the limits of what is to count as human for purposes of sport. So let's consider whether there are some reasonable stopping places on the slippery slope.

One place is the body's own basic boundary, the skin (though it is a porous and partial boundary at best). The differences between sports that are most evident are the differences in equipment and technical aids: the balls, bats, padding, skates, skis, cars, spikes, and other paraphernalia that define different sports, even the other animals who are used sometimes to augment human efforts. Changing the type of equipment in effect changes the identity of the sport. Changing the quality of the equipment also changes the sport, but not its identity, though it complicates efforts to compare performances across such equipment changes and sometimes requires minor changes in the rules. So where the slippery slope involves modifications of equipment, we can easily accept the new technologies as changing the sport.

The problem with performance drugs is that they are integrated into the body's own biosynthetic and metabolic pathways and so are intended to change the performance quality of the athlete, not the circumstances of the sport as defined by its goals, equipment, and rules. Here the slippery slope may yield the more difficult case where the last two possibilities come together, integration into the body of nonbiological technologies. If we condone the use of performance drugs, why not also the use of bionic implants, of artificial bones or organs? Most of the surgery available today for athletes is restorative, repairing the ravages of sports injuries. But not all. Some surgery may enhance performance, allowing greater muscle development or range of movement. And if this were possible on a wider scale, would we consider it, like performance drugs, to be liable to control? Should tissue implants to increase metabolic activity be forbidden? Should surgically improved visual acuity be outlawed? These are the stuff of science fiction for the most part, but we can begin to see the possibility of such procedures.

To some extent, we are at a loss to answer these questions, and not just for sports.[36] Our fears about such changes run deep. Would such procedures be fraught with severe side effects that would make their transient benefits pale by adverse comparison? Do they finally threaten our sense of human identity to a degree that we would find intolerable? Do they hold out the prospects of further divisions among us, not only by wealth, race, and belief, but also by health, talent, and access to biotechnology? I do not have adequate answers to these questions. Even after we satisfy ourselves of the reasonable safety of performance drugs or other performance enhancers (assuming that we could do that), many of these other questions would remain. But they are not limited to the case of sports. These fundamental issues are the spawn of biological technology in general and its possible future impact on our society. It is probably impossible to decide them in advance of the actual development of our knowledge and technology.

8. PERSONHOOD

I want now to look at an argument that is reminiscent of one I discussed earlier: the possibility that performance drugs may so affect athletes that their personal identities are threatened. There I looked at the risk that steroids in particular may change one's sexual identity. Here I want to look at a more general argument, that performance drugs, by stressing the physical competence of athletes, detract from their qualities as persons and hence corrupt the ideal of sport as competition among persons.[37] The gist of the argument seems to be that performance drugs somehow provide a physical boost to athletic ability that is totally separate from the personal qualities we often cherish in athletes, such as perseverance, good judgment, sportsmanship, grace

under pressure, and a striving for excellence. Sometimes, the argument goes further in stressing that when some athletes use performance drugs, they force others to use them, contrary to their desires and hence can corrupt their autonomy and freedom as persons.

These are serious claims, but are they cogent? Two considerations suggest that they are not. One is that the use of performance drugs is no different in these effects than are other ways that athletes develop their skills and capacities or enhance their competitive performance. The other is that none of these approaches to developing their excellence need undermine the athletes' qualities as persons. Consider the first of these two points. Athletes use a variety of means to improve their skills and extend their capacities to perform in their chosen sports. Training methods and diets are obvious ones, but many other techniques are common including psychological counseling and, above all, practice and competition which can develop mental toughness and tactical acuity. Performance drugs can also be used to promote training and the development of athletic skills. They are never a substitute for the hard work of general athletic preparation, and, if they are useful at all, are helpful in enhancing the effects of that work, not in substituting for it. Living at high altitude promotes the body's production of red blood cells, but it is worth little if training is absent. The same is true in actual performance. Performance drugs do not provide skill, stamina, and knowledge; at most, they give a boost to those already developed.

So far, then, performance drugs seem no more a threat to an athlete's "personhood" than any other technique of training or performance. Little is to be gained by stressing that performance drugs have effects on one's body: that's the point of them, as it is of most athletic training and practice. But it is worth noting that there are few other experiences in life outside of sports where we feel so unified in mind and body, where the distinction between being persons and having bodies seems so fatuous. And nothing, so far as I can see, in the use of performance drugs need threaten the development of those personal qualities that we often value in athletes. If it is true that some performance drugs can alter mood and outlook, then careful study is needed to determine how these can affect one's personality.[38] But pep talks, rivalries, and counseling can also affect mood and attitude, as can the sports themselves and are indeed relied on to do so as teams and individuals gear up for tough competition. If we are worried about performance drugs affecting moods, then we must also consider other tried and true methods for doing the same thing. Presumably it is only some moods, perhaps aggressive ones, that are said to be objectionable. If so, then much in the way certain sports are played and their players are developed must be changed as well. Performance drugs, like other athletic techniques, work primarily to enhance what is already there.

Again, it is said that athletes are coerced into choosing to use performance drugs, a curious contradictory claim in itself, by the fact that if some competitors use them, others must use them as well in order to compete successfully. But this is surely true of all changes in technique or training or tactics that athletes develop, as I have already noted. No one can introduce a successful change without others adopting it if they wish to compete successfully. We do not usually suggest that this denies athletes their autonomy. If you can't develop a good jump shot, or move to Colorado to train in the mountains, or develop a new tactical ploy, it is not your autonomy or free choice that is threatened. There may be an element of unfairness when the adoption of new techniques depends on wealth or special knowledge. But this may be the case for many features of dynamic and changing sports, not just for the use of performance drugs. The remedy would seem to be openness and research, not banning and secrecy.

9. CONSENSUS

Finally, it is sometimes urged that we should dismiss the contentions involved in many of the arguments discussed here, just agree on what we want to do about performance drugs, and then do it.[39] Whether there is such an agreement or consensus about drugs is of course an empirical matter, but, it is claimed, surely there is a widely accepted, though perhaps inchoate, sense of the ideals of sports, and these can be teased out, much the way linguists have teased out the unconscious rules governing our linguistic competence. This view would be a kind of democratic position, allowing a vote perhaps on whether or not performance drugs should be banned.

The strength of this position lies in its acknowledgment of the degree to which sports are arbitrary—the rules that constrain possible moves, time limits, equipment, scoring, numbers of players, courses, and contact being to a considerable degree artifacts of historical accident and whim. And it seeks to restore a sense of popular control over how our sports are played. But whatever the value of these points of view, the position also has important limits. For one, it isn't at all clear that its empirical premise is even plausible, no matter how difficult it might be to test. There is little reason to suppose that there is a consensus even about broad aspects of sports practices which would constitute an ideal of sport, let alone about specific issues such as using performance drugs. Further, where such a consensus has been present to some degree in the past, its effect has often been to exclude some from participation on grounds such as race or sex that few of us would tolerate, as I have noted.

In any case, surely once we grant the curious arbitrariness of some sports, or at least some aspects of them, it does not follow that all other aspects or changes in the sports are similarly arbitrary. (Many of our sports seem to have originated in their simulation of other human activities having little to do with play, for example, the techniques of war.) Most of the changes that come to be accepted are adopted to make sports more exciting to watch, to increase competitive challenge, or to ensure the relative safety of those participating in them. Sometimes, too, changes are designed to help preserve the identity of a sport across time, though changes in technologies often make this difficult. So far from being capricious or arbitrary, such changes often have a deeper rationale. Indeed, it has been the goal of this paper to examine some of the rationales given for prohibiting performance drugs. And at least some of these rationales seem to touch on more basic ethical principles of personal liberty and of not causing harm. So even if a consensus could be reached, there is no guarantee that it would represent a reasoned or moral ideal.

A more sophisticated variant on this position uses an argument based on the prisoner's dilemma.[40] Here the "prisoners" are athletes who must decide whether or not to use performance drugs (rather than whether or not to confess to a crime and receive a lesser penalty than their fellow prisoners). If one athlete does and the other does not (assuming that the drugs are actually effective), the one wins and the other loses. If both use performance drugs, neither has an advantage; if neither uses them, neither has an advantage. But the argument here assumes that it is better if both do not use performance drugs than if both do, though in either case the competition is balanced. But being unwilling to lose and not wanting to risk competing with someone who uses performance drugs, both competitors end up using them and therefore end up in the (assumed) worst situation rather than the (assumed) best one where no one uses the drugs. Like prisoners who are allowed to communicate and thus coordinate their silence or confession, athletes could, it is argued, find ways to arrive at a consensus about performance drugs (it is assumed it would be negative) and then ask that the consensus be enforced by sports organizations to avoid the consequences of the prisoner's dilemma.

However, independent arguments must be adduced to defend the main assumption of the dilemma matrix, namely that if everyone uses performance drugs, everyone is worse off than if no one uses them. These arguments tend to be the ones we have already considered and found to be lacking in cogency. So the argument from consensus depends on the other arguments to establish that the agreement or consensus should be against using performance drugs. Without these arguments, the prisoner's dilemma matrix only establishes that using performance drugs may be unfair if some athletes use them secretly or illicitly and that mutual use or nonuse would be equally balanced. And this, of course, brings us back to our starting point. We have come full circle.

Our sports have changed over the years. The days of the leisured amateur performing with elegant insouciance seem quaint and puzzling in an age of professionalism and "high-performance" skills driven by commerce and nationalism. There is much to deplore in these changes,[41] but much also to commend. We have seen the end to racism in American sport and positive efforts to resolve the problems of full participation in sports for women. Amateur and school sports flourish as never before. But because sports present so visibly to us a view of what it is to be human (though to be sure in only one of the many ways we understand ourselves), they are a focus of the concerns we have about the impact on human life of modern technologies, especially biomedical technologies. We should not, I believe, either reject or embrace these technologies uncritically, but study and reflect on the way they are changing our lives and our conceptions of who we are. They will continue to change us and our sports. I have argued not so much for the use of performance drugs as for the flourishing in sports of a critical exploration of their use and its impact on how we understand our skills and achievements.[42]

ENDNOTES

1. See John M. Hoberman, *Mortal Engines: The Science of Performance and the Dehumanization of Sport* (New York: The Free Press, 1992), and William Morgan's review essay of Hoberman in *Journal of the Philosophy of Sport* XIX (1992): 101–106.
2. See, for example, the study by Daniel Rudman and his colleagues, "Effects of Human Growth Hormone in Men over 60 Years Old." *The New England Journal of Medicine* 323 (July 5, 1990): 1–6.

3. Definitions are myriad, ranging from anything that changes any biological process to synthetic chemicals. The IOC sensibly just lists banned substances, though it fails to keep up with new products. For NCAA and USOC listings, see Allen & Hanburys *Athletic Drug Reference '94*, ed. Robert J. Fuentes, Jack M. Rosenberg, and Art Davis (Durham, N.C.: Clean Data, Inc., 1994).

4. See Thomas H. Murray, "Drugs, Sports, and Ethics." In Thomas H. Murray, Willard Gaylin, and Ruth Macklin, eds., *Feeling Good and Doing Better* (Clifton, N.J.: Humana Press, 1984), pp. 107–126. Ruth Macklin elaborates a bit on Murray's argument in her essay in the same volume, "Drugs, Models, and Moral Principles," pp. 197–200. Similar arguments are developed by Warren P. Fraleigh, "Performance-Enhancing Drugs in Sports: The Ethical Issue." *Journal of the Philosophy of Sport* XI (1984): 23–29, and by Angela J. Schneider and Robert B. Butcher, "Why Athletes Should Avoid the Use and Seek the Elimination of Performance-Enhancing Substances and Practices from the Olympic Games." *Journal of the Philosophy of Sport* XX–XXI (1993–4): 64–81.

5. See Gary I. Wadler and Brian Hainline, *Drugs and the Athlete* (Philadelphia: F. A. Davis Company, 1989), pp. 61 ff. It may be that steroids are very effective for athletes in some sports and not for others. Football linemen swear by them. But aside from the paucity of hard evidence, the issue is complicated by other factors. Steroids may accelerate training effects, for example, but not facilitate anabolic effects beyond what is possible without them.

6. The impression one gets in reviewing the literature is that both sides are much exaggerated: performance drugs are neither as dangerous nor as effective as their advocates are wont to claim. See the excellent series of reports on "Steroids in Sports," *The New York Times*, November 17–21, 1988.

7. Wadler and Hainline endorse this view (p. 67), though they note the practical problems of carrying it out. Presumably, careful study would also allow for greatly reduced risks of drug use. Perhaps the reason so few athletes are known to have been injured by performance drugs is that they are so often able to solicit professional medical advice.

8. Old standbys like caffeine seem to be somewhat effective and generally harmless, and new techniques like "blood doping" seem relatively effective and, if properly done, also harmless. See Melvin H. Williams, ed., *Ergogenic Aids in Sports* (Champaign, IL: Human Kinetics Publishers, 1983), Chs. 5 and 8. Robert Voy and Kirk D. Deeter, *Drugs, Sport, and Politics* (Champaign, IL: Leisure Press, 1991), pp. 21–23, briefly discuss the difficulties of research in this area.

9. See Voy and Deeter, pp. 20ff.

10. See Wadler and Hainline, p. 4ff.

11. The NCAA collects injury rates for intercollegiate sports in its Injury Surveillance System, a compilation of data voluntarily submitted by member schools. More serious injuries and fatalities are compiled by Frederick O. Mueller and Robert C. Cantu of the National Center for Catastrophic Sports Injury Research, University of North Carolina, Chapel Hill. See their "Eleventh Annual Report: Fall 1982–Spring 1993."

12. See Jonathan Schonsheck, "On Various Hypocrisies of the 'Drugs' in Sports Scandal." *The Philosophical Forum* XX/4 (Summer 1989): 247–285.

13. W. M. Brown, "Paternalism, Drugs, and the Nature of Sports." *Journal of the Philosophy of Sport* XI (1984): 14–22.

14. The Rudman study (see note 2) also warns against assuming that such supplements hold out hope for a general amelioration of the effects of aging.

15. John M. Hoberman and Charles E. Yesalis, "The History of Synthetic Testosterone." *Scientific American* (February 1995), 76–81.

16. One may be surprised to read that blood is a drug, but see H. G. Klein, "Blood Transfusions and Athletics: Games People Play." *New England Journal of Medicine* 312, 854 (1985): "Like other drugs, blood should be given only for medical indications." Quoted by Wadler and Hainline, p. 176.

17. For a good introduction to this issue, see Drew A. Hyland, *Philosophy of Sport* (New York: Paragon House, 1990), Chapter 1.

18. Schonsheck, p. 250.

19. See Schonsheck for a brief discussion of this point, pp. 275–281.

20. Alasdair MacIntyre, *After Virtue*, 2nd ed. (Notre Dame, Ind.: University of Notre Dame Press, 1984), Chapter 14; and Schneider and Butcher, pp. 95–97.

21. MacIntyre, p. 187.

22. As an aside, it may be noted that the association of skill and satisfaction in sports is a fluid one.

Many people who scarcely compare to high-performance athletes nevertheless take great satisfaction in the exercise of their more limited skills. The satisfactions lie here in improving and comparing skills, not just in having the finest developed ones and outdoing all others.

23. MacIntyre, p. 274.

24. Schneider and Butcher, p. 77.

25. Schneider and Butcher, p. 66.

26. See Hyland's discussion of this issue, pp. 61–63.

27. One individual out of 500 has sex-related genetic anomalies. See Joseph Levine and David Suzuki, *The Secret of Life: Redesigning the Living World* (Boston: WGBH Educational Foundation, 1993), p. 70.

28. Anecdotal evidence suggests that steroids have a greater effect in some sports, for example American football. But it is hard to judge the relative effects of drugs, training, selection, and other factors.

29. There may be other reasons why men and women will continue to find separate sports appropriate and satisfying. If Carol Gilligan and her followers are right, there may be striking differences in the development of moral sensibilities in boys and girls. Perhaps these different approaches to morality carry over to different values in competition and achievement in sports as well. See Carol Gilligan, *In a Different Voice: Psychological Theory and Women's Development* (Cambridge: Harvard University Press, 1982).

30. Levine and Suzuki, Chapter 3, note. 4.

31. For example, what would sports be like in a society traditionally dominated by women? Would they not emphasize strength, speed, and size? Would it be difficult for the average man to compete in them? Would men seek to emulate women's sports achievements? (No men seek to compete today on the balance beam, a sport in which women excel.) Perhaps it is with questions like these that the findings of Gilligan and others are most relevant. (See note 29.) On the other hand, it is not clear that in such a society women and men would develop the same characteristics that they tend to in societies like ours.

32. For an excellent discussion of slippery slope arguments, see David Lamb, *Down the Slippery Slope: Arguing in Applied Ethics* (New York: Croom Helm, 1988).

33. The history of the mile run is fascinating. The greatest miler in the nineteenth century, Walter George, ran at least once in 4:10.2 in 1885, shortly before his first professional race in the sport then called pedestrianism; his fastest racing time was 4:12.75 in 1886, a record that was not beaten until Paavo Nurmi ran 4:10.4 in 1923. It was only in the 1930s that Glenn Cunningham and others began to break the new 4:10 barrier, and in 1954 that Roger Bannister ran the mile in 3:59.4. See Cordner Nelson and Roberto Quercetani, *The Milers* (Los Altos, Calif.: Tafnews Press, 1985).

34. The device was motor driven and used slats attached to the legs to move them at great speed.

35. Robert Simon, "Good Competition and Drug-Enhanced Performance." *Journal of the Philosophy of Sport* XI (1984): 12.

36. See W. M. Brown, "Ability-Enhancing Drugs." In Steven Luper-Foy and Curtis Brown, eds., *Drugs, Morality and the Law* (New York: Garland Publishing, 1994), pp. 113–132, and Robert Simon's reply in the same book, "Better Performance Through Chemistry: The Ethics of Enhancing Ability Through Drugs," pp. 133–150.

37. See Robert Simon, "Good Competition and Drug-Enhanced Performance," p. 12, and "Response to Brown and Fraleigh," *Journal of the Philosophy of Sport* XI: 30–32.

38. Interestingly, Peter Kramer argues in *Listening to Prozac* (New York: Viking, 1993) that far from destroying one's personality, some new mood-alternating drugs allow it to be expressed more fully and authentically.

39. See Michael Lavin, "Sports and Drugs: Are the Current Bans Justified?" *Journal of the Philosophy of Sports* XIV (1987): 32–43, and Robert Simon, "Better Performance Through Chemistry . . . ," pp. 134–137.

40. See Schneider and Butcher, pp. 73–74; and Gunter Breivik, "Doping Games: A Game Theoretical Exploration of Doping," *International Review for Sociology of Sport* 27 (1992): 235–252.

41. See, for example, the fine book by William Morgan, *Leftist Theories of Sport: A Critique and Reconstruction* (Urbana and Chicago: University of Illinois Press, 1994).

42. My thanks to my colleagues, Drew Hyland and Maurice Wade, for their challenging criticisms of earlier drafts of this paper.

Bibliography

Breivik, G. "Doping Games: A Game Theoretical Exploration of Doping." *International Review for Sociology of Sport* 27 (1992): 235–252.

Brown, W. M. "Ability Enhancing Drugs." In Steven Luper-Foy and Curtis Brown, eds., *Drugs, Morality and the Law.* New York: Garland Publishing, 1994, pp. 113–132.

———. "Ethics, Drugs, and Sports." *Journal of the Philosophy of Sport* VII (1980): 15–23.

———. "Paternalism, Drugs, and the Nature of Sports." *Journal of the Philosophy of Sport* XI (1984): 14–22.

———. "Comments on Simon and Fraleigh." *Journal of the Philosophy of Sport* XI (1984): 33–35.

———. "Practices and Prudence." *Journal of the Philosophy of Sport* XVII (1990): 71–84.

Fraleigh, Warren P. "Performance-Enhancing Drugs in Sports: The Ethical Issue." *Journal of the Philosophy of Sport* XI (1984): 23–29.

Gilligan, Carol. *In a Different Voice: Psychological Theory and Women's Development.* Cambridge: Harvard University Press, 1982.

Hoberman, John M. *Mortal Engines: The Science of Performance and the Dehumanization of Sport.* New York: The Free Press, 1992.

Hoberman, John M., and Charles E. Yesalis. "The History of Synthetic Testosterone." *Scientific American* (February 1995): 76–81.

Hyland, Drew A. *Philosophy of Sport.* New York: Paragon House, 1990.

Kramer, Peter D. *Listening to Prozac.* New York: Viking, 1993.

Lamb, David. *Down the Slippery Slope: Arguing in Applied Ethics.* New York: Croom Helm, 1988.

Lavin, Michael. "Sports and Drugs: Are the Current Bans Justified?" *Journal of the Philosophy of Sport* XIV (1987): 34–43.

Levine, Joseph, and David Suzuki. *The Secret of Life: Redesigning the Living World.* Boston: WGBH Educational Foundation, 1993.

Luper-Foy, Steven, and Curtis Brown, eds. *Drugs, Morality and the Law.* New York: Garland Publishing, 1994.

MacIntyre, Alasdair. *After Virtue*, 2nd ed. Notre Dame, Ind.: University of Notre Dame Press, 1984.

Macklin, Ruth. "Drugs, Models, and Moral Principles." In Thomas H. Murray, Willard Gaylin and Ruth Macklin, eds., *Feeling Good and Doing Better: Ethics and Nontherapeutic Drug Use.* Clifton, N.J.: Humana Press, 1984, pp. 187–213.

Morgan, William J. *Leftist Theories of Sport: A Critique and Reconstruction.* Urbana and Chicago: University of Illinois Press, 1994.

Mueller, Frederick O., and Robert C. Cantu. *Eleventh Annual Report: Fall 1982–Spring 1993.* Chapel Hill, N.C.: National Center for Catastrophic Sports Injury Research, 1994.

Murray, Thomas H. "Drugs, Sports, and Ethics." In Thomas H. Murray, Willard Gaylin and Ruth Macklin, eds., *Feeling Good and Doing Better: Ethics and Nontherapeutic Drug Use.* Clifton, N.J.: Humana Press, 1984, pp. 107–126.

Murray, Thomas H., Willard Gaylin and Ruth Macklin, eds. *Feeling Good and Doing Better: Ethics and Nontherapeutic Drug Use.* Clifton, N.J.: Humana Press, 1984.

Nelson, Cordner and Roberto Quercetan. *The Milers.* Los Altos, Calif.: Tafnews Press, 1985.

Schneider, Angela J., and Robert B. Butcher. "Why Athletes Should Avoid the Use and Seek the Elimination of Performance-Enhancing Substances and Practices from the Olympic Games." *Journal of the Philosophy of Sport* XX–XXI (1993–4): 64–81.

Schonsheck, Jonathan. "On Various Hypocrisies of the 'Drugs' in Sports Scandal." *The Philosophical Forum* XX/4 (Summer 1989): 247–285.

Simon, Robert L. "Better Performance Through Chemistry: The Ethics of Enhancing Ability Through Drugs." In Steven Luper-Foy and Curtis Brown, eds., *Drugs, Morality, and the Law.* New York: Garland Publishing, 1994, pp. 133–150.

Simon, Robert L. "Good Competition and Drug-Enhanced Performance." *Journal of the Philosophy of Sport* XI (1984): 6–13.

Simon, Robert L. "Response to Brown and Fraleigh." *Journal of the Philosophy of Sport* XI (1984): 30–32.

"Steroids in Sports." *The New York Times* (November 17–21, 1988), pp. 1, et seq.

Voy, Robert, and Kirk D. Deeter. *Drugs, Sport, and Politics.* Champaign, Ill.: Leisure Press, 1991.

Wadler, Gary I., and Brian Hainline. *Drugs and the Athlete.* Philadelphia: F. A. Davis Company, 1989.

Williams, Melvin H., ed. *Ergogenic Aids in Sport.* Champaign, Ill.: Human Kinetics Publishers, 1983.

In this personal and searching testimonial to her former softball coach, Kathleen Pignatelli recounts the values that were imparted to her as well as the impact they have had on her personal and professional development.

Athletics as a Model for Ethical Living

Kathleen Pignatelli

We need role models so we can stop the abuses in athletics and so we can stop glorifying behavior without consequences.

As long as athletes are models for others, like it or not, they set an example others may follow. It is reasonable to expect ethical development from athletes if they are being coached by ethical role models.

Most dramatically, the great coaches are great teachers. There is no tolerance for players who taunt or bait other players. They are taught that such behavior will be penalized without warning. Officials are advised that they will be fired if they do not enforce the rules. Finally, coaches know that they will be suspended from a game if their players leave the bench to fight.

Sometimes we stand entirely alone, unaffiliated except with our conscience and beliefs.

What stands the test of time is total dedication to the truth. Competitive athletics is a microcosm of daily life. Money certainly seems to play too important a part in the way of life. It appears to me the very same is true in athletics—be that professional or amateur athletics.

Athletics, properly coached, provides a special arena for learning about oneself and about life. Athletic experiences are as important to the process of human development and to the building of character and leadership skills as any other worthwhile learning venture.

There is no better arena for evaluating your value system. A philosophy of sport is lived every day. Sport develops, teaches, and exposes our talents as well as our defects. There is no better proving ground for investigating and demonstrating character and integrity.

Young people want the demonstration of high standards. The approach is simple—just do what is right. It's right to be honest. It's right to be on time. It's right to be respectful. It's right to play by the rules.

The coach's goal is leadership, not popularity. May we all learn the endurance to accept the consequences of holding to what we believe to be right.

Athletics will speak to generations to come. It will reflect the level of commitment, ethical standards and role models of this generation.

Ethical standards are sadly lacking in our society on many levels. Take athletics, from the peewee leagues right through to the most prestigious collegiate or professional teams. Ugly situations have presented themselves that call for diplomatic or perhaps forceful handling so that integrity and ethics can be upheld in organized athletics.

Coaches never sacrifice their athletes for the purpose of winning. When the training for an intercollegiate team becomes so time-consuming, so intense and so exhausting that it is no longer possible for the student-athlete to participate in academia and a balanced life, something is wrong. The moral fiber gradually weakens and, by the time the intercollegiate competition is over, the athlete is a victim of the system. When ideals are obscured on the amateur level, there is potential of bruising the character of the athlete that may lead to other serious injuries. The violence in athletics is one such injury to the whole system of respectable sports participation.

While listening to the keynote speaker at my daughter's athletic banquet, my thoughts turned to the "life lessons" that inspired my days of athletic participation. The speaker, a professional basketball player, noted that being an athlete had taught him that some teammates are willing to work hard; others are lazy. Some cooperate for the good of all; others are selfish. Some are responsible and honorable and others are always looking for the shortcuts. The main ingredient that brings it all together is "heart." Someone on the team has to assume leadership. Hopefully, the coach is that responsible, caring leader who pulls everyone together through example and enthusiasm and demonstrates that "heart."

Young people have lost hope in many institutions, including athletics. Many have become blinded to the true nature and value of athletics. However, there are some who have had the vision of how athletics can make a positive difference in the lives of people.

This is a tribute to such a person. It could be anyone's coach. It happens to be my former coach. I am grateful for the example breathed and lived in the many cornerstones of her coaching philosophy.

Coach, thank you for the countless ways that you have made a difference in our lives. You never bawled us out or sweet-talked us. You taught us character by example. No matter what happened, on or off the playing field, you maintained your poise. You always conducted yourself like a lady. Coach, you always said the right things. We found ourselves wanting to be more like you. You were always there to share our defeats and praise our wins.

Coach, there are so many young people today floundering and crying out in so many different ways for a role model. They are crying out with violence, drug abuse, and the loss of purpose of commitment in their lives. Too many have not had the opportunity to see someone maintain a level of excellence on and off the playing field. They have not had the benefit of knowing that standards upheld do not interfere with athletic performance, but on the contrary, they produce citizens who have learned to commit themselves to rules and modes of conduct that become positively contagious.

It is apropos to mention how you expanded upon the potential values of sport as an adjunct to the educational process.

You always encouraged players to keep a balance in their lives. Knowing athletics were important to you did not diminish the rest of life. You emphasized preparation time, hard work, and responsibility on and off the field.

Coach, you always rose to the occasion. Whenever a player needed to talk, you did not play favorites. You simply gave of yourself and your time. You always seemed to know and live the motto that strengthening team members strengthens the team.

You encouraged all of your athletes to excel athletically as well as academically. You taught that capability determined talent but success is determined by attitude. Your attitude had the qualities of caring and respect.

We learned that everyone would not always play and every game would not be won, but everyone could be the best they could possibly be. Participation in athletics encourages success and happiness, regardless of the quality of performance or monetary rewards. In short, sport for sport's sake is a top social value.

We learned the agony of defeat as well as the ecstasy of victory. We were always encouraged to improve our past performances but never made to feel like failures. You fostered aggressive, skillful play without bending the rules of fair play. We witnessed the times you even fought for the rights of other athletes who were not even on your team.

You gave us a sense of pride not just in ourselves but in the bigger picture—as a team.

You lived that philosophy each day. All of us have seen people of average ability who strive to be something other than average and succeed in athletics. This fact has tremendous carryover value as a way to tap into human energy and potential.

The importance of an ethical standard that is fostered and upheld in sports has far-reaching benefits. The physical and mental strains of athletic competition prepare us for the ups and downs of life. Participation in athletics is a common thread in the personal and professional development of leaders. All the hype about making six-figure incomes or earning an athletic scholarship could diminish this positive image. However, as long as there are role models like you, Coach, excellence will emerge victorious in what really makes a difference. Coaches can be hard-driving; they demand commitment, concentration, and effort when they have demonstrated that daily. When athletics has lost the element of human respect, joy, and fun, it has lost perspective. Coach, thank you for living what you taught.

Coach, thank you for having the courage and wisdom to listen to that inner voice that strengthened all of us. Your integrity was an inner commitment that affirmed and developed each player's special talents and strengths. You taught us to care deeply about honesty and respect by showing the depth of your heart when such values were violated.

My hope is that some of what I have learned from my coach has been passed on to my athletes. Young people will have something to believe in as we approach the twenty-first century and that is their own worth and value demonstrated in their fair play.

Closing Questions

1. Should the use of performance-enhancing drugs such as anabolic steroids be banned from sports? If so, what about weight training? On what grounds should either be banned, if at all?

    _____

    _____

    _____

    _____

    _____

2. Are vitamins performance-enhancing drugs? Is coffee? What about medication that alleviates allergy symptoms? What about alcohol which, because it slows the heartbeat, improves performance in riflery because it allows a steadier hand?

    _____

    _____

    _____

    _____

    _____

3. Discuss what the requirements for sexual equality in sports should be.

    _____

    _____

    _____

    _____

    _____

4. Is excellence in competition for the few preferable to greater participation by the many?

    _____

    _____

    _____

    _____

5. Is boxing unethical? Consider the fact that 350 boxers, pro and amateur, have been killed in the ring since 1945. If boxing is unethical, how would you evaluate other "violent" sports such as football and hockey? Can you identify a morally relevant difference between boxing and these other sports? What about hunting for sport? Cock fighting and dog fighting?

_____

_____

_____

_____

_____

6. Do intercollegiate athletics belong on campus? Consider this question in the light of the nature and purpose of the university.

_____

_____

_____

_____

_____

7. Should athletes serve as role models for our youth?

_____

_____

_____

_____

_____

8. Just prior to the start of the 1995 major league baseball season, President Clinton asked a reluctant Congress for its help in settling the strike. Should Congress get involved in such matters?

_____

_____

_____

_____

_____

9. Discuss the claim that, far from having any positive moral influence, sports are symptomatic of our moral decline.

_____

_____

_____

_____

_____

10. Some of America's professional athletes (for example, Darryl Strawberry, John McEnroe, Mike Tyson, and O. J. Simpson) are notoriously bad role models, while others, such as Marty Lyons and Tony Gwynn, are good ones. Do professional athletes have a responsibility to serve as role models? Name some athletes you admire or dislike and list the virtues or vices that these athletes embody.

_____

_____

_____

_____

_____

11. Discuss the ethics of college recruitment practices in the area of sports.

_____

_____

_____

_____

_____

For Further Reading

————. *Sports and Social Values.* Englewood Cliffs, N.J.: Prentice Hall, 1985.

Brown, W. M. "Comments on Simon and Fraleigh." *Journal of the Philosophy of Sport* XI (1984).

————. "Ethics, Drugs, and Sport." *Journal of the Philosophy of Sport* VII (1980).

———— "Paternalism, Drugs, and the Nature of Sports." *Journal of the Philosophy of Sport* XI (1984).

Fraleigh, Warren P. *Right Actions in Sports: Ethics for Contestants.* Champaign, Ill.: Human Kinetics, 1984.

Hyland, Drew. *Philosophy of Sport.* New York: Paragon House, 1990.

Morgan, William, and Klaus Meier, eds. *Philosophic Inquiry in Sport.* Champaign, Ill.: Human Kinetics, 1988.

Postow, Betsy, ed. *Women, Philosophy, and Sport: A Collection of New Essays.* New Jersey: Scarecrow Press, 1983.

Simon, Robert L. *Fair Play: Sports, Values, & Society.* Boulder, Col.: Westview Press, 1991.

Weiss, Paul. *Sport: A Philosophic Inquiry.* Carbondale, Ill.: Southern Illinois University Press, 1969.

Will, George F. *Men at Work: The Craft of Baseball.* New York: Macmillan, 1990.

Chapter 11

Ethics and Science

Passages for Reflection

"Science has nothing to be ashamed of, even in the ruins
of Nagasaki."
—*Jacob Bronowski*

"In science, all facts, no matter how trivial or banal, enjoy
democratic equality."
—*Mary McCarthy*

"Science without religion is lame."
—*Albert Einstein*

Opening Questions

1. Is science a value-free enterprise?
2. Should science not try to answer some questions? Which ones?
3. What are the differences between science and morality?

The scientific community has been described as a community of rational inquirers openly engaged in the pursuit of truth untrammeled by considerations of value. This is the ideal of science put forward by its defenders against those who argue that science should be constrained by axiological considerations (considerations of value). We feel the force of this ideal when we learn, for example, that in the Soviet Union following the days of Stalin, Freudianism was considered a priori false since, according to the ruling authority, it could not be true that factors other than environmental ones motivate human behavior. We also feel its force when we hear religious fundamentalists argue that the world cannot possibly be Darwinian (and that there's no sense arguing about this) owing to the literal truth of the creation story.

At the same time, we have reason to believe that science is not wholly value-free. We distinguish between "good" and "bad" science and between real science and pseudoscience (for example, astronomy versus astrology). A foray into ethics and science, then, might begin by asking about the role of values *in* science. It might also begin by asking about the value *of* science. Whether or not science is a value-free enterprise, the uses to which science is put create grave moral problems. The most dramatic examples are the problems created by the control of nuclear fission, advances in medical technology, and genetic engineering. Consequently, beyond such questions as whether science is value-free, we need to look at the ethical implications of science's unbridled pursuit of knowledge.

Keeping in mind that not all values are moral ones, and that science may be morally neutral even if it's not value-neutral, let us proceed by asking, "What is the role of values in science?" and "What are the value implications of science?" We ask why there is or even should be any problems about the relationship between science and values, since just this distinction is at the heart of the relation between science and ethics.

The distinction between science and values is a new one, made following the scientific revolution of the seventeenth century. At that time, with the ascendence of Newtonian physics, a sharp distinction was drawn between scientific claims and axiological ones. Prior to that, the views of the ancient Greeks occupied the minds of learned men and women.

The ancient Greeks drew no distinction between science and values, between a descriptive account of the world and an evaluative one. In Plato's *Republic*, for instance, we are told that the cosmos is characterized by the idea of the Good, that is, of order, pattern, beauty, and purpose.[1] Plato maintained that in order to understand the world, we must understand the laws and structures that unify it into a coherent and meaningful whole. The knowledge this results in is not to be confounded with what we call knowledge, since we mean by "knowledge" *scientific* knowledge. For Plato, the empirical sciences provide us only with a limited insight into reality. What is most real—the Platonic Forms—are abstract ideas accessible only by means of cognition (*nous*). An "objective account" of things (*logos*) involves a unified picture of the world replete with purpose and norms.

In Aristotle, too, we are told that we cannot understand the world in the absence of a normative account. In his *Metaphysics*, Aristotle's concern is to account for the nature of change, which, for Aristotle, is a pervasive feature of reality. It is in answer to the question "How do things change?" that we get Aristotle's famous doctrine of four causes. He maintained that for anything that changes, we explain that change by showing: (1) what is changing (the material cause), (2) into what the thing is changing (the formal cause); (3) how the change is taking place (the efficient cause), and (4) why the change is taking place (the final or teleological cause). By including the final or teleological cause, Aristotle is assuming a normative view of nature according to which what happens in the world happens for a purpose.

Aristotle's world view influenced the world of science up until the seventeenth century when Newton (and the philosopher René Descartes) put forth a mechanical picture of the world. According to this picture, the world is a vast machine governed by quantitative laws and relationships (written in the language of mathematics) whose features are matter, motion, and magnitude. In this view, only such features are truly objective. This means, among other things, a sharp distinction between the objective world of nature and the subjective world of mind. Hence, a scientific explanation of the world could not be framed in terms of Plato's good or Aristotle's ends and purposes. Instead, the way to explain the world is to take into account only those features that can be quantified, or written in mathematical language. Everything else about the world—interpretations, purpose, and values—is not "objective" (unless they can be shown to be reduced to objective terms) and falls outside the purview of science.

To appreciate just how far we have moved from Aristotle's teleological conception of the world to the Newtonian mechanistic one, con-

---

[1] *Republic*, bks. 4–7.

sider how a modern scientist would go about explaining, say, the death of a person from an automobile accident. In addition to such biological factors as loss of oxygen to the brain, the scientist would cite the force with which the vehicle hit the other object, the velocity at which it was traveling, the vehicle's direction, and so forth. The scientist would give the objective and quantifiable features of the event—what Aristotle earlier had referred to as the event's efficient cause. What the scientist would not cite is the purpose of the accident, where by *purpose* is meant the reason for the event's occurring or the event's location in the overall scheme of things.

Objectivity, then, with its attendant emphasis on mathematics, became the hallmark of science following Newton. Anything that was not objective and quantifiable was to be denounced as "subjective," replete with biases, interpretations, emotions, and opinions. The objective/subjective dichotomy was made even more forcefully in the 1930s when logical positivism came into prominence. The logical positivists argued that the only utterances that had cognitive significance were those that could be verified. These included scientific ones, such as that water boils at 212 degrees Fahrenheit, or those that were true by definition, such as that parallel lines meet at infinity or that bachelors are unmarried males. This meant, by implication, that value assertions, such as those found in ethics, are meaningless in the literal sense of the word; they have no cognitive significance and merely express the attitudes and preferences of those who assert them. Since science, for the positivists, was the very paradigm of knowledge, they insisted that science could not possibly include value assertions. Writing for the logical positivists, Rudolph Carnap, in particular, was adamant on this point. He insisted that "the objective validity of a value cannot be asserted in a meaningful statement at all."[2] This mentality lies behind the claim that science is essentially a value-free enterprise.

In the years that followed, philosophers abandoned logical positivism owing, in part, to misunderstandings about the nature of both science and ethics alike. Although today it is considered thoroughly discredited, it nevertheless left its mark together with its Newtonian (and Cartesian) forebears. We still distinguish between the objective and subjective in terms of methodology, as well as between the "hard" and "soft" sciences. Much work in moral theory, too, has concerned itself with saving ethics from a scientific onslaught that would render it meaningless. Mindful of the claim that the scientific method is the only rational method for solving problems, moral philosophers have inferred either that ethics is not rational or that it is merely concerned with means-ends analysis. At the same time, many philosophers believe that assumptions regarding

---

[2]Rudolph Carnap, "The Elimination of Metaphysics through Logical Analysis of Language." Translated by Arthur Pap. In A. J. Ayer, ed., *Logical Positivism* (Glencoe, Ill: Free Press, 1959), pp. 60–81.

objectivity, subjectivity, and rationality result from inadequate conceptions of both science and ethics. Today, the claim that science is value-laden is the prevalent orthodoxy and is hardly considered controversial.

In his essay, "The Scientist *Qua* Scientist Makes Value Judgments,"[3] Richard Rudner argues that the need for scientists to decide when and if available evidence is good enough to warrant the acceptance of a hypothesis is an evaluative activity, implying that science as science is a normative discipline. Since, as Rudner sees it, scientists can never completely verify a hypothesis, they must decide when evidence is strong enough to warrant our acceptance of it. This, he argues, invariably depends on the implications of accepting a hypothesis as true.

Suppose, says Rudner, a hypothesis was under consideration to the effect that a toxic ingredient of a drug was not present in lethal quantity. We would require a high degree of confirmation before we would accept it, since the consequences of making a mistake are potentially lethal. On the other hand, if a hypothesis were being considered to the effect that a box of machine belt buckles was not defective, we would not require a great degree of confirmation. This proves to Rudner that our interest in accepting a hypothesis as true is a function of the value we place on what is tested.

Although Rudner's argument can be criticized, it does indicate one way in which values enter into the enterprise of science. Another way is suggested by the philosopher of science, Thomas Kuhn, in his 1973 essay, "Objectivity, Value-Judgment, and Theory Choice."[4] Kuhn asks what are the characteristic values of a good scientific theory, and he lists, as a start, five that are fairly uncontroversial: (1) predictive accuracy, (2) internal coherence (the absence of logical inconsistencies within the theory), (3) external consistency (the theory's ability to cohere with other theories), (4) unifying power (the theory's ability to bring together disparate areas of inquiry), and (5) fertility (the theory's ability to make novel predictions). Kuhn's point is that these criteria unmistakably function as values. He writes: "The criteria of choice function not as rules, which determine choice, but as values which influence it. Two men deeply committed to the same values may nevertheless, in particular situations, make different choices, as in fact they do."[5]

Kuhn uses the dispute between Neils Bohr and Albert Einstein over the acceptability of the new quantum theory of matter to illustrate his point. Einstein, says Kuhn, was skeptical of the theory. Even though he admitted its predictive accuracy, he felt it was lacking in coherence and

---

[3]Richard Rudner, "The Scientist *Qua* Scientist Makes Value Judgments." *Philosophy of Science* 20 (1953): pp. 1–6.

[4]Thomas Kuhn, "Objectivity, Value-Judgment, and Theory Choice." In *The Essential Tension* (Chicago: University of Chicago Press), pp. 320–339.

[5]Ibid., p. 331.

consistency with the rest of physics. Bohr was disposed to accept it. He admitted consistency but played down its importance. The predictive successes of the theory counted more for Bohr than they did for Einstein. The difference between their assessments, then, was due to differences in the values they employed in assessing theories.

Another characteristic—simplicity—is a favorite of many philosophers of science, and a discussion of this "virtue" will prove instructive. *Simplicity*, as used here, means a theory's ability to predict and explain phenomena in a facile way. More formally, between any two theories, T-1 and T-2, T-1 is preferable to T-2 if T-1 can explain and predict all that T-2 can, but T-1 is simpler. We can easily illustrate how this virtue operates if we call upon the history of science, namely the famous contrast between Copernicus' heliocentric system of planetary orbit and Ptolemy's geocentric one.

As Ptolemy understood it, the earth was the center of the universe and the planets revolved around it in circular motion. On this supposition, Ptolemy should have been able to predict the location of the planets at any given time. However, Ptolemy's predictions were wrong. Instead of a planet being where it was supposed to be at a chosen time, it was at a different place. Not willing to abandon his theory for an erroneous prediction, Ptolemy hypothesized that planets took circular detours (called *epicycles*) to get to the spot his theory initially predicted. While this ad hoc hypothesis had the virtue of saving Ptolemy's theory, the theory became increasingly complicated as more and more epicycles were employed to save more and more appearances from going awry.

Copernicus abandoned the geocentric theory and hypothesized that the planets do not go around the earth but that they go around the sun. (In an effort to explain the apparent retrograde motion of Mars, Kepler added that the planets rotate in elliptical, not circular, motion.) This theory was finally accepted not because Ptolemy's theory was false, which it was not if one added enough epicycles, but because Copernicus' theory did all that Ptolemy's did and had the virtue of simplicity—an aesthetic characteristic!

One of the main reasons behind science's reluctance to abandon the geocentric system was the deeply held conviction that the universe revolved around the earth in circular motion. The Roman Catholic Church maintained that the universe was created for the sake of humankind and that any orbit God might prescribe for planets are circular ones—the symbol for eternity. Galileo, who subscribed to the heliocentric system, was persecuted by the Church for believing otherwise and was forced to retract his views at the threat of death even though he recanted on his deathbed.

The more modern controversy between Darwin and his critics over the origin of the species is reminiscent of Galileo's conflict with the Church. Theologians and some moralists have worried that evolution is incompatible with religion. Even first-rate scientists have struggled with the theory of evolution because of the threat it has posed to their beliefs about the sanctity and value of human life. You can see this controversy in the competing theories of the Burgess Shale, a region in British Columbia containing a gold mine of fossils.

Discovered in 1909 by paleontologist Charles Walcott, the Burgess Shale was significant in that it contained fossilized animals that did not obviously belong to any known groups. This was astounding, inasmuch as taxonomists had been able to fit almost a million species of arthropods into four known groups prior to that discovery. In an effort to explain these peculiar fauna, Walcott, a first-rate scientist, surmised that they belonged to familiar groups, believing them to be primitive versions of later, more improved forms.

The fit, however, was not tight. Harvard paleontologist Stephen Jay Gould has contended that the Burgess fauna are unfortunate losers in the story of life whose pattern is determined largely by chance.[6] For Gould, evolution is nothing but adaptation to changing local environments coupled with sheer, downright luck. But for an asteroid hitting the earth millions of years ago, leading to the massive removal of dinosaurs, mammals would not have left the sea and we would not be here. For Gould, then, *homo sapiens* is the fortunate beneficiary of evolution. Walcott, in contrast, was a staunchly devout Presbyterian who saw evolution as moving in a predictable pattern of steadily increasing excellence with the most superior species, *homo sapiens*, inevitably appearing at the end. It did not occur to Walcott to interpret the Burgess fauna in any other way. In a personal correspondence one year after the Scopes trial took place—a trial that questioned the legitimacy of teaching Darwinism in public schools—Walcott says this about the value of orderly progress:

> I have felt for several years that there was a danger of science running away with the orderly progress of human evolution and bringing about a catastrophe unless there was some method found of developing to a greater degree the altruistic or, as some would put it, the spiritual nature of man.[7]

As the examples of Galileo and Walcott illustrate, the question is not *whether* values play a role in science, but *where* values play a role in science.

Beyond questioning the place of values in science, we can question the value of science. From one perspective, this is peculiar since the virtues of science are commonly extolled. The growth of scientific knowledge and its practical applications have not only reduced such formida-

---

[6]Stephen Jay Gould, *Wonderful Life: The Burgess Shale and the Nature of History* (New York: W. W. Norton, 1989).

[7]Ibid., p. 261.

ble plagues as famine and pestilence, but they have raised humankind's material standard of living to an unparalleled level. As a result of scientific knowledge, we have within our reach the realization of visions which would have appeared fantastic not too long ago. At the same time, scientific knowledge has given rise to never before imagined ethical problems, evinced by our ability to harvest nuclear fission.

The popular film *Jurassic Park* is the latest in a series of films, including *Frankenstein*, *Dr. Jekyll and Mr. Hyde*, *The Fly*, and *Species*, that have brought home the perils of scientific research. In each of these stories, we are warned that unless science is constrained by ethical considerations, its unbridled search for truth (and power) may prove disastrous. The dispute between Arnold and Malcolm in *Jurassic Park* is an example of just how far science should go in its pursuit of truth. Arnold holds that modern science is fundamentally a moral activity and that scientists ought to do anything they wish in the name of knowledge. Malcolm (Jeff Goldblum) on the other hand disagrees. Seeing the world as chaotic, he argues that the dream of total control that once drove science is no longer viable and so too our justification for relying on it to guide our lives. Malcolm says:

> We are witnessing the end of the scientific era. Science, like other outmoded systems, is destroying itself. As it gains in power, it proves itself incapable of handling the power. Because things are going very fast now. Fifty years ago, everyone was gaga over the atomic bomb. That was power. No one could imagine anything more. Yet a bare decade after the bomb, we began to have genetic power. And it will be in everyone's hands. It will be in kits for backyard gardeners. Experiments for school children. Cheap labs for terrorist dictators. And that will force everyone to ask the same question—what should I do with my power—which is the very question science says it cannot answer.

We need not resort to film or fiction to argue that science ignores ethics at its peril. Consider, for example, how much we could learn about human cancers if we experimented on people regardless of informed consent. We might well discover how to cure them. In the animal world, veterinarians are able to vaccinate cats against leukemia precisely because scientists have conducted experiments on cats. But we value our freedom and autonomy at least as much as we value our health. Although we might gain a wealth of knowledge by ignoring ethical considerations, the risks of doing this are as great as the benefits obtained. Think also of how much we might gain if we mated a human being with a chimpanzee—an experiment Stephen Jay Gould has called the most horrific imaginable. Assuming such mating to be possible, we would stand to learn a considerable amount about chimpanzee consciousness. But we would do so by deliberately creating a defective human being which is something we must never do.

Considerations like these would be fantastic and far-fetched were it not for the Nazi experiments during the Holocaust. Even so, we need look no further than home to see the perils of a science unconstrained by ethics. Consider the implications of the human genome project, a project investigating human DNA. Apparently, it is easy to determine the sex of a child since it involves only one chromosome. However, if everyone were free to do so, we would have a dearth of females, since polls consistently show that if given the choice between having a boy or a girl, 80 percent of people would prefer to have boys. We cannot afford too many generations of this.

Other issues related to the genome project will arise if scientists can find a genetic relationship to talents and abilities. Suppose, for instance, it were possible to inexpensively manipulate the genes of our children so that they could have IQs significantly higher than they would otherwise have, or musical abilities they would not have by nature. Imagine the pressures this might put on upwardly mobile couples whose peers opt for gene manipulation in an effort to send their children to elite schools. Although such pressures are similar to the ones couples feel when they buy computers for their children or provide them with piano lessons, many people perceive that gene manipulation is morally repugnant.

Consider, as well, some of the ethical issues that result from the new reproductive technologies. To what extent is it permissible for a married woman to be impregnated with the sperm of a donor? Is this a form of adultery? Or, considering the practice of surrogate motherhood, to what extent is it permissible to become pregnant with the intention of donating the child to another? Is this an instance of baby selling? Suppose, as might be the case in the near future, it were possible not only to fertilize an ovum *in vitro*, but to maintain the ovum in an incubator for most of the gestation period. How might we look upon the woman who, not willing to compromise her professional career, opts for this route in lieu of pregnancy? We are already facing such questions and are likely to do so even more in the future.

In his ethical writings, the American pragmatist John Dewey envisioned science as one day able to serve the many needs of humankind. That vision is a salutary one if science is used for the good. But what we must never forget is that science can provide us with Chernobyl just as it can provide us with the microwave oven. The value of science greatly depends on the uses to which it is put—a moral we must never forget.

Lowell Kleiman is Professor of Philosophy at Suffolk Community College. A former Fellow at Princeton University, he is the co-editor of *Ethical Issues in Scientific Research* (Garland, 1994).

Video Presentation

Guest: Lowell Kleiman, Professor of Philosophy, Suffolk Community College

Student Panel: Christy Amaru, Yahav Shoost, Gary Louizides

I begin my discussion with Lowell Kleiman by asking him to comment on the perception of scientists as a community of researchers openly engaged in the pursuit of truth. Remarking that this picture of scientists is both fact and fiction, Kleiman picks up my reference to the scientific *community* and talks of how the social aspect of science makes it noteworthy to the moral philosopher.

Unlike in the past when scientific discoveries were made by individual people of genius, Kleiman tells us that today's scientist relies heavily on the findings of his or her peers. This means that fraud has implications in science that it does not have in other disciplines. Compare, says Kleiman, fraud in art and science. If the curator of a museum happens to purchase a fraudulent painting, only the museum and some art aficionados suffer as a result. By contrast, if a scientist publishes fraudulent research, the entire enterprise of science suffers since scientists rely on the findings of other scientists in order to go forward with their research. Likening fraud in science to an infectious virus, Kleiman contends that in the presence of fraud, no scientist could ever be sure of his or her research.

In connection with fraud, I ask Kleiman to discuss the David Baltimore affair. Baltimore, he says, was a Nobel laureate who, in 1986, had his name affixed to a paper published in the prestigious journal, *Cell*, concerning research undertaken on transgenetic mice. One of the research assistants—though not Baltimore himself—suggested afterward that some of the data had been fabricated. Although the investigating authorities ultimately exonerated the research team, Kleiman tells us how they came to that conclusion partly because they lacked a viable theory of scientific fraud. Following some discussion of cold fusion and the charge of fraud connected with it, Kleiman discusses some of the problems with delineating a satisfactory theory.

At this point in the show, we move away from the discussion of fraudulent research to the topic of animal experimentation. I ask Kleiman to discuss Peter Singer's claim that much research on animals is both avoidable and useless—a claim with which Kleiman apparently agrees. I suggest that if Singer is right, then a hidden agenda is likely behind animal research. In addition to scholars publishing research to secure further grants, get promotions, and so on, some scientists whose research is funded by corporations have a vested interested in the findings. I mention the research funded by the makers of Rogaine who have found a causal connection between baldness and heart disease. As manufacturers of a leading hair loss product, Rogaine would be interested in this result. Kleiman agrees that we must be skeptical of scientific research funded by manufacturers with vested interests, but reminds us to distinguish between where research comes from and whether it is valid.

Just before the break, the conversation turns to ethical issues in genetic research. Kleiman points out that much of the public's fears in this area are unfounded since the concern has not been with creating better human beings—evoking images of Hitler's super race—but with eliminating genetic disorders.

After the break, Gary Louizides asks Kleiman about artificial intelligence. Yahav Shoost asks him whether the Food and Drug Administration is right to withhold its approval of medications that might otherwise save lives. Christy Amaru asks Kleiman about research on prisoners. The show ends with Kleiman and I discussing the concept of informed consent.

In this article, written expressly for this book, Lowell Kleiman marks out what he perceives to be the major issues that science faces in the years ahead: the nature of fraud in science, the use of human beings as experimental subjects, the treatment of animals in scientific research, and the human genome project. Not claiming to answer the questions he raises, Kleiman critically examines them while arguing against the thesis that the path of science is fraught with dangers—a thesis raised by the specter of Frankenstein. Quite to the contrary, Kleiman's view is that science provides us with the best hope of solving humankind's most urgent problems.

Science and Morality

Lowell Kleiman

INTRODUCTION

Scientists stand on the threshold of new discoveries that will not only alter the nature of life as we know it, but will provide insights for the creation of life itself. Will the new developments be beneficial, or will we create monsters to destroy us? The great questions facing science today are not just theoretical and technical, but ethical and moral.

In the discussion to follow, I will try to illuminate the moral dimension of science by examining four areas of concern: the nature of fraud in science, the use of human beings as experimental subjects, the treatment of animals in research, and the new genetics. I will not try to solve the issues raised; that would go beyond the scope of this discussion. Rather, I will attempt to describe simply what the issues are. However, my main point is critical: unlike the grim picture of the scientist depicted in the tale of Frankenstein, and contrary to the dire assessment of scientific practice by contemporary critics, scientific achievement remains the best hope of the future.

Before we start, however, we must address a preliminary question: "What sort of achievement can we expect from science?" In the past, scientists provided cures for disease as well as the means for widespread destruction. If the future promises more of the same, then scientific achievement by itself need not be beneficial. Something more is needed if science is to provide not just technical progress, but moral advancement as well. What can that be?

Two answers to this question have emerged. The first is that science is morally neutral and, by itself, can offer no moral guidance. In this view, either scientists are isolated dreamers removed from the everyday concerns of ordinary life (like Dr. Frankenstein), or they are little more than technicians at the employ of giant corporations or big government doing the bidding of corporate executives and politicians. In either case, scientists are not themselves responsible for the results of their labors, any more than is Wagner for the Nazification of his music, or the worker for welding the gas tank onto the Ford Pinto. Someone else is responsible—the executive, the politician, society at large—an authority independent of science that must decide how the work of science is to be used. In this skeptical view, the scientists that produced the first atomic bomb were not responsible for the destruction of Hiroshima and Nagasaki. The use of those weapons was, in part, a military decision. If the decision was right, the credit goes to the political leaders and their generals; if wrong, the scientists are off the hook.

However, Robert Oppenheimer and the others who worked on the Manhattan Project were not oblivious to the potential power of the device they were creating. They knew that the sole purpose of their research was to produce a destructive weapon of unprecedented magnitude. It is difficult to understand how anyone, especially people of science, could be morally neutral about developing an atomic bomb. Parents are not indifferent to children using firecrackers. How could scientists be indifferent to politicians using atomic weapons? If the leaders get credit for ending a war, then the scientists who helped them should receive credit as well. And if the decision to bomb civilians is a mistake, then those who allowed for that mistake also must be blamed. Contrary to the skeptic, science is not morally neutral.

The second view concerning the relationship between science and morality is that the institution of science, like every human enterprise, is governed by a set of rules of conduct peculiar to it. Just as parenting includes the special obligation to feed and clothe one's own offspring, so science includes the obligation to seek the truth.

How much leeway does a scientist have in pursuing the truth? Can a parent, for example, steal in order to protect his or her family? Can a scientist deceive research subjects to gain insight into human behavior? These are difficult questions that are not answered simply by embracing a philosophy of relativism, the view that all rules of conduct, like rules of etiquette, are valid only within a special social context. For example, just as eating with one's fingers is acceptable as a formal mode of dining within the Brahman culture of southern India, so it might be felt that lying to patients is acceptable in the pursuit of medical research.

However, not all lying *is* acceptable even in the pursuit of research, just as not all fingers are acceptable in Brahman dining. For reasons of sanitation and health that extend beyond Indian culture, only right hands are used at the dining table (the left hand is reserved for toilet hygiene); so, too, for reasons that extend beyond the special goals of science, only subjects that have given voluntary and informed consent can be used for medical research. Hence, the idea of relativism does not adequately account for the broader perspective in which we make our judgments about conduct whether at the table or in the laboratory.

In opposition to both skeptic and relativist, I propose that scientists are subject to the same basic rules of decency as everyone else—corporate executive, automobile worker, southern Indian Brahman, military general, and natural leader alike. If the executive of a chemical plant is responsible for allowing his factory to pollute the environment, then the research chemist bears some of the responsibility for creating the noxious chemicals; if the assembly worker is partly responsible for contributing to the manufacture of an unsafe automobile, then so is the engineer who designed the product; and if the military leader is responsible for deciding to drop the bomb,

the nuclear scientist bears some of the responsibility as well.

There is, however, at least one difference between science and other professions. Scientific research is at the forefront of technology. If food production can be increased by genetically altering vegetables, AIDS eliminated by a new vaccine, criminal conduct altered by behavior modification, and world peace insured by the development of greater weapons of destruction, the scientist will be the first to know. The research scientist is in a morally privileged position to see where our research is going, and the view is not limited to the specialist. One need not be an endocrinologist to appreciate the elimination of Parkinson's disease, nor need one be a rocket scientist to contemplate the destruction of all humanity. The scientist, with his or her special training and expertise, is privileged to witness not just a horizon of new technology, but a better world that may eventually be opened for all to see.

In what follows I will assume that scientists bear moral responsibility for their work and that scientific and moral judgment are often inseparable. If the question is "What guarantees that the future of science will be for the good?," the preliminary answer is the morality of scientists themselves. However, this answer raises another question. Since scientists are only human, what guarantee is there that scientists will pursue their occupation faithfully and not be corrupted by greed or the lure of fame? If science is no less moral than any other institution, is it any less corruptible? We will turn to this question in the next section.

FRAUD

Are scientists greedier, more ambitious, more competitive, more ruthless, or more prone to cut moral corners than the rest of us in their pursuit of fame and professional glory? National newspaper headlines in recent years would have us think so.

The Baltimore affair is a good case in point. David Baltimore is a well-known molecular biologist who received the Nobel Prize in 1975 for his work on tumor viruses. In 1986, as director of the Whitehead Institute for Biomedical Research at the Massachusetts Institute of Technology, he lent his name to a paper on immunological research which was published in the journal *Cell*. That one of Baltimore's assistants did most of the research was not the cause of the ensuing scandal. It is common practice today for the heads of graduate departments and research programs to receive credit as coauthors of professional articles written by others. Rather, the author, Thereza Imanishi-Kari, was accused by another assistant of fraud.

The story made national headlines in 1988 when a congressional committee, the House Subcommittee on Oversight and Investigations, opened hearings on fraud in science focusing on the charges against Imanishi-Kari. The main question before the committee was: "Could research programs in science, heavily funded by the National Institutes of Health and other agencies of government, police themselves against misconduct?"

The problem facing the committee members was not just sorting through the details of a highly technical paper. The deeper issue was the nature of fraud itself, especially in contemporary science. One of the reasons that no formal charges were brought against Imanishi-Kari was that the idea of misconduct in science is not well defined.

At one extreme is plagiarism, the theft of someone else's intellectual work, which is a problem in contemporary science as it is in other academic and literary areas. Plagiarism, however, was not the main concern for the members of Congress that investigated the Baltimore case. Imanishi-Kari was not accused of theft but of fabricating data. Had the charge been stealing, there might not have been any hearings. *Who* did the work is one thing. Whether the work is valid is something else. The main issue for contemporary science is whether there are sufficient controls on the myriad papers published yearly in the professional journals to insure the integrity of current scientific belief. Mary Shelley's story of the mad scientist who makes an astounding breakthrough in complete isolation from his

peers is a myth, certainly as science is practiced today. Science is a social enterprise; each practitioner is intimately dependent on the previous work of others. If fraud in science is as "endemic" as William Broad and Nicholas Wade claim in their recent book, *Betrayers of the Truth*, the whole structure would be undermined. No researcher can be expected to investigate all the work that went before. Contrary to what we were taught in high school science class, surprisingly little scientific research is actually duplicated. Unless scientists can trust the competence and integrity of their predecessors, the results of even honest practitioners would be tainted.

Is fraud widespread in science? Besides plagiarism, the answer depends on what else can be meant by *fraud*. Imanishi-Kari was accused of manipulating data, but is the manipulation of data always wrong? The physicist Robert Millikan failed to publish data contained in his notebooks that would have undermined the results of his Nobel-winning experiments on electron charge. He manipulated the data, yet historians do not accuse him of misconduct—and not just because later independent research confirmed his findings. If we think of Millikan as a hero, as history suggests we should, we must suppose that he had reason to leave out certain data apart from whatever motivations he might have had to win the Nobel Prize. A chemist whose cat jumps onto his workbench at a crucial juncture in a key experiment has the right to judge the results invalid. He violates no apparent cannon of scientific ethics when he fails to include the data in his final report. Omitting data is not always wrong.

What about "fabricating" data, one of the charges against Imanishi-Kari? Is there misconduct when an investigator includes material that was not obtained in the study? Not always. It is common practice in both the so-called hard and social sciences to represent the results of studies by a graph. Plotting a line that represents, for example, the relationship between changing demographics in local school districts and the rejection of school budgets is an effective way of showing certain trends between an aging population with fewer school-age children and the increasing lack of support for public school education. The raw data alone would fail to illustrate the total picture as poignantly. Yet in plotting the curve, many more data points are included than were revealed in the study. The same is true for all graphic representation of data, yet the use of a graph by itself violates no rules of ethics. Including in a final report data not otherwise obtained in a study is a part of standard scientific practice.

Why then should the manipulation of data be thought a crime? Learning to do research in science, in part, consists in developing certain intuitions for distinguishing between results that are far-fetched and those that are merely unexpected. Galileo, to his scientific credit, was the first to appreciate telescopically observed points of light as satellites of Jupiter. Unlike the Aristotelians of his day, he did not reject the observations as optical aberrations of the glass. Who was the fraud, Galileo or his critics? Perhaps in the seventeenth century, there was room for honest disagreement.

What then is the difference between a faulty interpretation and fraud? It may be thought that besides the manipulation of data, fraud must include the intent to deceive. The British psychologist Cyril Burt, for example, knowingly deceived his contemporaries by faking reports of IQ scores among British school children of different economic and social backgrounds. His work is discredited today as fraudulent.

However, the use of deception in science is not always fraud. Medical researchers commonly administer placebos to unwitting subjects enrolled in drug-testing programs, and social scientists also deceive those enlisted in their studies. Stanley Milgram's investigation of aggression and authority is a classic example.

If Milgram's work is acceptable, why not Cyril Burt's? Part of the answer seems to be that Burt withheld relevant details from colleagues, professionals for whose instruction the study was undertaken. By contrast, subjects in an experiment expect to have some details withheld. Otherwise, only those with a tech-nical background in the field would be eligible to participate, which need not be the case.

But professionals also allow researchers some leeway in reporting details. Otherwise every oversight, slip, and misprint would be fraud, which seems excessive. Sloppy science is one thing; fraud is something else.

Wade and Broad may be right that the manipulation of data in science is endemic; but without a clearer definition of fraud, and except for certain individuals, it is not clear that scientists are betrayers of the truth.

If scientists are no worse than anybody else, is their practice any better? Human experimentation plays a key role in modern scientific research. Progress in medicine, psychology, biology, and a host of other disciplines would be seriously hampered if human beings were not subjects of scientific studies. To avoid abuses of the past, such as the Nazi experiments on concentration camp victims, or recently revealed radiation experiments on children, certain protocols are observed, for example, that subjects participate freely and be informed of personal risks. Despite proposed safeguards, however, researchers face a moral dilemma to which we will turn in the next section.

HUMAN EXPERIMENTATION

Human beings are not guinea pigs and should not be treated as such. Immanuel Kant's eighteenth-century "Categorical Imperative," that a person must not be enslaved to the interests of others, helped to enshrine in Western philosophy the ideal of autonomy and respect for the individual as a cannon of moral reasoning. But Western thought also includes the utilitarian prescription that individual interests can be sacrificed for the common good. How to reconcile these apparently conflicting moral demands is an underlying issue in much contemporary debate.

The problem is particularly acute in picking subjects for medical research. During the 1980s, for example, the National Cancer Institute funded an international study on breast cancer, the National Surgical Adjuvant Breast and Bowel Project, the findings of which helped to alter treatment from mastectomy to the less radical lumpectomy, now more commonly practiced. In the initial stages of the study, researchers assigned volunteers randomly to different treatment. Random assignment helps to insure statistical validity by minimizing influences such as age, race, and socioeconomic background on the therapeutic benefit of one surgical procedure compared to another.

The method of random assignment, however, failed to enlist enough subjects. Researchers could have solved the problem by reviewing past records of cancer patients on file in the medical archives. However, historical review is less reliable in controlling for the same distorting influences that randomizing is designed to avoid.

Investigators introduced a new procedure, *prerandomization*, which seemed to achieve the best of both worlds. The method works like this: the clinician invites his patient to participate in the study *after* the individual is randomly assigned to a treatment. Patients seem more willing to participate when they know in advance which treatment they will receive.

The new procedure, however, created another problem: when told that they were selected to receive mastectomy, some patients preferred the less radical procedure. Clinicians were in a bind. Having disclosed an alternative treatment, physicians felt compelled to allow the patient a choice. However, whatever the patient's preference, to insure that selection remained random, the subject was counted for purposes of the study as receiving the originally selected treatment. To overcome this statistical anomaly, the study was expanded.

Again, researchers needed more subjects. However, the solution seemed simple: *don't tell* the patient that she is a subject of medical research especially if she is preselected to receive the standard treatment. The rationale is that since the patient is to receive the same treatment she would otherwise receive if she were not part of the study, she need not be informed of alternative treatment, just as a patient who is not part of the study need not be informed of alternative treatment.

Ethical issues abound. There is at least one difference between the patient who is used for medical research and the one who is not: the one used, if informed, would have the right to choose the alternative treatment. Otherwise, why did the clinicians feel compelled to allow the subjects to choose? If the subjects have the right to choose, what right does the clinician have to keep that information from them?

Without additional argument to justify violating patients' rights, can prerandomization be both effective and ethical? Exactly why did prerandomization prove effective in getting volunteers to undertake the National Surgical Adjuvant Breast and Bowel Project? Were the patients fully informed? Did they understand that the treatment proposed to them by their physician was selected by chance? If so, why were more women willing to take that chance than were willing to submit to a random selection after volunteering? These are difficult questions that should be further explored. If left unanswered, they may tempt us to speculate that prerandomization as a technique for accruing subjects in scientific experimentation is effective only if it is unethical. That would be a harsh indictment of a widely accepted practice in scientific research today.

Without prerandomization, researchers could opt for randomization; the method used initially in the breast cancer study. Would that help?

Physicians have an obligation to provide their patients with sound medical advice and health care commensurate with acceptable current practice. Otherwise, they are violating the ethics of their profession. However, the medical profession also has an obligation to increase understanding of disease and provide more efficient and effective means of controlling illness and alleviating pain and suffering. Clinicians no less than medical theorists share this obligation to provide treatment of the highest caliber.

The question is, can the medical practitioner satisfy both obligations, especially if, as part of a study, he or she allows treatment to be selected randomly? In the breast cancer study, physicians allowed some of their patients to be selected randomly for lumpectomy though the standard treatment at the time was mastectomy. Lumpectomy was an experimental procedure which, to the benefit of many patients, has since proven effective. However, at the time, physicians were unsure, which was why the study was undertaken. Without established medical opinion, how can a physician allow his or her patient to subject herself to treatment that may prove less effective? How can a physician abrogate his or her medical responsibility to chance? It may be suggested that the patient was aware of the possibility of receiving experimental treatment but volunteered anyway. People have the right to compromise their immediate interests for long-term gains, even to benefit others.

In any experiment, however, the gains are iffy. The medical expert more than the patient should be aware of that, which is why the physician is not relieved completely of responsibility. If the study succeeds, then participating physicians and their patients are to be commended. If the experiment fails, the doctor's judgment should be questioned.

How then can the clinician satisfy his or her therapeutic obligation? Might he or she refuse to participate? Perhaps the clinician should forego participation even at the expense of personal prestige. His or her interest in the patient should take precedence over professional glory.

But what of the obligation to the profession and the greater interests of society to extend learning and improve medical care? If physicians ceased to allow their patients to participate in medical studies, advances in medical science would stop.

Besides historical review of clinical records, are there effective methods of study other than human experimentation? In the next section, we will turn to the ethics of animal research.

ANIMAL RESEARCH

Animals, dogs and cats, are not human beings. They do not have forty-six chromosomes nor do they act as we do. They do not wear clothes, carry credit cards, drive automobiles, shop at malls, or do any of the other things we commonly associate with being human. Partly for this reason, we do not feel compelled to treat them as we treat ourselves. We do not protect them with the same legislation or extend to them the same rights and privileges. Murder is a capital offense in many states, but poaching is a misdemeanor; voting is reserved for citizens, a status that even the highest order of animal will never achieve.

Despite the obvious differences, however, some animals are very much like us. Apes have been taught to use sign language, and recently biologists have discovered genetic ties between us and chimpanzees. Animals are conscious of their surroundings; they can experience hunger and thirst and exhibit sexual as well as familial instincts. The more familiar we become with animal behavior, the more human they seem.

Why then do we treat them so differently from how we treat ourselves, especially in scientific and industrial research? We sacrifice close to a half-billion animals a year for product testing, behavioral research, instructional purposes, pharmaceutical investigations, and medical study. The number does not include the vast array of other creatures raised or otherwise obtained for food. If an equivalent number of people were destroyed, we would experience a holocaust unprecedented in all human history. Yet we do not read or hear much about this slaughter except for the articles published in professional journals or the occasional text that finds a wider audience. Ted Koppel does not devote much air time to the subject, nor does MacNeil-Lehrer or any of the other nightly or feature news programs. Radio broadcasts, too, lack serious coverage. Except for the report of some ritual sacrifice by an otherwise secret religious cult, animal killing is not a major story.

Can it be that we accept the sacrifices of animals as a necessary evil, something we would prefer to eliminate eventually? Mathematical and computer models, the use of lower organisms such as bacteria and fungi, and tissue cultures are alternatives, but they cannot yet replace the use of whole living organisms, for example, in testing for toxicity or analgesic effect.

Should we just shrug our shoulders? Maybe next year the prospects for a capuchin monkey living its entire life in a back shelf cage wired to an arrhythmia monitor will improve. For the moment, its life along with many others of its species, is confined to the laboratory and consigned to the interests of medical science.

We are not, however, so sanguine about all species leading lives of forced misery. A human being in place of that capuchin would cause not just a storm of protest, not just a series of news reports, but an FBI raid, congressional hearings, and criminal indictments.

Why the difference? Are we *speciesists?* Are we biased in favor of human beings, prejudiced toward others, in the way that white supremacists reject blacks and sexists women?

But racism and sexism are not the same. The white supremacist will not live or work with blacks, will not send his or her children to the same schools that black children attend, nor worship with blacks in the same church. Black supremacists feel the same way about whites. The racist, whether black or white, is a bigot who ideally seeks complete separation as if the other group were subhuman.

Male chauvinists fall into a different category since many are married and have no problem living with women, sending their children (often the same children) to the same school, or worshipping in the same church. They do not seek separation but *domination* of one gender over the other. The sexist is a not a bigot but a "pig," a lowlife of diminished sensibility who treats mature women as if they were children.

What of the speciesist? If by *speciesism* we mean separating, for example, farm animals from human beings, then we are all speciesists. Why is that bad? People are not expected to share living quarters with sheep, goats, and chickens. The habits of barnyard creatures would make our living space uninhabitable. They defecate and urinate where they eat and sleep, and they need materials such as straw for their comfort that is unsuitable for us. Treating a person like a farm animal is wrong; treating a farm animal like a farm animal is not. In this sense, speciesism is not bad.

On the other hand, if a "speciesist" is a lowlife with diminished sensibility, then speciesism is bad. However, a farmhand need not have diminished sensibility to command oxen to pull a cart. An ox is bred for pulling heavy loads and is capable of little else. It is a beast of burden and, in the sense under consideration, one need not be a speciesist to treat an ox as such.

Where does this leave us? We treat animals in research, as in other areas, differently than we treat ourselves. Human subjects volunteer; animals do not. Different treatment by itself does not mean that scientific research is unethical. Why then are organizations such as People for the Ethical Treatment of Animals (PETA) opposed to the use of laboratory animals?

Part of the answer is that some of the methods of science are cruel. The Noble-Collip Drum is a particularly odious device which "crushes bones, destroys tissues, smashes teeth and ruptures internal organs," while the Draize Test is a fiendish procedure for testing primarily new cosmetics for irritants by placing the substance in the eyes of restrained albino rabbits.

Cruelty can be abolished, abuse corrected, yet critics encourage alternatives to animal experimentation even if they prove more costly. We can agree with the critics that if we are not to mistreat animals, perhaps we should just leave them alone. However, without available alternatives, the use of animals in research is difficult to avoid.

So far we have been discussing the ethics of scientists and their past and present methods. In the next and final section, we will examine the new genetics and attempt to get a glimpse into the future.

GENETIC ENGINEERING

Victor Frankenstein was a good theorist and technician. Mary Shelley tells us that he created in the laboratory a new living being. But he lacked moral vision and failed to foresee the monster that his being would become.

Are scientists today, especially those working in the new genetics, better able to foresee the outcome of their work? Our discussion of fraud suggests that scientists are no worse than anybody else. That some scientists have betrayed their calling does not mean that fraud is endemic. Nor should we allow the dilemma of using human beings or the reservations we may have of using animals as research subjects to stand in the way of progress. Scientists in the past faced similar dilemmas and may have shared our reservations, yet we do not condemn their practice, especially considering the progress they made in attacking and even eliminating diseases such as smallpox. If medical science can eradicate the afflictions of the late twentieth century—painful and debilitating genetic disorders such as sickle-cell anemia, Tay-Sachs disease, Lesch-Nyhan disease, Huntington's chorea, and cystic fibrosis, and even heart disease and cancer—then perhaps we should suspend judgment on some of their methods.

However, the prospects of the new genetic techniques extend beyond the treatment of disease. The Human Genome Project, a multi-billion-dollar, fifteen-year undertaking subsidized by the National Institutes of Health (NIH) and Department of Energy (DOE), is an ongoing attempt to map the 100,000 human genes and determine the sequence of the three billion nucleotides that define human DNA. Although the immediate goal is therapeutic, eventually the knowledge gleaned from basic research may be used for eugenics, the attempt to improve the whole of homo sapiens. Through the lens of modern eugenics we can glimpse a world of strong and healthy men, women, and children genetically engineered to lead athletically and intellectually active lives, eating cheap but nutritional and satisfying recombinant fruits, vegetables, and other genetically designed foods A biblical paradise—in a future here-and-now.

The problem is that treating an individual's ailment is one thing; playing God by altering the gene pool is something else. Are we wise enough to decide whether aggression, like smallpox, should be eliminated? Except in certain cases like hemophilia, genes do not act discretely. The gene for sickle-cell anemia confers on the individual who carries it immunity to malaria. Eradicating the disease eliminates the immunity. Altering the genetic underpinnings of a human trait like aggression should prove at least as complex. Would violent street crime be diminished? War eliminated? Remember that George Bush shed his wimpy reputation only *after* he led the allied confrontation with Iraq in the Persian Gulf War.

Is the question of human wisdom premature? Geneticists are only beginning to understand the function of individual genes, like the "suicide gene" that may be the key to Alzheimer's disease. Perhaps when geneticists know more about the complex genetic underpinnings of aggression, moralists will know what to do about it.

Other fears, however, abound. Should geneticists be allowed to interfere with the food supply? Partly in response to the dangers of DDT, people are weary of the use of pesticides to increase fruit and vegetable yields, of hormones to enhance animal growth, and enzyme additives to increase egg and milk production. We can understand why consumers are apprehensive of new transgenetic vegetables, like the tomato with a flounder gene spliced into its DNA to increase its resistance to frost. That genetically altered food today may be as safe as frozen food was when first introduced in the 1920s does not allay people's fears.

If we are concerned about genetically altered tomatoes, how much more concerned should we be with the prospect of genetically designed children? That parents will be able to pick their offspring's eye and hair color, body type, and personality does not seem to arouse as much concern as the power to determine gender. Why that is, however, is not clear.

Will the sex ratio be skewed in favor of males? Why is that bad? That prospective parents *prefer* male offspring may be an unfortunate residue of our chauvinistic past; but that people can *have* whatever gender they want, especially for the first or second child, might benefit society by limiting unnecessary population growth.

The concern for genetically engineered children may go deeper. Who will decide the genetic makeup of the next generation, parents or government? Individuals have a right to decide whether to have children. Perhaps they should also have the right to determine what type of child to have.

But parents do not have complete control over the fate of their offspring. The state mandates education and the courts have ordered blood transfusions in opposition to the Jehovah's Witnesses. Perhaps the state should have the power to remove the gene for Huntington's disease and other genetic disorders, whether or not parents agree. But what of aggression? Should an agency of the state have the authority to order the genetic equivalent of lobotomy?

These questions are not new. Social policy in a democratic society always must contend with the delicate balance between the rights of individuals and the needs of the group. Genetic research merely brings greater urgency to the debate. If social issues cannot be postponed, genetic research should not be postponed either.

CONCLUSION

Science has many moral pitfalls. Its history includes questionable practices, excesses, and unsolved moral dilemmas. If scientists have special responsibility because of their privileged position at the forefront of human knowledge, then, perhaps, like the rest of us, they are only human and on occasion succumb to temptation. As a group, however, scientists are no worse than the rest of us, nor is there anything special about their practice that should make them particularly suspect. Recognizing that many moral issues within science remain to be solved, nevertheless, unless we are to embrace an unnecessary moral skepticism or an unwarranted relativism, science still remains the best hope of the future.

Closing Questions

1. Is the morally neutral scientist a poorer scientist because of his or her neutrality?

   _____

   _____

   _____

   _____

2. In his magnum opus, *A Treatise of Human Nature*, British Empiricist David Hume remarks: "Tis not contrary to reason to prefer the destruction of the whole world to the scratching of my finger." One of the things he meant by this is that morality has its source in sentiment rather than reason. Later in history, the logical positivists argued for a similar thesis. They thought that, unlike scientific judgments, moral judgments were cognitively meaningless. Is this portrayal of morality correct?

   _____

   _____

   _____

   _____

3. In Thorton Wilder's *The Bridge Over San Luis Rey*, the narrator seeks to explain the fate of several men and women who fell to their deaths while crossing a bridge. He does this by reconstructing the lives of each individual up until the moment when each character walked across the bridge. In your judgment, how scientific a methodology is this? What presuppositions does the narrator make about the place of values in the world?

   _____

   _____

   _____

   _____

4. Several years ago, scientists at the University of Minnesota debated whether they should look at the results of Nazi research. The dilemma was this: on the one hand, such research might prove invaluable since it was conducted on human beings and therefore did not involve the kinds of inferences scientists must make when they

experiment on animals. On the other hand, the research was conducted in gross disregard of human rights. Thinking that the benefits of such research outweighed the costs, especially since the research was a *fait accompli*, scientists decided to study the results. As it turned out, they were of little value since Nazi science was bad science. Do you think the scientists were right to look at these experiments?

_____

_____

_____

_____

5. Advances in scientific technology are often said to have resulted in an increase of our material level of being. Many households in North America now possess microwave ovens, personal computers, fax machines, cellular phones, and so on. In your experience and observation, has the availability of these items truly made life better?

_____

_____

_____

_____

6. Is it permissible to experiment on prisoners without first obtaining their informed consent?

_____

_____

_____

_____

7. Discuss some of the value implications in the social sciences, particularly in psychology and sociology.

_____

_____

_____

_____

8. Sociobiologists, such as Edward O. Wilson of Harvard University, have argued that any moral institution that ignores evolution does so at its peril. Monogamy, for instance, is such an institution. As some sociobiologists see it, we cannot afford to remain monogamous if we are to survive as a species because (1) women outnumber men two to one and (2) men are more able (and willing) to procreate than women. The same considerations do not argue for one wife having several husbands (polyandry)—a conclusion that has upset many feminists. To what extent should science respect findings that are morally objectionable? Would you support research into the differences between blacks and whites not knowing what the research might yield?

_____

_____

_____

_____

9. Is research on animals justifiable?

_____

_____

_____

_____

10. One of the discoveries of modern science has been the RU 486 morning-after abortion pill which, like the Intra Uterine Device (IUD), destroys a fertilized ovum. While widely available in France, the RU 486 pill has met with considerable opposition in the United States. Do you support the availability of this pill?

_____

_____

_____

_____

For Further Reading

Baumrin, Bernard, and B. Freedman, eds. *Moral Responsibility and the Professions*. Section III: "Ethics and the Sciences." New York: Haven, 1983.

Bronowski, John. *Science and Human Values*. New York: Harper, 1965.

Caws, Peter. *Ethics from Experience*. Boston, Mass.: Jones and Bartlett, 1996.

Engelhardt, H. Tristram, and Daniel Callahan, eds. *Morals, Science, and Society*. New York: Hastings Center, 1978.

Haan, N., R. Bellah, et al., eds. *Social Science and Moral Inquiry*. New York: Columbia University Press, 1983.

Hook, Sidney, Paul Kurtz, and Miro Todorovich, eds. *The Ethics of Teaching and Scientific Research*. Buffalo: Prometheus Books, 1977.

Milgram, Stanley. *Obedience to Authority*. New York: Harper, 1974.

Polyani, M. *Personal Knowledge*. New York: Harper, 1958.

Rolston, Holmes III, ed. *Biology, Ethics, and the Origins of Life*. Boston, Mass.: Jones & Bartlett, 1995.

Shrader-Frechette, Kristin. *Ethics of Scientific Research*. Lanham, Md.: Rowman & Littlefield, 1994.

Chapter 12

Racism and Anti-Semitism

Passages for Reflection

"The problem of the twentieth century is the problem of the color line."

—*W. E. B. Du Bois*

"The Jews are not hated because they have evil qualities; evil qualities are sought for because they are hated."

—*Max Nordau*

"Racism is a bacterium, potentially curable but presently deadly; anti-Semitism is a virus, potentially deadly but presently contained."

—*Letty Cottin Pogrebin*

"Jew me, sue me, everybody do me. Kick me, Kike me, don't you black or white me."

—*Michael Jackson*

Opening Questions

1. What differences, if any, exist between racism and anti-Semitism?
2. Should you support affirmative action for racial minorities?
3. Is black racism against whites possible?

Racism and anti-Semitism are morally wrong practices and pernicious evils. In their more modest embodiments, racism as practiced against blacks and anti-Semitism are morally wrong since they deny to blacks and Jews such primary goods as housing, employment, and education. In their more extreme representations, racism and anti-Semitism led to such horrific evils as American slavery and the Nazi Holocaust. While the truth of this claim is beyond dispute, what is not obvious are the reasons why racism and anti-Semitism are the evils we know them to be and what ought to be done to eradicate them.

Before we address each of these questions, let us specify what is meant by *racism* and *anti-Semitism*. Although *racism* has been used to refer to such disparate phenomena as actions, practices, and attitudes, each of these have common assumptions. The most common of these is that human beings are divided into races, and that some of these races are morally, intellectually, or physically superior to others owing to inherited biological differences. These theses are then used to derive moral and political claims such as that the superior race has a right to rule over the inferior ones, and that the superior race has a duty to preserve its purity by such strategies as segregated housing and education and, if all else fails, extermination.

Each of these claims is disputable. With respect to the claim that human beings are divided into races, the prevailing consensus among enlightened men and women is that the view is false. Although not uncontested, many philosophers, biologists, and anthropologists maintain that the notion of "race" implies that visible differences between population groups, such as skin color, correlate with deeper genetically based traits such as character, intelligence, and personality. However, the consensus is that no such correlations occur and consequently that there are no races.[1]

Even if this consensus did not exist, even if the prevailing view were that races do exist, it would not follow that some races are superior to others owing to inherited biological features. This is true even if we could show that some races are superior to others in some respects. Even though, for instance, a fifteen point mean difference in IQ occurs be-

---

[1]See Stephen Jay Gould, *Ever Since Darwin* (New York: W. W. Norton, 1977), ch. 29.

tween and blacks and whites, it does not follow that any white is biologically superior to any black for the simple reason that some blacks have higher IQs than whites. It also does not follow because we cannot rule out that the difference between mean scores of the relative groups is an effect of socialization and not biology.

Yet a further problem concerns the attempt to derive the conclusion that superior races ought to dominate inferior ones from the premise that races exist and that some races are superior to others. Even if races did exist and some were superior to others in a biologically inheritable way, it would not follow that the superior race would have a right or duty to dominate the inferior one. As David Hume showed a few centuries ago, we cannot infer what should be the case from what is the case. (Citing Hume to repudiate the racist's claim is ironic. In a notorious footnote to his essay, "National Character" (1748), Hume proclaimed that Negroes (sic.) were of low intelligence.") What he meant by this can be explained as follows.

Given that all women are mortal and Whoopi Goldberg is a woman, it follows that Whoopi Goldberg is mortal. Similarly, we may infer that the Prelude is made in Japan if we assume that all Hondas are made in Japan and the Prelude is made by Honda. What does not make sense is inferring that Whoopi Goldberg *should* be mortal in the first example, and that the Prelude *should* be made in Japan in the second, in the sense that Whoopi Goldberg has an obligation to be mortal and the Prelude has an obligation to be made in Japan. These inferences make no sense because the ethical obligations that are being inferred are not contained in the statements from which they are allegedly inferred. Analogously, even if we assume that whites are inferior to blacks and Jones is black, it does not follow that Jones ought to be dominated by whites. Thus, even if it were true that some races are superior to others in a biologically inheritable way, no moral agenda may be inferred from this. (Many *Star Trek* episodes address this theme.) Racism, then, is a disreputable theory whose appeal lies not in its intellectual attractiveness but, as Bernard Boxill has pointed out, in its ability to serve as a potent weapon in the competition over scarce resources.[2]

Having discussed racism, it remains for us to analyze anti-Semitism. I begin by pointing out that *racism,* as just defined, is broad enough to cover anti-Semitism, construed as racism toward Jews. Some philosophers maintain this implicitly. Philip Cummings's entry on racism in the *Encyclopedia of Philosophy*[3] mentions Hitler's *Mein Kampf* as containing racist views, and Lawrence Blum speaks of racism and anti-Semitism in

---

[2]Bernard R. Boxill, "Racism and Related Issues." In Lawrence C. Becker and Charlotte B. Becker, eds., *Encyclopedia of Ethics* (New York: Garland Press, 1992).

[3]Philip W. Cummings, "Racism." In Paul Edwards, ed., *The Encyclopedia of Philosophy* (New York, Macmillan, 1967).

the same breath,[4] as does Cornell West.[5] While not denying that *racism* is broad enough to incorporate anti-Semitism, we can point to enough historical differences between the two to warrant treating them as distinct phenomena to the extent that racism is regarded as a white ideology directed against blacks.

The coining of the word *anti-Semitism* is usually attributed to the German journalist Wilhelm Marr who, in 1873, published his anti-Semitic best seller, *The Victory of Judaism over Germanism*. The term *anti-Judaism* is preferable inasmuch as Arabs are Semites, while anti-Semitism is an ideology directed against Jews. In this light, we can understand a remark made by chess champion Bobby Fisher who reportedly is rabidly anti-Semitic. When asked if he was in fact anti-Semitic, Fisher remarked, "Well, I don't dislike Arabs."[6] These kinds of word games go a long way in explaining the insistence of many Arabs that it is not anti-Semitic of them to oppose the Jewish State of Israel. *By definition*, they cannot be anti-Semitic. Of course, they *can* be anti-Israel, which they have been, historically, and to the extent they believe that Zionism (support for the State of Israel) is racism, they can be antiracist. Word games aside, the term *anti-Semitism* is deeply embedded in the English language and we can safely say that anti-Semitism has its source in the idea that Jews, as descendants of Lucifer, are morally responsible for the death of Jesus Christ.

The source for the idea that Jews are responsible for the death of Christ is the New Testament, particularly the Gospel of John. There, Jews are portrayed as nothing less than malevolent creatures explicitly rejecting what is manifestly good. Beyond that, the Gospel of John has Jesus accusing Jews of having the devil himself as their father (*John* 8:42–47). This makes Jews not only evil, but irredeemably so.

The eminent historian Gavin I. Langmuir has identified three features of anti-Semitism that deepen the preceding account; each owes its appeal to what he maintains are repressed doubts by Christians regarding the veracity of their religious beliefs. The first is the belief that Jews are in some mysterious way incapable of properly understanding history and their roles within it, that they suffer from a "supernatural blindness." This, says Langmuir, has been used to explain why Jews are able to reject Jesus as the Messiah. The second is the belief that Jews are responsible for the death of Jesus. As Langmuir explains it, it has seemed so implausible to some Christians that Jews encountered Jesus and did not recognize that he was God, that some have found it easier to attribute

---

[4]Lawrence Blum, "Moral Asymmetry in Manifestations of Racism." Unpublished paper presented at Oberlin Philosophy Colloquium, April 21–23, 1995.

[5]Cornell West, *Race Matters*. (Boston: Beacon Press, 1993). West writes: "Black anti-Semitism—along with its concomitant xenophobias, such as patriarchal and homophobic prejudices—. . . plays into the hands of the old style *racists*. . . ." (emphasis mine).

[6]Chalmers Clark brought this to my attention.

ill-will, as opposed to ignorance, to Jews. The third feature is the belief that historical events have demonstrated that God punished Jews for their deicide, events which—ironically—were often initiated by anti-Semites themselves.[7]

As Langmuir explains it, this conception of Jews helps explain many of the irrational beliefs that people have had about Jews, such as holding that Jews use the blood of children in commemorating Passover, a libel vividly portrayed in literature by Bernard Malamud in *The Fixer*.[8] The stereotype has it that Jews are sly, greedy people and that such vices are inheritable. Small wonder, then, that the Nazis believed it was their right as well as their duty to exterminate Jews to "purify" the Aryan race. If Jews are perceived as irredeemably evil, then neither assimilation nor deportation can serve the anti-Semite's ends.

Other accounts of anti-Semitism include that of Jean-Paul Sartre whose account owes much to existentialism.[9] As Sartre sees it, the anti-Semite is a person who, in bad faith, creates a person with qualities that the anti-Semite can hate in order to escape from the responsibilities that come with freedom. In blaming the Jews for killing Jesus, the anti-Semite is able to avoid the awesome responsibilities that come from a radically-free self. In this regard, Sartre sees anti-Semitism as no different from racism which also serves as an escape from freedom. Consequently, Sartre is able to say that "the Jew only serves him [the anti-Semite] as a pretext; elsewhere his counterpart will make use of the Negro or the man of yellow skin. . . . Anti-Semitism, in short, is fear of the human condition."[10]

Sartre's explanation of anti-Semitism is predicated on his philosophy and because of that suffers from the failure to account for anti-Semitism's historical conditions. The important differences between racism and anti-Semitism, however, are made clearer if we examine the racist underpinnings of the pinnacle of white racism against blacks: the institution of American slavery.[11] Far from viewing blacks as irredeemably evil, slave owners viewed blacks as moral simpletons, incapable of full membership in the moral community and unable to contribute in any important way to the development of humankind. The stereotypical black was an individual who, though not without physical prowess, was devoid of moral and intellectual prowess. To the slave owner, the

---

[7]Gavin I. Langmuir, *History, Religion, and Anti-Semitism* (Los Angeles: University of California Press, 1990), Chap. 14.

[8]Penguin Books, 1961.

[9]Jean-Paul Sartre, *Anti-Semite and Jew*, translated by George J. Becker. (New York: Schocken Books, 1965.)

[10]Ibid., p. 54.

[11]This account is indebted to Laurence Mordekhai Thomas, *Vessels of Evil: American Slavery and the Holocaust* (Philadelphia: Temple University Press, 1993).

black slave was a sexually overactive individual who was capable of excelling at singing and dancing, but not at more cultured pursuits. The stereotypical Uncle Tom speaks to this conception.

These differences between white racism and anti-Semitism go far toward explaining why the Holocaust took its particular form and why American slavery took its particular form. If, in the eyes of the anti-Semite, Jews are regarded as irredeemably evil whose aim is to overthrow God himself, then genocide is the logical solution to "the Jewish problem." Assimilation, conversion, and deportation are no answers to the existence of a people regarded as malevolent. Since blacks were regarded as simpletons as opposed to evildoers, subordination in the form of slavery made sense. Because slave owners denied blacks their full humanity, regarded them as incapable of actively participating in social arrangements, the slave owners had no reason not to treat slaves as so much utility like some animals are regarded. For all of these reasons, we should not construe anti-Semitism as a species of racism.

Having discussed what racism and anti-Semitism are about, we should say a few words to explain why they are wrong. That they are wrong or bad is hardly contestable. The reason they are wrong, aside from the appalling consequences that have resulted from them, is usually explained via the principle of equality. According to the principle of equality, equals should be treated equally and unequals should be treated unequally. This principle, which dates back to Aristotle, is sometimes referred to as the "formal principle of justice"—*formal* because it concerns form as opposed to content. It does not, however, specify in what ways people must be alike before they receive the same treatment and in what ways people must be unalike before they receive unequal treatment. We need to inquire, then, about content; we need to ask in what ways people must be alike or different before we can claim that they should receive equal or unequal treatment.

Usually, the way to answer this question is to say that the differences between people must be relevant to the treatment in question. If, for instance, the issue concerns a kind of employment, what is relevant is having the appropriate skills, competencies, and abilities relative to the employment opportunity. We do not unjustly discriminate against a male, for example, if we are looking to hire a wet nurse; we do unjustly discriminate against a woman if we are hiring for the position of accountant and the woman candidate has the same mathematical abilities as the male. Thus, we violate the principle of equality and hence unjustly discriminate against an individual when we rely on features that are morally irrelevant. In the case of blacks, this feature is color; in the case of Jews, this feature is religious belief. Simply put, color and religious belief are features that are irrelevant to such practices as employment, education, and housing. Therefore, treating people as if these features are relevant violates the principle of equality.

Having explained why racism and anti-Semitism are bad, we now want to ask what should be done about them. The discrimination of the past was unjust insofar as it involved gross violations of the principle of equality. But discrimination is ongoing and equally wrong. In fact, past discrimination is very much responsible for many of the inequalities that exist today. One reason blacks today are denied preferred positions in society is because they have been historically denied quality education.

Before examining some answers to our question, we note that discussions about discrimination are often confined to blacks and minorities other than Jews. This is unfortunate, inasmuch as discrimination against Jews has been and continues to be no less pervasive than discrimination against other minorities, although it is typically so subtle as to go unnoticed.[12] The reason usually given for this is the "social invisibility thesis" that makes discrimination against Jews less obvious than discrimination against blacks. In the 1920s, the president of Harvard University implicitly appealed to this thesis when he remarked: "Cambridge could make a Jew indistinguishable from an Anglo-Saxon; but not even Harvard could make a black man white."[13] Partially for this reason, much of the literature often ignores discrimination against Jews.

While not going so far as to claim that bypassing Jews is itself a form of anti-Semitism, one has to wonder why Jews are often omitted from discussions of this nature. Few, if any, textbooks on ethics address the issue of anti-Semitism alongside questions of racism and sexism. Part of the reason undoubtedly concerns the fact that discriminating against minorities—blacks, in particular—is a distinctively though (not uniquely) American phenomenon. Blacks were the victims of slavery and they have systematically and institutionally been denied housing, employment, and educational opportunities. Jews, in contrast, have been the victims of discrimination, but they have not suffered it institutionally in America. Otherwise put, blacks have been the victims of *de jure* discrimination, while discrimination against Jews has largely been *de facto*.

Yet another reason for the asymmetrical treatment of blacks and Jews in America is the fact that Jews have flourished in America whereas blacks have not. By and large, Jews have prospered economically, have ascended to political office, have gained admission to prestigious universities, and have obtained adequate housing. Finally, since the horrors of the Holocaust have become known, it is socially unacceptable to be overtly anti-Semitic. The association of anti-Semitism with Hitler has led to an almost worldwide condemnation of anti-Semitism, especially in the minds of Western society. The upshot, then, is that anti-Semitism in

---

[12]For a disturbing account of anti-Semitism in the West, see John Loftus and Mark Aarons, *The Secret War Against the Jews* (New York: St. Martin's Press, 1994).

[13]Quoted in Bruce Kuklick, *The Rise of American Philosophy* (New Haven: Yale University Press, 1977), p. 456.

America has not achieved proportions equal to antiblack racism, however prevalent it has been elsewhere. For this reason, we shall follow convention and limit our discussion of rectifying antiblack racism. When what is said pertains to racism against Jews and other minorities as well, it applies with equal force. As for discrimination against women, the reader is referred to Chapter 8 where that issue is taken up alongside other feminist issues.

What then should we do about current ongoing discrimination as well as the inequalities that have resulted from past discrimination? What obligations, if any, does society have to rectify present wrongs as well as the wrongs that are the result of past discrimination? By far the most provocative answer to this question centers around government-required affirmative-action programs. Initiated in 1965 by President Lyndon B. Johnson, affirmative action policy was originally put forward to correct past discrimination. Its purpose was to actively seek out black candidates for jobs, college, or promotions, without treating them differently in the decision to hire, admit, or promote. In the 1970s, however, affirmative action took on a new meaning as good-faith efforts to recruit blacks would not withstand a Title VII challenge of the Civil Rights Act of 1964. Employers and admission committees had to actually hire or admit black applicants to withstand challenges of racial discrimination. The tack most frequently employed was to select the best available black candidate even if the best was not good enough for the position.

Affirmative-action programs, especially in institutions of higher education, have led to landmark lawsuits, the most important of which is *University of California v. Bakke* [438 U.S. 265 (1978)]. The case concerned Allen Bakke, a white male, who applied for admission to the University of California at Davis Medical School. The school had set aside 16 of its 100 places in its first-year class for minority students. Despite having a significantly higher grade point average and medical school admission test scores than the sixteen minority students, Bakke was denied admission. He then challenged the constitutionality of the University's admission procedures. In a 5–4 decision, the Supreme Court, led by Justice Lewis F. Powell, ruled in favor of Bakke that quota systems such as the one used at the University of California Medical School were unconstitutional. At the same time, the Court held that colleges and universities can consider race as a factor in the admissions process. While inroads have been made against affirmative action in the past few years, *Bakke*, to this day, remains valid law.

The rationale most frequently given for affirmative-action programs is "the principle of compensatory justice." This principle states that whenever an injustice has been committed, just compensation or reparation must be made to the injured party. It is this principle that is the rationale behind tort law's compensating victims for injuries for individual harms. Thus, if, as a result of a homeowner's not posting a warning sign around a hole he had been digging on the sidewalk in front of his house, a passerby fell in and broke her leg, the law requires the homeowner to make the passerby whole again insofar as it is in his power to do so. Ordinarily, this translates into the homeowner's being made to pay the passerby's medical bills, her salary for the time she missed at work, and loss of consortium (the monetary value placed upon the passerby's value to her family). This principle of compensatory justice also explains why Germany pays Jews money for the harms it caused them in World War II, and it is the principle behind the claim that American Indians should be compensated for the past unjust deprivation of their tribal land.

While supporters of affirmative action cite the principle of compensatory justice to justify that policy, the policy has many detractors including, at the time of this writing, the Republican-led U.S. Congress and the U.S. Supreme Court. The arguments made are diverse and many. First, it is argued that affirmative action is racism in reverse. Using race as a criterion to make hiring or admission decisions violates the very principle of equality that is the basis of the claim that racism is wrong. Second, individuals receiving preferential treatment may not themselves have suffered unjust treatment. A third argument is that individuals who lose out because others receive preferential treatment may themselves have been disadvantaged. A fourth and perhaps the most powerful argument against affirmative action is that it is self-defeating. The claim is made that in admitting or hiring the most qualified blacks, the agencies doing the hiring or admitting are benefiting those individuals with middle-class backgrounds instead of those from lower-class backgrounds who presumably need affirmative action the most.[14] But, if the most qualified blacks are those least harmed or wronged, so the argument goes, then affirmative action only helps those who are best able to help themselves.

Most of the arguments discussed so far are deontological in nature. Utilitarian arguments are found on both sides as well. Proponents of affirmative action sometimes argue that the "backward-looking" principle of compensatory justice is beside the point. The issue, they argue, is not so much that of rectifying past injustices, but creating an environment that is free of racial inequality. Accordingly, even if affirmative action did discriminate in reverse or favor blacks who have not been the victims of past injustices, the policy would nonetheless be justified. Utilitarian opponents, on the other hand, argue that if the goal of affirmative action is to move toward a more equal society, the effect is to create Balkanized campuses and businesses obsessed with racial and ethnic divisions.

Affirmative action is but one solution to the problem of racism. Other solutions range from passive nondiscrimination (requiring deci-

---

[14]See Bernard R. Boxill. *Blacks and Social Justice*, rev. ed. (Savage, MD: Rowman & Littlefield, 1992), p. 4.

sions about hiring and admission to disregard race) to total emigration such as to Israel for Jews or to Africa for blacks.

Having examined racism and anti-Semitism as well as some of the strategies employed as responses to them, we conclude by asking why, in recent history, have Jews and blacks not gotten along when, given that both have been targets of discrimination, they should be natural allies. That they have not gotten along since the Civil Rights Bill was passed is painfully obvious. The Crown Heights incident is one of many that exemplify the tension between the two communities. In August 1991, the Crown Heights section of Brooklyn erupted in three days of anti-Jewish rioting after a Hasidic motorist accidentally killed a black child. Over eighty Jews were injured and rabbinic student Yankel Rosenbaum was stabbed to death by a mob shouting, "Kill the Jew." Lemrick Nelson, the assailant identified by Rosenbaum before he died, was later acquitted by a predominately black jury.

But black-Jewish relationships have also languished in a more "cerebral" environment. Witness the following excerpt from Nation of Islam spokesperson Khalid Abdul Muhammed at a speech he delivered in November 1993 at Kean College, New Jersey:

> Who are the slumlords in the black community? The so-called Jew. . . .
> Who is sucking our blood in the black community? A white imposter Arab and a white imposter Jew. Right in the black community, sucking our blood on a daily basis. . . . Professor Griff was right when he spoke here . . . and when he spoke in the general vicinity of Jersey and New York, and when he spoke at Columbia Jewniversity over in Jew York City. He was right. . . ."

The insidious comments of Professor Leonard Jeffries of the City University of New York constitutes another example of black-Jewish tension. Jeffries has publicly charged that "rich Jews . . . helped finance the slave trade." Then we have the Nation of Islam leader Louis Farrakhan who has charged Jews with "monumental culpability" for the evils of slavery, and the Reverend Jesse Jackson who has referred to New York as "Hymie Town." The list goes on. While Jackson has apologized for this careless remark, we have to wonder whether he would have apologized had it not been politically advantageous for him to do so.

Cornell West cites two major issues that divide the black and Jewish communities.[15] The first concerns the question of what constitutes the most effective means for black progress in America. Blacks, says West, blame Jews for sometimes opposing affirmative action, which many blacks see as essential to their survival. And while Jewish opposition is not as strong as that of other groups in the country, West maintains that

---

[15]See Cornell West, *Race Matters* (Boston: Beacon Press, 1993), Ch. 6.

it is most visible to blacks inasmuch as Jews historically have supported black progress.

The second issue that West believes divides blacks and Jews concerns the significance of Israel for Jews. Lacking a sympathetic understanding of the historic sources of Jewish anxieties about group survival, West thinks blacks do not grasp the attachment Jews have to the State of Israel. At the same time, he thinks that Jews fail to acknowledge the status of blacks as permanent underdogs in American society by not comprehending what the symbolic predicament of Palestinians in Israel means to blacks. He claims that the Jewish defense of Israel smacks of dogmatic group interest to the detriment of substantive moral deliberation.

Whether or not West is right in diagnosing what ails black-Jewish relations, we cannot deny that the alliance between blacks and Jews that had flourished from 1910 to 1967 has faltered in recent years with the rise of black anti-Semitism. As West sees it, black anti-Semitism rests on three foundations. First, it is a species of antiwhitism. Although Jewish complicity in American racism has been less extensive than that of other white Americans, the black perception is that Jews are identical to any other group that benefits from white privileges. Second, it is a result of higher expectations some blacks have of Jews. This perspective, says West, holds Jews to a higher moral standard than other white ethnic groups. Finally, black anti-Semitism results from resentment and envy directed at a fellow underdog who has achieved success in American society.[16]

Denouncing the rhetoric of the Farrakhans and Jeffrieses, West's solution to what divides the black and Jewish communities is self-critical exchanges within both communities about what being black or Jewish means in ethical terms. Insisting that the black freedom struggle is the major buffer between the David Dukes of America (Duke was a Ku Klux Klan stalwart who got considerable support in the 1992 presidential election) and a future in which Americans can take justice and freedom seriously, West sees black anti-Semitism as weakening this buffer while catering to old-style racists. "If," as he says, "the black freedom struggle becomes simply a power driven war of all against all that pits xenophobia from below against racism from above, then David Duke's project is the wave of the future—and a racial apocalypse awaits us."[17]

You would think that the David Dukes of the world would unite the black and Jewish communities rather than divide them; that having a common enemy would work to bring together the two oppressed groups. However, as Laurence Mordekhai Thomas has pointed out, to think this is a mistake.[18] Borrowing the prisoner's dilemma from game theory,

---

[16]Ibid, pp. 76–77.

[17]Ibid, p. 75.

[18]Laurence Mordekhai Thomas, *Vessels of Evil*, pp. 190–205.

Thomas argues that having a common enemy is not enough to bring together two groups in a hostile society.

The prisoner's dilemma works as follows. At times it is rational for two people not to work together, although for each the benefit from working together would exceed the benefit from going it alone. What accounts for the rationality of not working together is uncertainty with respect to the other person's conduct. If neither party can be sure that the other party will work together, and if either does her part while the other does not, then the one who contributes her share will be worse off than if she had gone it alone.

To understand this better, suppose that you and an accomplice have committed a crime. The police have only enough evidence to give each of you a two-year sentence, but they want to get at least one of you in prison for longer. If one of you confesses, giving evidence against the other, they could do this. So they put you in separate cells where you can't communicate, and then the police come to talk to you in your cell. They offer you this deal: If both of you keep silent, you yourself will get two years; but if you confess and your accomplice doesn't, then you'll get only one year. If you confess and she does too, then you'll get three years. The police also say that the same deal is being offered to your accomplice. You're only interested in minimizing your own sentence and don't care how long your accomplice stays in jail. Not knowing what she will do, reason demands confessing even though, if you both refused to confess, you'd be better off. The moral of the story, then, is that cooperation is more profitable than isolation.

Thomas's point, in drawing upon the prisoner's dilemma, is that having a hostile common enemy is not, by itself, sufficient to bring blacks and Jews together. Not knowing or trusting how Jewish groups will behave, Thomas points out that the interest of blacks is to go it alone even though blacks would benefit by cooperating with Jews in combatting racism. As for what it would take for blacks to trust Jews so as to facilitate cooperation, Thomas suggests the possession of a narrative—something blacks were systematically denied during their years of bondage and from whose effects they still suffer. A narrative, he says, would consist of a sense of the good giving meaning to black existence. It would also contain ennobling rituals like those inherent in Jewish practice. By having a sense of the good and accompanying rituals, Thomas is convinced that blacks will be able to flourish in a hostile society and cooperate with Jews in an affirming rather than coercive way.

Robert H. Robinson is past president of the Bergen County chapter of the National Association for the Advancement of Colored People.

Mark Weitzman is National Associate Director of the Simon Wiesenthal Center's Educational Outreach Program.

Video Presentation

Guests: Mark Weitzman, National Associate Director of the Simon Wiesenthal Center's Educational Outreach Program

Robert H. Robinson, past president, National Association for the Advancement of Colored People (Bergen County, New Jersey)

Student Panel: Ursula Selbach, Marc Gussen, Krystal Eichelberger, Harold Edgar, Brenda Rubenfeld

I begin the hour-long interview by asking both Weitzman and Robinson to address the similarities and differences between racism and anti-Semitism. Robinson's answer addresses similarities between them; he thinks that competition for scarce resources lies behind both evils. Weitzman's answer speaks more to their differences. He points out that Jews have historically blended into society in a way that blacks have not. This response prompts me to ask whether blacks and Jews have different strategies for countering racism and anti-Semitism, respectively, with blacks being more vociferous about racial injustices. Weitzman's response is that the Simon Wiesenthal Center's very existence is evidence that Jewish protest against anti-Semitism is more public than my question suggests. Against this, I point out that the black community's protest over the Rodney King incident (white Los Angeles police officers were videotaped beating King excessively) was more unruly than the Jewish community's protest over Yankel Rosenbaum. This occasions further discussion as to what strategies are best suited to combat discrimination.

The conversation then turns to ex-Ku Klux Klan member David Duke's presidential bid. I ask both Robinson and Weitzman whether Duke was an anomaly or whether he and his ilk pose a veritable threat to liberal values. Both agree that Duke was no anomaly, pointing out that he drew significant support from the Northeast. This occasions discussion of why blacks and Jews have not gotten along in the recent past inasmuch as they have a common enemy. Weitzman's response is that is a mistake to think that a monolithic Jewish community exists and that "it" does not get along with the black community or communities. He also brings attention to what he believes is resentment by blacks of Jews who have achieved a modicum of success.

Following the break, Harold Edgar solicits advice on how to combat racism to which Robinson responds, through education. At this point, I ask what is meant by racism, whether it is an attitude or a set of behaviors. Following a discussion of that question, Mark Gussen asks whether the prevalence of racism in America is due either to the loss of moral fiber or some warped sense of self-preservation. Weitzman remarks that it is the second, pointing out that the Nazis became empowered following the great depression in Germany between 1929–1937. Just prior to the end of the first half-hour, Krystal Eichelberger asks Robinson to comment on the value of public educational programs which teach black history as opposed to "white man's history." Robinson says he supports this approach and gives his reasons why.

The second half-hour begins with my asking Weitzman to expand upon a theme I had raised during the previous interview: whether Jews intentionally employ a quiet strategy in combating anti-Semitism as opposed to a more vociferous strategy apparently favored by blacks for opposing racism. I raise the Jonathan Pollard case in connection with this question which, as Weitzman explains, concerns an American Defense Department employee who passed secret information to Israel. After being tried and convicted for treason, Pollard was sentenced to an extremely harsh prison term—significantly more severe than agents who have traded secrets in similar cases with hostile governments. According to Weitzman,

Jews had initially not seen fit to voice their complaints about what they perceived to be unfair treatment of Pollard, fearing the charge of dual loyalty to Israel and the United States—a charge traditionally leveled by anti-Semites at Jews. This fear was fueled, says Weitzman, when then-President George Bush alluded to such an accusation. But when the fears subsided, the Jewish community realized that they, as Americans, have the right to voice their moral indignation. Talk of Pollard then occasions talk of whether the State Department is anti-Semitic and whether an analogue exists in the black community to anti-Zionistic anti-Semitism (prejudice against Jews under the guise of prejudice against the State of Israel).

The discussion turns to the activities of Leonard Jeffries and Michael Levin, professors at the City University of New York notorious for their racist or anti-Semitic assertions. Surprisingly, Robinson defends Jeffries's infamous speech in Albany in which Jeffries claimed that Jews had a more than incidental role in the slave trade. Taking issue with Robinson's apologetic, Weitzman points out how Jeffries is a pseudo-scholar whose primary source of information is the notorious *The Secret Relationship Between Blacks and Jews*—an anti-Semitic monograph published by the Nation of Islam containing pernicious lies and half-truths. And while Weitzman argues that Levin, too, is a racist who doesn't deserve a tenured position in a public university, he points out that Levin's racist writings have never entered Levin's classrooms.

The conversation turns to a discussion of affirmative action, at which point I ask Robinson whether he thinks a time limit should be imposed on affirmative measures to correct past wrongs. He does not think there should be, and points out that blacks, unlike Jews, lack the support system needed to succeed in the absence of affirmative action. This occasions discussion of what kind of support system Robinson has in mind. Following this, Brenda Rubenfeld asks Robinson how to overcome xenophobia, and Ursula Selbach and I invite Weitzman to comment on the notion of collective responsibility vis-à-vis the Nazis.

In this article, written expressly for this book, David Theo Goldberg explores several theses that people have put forward in talking about racism: it is irrational; it is predicated upon biological characteristics; it is an ideology; and its design and effects are domination. Arguing that these theses provide an incomplete or misleading picture of racism, Goldberg urges that we conceive of racism—or racisms, as he insists—in terms of the power to exclude. Conceived this way, Goldberg contends that the disparate attitudes, practices, and institutions that go under the common name of racism make greater sense than a concept depicting racism as a unified idea.

David Theo Goldberg teaches philosophy in the School of Justice Studies, Arizona State University. He is the editor of Anatomy of Racism *(Minneapolis: University of Minnesota Press, 1990) and the editor of a double issue of* The Philosophical Forum *on apartheid.*

Re-Viewing the Nature of Racisms

David Theo Goldberg

Racism has been construed in a wide variety of ways in social theory and science. Nevertheless, it is possible to identify broad if implicit agreement among social scientists and philosophers on a range of standard features marking racism. So, racism tends to be construed most generally as the irrational (or prejudicial) belief in or practice of differentiating population groups on the basis of their typical phenomenal characteristics, and the hierarchical ordering of the racial groups so distinguished as superior or inferior. "Typical phenomenal characteristics" are interpreted largely in biological terms. Consistent in either case with this biological construal, the most usual and significant qualifications of the general characterization are twofold. On the one hand, racism is considered exclusively as an ideology. On the other hand, racism is considered necessarily to involve the domination and subordination of those groups deemed inferior.

FIVE THESES ON THE NATURE OF RACISM

Accordingly, we can distinguish five theses usual to the specification of the nature of racism (or what, for the sake of convenience, I am taking to be its terminological equivalents).[1] First, racism is irrational;[2] second, the ordering of races it necessarily presupposes is predicated upon biological characteristics;[3] third, this ordering is hierarchical;[4] fourth, racism is an ideological phenomenon;[5] and fifth, its design and effects are domination.[6] This widely accepted way of construing the nature of racism is incomplete at best, misleading at worst.

Irrationality

Some appeals to racial distinction are not inherently arbitrary but are carefully designed to achieve well-defined ends. In South Africa, for example, distinguishing people in racial terms has served historically to maintain political and economic power in the hands of the white minority. It follows that defining racism as irrational will fail to illuminate the full range of what I am going to insist is central to the condition, namely, racialized relations of power. It is at least reasonable to inquire, as others have, whether some occurrence or interpretation of racism may be rational. (This inquiry, it should be emphasized, in no way commits us to acknowledging that some or other form of racism may be socially or morally acceptable.) The question of racism's rationality, at least intuitively, is not an ill-conceived one. That prominent sociologists have analyzed racism in terms of rational choice theory should suffice here as evidence.[7] It follows that as a matter of *definition* racism must be neutral in respect of its rational status.

Biology and Hierarchy

We may press a similar point with respect to the claimed necessity of biological reference. Racisms of any kind *ex hypothesi* presuppose reference, however veiled or implicit, to race. Racial characterization and reference have long ceased to be exclusively—and sometimes not at all—in terms of biological considerations. Those who insist by way of the imperative of definition that biological presupposition is conceptually central to racism will ignore those racisms predicated upon nonbiologically defined racial constructions. It should be clear, moreover, that racisms need not be premised upon hierarchical racial orderings of superiority and inferiority. For though this claim is historically prevalent, there are many instances (especially recently) of discriminations based simply upon racially defined *differences*. For example, Robin Page, a British MP at the beginning of the 1980s, argued that "the whole question of race is not a matter of being superior or inferior, dirty or clean, but of being different."[8] Similarly, the South African government changed the rationalization of its "Homelands" policy in its yearbook of 1976 from earlier appeals to "natural white superiority" to "ethnic difference." If these examples are considered disingenuous appeals to difference as a way of veiling implicit claims of hierarchy, one could cite as nonhierarchical claims to racial apartness those of some African-American Pan-Africanists (the early Du Bois is arguably a case in point), or of principled *apartheid* purists like the son of H. F. Verwoerd who insisted on strict race-based segregation with South Africa's social resources equitably divided and whites committed to undertaking their own manual labor.

Ideology

The claim that racism is nothing more than ideological is confusing or delimiting in a different way. It leaves the deleterious effects of racist practices and institutions to be captured by some other term like *racialism* or *racist discrimination*. If ideology is necessarily tied up with domination, if it is only the rationalization of or the cover for domination, then it is misleading to conceive of racism merely as ideology in this sense. By insisting that the point of racist ideological structure is to hide some underlying form of economic, social, or political oppression, this widely shared ideological claim refuses to acknowledge the materiality of racially defined effects in their own right. It fails to acknowledge, and so leaves unexplained, the fact that racist expressions may at times define and promote rather than merely rationalize social arrangements and institutions. By contrast, I will undertake to incorporate the distinctions between belief structure, aims, practices, institutions, principles, and effects into a coherent characterization of the concept of racisms.[9]

Domination

The claim concerning the centrality of domination, oppression, and subjugation does seem to capture a feature central to racism, namely, the relationships of power that racisms promote. And clearly, racisms may serve narrowly as ideological rationalizations of relations of domination, or they may serve practically to effect such domination by defining who are its objects and what they may be subjected to. Racisms may be taken most broadly as the condition of this domination and subjection, the mode and fact of racialized, of racially defined and articulated, oppression.

This point should not conceal a wider feature of racisms that we need to hold firmly in view. At the very least, generically speaking, racisms need not be about domination so much as they are about racially predicated *exclusions*. And exclusions, even racially defined ones, need not necessarily involve domination and subjugation. Indeed, some exclusions may be for the sake of nothing else than holding the racially different at a distance. The reasons for such exclusion may be various. They have been made to include cultural preservation, or maintaining the size of relative economic distributions and benefits of the included, or fear of the unknown, and so forth. While domination may be more or less directly at the heart of most racialized exclusions, it is not necessary to, or necessarily a part of, all.

My concern here is not simply to contest the definition of a well-worn concept in social theory and everyday discourse. Rather, it is primarily to furnish a different way of thinking about social relations that in very fundamental but often silent ways have come to prevail in contemporary social life. It is therefore not wrong to think of racism primarily in terms of the drive to domination especially by whites—that is, by those defined as white and who are conceived as European or somehow related to Europeans. Nevertheless, I will argue that it helps to conceive of racism more broadly and fluidly as generally engaged in the articulation of modern relations of power—of the power not only to dominate, conquer, and destroy, but of the basic power to exclude, distance, and ignore.

Thus, the standard view of racism seems for the most part not to cover genuine cases. We might be tempted, as Frank Reeves suggests, simply to differentiate between more or less severe and extreme kinds of racist expression. Reeves distinguishes between a weak, medium, and strong form of racism. *Weak racism* consists minimally in the set of claims that enduring races of human beings exist, and that the differences are significant both because they explain existing social structures and because they have consequences for social policy. *Medium racism* adds to this the evaluation in terms of a scale of superiority and inferiority of the different races identified by weak racism. This qualification obviously involves implications for both explanation and policy recommendation. Where the rank ordering is taken to entail that the superior races should be entitled to more favorable treatment, Reeves thinks we have a case of *strong racism*.[10]

These distinctions are clearly in keeping with the growing recognition that there are different kinds of racism, or different racisms. However, they fail to reflect (upon) an equally important consideration tying different racisms together. The theories of racial difference, hi-erarchical evaluations, and related imperatives for differential treatment distinguishing Reeves's racisms from each other are basically all of a larger piece. Racial distinction, evaluation, and recommendation sustain each other both within sociosystemic constructions at specific historical moments and across the long historical duration of racialized discourse and racisms. So, although the sorts of distinction suggested by Reeves may at times suffice to order priorities of response or resistance, they are potentially misleading. Both the micro expressions that constitute a racialized social formation—the epithets, glances, avoidances, characterizations, prejudgments, dispositions, rationalizations, and so on—and the racialized theories, evaluations, and behavioral recommendations enable perpetuation of the social formation in its racialized determination. They enable, in other words, common sense to be racialized and so the easiness, the natural familiarity, of racist expression.

This is something to which Zygmunt Bauman is sensitive in his stimulating and provocative analysis of the Holocaust. However, trapped in a sense by the object of his study, Bauman narrows the range of racisms in another direction. Racism, he insists, is "inevitably associated with" the estranging strategies of expulsion or extermination. These strategies, Bauman argues, are necessitated by racism's inherent commitment to the "design of the perfect society and intention to implement the design." Racism, in this picture, is conceived only as an end in itself, pursued for its own sake and never simply as a means for instituting other ends such as profit or power.[11] This restriction of the range of racisms follows only if we accept something like the Holocaust as the paradigm case providing criteria against which to establish any other racist occurrence, and not simply as an extreme, one of racism's most dire historical manifestations. Once we admit that there are racist occurrences having nothing to do with (territorial) expulsion or extermination from the perfectly designed society, we are well along the way to admitting the proliferation of kinds of racism, of racisms.

RACISMS

We cannot avoid asking what characteristics are common to racisms in virtue of which a racist expression may be differentiated from other kinds across historical time. In this sense, not much hangs on the difference between claiming that there are racisms of many kinds and the claim that racism takes many forms, provided we keep clearly in mind that the singular conception of racism is simply a conceptual abstraction, nothing more than a convenient way of referring to racisms' common identifying conditions, rather than an ontologically universal transhistorical social phenomenon. However, unless we have some idea of the commonalities among different kinds of racist expression, we cannot identify any as such; nor can we comfortably characterize what makes one kind of historically specific *racist* expression differ from another.

Examples of the varying types of racism(s) abound. The racisms that sustained as well as those that informed opposition to slavery in the United States differ from postslavery segregationism, and each differs substantially from contemporary racist expressions. The racisms that buttressed British colonial rule in South Africa differ in some fundamental ways from the establishment of *apartheid* since the 1940s, as well as from the sort of racisms indigenous to life in Britain now that "the empire has struck back." And formalized *apartheid* will contrast increasingly sharply from the racisms now emergent in South Africa with the dismantling of *apartheid*'s more overt and formal institutions. I am not claiming that any one racism cited here emerged directly from the preceding one; nor am I contesting the fact that in each case the earlier racist formations enabled the later expressions in some direct or extended way. Causal relations in any microanalysis need to be distinguished from the natures of the conditions themselves. Thus, too, as Antonio Gramsci makes clear in his suggestive analysis, the racism in Mussolini's Italy differed significantly in its longstanding background conditions and in its manifestations from those of Hitler's Ger-

many.[12] And as Bauman convincingly argues, the anti-Semitism of those designing and managing the Holocaust took quite another form from that of the general German population at the time.[13] This variety highlights the difficulty of definition.

Context of Definition

We require a characterization of the condition that does not commit us vacuously to finding racism everywhere, but that nevertheless takes it systemic nature as basic. We need clear criteria for identifying individual responsibility for the various sorts of racist expression, but that do not tie the changing conditions of racisms too restrictively to individual intentionality. And we need an account that properly distinguishes between racialized reference or characterization and racist expression, for the burden of proof must rest with those wanting to hold that the former reduces inherently to the latter.

The definition of racism offered by Michael Omi and Howard Winant clearly takes in too much. Racism, they suggest, consists of those "social practices which (implicitly or explicitly) attribute merits or allocate values to members of racially categorized groups, solely because of their race."[14] So, racist expressions include statements such as, "Blacks appreciate good music," or "Blacks are as hardworking or intelligent as any other racial group," or "I think highly of American Indian culture." Omi and Winant's definition comes close to dismissing racism as unjustifiable in virtue of conceiving race as a morally irrelevant category, and the sorts of examples offered here suggest the conceptual overextension involved. Perhaps in some idealized possible world it would be better not to use racialized expressions at all. Indeed, where discriminatory structures and effects are historically absent from a social formation, it may be that racialized reference should be discouraged where possible while acknowledging *and* appreciating human difference. But in *this* world, racialized reference is widely used in ordinary speech, and insistence upon its absence or silence may serve simply to disguise discriminatory practices and institutions, or at least to repress socially significant self-identification. Thus, any reasonable definition of racism must be able in principle to distinguish between racialized expressions that are more or less benign.

If race is a conception, then racism is a condition; or more precisely, where race is a set of conceptions, racisms are sets of conditions. Terminologically, the word *racism* was first used in English by Ruth Benedict in the 1940s. Benedict, in turn, was influenced by the first use of *racisme* in France in the title of a book published in 1938. The use and meanings of both terms were strongly influenced by the wartime experience of anti-Semitism. *Racialism*, it is true, was used in the late nineteenth century. However, racist conditions clearly predate by a considerable time the emergence of a word in any language to refer to them: conditions may exist whether named or not. By contrast, historically specific racisms necessarily presuppose and so cannot predate some or other conception of racial difference prevailing at the time. Thus, whereas the connotations of *race* can only be established in terms of actual historical usage, any viable definition of *racisms* must be stipulated.

So, *racisms* involve promoting exclusions, or the actual exclusions of people in virtue of their being deemed members of different racial groups, however racial groups are taken to be constituted. It follows that in some instances expressions may be racist on grounds of their effects. The mark of racism in these cases will be whether the discriminatory racial exclusion reflects a persistent pattern or could reasonably have been avoided.

Racists are those persons who explicitly or implicitly ascribe racial characteristics of others which purportedly differ from their own and others like them. These ascriptions, whether biological or social in character, must not merely propose racial differences; they must assign racial preferences (*desired* inclusions or exclusions) or express intended or actual inclusions or exclusions, entitlements, or restrictions.[15] Expression or racial preferences need not be identical to actual inclusions or exclusions, and may not even amount to intended ones. They are all—desired or preferred, intended, or actual exclusions—racist in the view offered here. But it may be that such ascriptions are offered only to "explain" racial differences as natural, inevitable, and therefore unchangeable. Such putative explanations are likewise to be regarded as racist.

Persons may be judged (more or less) racist, then, not only on the narrow basis of intentions but also where the effects of their actions (or implications of their explanations) are (more or less) racially discriminatory or exclusionary. That is, persons may be racist also where their expressions fit a historical legacy or where the effects exhibit a pattern of racialized exclusion. These are effects the persons should reasonably be clear about or it is a historical legacy to which they should reasonably be sensitive. The tendency to hold agents accountable in these cases will harden the more reasonable it is to insist that they should have known better, and especially once the nature of the effects or the tradition are brought to their notice and they refuse to acknowledge that it is racist because they did not intend it so. This suggestion, it should be emphasized, is offered as a way of assessing agent accountability for the expression, not of establishing the presence or absence of racist intention. Clearly, one may express oneself in racist fashion whether one recognizes and acknowledges it or not. Accountability will be especially difficult for someone to avoid where there are no other obvious grounds for the differential treatment than racial ascription, or where no other grounds could have been known to the one differentiating in that way. Moreover, where persons deny racist intent to bring about the racially differential effects in some case, their behavior can be checked in other cases to assess whether similar racially defined outcomes resulted, whether they apply in other cases the nondiscriminatory principles they claim to be instituting in this case, and so on. Thus, there are ways of assessing accountability for racist acts or policies, the (claimed) absence of individual racist intentionality notwithstanding.[16]

Racist institutions, by extension, are those whose formative principles incorporate and whose social functions serve to institute and perpetuate the racist beliefs and acts in question. Again, it is too restrictive to claim that institutions can be judged racist only if the institutional aim is racial discrimination.[17] If it is reasonably clear that some institutional practice gives rise to racially patterned exclusionary or discriminatory outcomes, no matter the institutional aims, and the institution does little or nothing to avoid, diminish, or alleviate these outcomes, the reasonable presumption must be that the institution is racist or effectively promotes racism of a sort. If the effect of an oil company's practices is a damaging spill despite stated aims, but the company does little to avoid, diminish, or alleviate these outcomes, we do not hesitate to accuse the culprit of engaging in hazardous behavior, indeed, of being environmentally culpable. The burden of proof rests with those who argue that the racist effects are unavoidable contingent and coincidental outcomes of otherwise permissible nonracist practices, aims, or institutional structures. For example, officers of a homeowners' association who work to prevent low-cost housing in their district for members of a racially defined group other than their own may not simply be concerned, as Baier insists they are, about their own (nonracist) economic interests. To escape the charge of racism, they must be prepared also and equally to exclude low-cost housing for members of their own race, and it must be clear that they engage in such exclusion for reasons that are in no way related to some underlying racially segregationist end.[18]

Where there is a recognizable, institutionally governed pattern of racially predicated discrimination or exclusion, ongoing because unrectified, the presumption must be that the continuing exclusions are considered permissible by those institutionally able to do something about them. Similarly, the institutional officers who knowingly implement existing racist institutional rules, even if not for the sake of self-advantage, are implicated in the racism if they fail in some reasonable way to resist at least implementation of the racist rules.[19]

Consider the case of a student newspaper that publishes cartoons stereotyping blacks as cannibals or as monkeys. The material continues to appear even after vocal complaints by the university community of the harm promoted by or the offensiveness of it. The newspaper cannot escape being characterized as racist by claiming that it has no racist rules governing its operation; or on grounds that the editorial board denies that its members individually or collectively have any racist intention; or by denying that the cartoons are meant to represent a generic image of blacks. For, no matter the claimed intention, the perceived and actual effects of their publication are perpetuation of exclusionary racial difference. The editorial board's insistence upon publishing the material, even after the standing of such images in the history of racist expression has been explained to the members, may turn on the nonracist intention of its members to buck authority or to exercise their First Amendment rights to free expression. Nevertheless, this insistence does not simply suggest insensitivity to the interests and concerns of a group traditionally excluded on racial grounds. It indicates the continued promotion of such exclusion, no matter the intentions. Here, then, is an instance of a racist practice whose necessary and sufficient conditions for being defined as such do not turn on the presence of racist intentions or racist rules.[20]

The dominant feature in this characterization of racist expression—whether belief, practice, or institution—is promotion of exclusion on the basis of (purported) racial membership. The exclusion may be intended, actual (even if unintended), or (implicitly) rationalized. This raises the question concerning the link between racialized conception and racist exclusion. Exclusion may be race-based either explicitly, where the grounds of the exclusion are more or less openly declared to be racial, or by way of historical and implied connection to race. Historically, race has been coded in terms of socially defined categories such as national characteristics, language, culture generally, and even religion or gender. Here, situational analysis will have to reveal whether race is implicitly involved, whether it is veiled as the actual basis for the exclusion in question.

Jews, for example, are sometimes characterized as a race and at other times as a religion, a nonracialized culture, or a nation. It would seem an odd implication to have discriminatory exclusion of some population group, in this case Jews, count as racist only where that group is directly racialized. In my view, exclusion of Jews will be racist where the underlying characterization of Jews is racialized either explicitly or by being linked to a history of racialized characterization. The characterization in question can then be said to stand in the tradition of such reference. The more central to the racist tradition are the categories invoked, the more fully can one say that their use is racist. Similarly, religious antagonism in Northern Ireland has sometimes been racialized, just as the Irish generally have been by the English. So, an exclusion of Catholics by Protestants in Northern Ireland from holding some office, say, may be racist where there is evidence at least that the exclusion is racially articulated. Moreover, women in the nineteenth century were racialized by being analogically identified with/as blacks. Accordingly, exclusion of women in these terms at the time would count as a case of racism.[21]

These are extreme cases. In general, an expression will be more centrally and seriously racist the more directly, effectively, and usually it serves to exclude racially defined persons. Racist exclusion involves relative lack of access to, absence from the distribution of, or lack of availability of goods or services, opportunities, or privileges; rights and powers; and even social responsibilities and burdens. These absences, lacks, and impediments by means of which exclusions are instituted must be manifest in racially significant terms. By extension, social subjects' exclusionary acts can be racist without their quite realizing or intending it. As in the general formulation, they will be racist here to the extent they con-

tinue so to characterize and act, especially once informed that these expressions stand in a racist tradition, or where they refuse to acknowledge their racism and character once properly apprised of it, or where they should reasonably have been aware of it.

This captures in the most conceptually minimal form the sense of social power—again whether desired, actual, or rationalized—that centrally marks racist beliefs, practices, and institutions. Racist exclusions are not only done for the sake of gaining power in economic, political, or personal terms. Power is exercised in the promotion and execution of the exclusions, whether intended or not. So, racist exclusions need not be sought only instrumentally to control the socioeconomic resources; they may be sought for the recognition of some imputed value in the exclusions themselves, or for the sake of power in the execution of the exclusion.[22] This suggests that the proper yardstick against which to assess the degree of racist exclusion, the depth of the condition, is not simply the level of inclusion in and access to social resources. It is rather the fuller measures of incorporation into *and* influence upon the body politic, whether economically, politically, legally, or culturally.

In summary, racism excludes racially defined others, or promotes, secures, or sustains such exclusion. Often, racist exclusions will serve as a means to some form of exploitation, but there are times when the exclusions will be undertaken or expressed for their own sakes, for the recognition of the putatively inherent value the expressions are claimed to represent. In the latter case, where persons insist that they are acting for the sake of the racist principles themselves, it is conceivable that exploitative acts will be a means to sustaining the racist principles.

Two more general examples should serve to elucidate the scope of my account of racisms and of their modes of applicability. The first concerns immigration restrictions. Maintenance and promotion of cultural tradition are widely considered morally acceptable ends. A general policy to foster these ends preserves prima facie regard for members of the various cultures in question. Some societies claim to find as a necessary means for realizing these ends the enforcement of immigration restrictions on members of "alien" cultures. Quotas of this kind need not be overtly racist in formulation: Consider the ruling that "Only persons with families domiciled in Britain in 1850 will be granted British citizenship." It is possible to universalize the policy without contradiction, for Tory parliamentarians have readily acknowledged that "alien" cultures may want to protect their own heritage, that they ought to do so, and that this would necessitate similar immigration restrictions on their behalf.[23]

Consider also the case of a white district attorney in the United States who uses the majority of her preemptory challenges to exclude blacks from the jury in trials involving black defendants. She correctly believes from long experience and statistical studies that the more black jury members there are the less likely she is to obtain a jury decision in such cases.[24]

It might be argued that neither case is racist. There is no attribution to the excluded group of biologically determined characteristics that purports to render its members inferior or inept. However, this restricts racism to its older forms. Though neither case need be overtly racist in formulation, both turn out racist on my characterization. The first is racist in intending to exclude racial others; the second in effect. The prosecutor's professional aim is to secure prosecution. Should social statistics about black jury members change, the prosecutor would be willing to change her strategy accordingly. So, she is clearly aware of the effects. Both cases pointedly involve exclusion of members of the racial group involved, and as policy both would affect the excluded group adversely. Group members are (to be) excluded because of racial membership from entitlements available to others in a different racially defined group. In neither case is the policy self-defeating. Each is consistent and coheres with interests central to the society in question.

These cases surely involve morally invidious undertakings. The former aims to and the latter does exclude on the basis of racial membership. The first case is tied to a pattern of historical exclusion, exploitation, and invidious treatment. The second case, if generalized as a policy, would go far in perpetuating blacks' exclusion from access to and active participation in the institutions of justice. The rights to equal protection of the law and trial by fair cross-section of the community would be violated. Such a policy would increase the probability of procedural unfairness. In general, black defendants would be open to penalties in ways whites would not. Trial outcomes might be skewed by undermining the likelihood of jury divergence, for example, in interpreting the facts. Such was the charge of many criticizing the criminal acquittal of the police officers in the beating of Rodney King.

These examples suggest what I have insisted upon throughout, namely, that a very wide set of conditions, often quite different from one another, make up the range of racisms. They can be combined under the common rubric of racism only by viewing them as racially conceived, produced, or effected exclusions.

ENDNOTES

1. The disjunction between an ideology of racial inferiority and discriminatory practices for the sake of domination is sometimes signified by the use of different terms. So, some analysts distinguish between *racism* and *racialism* (sometimes the former is made to signify the theory; at others it refers to the practice), or between racialist beliefs or prejudices and racist or discriminatory practices.

2. The presumption that racism is irrational is widespread. It is reflected not only in the popular political rhetoric that refers to racism as a cancer or social pathology, but more deeply in the prevailing liberal philosophical conception of "race" as a "morally irrelevant category," as arbitrary. Any appeal to "race" accordingly would make ungrounded distinctions between people so referenced. Racism necessarily presupposes racial distinction, and so it is taken to rest on arbitrary differentiations between people. The baldest articulation of this view appears in Rawls (1971, p. 19) and Feinberg (1973, p. 103). Appiah (1985, pp. 23–29) offers

a more subtle version of this argument, and Walter Benn Michaels (1992) appears to be persuaded. Some theorists dismiss racism as irrational on more straightforward grounds. Thus, Kurt Baier (1978, p. 126) deems racists irrational because their beliefs are "hypothetical or deluded" and Marcus Singer (1978, p. 176) insists that "the theory of racism . . . is self-contradictory as well as confused." I have discussed the claim that racism is inherently irrational at considerable length in Goldberg (1990a).

3. See Appiah (1985, pp. 26–27), and Kwame Anthony Appiah, "Racisms," in Goldberg, ed. (1990, pp. 4–5); Miles (1989, p. 76); Barker (1981, p. 4), and Susan Smith (1989, p. 5).

4. For one among many on the point of superiority and inferiority, see Richter (1986, pp. 785–794).

5. Miles (1982, p. 78), Miles (1989, pp. 42–50, 87), and Barrett (1987, p. 5).

6. Miles (1989, p. 66), John Hodge, "Domination and the Will in Western Thought and Culture" in Hodge et al. (1975, pp. 10–11); Carmichael and Hamilton (1967), p. 3; Dominguez (1977, p. 262); and Weinroth (1979, p. 68). For examples of those articulating the general definition, see Michael Banton, "The Concept of Racism," in Zubaida, ed. (1970, p. 18); Barrett (1987, p. 5); and Dominguez (1977, pp. 262–263).

7. Cf. Banton (1983); Hechter et al. (1982); Mason (1984); McClendon (1983). See also "Rational Choice Revisited," the Special Issue of *Ethnic and Racial Studies* 8, 4 (October 1985). I have addressed the issues involved here in Goldberg (1993), Chapter 6.

8. Page is quoted in Barker (1981, p. 20).

9. For the clearest example of one committed to this narrow construal of racism as ideology, see Miles (1989, pp. 42–50, 87–90). See also Immanuel Wallerstein's contributions on racism to Balibar and Wallerstein (1991). On racisms as discursive practices, see my "The Social Formation of Racist Discourse," in Goldberg, ed. (1990, pp. 295–318).

10. Reeves (1983, pp. 12–13). If Reeves's categories are assumed, strong racism seems possible without the evaluative ordering into superior and inferior races. It may be recommended that members of a specified race deserve privileges others are denied simply because of some pertinent difference, say, in historical or cultural experience. Reeves fails to acknowledge this.

11. Bauman (1989, pp. 65–66). This is a view widely held. Cf. Baier (1978, p. 129). Janet Radcliffe Richards (1985, pp. 53–82) insists on the point more generally in defining *discrimination* as "a rule that treats two groups differently as an end in itself."

12. Antonio Gramsci (1952, p. 185). See N. Cheboksarov, "Critical Analysis of Racism and Colonialism," in UNESCO (1980, p. 363).

13. Bauman (1989, p. 33).

14. Omi and Winant (1987, pp. 145, 172).

15. Disjuncts are intended inclusively here, as elsewhere.

16. Harry Lesser (1984, pp. 253–256) develops this point helpfully at some length. Unfortunately, given the insightfulness of his theoretical analysis, the account of the tenure example at the end of his paper is less than convincing. Michael Philips (1984, pp. 78–79) contrasts two theories for attributing racism: the standard "agent-centered" and the "act-centered" theories, respectively. The former attributes racism in terms only of the presence of appropriate beliefs, feelings, and intentions of agents. By contrast, Philips defends the latter, which adjudges acts racist in terms of "the meaning of the act for the victims," that is, in terms of the (racialized) victims' judgments of their "mistreatment." Nevertheless, it does seem that an act may turn out racist no matter the victim's consideration, which after all may be mistaken. This suggests that a more comprehensive account needs to be offered than either the "agent" or "act-centered" theories alone can furnish.

17. Baier (1978, p. 129).

18. Even if not racist, the officers may be guilty of (extra economic) class discrimination. Robert Miles (1989, pp. 84–85) may be right, to take another case, that the disproportionate laying off of black workers in recessionary conditions may be a function not of a racist institutional aim but of the hard-fought union principle of seniority. Hired last, blacks will be fired first. But if the union and employer do little to alter the discriminatory effects of the principle over time, the suspicion must arise of racist collusion. The U.S. Supreme Court, while stressing a state's intentionality, has permitted racially discriminatory impact of a statute as a standard for unconstitutionality. "Sometimes a clear pattern, unexplainable on grounds other than race, emerges from the effect of state action." (*Village*

of *Arlington Heights v. Metropolitan Development Housing Corp.* 429 U.S. at 266, 267). See Diamond and Cottrol (1983, pp. 274–275).

19. Contra Baier (1978, p. 129), and Richards (1983, p. 71). The obligations of the institutional officer here can be likened to those of a knowing employee whose employer is engaged in committing egregious social harms. For more on whistle-blowing, see Goldberg (1990).

20. Examples of institutional racism can easily be multiplied. A recent study of mortgage practices by banks in the United States showed that blacks are more than twice as likely to be denied home loans even after disaggregating for obvious casual factors like class and home location differences. The kind of analysis pursued in the student newspaper case should be followed to establish whether cases like these exhibit institutional racism.

21. For a fuller analysis of the conception of race at work here, see Goldberg (1992). On Irish racism, see McVeigh (1992); on the identification of women with blacks in nineteenth-century science and the implications for racism, see Nancy Leys Stepan, "Race and Gender: The Role of Analogy in Science," in Goldberg, ed. (1990, pp. 38–57). These examples run strongly counter to the essentialized understanding of race in the standard view, most clearly represented by Miles (1989, pp. 58–61).

22. Cf. D. Baker (1978, pp. 316–321).

23. For a popular expression of this kind of claim, see Enoch Powell, "Introduction" in Lewis (1988). For critical analysis, see Barker (1981, pp. 16–20); and A. Dummett and M. Dummett, "The Role of Government in Britain's Racial Crisis" in Husband (1982, pp. 58–92).

24. Cf. *Batson v. Kentucky*, 1986.

References

Appiah, Anthony. "The Uncompleted Argument: Du Bois and the Illusion of Race." *Critical Inquiry* 12 (1985): 121–137.

Baier, Kurt. "Merit and Race." *Philosophia* 8, 2, 3 (1978): 121–151.

Baker, Donald. *Race, Ethnicity, and Power*. London: Routledge and Kegan Paul, 1983.

Baker, Donald. "Race and Power: Comparative Approaches to the Analysis of Race Relations." *Ethnic and Racial Studies* 1, 3 (1978): 316–335.

Balibar, Etienne, and Immanual Wallerstein. *Race, Nation, Class*. London: Verso, 1991.

Banton, Michael. *Ethnic and Racial Competition*. Cambridge: Cambridge University Press, 1983.

Barker, Martin. *The New Racism*. London: Junction Books, 1981.

Barrett, Stanley. *Is God a Racist? The Right Wing in Canada*. Toronto: University of Toronto Press, 1987.

Bauman, Zygmunt. *Modernity and the Holocaust*. Ithaca, N.Y.: Cornell University Press, 1989.

Carmichael, Stokely, and Charles Hamilton. *The Politics of Black Liberation in America*. New York: Random House, 1967.

Diamond, Raymond, and Robert Cottrol. "Codifying Caste: Louisiana's Racial Classification Scheme and the Fourteenth Amendment." *Loyola Law Review* 29, 2 (1983): 255–285.

Dominguez, Majel. "The Ideologies of Racism and Sexism: A Comparison." *Review Journal of the Philosophy of Social Science* 1 (1977): 261–271.

Feinberg, Joel. *Social Philosophy*. Totowa, N.J.: Prentice-Hall, 1973.

Goldberg, David Theo. *Racist Culture: Philosophy and the Politics of Meaning*. Oxford: Basil Blackwell, 1993.

———. "The Semantics of Race." *Ethnic and Racial Studies* 15, 4 (October 1992): 543–569.

———. "Racism and Rationality: The Need for a New Critique." *Philosophy of the Social Sciences* 20, 3 (Sept. 1990a): 317–350.

Goldberg, David Theo, ed. *Anatomy of Racism*. Minneapolis: University of Minnesota Press, 1990.

Gramsci, Antonio. *Gli intellettuali e l'organizzazione della culture*. Torino: Einaudi, 1952.

Hechter, M., D. Friedman, and M. Appelbaum. "A Theory of Ethnic Collective Action." *International Migration Review* 16, 2 (1982): 412–434.

Hodge, J., D. Struckmann, and L. Trost. *Cultural Bases of Racism and Group Oppression*. Berkeley, Calif.: Two Riders Press, 1975.

Husband, Charles, ed. *Race in Britain*. London: Open University Press, 1982.

Lesser, Harry. "Can Racial Discrimination Be Proved?" *Journal of Applied Philosophy* 1, 2 (1984): 253–261.

Lewis, Russell. *Anti-Racism: A Mania Exposed*. London: Quartet Books, 1988.

Mason, T. David. "Individual Participation in Collective Racial Violence: A Rational Choice Synthesis." *The American Political Science Review* 78 (1984): 1040–1056.

McVeigh, Robbie. "The Specificity of Irish Racism." *Race and Class* 33 (1992): 31–45.

McClendon, M. "Racism, Rational Choice, and White Opposition to Racial Change: A Case Study of Busing." *Political Opinion Quarterly* 49 (1983): 214–233.

Michaels, Walter Benn. "Race into Culture: A Critical Genealogy of Cultural Identity." *Critical Inquiry* 18 (Summer 1992): 655–685.

Miles, Robert. *Racism*. London: Routledge, 1989.

———. *Racism and Migrant Labor*. London: Routledge and Kegan Paul, 1982.

Omi, Michael, and Howard Winant. *Racial Formation in the United States: From the Sixties to the Eighties*. New York: Routledge, 1987.

Philips, Michael. "Racist Acts and Racist Humor." *Canadian Journal of Philosophy* XIV, 1 (March 1984): 75–96.

Rawls, John. *A Theory of Justice*. Cambridge, Mass.: Harvard University Press, 1971.

Reeves, Frank. *British Racial Discourse*. Cambridge: Cambridge University Press, 1983.

Richards, Janet Radcliffe. "Discrimination." *Proceedings of the Aristotelian Society: Supplement* V, 59 (1985): 53–82.

Richter, Reed. "On Philips and Racism." *Canadian Journal of Philosophy* 16, 4 (December 1986): 785–794.

Singer, Marcus. "Some Thoughts on Race and Racism." *Philosophia* 8 (1978): 2–3.

Smith, Susan. *The Politics of 'Race' and Residence: Citizenship, Segregation, and White Supremacy*. New York: Oxford University Press, 1989.

UNESCO, ed. *Sociological Theories: Race and Racism*. London, Author, 1980.

Weinroth, Jay. "Nation and Race: Two Destructive Concepts." *Philosophy Forum* 16 (1979): 67–86.

Zubaida, Sami, ed. *Race and Racialism*. London: Tavistock, 1970.

In this essay, written expressly for this book, Mark Weitzman documents the dangers of revisionist efforts at distorting history. Citing the efforts of the Nation of Islam as well as the more subtle Institute of Historical Review, Weitzman reveals how revisionist historians distort facts in the service of promoting anti-Semitism.

Mark Weitzman is affiliated with the Simon Wiesenthal Center, an institution committed to monitoring anti-Semitic activities throughout the world.

The Blinded Muse: Ethics, Anti-Semitism, and the Abuse of History

Mark Weitzman

Ethical behavior, is by common definition, behavior that "relates to morals"[1] By this is meant, again, according to the *Oxford English Dictionary*: "of or pertaining to character or disposition considered as good or bad, virtuous or vicious; of or pertaining to the distinction between right and wrong, good or evil, in rela- tion to the actions, volitions or character of responsible beings."[2] Morals and ethics have to be linked to behavior, as Aristotle, in his *Nicomachean Ethics* recognized: "Now if discourses on the theory of ethics were enough in themselves to make men good, many and great the rewards they would win . . . but the plain truth is . . . they are unable to push the many."[3]

Despite all that has been written on the subject, no one could say that our world is one dominated by ethics by any definition. Everywhere we look, from Bosnia to China, from Rwanda to Washington, issues of human rights and ethics dominate. If our century has been one rightfully characterized as a century of genocide, then it is clear that ethical behavior has been noticeably absent. Earlier generations did not even have a word to describe murder on such a scale as the word *genocide* itself did not exist until the midway point of our century. (The word was originally coined by Polish jurist Raphael Lemkin and was not accepted into regular usage until after World War II, when it was adopted by the United Nations in the Genocide Convention of December 9, 1948.) The need for the word grew out of the need to adequately describe the atrocities of our century, beginning in Armenia, shifting to the Stalinist actions in the Ukraine, peaking in the Holocaust (and continuing in our time, numbering the Kurds, the Bosnians, and the Rwandan Tutsis, among others, as victims).

If we are, quoting Aristotle's famous definition, "political animals,"[4] it is in the sense of needing to function, to live, not only as individuals but as a collective whole. This collective begins with family and extends through various groupings up to the global level. Our history tells us we have not yet mastered this ability to live and function together, but it also tells us that we must, for all our sakes. And, furthermore, the responsibility for this effort must also be shared, both by all of us as individuals and by those we choose to follow or to set up in leadership roles.

Martin Buber, in an essay entitled *People and Leader,* originally published in 1942, discussed leadership in this century. Buber stated that the ultimate accomplishment for a leader is not whether the people, or the leader, achieve specific immediate goals, but what ultimately becomes of them both. In Buber's words: "He who increases the power of his people in ways whereby the people loses its capacity to do the right thing with its power, he who leaves the people powerful but evil, stands before the living court before which he is responsible, with or without fore knowledge, as the corrupter of those he has led."[5] Buber is pointing out the responsibility of leadership: it is not only the practical, but the ethical, that is necessary. Especially for one who claims to bring a greater vision to the people, "power without responsibility is a dazzling-clothed impotence."[6] Buber wrote these words specifically in reference to leaders like Mussolini and Hitler, but his words could be applied just as well to some of today's leaders.

It was specifically in the applications of their anti-Semitism that the Nazis expressed their anti-ethics, a thought brought to life in Hitler's famous outburst "Conscience is a Jewish invention."[7] While our century has justly been described as a century of genocide,[8] it is the Holocaust, with its implications of a state-run, bureaucratically organized Final Solution that has come to symbolize the ultimate rupture of our moral fabric.[9]

Thus, in a post-Holocaust world, incidents of anti-Semitism are taken very seriously; they represent not only the isolated outbursts of lonely haters, but symbolize as well the potential for reenactment of our darkest nightmares. In some fundamental manner, we feel a sense of amazement or outrage that people, having seen the results of Nazi anti-Semitism, could opt to follow the same path in a post-Auschwitz world. If ethical behavior can have any meaning, or any reality, then it must be grounded in *historical* reality—not just the reality of the past, but also the reality of the present. Those who knowingly opt to follow in the path of the Nazis are consciously choosing to avoid the ethical imperative built upon the experiences of our century. They truly follow the Hitlerian maxim cited earlier in their rejection of conscience as "a Jewish invention." And, without conscience,[10] without moral responsibility, any discussion of ethics (as in the Aristotelian sense of "doing good"[11] is irrelevant and futile.

So, then, why or how does anti-Semitism still exist after Auschwitz? The only way to answer that question is to examine today's anti-Semites, their claims, and their motives.

One of the favorite methods of today's anti-Semite is to distort history. If we examine more closely two versions of this phenomenon, we will see exactly how history can be distorted, or even reversed.

The Reverend Louis Farrakhan and his Nation of Islam have provided many newspaper headlines and media sound bites over the past decade (and more). Splitting off from the established Black Muslim movement founded by Elijah Muhammad and continued by Elijah's son Wallace, the Nation of Islam began to make headlines in the 1980s.[12] Farrakhan had first made headlines when he led the attack on the "new" Malcolm X. Writing in the Nation of Islam's newspaper in 1965, Farrakhan said, "Only those who wish to be led to hell, or to their doom, will follow Malcolm. The die is set, and Malcolm shall not escape, especially after such evil, foolish talk. . . . such a man as Malcolm is worthy of death."[13] Less than a year later, Malcolm X was assassinated, a murder that Malcolm's widow Betty Shabazz has insisted involved Farrakhan.[14]

Basic Black Muslim ideology includes elements of traditional Muslim belief, built upon the Koran. Innovations include the "metaphysical view that identifies whiteness with evil and white people with the devil. . . . Black Muslims are taught that Mr. Yakub, a black mad scientist in rebellion against Allah, created the white race, a weak hybrid race devoid of any humanity."[15] Also taught is a social message that includes separation from whites, affirmation of black history, self-discipline, avoidance of drugs, and strict traditional sexual standards.

The roots of the movement began with "a shadowy mysterious evangelist" known as Wali Farrad or Wallace Fard. Fard taught that "Black debasement had occurred over the centuries because Blacks were separated from the knowledge of Allah and knowledge of self. . . . The problem was to restore to the Lost-found Nation the truth, the only truth that could make them free."[16] After Fard mysteriously vanished, his disciple Elijah Muhammad (originally Poole) succeeded him. Elijah did not aim to build an orthodox Muslim movement; as the historian C. Eric Lincoln put it, "he created his own supplement to fix the limited understanding of his followers. . . . he achieved a pronounced American awareness" and he did it by, in Elijah's own words, "cutting the cloak to fit the cloth."[17]

For the new Nation of Islam, anti-Semitism has become a central tenet. In 1984 Louis Farrakhan labeled Judaism as a "gutter religion." By the 1990s the emphasis had grown into not only the denigration of Judaism, but also into the blaming of Jews and Judaism for both the present (holes in the ozone layer, AIDS) and past (slavery) ills of society.[18]

It is this aspect of blame, of looking for a conspiracy that would yield an individual or a group who could be blamed for either the real of perceived oppression of the victim or their group, that helps identify some of these extremists as propagandists interested in scapegoating, instead of as historians interested in uncovering the complex interplay of past events.

The myth of Yakub, of labeling whites as devils, has been described as "a theodicy, as an explanation and rationalization for the pain and suffering inflicted upon Black people in America."[19] Malcolm X's conversion from Malcolm Little began when a fellow convict whispered, "The white man is the devil." This, in one scholar's words, "made sense of his experience."[20]

But since part of this "making sense" involved looking for others to blame, these others needed to be found and identified. While questions regarding Black Muslim anti-Semitism are not new, for Elijah and his followers, the generic term *devil* applied to *all* whites, Christian and Jew. His son and successor Warith Deen Muhammad, has sought to bring the movement away from this "racial" view to one closer to traditional Sunni Islamic Orthodoxy,[21] one where whites are no longer automatically devils.

However, for Louis Farrakhan and the new Nation of Islam, Jews are "the blood suckers of the black nation and the black community."[22]

The evidence for this view of history is laid out in *The Secret Relationship Between Blacks and Jews,* a tract that has become as important as the Koran in Nation of Islam ideology. Indeed, the black scholar Henry Louis Gates, Jr., described it as "the bible of the new anti-semitism.[23] Published in 1991, *The Secret Relationship* is 334 pages long, with over 1,200 footnotes.[24] The premise of the work can be found at the very beginning: "Jews have been conclusively linked to the greatest criminal endeavor ever undertaken against an entire race of people—The Black African Holocaust."[25] It purports to disclose "hidden history" and "facts known only to a few . . . hidden and misunderstood," kept "deep within the recesses of the Jewish historical record.[26] These "hidden" facts were uncovered by using Jewish historians and scholars as its sources, an assertion that also is meant to buttress the legitimacy of its claims.

The historian Harold Brackman has exposed the spurious scholarship and blatant distortions and lies that make up the bulk of *The Secret Relationship*.[27] David Brion Davis, the acknowledged expert on American slavery, has also called *The Secret Relationship* "the extreme example of anti-semitic accusations masquerading as a documented history of Jewish involvement in the slave trade and American slavery."[28]

Brackman finds that *all* of the book's claims fall apart when confronted. He concludes that the book consists of "deliberate falsification(s) for antisemitic purposes".[29] Identifying four major methods of falsification: "1. deliberate misquotation of legitimate scholars; 2. misleading citation of scholarly works as if they supported antisemitic conclusions, which, in fact they refute; 3. the cynical explosion of sources that are not authoritative including outdated studies, general textbooks, amateur histories and journalistic non-histories; and, 4. the shameless reliance on blatant antisemitic polemics."[30] For example, one historian (Philip Curtin) is quoted by *The Secret Relationship* as saying that an estimated "oft repeated figure of 15 million" slaves is "conservative," but Curtin actually wrote that it is "extremely

unlikely that the ultimate total will . . . be less than 8,000,000 or more than 10,500,000,"[31] thus not even approaching the numbers attributed to him by *The Secret Relationship*. Misleading citations used in *The Secret Relationship* include mention of two eminent Jewish historians (S. D. Gotein, and Jacob R. Marcus). Both conclude that for their periods of study (Medieval Mediterranean and Colonial American Jewish History), "the Jews had no share in the slave trade" (Gotein) and "Jewish participation was minimal" (Marcus). Neither conclusion is ever mentioned in *The Secret Relationship,* let alone refuted.[32] *The Jewish Encyclopedia* of 1904 is cited, but not the much more current *Encyclopedia Judaica* of 1971. A 1937 book on Dutch Jewish economic history is listed, but again, a more recent 1985 work on the same subject is omitted.[33] Even though *The Secret Relationship* claimed to have "excluded . . . sources considered (to be) antisemitic and/or antiJewish,"[34] Brackman demonstrates that this promise is "violated in every chapter if not on every page."[35]

The influence of the Nation of Islam today cannot be underestimated. Writing in *The New York Times* (July 20, 1994), Henry Louis Gates, Jr., finds "that it is among the younger and more educated blacks that anti-semitism is most pronounced" and, as described earlier, *The Secret Relationship* is its "bible." Gates adds that the purpose of *The Secret Relationship* is, according to Louis Farrakhan "to rearrange a relationship" that "has been detrimental to us." But, if the nature of the relationship is detrimental, Gates points out the best response is to "sever it as quickly as possible." However, attempts to "rearrange a relationship" indicate the maintenance of a relationship, not the severing of it; and so all that is changed in effect is the nature of an ongoing relationship. Since Gates is aware that *The Secret Relationship* "massively misrepresents the historical record," he knows that true history is really reflected in a picture reversed from *The Secret Relationship's* portrayal.

Gates suggests that the reason certain African-American leaders have "engineered and promoted" this "anti-semitism from the top down" is as part of a struggle for "who will speak for Black America," and that those who choose to use anti-Semitism do so in an effort to further isolate African Americans from all allies, from sources of mainstream influence and power, and with the resulting misery and poverty hope to find a more receptive audience for their message of "racial authenticity."[36] In other words, Gates presents this anti-Semitism as a cynical card being played by the followers of Louis Farrakhan, Tony Martin, and Leonard Jeffries against the followers of Martin Luther King, Jr., the later Malcolm X, and Warith Deen Muhammad.

This belief in racial ideology is a connecting factor between the African-American extremists represented by the Nation of Islam and the Neo-Nazi movement in the United States. It is not the only one. Another connection can be found in the abuse of history, as also described earlier. The Neo-Nazi, or far right, version of this abuse of history is Holocaust denial.

Holocaust denial in the United States is centered around a little known institution in California, The Institute of Historical Review.[37] The Institute was created in 1978 and was the brainchild of Willis Carto. Establishing, bank-rolling, and providing ideological guidance to the Institute, Carto has been the dominant or organizing figure of Holocaust denial for almost forty years. Born in 1926, Carto cut his teeth in the John Birch Society, founded The Liberty Lobby for extreme right-wing lobbying in Washington, and reestablished the Populist Party, where David Duke ran his first presidential campaign. Carto's ideology is not fixated only on Holocaust denial. He compounds it with mixtures of anti-Semitism ("If Satan himself had tried to create a permanent disintegration and force for the destruction of nations, he could have done no better than to invent the Jews."), racism (a complaint in 1955 letter that enough Americans are not concerned about "the inevitable niggerfication of America"), and outright admiration for Hitler and Nazism ("Hitler's defeat was the defeat of Europe and America").[38] Featuring a journal (*The Journal of Historical Review*), an annual conference, and a publishing house

(Noontide Press) that specializes in racist, anti-Semitic, and Holocaust denial literature, the Institute has attempted to pass itself off as an academic institution. A new generation of writers, such as Robert Faurisson of France, David Irving of Britain, and Arthur Butz, Bradley Smith, Fred Leuchter, and Mark Weber from the United States, are featured. Video has also become a regular tool.

Recently, Carto and some of his staff members have become embroiled in a power struggle over control of the IHR. Mark Weber was quoted as saying that Carto wanted to make the Institute "more clearly white racist." As of this writing, it appears that the rebels who want to continue the Institute's current focus on Holocaust denial have succeeded in ousting Carto. What this means for the future of the movement is unclear, although the apparent victory of the professional deniers would indicate continued focus on this subject.[39]

We can see some of the basic elements of Holocaust denial if we look at the work of the former head of the IHR's radio project and the contributing editor of its newsletter, Bradley Smith. Smith is better known today as the focus of CODOH, the Committee for Open Debate on the Holocaust. Smith's primary activity for the last three years has been the placement of a series of full-page advertisements in college newspapers. So far, three advertisements have run. The first is a basic explanation of the tenets of Holocaust denial. It relies on the technical expertise of Fred Leuchter (who claimed to be an engineer and an expert on gas chamber technology, and who wrote a report that "proved that there were no gassings in Auschwitz Birkenau). Smith relied on Leuchter's report in his advertisement throughout the fall of 1991 into the winter of 1992.[40] "It (The Leuchter Report) concludes that no mass gassings ever did or ever could have taken place in the so-called gas chambers." It is worth noting that Leuchter signed a consent agreement with Massachusetts in June 1991, in which he agreed that he was "not and never had been" a professional engineer, that he had fraudulently represented himself as such on matters in regard to "execution technology" and the death camps, and he would agree to "cease and desist" doing so in the future.[41]

Along with Leuchter, Smith relied on the historical expertise of David Irving[42] who claimed "there were no gas chambers at Auschwitz" in an attempt to counter "the rise of a Holocaust story which reads more like the success of a P.R. campaign then anything else."[43] Irving was described in 1989 by the London *Times* as a "man for whom Hitler is something of a hero." Thus Irving earned his banishment from many countries, including Canada and Germany, as well the description passed by the House of Commons in London of himself as a "Nazi propagandist and long-time Hitler apologist."[44]

Smith's first advertisement touched on the major themes of Holocaust denial: "Jews were considered to be enemies of the (Nazi) state, thus Jews under Nazi control, including women and children, deserved their harsh treatment"; the denial "that the German state had a policy to exterminate the Jewish people"; that photographs of Nazi atrocities have been put to "base", that is, false, use; that there are no documents, no valid eyewitness testimonies, no confessions, no evidence, and ultimately, no reality to the "Holocaust story."[45] The reasons that Jews created this myth is because they wanted to "drum up world sympathy and political and financial support for Jewish causes, especially the State of Israel."[46]

Smith's campaign is part of a campaign to make racism and denial respectable. The attempt to reach the campus is based on two premises; the first being that anything that lends legitimate intellectual or academic cover to the denial movement is a gain for the movement. (Throughout its history, the IHR has approached historical organizations. It attempted to purchase mailing lists to distribute the *Journal* to the membership of the Organization of American Historians in 1980 and gleefully printed the resulting letters of dismay and disgust through the next year.[47] The IHR also sent out mailings to university history departments and applied to the convention of the American Historical Association for permission to display its material (permission which has so far been denied).[48] The second premise is obviously an attempt to reach a group that is one more generation removed from the events under discussion, that is open to questioning established and received beliefs, that is sympathetic to perceived anti-establishment voices, and from which the leaders of tomorrow's society will come.

The historian Gavin Langmuir has noted that "the rapid change in the meaning of 'Jews' or 'antisemitism' for many non-Jews after 1945 owed more to Hitler than to scholarship before 1945."[49] Thus, the demise of anti-Semitism as an acceptable or respectable belief can be traced directly to feelings of repugnance and aversion to the Holocaust and its perpetrators.

If the Holocaust can be erased, history can be negated and prejudice and irrationality can return. That is the goal of the denier. To quote Langmuir again: "If I encounter individuals who deny that anything like that (the Holocaust) happened, I can only assume their individual irrationality, their cynical political immorality, or the irrationality of their social indoctrination."[50]

For both the Nation of Islam and the Holocaust deniers, history exists as a vast conspiracy theory. There is not much difference between the words of Khalid Muhammad ("You can believe that Jews control that seat [the White House] that they sit in behind the scenes. They control the finance and not only that, they influence the policy-making")[52] and the words of William Grimstad, the author of *The Six Million Reconsidered* "The American people sodden with persecution propaganda from the . . . Zionist-controlled radio and television networks and the overwhelmingly pro-Zionist print media, have become confused and inert."[53]

To see all of history as a conspiracy is different from seeing some conspiracies in history. Conspiracies do exist, as, for example, demonstrated by political revolts or assassinations.[54] But when the real facts are known, and the purveyors still insist on spinning their lies, then history is not only a matter of what happened in the past, but is a cause for ethical concern in the present. The Nazis specialized in the "Big Lie" technique, which involved repeating an assertion that is based on some facts but involved other invented or misrepresented claims to produce a false conclusion. By using this method, the Nazis achieved unparalleled success in propaganda.[55]

The modern abusers of history have learned their lesson well. What they share marks them as true inheritors of the Nazi perspective. They both find race to be a dominant factor. Gates describes the Nation of Islam as teaching the doctrine of "racial evil"[56]; or as Louis Farrakhan said about the Ku Klux Klan, "They don't want to see integration and mongrelization of the races. They want to see black folk separate. In that sense we have some common grounds."[57] This statement invokes memories of Willis Carto (the force behind Holocaust denial), who had written in 1955 that not enough Americans were concerned about "the inevitable niggerfication of America."[58] It is thus not surprising to find Arthur Butz, the author of the single most important text of Holocaust denial, as presenting his "ideas at the Savior's Day meeting of Louis Farrakhan's Nation of Islam" in 1985.[59] Nor was it surprising to find Leonard Jeffries, the anti-Semitic chair of City College's Black studies program, agreeing to speak at a Holocaust denial conference with "backers of David Duke and suspected Neo-Nazi and KKK types.[60] Finally, a world anti-Semitic, anti-Zionist, and Holocaust denial conference took place for Sweden in 1992. Farrakhan, Holocaust deniers Robert Faurisson and Fred Leuchter, and representative from extremists terrorist groups such as the Russian Pamyat, the Iranian Hezbollah, and the Islamic Hamas appeared at the conference.[61]

Obviously, what unites all the above is anti-Semitism. This anti-Semitism is based on lies, based on manipulations and distortions of history. It is an attempt to corrupt our view of the past in order to achieve a racist present and future. George Santayana wrote that "those who cannot remember the past are condemned to repeat it" or, in its more popular form, "Those

who ignore the past are condemned to repeat it."[62] What then should be our fate if we allow the past not to be ignored, but rather to be distorted and manipulated?

Our century has been the century of genocide, in part because history was twisted and perverted in order to provide a justification for discrimination. If the great ethical issues of our time revolve around human rights, if genocide is to be rejected as "solution," "final" or otherwise, then our reactions to anti-Semitism and other forms of racism stand as perhaps the clearest indication of where we stand as individuals and where we are heading as a society.

ENDNOTES

1. *Oxford English Dictionary*, entry on Ethic.
2. *Oxford English Dictionary*, entry on Moral.
3. *Nicomacean Ethics,* translated by J. A. K. Thompson, Middlesex, 1959, pp. 309–310.
4. Politics i.v. 1253a
5. Martin Buber, *People and Leader* reprinted in, *Pointing the Way*, New York, p. 157.
6. Ibid.
7. Ibid., p. 153.
8. For comparisons between the Holocaust and other historical tragedies, see Steven Katz, *The Holocaust in Historical Context*, New York, 1994.
9. See Arthur Cohen in his *The Tremendum*, 1991, pp. 52–53.
10. Defined by the *Oxford English Dictionary* as "consciousness of right and wrong, moral sense: Internal acknowledgment or recognition of the moral quality of one's motives and actions; the sense of right and wrong as regards things for which one is responsible."
11. Aristotle, *Nicomachean Ethics*, p. 25. "The good is that at which all things aim"—leaving aside detailed descriptions and discussions over exactly what is meant by "good."
12. For a basic overview of the Black Muslims, see, for example, the early work by C. Eric Lincoln, *Black Muslims in America* (originally published in Boston, 1951) which contains a basic account that has since been updated. For a recent, more popular look, see Steven Barboza, *American Jihad* (New York, 1993). Both these works are sympathetic to their subject. The split between Warith Deen Muhammad and Louis Farrakhan is discussed in Lawrence H. Mamiya's essay, "Minister Louis Farrakhan and the Final Call:

Schism in the Muslim Movement," pp. 234–255, in *The Muslim Community in North America*, ed. Earle H. Waugh, Baha Abu-Laban, and Regula B. Qureshi (Edmonton, 1983).

13. Mamiya, p. 236.
14. For example, "Malcolm X's widow, Betty Shabazz, said recently she believes Farrakhan had some role in her husband's murder" in *Farrakhan Admits He Turned Tide on Malcolm*, Associated Press, April 23, 1994.
15. Mamiya, p. 240.
16. C. Eric Lincoln, "The American Muslim Mission in the Context of American Social History" in Waugh, Abu-Laban, Qureshi, eds., *The Muslim Community in North America* (Edmonton, 1983), p. 221.
17. Ibid., p. 225. The quote from Elijah is brought by Lincoln, p. 224.
18. Harold Brackman, *Ministry of Lies: The Truth Behind the Nation of Islam's "The Secret Relationship Between Blacks and Jews,"* New York, p. 32, and see pp. 124–125, n. 23 for sources.
19. Mamiya, p. 240.
20. Ibid.
21. Ibid., p. 236.
22. Khalid Abdul Muhammad, Nation of Islam spokesman, *Newsday*, January 24, 1994, excerpted from ad printed by Anti-Defamation League, January 16, 1994.
23. *The New York Times*, July 20, 1992.
24. *The Secret Relationship Between Blacks and Jews*, the Historical Research Department of the Nation of Islam, Chicago, 1991.
25. Ibid., p. VII.
26. Ibid., pp. VII–VIII.
27. Brackman, 1994.
28. David Brion Davis, *The Slave Trade and the Jews*, *New York Review of Books*, December 22, 1994.
29. Brackman, p. 90.
30. Ibid., p. 46.
31. Ibid., pp. 48–49.
32. Ibid., pp. 50–51.
33. Ibid., p. 51.
34. *The Secret Relationship*, p. IV.
35. Brackman, pp. 58–59.
36. All preceding quotes from Henry Louis Gates, *The New York Times*, July 20, 1992.
37. I have taken much of this analysis of Holocaust denial from my (unpublished) paper, *Holocaust Denial: Method and Motive*, presented at a conference held on March 3–4, 1994, at Wilfred Laurier University, Waterloo, Ontario, Canada.
38. Letters cited in Deborah Lipstadt *Denying the Holocaust*, New York, 1993, p. 146. This is the best available overview of Holocaust denial. Copies also in possession of Simon Wiesenthal Center Archives.
39. See the summary in *The Los Angeles Times*, Sunday, May 5, 1994, p. A3.
40. Advertisement run under the headline: *The Holocaust Controversy, Michigan Daily,* November 11, 1991.
41. For consent agreement and other issues regarding Leuchter, see Lipstadt, *Denying the Holocaust*, pp. 170–171.
42. Advertisement run under the headline: *The Holocaust Controversy, Michigan Daily*, November 11, 1991.
43. Ibid.
44. Lipstadt, *Denying the Holocaust*, New York, 1993, p. 180.
45. *The Holocaust Controversy, Michigan Daily*, November 11, 1991.
46. Ibid.
47. Lipstadt, p. 204, on the OHA. Examples of letter from Dr. Peter O'Keefe, Professor. R. J. Dicenzo in *The Journal of Historical Review* 2, 1 (Spring 1981): 9.
48. Lipstadt, pp. 204–205.
49. Gavin Langmuir, *History, Religion and Antisemitism*, Berkeley University of California Press, 1990, p. 4.
50. Ibid., p. 350.
51. Omer Bartov, "Intellectuals on Auschwitz," *History and Memory* 5, 1: 108.
52. *New York Newsday*, January 24, 1994.
53. William Grimstad, [identified as the book's research editor] *The Six Million Reconsidered*, Torrance, 1979, p. 53.
54. Brackman cites (pp. 28–29) Richard Hofstadter's assertion that "The distinguishing thing about the paranoid style (of thinking)" is that according to its adherents "history is a conspiracy, set in motion by demonic forces of almost transcendent power." Richard Hofstadter, *The Paranoid Style in American Politics and Other Essays*, Chicago, 1964, p. 29.
55. See, for example, Hitler's discussion in *Mein Kampf:* "The magnitude of a lie always contains a certain factor of credibility, since the great masses of the people in the very bottom of their hearts tend to be corrupted rather than consciously and purposely evil, and that, therefore . . . they more easily fall victim to a big lie than to a little one." Adolf Hitler, *Mein Kampf* [translation Mannheim], Boston, 1971, p. 231.

56. *The New York Times*, July 20, 1992.

57. Barboza, *American Jihad*, p. 147.

58. Letters cited in Lipstadt, p. 146. Copies also in the possession of Simon Wiesenthal Center Archives.

59. Lipstadt, *Denying the Holocaust*, p. 126. Savior's Day, the birthday celebration of Farad, is perhaps the most important day on the Nation of Islam's liturgical calendar.

60. *New York Daily News*, January 30, 1992. Jeffries, after the publicity, backed out of the engagement. *New York Newsday*, January 31, 1992.

61. Lipstadt, *Denying the Holocaust*, p. 14.

62. George Santayana, "Flux and Constancy in Human Nature," in his *Life of Reason*, 1905–1906.

Questions for Discussion

1. Critically comment on the following: "Racialism (*sic*) is a universal; anti-Semitism an exclusively Christian disease" (R. H. S. Crossman).

   _____

   _____

   _____

   _____

2. Critically comment on the claim that blacks cannot be racist in America since racism presupposes a degree of empowerment that blacks have historically not enjoyed.

   _____

   _____

   _____

   _____

3. Is Zionism racism? Discuss.

   _____

   _____

   _____

   _____

4. In some views of what counts as racism, America will not be racist-free until we no more notice skin color than we notice eye color. Assess this claim. How would you analyze a film producer who, in casting for the role of Martin Luther King, Jr., chooses, say, Louis Gossett, Jr., over Gene Hackman, assuming each can play the role equally well? How would you analyze a producer who, in casting for the role of former Israeli prime minister Golda Meir, chooses Debra Winger (who is Jewish) over Meryl Streep (who is not), assuming both can play the role equally well?

   _____

   _____

   _____

   _____

5. Suppose an employer refuses to hire an Orthodox Jew who is more than qualified for a particular job but cannot work on Jewish holidays and that is the reason he or she is not hired. Would this be anti-Semitic?

_____

_____

_____

_____

6. Does affirmative action work to make society more tolerant of diversity or does it racially divide society even further?

_____

_____

_____

_____

7. Professor Michael Levin of the City College of New York has argued that nothing is wrong with racial discrimination making it worthy of rectification. He thinks that if we should rectify the wrongs of racial discrimination, we should rectify the wrongs of theft, murder, fraud, and so on. Is he right?

_____

_____

_____

_____

8. Should scientists be free to study possible correlations between race and intelligence?

_____

_____

_____

_____

9. In recent years, some universities have permitted speakers such as Louis Farrakhan and Leonard Jeffries to advance blatantly anti-Semitic notions in the name of free speech. At the same time, little or no instances of speakers discussing antiblack racist ideas have oc-

curred. Does this lack of symmetry bespeak a subtle anti-Semitism? What are the limits of free speech?

_____

_____

_____

_____

_____

10. Someone once suggested that one approach to racism is "passive nondiscrimination"—the practice of disregarding race in making all decisions about hiring, promotion, and so on. Discuss the pros and cons of this policy.

_____

_____

_____

_____

_____

11. Former Israeli Jonathan Pollard has been convicted of espionage against the United States and sentenced to several years of imprisonment (including years of solitary confinement) even though Israel is an ally of the United States and the material he "leaked" did not include vital information. Despite protests from the Jewish community that his sentence should be reduced and that more egregious acts of espionage have resulted in less severe punishments, his sentence has not been commuted by Presidents Bush or Clinton. Is this a form of anti-Semitism?

_____

_____

_____

_____

_____

12. Henry Ford, the founder of the Ford Motor Company, was said to have been virulently anti-Semitic before he was approached by a member of the Jewish community who pointed out the error of his beliefs, at which time Ford recanted and went out of his way to ap-

pease the Jewish community. Is the Ford case an anomaly? What is the best way to counter racism and anti-Semitism?

_____

_____

_____

_____

_____

13. Beside blacks and Jews, what other minorities can you identify that have been the victims of prejudice? How does prejudice against the groups you have identified differ from prejudice against blacks and Jews?

_____

_____

_____

_____

_____

For Further Reading

Cahn, Steven M. *Affirmative Action*. Philadelphia: Temple University Press, 1995.

Feagin, Joe, and Hernan Vera. *White Racism*. New York: Routledge, 1995.

Goldberg, David Theo, ed. *Anatomy of Racism*. Minneapolis: University of Minnesota Press, 1990.

Herrnstein, Richard J. and Charles A. Murray. *The Bell Curve*. New York: Simon & Schuster, 1994.

Langmuir, Gavin I. *History, Religion, and Anti-Semitism*. Los Angeles: University of California Press, 1990.

———. *Toward a Definition of Anti-Semitism*. Los Angeles: University of California Press, 1990.

Levin, Michael. "Is Racial Discrimination Special?" *Journal of Value Inquiry* 15 (1981): 225–232.

Popkin, Richard H. *The High Road to Pyrrhonism*. San Diego, CA: Austin Hill, 1980.

Sartre, Jean Paul. *Anti-Semite and Jew*. Translated by George J. Becker. New York: Schocken Books, 1965.

Thomas, Laurence Mordekhai. *Vessels of Evil: American Slavery and the Holocaust*. Philadelphia: Temple University Press, 1993.

Wasserstrom, Richard. "On Racism and Sexism." In Richard Wasserstrom, ed., *Today's Moral Problems*. New York: Macmillan, 1979, pp. 75–105.

Zack, Naomi. *Race and Mixed Race*. Philadelphia: Temple University Press, 1993.

Chapter 13

Ethics in Advertising

Passages for Reflection

"You can tell the ideals of a nation by its advertisements."

—Norman Douglas

"We grow up founding our dreams on the infinite promise of American advertising. I still believe that one can learn to play the piano by mail and that mud will give you a perfect complexion."

—Zelda Fitzgerald

"Promises, large promises, is the soul of advertising. . . . I cannot but propose it as a moral question to these masters of the public ear, whether they do not sometimes play too wantonly with our passions."

—Samuel Johnson

Opening Questions

1. What standards of honesty, if any, are obligatory in marketing practices?
2. Do people have a right not to be lied to or deceived?
3. Are manufacturers obligated not to offer products that are harmful or addictive, such as guns, tobacco, and alcohol?

In 1988, the Beech-Nut Corporation admitted that it had knowingly sold adulterated apple juice. The baby juice, which putatively contained "100% fruit juice," in fact contained little if any apple juice but was made of a synthetic concentrate that resembled apple juice. The fraud (and subsequent coverup) was a consequence of intense financial pressures brought upon Beech-Nut following a merger with the Nestlé Corporation in 1979. Having lost $2.5 million in 1981, Beech-Nut's chief executive officer promised to show a profit the following year.

Instances like this are not unique. In 1992, Sears, Roebuck and Company was inundated with complaints that its automotive service division was misleading customers and selling them unnecessary parts and services. In the face of declining revenues and an increasingly competitive market for car services, Sears spurred the performance of its auto centers by introducing goals and incentives for employees. Among the perks it introduced were commissions based on sales of such items and services as brakes, springs, shocks, and front-end alignments. Failure to meet these goals were accompanied by threats of transfers or reduced work hours.

When we consider that personal selling accounts for more than eight million jobs in the United States and that for every position in advertising there are more than thirty jobs in sales, you may be surprised that scandals like those surrounding Beech-Nut and Sears are not heard of more often. The problem is magnified when we consider that the purpose of selling is to convince the consumer that the product or service is the best solution to the customer's needs. Given the financial magnitude of U.S. corporations and the persuasive power of advertising, we may little wonder that advertising generates serious ethical issues. In what follows we will examine some of the issues that pertain to advertising products and services generally, and then discuss some specific issues pertaining to professionals who market their services.

The most obvious ethical issue confronting the world of advertising is deceiving or lying to potential consumers. The Beech-Nut Corporation was guilty of lying to consumers when it replaced apple juice with synthetic concentrate, Sears was guilty of lying when it informed its customers that they needed unnecessary parts and services. But compare the Beech-Nut and Sears cases with the marketing strategy of some house-hold laundry detergents (say, Cheer) which, in recent years, announced that such products were effective in removing odors from clothes in addition to removing stains. This feature was put forward as a virtue in that product when in fact *all* laundry detergents eliminate odors. Is this a case of lying? Did the makers of deodorizing laundry detergents behave improperly by highlighting a feature of their product that was shared by their competitors' products?

Before we answer these questions, we need to clarify the concepts of lying and deception. Surprisingly, not until the appearance of Sissela Bok's *Lying: Moral Choice in Public and Private Life* in 1978 did philosophers turn their attention to the moral significance of lying even though Immanuel Kant paid it some thought in his work on moral theory. Prior to that, philosophers were primarily concerned with truth and its role in theory of knowledge. Our analysis, accordingly, owes much to Bok.

I am tempted to define a *lie* as a stated falsehood, since so many lies fit that bill. This will not do, however, because not all falsehoods are lies and because lies need neither be false nor stated. That not all falsehoods are lies is demonstrated by imagining a psychology professor uttering a falsehood in class—for example, that Freud was a famous opera singer—for the purpose of seeing whether students are awake. That lies need not be false is demonstrated by imagining your friend calling you one Saturday evening inquiring whether you are busy, implying an interest in going to a movie. Not desiring his company but doing nothing of interest, you inform him that you *are* busy, thinking to yourself that you are busy doing nothing. Finally, that lies need not be stated (at least explicitly) is demonstrated by imagining a sinister stranger inquiring whether you have the correct time. Knowing the time but suspecting that the stranger might misappropriate your watch, you politely shrug your shoulders without uttering a word.

This analysis of what a lie is not throws into relief what a lie is. A lie is a message that is communicated with the intention to deceive. Some philosophers distinguish between deceiving and lying. They construe lying as a species of deception with lying functioning as a stated form of deception. Taking a cue from Bok, who allows us to collapse the distinction,[1] my own analysis construes lying to be any message that is *communicated*, which makes the difference between my view and others semantic. So construed, our psychology professor did not lie because his intention was to gain the students' attention, whereas telling a friend that you are busy when you are not *is* a lie since your aim is to deceive that person. So, too, conveying a message to a sinister stranger that you have

---

[1] Sissela Bok, *Lying; Moral Choice in Public and Private Life* (New York: Vintage Books, 1979), page 14.

no watch in your possession is a lie inasmuch as you are intending to deceive the stranger into believing otherwise.

Sometimes, as the example of the sinister stranger shows, we have good reasons for lying. But a presumption exists against it. Utilitarians argue that the presumption against lying is explained by the harmful consequences to which lying might lead. When cigarettes, for example, are associated with fun and amusement—which is the message advertised by Old Joe Camel—the outcome could be extremely harmful. And even when Wheaties is put forward as the "breakfast of champions" consumers are harmed by buying it when alternative cereals are equally or more nutritional and cheaper in price. (The benefits to General Mills offset this cost.)

Bok argues that the presumption against lying is explained by the fact that lying lowers the general level of trust and truthfulness that is essential to the proper functioning of society. Truth-telling, she says, is a foundation of relations among people. Without our trust that people speak truthfully, institutions collapse and communication is imperiled.[2] Ponder, if you will, the enormous extent to which we trust our fellow human beings to speak the truth. In addition to such trivial instances as relying upon people to give us accurate directions when we are lost, think of the consequences of our professors intentionally deceiving us by providing bad information, of our physicians knowingly prescribing bad medications yet telling us they are helpful, and of our lawyers deceitfully providing us with deleterious advice. Think also of the extent to which we rely upon the guidance of salespersons to provide us with good information in an increasingly complex marketplace. Beyond consulting *Consumer Reports*, we have little choice but to place our trust in the veracity of the salesperson who extols the virtues of Windows 95 or an automobile's antilock braking system.

Finally, some philosophers explain the presumption against lying by arguing that lying is wrong apart from its consequences. The deontologist W. D. Ross held this position. He claimed that lying is prima facie wrong apart from the bad consequences that might ensue. In this view, even if no one were hurt being deceived into thinking that M&Ms melted in your mouth and not in your hands, it would still be morally wrong to represent it as such.

We see more plainly now why Beech-Nut was wrong in mislabeling its baby food product as apple juice, and why Sears was wrong in claiming that its automotive services were needed when they were not. But such companies would not stay in business long if they consistently lied to consumers. This is why companies resort to more subtle marketing tactics typified by the deodorizing laundry detergent. The question is

---

[2]Richard De George, *Business Ethics* (New York: Macmillan, 1982), and Norman Bowie, *Business Ethics* (Englewood Cliffs, N.J.: Prentice Hall, 1982) appeal to similar reasons.

whether these techniques constitute lying. On the analysis put forward, the answer is yes, since marketing a detergent as deodorizing deceives the consumer into thinking that the product has a virtue that is unique to it. The same is true for bread manufacturers who advertise bread as cholesterol-free. *All* bread is cholesterol-free!

To bolster this point, think of the company that sold canned tuna, advertising that "It Never Turns Black in the Can." The company's sales increased dramatically as millions of consumers chose that brand, visualizing the blackened mess they might encounter if they opened a can of a competing brand. This slogan was misleading since no tuna *ever* turned black in the can even though what the company said was true. Suppose the company had advertised that its fish did not turn indigo or mauve. That would not have been misleading since no consumer would have thought that it did.

Beyond lying to consumers, marketing strategies have been criticized as undermining consumer autonomy. More precisely, critics contend that advertising undermines the right of consumers to make decisions that fully express their free wills. In an oft-discussed criticism, economist John Kenneth Galbraith has charged that advertising creates needs rather than responds to them.[3] When consumers are manipulated into purchasing products they think they need when they do not, their autonomy is violated; they are controlled and exploited. Galbraith coins the term "the dependence effect" to designate the way needs depend on the very process by which they are satisfied, and David Braybrooke argues that many consumers would want different products if they had good information rather than the information provided by manipulative advertisements.[4]

Violations of autonomy are commonplace in the advertising world. We are often reminded that we "need" deodorizing soap in addition to deodorants. We are told that we "need" to launder our clothes not only with Bold Three which has the virtues of being a detergent, bleach, and fabric softener, but that we "need" to add to our laundry both bleach and fabric softener. And just in case we are lost in the desert and have "need" to traverse mountainous terrains, we are reminded of the virtues of four-wheel drive vehicles such as the Jeep Eagle Cherokee.

In his popular book, *The Hidden Persuaders*, Vance Packard notes that a number of people in the advertising world admit to manipulating consumer behavior:

> As early as 1941 Dr. Dichter (an influential advertising consultant) was exhorting ad agencies to recognize themselves for what they ac-

---

[3]John Kenneth Galbraith, *The New Industrial State* (Boston: Houghton Mifflin, 1967), pp. 198–218.

[4]David Braybrooke, "Skepticism of Wants, and Certain Subversive Effects of Corporations on American Values." In Sidney Hook, ed., *Human Values and Economic Policy* (New York: New York University Press, 1967).

tually were—"one of the most advanced laboratories in psychology." He said the successful ad agency "manipulates human motivations and desires and develops a need for goods with which the public has at one time been unfamiliar—perhaps even undesirous of purchasing. The following year *Advertising Agency* carried an ad man's statement that psychology not only holds promise for understanding people but "ultimately for controlling their behavior."[5]

Beyond manufacturing felt needs, advertisers manipulate consumers by "puffery," "indirect information transfer," and "subliminal advertising." "Puffery" refers to the practice of exaggerating claims that have a grain of truth to them. Consider the cholesterol-reducing virtue that marketers of oat bran claimed for it after a medical journal refuted that oat bran was "correlated" with low cholesterol. Notwithstanding that this was an isolated study lacking the widespread consensus of the medical establishment, makers of oat bran marketed the product as though it were an elixir for countering high cholesterol. This resulted in a frenzy of consumer spending that benefited the manufacturers of oat bran far more than the consumers who purchased it. Similar techniques are employed by health food manufacturers who claim much more for their products than their products deliver. The problem is acute in the health food industry since health food manufacturers know all too well that their customers include hypochondriacal individuals looking for simple solutions to complex health problems.

"Indirect information transfer" refers to the practice of providing consumers with information that is not derived from the content of what is said but from the fact that it is said so often as to vividly remain in the consumer's mind. Pepsi and Coke commercials come to mind here, as do those for Budweiser beer. Finally, "subliminal advertising" refers to the practice of advertising messages that are targeted at the consumer's unconscious needs, desires, and fears. That the tire manufacturer Michelin portrays a baby to the tune of "a lot is riding on your tires" is an obvious example. Less obvious ones include movie theaters flashing ice cream ads and scantily clad women advertising brands of cars meant to appeal to men on screens during regular showings of feature films.

For each of these techniques, we can ask whether we are being manipulated into acting in a way that is hostile to our autonomy, or whether the advertising world is giving the consumer what he or she wants. Those who maintain that we are manipulated and not acting autonomously argue that a fully informed and rational consumer would not make purchases induced solely by these ads. Advertising, in this view, is no different from brainwashing. Just as in brainwashing, the brain-

---

[5]Vance Packard, *The Hidden Persuaders* (New York: Pocket Books, 1958), pp. 20–21. Cited in Robert Arrington, "Advertising and Behavior Control," *Journal of Business Ethics*, 1, 1 (February 1982): 3–12.

washers employ subtle techniques to cause their victims to have beliefs, wants, and attitudes they would not otherwise have, so, too, advertisers manipulate consumers into holding beliefs, wants, and attitudes they would not otherwise have. And having the relevant beliefs, wants, and attitudes serves the economic interests of corporations much more than the individual consumer.

Defenders of such advertising techniques argue along different lines. They claim that even if marketing strategies are manipulative in the ways their critics suggest, the consumer always has the freedom to resist the product or service promoted. Consumers are not coerced into purchasing Michelin tires, Levi's jeans, or Maxwell House coffee, and the ads for any brand are countered by ads for other brands. This argument would be compelling but for the pervasiveness of advertisement and the pressures it exerts on each of us starting with the young and impressionable.

A more compelling defense of advertising techniques is made by Theodore Levitt of the Harvard Business School.[6] Imagine, says Levitt, what the world would be like if we eliminated the exaggerated and fanciful claims that advertisement provides. We would be left with literal descriptions of the empirical characteristics of products and their functions. Rather than the adventure that accompanies the purchase of a Mazda Miata or the intrigue and sex appeal that accompanies the purchase of Calvin Klein's Obsession, we would be left with a crass and unpleasant description of cars and colognes. In other words, says Levitt, we want the dreams and fancies that accompany the products we purchase. Levitt makes another interesting point that commerce is doing nothing different in this way than art and theology. Just as art and theology influence their audiences by creating illusions that promise more than functionality, "embellishment and distortion are among advertisement's legitimate and socially desirable purposes."

Levitt's defense of puffery is related to the claim made by marketing apologizers that marketing has the noble purpose of satisfying human needs and wants and helping people through the commercial exchange process. In this view, we are mistaken to equate the unethical practices of some unscrupulous marketing firms with the respectable role of marketing generally. At its best, marketing involves the coordination of such variables as product, price, and promotion to effectively address the needs of consumers.

You can easily be a skeptic about this defense, given the tobacco companies denial of the proven connection between tobacco and lung cancer, Calvin Klein's erotic use of adolescents to promote its line of underwear (labeled "kiddy porn" by the American Family Association), and the abuse of the word *light* by food manufacturers who market their

---

[6]Theodore Levitt, "The Morality (?) of Advertising." *Harvard Business Review* 48 (1970): 84–92.

products as healthy when they are not. You can also be a skeptic in the absence of rational ways to adjudicate among competing products. How, for instance, are we to weigh the costs and benefits of competing brands of diapers when one diaper fits 22- to 35-pound infant boys and a competing brand fits 17- to 30-pound infant boys and girls? Not being similar in relevant respects, products leave us no rational way to decide which is the better for the money.

Being skeptical about marketing is also easy once you know the subtle techniques that supermarkets employ in arranging their products. Supermarket aisles are strategically arranged to maximize the purchase of products by consumers during any one visit. They are the brainchildren of industrial psychology, with the consumer playing the role of the rat in the maze. Note how the dairy aisle is invariably located at the point furthest from the entrance. This is because we usually need products such as milk, eggs, and butter, and so in making our way over to the very last aisle, we have ample opportunity to purchase products we might not otherwise need. Note also how breakfast cereals are arranged according to those most interested in purchasing them, with children's cereals on the bottom shelves and adult cereals on top. And note how items that appeal to children such as candy and balloons are located at the cash registers, thereby encouraging parents with impatient children to pacify them as they check out.

Advertisement of supermarket products also raises doubts about advertising's claim to nobility. Typically, supermarkets will discount products like hot dogs or hamburgers while raising (or not discounting) the products we typically use with them such as condiments and buns. Spurred on by the advertised discount, we usually wind up paying more than we had bargained for when the advertisement first caught our eye. Some supermarkets go so far as to award special discounts to those individuals who have been graced with the privilege of being "members" of their "clubs." For all of these reasons, we look askance when told that consumers are the ultimate authority about what they purchase and that advertising has the very noble purpose of satisfying human needs by helping us through the commercial exchange process.

Advertising raises other issues including personal privacy in the face of telemarketers who always seem to call as we relax over dinner. It raises issues in ecology such as when it promotes compact discs in environmentally unfriendly packages. And it raises issues of obscenity such as when Calvin Klein portrays seminude models in suggestive positions promoting its line of sportswear and cosmetics. Finally, advertising raises issues that speak to the morality of capitalism itself as when manufacturers promote gourmet pet foods. Before the collapse of the Soviet Union, communist propaganda showed pictures of aisles of gourmet pet food alongside pictures of homeless and destitute Americans, suggesting that Americans care more about profit making than they do about people. The counterargument to this is that people prefer a wide range of choices even if this entails social difficulties. Proponents of this view ask us to imagine how dull life would be if we lacked the wide range of products to which we have access.

Whatever your view on these issue are, you cannot deny that advertising, which is the lifeblood of profit making, raises issues of social responsibility that cannot be lightly dismissed. I suggest we address these issues by considering Susan Wolf's claim that the good advertiser is the one who does the best advertising job with the material he or she has to work with subject to the constraints that apply inside and outside the context of the job.[7] But contenting ourselves just to raise these issues and offer this advice, we will conclude by taking a brief look at some special problems that professionals encounter in advertising their services.[8]

Up until 1978, when, in the case of *Bates v. State Bar of Arizona*, the Supreme Court ruled that attorneys have the First Amendment right to advertise fees for their services, the professions considered it unethical for lawyers, doctors, and other professionals to engage in the practice of advertising. The reasoning was that it was "unprofessional" for individuals who consider themselves members of a professional community to lower themselves to using common business practices. Resorting to the gimmicks typified by the business world was considered a cheapening of the professions. In this light, we can understand former Chief Justice Warren Burger who insisted that "the public should never, never, employ a lawyer or doctor who finds it necessary to advertise." And while professionals today routinely advertise their services, the techniques of their advertising raise new controversial issues.

You can understand why some people believe it to be unprofessional for doctors and lawyers to market their services. Professionals are typically thought to be driven by the desire to help people as opposed to making a profit. This is not to deny that professionals are interested in making a profit; it is to deny that the profit motive is what fundamentally drives them. Professionals, in this sense, are to be contrasted with businesspeople who are thought to be driven first and foremost by the desire to make money.

For the legal community, the case against advertising is due to the negative image from which lawyers have historically suffered. When lawyers are perceived by the public as greedy and self-interested ambulance chasers, advertising adds to this image when it is in poor taste, as when an ad seeking drunk driving cases shows a liquor bottle, a

---

[7]Susan Wolf, "Ethics, Legal Ethics, and the Ethics of Law." In David Luban, ed., *The Good Lawyer: Lawyer's Roles and Lawyers' Ethics* (Savage, Md.: Rowman and Littlefield, 1983), p. 47.

[8]See Patrick E. Murphy and Gene R. Laczniak, "Marketing by Professionals: Some Ethical Issues and Prescriptions." *Business Insights* (Spring-Summer 1990): 5–9.

wrecked car, and a drunk, or when a TV ad for personal injury cases shows an accident victim, flashing lights, and injured persons being loaded into ambulances.[9]

For the medical community, the case against advertising is due to the even stronger perception that marketing is primarily a selling activity, far removed from the portrait of the physician's responsibilities as dictated by the Hippocratic Oath. Although patients are now sometimes thought of as "health care consumers" and physicians as "health care providers," you would not want to shop for the lowest price for a heart transplant as you would for a used car. At right angles to this is the fear that marketing will result in undue emphasis on price at the expense of quality of care.

Despite these arguments against advertising, lawyers and physicians now market their services to an unprecedented extent. The reasons for this include the growing level of competition among practitioners. A glut of practicing attorneys has occurred, especially in geographically desirable areas, and law schools continue to graduate large numbers of students year after year. This means that young attorneys have to use marketing techniques to compete with more established firms. With respect to physicians, the changing nature of how medicine is practiced explains the increase in advertising. Medicine is no longer dominated by private practitioners who did not see themselves as competing with their colleagues. Instead, such individuals compete with clinics, Health Maintenance Organizations, and hospitals. The pressure, then, is on private practitioners to market themselves more aggressively against these new competitive forms.

Beyond these professional-specific reasons are four reasons that argue in favor of professional advertising. The first is that consumers demand information about legal and medical services. At a minimum, consumers want to know the location and range of service provided, and advertising provides them with this knowledge. A second reason concerns the right of professionals to communicate with the public in any nondeceptive manner they choose. Citing the First Amendment as a basis, professionals claim that free speech guarantees them the right to advertise no less than nonprofessionals. A third reason is the economic one that costs to consumers are lower when advertising is present than when it is absent. A fourth reason is that advertising allows new entrants to gain access to the market more easily.

Despite the number of developments in the last two decades that have moved professionals out of their usual way of doing business, the use of marketing techniques continues to be an emotional and controversial issue. Time will tell whether the foray into the advertising world will work to the betterment or detriment of their professions.

---

[9]See "Lawyer Advertising—Marketing, Professionalism, the Future." *Res Gestae* (August 1988): 63.

Michael G. Helliwell is Professor of Marketing at Kean College and Coordinator of its International Business Program. He has taught marketing for over twenty years.

Video Presentation

Guest: Michael G. Helliwell, Professor of Marketing, Kean College

Student Panel: Joanne Grand, Mark Espositio, Jack Tancos

I begin my discussion by asking Helliwell to respond to a remark Susan Wolf once made concerning what makes an advertiser a good one. Wolf's opinion is that a good advertiser does the best job promoting a product within the limits of that product's capabilities. A so-called better advertiser, making claims about a product that are exaggerated and even false, is not better, just unscrupulous. Helliwell's answer, not quite on point, is to distinguish the various constituencies involved in advertising a product or service. After I press him to respond more directly to Wolf's comment, Helliwell reluctantly commits to the position that what is not legally forbidden is ethically permissible.

At this point, I ask Helliwell whether he thinks businesses have an obligation to be truthful to consumers, offering two examples of what I feel are misleading cases of advertising. The first concerns aerosol products which advertise the lack of fluorocarbons when no aerosols contain fluorocarbons since containing them is illegal. The second concerns the cough suppressant Triaminic which advertises that it is now available in half-strength dosages even as it requires twice the amount of its displaced version. While not addressing these products per se, Helliwell talks about the need for social responsibility while defending the rights of advertisers to market their products within the boundaries set by law. Underscoring his point is his confidence in what he perceives to be an educated consumer—a confidence I tell him I do not share.

At this point in the show, I ask Helliwell to comment on the tobacco companies minimizing the hazards of cigarette smoking as suggested by their use of Joe Camel. I point out, and Helliwell concurs, that Joe Camel has been found to be more famous than Mickey Mouse among portions of the population. Noting the need to be creative when faced with diminishing profits, I ask Helliwell if "creative" is not a euphemism for "wrong." This occasions discussion of subliminal advertising, followed by questions concerning the ethics of advertising condoms and the issues generated by different media.

Following the break, Jack Tancos asks Helliwell to comment on the ethics of marketing pharmaceutical products. Mark Esposito asks him about the direction condom advertisements will take. And Joanne Grand asks him about the role of government in regulating the marketing of tobacco. To this last question, Helliwell points out how government wants both to control noxious substances and reap the profits brought in by taxation.

In this widely discussed article, Albert Z. Carr argues that lying in business is analogous to bluffing in poker. Both are strategies that are acceptable because they are permissible within the rules of the game. Just as the rules of poker permit bluffing and every one understands that, the rules of business permit exaggeration and the promotion of products that are obsolete.

Is Business Bluffing Ethical?

Albert Z. Carr

A respected businessman with whom I discussed the theme of this article remarked with some heat, "You mean to say you're going to encourage men to bluff? Why, bluffing is nothing more than a form of lying! You're advising them to lie!"

I agreed that the basis of private morality is a respect for truth and that the closer a businessman comes to the truth, the more he deserves respect. At the same time, I suggested

Albert Z. Carr, "Is Business Bluffing Legal?" *Harvard Business Review,* vol. 46, 1968, 143–153. © President and Fellows of Harvard College.

that most bluffing in business might be regarded simply as game strategy—much like bluffing in poker, which does not reflect on the morality of the bluffer.

I quoted Henry Taylor, the British statesman who pointed out that "falsehood ceases to be falsehood when it is understood on all sides that the truth is not expected to be spoken"—an exact description of bluffing in poker, diplomacy, and business. I cited the analogy of the criminal court, where the criminal is not expected to tell the truth when he pleads "not guilty." Everyone from the judge down takes it for granted that the job of the defendant's attorney is to get his client off, not to reveal the truth; and this is considered ethical practice. I mentioned Representative Omar Burleson, the Democrat from Texas, who was quoted as saying, in regard to the ethics of Congress, "Ethics is a barrel of worms"[1]—a pungent summing up of the problem of deciding who is ethical in politics.

I reminded my friend that millions of businessmen feel constrained every day to say *yes* to their bosses when they secretly believe *no* and that this is generally accepted as permissible strategy when the alternative might be the loss of a job. The essential point, I said, is that the ethics of business are game ethics, different from the ethics of religion.

He remained unconvinced. Referring to the company of which he is president, he declared: "Maybe that's good enough for some businessmen, but I can tell you that we pride ourselves on our ethics. In thirty years not one customer has ever questioned my word or asked to check our figures. We're loyal to our customers and fair to our suppliers. I regard my handshake on a deal as a contract. I've never entered into price-fixing schemes with my competitors. I've never allowed my salesmen to spread injurious rumors about other companies. Our union contract is the best in our industry. And, if I do say so myself, our ethical standards are of the highest!"

He really was saying, without realizing it, that he was living up to the ethical standards of the business game—which are a far cry from those of private life. Like a gentlemanly poker player, he did not play in cahoots with others at the table, try to smear their reputations, or hold back chips he owed them.

But this same fine man, at that very time, was allowing one of his products to be advertised in a way that made it sound a great deal better than it actually was. Another item in his product line was notorious among dealers for its "built-in obsolescence." He was holding back from the market a much-improved product because he did not want it to interfere with sales of the inferior item it would have replaced. He had joined with certain of his competitors in hiring a lobbyist to push a state legislature, by methods that he preferred not to know too much about, into amending a bill then being enacted.

In his view these things had nothing to do with ethics; they were merely normal business practice. He himself undoubtedly avoided outright falsehoods—never lied in so many words. But the entire organization that he ruled was deeply involved in numerous strategies of deception.

PRESSURE TO DECEIVE

Most executives from time to time are almost compelled, in the interest of their companies or themselves, to practice some form of deception when negotiating with customers, dealers, labor unions, government officials, or even other departments of their companies. By conscious misstatements, concealment of pertinent facts, or exaggeration—in short, by bluffing—they seek to persuade others to agree with them. I think it is fair to say that if the individual executive refuses to bluff from time to time—if he feels obligated to tell the truth, the whole truth, and nothing but the truth—he is ignoring opportunities permitted under the rules and is at a heavy disadvantage in his business dealings.

But here and there a businessman is unable to reconcile himself to the bluff in which he plays a part. His conscience, perhaps spurred by religious idealism, troubles him. He feels guilty; he may develop an ulcer or a nervous tic. Before any executive can make profitable use of the strategy of the bluff, he needs to make sure that in bluffing he will not lose self-respect or become emotionally disturbed. If he is to reconcile personal integrity and high standards of honesty with the practical requirements of business, he must feel that his bluffs are ethically justified. The justification rests on the fact that business, as practiced by individuals as well as by corporations, has the impersonal character of a game—a game that demands both special strategy and an understanding of its special ethics.

The game is played at all levels of corporate life, from the highest to the lowest. At the very instant that a man decides to enter business, he may be forced into a game situation, as is shown by the recent experience of a Cornell honor graduate who applied for a job with a large company.

This applicant was given a psychological test which included the statement, "Of the following magazines, check any that you have read either regularly or from time to time, and double-check those which interest you most. *Reader's Digest, Time, Fortune, Saturday Evening Post, The New Republic, Life, Look, Ramparts, Newsweek, Business Week, U.S. News & World Report, The Nation, Playboy, Esquire, Harper's, Sports Illustrated.*"

His tastes in reading were broad, and at one time or another he had read almost all of these magazines. He was a subscriber to *The New Republic*, an enthusiast for *Ramparts*, and an avid student of the pictures in *Playboy*. He was not sure whether his interest in *Playboy* would be held against him, but he had a shrewd suspicion that if he confessed to an interest in *Ramparts* and *The New Republic*, he would be thought a liberal, a radical, or at least an intellectual, and his chances of getting the job, which he needed, would greatly diminish. He therefore checked five of the more conservative magazines. Apparently it was a sound decision, for he got the job.

He had made a game player's decision, consistent with business ethics.

A similar case is that of a magazine space salesman who, owing to a merger, suddenly found himself out of a job.

The man was 58, and, in spite of a good record, his chance of getting a job elsewhere in a business where youth is favored in hiring practice was not good. He was a vigorous, healthy man, and only a considerable amount of gray in his hair suggested his age. Before beginning his job search he touched up his hair with black dye to confine the gray to his temples. He knew that the truth about his age might well come out in time, but he calculated that he could deal with that situation when it arose. He and his wife decided that he could easily pass for 45, and he so stated his age on his résumé.

This was a lie; yet within the accepted rules of the business game, no moral culpability attaches to it.

THE POKER ANALOGY

We can learn a good deal about the nature of business by comparing it with poker. While both have a large element of chance, in the long run the winner is the man who plays with steady skill. In both games ultimate victory requires intimate knowledge of the rules, insight into the psychology of the other players, a bold front, a considerable amount of self-discipline, and the ability to respond swiftly and effectively to opportunities provided by chance.

No one expects poker to be played on the ethical principles preached in churches. In poker it is right and proper to bluff a friend out of the rewards of being dealt a good hand. A player feels no more than a slight twinge of sympathy, if that, when—with nothing better than a single ace in his hand—he strips a heavy loser, who holds a pair, of the rest of his chips. It was up to the other fellow to protect himself. In the words of an excellent poker player, former President Harry Truman, "If you can't stand the heat, stay out of the kitchen." If one shows mercy to a loser in poker, it is a personal gesture, divorced from the rules of the game.

Poker has its special ethics, and here I am not referring to rules against cheating. The man who keeps an ace up his sleeve or who marks the cards is more than unethical; he is a crook, and can be punished as such—kicked out of the game, or in the Old West, shot.

In contrast to the cheat, the unethical poker player is one who, while abiding by the letter of the rules, finds ways to put the other players at an unfair disadvantage. Perhaps he unnerves them with loud talk. Or he tries to get them drunk. Or he plays in cahoots with someone else at the table. Ethical poker players frown on such tactics.

Poker's own brand of ethics is different from the ethical ideals of civilized human relationships. The game calls for distrust of the other fellow. It ignores the claim of friend-ship. Cunning deception and concealment of one's strength and intentions, not kindness and openheartedness, are vital in poker. No one thinks any the worse of poker on that account. And no one should think any the worse of the game of business because its standards of right and wrong differ from the prevailing traditions of morality in our society.

DISCARD THE GOLDEN RULE

This view of business is especially worrisome to people without much business experience. A minister of my acquaintance once protested that business cannot possibly function in our society unless it is based on the Judeo-Christian system of ethics. He told me:

> I know some businessmen have supplied call girls to customers, but there are always a few rotten apples in every barrel. That doesn't mean the rest of the fruit isn't sound. Surely the vast majority of businessmen are ethical. I myself am acquainted with many who adhere to strict codes of ethics based fundamentally on religious teachings. They contribute to good causes. They participate in community activities. They cooperate with other companies to improve working conditions in their industries. Certainly they are not indifferent to ethics.

That most businessmen are not indifferent to ethics in their private lives, everyone will agree. My point is that in their office lives they cease to be private citizens; they become game players who must be guided by a somewhat different set of ethical standards.

The point was forcefully made to me by a Midwestern executive who has given a good deal of thought to the question:

> So long as a businessman complies with the laws of the land and avoids telling malicious lies, he's ethical. If the law as written gives a man a wide-open chance to make a killing, he'd be a fool not to

take advantage of it. If he doesn't, some-body else will. There's no obligation on him to stop and consider who is going to get hurt. If the law says he can do it, that's all the justification he needs. There's nothing unethical about that. It's just plain business sense.

This executive (call him Robbins) took the stand that even industrial espionage, which is frowned on by some businessmen, ought not to be considered unethical. He recalled a recent meeting of the National Industrial Conference Board where an authority on marketing made a speech in which he deplored the employment of spies by business organizations. More and more companies, he pointed out, find it cheaper to penetrate the secrets of competitors with concealed cameras and microphones or by bribing employees than to set up costly research and design departments of their own. A whole branch of the electronics industry has grown up with this trend, he continues, providing equipment to make industrial espionage easier.

Disturbing? The marketing expert found it so. But when it came to a remedy, he could only appeal to "respect for the golden rule." Robbins thought this a confession of defeat, believing that the golden rule, for all its value as an ideal for society, is simply not feasible as a guide for business. A good part of the time the businessman is trying to do unto others as he hopes others will *not* do unto him.[2] Robbins continued:

> Espionage of one kind or another has become so common in business that it's like taking a drink during Prohibition—it's not considered sinful. And we don't even have Prohibition where espionage is concerned; the law is very tolerant in this area. There's no more shame for a business that uses secret agents than there is for a nation. Bear in mind that there already is at least one large corporation—you can buy its stock over the counter—that makes millions by providing counterespionage service to indus-

trial firms. Espionage in business is not an ethical problem; it's an established technique of business competition.

"We Don't Make the Laws."

Wherever we turn in business, we can perceive the sharp distinction between its ethical standards and those of the churches. Newspapers abound with sensational stories growing out of this distinction:

- We read one day that Senator Philip A. Hart of Michigan has attacked food processors for deceptive packaging of numerous products.[3]
- The next day there is a Congressional to-do over Ralph Nader's book, *Unsafe At Any Speed*, which demonstrates that automobile companies for years have neglected the safety of car-owning families.[4]
- Then another Senator, Lee Metcalf of Montana, and journalist Vic Reinemer show in their book, *Overcharge*, the methods by which utility companies elude regulating government bodies to extract unduly large payments from users of electricity.[5]

These are merely dramatic instances of a prevailing condition; there is hardly a major industry at which a similar attack could not be aimed. Critics of business regard such behavior as unethical, but the companies concerned know that they are merely playing the business game.

Among the most respected of our business institutions are the insurance companies. A group of insurance executives meeting recently in New England was startled when their guest speaker, social critic Daniel Patrick Moynihan, roundly berated them for "unethical" practices. They had been guilty, Moynihan alleged, of using outdated actuarial tables to obtain unfairly high premiums. They habitually delayed the hearings of lawsuits against them in order to tire out the plaintiffs and win cheap settlements. In their employ-

ment policies they used ingenious devices to discriminate against certain minority groups.[6]

It was difficult for the audience to deny the validity of these charges. But these men were business game players. Their reaction to Moynihan's attack was much the same as that of the automobile manufacturers to Nader, of the utilities to Senator Metcalf, and of the food processors to Senator Hart. If the laws governing their businesses change, or if public opinion becomes clamorous, they will make the necessary adjustments. But morally they have, in their view, done nothing wrong. As long as they comply with the letter of the law, they are within their rights to operate their businesses as they see fit.

The small business is in the same position as the great corporation in this respect. For example:

> In 1967 a key manufacturer was accused of providing master keys for automobiles to mail-order customers, although it was obvious that some of the purchasers might be automobile thieves. His defense was plain and straightforward. If there was nothing in the law to prevent him from selling his keys to anyone who ordered them, it was not up to him to inquire as to his customers' motives. Why was it any worse, he insisted, for him to sell car keys by mail, than for mail-order houses to sell guns that might be used for murder? Until the law was changed, the key manufacturer could regard himself as being just as ethical as any other businessman by the rules of the business game.[7]

Violations of the ethical ideals of society are common in business, but they are not necessarily violations of business principles. Each year the Federal Trade Commission orders hundreds of companies, many of them of the first magnitude, to "cease and desist" from practices which, judged by ordinary standards, are of questionable morality but which are stoutly defended by the companies concerned.

In one case, a firm manufacturing a well-known mouthwash was accused of using a cheap form of alcohol possibly deleterious to health. The company's chief executive, after testifying in Washington, made this comment privately:

> We broke no law. We're in a highly competitive industry. If we're going to stay in business, we have to look for profit wherever the law permits. We don't make the laws. We obey them. Then why do we have to put up with this "holier than thou' talk about ethics? It's sheer hypocrisy. We're not in business to promote ethics: Look at the cigarette companies, for God's sake! If the ethics aren't embodied in the laws by the men who made them, you can't expect businessmen to fill the lack. Why, a sudden submission to Christian ethics by businessmen would bring about the greatest economic upheaval in history!

It may be noted that the government failed to prove its case against him.

Cast Illusions Aside

Talk about ethics by businessmen is often a thin decorative coating over the hard realities of the game:

Once I listened to a speech by a young executive who pointed to a new industry code as proof that his company and its competitors were deeply aware of their responsibilities to society. It was a code of ethics, he said. The industry was going to police itself, to dissuade constituent companies from wrongdoing. His eyes shone with conviction and enthusiasm.

The same day there was a meeting in a hotel room where the industry's top executives met with the "czar" who was to administer the new code, a man of high repute. No one who was present could doubt their common attitude. In their eyes the code was designed primarily to forestall a move by the federal government to impose stern restrictions on the industry. They felt that the code would hamper them a good deal less than new federal laws would. It was, in other words, conceived as a protection for the industry, not for the public.

The young executive accepted the surface explanation of the code; these leaders, all experienced game players, did not deceive themselves for a moment about its purpose.

The illusion that business can afford to be guided by ethics as conceived in private life is often fostered by speeches and articles containing such phrases as, "It pays to be ethical," or, "Sound ethics is good business" Actually this is not an ethical position at all; it is a self-serving calculation in disguise. The speaker is really saying that in the long run a company can make more money if it does not antagonize competitors, suppliers, employees, and customers by squeezing them too hard. He is saying that oversharp policies reduce ultimate gains. That is true, but it has nothing to do with ethics. The underlying attitude is much like that in the familiar story of the shopkeeper who finds an extra twenty-dollar bill in the cash register, debates with himself the ethical problem—should he tell his partner?—and finally decides to share the money because the gesture will give him an edge over the s.o.b. the next time they quarrel.

I think it is fair to sum up the prevailing attitude of businessmen on ethics as follows:

We live in what is probably the most competitive of the world's civilized societies. Our customs encourage a high degree of aggression in the individual's striving for success. Business is our main area of competition, and it has been ritualized into a game of strategy. The basic rules of the game have been set by the government, which attempts to detect and punish business frauds. But as long as a company does not transgress the rules of the game set by law, it has the legal right to shape its strategy without reference to anything but its profits. If it takes a long-term view of its profits, it will preserve amicable relations, so far as possible, with those with whom it deals. A wise businessman will not seek advantage to the point where he generates dangerous hostility among employees, competitors, customers, government, or the public at large.

But decisions in this area are, in the final test, decisions of strategy, not of ethics.

THE INDIVIDUAL AND THE GAME

An individual within a company often finds it difficult to adjust to the requirements of the business game. He tries to preserve his private ethical standards in situations that call for game strategy. When he is obliged to carry out company policies that challenge his conception of himself as an ethical man, he suffers.

It disturbs him when he is ordered, for instance, to deny a raise to a man who deserves it, to fire an employee of long standing, to prepare advertising that he believes to be misleading, to conceal facts that he feels customers are entitled to know, to cheapen the quality of materials used in the manufacture of an established product, to sell as new a product that he knows to be rebuilt, to exaggerate the curative powers of a medicinal preparation, or to coerce dealers.

There are some fortunate executives who, by the nature of their work and circumstances, never have to face problems of this kind. But in one form or another the ethical dilemma is felt sooner or later by most businessmen. Possibly the dilemma is most painful not when the company forces the action on the executive but when he originates it himself—that is, when he has taken or is contemplating a step which is in his own interest but which runs counter to his early moral conditioning. To illustrate:

- The manager of an export department, eager to show rising sales, is pressed by a big customer to provide invoices which, while containing no overt falsehood that would violate a U.S. law, are so worded that the customer may be able to evade certain taxes in his homeland.
- A company president finds that an aging executive, within a few years of retirement and his pension, is not as productive as formerly. Should he be kept on?
- The produce manager of a supermarket debates with himself whether to get rid of a lot of half-rotten tomatoes by including one, with its good side exposed, in every tomato six-pack.
- An accountant discovers that he has taken an improper deduction on his company's tax return and fears the consequences if he calls the matter to the president's attention, though he himself has done nothing illegal. Perhaps if he says nothing, no one will notice the error.
- A chief executive officer is asked by his directors to comment on a rumor that he owns stock in another company with which he has placed large orders. He could deny it, for the stock is in the name of his son-in-law and he has earlier formally instructed his son-in-law to sell the holding.

Temptations of this kind constantly arise in business. If an executive allows himself to be torn between a decision based on business considerations and one based on his private ethical code, he exposes himself to a grave psychological strain.

This is not to say that sound business strategy necessarily runs counter to ethical ideals. They may frequently coincide; and when they do, everyone is gratified. But the major tests of every move in business, as in all games of strategy, are legality and profit. A man who intends to be a winner in the business game must have a game player's attitude.

The business strategist's decisions must be as impersonal as those of a surgeon performing an operation—concentrating on objective and technique, and subordinating personal feelings. If the chief executive admits that his son-in-law owns the stock, it is because he stands to lose more if the fact comes out later than if he states it boldly and at once. If the supermarket manager orders the rotten tomatoes to be discarded, he does so to avoid an increase in consumer complaints and a loss of goodwill. The company president decides not to fire the elderly executive in the belief that the negative reaction of other employees would in the long run cost the company more than it would lose in keeping him and paying his pension.

All sensible businessmen prefer to be truthful, but they seldom feel inclined to tell the *whole* truth. In the business game truth-telling usually has to be kept within narrow limits if trouble is to be avoided. The point was neatly made a long time ago (in 1888) by one of John D. Rockefeller's associates, Paul Babcock, to Standard Oil Company executives who were about to testify before a government investigating committee: "Parry every question with answers which, while perfectly truthful, are evasive of *bottom* facts."[8] This was, is, and probably always will be regarded as wise and permissible business strategy.

For Office Use Only

An executive's family life can easily be dislocated if he fails to make a sharp distinction between the ethical systems of the home and the office—or if his wife does not grasp that distinction. Many a businessman who has remarked to his wife, "I had to let Jones go today" or "I had to admit to the boss that Jim has been goofing off lately," has been met with an indignant protest. "How could you do a thing like that? You know Jones is over 50 and will have a lot of trouble getting another job." Or, "You did that to Jim? With his wife ill and all the worry she's been having with the kids?"

If the executive insists that he had no choice because the profits of the company and his own security were involved, he may see a certain cool and ominous reappraisal in his wife's eyes. Many wives are not prepared to accept the fact that business operates with a special code of ethics. An illuminating illustration of this comes from a Southern sales executive who related a conversation he had had with his wife at a time when a hotly contested political campaign was being waged in their state:

"I made the mistake of telling her that I had had lunch with Colby, who gives me about half my business. Colby mentioned that his company had a stake in the election. Then he said, 'By the way, I'm treasurer of the citizens'

committee for Lang. I'm collecting contributions. Can I count on you for a hundred dollars?'

"Well, there I was. I was opposed to Lang, but I knew Colby. If he withdrew his business, I could be in a bad spot. So I just smiled and wrote out a check then and there. He thanked me, and we started to talk about his next order. Maybe he thought I shared his political views. If so, I wasn't going to lose any sleep over it.

"I should have had sense enough not to tell Mary about it. She hit the ceiling. She said she was disappointed in me. She said I hadn't acted like a man, that I should have stood up to Colby.

"I said, 'Look, it was an either-or situation. I had to do it or risk losing the business.'

"She came back at me with, 'I don't believe it. You could have been honest with him. You could have said that you didn't feel you ought to contribute to a campaign for a man you weren't going to vote for. I'm sure he would have understood.'

"I said, 'Mary, you're a wonderful woman, but you're way off the track. Do you know what would have happened if I had said that? Colby would have smiled and said, 'Oh, I didn't realize. Forget it.' But in his eyes from that moment I would be an oddball, maybe a bit of a radical. He would have listened to me talk about his order and would have promised to give it consideration. After that I wouldn't hear from him for a week. Then I would telephone and learn from his secretary that he wasn't yet ready to place the order. And in about a month I would hear through the grapevine that he was giving his business to another company. A month after that I'd be out of a job.'

"She was silent for a while. Then she said, 'Tom, something is wrong with business when a man is forced to choose between his family's security and his moral obligation to himself. It's easy for me to say you should have stood up to him—but if you had, you might have felt you were betraying me and the kids. I'm sorry that you did it, Tom, but I can't blame you. Something is wrong with business!'"

This wife saw the problem in terms of moral obligations conceived in private life; her husband saw it as a matter of game strategy. As a player in a weak position, he felt that he could not afford to indulge an ethical sentiment that might have cost him his seat at the table.

Playing to Win

Some men might challenge the Colbys of business—might accept serious setbacks to their business careers rather than risk a feeling of moral cowardice. They merit our respect—but as private individuals, not businessmen. When the skillful player of the business game is compelled to submit to unfair pressure, he does not castigate himself for moral weakness. Instead, he strives to put himself into a strong position where he can defend himself against such pressures in the future without loss.

If a man plans to take a seat in the business game, he owes it to himself to master the principles by which the game is played, including its special ethical outlook. He can then hardly fail to recognize that an occasional bluff may well be justified in terms of the game's ethics and warranted in terms of economic necessity. Once he clears is mind on this point, he is in a good position to match his strategy against that of the other players. He can then determine objectively whether a bluff in a given situation has a good chance of succeeding and can decide when and how to bluff, without a feeling of ethical transgression.

To be a winner, a man must play to win. This does not mean that he must be ruthless, cruel, harsh, or treacherous. On the contrary, the better his reputation for integrity, honesty, and decency, the better his chances of victory will be in the long run. But from time to time every businessman, like every poker player, is offered a choice between certain loss or bluffing within the legal rules of the game. If he is not resigned to losing, if he wants to rise in his company and industry, then in such a crisis he will bluff—and bluff hard.

Every now and then one meets a successful businessman who has conveniently forgotten the small or large deceptions that he practiced on his way to fortune. "God gave me my money," old John D. Rockefeller once piously told a Sunday school class. It would be a rare tycoon in our time who would risk the horse laugh with which such a remark would be greeted.

In the last third of the twentieth century even children are aware that if a man has become prosperous in business, he has sometimes departed from the strict truth in order to overcome obstacles or has practiced the more subtle deceptions of the half-truth or the misleading omission. Whatever the form of the bluff, it is an integral part of the game, and the executive who does not master its techniques is not likely to accumulate much money or power.

Endnotes

1. *The New York Times*, March 9, 1967.
2. See Bruce D. Henderson, "Brinkmanship in Business," HBR, March-April 1967, p. 49.
3. *The New York Times*, November 21, 1966.
4. New York, Grossman Publishers, Inc., 1965.
5. New York, David McKay Company, Inc., 1967.
6. *The New York Times*, January 17, 1967.
7. Cited by Ralph Nader in "Business Crime" *The New Republic*, July 1, 1967, p. 7.
8. Babcock in a memorandum to Rockefeller (Rockefeller Archives).

Closing Questions

1. What effect would a wholesale adoption of Kantian ethics have on the advertising community?

2. Is an organization duty-bound to reveal product defects to consumers?

3. Which area of marketing strategy is most subject to ethical scrutiny?

4. Discuss whether marketing personnel can behave ethically and at the same time prosper.

5. Are Calvin Klein ads obscene? Discuss pro or con.

6. Sometimes, large concerns employ "bait and switch" techniques whereby consumers are baited into purchasing a product because of an advertised price but are then talked into purchasing a more expensive product. Tops electronics, for instance, often advertises stereos at extremely low prices only to encourage their sales representatives to convince consumers to purchase a better and more expensive model. The same is true of All-Tune and Lube. Is this practice ethical?

_____

_____

_____

_____

_____

7. Former Chief Justice Warren Burger once remarked, "The public should never, never employ a lawyer or doctor who finds it necessary to advertise." Is this statement defensible? Compare it with the statement made by a Federal Trade Commission official who said: "At bottom, the prejudice against advertising is that it creates pressure to compete."

_____

_____

_____

_____

_____

8. Attorneys typically get paid "contingency fees" when handling personal injury cases in which case the attorney receives one-third of the award *minus litigation costs*. Is a personal injury ad that reads "No recovery—no fee" misleading for failing to mention that the client is responsible for litigation costs?

_____

_____

_____

_____

_____

9. Companies have been accused of advertising to create needs in consumers that the companies' products will then meet. Is this accusation plausible? Is anything wrong with it if it is true?

_____

_____

_____

_____

_____

10. It has been said that any publicity is good publicity. What sense can that have? What ethical limits should apply?

_____

_____

_____

_____

_____

For Further Reading

Beauchamp, Tom L. "Manipulative Advertising." *Business and Professional Ethics Journal* 3, 3 & 4 (1983): 1–22.

Bok, Sissela. *Lying: Moral Choice in Public and Private Life*. New York: Vintage Books, 1978.

Carson, Thomas. "On the Definition of Lying: A Reply to Jones and Revisions." *Journal of Business Ethics* 7 (1988): 509–514.

Fallows, James. *Breaking the News: How the Media Undermine Democracy*. New York: Pantheon Books, 1996.

Goldman, Alan. "Ethical Issues in Advertising." in Tom Regan, ed., *Just Business*. New York: Random House, 1983, pp. 235–270.

Leiser, Burton. "The Ethics of Advertising." In Richard T. De George and Joseph A. Picheler, eds., *Ethics, Free Enterprise, and Public Policy*. New York: Oxford University Press, 1978, pp. 173–186.

Machan, Tibor R. "Advertising: The Whole or Only Some of the Truth?" Public *Affairs Quarterly* 1, 4 (October 1987): 59–71.

Michelman, James H. "Deception in Commercial Negotiation." *Journal of Business Ethics* 2 (1983): 255–262.

Sullivan, Roger J. "A Response to 'Is Business Bluffing Ethical?' " *Business and Professional Ethics Journal* 3, 2 (1983): 1–18.

Wokutch, Richard E., and Thomas L. Carson. "The Ethics and Profitability of Bluffing in Business." *Westminster Institute Review* 1, 2 (May 1981, rev. 1986). In Thomas Donaldson and Patricia Werhane, eds., *Ethical Issues in Business: A Philosophical Approach*. Englewood Cliffs, N.J.: Prentice Hall, 1988, pp. 77–83.

———. "The Moral Status of Bluffing and Deception in Business." In Wade L. Robison, Michael S. Pritchard, and Joseph Ellin, eds., *Profits and Professions*. Clifton, N.J.: Humana Press, 1983, pp. 141–155.

Chapter 14

Ethics in Journalism

Passages for Reflection

"No news is good news."
—*Unknown*

"The function of the press is very high. It is almost holy. To misstate or suppress the news is a breach of trust."
—*Louis D. Brandeis*

"The press is the hired agent of a monied system, and set up for no other purpose than to tell lies where their interests are involved."
—*Henry Brooks Adams*

Opening Questions

1. What is news?
2. What is the role of the press in a democratic society?
3. To what extent can news reporters be objective?

Conventional wisdom has it that the press and the government are natural adversaries. On the one hand, democratic government needs the support of its citizenry in order to ensure its effective operation. Without the good opinion of its people, and without the consent of the governed, state policy cannot be carried out smoothly and the obligations the state imposes (such as taxes and conscription) can hardly be secured. The press in the United States, on the other hand, sees itself as a guardian of the people, as a "fourth branch of government" comparable to the legislative, executive, and judicial branches. Always on the lookout for tyranny and oppression, its self-appointed task is to subject the government to scrutiny and criticism.

The government and press are adversaries only in a democracy where the press functions as a check against abuse. In a totalitarian government, the press is a conduit of the powers that be. Accordingly, if the press is to serve its appointed function in a democracy, it is imperative that the press be fair, truthful, and unbiased. Otherwise, the propaganda the press is designed to protect us from is replaced by the propaganda the press provides us with.

Is the press the objective watchdog that American citizens suppose it to be? Is what it reports fair, truthful, and unbiased? After examining the role of the press in a democracy, particularly as it has evolved historically in the United States, we will discuss these questions and critically ask whether the press is as objective and impartial as it asserts itself to be.

The history of the freedom of the press, like so many of the freedoms the United States Constitution protects, dates back to the time when nation-states emerged from the Middle Ages.[1] During that time, political authority derived its legitimacy from religious authority, and truth was determined by divine revelation. If controversies existed, they were resolved by God through God's infallible human agents, and dissenters were damned as well as ostracized. When governments changed, their focus and moved from religious to political concerns, they barely toler-

---

[1]For a history of the First Amendment's freedom of speech and press clause, see John E. Nowack, Ronald D. Rotunda, and J. Nelson Young, *Constitutional Law.* (St. Paul, Minn: West Publishing Co., 1980).

ated dissent since, in the absence of religious authority, government needed the approval of its populace.

In fifteenth-century England, the situation was aggravated by the split between the Church of England and the Catholic Church as well as the struggle for supremacy between the King and Parliament. Consequently, in the centuries prior to the Declaration of Independence, the battle for the hearts and minds of the English required the suppression of ideas inimical to the controlling power. The two methods by which this suppression took place were through licensing regulations and the doctrine of seditious libel. Regulations required the licensing of all writing prior to publication, and the doctrine of seditious libel made criminal any published statements that were critical of the ruling power.

In America, at the time the Constitution was framed, the practice of censorship had ceased to exist although the doctrine of seditious libel was alive and well. When the First Amendment was written prohibiting Congress from abridging the freedom of speech and press, the concern was with the power of the government to punish publications that were critical of it. Matters crystalized in the 1790s when President John Adams' Federalist administration invoked the Sedition Act of 1798 against Thomas Jefferson's Democratic-Republican party for their criticism of Adams' administration. The Sedition Act prohibited "publishing any false, scandalous and malicious writing or writings against the government of the United States, or either house of Congress . . . or the President . . . with intent to defame . . . or to bring them . . . into contempt or disrepute." While the Sedition Act was never explicitly ruled to violate the First Amendment, the attack on its validity gave the Amendment its central meaning. Writing for the Supreme Court in 1964, Justice Brennan declared that the attack on the Sedition Act "reflected a broad consensus that the Act, because of the constraint it imposed upon criticism of government and public officials, was inconsistent with the First Amendment."[2]

While Brennan did not say why the Sedition Act is inconsistent with the First Amendment, it is presumably because of the conviction that the truth of an idea can only be determined in the "marketplace" of competing ideas. This conviction was forcefully defended by John Stuart Mill in his 1859 essay *On Liberty,* where Mill warned us of the dangers of suppressing dissenting opinions. He argued that only an enlightened citizenry can make the informed decisions required in an effective democracy. While Mill was more fearful of the tyranny of the majority than he was of the tyranny of the state, his argument against censorship was no less compelling. We have more to fear, he said, from controlling the free and open exchange of ideas than anything we might learn by honest discussion. Against these considerations, we can understand that

---

[2]376 U.S. 254, 276 (1964).

the purpose of the press is to inform the people and serve as an antidote to established power. As Justice Black put it, writing for the Supreme Court in *New York Times Co. v. United States,* "Paramount among the responsibilities of a free press is the duty to prevent any part of the government from deceiving the people."[3]

Does the press fulfill this "paramount duty?" The linguist and social critic Noam Chomsky has vociferously argued that it does not, although his criticism is directed more against government for slanting the news than at any bias of the press itself. In his controversial essay "Propaganda, American Style,"[4] Chomsky discusses the subtle mechanisms the American government employs in its efforts to control the press. He begins by favorably citing journalist Walter Lippmann's remark that the art of democracy requires "the manufacture of consent," noting that Lippmann's term is an Orwellian euphemism for "thought control." The idea is that since, in a democracy, the government cannot control people's behavior, it resorts to controlling what people think. And it does this by manipulating the press.

To illustrate, Chomsky cites the government's efforts at creating political debate that appears to embrace many opinions but really stays within narrow bounds. Using the Vietnam War for an example, Chomsky argues that in the mainstream media—for instance, *The New York Times*—a lively debate took place during the war between "hawks" and "doves." The hawks argued that America could win the war if America sustained the war effort. The doves argued that the war was not winnable and that America had been killing too many people. But both sides unwittingly accepted the premise that America had the right to carry out aggression against North Vietnam, although they used the term *defense* in lieu of *aggression.* In reality, says Chomsky, America attacked North Vietnam just as the Soviets later attacked Afghanistan. Despite numerous instances of heavy bombing and defoliation, Chomsky points out that not one book in American history lists an American "attack" on Vietnam. What this shows, he concludes, is that the U.S. propaganda system subtly shaped the contours around which the debate took place. Lacking the authority to say, "It is right that America go into Vietnam. Do not argue with it," the government nonetheless indoctrinated its citizens through subtle practices and mechanisms, marginalizing or eliminating those ideas dangerous to the security of the state.

To appreciate Chomsky's point, compare what he is saying about our government's relationship with the press to a government such as the former Soviet Union which overtly used the state-sponsored news, *Pravda* (the Russian word for "truth"), to put forward ideas it endorsed.

---

[3]403 U.S. 713 (1971).

[4]See Noam Chomsky, "Propaganda, American Style." *Utne Review* (Sept.–Oct. 1988): 78–83.

Overseen by the Ministry of Truth, the state-controlled news implicitly warned people not to disobey official doctrine no matter what they might think. A democratic society like the United States has no Ministry of Truth and the state lacks the authority to control behavior. Since the voice of the people is given free reign, Chomsky accuses those in power of seeing to it that what people think is politically determined.

We cannot deny that politicians at least attempt to control the press through subtle manipulation of facts, clever presentation of ideas, and careful timing of press releases and leaks. We also cannot deny the narrow range of acceptable positions Americans may take on political issues. Although some publications, such as the *Nation*, are extremely liberal, and some, such as *Insight Magazine*, are extremely conservative, anything more left or right is effectively marginalized. Witness how few communist and fascist publications are available on newsstands. Seeing this as thought control similar to that feared by George Orwell in *1984*, Chomsky thinks this blatant propaganda is no less dangerous to a democracy than violence is to a totalitarian state.

Chomsky aside, some critics of the press have argued that the press is biased in its coverage of political events, that it is not objective, and that it has an agenda of its own. To the extent any of this criticism is true, the political corruption from which the press has the duty to protect us is supplanted by the bias it has an interest in promoting. If the press does have a political agenda, it would be a serious iniquity owing to the presumption of press objectivity. Since, in the post-Watergate world of the 1990s, we presume the press to be honest in a way we do not presume of the government, the press carries a great moral burden and the charge of bias is deadly serious.

But why think that the press is biased, or that it has an agenda to promote? For one thing, the press is often owned by huge conglomerates that have an interest in controlling what is reported. The Time-Life merger with Warner Brothers in the 1980s is a case in point. Although the merger created a corporate giant controlling huge areas of news, it was a big news event in all the news magazines with the single exception of *Time* magazine, which gave it only the briefest mention. The lack of attention was so glaring that afterwards *Time* itself attempted to explain its behavior.

Another reason the press may be biased is that the press often has ideological leanings. *The New York Times*, for instance, has historically had a liberal bent which has shaped its coverage of political events. In recent years the *Times* has given unbalanced reports of the peace negotiations in the Middle East: it gave front-page preference to news casting Israel in a negative light while making short shrift of news detrimental to the Palestinian cause. The anti-Israel bent is reflected not only in the paper's editorial positions, but in the very terms and depictions of the news itself. By referring to Israel's West Bank as "occupied territory," for instance, the *Times* implicitly exposes its ideological commitments. From Israel's point of view, the West Bank is and has always been Israeli territory.

Other examples of liberal bias abound, especially in the television news media. Journalism professor H. Joachim Maitre reports that President Clinton had not been in office one month when CBS News anchorman Dan Rather reported that Clinton's program "will include money to put people back to work repairing this country's infrastructure, roads, bridges, and other public works." Maitre interprets Rather's unspoken message to be the partisan one that the Clinton administration was committed to rebuilding an America that had been run down through years of neglect by Clinton's Republican predecessors.[5]

Others blame press distortions on a staunchly *conservative* hierarchy as well as on the press's profit motivations.[6] Robert Cirino has argued that the press's conservative slant leads it to produce an establishment view of reality which, in turn, encourages such atrocities as the Vietnam War which the press helped cause and support. Cirino maintains that if the press did not suppress antiestablishment information and opinion, but presented it in a favorable light alongside conservative propaganda, Americans would support responsible activity and condemn activity it thought was immoral. Cirino's claim is bolstered if we think about the press's coverage of America's war against Iraq (1991) which, despite much death and destruction, was portrayed by the press with antiseptic clarity. Instead of seeing scenes of ruin and devastation, we saw computer simulations of smart bombs hitting fabricated targets. As for the press's profit motivation, we need look no further than to President Clinton's former press secretary Dee Dee Myers who, in a speech delivered at the University of Nevada in March 1995, recited what she sees as the four rules of the news trade: No. 1: Be first rather than right. No. 2: Never let the facts stand in the way of a good story. No. 3: When in doubt, analyze. No. 4. Good news is no news, so create conflict.[7]

But criticism of the press makes sense only against a realistic assessment of what the press is capable of reporting. It is one thing to say that the task of the press is "to report the news the public needs to know, as honestly and as fully as possible,"[8] or that the job of journalism is

---

[5]H. Joachim Maitre, "The Title to the News: How American Journalism Has Swerved from the Ideal of Objectivity." *The World and I* (December 1993). Reprinted in Alison Alexander and Jarice Hanson, eds., *Taking Sides: Clashing Views of Controversial Issues in Mass Media and Society,* 3rd ed. (Guilford, Conn.: Dushkin Publishing Group, 1995).

[6]Robert Cirino, *Don't Blame the People: How the News Media Use Bias, Distortion, and Censorship to Manipulate Public Opinion* (New York: Vintage, 1972).

[7]*Rockland Journal News* (March 3, 1995).

[8]John L. Hulteng, *The Messenger's Motives: Ethical Problems of the News Media* (Englewood Cliffs, N.J.: Prentice Hall, 1976), p. 23.

merely to "state the facts."[9] It is another thing to decide what counts as newsworthy, and to expect journalists to remain neutral when all perception is at least partially biased. What is needed, then, is a discussion of the concept of "newsworthiness" as well as discussion of what journalists refer to as "the problem of objectivity."

Given the vast number of items competing for limited news space, why are some items included but others not? What makes one item *newsworthy* and another item not? Although a paucity of literature speaks to this question, it is important and underlies many of the criticisms of editorial policies governing news selection. Joshua Halberstam (See Chapter 1) is one of the few philosophers who have attempted to answer this question.[10] After Halberstam points out that news is: (1) about events as opposed to facts, (2) aims at current as opposed to past events, and (3) is the report of an event rather than the experience of an event, he then cites three theories that explain newsworthiness.

(1) According to what Halberstam calls the "speech act" theory, news is whatever is reported by the press. While much is to be said in this theory's favor (for example, studies show that voters believe that the important issues in an election are those receiving the most media coverage), Halberstam rejects the view as too relativistic. Surely, he says, some newsworthy items are not reported by the press. (2) Another theory construes news in terms of the degree of importance of the item in question. This theory is preferable to the first as it connects newsworthiness to consumer needs, but it suffers from ambiguity. How, for instance, are we to understand "importance"? If *moral* importance is what is meant, then a murder in Brooklyn would be more newsworthy than the destruction of the Mona Lisa. (3) The theory with which Halberstam has most sympathy analyzes newsworthiness in term's of people's actual interests, especially those we share with others, marking us out as members of a community of shared interests. Against Robert Nozick who argues that people spend far too much time reading news relative to reading high-brow literature,[11] Halberstam argues that the purpose of news is not to provide information but to connect the reader to the world community. This explains, for instance, why news is predominantly about recent developments and current events.

A theory of news, while providing some standard for journalistic assessment, does not solve the problem of objectivity. Even if the purpose

---

[9]Anthony Serafini, "Objectivity, Epistemics, and an Ethic of Journalism." In Anthony Serafini, ed., *Ethics and Social Concern* (New York: Paragon House, 1989), p. 579.

[10]See Joshua Halberstam, "A Prolegomenon for a Theory of News." *The International Journals of Applied Philosophy* 3, 3 (Spring 1987). Reprinted in Elliot D. Cohen, ed., *Philosophical Issues in Journalism* (New York: Oxford University Press, 1992).

[11]See Robert Nozick, *Philosophical Explanations* (Cambridge, Mass.: Harvard University Press), p. 525.

of news is to connect the reader to the world at large, the journalist who does the connecting must still be objective and impartial. Otherwise, the journalist connects the reader not to the world as it is, but to the world as perceived through the journalist's eyes. Here we are on dangerous if fertile philosophical terrain. For implicit in insisting that journalists be neutral in reporting events, we encounter issues that concern our perception of the world. We also have some interesting questions in the philosophy of language since the journalist's words are used to communicate what is reported. Although what meager literature there is in journalistic ethics speaks to just these issues, we cannot provide anything like a systematic account. I will provide a brief schematization focusing on the vexing problem of objectivity.

Objectivity is a demand that reporters be objective in their account of the facts, that they keep their biases, interpretations, and other subjective factors out of news reports. So construed, the journalist's job is to report news, not make news. Several philosophical questions are connected with this claim. First, it assumes that reporters (and human beings generally) can transcend their subjectivity in describing "the facts" as they present themselves independent of the observer. But can they? According to the celebrated journalist Walter Lippmann, "a report is the joint product of the knower and the known, in which the role of the observer is always selective and usually creative. The facts we see depend on where we are placed, and the habits of our eyes."[12]

Lippmann is not unique in asserting this claim, as you know if you have heard more than one witness describe the same event. A long-standing philosophical tradition sees all observation as "value-laden" or "theory-laden." Consider, for instance, the figure below, courtesy of Ludwig Wittgenstein. From one perspective, the figure is of a duck, while from another perspective, it is of a rabbit. What observers will report in setting down what they see will vary depending on whether they see a duck, a rabbit, or both. Consider as well how an Eskimo observes snow as opposed to non-Eskimos. Eskimos reportedly list fifty-two different kinds of snow, while non Eskimos list just one. And it is not as if Eskimos observe fifty-two modifications of one snow: they observe fifty-two snows!

---

[12]Walter Lippmann, "Stereotypes, Public Opinion, and the Press." In W. Lippmann, *Public Opinion* (New York: Macmillan, 1946). Reprinted in Elliot D. Cohen, *Philosophical Issues in Journalism* (New York: Oxford University Press, 1992), pp. 161–175.

The claim that observation is "theory-laden" has received extensive discussion in the philosophy of science. What might be called the orthodox view of observation supposes an observational given, or a neutral database, against which scientific theories can be proved or falsified. In other words, a world is out there, independent of observers, and theories are better or worse according to whether or not they account for what is given. In the view that holds observation to be theory-laden, no "there" is out there, but what we observe depends on our theoretical commitments. As the philosopher Norwood Russell Hanson once put it, Tycho Brahe and Johannes Kepler would really see different things in the west at dusk rather than seeing the same thing and drawing different inferences. According to Hanson, Brahe would see the sun setting as he believed the sun revolved around the earth, while Kepler would see the earth rising as he believed the earth revolved around the sun. If this is so, then it will not do to expect journalists to simply report the facts of the matter, since in this view there are no facts of the matter. From the host of details of an event or situation, reporters select those which seem to them important, investigate and ask questions to clarify the meaning of what they have perceived, and then organize their knowledge. What they select for attention, how they weigh various elements, and the kinds of questions they ask are all influenced by the personal history reporters bring to their work.[13]

Another problem with objectivity concerns the language reporters use to describe what they report. Even if reporters were somehow able to observe events in a value-neutral way, it is not clear how they can report these events in a value-neutral way. Philosophers of language are fond of pointing out the constraints that language places on our ability to describe what we think and feel. Consider the function of euphemisms: a garbage truck is described as a sanitation truck, a doorman as an access controller. A journalist, consequently, who speaks of the CIA "disposing" of Fidel Castro says something different than the journalist who speaks of "murdering" Castro. In this connection, Hugh Rawson, author of the *Dictionary of Euphemisms and Other Doubletalk*, tells the story of Col. David H. E. Opter, who served as air attaché at the U.S. Embassy in Phnom Penh, Cambodia, in 1973. He complained one day to reporters: "You always write it's bombing, bombing, bombing! It's not bombing. It's Air Support."

Examples like these should suffice to question the view that we have wordless thoughts and the purpose of language is to expresses these thoughts. If we are sensitive to the nuances of language and to the many ways in which words have meaning, we see how difficult it is to describe the world with absolute impartiality. Reporters must choose words to describe what they report but the words they choose shape that very world.

---

[13]Donald McDonald, "Is Objectivity Possible?" In Serafini, *Ethics and Social Concern* p. 633.

In a provocative essay, Theodore L. Glasser argues that the premium placed on objectivity is itself a value judgment.[14] As Glasser sees it, the commitment to objectivity is biased against the watchdog role of the press in favor of the status quo. In an effort to remain objective, journalists embrace the convention of quoting news sources with "impeccable credentials." Such sources inevitably turn out to be prominent members of society such as government officials, civic leaders, and wealthy businesspeople. The effect this has is to exclude the participation of more marginalized members of society. Yet another value judgment presupposed by the commitment to objectivity is a bias against the journalist's assumption of responsibility for what is reported. On the ideology in question, news exists "out there," independent of the reporter. Hence, journalists are not responsible for reporting as they are not social engineers.

If we keep in mind that reporters are preparing the first draft of history, the challenge that faces responsible journalism is not so much to be as objective as possible as it is to responsibly report the news in a way that furthers the aims of democracy. Since the aim of a democracy is to effectuate the diversity of views of those who comprise it, the way to do this is to provide a great range of opinions on a great number of views. Rather than hiding values behind a mask of neutrality, the answer to the problem of objectivity is to take a multiperspective approach to news, giving effect to the belief that truth is not the exclusive province of an omniscient government but emerges from the free and open interchange of ideas.

---

[14]Theodore L. Glasser, "Objectivity Precludes Responsibility." *The Quill* 72 (February 1984): 13–16. Reprinted in Elliot D. Cohen, *Philosophical Issues in Journalism* (New York: Oxford University Press, 1992), pp. 176–185.

Chuck Strum is a staff reporter with *The New York Times*.

Video Presentation

Guest: Chuck Strum, Staff Reporter, *The New York Times*

Student Panel: Mark Esposito, Elizabeth Daskalakis, Kathy Poliey

I begin my discussion with Chuck Strum by asking him to comment on a paid advertisement in *The New York Times* criticizing the press for unfair reporting, distorting facts, inciting riots, and a host of other wrongdoing. The ad mentions the media's use of the Rodney King videotape as a contributing factor in the Los Angeles riots of the 1990s. Speaking to the King tapes in particular, Strum takes the position that the press is obligated to convey the best they have at the time they report the news. After I press him on the deeper issue of what responsibilities journalists have to the public generally, he reiterates the view that the press is responsible for reporting news insofar as it is possible to do so, adding that people have a plurality of news sources to consider if they want a balanced opinion on any one issue. Strum also points out that *The New York Times*, at least, has self-consciously undertaken to report on itself. This leads to a discussion on whether reporters find news or make news.

I suggest that "facts" often have a value component and that the distinction between facts and values is not a hard and fast one. I then question whether journalists can be objective in reporting the news. Strum agrees that journalists must often make decisions based on what they consider important. He remarks that in the world of journalism, the "truth is what you know on deadline." He does not see this as an acute problem since journalists have the opportunity to amend the record the next day as answers to the previous day's questions become clear and new information comes to light. When I ask Strum if his readers understand this, his only answer is that he wishes they would. He does say that unlike TV and radio news which preselects what you will hear, the print media is put together in such a way that readers can "shop" for what they want to read about in an effort to get a fair account.

Not satisfied with Strum's apologetic, I suggest that even on his supermarket model of news items, readers can get slanted reports. I also suggest that, in this regard, the *Times* may be more "dangerous" than tabloids that compete with it inasmuch as the *Times* has the reputation of unbiased reporting and is taken seriously in a way that tabloids are not. When asked to exemplify what I consider to be biased reporting, I point to events in the Mideast which the *Times* slants against Israel. Besides saying that he does not report on foreign affairs, Strum's comment is that the reporting is not biased given the significance of what happens in the Mideast.

The conversation turns from biased reporting to the question of peephole journalism. After some brief discussion concerning the media's coverage of Amy Fisher (convicted of shooting her lover's wife) and former athlete Arthur Ashe who died of AIDS, we discuss yellow journalism. Strum tells us that the term *yellow journalism* originated in the 1890s when William Randolph Hearst sent a news illustrator to Havana to cover the Spanish-American war. Finding no war to report on, the illustrator wired Hearst that there was "no war here," at which time Hearst wired back: "You supply the pictures, I'll supply the war." Hearst's reporting on the "war" was to drum up support for American foreign interests—a decision that has ramifications to this day. We discuss the ethics of such behavior and, just before the break, whether codes of professional responsibility speak to what the press may and may not do.

Following the break, Mark Espositio, the editor of the student newspaper at Bergen Community College, shares with Strum some ethical dilemmas he has faced while running a college newspaper. Elizabeth Daskalakis asks Strum questions about peephole journalism. And Kathy Poliey, also an editor of the Bergen student newspaper, asks Strum whether he has ever been personally affected by any articles he has written. Regarding this last question, Strum discusses a quandary he faced when the *Times* struggled with whether to publish the name of the woman who accused William Kennedy Smith of raping her.

Interview with Jerry Milton Gray, State House Bureau Chief, The New York Times, and Professor of Journalism, Rutgers University (Newark)

Haber: What makes a story newsworthy?

Gray: The idea of a hard and fast rule or test of what makes a story newsworthy goes against the grain of what journalism is all about. But there are some elements and conditions that most newsworthy stories share.

A newsworthy story should enlighten as well as inform. The answer to the question why or how something occurred is frequently the most difficult one and not readily apparent or even available. But the answer can frequently elevate a story.

Circumstances also dictate what is newsworthy. An example: During the 1993 race for governor in New Jersey, two staffers from Governor Jim Florio's campaign—one with a camcorder and the other with a tape recorder—constantly shadowed his Republican opponent, Christine Todd Whitman, at public events, hoping to catch her stumbling. On one occasion, they followed Mrs. Whitman to her family farm, Pontefract, in an effort to make her wealth an issue in the campaign. Reporters, for the most part, ignored this campaign psyche game or only mentioned it in passing until Mrs. Whitman spotted the Florio spies on her property and she and a bodyguard jumped into a car and chased them for several miles. The incident was related on the front pages of nearly every newspaper in the state.

Then there is the long-standing test of when man bites dog, then it's news. Trite as it is, the concept is still valid: the unusual is always newsworthy. Thus, much to the chagrin of the reporters who covered the story (including yours truly), the saga of "Taro, New Jersey's death row dog," became an international story and made the front page of *The New York Times* when Governor Whitman extended the animal a pardon on the condition that it be banished from New Jersey.

Haber: How far should reporters go in protecting the privacy of their news sources?

Gray: Reporters are not paid to be martyrs, neither should it be their mission. But protecting the privacy of their news sources should be one of their paramount tenets. Reporters should hold fast to that ideal, even if refusal to divulge a source threatens jail. There is a larger issue at play than just protecting a source.

Electricians and plumbers are licensed, lawyers must pass the bar, accountants are certified, but a journalist's livelihood is based on public trust. Anything that shakes that trust undermines the journalist.

Allowing a source the cloak of privacy should never be automatic or taken lightly, but once having offered that protection, it should be fiercely maintained.

Haber: Is journalistic objectivity possible?

Gray: I believe journalistic objectivity is possible, but I question whether achieving that goal best serves the reader in all cases. Sticking hard and fast to the rules of objective reporting, would Watergate have been reported? Would the public have a true sense of what the carnage is like in Bosnia, Rwanda, or Somalia? I think readers rightfully mistrust any journalist who insists that he or she or the media is bias-free. The standard in reporting ought to be fairness. (I am a black American and among my early assignments was coverage of a Ku Klux Klan rally in Tennessee. Was I biased? Most certainly. But did I faithfully report what occurred? I would again answer, most certainly.)

Haber: When, if ever, are attempts to suppress the free expression or free publication of ideas justified?

Gray: Never, especially in regard to the truth. There are times when the free expression or free publication of ideas tears at our social fabric, possibly threatens our national security, divides communities, and offends. But it is the unfettered right of free expression and free publication that also keeps things in balance and exposes the half-truths or lies.

Haber: Is a multiperspectival approach to the news a viable answer to the problem of news bias and news distortion?

Gray: The question is loaded. It assumes that news bias and news distortion are an institutional problem and intentional, positions which I would argue against. Diversity in a newsroom and a news report is the answer to many problems that plague the media. Many of the perceived biases and distortions for which the media is criticized are largely a function of ignorance of other cultures. While it may not be intentional, at the end of the day a slight remains a slight.

Haber: What logical standards are possible for the detection and/or elimination of cognitive errors and prejudices in news reporting?

Gray: The logical standard already exists; it is called the public: the newspaper reader, the television viewer, and the radio listener. Within the community of journalists there is also peer pressure. I, and I believe most other journalists, would object to the idea of some authoritative body that would act as a word policeman.

Haber: Comment on the claim that the media unfairly reports events, particularly in the Middle East.

Gray: Another loaded question and overly general. Does the media unfairly report events at times? Yes. Does it occur "particularly in the Middle East?" Israel thinks so, as does Egypt, Jordan, Syria . . . . In that aspect, the Middle East is no different than the United States Congress, a professional sports league, or a political campaign where the media is routinely and roundly criticized for unfairly reporting events, frequently by both sides. Are there times when the media is totally off the mark as to be unfair? Did any of the thousands of reports by American journalists on "Operation Desert Storm" smack of U.S. boosterism? Most certainly.

Haber: In his posthumously public book *Beyond Peace*, Richard M. Nixon wrote that the news media "bear a large share of responsibility for the current loss of faith in American political institutions" and that an institutional bias in the press "makes for excessively harsh criticisms of all political and public officials." Your reaction to these comments.

Gray: My first reaction is consider the source. But having said that, I fully agree with many of Mr. Nixon's observations. If Watergate had gone unreported, the public faith in the presidency would likely have been much stronger.

I do agree that the media glare is normally harsh and sometimes too intense on our elected leaders, that pack journalism does not serve the reader or the profession. But I find it personally insulting that politicians would harp about "an institutional bias" in the press.

Haber: What political powers and responsibilities do the media bear?

Gray: Given the issue, the political powers of the media can be considerable. But it all eventually comes down to the public and whether they entrust the media enough with that power and whether they trust what is being reported. The media has the responsibility to be fair, accurate, and responsible in the use of its powers.

Haber: What value might the study of ethics itself have for journalistic education?

Gray: The value of the study of ethics, like every other facet of a journalistic education, is that it exposes a student to what life will be like as a journalist. But only that. The most useful education will come when that student-turned-journalist is faced very quickly with the ethical issues that are so much a part of life in the real world.

I don't think you can teach ethics.

You can establish standards of fairness and accuracy and train students to think through problems, things that will act as guides to ethical behavior.

Closing Questions

1. Is the press biased? If so, how?

    _____

    _____

    _____

2. Comment on the claim that journalists are relatively uniformed people inasmuch as, unlike in law or medicine, there is no body of knowledge that constitutes the field of journalism.

    _____

    _____

    _____

3. Are the press and government natural adversaries?

    _____

    _____

    _____

4. What makes a story newsworthy? (What is "all the news that's fit to print?")

    _____

    _____

    _____

5. How far should reporters go in protecting the privacy of their news sources?

    _____

    _____

    _____

6. When, if ever, are attempts to suppress the free publication of ideas justified?

    _____

    _____

    _____

7. Discuss some of the ways good journalism might conflict with the demands of morality.

_____

_____

_____

_____

8. What is the role of the press in a democratic society?

_____

_____

_____

_____

9. Is Noam Chomsky right that, through subtle means of manipulation, the American government influences the press and that in its own way it is as coercive as the former Soviet Union?

_____

_____

_____

_____

10. According to former president Richard Nixon, "Competitive pressures too often push the media past the limits of responsibility, destructively and unnecessarily undermining the authority and credibility of government." And while the news media would not have physicians certify themselves or politicians investigate themselves, the thirty-seventh president noted how "we are taught to expect that editors, reporters, and broadcasters have a unique capacity to ensure that they themselves act responsibly." In the light of these remarks, do you think reporters should be governed by a code of ethics? What might such a code look like?

_____

_____

_____

_____

_____

For Further Reading

Chomsky, Noam. "Propaganda, American Style." *Utne Review* (Sept.–Oct. 1988): 78–83.

Cohen, Elliot, D. *Philosophical Issues in Journalism.* New York: Oxford University Press, 1992.

Elliston, Frederick A. "Whistle-Blowing: The Reporter's Role." *The International Journal of Applied Philosophy* 3, 2 (Fall 1986).

Hutchins, Robert A. *A Free and Responsible Press* (Chicago: University of Chicago Press, 1947).

Lee, Martin A., and Norman Solomon. *Unreliable Sources: A Guide to Detecting Bias in News Media.* Carol Publishing Co., 1990.

Liebling, A. J. *The Press.* New York: Ballantine Books, 1961.

Michener, James A. "On Integrity in Journalism." *U.S. News and World Report,* May 4, 1981.

McDonald, Donald. "Is Objectivity Possible?" *The Center Magazine* 4, 5 (Sept.–Oct. 1971).

Postman, Neil. *Amusing Ourselves to Death.* New York: Viking Penguin, 1985.

Silvers, Anita. "How to Avoid Resting Journalistic Ethics on a Mistake?" *Journal of Social Philosophy* (Fall 1985): 20–35.

Walsh, Kenneth T. *Feeding the Beast: The White House versus the Press.* New York, Random House, 1996.

Chapter 15

Ethics and Literature

Passages for Reflection

"Man is in his actions and practice, as well as in his fictions, essentially a story-telling animal."
—*Alasdair MacIntyre*

"Surely philosophy is no other than sophisticated poetry."
—*Montaigne*

"I spoke of the novel as an especially useful agent of the moral imagination, as the literary form which most directly reveals to us the complexity, the difficulty, and the interest of life in society, and best instructs us in our human variety and contradiction."
—*Lionel Trilling*

Opening Questions

1. What is the difference between philosophy and literature?
2. Does literature give us knowledge?
3. What philosophers would you include as literary figures? What literary figures would you include as philosophers?

"Let us observe," says Plato's Socrates, "that there is a quarrel of long standing between philosophy and poetry."[1] While Plato specifically mentions a quarrel between *poetry* and philosophy, there is little doubt that had the novel been extant in Plato's time, a quarrel would have existed between philosophy and it. It is Plato, in fact, to whom we owe the categories of philosophy and literature on account of his setting the one against the other. And to Plato we owe philosophy and literature's having come to occupy distinct disciplines in the modern university. The quarrel, as Plato refers to it, is about truth and education. Which "contender," he asks, is best capable of knowing reality and whose influence should be decisive in shaping human lives? As we shall see, he ruled decisively in the philosopher's favor—a ruling which until recently was to influence the course of philosophy for centuries to come.

As Plato understood it, the world consists of physical objects in which ideas (or forms) are embodied that make these objects what they are. To take a trivial example, there are chairs in the world only because the idea of "chair" is embodied in them. Were some other idea embodied in the material out of which chairs are composed, say, the idea of "table," then, far from being chairs, these physical objects would be tables instead. So, too, for any physical object, it is what it is only because it embodies an idea or form that is different from other ideas or forms.

While the objects in the physical world are distinct and many, says Plato, the ideas embedded in them are one and the same. Though each particular chair in the world is unique in its peculiar way, every object that we identify as a chair is identified as one because it shares some features of a model case. (Even two chairs that are identical in all perceivable respects are different. If they were identical in *every* respect, they would be one and the same chair.) In other words, we need a model of a chair in order to identify something as a chair at all. It will not do to say that the model is itself a physical chair that stands as the model for all other chairs, for how would we know what was to count as the model case? For this reason, Plato concludes that the model case is not a physical object, but a concept that stands apart from the physical objects that "partake" of it. Un-

---

[1] *Republic*, 607D.

like the physical objects which are distinct and many, the model applies universally to all things of which it is a model, and for this reason it is said to be one. Thus, for all the many chairs in the world, each partakes of the one Idea (or Form) of Chair (with an upper case "C").

Having distinguished between the one idea and its many representations, the universal concept and its particular objects, Plato asks which of the two has greater reality? Which, that is, is really real? The intuitive answer is that the physical objects are more real since they are immediately available to the senses. A wooden chair, after all, is not only tangible and more easily accessible to the senses, but is better to sit on than its conceptual counterpart. But Plato's answer is that ideas have more reality than the physical objects partaking of them. For one thing, ideas are not tangible but they are immune to the wear and tear that inevitably destroys physical objects. They are, that is, not subject to the imperfections that befall objects in the material world. (The most perfect chair we can produce has defects even if on some microscopic level.) In contrast, the idea of chair has no such defects. For another thing, ideas are fixed, permanent, and stable (have being), while objects are changing and in constant flux (are becoming). Even as we view what is an apparently stationary chair, the chair is imperceptibly going out of existence. We would see this clearly if we videotaped the life of the chair and then played back the tape in the fast forward mode. (Needless to say, there are better films to watch.) Ideas, on the other hand, are not subject to the vicissitudes of space and time. To put the matter another way, ideas are necessary, whereas objects are contingent. Unlike tangible chairs whose existence is contingent upon trees, wood, chair manufacturers, and so on, the idea of "chair" is not dependent on anything at all: it necessarily is what it is.

Plato's Ideas—because they are ideas—are known by reason rather than perception. It is true that perception enables us to become acquainted with the features of physical objects such as their size, texture, color, shape, and location, but strictly speaking, perception does not enable us to "know" the object. To understand why, let us suppose that we were visited by a space traveler who spoke our language and had every idea we had save for the idea of "chair." (Ignore such question as how this might come about.) Suppose we wished to impart to the traveler this idea and did so by pointing to a chair—what philosophers call definition by ostension—and saying: That is what we mean by "chair." Presumably, the traveler would think that by "chair" is meant the particular chair to which we had pointed. And if he exhibited this mistake, say, by referring to that chair in speaking of chairs generally, it would not help to say that by "chair" is meant not only that one, but this, that, and every other one we point to. For then, he would presumably think that "chair" refers to the set of chairs which we had gathered together. And even if, perchance, we gathered together all the chairs in the world, he would still not know what is meant by "chair." He would understand what is meant only when he understood the features in virtue of which something is a chair—that is, when he understood what is meant by the *idea* of chair. Equipped with the idea, he would then never have to perceive that to which the idea refers. He would "know" what it means to be a chair and not merely "believe" that what he perceives are chairs. For Plato, knowledge is "justified true belief."

But we need not resort to space travelers to make this point. For Plato, the typical nonphilosopher will do just fine as illustrated by Plato's famous Allegory of the Cave. In his *Republic* (Book VII), Plato likens nonphilosophers to people who have lived all their lives in a cave and who have been chained in such a way as to see only the shadows of the objects that exist at the mouth of the cave which are illuminated by the sun. Seeing only the shadows and not the objects that create the shadows, these people insist that what they perceive is real whereas what they perceive is only a reflection of reality. The philosopher, by contrast, is the one who ascends from the cave and confronts the objects face to face. The objects at the mouth of the cave represent Platonic ideas; the shadows of the objects in the cave represent physical objects. Having "seen the light," the philosopher is then able to return to the cave and educate the nonphilosophers about the true nature of the world.

Plato notes that the philosopher is sure to meet with resistance as he attempts to explain to the cave people that what they are convinced is real is a shadow of reality. Think how resistant you would be to someone who insisted that the objects of the world—this very book, the chair on which you sit, the pen in your hand—are pale reflections of a more real world that is abstract and ethereal. Small wonder that philosophers have a reputation for having their heads in the clouds and being "out of this world." Small wonder, too, that philosophers have had a strained relationship with materialistic types. In my travels through life, I have consistently found that identifying myself as a philosopher is an effective way to end a conversation (although calling myself a *professor* of philosophy is a conversation starter). Among the more amusing reactions to my identifying myself as a philosopher have been: "Oh? I've read Freud, too" (Freud was a psychiatrist), and, after a very long pause, "You don't meet many of those." Then, too, calling myself a philosopher in order to end a conversation sometimes backfires. I recall attending a wedding and being forced to listen to an amateur philosopher pontificate on the meaning of life over filet mignon for an entire evening.

We need only to situate the emotions in Plato's scheme to complete the picture and understand his distinction between philosophy and literature. This will not be hard to do. Having maintained that reason alone can be acquainted with the world of ideas where knowledge alone is possible, and having argued that the physical world is a mere shadow of the real world, we should not be surprised that Plato regards emotions as impediments to good philosophizing. They are, as Plato sees them, irrational forces likely to make us act on other than the Idea of the Good. In this light, we can appreciate Socrates' attitude toward his wife, Xanthippe, as he sits reflectively awaiting his executioner after having been sentenced to death: he has her hauled away for wailing and interfering with his wish to discuss death in a detached and impartial manner. Similarly, he chides Crito, in the dialogue by that name, for appealing to emotion in an effort to tell him why he should escape from prison.

Having drawn battle lines around universals and particulars as well as necessity/contingency, knowledge/belief, being/becoming, and reason/emotion, we are now at the point where we can begin to appreciate Plato's distinguishing philosophy from literature. The more precise reason concerns Plato's conception of the good life relative to the form the tragic drama took during Plato's era.

Plato, as we have seen, placed a premium on reason, knowledge, necessity, and being. Because of this, he viewed the moral life as a life of self-sufficiency, whereby a person rationally seeks the good (understood as knowing the Idea of Good) independent of what chance circumstances he or she encounters. In this light, we find Socrates insisting that "a good person cannot be harmed" even after he has been falsely accused of betraying Athens. At the same time, during Plato's youth, tragic dramas were considered by Athenians to be the city's primary source of moral reflection. These dramas centered around the idea that good people can be harmed or benefited by reversals of fortune that were not of their making. Good people, for instance, could lose their children or their country through no fault of their own. Such tragedies as *Antigone* and *Oedipus* cultivated in their audiences the idea that such events have moral significance and that the hero can respond with appropriate emotions when they are present. To the extent that the emotions that hold the audience to the dramas (pity for the hero, fear for themselves) are themselves based on the recognition that such events have moral significance, these too were thought to be important. Here then lies one source of "the quarrel": if you hold the view that the moral life is a matter of rational self-sufficiency, then tragic drama will immediately appear morally suspect. Since we know that Plato held strong to this view, it is not surprising that Plato thought tragedy to be deceptive and objectionable.[2]

But beyond Plato's objection to Athenian drama, a more general source of his distinction lies in the fact that philosophy is abstract and speaks in an impersonal tongue whereas literature is particular and has a more personal tone. The plots of dramas, for instance, are often about particular people finding themselves in particular circumstances—

---

[2]The Stoics were later to have this same view. See Martha C. Nussbaum, *The Therapy of Desire: Theory and Practice in Hellenistic Ethics* (Princeton, N.J.: Princeton University Press, 1994), esp. pp. 9 and 10.

circumstances, we might add, that are based on serendipitous events. Milan Kundera's *The Unbearable Lightness of Being*, for instance, is a novel that addresses the element of contingency in a particularly effective way. The protagonist of the book, a Czech physician named Tomas, meets the woman with whom he is to share his life (Tereza) under wholly accidental circumstances: he meets her because she happened to be serving his table after he happened to be called in to perform surgery after his chief surgeon happened to come down with sciatica. Later, during one of those tender moments that occur between lovers, Tereza tells Tomas that had she not met him, she certainly would have fallen in love with Tomas's friend and gone on to share a life with the friend. After this, Tomas refers to Tereza as the "personification of absolute fortuity."[3] In this way, Kundera emphasizes the nature of the contingent in life itself. He also emphasizes what he perceives as "the unbearable lightness (read: contingency) of being." But compare Kundera with paleontologist Stephen Jay Gould who never fails to point out that contingency does not imply meaninglessness. Gould cites the life of George Bailey (Jimmy Stewart) in Frank Capra's classical film, *It's a Wonderful Life*, which is not less meaningful because of its fortuity.[4]

Literature also elicits an emotional response to the circumstances it portrays. We vicariously experience, for example, the trials and tribulations of the characters we meet in our novels and plays: we weep, for instance, when Tolstoy's Anna Karenina kills herself; we are frustrated at K's efforts to reach Kafka's castle; and we thrill with Hemingway's fisherman as he does battle with the marlin. To the extent, then, that literature focuses its attention on fortuitous events while eliciting our emotional responses, it detracts from what Plato perceived to be the philosopher's more bona fide attempt to understand the world. We must not forget that for Plato the good life is the life of reason.

Even after Plato placed the philosophy/literature dichotomy within his more general theories of knowledge and reality, the split between philosophy and literature was to follow the reason/emotion dichotomy as philosophy sought to distant itself from literature and align itself with science and mathematics. From Aristotle to Bertrand Russell, philosophers typically viewed science as providing us with an objective picture of reality and mathematics as a procedure which philosophy should emulate in its pursuit of truth. Literature, on the other hand, was thought to distort truth in its reliance upon emotion. In Descartes, for example, we find philosophy's clear and distinct ideas winning out over the input of sense perception in the search for truth and certainty. In Spinoza, we find phi-

---

[3]Milan Kundera, *The Unbearable Lightness of Being*, translated from the Czech by Michael Henry Heim (New York: Harper and Row, 1984), p. 35.

[4]Stephen Jay Gould, *Wonderful Life: The Burgess Shale and the Nature of History* (New York: W. W. Norton, 1989), pp. 287–88.

losophy employing the method of geometry, with the emotions relegated to the status of confused ideas. In Kant, despite the autonomy of aesthetics, we find pure reason gaining the upper hand against the empirical psychological self, and in the early half of the twentieth century, we find the logical positivists celebrating science and mathematics, while viewing poetry as a pleasant diversion devoid of cognitive meaning. Not until recently have philosophers viewed emotions as possibly rational and as having moral significance. Not until recently did philosophers begin to view literature as being relevant to ethics. Voltaire, Diderot, and Rousseau were eighteenth-century exceptions.

Identifying the factors contributing to recent efforts at taking emotions seriously and with them the value of literature is difficult. Perhaps nothing other than a perceived failure of philosophy understood along traditional rationalistic lines accounts for this. More probably, it is this in combination with a growing interest in virtue-theory, feminism, and particularism, which themselves may be understood as reactions to philosophy in its traditional sense.

Originally associated with Aristotle, virtue-theory came of age in the twentieth century when the British philosopher G. E. M. Anscombe pointed out that moral philosophers have been asking the wrong question when theorizing about ethics.[5] Instead of asking, What should we do when confronted with questions of right and wrong?, Anscombe argued that we ought to be asking, 'What kind of person should we strive to be?' Then, instead of rationally delineating principles that could guide right and wrong conduct—a procedure that had modest success—we would emphasize traits of character that ought to be cultivated in an effort to live a morally good life. The starting point for such a virtue-based approach would be individuals we could confidently identify as moral saints. Many of these people would come from life (for example, Mother Theresa), but many, too, would come from literature (for example, Jean Valjean). In this light, we find the virtue-theorist Bernard Mayo saying:

> Attention to the novelists can be a welcome correction to a tendency of philosophical ethics of the last generation or two to lose contact with the ordinary life of man which is just what the novelists, in their own way, are concerned with. Of course there are writers who can be called in to illustrate problems about Duty (Graham Greene is a good example). But there are more who perhaps never mention the words duty, obligation or principle. Yet they are all concerned—Jane Austen, for instance, entirely and absolutely—with the moral qualities or defects of their heroes and heroines and other characters.[6]

---

[5]G. E. M. Anscombe, "Modern Moral Philosophy." *The Journal of the Royal Institute of Philosophy* 33 (January 1958): 1–19.

[6]Bernard Mayo, *Ethics and the Moral Life* (1958). Reprinted in my *Doing and Being: Selected Readings in Moral Philosophy* (Englewood Cliffs, N.J.: Prentice Hall, 1993), pp. 159–160.

Many feminist philosophers have argued against what they have perceived to be a male bias in moral philosophy which is nothing other than the one-sided emphasis on reason to the neglect of the emotions. During the late 1970s and early 1980s, several feminists expressed doubts about the conceptual apparatus supplied by traditional moral theory with its emphasis on abstract reason, principle, and impartiality. Such doubts were fueled by the work of Carol Gilligan, whose book *In a Different Voice*[7] seemed to demonstrate that the moral development of women is significantly different from that of men. Gilligan described females as less likely than males to make moral decisions by the application of abstract rules; instead, she claimed that girls and women were more likely to act on feelings of love and compassion. While previously, theorists argued that this showed women to be morally *immature*,[8] Gilligan argued that this showed women to be morally *different*. Gilligan's thesis was that while men typically adhere to an ethic of justice whose primary values are fairness and equality, women often adhere to an ethic of care whose primary values are inclusion and protection from harm.

With respect to particularism, an increasing number of philosophers[9] have come to hold the view that particular features of a person or situation display an important dimension of morality. These particulars are made up of repeatable properties (those that taken singly appear in other situations) as well as nonrepeatable properties (those that are rooted in historical singularity). The perception of both requires a power of discernment different from the application of general rules and principles characteristic of traditional rationalistic philosophy. From the particularist perspective, moral perception is an activity essentially concerned with the apprehension of concrete particulars in addition to general features. Compare this view with consequentialist philosopher Jonathan Bennett's notion (said in conversation) that it is not people that are important in moral philosophy but *features* of people.

Against the backdrop of virtue-theory, feminism, and particularism, then, the emotions became the subject of serious philosophizing. And, since literature renders active such emotions as love, hope, and compassion, it too became philosophically important again. In this light, we can understand Iris Murdoch's reference to literature as "a sort of disci-

---

[7]Carol Gilligan, *In a Different Voice: Psychological Theory and Women's Development* (Cambridge, Mass.: Harvard University Press, 1982).

[8]See, for example, Lawrence Kohlberg, "Indoctrination v. Relativity in Value Education," in his *The Philosophy of Moral Development*, Vol. 1 (New York: Harper & Row/Chicago: University of Chicago Press, 1971).

[9]See Iris Murdoch, *The Sovereignty of Goodness* (London: Routledge and Kegan Paul, 1970); Martha Nussbaum, *Love's Knowledge: Essays on Philosophy and Literature* (New York: Oxford University Press, 1990); and Lawrence Blum, *Perception and Particularity* (New York: Cambridge University Press, 1994).

plined technique for arousing certain emotions." Once the significance of the emotions is asserted, as well as the fortuitous circumstances and the particular situations in which ethical choices are made, we need but a short step to see literary forms as embodying a moral vision in which these features are prominent. Not surprisingly, therefore, philosophers—especially ethicists—have turned to literature in an effort to augment their understanding of morality.

The contemporary philosopher Martha Nussbaum has taken the lead in this area. She maintains that literature, especially the novel, embodies in its form a content that cannot be expressed (or expressed as well) in any other way.[10] Insisting on the ethical value of the emotions, of uncontrolled happenings, and the circumstances in which ethical choices are made, she has argued that the novel embodies a moral vision in which these features have high importance.

We cannot deny that literature provides vivid illustrations of the meaning and poignancy of abstract thought. Compare, for instance, the following two sentences, courtesy of Ray G. Wright:[11] (1) I watched a man pick up his guitar and begin to play, and (2):

> With what attentive courtesy he bent
> Over the instrument
> Not as a lordly conqueror who could
> Command both wire and wood,
> But as a man who loved a woman might
> Inquiring with delight
> What slight essential things she had to say
> Before they started, he and she, to play

No one can deny the eloquence in (2) that is absent in (1). Nussbaum, however, goes beyond celebrating the eloquence of colorful literary expressions. Speaking of the novel, she argues that the form in which sentences are put makes a statement about what is significant and what is not, and that some philosophical contents exist that cannot be expressed without the use of literary forms. Leaning upon such literary figures as Henry James and Marcel Proust, as well as such philosophical figures as Aristotle, much of Nussbaum's work consists of trying to show the value of taking form seriously in its expressive and statement-making functions.

Nussbaum provides many examples of how literary form determines philosophical content.[12] One example is the use Nussbaum makes

---

[10]See Nussbaum, *Love's Knowledge: Essays on Philosophy and Literature* (New York: Oxford University Press, 1990).

[11]Ray G. Wright, "Teaching Philosophy Through Literature." *American Association of Philosophy Teachers News* (November 1994): 9–11.

[12]See Nussbaum, *Love's Knowledge.*

of the antipornographer Andrea Dworkin's novel, *Mercy*.[13] Beginning with the observation that this novel is not a novel in any traditional sense, Nussbaum points out that the book is a series of events in which its narrator, also named Andrea, is repeatedly subjected to episodes of male cruelty: at the age of nine, she is molested by an anonymous man in a movie theater; at fourteen, she is cut with a knife by a sadistic lover; at eighteen, she is raped by her lover's roommate; at twenty-two, she marries someone who turns out to be a sadomasochist; and so forth and so on. After some twenty-odd years of being victimized in this way, Andrea learns karate and becomes adept at kicking drunken homeless men to death. She writes:

> We stomp on the rape magazines or we invade where they prostitute us, where we are herded and sold, we ruin their theaters where they have sex on us, we face them, we scream in their fucking faces, we are the women they have made scream when they choose. . . . We're all the same, cunt is cunt is cunt, we're facsimiles of the ones they done it to, or we are the ones they done it too, and I can't tell him from him from him . . . so at night, ghosts, we convene; to spread justice, which stands in for law, which has always been merciless, which is, by its nature, cruel.[14]

This passage, says Nussbaum, illustrates Andrea's determination to exact retribution without concern for the identity of her victims—a perception endorsed by the novel as a whole. (Compare: "cunt is cunt is cunt" with "I can't tell him from him from him.") By refusing to perceive any of the male offenders as an individual with a unique history, the book refuses to invite the reader into the story of their lives which might allow us to understand their motivations for acting. This connects with the narrator's refusal to be merciful to any of the individuals she encounters. Believing all heterosexual men to be rapists and all heterosexual sex to be rape, Dworkin exacts a form of "justice" she is convinced must be cruel and hard. The very form of Dworkin's "novel" helps make this argument: it causes the reader to inhabit a retributive frame of mind with little viable alternatives. Against this view, Nussbaum argues that if we open our heart to admit the life story of someone else, it becomes far more difficult to finish that person off with a karate kick. Thus, a different form of novel might well construct a reader who, while judging justly, remains capable of love in a way that Andrea is not. Think in this context of Iris Murdoch's observation that "the central concept of morality is "the individual thought of as knowable by love."

---

[13]Martha Nussbaum, "Equity and Mercy," *Philosophy and Public Affairs*, 22:2 (1993). Reprinted in Jeffrie Murphy, ed., *Punishment and Rehabilitation*. 3rd ed., (Belmont, Cal: Wadsworth Publishing Co., 1995), pp. 212–248.

[14] Cited in "Equity and Mercy," Ibid., p. 213.

We see Nussbaum's point in Gary Watson's essay, "Responsibility and the Limits of Evil: Variations on a Strawsonian Theme."[15] While not addressed specifically to the relationship between ethics and literature, this essay is nonetheless interested in examining the relevance of historical considerations for our ascriptions of mercy and blame. He begins with a newspaper description concerning the murderous life of one Robert Harris. It is fascinating to read, so I will repeat it in its entirety.

> On the south tier of Death Row, in a section called "Peckerwood Flats" where the white inmates are housed, there will be a small celebration the day Robert Alton Harris dies.
>
> A group of inmates on the row have pledged several dollars for candy, cookies and soda. At the moment they estimate that Harris has been executed, they will eat, drink and toast to his passing.
>
> "The guy's a misery, a total scumbag; we're going to party when he goes," said Richard (Chic) Mroczko, who lived in the cell next to Harris on San Quentin Prison's Death Row for more than a year. "He doesn't care about life, he doesn't care about others, he doesn't care about himself.
>
> "We're not a bunch of Boy Scouts around here, and you might think we're pretty cold-blooded about the whole thing. But then, you just don't know the dude."
>
> San Diego County Assistant Dist. Atty. Richard Huffman, who prosecuted Harris, said, "If a person like Harris can't be executed under California law and federal procedure, then we should be honest and say we're incapable of handling capital punishment."
>
> State Deputy Atty. Gen. Michael D. Wellington asked the court during an appeal hearing for Harris, "If this isn't the kind of defendant that justifies the death penalty, is there ever going to be one?"
>
> What crime did Robert Harris commit to be considered the archetypal candidate for the death penalty? And what kind of man provokes such enmity that even those on Death Row . . . call for his execution?
>
> On July 5, 1978, John Mayeski and Michael Baker had just driven through [a] fast-food restaurant and were sitting in the parking lot eating lunch. Mayeski and Baker . . . lived on the same street and were best friends. They were on their way to a nearby lake for a day of fishing.
>
> At the other end of the parking lot, Robert Harris, 25, and his brother Daniel, 18, were trying to hotwire a [car] when they spotted the two boys. The Harris brothers were planning to rob a bank that afternoon and did not want to use their own car. When Robert Har-

From Miles Corwin, "Icy Killer's Life Steeped in Violence," copyright 1982, *Los Angeles Times*. Reprinted by permission.

[16]Gary Watson, "Responsibility and the Limits of Evil: Variations on a Strawsonian Theme." In Ferdinand Schoeman, ed., *Responsibility, Character, and the Emotions: New Essays in Moral Psychology* (New York: Cambridge University Press, 1987), pp. 256–286.

ris could not start the car, he pointed to the [car] where the 16-year-olds were eating and said to Daniel, "We'll take this one."

He pointed a . . . Luger at Mayeski, crawled into the back seat, and told him to drive east. . . .

Daniel Harris followed in the Harrises' car. When they reached a canyon area. . . , Robert Harris told the youths he was going to use their car in a bank robbery and assured them that they would not be hurt. Robert Harris yelled to Daniel to get the .22 caliber rifle out of the back seat of their car.

"When I caught up," Daniel said in a recent interview, "Robert was telling them about the bank robbery we were going to do. He was telling them that he would leave them some money in the car and all, for us using it. Both of them said that they would wait on top of this little hill until we were gone, and then walk into town and report the car stolen." Robert Harris agreed.

"Michael turned and went through some bushes. John said, 'Good luck,' and turned to leave."

As the two boys walked away, Harris slowly raised the Luger and shot Mayeski in the back, Daniel said. Mayeski yelled: "Oh, God," and slumped to the ground. Harris chased Baker down a hill into a little valley and shot him four times.

Mayeski was still alive when Harris climbed back up the hill, Daniel said. Harris walked over to the boy, knelt down, put the Luger to his head and fired.

"God, everything started to spin," Daniel said. "It was like slow motion. I saw the gun, and then his head exploded like a balloon, . . . I just started running and running. . . . But I heard Robert and turned around.

"He was swinging the rifle and pistol in the air and laughing. God, that laugh made blood and bone freeze in me."

Harris drove [the] car to a friend's house where he and Daniel were staying. Harris walked into the house, carrying the weapons and the bag [containing] the remainder of the slain youths' lunch. Then, about 15 minutes after he had killed the two 16-year-old boys, Harris took the food out of the bag . . . and began eating a hamburger. He offered his brother an apple turnover, and Daniel became nauseated and ran to the bathroom.

"Robert laughed at me," Daniel said. "He said I was weak; he called me a sissy and said I didn't have the stomach for it."

Harris was in an almost lighthearted mood. He smiled and told Daniel that it would be amusing if the two of them were to pose as police officers and inform the parents that their sons were killed. Then, for the first time, he turned serious. He thought that somebody might have heard the shots and that police could be searching for the bodies. He told Daniel that they should begin cruising the street near the bodies, and possibly kill some police in the area.

[Later, as they prepared to rob the bank.] Harris pulled out the Luger, noticed blood stains and remnants of flesh on the barrel as a result of the point-blank shot, and said, "I really blew that guy's brains out." And then, again, he started laughing.

. . . Harris was given the death penalty. He has refused all requests for interviews since the conviction.

"He just doesn't see the point of talking," said a sister, . . . who has visited him three times since he has been on Death Row. "He told me he had his chance, he took the road to hell and there's nothing more to say."

. . . Few of Harris' friends or family were surprised that he ended up on Death Row. He had spent seven of the previous 10 years behind bars. Harris, who has an eighth-grade education, was convicted of car theft at 15 and was sentenced to a federal youth center. After being released, he was arrested twice for torturing animals and was convicted of manslaughter for beating a neighbor to death after a dispute.

Barbara Harris, another sister, talked to her brother at a family picnic on July 4, 1978. He had been out of prison less than six months, and his sister had not seen him in several years.

. . . Barbara Harris noticed his eyes, and she began to shudder. . . . "I thought, 'My God, what have they done to him?' He smiled, but his eyes were so cold, totally flat. It was like looking at a rattlesnake or a cobra ready to strike. They were hooded eyes, with nothing but meanness in them.

"He had the eyes of a killer. I told a friend that I knew someone else would die by his hand."

The next day, Robert Harris killed the two youths. Those familiar with the case were as mystified as they were outraged by Harris' actions. Most found it incomprehensible that a man could be so devoid of compassion and conscience that he could kill two youths, laugh about their deaths and then casually eat their hamburgers. . . .

. . . Harris is a dangerous man on the streets and a dangerous man behind bars, said Mroczko, who spent more than a year in the cell next to Harris'. . . .

"You don't want to deal with him out there," said Mroczko, . . . "We don't want to deal with him in here."

During his first year on the row, Mroczko said, Harris was involved in several fights on the yard and was caught trying to supply a prisoner in an adjacent yard with a knife. During one fight, Harris was stabbed and the other prisoner was shot by a guard. He grated on people's nerves and one night he kept the whole cell block awake by banging his shoe on a steel water basin and laughing hysterically.

An encounter with Harris always resulted in a confrontation. If an inmate had cigarettes, or something else Harris wanted, and he did not think "you could hold your mud," Mroczko said, he would try to take them.

Harris was a man who just did not know "when to be cool," he said. He was an obnoxious presence in the yard and in his cell, and his behavior precipitated unwanted attention from the guards. . . .

He acted like a man who did not care about anything. His cell was filthy, Mroczko said, and clothes, trash, tobacco and magazines were scattered on the floor. He wore the same clothes every day and had little interest in showers. Harris spent his days watching television in his cell, occasionally reading a Western novel.

Unlike Dworkin's faceless males for whom Andrea has contempt but whom we do not judge less harshly, we feel moral outrage and loathing for Robert Harris's heartlessness and viciousness. At the same time, our outrage is mollified (though our judgment remains intact) when we learn the historical considerations relevant to our "reactive attitude."[16]

[During the interview] Barbara Harris put her palms over her eyes and said softly, "I saw every grain of sweetness, pity and goodness in him destroyed. . . . It was a long and ugly journey before he reached that point."

Robert Harris' 29 years . . . have been dominated by incessant cruelty and profound suffering that he has both experienced and provoked. Violence presaged his birth, and a violent act is expected to end his life.

Harris was born Jan. 15, 1953, several hours after his mother was kicked in the stomach. She was 6½ months pregnant and her husband, an insanely jealous man, . . . came home drunk and accused her of infidelity. He claimed that the child was not his, threw her down and kicked her. She began hemorrhaging, and he took her to the hospital.

Robert was born that night. His heartbeat stopped at one point . . . but labor was induced and he was saved. Because of the premature birth, he was a tiny baby; he was kept alive in an incubator and spent months at the hospital.

His father was an alcoholic who was twice convicted of sexually molesting his daughters. He frequently beat his children . . . and often caused serious injury. Their mother also became an alcoholic and was arrested several times, once for bank robbery.

All of the children had monstrous childhoods. But even in the Harris family, . . . the abuse Robert was subjected to was unusual.

Before their mother died last year, Barbara Harris said, she talked incessantly about Robert's early years. She felt guilty that she was never able to love him; she felt partly responsible that he ended up on Death Row.

When Robert's father visited his wife in the hospital and saw his son for the first time, . . . the first thing he said was, "Who is the father of that bastard?" When his mother picked him up from the hospital . . . she said it was like taking a stranger's baby home.

---

[16]The phrase is P. F. Strawson's. See Strawson, "Freedom and Resentment." *Proceedings of the British Academy*, 48 (1962). Reprinted in P. F. Strawson, ed., *Freedom and Resentment and Other Essays*. (Oxford, England: Methuen, 1974).

The pain and permanent injury Robert's mother suffered as a result of the birth, . . . and the constant abuse she was subjected to by her husband, turned her against her son. Money was tight, she was overworked and he was her fifth child in just a few years. She began to blame all of her problems on Robert, and she grew to hate the child.

"I remember one time we were in the car and Mother was in the back seat with Robbie in her arms. He was crying and my father threw a glass bottle at him, but it hit my mother in the face. The glass shattered and Robbie started screaming. I'll never forget it," she said. . . .

"Her face was all pink, from the mixture of blood and milk. She ended up blaming Robbie for all the hurt, all the things like that. She felt helpless and he was someone to vent her anger on."

. . . Harris had a learning disability and a speech problem, but there was no money for therapy. When he was at school he felt stupid and classmates teased him, his sister said, and when he was at home he was abused.

"He was the most beautiful of all my mother's children; he was an angel," she said. "He would just break your heart. He wanted love so bad he would beg for any kind of physical contact.

"He'd come up to my mother and just try to rub his little hands on her leg or her arm. He just never got touched at all. She'd just push him away or kick him. One time she bloodied his nose when he was trying to get close to her."

Barbara Harris put her head in her hands and cried softly. "One killer out of nine kids. . . . The sad thing is he was the most sensitive of all of us. When he was 10 and we all saw 'Bambi,' he cried and cried when Bambi's mother was shot. Everything was pretty to him as a child; he loved animals. But all that changed; it all changed so much."

. . . All nine children are psychologically crippled as a result of their father, she said, but most have been able to lead useful lives. But Robert was too young, and the abuse lasted too long, she said, for him ever to have had a chance to recover.

[At age 14] Harris was sentenced to a federal youth detention center [for car theft]. He was one of the youngest inmates there, Barbara Harris said, and he grew up "hard and fast."

. . . Harris was raped several times, his sister said, and he slashed his wrists twice in suicide attempts. He spent more than four years behind bars as a result of an escape, an attempted escape and a parole violation.

The centers were "gladiator schools," Barbara Harris said, and Harris learned to fight and be mean. By the time he was released from federal prison at 19, all his problems were accentuated. Everyone in the family knew that he needed psychiatric help.

The child who had cried at the movies when Bambi's mother dies had evolved into a man who was arrested several times for abusing animals. He killed cats and dogs, Daniel said, and laughed while torturing them with mop handles, darts and pellet guns. Once he stabbed a prize pig more than 1,000 times.

"The only way he could vent his feelings was to break or kill something," Barbara Harris said. "He took out all the frustrations of his life on animals. He had no feeling for life, no sense of remorse. He reached the point where there wasn't that much left of him."

. . . Harris' family is ambivalent about his death sentence. [Another sister said that] if she did not know her brother's past so intimately, she would support his execution without hesitation. Barbara has a 16-year-old son; she often imagines the horror of the slain boys' parents.

"If anyone killed my son, I'd try my damnedest, no matter what it took, to have my child revenged," Barbara Harris said. "I know how those parents must suffer every day.

"But Robbie in the gas chamber. . . ." She broke off in mid-sentence and stared out a window. "Well, I still remember the little boy who used to beg for love, for just one pat or word of kindness. . . . No I can't say I want my brother to die."

. . . Since Harris has been on Death Row, he has made no demands of time or money on his family. Harris has made only one request; he wants a dignified and serene ceremony after he dies—a ceremony in marked contrast to his life.

He has asked his oldest brother to take his ashes, to drive to the Sierra, hike to a secluded spot and scatter his remains in the trees.

I introduce these passages to show that Dworkin's description of her victims causes her reader to inhabit a retributivist frame of mind in a way that the newspaper account of Harris does not. Harris's history cannot help but give pause to our attitude of moral outrage. If that is so, then Nussbaum is correct to insist that form determines content, and that attention to the novel can be of great value for moral philosophy. If, as Iris Murdoch has pointed out, "the central concept of morality is the individual thought knowable by love," then this vision is best explored not in abstract philosophical language in which individuals succumb to features thereof, but in "the messy accidental world of the novel" and other literary devices where people are taken seriously in the full context of their richly textured particularity.

We can make Nussbaum's point in other ways. Consider the way philosophers are prone to using the *ceteris paribus* (all things being equal) clause in moral philosophy. Utilitarians, in particular, use the clause to test "the greatest happiness principle" against our moral intuitions. Take the case of the runaway roller coaster, discussed in Chapter 1. We are asked to imagine that we are at the helm of a runaway roller coaster encountering a fork on the track. To the left are two to three individuals, while to the right is a crowd. We are advised that we should turn left since, *all things being equal*, many alive and one dead is preferable to one alive and many dead.

Now suppose we were given not a "thinly" written story in which the only relevant considerations are the number of people on the track, but a "thickly" written one where the characters are richly described in their individuality. Suppose, as philosophers Grisez and Shaw have pointed out, we know something about the individuals and the circumstances they are in. Suppose the few people to our left consist of decent citizens—a mother with a baby in a stroller, an elderly rabbi—crossing the street on a green light, while the crowd on our right consists of hoodlums who regularly ignore the rules of society. Grisez and Shaw use this example to illustrate how diverse a mix human goods are, and how it will not suffice to employ a *ceteris paribus* clause to prove the greatest happiness principle.[17] My point in using this illustration is to show how the form in which a moral choice is offered makes a statement that becomes part of the choice. Furthermore, if we do rest content with what are still thinly written descriptions (a mother, a rabbi, some hoodlums) but insist on more richly textured stories (How old is the rabbi? What kind of childhoods did these hoodlums have? What are their chances for rehabilitation?), then, depending on how much description we require, we might demand a full-blown novel.

Yet other philosophers argue that the very meaning of moral terms can only be understood when embedded in narratives. Alasdair MacIntyre, for one, has pointed out that the ways in which people make sense of the meaning and unity of their lives is only by thinking about narratives.[18] And Laurence Mordekhai Thomas, in a more specific context, has argued that the primary reason why African-Americans have languished as a community (following slavery) in contrast with American Jews (following the Holocaust) is their failure to develop a uniquely black narrative.[19]

We need only to consider some of the ways we are typically asked how we are and what we are to see how pervasive the narrative is. In colloquial English, someone may inquire about our welfare by asking "What's doing?" or "What's happening?" which is nothing less than a request for a narrative. Even when we answer "nothin' " in response to this question, what we mean is something like "nothing of importance in our life story." And it is also not unusual to define ourselves in reference to "our stories." In Giacomo Puccini's great opera *La Boheme*, for instance, we find the poet Rodolfo telling Mimi his story upon meeting her. He says:

Wait, mademoiselle,
I will tell you in two words

[17]See Germain Grisez and Russell Shaw, *Beyond the New Morality: The Responsibilities of Freedom*, 3rd ed. (Notre Dame, Ind.: University of Notre Dame Press, 1988), pp. 132–133.

[18]Alasdair MacIntyre, *After Virtue* (Notre Dame, Ind.: University of Notre Dame Press, 1981).

[19]Lawrence Mordekhai Thomas, *Vessels of Evil: American Slavery and the Holocaust* (Philadelphia: Temple University Press, 1993).

who I am, what I do,
and how I live. May I?
Who am I? I'm a poet.
What do I do? I write.
And how do I live? I live.

Following some further verses (sung to a mesmerizing tune, especially by Luciano Pavarotti), Rodolfo remarks:

Now that you know all about me,
you tell me now who you are

at which time Mimi sings the enthralling aria, *Si. Mi chiamano Mimi*.

The subject of ethics and literature is large and multifaceted. Our concern has been limited to showing how the development of the relationship between the two disciplines is intertwined in the history of philosophy, as well as sampling various ways that literature bears upon ethics. We have not explored all the ways in which philosophy and literature interact but have discussed some stimulating ones.

Rebecca Goldstein is a philosopher and novelist. She is the author
of *The Mind-Body Problem, The Late Summer Passion of a Woman of
Mind, The Dark Sister, Strange Attractors*, and *Mazel*. A 1996 recipient
of the MacArthur Award, she presently teaches creative writing at
Columbia University.

Video Presentation

Guest: Rebecca Goldstein, Philosopher/Novelist

Student Panel: Brenda Rubenfeld, Kelley Greene, Heidi Bukler

Knowing that she has feet in both doors, I begin by asking Rebecca Goldstein to compare philosophy with literature. She does this by pointing out that whereas philosophy is objective, rational, and dispassionate, literature is concrete, particular, subjective, and irrational. To underscore this point, she tells of how Renee Feuer, the protagonist of her novel *The Mind-Body Problem*, came to occupy her mind when she was writing the book, almost against her will. Incidents like this, she points out, led Plato to rail against artists, although he believed that artists were possessed by the gods, whereas we believe the unconscious takes control of the artist/novelist.

After pointing out how the work of Martha Nussbaum has inspired interest in ethics and literature, I ask Goldstein whether she believes reading literature has moral value. Convinced that it does, she makes her case by pointing out the obvious truth that each individual occupies a point of view that is not wholly accessible to other individuals. This being so, we need the imagination to train ourselves to see the world the way other people see it. We need, that is, to learn how to occupy other people's points of view. Herein lies the value of the novel for Goldstein, for it, more than any other art form, helps us to see the world from other points of view. Claiming never to have understood Plato's conception of the Good as something abstract and impersonal, Goldstein claims that the key to ethics is the ability to perceive the world as others perceive it, to come to occupy a world view that is different from our own.

Goldstein mentions Plato to point out yet another difference between philosophy and literature. For Plato as well as Spinoza, she says, the good life is a self-sufficient life of reason in which luck and contingency have no rightful place. The novelist, by contrast, embraces contingency and moral luck. We see this, I point out, in Eva Mueller of Goldstein's *The Late*

Summer Passion of a Woman of Mind. There, Eva tries to live a self-sufficient life of reason, learns that her father was a Nazi, and then tries to see the world the way he might have seen it. When Goldstein claims that this is what she herself does when writing a novel, we discuss whether this is dangerous inasmuch as the novelist might inadvertently come to occupy the mind-set of her evil characters.

At this point, I steer the conversation to Martha Nussbaum's observation that the novel is a preparation for the moral life inasmuch as the reader can become involved in the novel's character conflicts and at the same time remain detached and critical. Goldstein agrees with this and adds that while the novel is not ethics itself, it is like ethics in that we become accustomed to seeing the world from different perspectives. She is quick to point out that she does not mean to deny objectivity in the world.

Although Goldstein believes that subjectivity is the most important ethical fact, she does not imply that we cannot generate an objective ethics. To the contrary, she believes that we can get such objectivity by coming to appreciate that each world view is rich and inexhaustible. Simultaneously, we quote Henry James who claimed that reading novels makes one "finely aware and richly responsible," after which Goldstein points out how James, in response to a critic who claimed that no real person could possibly have all the perceptions that James's characters have, says "no, but they ought to."

Following the break, Brenda Rubenfeld asks Goldstein how reading novels can help develop a person philosophically, to which Goldstein reiterates her point about seeing the world from different perspectives and adds how this is helpful in epistemology as well as in ethics. Kelley Greene asks whether Goldstein feels novelists are morally responsible for the ethical views presented in their novels, knowing that readers live vicariously through them. And Heidi Bukler asks Goldstein what her philosopher colleagues think of her foray into the world of literature.

In this short essay written exclusively for this book, philosopher/novelist Rebecca Goldstein contrasts the philosopher's art (especially Plato's) with the art of the modern novelist. Against philosophy's concern with using abstract reasoning in the service of the good life, Goldstein recommends the novelist's approach, arguing that the novelist's endeavor to understand life from within makes it particularly appropriate for moral philosophy. Referring to the novel as "the handmaiden" to ethics, she calls for a need to imagine experiences and narratives that are distinct from our own, which the novel uniquely provides. Our reactions to these experiences enable us, in turn, to rehearse our reactions to other people.

Imagination and the Moral Life
or Why Plato Would Have Really Hated the Modern Novel

Rebecca Goldstein

> A man, to be greatly good, must imagine intensely and comprehensively; he must put himself in the place of another and of many others; the pains and pleasures of his species must become his own. The great instrument of moral good is the imagination.
>
> —*Percy Bysshe Shelley*, A Defense of Poetry

> Suppose, then, that an individual clever enough to assume any character and give imitations of anything and everything should visit our country and offer to perform his compositions, we shall bow down before a being with such miraculous powers of giving pleasure; but we shall tell him that we are not allowed to have any such person in our commonwealth; we shall crown him with fillets of wool, anoint his head with myrrh, and conduct him to the borders of some other country.
>
> —*Plato*, The Republic, III, 3981

The difference of opinion here couldn't really be any starker. On the one hand, we have the poet, claiming that a certain type of imagination is paramount in moral life. On the other hand, we have the philosopher protesting (with literary style enough to make a poet swoon) that the protean gifts of that imagination are downright pernicious to the moral well-being of individuals.

Becoming a better person—acting in terms of a view that takes into account considerations in addition to those of narrow self-interest—is, quite obviously, extremely hard work. It is hard to know what to do, and it is then hard to do it. What is the content of this wider moral point of view that has within it the power to offer (some) resistance to the centripetal forces of the ego? What are the faculties of the mind that we call upon in arriving at this view? Is the faculty (solely) the philosopher's power of conceptual reasoning, or is it

(also?) the poet's power of imagining "intensely and comprehensively?"

Neither the poet nor the philosopher is speaking here specifically of the novel, although it is of the novel that I want specifically to speak. I think that had there been anything remotely like the modern novel around in Plato's day he would have reviled it beyond any of the literary forms he found cause to abuse. There is no other art form that pays closer attention to the vast intricacies and subtleties of the subjective side of life, and Plato had precious little use for subjectivity. He conceives of intellectual and moral progress as an ascent out of narrow subjectivity, egocentric and fantasy-infested, into the realm of the purely objective and general, the abstract and impersonal. At the highest level of this ascent lies our apprehension of the Good, the content of the moral point of view.

And yet I also think that, in spite of the

(projected) Platonic disdain, the novel possesses a very special sort of moral relevance, a way of thinking that helps to fill in the blanks of what Plato has to tell us about the Good. I think that if there is any aspect of the imagination that has an essential moral role to play, it is precisely the sort of imagination that receives its most vigorous and expansive employment in the modern novel.

No matter at what date we choose to fix the birth of the modern novel—perhaps in the early seventeenth century with the publication of Cervantes' *Don Quixote*, perhaps later— there is no doubt that the form undergoes a most remarkable development in the course of the nineteenth century. One of the more significant aspects of what comes to distinguish it is the unique ease and naturalness with which it manages to "get behind" (the expression is Henry James's) the outward actions of its characters and represent that inner life—endlessly shifting, endlessly nuanced— from which these actions issue. The novel, as it develops over the course of the nineteenth century, becomes more and more an exploration of subjectivity, so that by the time we get to such masters of the form as Henry James, George Eliot, Marcel Proust, and James Joyce, outward actions are sometimes almost beside the point. The novelist creates her characters from the inside, struggling to render the qualities of their felt realities, to offer fistfuls of the diaphanous stuff of the individual consciousness. To grasp a character in a novel is to imaginatively inhabit his subjectivity, to live the world as he lives it. No other art form melds together so seamlessly (just as they are in life) the internal and external aspects of human existence.

There was nothing like the novel as we know it around in Plato's day. The literary artists that Plato is politely (more or less) escorting to the far side of his utopian borders are dramatic poets, who are not given to "getting behind" their characters in any significant way. Epic poetry, the supreme literary achievement of ancient Greece, narrates the adventures of heroically cast mortals, their dramas shaped by the designs of the ever-attentive gods. The heroes of Homer's *Iliad* and *Odyssey* are defined by their actions, not their points of view, for it is by the gods that they are typically moved. What is it that Plato found worthy of exile in these narratives?

The reasons behind Plato's hostility to the poets are complex and diverse, evolving with his ever-changing views of the way things are (metaphysics) and the way things ought to be (ethics). Plato has always a preference for stasis over change; for control and foreseeability over upsets and reversals of fortune; for the closed, the countable, and the explicable over a universe forever springing leaks into infinity and escaping from our grasp. In short, Plato is committed to the world's being deeply and inviolably rational, and he (rightly) believes that art rarely has it so.

Art, in both its circumstances and its content, must submit itself to chance. There is, first of all, the matter of circumstance, the tricky business of inspiration, over which the poet never has complete control. "It" comes over him, and he in turn comes out of himself, stands beside himself and raves in immortal stanzas. (The word *ecstasy* comes from the Greek, meaning "to stand beside.") Hesiod was a shepherd until the Muses made their sudden appearance and bid him "sing of the race of the blessed gods immortal." In the *Ion*, Plato likens the poet's state to divine madness or drunkenness and says that the inspired artist is out of his senses, which is why the poet is often at a loss to explain his meaning.

We, of course, would speak—perhaps only slightly less metaphorically—more in terms of the unconscious than of the gods in describing this aspect of creativity, but the aspect itself is real enough. Plato knows all about inspiration and its ecstasies, enough to mistrust it all profoundly.

But more serious for Plato than the dubious circumstances in which poetry begins is the problematic content in which it issues. The stories that the epic poets and tragic playwrites give us are drenched through and through in the cold chanciness of life. Stasis and predictability do not make for interesting plots. In order for these works of art to do what they are meant to do, in order for them to move us to pity and terror, we must feel with the characters that the reversals they suffer do in fact matter, that events beyond our control can shape our lives, can determine whether they are good or bad lives. That this is so is of the essence of what is called the tragic sense of life, and it is one of Plato's deepest objectives to demonstrate to us that this is not so. No external events can really harm us, because the only thing that really matters is our intellectual/ethical ascent through life, over which we, and only we, exert control. Plato's aim is to make our lives impervious to what seems to be life's truly awful precariousness, which does indeed make that aim incompatible with almost all literary art.

Spinoza, who shared Plato's aim, put it like this:

> After experience had taught me that all the usual surroundings of social life are vain and futile; seeing that none of the objects of my fears contained in themselves anything either good or bad, except in so far as the mind is affected by them, I finally resolved to inquire whether there might be some real good, having the power to communicate itself, which would affect the mind singly, to the exclusion of all else; whether, in fact, there might be anything of which the discovery and attainment would enable me to enjoy continuous, supreme, and unending happiness.—*On the Improvement of the Understanding*

The aim here might sound baldly selfish—"continuous, supreme, and unending happiness"—but in fact the enterprise consists, for both Plato and Spinoza, of a struggle toward the most egoless sort of apprehension conceivable. For both these philosophers, moral ascent and intellectual ascent are one and the same, accomplished through the rigors of the truth-considering, argument-evaluating, analytic and dispassionate faculty of reason, which will lead us out of the narrow confines of our own densely detailed, purely personal,

particular, and contingent subjectivity. Moral sight comes, eventually, after we have emerged from that dark place of our ego-determined view of the world (the cave, in Plato's famous allegory), the opaque perspective that lets in nothing else, so that it seems to constitute the whole of reality.

And it *isn't* the whole of reality, of course. Plato says that all of us begin in that dark place, and I think it is also true that the forces of the ego are such—in the *Timeus* he speaks of the "dreadful and necessary" elements that had to be conferred on humanity—so that most of us return to it periodically. (The psychological/moral disease of narcissism consists of never once leaving it.)

But when we do emerge from that cramped space, what is it, precisely, that we see? What is the vision that will tell us *what* to do, and will it also contain within itself some impetus so that we will *want* to do it?

Plato conceived of that version as consisting of the most rarified and purified objectivity, which he dubbed the Good, and which is formulated in terms of his Theory of Forms. The Forms, which are postulated as the objects of all knowledge, are conceived of as changeless, eternal, nonsensible, essences grasped by the rational soul. The Good exists at a level of objectivity and abstraction at least equal to that of the Forms, which themselves exist at a level of objectivity and abstraction at least equal to that of mathematics. The rational soul, on its pilgrim's progress, passes from the subjective and personal particulars, to the objective and impersonal particulars, and from thence (by way of mathematics) to the general and abstract, of which the Form of the Good is (in some sense[2]) the highest. The only faculty that is employed in this work of ascent is the faculty of reason. Insofar as we can know what to do and want to do it, we must be, must think as, philosophers.

What Plato has to say about the vision of the Good and its power to move us leaves us, or so it has always seemed to me, begging for more. Spinoza is, I think, the philosopher who tries the hardest to deliver on what Plato has so magnificently but, when all is said and done, only metaphorically, suggested: an ascent by way of pure reason through regions perfectly objective and general, that will end in making us better people, seeing what is right (yielding moral sight) and wanting to do it (yielding moral will). The goal is to arrange concepts into abstract propositions that will make an appeal on our will and desire. Like Plato, Spinoza tells us the faculty of mind we must call upon to make this ascent to the moral point of view is the philosopher's—or for that matter the mathematician's—power of abstract reason, constructing formal proofs and operating in a realm perfectly objective and impersonal. "I shall consider human actions and desires in exactly the same manner as though I were concerned with lines, planes, and solids," Spinoza tells us in one startling passage.[3]

It is high time we let the poet[4] speak his piece (or the novelist hers.) In almost all of the most important ways in which the poet and the philosopher might disagree, they, in fact, agree. The poet, too, believes that there is a moral point of view, that the apprehension of it involves escaping from that dark, cramped space where the only reality is the one projected before one's eyes by one's own entirely personal circumstances (the shadowplay in Plato's cave.) It is true, agrees the poet, that there is more, far more, to reality than *that* (pity the narcissist), and that this "more" must be incorporated into one's point of view in order for it to become a moral point of view.

Where the poet disagrees with the philosopher is on the nature of what must be seen and the type of thinking that will get us to see it. More to the point, he is convinced that the moral point of view is a way of apprehending not abstract entities but other human beings, and that its content, therefore, is irreducibly particular and has irreducibly to do with subjectivity. Arguments perfectly formal and general may have their place, but they can never, in themselves, express all that we must see in order that we be moved to act with a view extending beyond ourselves.

The poet, after all, isn't all *that* fond of

mathematics. What the poet likes are stories, *human* stories, filled with the vast wide wonder of the endless varieties of human beings to be found on this planet, and he believes that the rigorous exertions of imagination that are called upon in trying to grasp something of the inner reality of these lives is the faculty that will get us to see what must morally be seen. We must think not as mathematicians and philosophers seeking a vision purged of the subjective and particular, which is a vision purged of the knowledge of what it is like to live a human life, but rather as poets and novelists seeking to imagine our way into experiences distinct from our own.

The faculty of the mind that needs strengthening, if we are to treat each other as we ought to, is the empathetic imagination, which is a storytelling imagination, attempting to construct a narrative context for what we observe in others. And the material supplied by this faculty is as unlike the static, eternal, nonhuman objects of the truth-seeking faculty of reason as it is possible to be. And unlike those objects, says the poet, this material has the demonstrable capacity to *move* us, to make so powerful an appeal on our emotions that it provides us with motives for actions having nothing at all to do with narrow concerns of self-interest. The more vivid our imaginatively given apprehensions of the full humanity of others'—and after all, that humanity *is* there for the imagining—the more powerful an appeal that humanity makes on us.

And that is why the modern novel is a handmaiden to ethics. To read a novel with the proper attention and response is to leave off one's own subjectivity and to move off into others.' This movement of the mind is a sort of moral exercise, if not exactly morality itself, since morality itself takes place (or doesn't) in our reactions to, our interactions with, real people, not fictional characters. The moral point of view is brought to bear when the insistently clamoring realities of one's own inner life, the "dreadful and necessary" elements that make for survival, are tempered by whatever little one can apprehend of how it is for others. What one imagines and feels while reading a novel isn't in itself moral behavior, but it is something like at least one of the essential components of morality, a kind of shadowing of the real thing.

Literary genres, the various forms the art of the written word can take, have sometimes within themselves their own kind of extratextual voice. There are ways in which a writer asserts certain extratextual claims simply by the form of writing she undertakes. This is what Plato was telling us by banishing the dramatic poets from his utopia. The style of writing that Plato himself countenanced and practiced was one which asserts, not just in its content but in its form, the singular position of the truth-seeking, argument-evaluating faculty of reason in the all-important task of living the good life. The novel, by virtue of its very form, puts before us the claim that people of every conceivable sort are deserving of acts of supreme attention, intensive and comprehensive.

ENDNOTES

1. The translation here is by Francis McDonald Cornford (Oxford University Press: 1945).
2. One of the senses is this: The ascending levels of reality Plato lays down are a ladder of explication. One can only come to know the nature of any one level by ascending to the next, for it is only there that one can grasp the explanation for what one has just left behind. For example, we only know what the particulars are when we have grasped the Forms, for it is the Forms which make the particulars what they are. Therefore, Plato, in placing the Good at the highest level on his ladder of explication, is asserting that the ultimate explanation for the entire universe is a moral one. Philosophers have long debated whether one can derive "ought" from "is." Plato's position is to stand this question on its head.
3. *The Ethics*, Part III, "On the Origin and Nature of the Emotions."
4. "The poet" is now, quite obviously, being used in a more abstract fashion than before, where it was meant, quite literally, to refer to Percy Bysshe Shelley.

Closing Questions

1. In your judgment, how might reading novels enhance our understanding of life and contribute to a better understanding of ethics?

   _____

   _____

   _____

2. What might Alasdair MacIntrye mean when he says that "man is in his actions and practice, as well as in his fictions, essentially a storytelling animal?"

   _____

   _____

   _____

3. Knowing that readers live vicariously through novels, should novelists be held accountable for the ethical views presented in their novels?

   _____

   _____

   _____

4. What novels, poems, or films have you read (or seen) that have made philosophical points? Discuss these points and the way the genre made them.

   _____

   _____

   _____

5. A person might hold that some truths can be adequately stated in theoretical language and also hold that they are most efficiently communicated to readers through colorful and moving narrative. Martha Nussbaum argues that some truths are only expressible in literature and are not expressible in philosophy. Is her claim sound? What might such truths be?

   _____

   _____

   _____

6. We talk not only of enjoying music, but of understanding it. Does this mean that music can have meaning? Discuss critically.

_____

_____

_____

7. Are Plato and Spinoza right that the emotions are irrational? If you believe they are rational, discuss how they can be so using one emotion such as anger or jealousy.

_____

_____

_____

8. Jonathan Bennett once remarked that it is not people that are important in moral philosophy, but features of people. Critically discuss this remark in light of particularism.

_____

_____

_____

9. William Styron is a novelist who has been criticized for writing novels about American slavery (*The Confession of Nat Turner*) and the Nazi genocide (*Sophie's Choice*) although as he is neither black nor Jewish. Does Styron have a right to write about these institutions? Are there moral limits to the poetic license?

_____

_____

_____

10. Plato objected to putting thoughts down on paper, since he thought that writing would stifle thinking. George Bernard Shaw once remarked that reading is an enemy of thinking. Are Plato and Shaw right? Should you write your thoughts on this topic?

_____

_____

_____

_____

For Further Reading

Aristotle. *The Poetics of Aristotle*. Translated by Halliwell. Chapel Hill: University of North Carolina Press, 1986.

Becker, Lawrence C., ed. "Symposium on Morality and Literature." *Ethics* 98 (1988): 223–340.

Booth, Wayne C. *The Company We Keep: An Ethics of Fiction*. Berkeley: University of California Press, 1988.

Cavell, Stanley. *Conditions Handsome and Unhandsome*. Chicago: Open Court, 1990.

Gaarder, Jostein. *Sophie's World: A Novel About the History of Philosophy*. Translated by Paulette Moller. New York: Farrar, Strauss and Giroux, 1994.

MacIntyre, Alasdair. *After Virtue*. Notre Dame, Ind.: University of Notre Dame Press, 1981.

Murdoch, Iris. *The Sovereignty of Good*. London: Routledge and Kegan Paul, 1970.

Nussbaum, Martha. *Love's Knowledge: Essays on Philosophy and Literature*. New York.: Oxford University Press, 1990.

Rosenstand, Nina. *The Moral of the Story*. Mountain View, Calif.: Mayfield, 1994.

Sesonske, Alexander. "Truth in Art." *The Journal of Philosophy* 53, 11 (May 24, 1956): 345–353.

Chapter 16

Ethics in Academia

Passages for Reflection

"To impose any straightjacket upon the intellectual leaders in our colleges and universities would imperil the future of the nation."
—*Sweezy v. New Hampshire (1957)*

"A university is what a college becomes when the faculty loses interest in students."
—*John Ciardi*

"A professor is one who talks in someone else's sleep."
—*W. H. Auden*

Opening Questions

1. Should professors and students be friends outside the classroom? Should they be lovers?
2. Should the tenure system be abolished?
3. What is a good professor?

In his edifying book, *Saints and Scamps: Ethics in Academia,* Steven M. Cahn recalls how he was once asked to deliver a lecture on the subject of "Ethics in the Academic World" when a colleague of his remarked, "It'll be a short talk."[1] After that, Cahn laments how little has been written on the responsibilities of faculty members while much has been written on their rights and privileges. Yet surely, says Cahn, professors should be expected to adhere to high standards of professional conduct. Taking our cue from Cahn, we will examine these standards and the issues generated by them. We will also examine some issues faced by students since, like faculty, administrators, staff, and trustees, they form a vital part of the educational process.

Let us begin with the question of academic freedom. The university is a bastion of liberal ideas, championing the unfettered pursuit of knowledge and truth. Because of this, defenders of academic freedom argue that faculty within the university must be free to seek, teach, and publish the truth as they see it within their respective fields of competency. If the pursuit of knowledge were obstructed by political or religious ideologies—if professors were made to tailor their research to some proffered ideal—then the aims of the university would be foiled and subverted. For this reason, professors must be allowed the freedom to develop and teach even the most unpopular ideas.

Beyond the commitment to truth as an intrinsic value, academic freedom is needed if the university is to contribute to the welfare of humankind. Humankind has a greater chance of flourishing if professors are left to their own devices without having a conception of the Good determined for them. While some things discovered and taught might endanger the welfare of humankind, such as accidents in genetic engineering and scientific research (see Mary Shelley's *Frankenstein*), history has shown that we have more to fear from the repression of ideas than from the unfettered pursuit of knowledge. Witness, in this regard, Socrates, who was put to death for corrupting the youth of Athens; Galileo, who was placed under house arrest for promulgating the helio-

---

[1] Steven M. Cahn, *Saints and Scamps: Ethics in Academia.* Savage, Md.: Rowman and Littlefield, 1986.

centric theory of planetary motion; and Darwin, whose views on evolution have often been suppressed.

John Stuart Mill is history's most celebrated champion of liberal causes in the service of human welfare, and what he says in support of democracy generally applies to the university, our most democratic institution. As a utilitarian moralist, Mill was convinced that happiness was the sole guide for determining right conduct. An action is right, he argued in *Utilitarianism*, if it increases the welfare of humanity; otherwise, it is wrong. Saying this, however, leaves open the question of how best to bring about happiness. Here is where Mill's celebrated defense of liberty comes in.

In his essay, *On Liberty*, Mill argued that humankind will flourish if individuals are left to examine competing conceptions of the good life unfettered by ideological considerations. As Mill saw it, since "we can never be sure that the opinion we are endeavoring to stifle is a false opinion," our pursuit of the Good must include experimenting with ideas and lifestyles even if they conflict with the prevailing orthodoxy.

The chief danger of a democratic society, said Mill, and the one to fear even more than unorthodox lifestyles, is its tendency to suppress individuality and to override its more marginalized members. We have more to fear from the "tyranny of the majority," he said, than from the tyranny of despots, since the tyranny of the majority is a more effective means of coercion. For this reason, Mill urged that society develop personalities strong enough to resist social pressures. This, in turn, meant developing citizens who were reasonably educated, tolerant of diversity, and armed with the fortitude to resist the pressure to conform to public opinion.

Champions of academic freedom in the university often take their cue from Mill. In defending the rights of professors to explore or defend even the most unpopular heresies, they make the claim that humankind will be the ultimate beneficiary. If an unpopular view turns out to be true, it will ultimately win out over competing views. Conversely, if an unpopular view is false, it will die a natural death. But we cannot know whether a view is true or false unless we are free to examine it. In this sense, to be denied the right to entertain a falsely held view is more tragic than to be denied the right to espouse it.

But just because academic freedom is vital to the pursuit of truth does not imply that academic freedom is inviolable. Even the most staunch defender of academic freedom admits values to which it must yield. We must not, for instance, experiment on people without their informed consent although such experimentation might prove to be tremendously valuable. More controversial is whether academic freedom should protect campus speakers whose views are unpalatable. In recent years, the issue has been raised in connection with the racist activities of Nation of Islam leader Louis Farrakhan and City College of New York professors Michael Levin and Leonard Jeffries. Closely connected with this controversy, though presenting different issues, is the right of student newspapers to publish material offensive to certain groups of people. The right of newspapers to publish offensive material involves the constitutionally protected freedom of the press as well as freedom of speech.

Champions of academic freedom who rely on John Stuart Mill might do well to pay more careful attention to his writings than they do. While Mill undeniably championed freedom of thought and discussion, it was always in the light of what such freedom meant for social action. Contrary to the way he is often portrayed, Mill did not champion freedom of expression for its own sake; he championed it for the sake of human happiness. The Mill who wrote *Utilitarianism* is the same Mill who wrote *On Liberty*. Having argued in *Utilitarianism* that ethics is concerned with maximizing happiness, Mill argues in *On Liberty* that freedom of thought and action are instrumental to achieving happiness. Where humankind has learned that certain ideas or actions impede this goal, there is no point to enduring them. Thus, while Mill was a patron of tolerance, he was not tolerant of views that history had proven were inimical to achieving happiness. For this reason, he would presumably not approve of racist ideas hiding behind the veil of academic freedom.

The freedom to develop and teach new ideas can be encouraged or discouraged in many ways. The most prominent way the university encourages it is in the granting of tenure. Many go so far as to equate academic freedom with tenure. The granting of tenure amounts to a lifetime contract for professors. It is typically granted after a six-year probation period during which time the professor has demonstrated excellence in teaching, scholarship, and service.

In recent years, the tenure system has come under critical attack. Opponents of tenure argue that the aims of academic freedom are best accomplished without tenure. Citing cases where tenured professors do little work after tenure is conferred, opponents argue that it encourages laziness, does not encourage research and publication, and sometimes results in uncooperative employees. Tenured professors are thus sometimes compared to professional athletes whose long-term contracts have diminishing returns. For this reason, opponents of tenure call for more short-term contracts with incentives for research and good teaching, or other measures such as increased release time and sabbatical leaves.

Opponents of tenure also argue that even if tenure is desirable, it is usually withheld from those individuals who need it most: junior faculty whose views are most likely to be unorthodox and a threat to existing paradigms. Many junior scholars lose their positions because their senior colleagues do not support their research or teaching material. Junior scholars—sometimes referred to, disparagingly, as "gypsy professors"[2]—

---

[2]See Viva Hardigg, Anna Mulrine, and Geoffrey Sanoff, "Gypsy Profs." *U.S. News and World Report* (March 20, 1995): 106.

commonly go from one untenured position to another with no job security and little of the benefits (for example, health care and a pension) that attach to full-time tenure.

Here is where Mill's insistence on developing individual character is at its strongest. In recent years, pressure has been exerted by senior faculty or administrators to defend views that are "politically correct," by which I mean views that conform to the prevailing liberal orthodoxy. An inordinate amount of "tyranny" of opinion has been brought to bear on being "politically correct," so that in many institutions not being politically correct is a substantial threat to the professional security of faculty members.

Opponents of tenure sometimes argue that no analogue can be found to it in any other profession and that academic life should be no exception. Just as in business, law, and medicine, the professional is not guaranteed job security, neither should academics have any. Security, so the argument goes, must always be tied to performance.

None of these arguments is persuasive. The argument that tenure leads to laziness is really an argument from abuse. Some professors do abuse the tenure system and construe the awarding of tenure as a license to slack off. In my institution, tenure is sometimes referred to as "partial retirement," and I cannot deny some truth to this. In an institution in which I previously taught, I had a tenured colleague who would go so far as to cancel a course in mid-semester on account of his losing his creative inspiration. This same professor would indiscriminately assign A's and B's to anyone who took his course.

But those who abuse the tenure system do not prove that the system is bad. For every professor who abuses the system, we can identify numerous professors whose research and teaching are protected by it. Beyond this, the desire to excel is motivated not only by such perks as promotion and recognition both within and without a professor's institution, but also by personal integrity. The desire to research, write, and teach should not be shortchanged since few people enter academia for its financial rewards.

The argument that tenure is a benefit conferred on those who need it least is also unpersuasive. Rather than arguing against the tenure system, the argument argues for protection of junior scholars in addition to senior ones. As for the argument that academics should not be entitled to security any more than other professionals, that too is without merit. Unlike lawyers, physicians, and most businesspeople, academics are severely limited in mobility. For every departmental opening in the field of philosophy, maybe 300 or more applicants are eager and qualified to fill it. One colleague of mine who recently was an interviewer for a position in philosophy was so inundated by qualified applicants that he challenged me to name an institution not represented in his pool of applicants! In other academic fields, the ratio is higher. In English, it is 600 to 1! We cannot then make a straightforward comparison between academia and other professions (which is why the analogy to athletes with long-term contracts is also misleading). Beyond this, some thinkers argue that tenure has come to serve as a replacement for the financial rewards of other professions.

Because the tenure system is steeped in history and has much to recommend it, and because of the presumption of freedom which the abolition of tenure must overcome, universities wishing to defeat tenure have gone to great lengths to avoid awarding it. In addition to creating nontenure track positions and filling courses with part-time adjuncts, some institutions have used innovative means to defeat tenure. One such means is to encourage minority candidates to apply for low-salaried, entry-level positions, knowing that in an age of preferential treatment, such mobile candidates have a better than average chance of moving elsewhere and not completing the tenure track. In this way, professors themselves are made to account for the low ratio of tenured to nontenured faculty rather than the institution that does the hiring.

Tenure, finally, is not just the reward of a lifetime contract for work well done in a six-year probation. Neither is it more than the freedom to keep on working. Tenure is a means to protect the academic freedom of the scholar-teacher against the values of the institution, the field, and the larger society. It is an intellectual freedom, but also a political one. Tenure is granted now by the institution so that the well-qualified person may one day be safely opposed to the institution. Without that protection, scholars would be intimidated, major errors would be institutionalized, and learning would not advance. Even with tenure, scholars still may be intimidated say, by being assigned undesirable schedules, but it is the most surefire means of safeguarding the values it is designed to protect.

Academic freedom is but one issue in academic ethics. Even if we grant that the essence of the professor's life is the pursuit of knowledge, the ability to convey that knowledge is equally important. Professors must distinguish between education and indoctrination and provide students with accurate information based on current research. This means keeping abreast of the literature and honing the skill to convey it with clarity and precision. While some professors see teaching as interfering with their scholarship, others recognize that teaching is an essential dimension of a professor's life. Accordingly, an eminent scholar who cannot teach well is as defective a professor as a minimally competent scholar with a keen ability to convey ideas.

Being able to effectively communicate material (or cultivate skills) begets its own set of questions that speak to what and how to teach. Having made the point that a good professor is one who teaches well in addition to knowing his or her field, we want to know how a professor should teach a course. In any given class, a professor will have students with diverse skills and abilities. If the professor "pitches" to the top of the class, she will lose the bottom of the class; if she pitches to the bottom, she will bore the top. Thus, she may be tempted to pitch to the middle. But pitching to the middle is no panacea. It fails to provide a realistic challenge to both the top and the bottom of the class.

Another question we want to ask is how much leeway a professor should have who is convinced that he is on the cutting edge of his field and wants to color his classes with his insights. The issue becomes sensitive when his colleagues insist that he teach more traditional topics. Should his academic freedom be limited by his colleagues' expectations? Is it permissible to teach a traditional course in a way that expresses a person's idiosyncrasies?[3]

Questions such as these speak to *what* one should teach. Regarding *how* one should teach, we want to ask, "What obligation do professors have to avoid offending their students?" Offending students is inevitable, as any professor knows who has taught philosophy of religion and has criticized the ontological argument for the existence of God. I was once accused of being the anti-Christ for having debunked this argument before a religious zealot, and I've offended more than my share of students when I've argued that animals cannot think in any real sense. My most memorable incident in class occurred when I was teaching a class in applied ethics and the topic of discussion was pornography and censorship. I had asked the class for a definition of pornography, when a student volunteered that pornography was "literature that contained lewd behavior and obscene language." Not having considered the question of obscene language, I addressed this definition and in doing so I made reference to the word *fuck*. Seeing one of my students become irate at my use of this word, I explained that I was mentioning this term rather than using it and was sorry if I had offended her. My explanation was to no avail.

Teaching well means also taking care not to abuse authority. The good professor must grade fairly, although what it means to grade fairly is not always clear. How, for example, should a professor of English account for a poorly written paper by a student whose native language is not English? How should a professor of philosophy account for such a paper?

Fairness in grading also requires the absence of partiality. Does this mean that a professor must grade anonymously? Does it mean that a professor may never befriend a student? Does it preclude romantic involvement? What exactly are a professor's obligations when examining and grading students?

The answers to these questions presuppose that grading students is desirable in the first place. Not everyone accepts this. Robert Paul Wolff,

---

[3]For more on these issues, see Peter J. Markie, *Professor's Duties: Ethical Issues in College Teaching* (Savage, Md.: Rowman and Littlefield, 1994), Part One.

for one, argues that grades serve no educational purpose and are harmful to education, especially when students fixate on grades and forget about learning. As he sees it, the purpose of grades is the economic one of facilitating the allocation of scarce resources inasmuch as good grades are tickets to further study and to careers with economic benefits.[4] If Wolff is right, then the good teacher may be one who does not grade at all.

A delicate question concerning fairness in grading concerns the grading procedures of adjunct professors. At a time when the supply of professors far exceeds demand and colleges and universities employ adjunct to full-time professors at ratios of 60 to 40, we are naive to insist that adjuncts comply with the requirements of fair grading. For the adjunct who relies on course enrollment in order to teach during a particular semester, inflating grades rather than grading fairly is imperative. The fair grader, in contrast to the inflated grader, runs the risk of becoming known as a hard grader. This, in turn, sometimes results in low enrollment—a luxury adjuncts can ill afford. Fair graders also invite students to complain to deans more frequently than inflated graders, further jeopardizing the adjunct's job security. As one ex-dean told me, deans don't like to hear complaints no matter how justified they are. The admonition to grade fairly, on this account, can fail to do justice to the realities of teaching.

The upshot of this discussion is that saying a professor must be a good teacher leaves open more questions than it answers. Beyond that is the question of how to evaluate a teacher's performance. Typically, colleges and universities rely both on peer review and student opinion. While each of these methods has much to recommend it for a sound evaluation, neither of these methods is without its flaws. Regarding peer reviews, the possibility is that a professor will receive a substandard review for other than academic reasons, and we want to control for this possibility. Regarding student reviews, the possibility (likelihood?) is that students will evaluate teachers on such irrelevant grounds as personality or the student's expected grade in a course. Some students will evaluate professors using no grounds at all. In a recent evaluation of my teaching—an evaluation, I might add, that was favorable—one student complained that I lectured too often from my notes when in fact I made no use of notes at all!

Having discussed ethical issues from the professorial side, some discussion is in order about the responsibilities of students. In addition to the usual strictures against cheating and plagiarism, one issue that is cause for concern involves the practice of buying and selling textbooks. Students commonly purchase used textbooks at a reduced price and subsequently sell them back to the campus bookstore. This practice is blatantly unethical and uneconomical for the student. That it is unethical

---

[4]Robert Paul Wolff, *The Ideal of the University* (Boston: Beacon Press, 1969), pp. 64–65.

is evinced by the fact that the profits rightfully belonging to the author and publisher are instead placed into the pockets of the bookstore. The bookstore does deserve its share in the profits, but it is not entitled to more than its rightful share. Thus, to the extent that students buy and sell used textbooks, they are participating in an institution that is unethical. Beyond this appeal to justice—an appeal that speaks to capitalism itself—we have an argument from integrity that argues for keeping your books in the form of a personal library.[5] The books you read should be a record and reminder of your personal and intellectual growth.

But maybe I've passed too quickly over the reference to capitalism. After all, if it is unethical to buy and sell used books, is it not unethical to buy and sell used cars? Used-clothes? Should flea-markets also be prohibited? I answer this question by pointing out that books differ from other products in a significant way. Books themselves may be transferred from one person to another through the economic process, but the ideas contained in books remain with their authors. This is why, for instance, you do not have the liberty to treat software as you please even when you purchase it legally. Thus, while the law allows the sale of used books in a way that it prohibits the sale of used software, justice requires a similar practice.

You as reader will be impatient with this: "You just want to maximize your profits," you might say. Aside from the irrelevancy of this rebuttal—logicians call this an *ad hominem* argument or attack on the person instead of the argument—I had mentioned that the buying and selling of used textbooks was uneconomical as well as unethical. In an effort to defeat the used-book market, publishers of college textbooks sometimes artificially create new editions that only nominally differ from previous ones. In such cases, the author of a book will, for example, add an article or two to an existing anthology or change the number of study questions at the end of a chapter. This manufacturing of new editions renders previous editions obsolete. And since the prices of textbooks go up and not down, the cash in hand from the sale of used textbooks is outweighed by the costlier new editions. This is especially so if we quantify the cost of textbooks over the expected life of a college career.

Some publishing companies are going to extremes in an effort to defeat the used-textbook market. The editor of a major publishing company recently told me that the trend is toward packaging software together with textbooks in such a way that one is useless without the other. The reason for this is that software cannot be resold as used without violating federal laws. And since, as anyone who has a personal computer knows, the cost of software is prohibitive, the price of textbook-software packages is likely to double in the near future if the used textbook market continues to flourish.

---

[5]I owe this point to Richard Hull.

Let me not be so quick to put the blame on bookstores and students alone. Professors, too, share some of the blame inasmuch as they too sell unwanted textbooks to the dealers (often disgruntled academics) who appear on campus from semester to semester. Then, too, publishers are themselves to blame to the extent that they provide instructors with unwanted examination copies which clutter bookshelves after time. In defense of publishing companies, many have adopted the policy of including return postage with examination copies and ask that unwanted copies be returned instead of sold.

Steven M. Cahn is Professor of Philosophy at the Graduate School of the City University of New York. He is the author of *Saints and Scamps: Ethics in Academia* (1986) and general editor of *Issues in Academic Ethics* (Rowman and Littlefield). He is also the editor (along with Joram G. Haber) of *Twentieth-Century Ethical Theory* (Prentice-Hall, 1995).

Video Presentation

Guest: Steven M. Cahn, Graduate School of the City University of New York

Student Panel: Catherine Morrow, Anthony De Prospero, Claudia Stevens

I begin by commenting on a story Cahn tells at the start of his book, *Saints and Scamps*. When informing a colleague that he was writing a book on academic ethics, Cahn's colleague remarked, "It'll be a short book." Pointing out that he had heard this response several times, Cahn talks about how, since the early 1970s, philosophers have scrutinized virtually every profession other than their own. They have examined such professions as medicine, law, business, and engineering, but have not turned their efforts to academia itself. I ask Cahn why he thinks this is so. He suggests that an analysis of the ethics of academic life tends to makes academics uncomfortable; it points to standards professors might not be living up to.

The discussion turns to Cahn's book where he discusses ethical issues under the headings of Teaching, Scholarship, and Personnel Decisions. I announce my goal to ask questions under each of these headings.

With respect to teaching, I ask Cahn what he thinks makes a teacher a good one. He answers with four criteria. A good teacher motivates students, discusses material clearly, is organized, and is able to put his or her subject matter into a larger perspective. A fifth criterion Cahn mentions that distinguishes a great teacher from a good one is the ability to project a vision of excellence. When I point out that this fifth feature might run counter to student relativism, Cahn quips that in the absence of a commitment to excellence, the university has no reason for being.

Regarding scholarship, I ask Cahn to respond to a moral dilemma I personally had concerning a friend I had asked to contribute to an anthology that I was editing. The anthology, for the most part, was to consist of well-known selections by prominent philosophers. My friend, whose philosophical abilities I greatly admired, produced a paper of substandard value which would have detracted from the value of the book. Even the revised paper he ultimately wrote lacked the virtues for which I was looking. I was torn between loyalty to my friend and my commitment to construct a high-quality anthology. Cahn, who indicated that he has had similar dilemmas, decided, like me, not to include such a piece inasmuch as doing so would undermine the integrity of the book and be a disservice to the academic community, the students who would use such a text, and ultimately (I add) to the author of the article.

I next ask Cahn how he would have responded to another dilemma I had, although this dilemma speaks to scholarship as well as to personnel decisions. I had been asked to review a nontenured colleague whose lecture indicated that the professor might be less than qualified to teach the course she was assigned. Knowing that a poor evaluation might have resulted in her termination, I agonized for two weeks and finally gave her the review I felt she deserved. Glad that I did, Cahn points out that students of this professor are entitled to quality instruction and that a sugar-coated evaluation would have been a disservice to them.

Finally, I ask Cahn how he would respond to a case I knew of a professor hired when the hiring body knew for a fact that this professor had been expelled from graduate school on account of plagiarism. The instructor was hired on account of his ethnicity so as to comply with affirmative-action pressures. Cahn says that ethnicity should not be a primary consideration in any personnel decision. This leads to a discussion of hiring practices where phantom ads have been known to appear when the advertised position has already been filled and the ad is placed to comply with federal regulations.

After the break, Anthony De Prospero (representing the Student Government Association of Bergen Community College) asks Cahn whether he thinks it is inappropriate for professors to date their students. Cahn remarks that it is inappropriate inasmuch as professors are duty-bound to treat all students equally and fairly. He likens professors dating students to judges dating attorneys. Catherine Morrow (representing the Phi Theta Kappa Honors Society) asks Cahn how a student is to behave when he or she is aware that a fellow student intends to cheat on an exam. Cahn remarks that this is a hard question for which he has no answer, at least in schools that do not have honor codes. Finally, Claudia Stevens (representing the philosophy club at Bergen) asks Cahn about professors who show favoritism to students for whom they have a fondness, perhaps on account of that student's having excelled in a prior course with that professor. This occasions discussion about anonymous grading and related issues.

In this previously unpublished paper, Steven M. Cahn addresses the dearth of literature in the field of academic ethics. Writing in a casual and anecdotal style, Cahn notes how most professions have been examining standards of conduct relative to their field for nearly two decades with the notable exception of academia. Bemoaning this omission, he provides reasons why a foray into this field would be fruitful and helpful for academicians, students, and others connected with academia.

Ethics on Campus

Steven M. Cahn

For almost two decades, academics have been explaining in depth the standards of conduct appropriate to a variety of professions. The activities of physicians, nurses, lawyers, business managers, journalists, engineers, and government policy makers have all been subjected to critical scrutiny. Indeed, I learned recently[1] of the formation of a new scholarly journal devoted to the ethics of agricultural workers. Yet the conduct of one group of professionals has thus far escaped detailed investigation. No one has carefully examined the examiners: college and university members. What are the standards of conduct appropriate in teaching and grading students, appointing and assisting colleagues, and conducting and evaluating research? About these important matters we hear little.

Much has been written about the rights of professors, but comparatively little has been given to their corresponding responsibilities. Indeed, even to raise the subject of a professor's obligations strikes some members of the profession as an inappropriate intrusion into academic life.

I recall some years ago, at a meeting of the American Philosophical Association, seeing an old friend who had recently moved from one university to another. When I inquired how things were going in his new position, he looked glum and told me that one of his colleagues was causing a problem. This professor, it turned out, was regularly missing classes, failing to turn in grades, and generally ignoring department business. I sympathized with the problem, remarking that it was too bad when a tenured professor acted this way. But my friend said, "Oh no, the professor isn't tenured." "What's the problem then?" I asked. "It's the administration," my friend replied. "The administration," I said, "they're forcing you to reappoint this fellow." "Oh no," said my colleague," "They're forcing us to let him go. We all want to keep him. He's a very good philosopher."

I should mention, by the way, what my friend's specialty is in philosophy: he works in the field of professional ethics. There is one footnote to this story. When I met the fellow later that day, he asked me whether, given my administrative duties, I still found time to write any books. "Yes," I said. "In fact, I'm working on a book in your field, professional ethics." "Any particular profession?" he asked. "Yes," I replied," the ethics of professors." He seemed surprised. "That's very interesting," he said." "I've never thought much about that."

But why is this subject so neglected? One answer was offered at a meeting I attended some years ago while I was working at the

Rockefeller Foundation. After listening to specialists in professional ethics spend many hours discussing the ethics of doctors and lawyers, I suggested that perhaps the time had come to consider the ethics of teachers. One professor immediately responded that we should instead examine the ethics of those who worked at foundations. While agreeing that this subject might prove of interest, I reiterated my concerns about the importance of academic ethics. At that point, another participant remarked, "I agree with you. We need to examine the ethics of administrators." I then explained that what I proposed was not the ethics of administrators but the ethics of faculty members. A professor then raised his hand and expressed puzzlement at my suggestion. "After all," he said, "Why discuss the ethics of professors? We can't harm anyone."

I presume this professor would have agreed that his efforts could help others. But those who can help us can also harm us. This is why we need to choose carefully who will be our physician, our lawyer, or our teacher.

This point was made eloquently by Plato in the *Protagoras* dialogue.[2] A young man named Hippocrates implores Socrates to arrange for him to study with the famed Sophist Protagoras, who just arrived in town. Socrates urges Hippocrates to be careful, saying to him:

> If it were a case of putting your body into the hands of someone and risking the treatment's turning out beneficial or the reverse, you would deeply ponder whether to entrust it to him or not, and would spend many days over the question, calling on the counsel of your friends and relations. But when it comes to something which you value more highly than your body, namely your soul, something in whose beneficial treatment your whole welfare depends, you have not consulted your father or your brother or any of use who are your friends on the question of whether to entrust your soul to this stranger who has arrived among us.

A related insight was offered by the famed essayist Montaigne, who wrote:

> The acquisition of learning is much more dangerous than that of any other food or drink. For with other things, we carry home what we have bought in some vessel; and there we have leisure to examine its value and decide how much of it we shall use, and when. But learning, we cannot at the outset put in any other vessel but our minds; we swallow it as we buy it, and by the time we leave the market we are already either infected or improved. There is some that only obstructs and burdens us instead of nourishing us; and some too that, while pretending to cure us, gives us poison.[3]

A professor has the opportunity to affect what students believe, to alter their perception of the world, to change the way they think. And not only for the better. Indeed, I am convinced that after studying with particular instructors, students are likely to emerge less open-minded, less common-sensical, less tolerant, less flexible, less aware. Professors can frustrate students, mislead them, miseducate them, destroy their will to learn. Surely, then, professors can harm as well as help their students.

But the actions of professors do not only affect their students. The actions of professors can create good will among their colleagues or can cause discord, interfering with the efforts of others to concentrate on their work. Professors can be helpful in forwarding the careers of other scholars or, through malice or neglect, can cause careers to be derailed or even destroyed. Professors can act to benefit their own institutions, making them stronger, or they can act to undermine those institutions, contributing to their gradual decline.

Why are these obvious points so rarely made? Why do professors not like to be reminded of their potential for causing harm to others? The answer, I think, lies in the constraints that morality imposes. For professors are not accustomed to constraints. After all, typical tenured professors more or less set their own schedules. They teach virtually when they want and what they want. They keep whatever office hours they want, they attend such faculty meetings as they want, they accept committee assignments to the extent they want. They teach in whatever style they want, they evaluate students' work as they want, they give grades as they want. If anyone should attempt to interfere with these options, such intruders are apt to be viewed at best as naive or at worst as attackers of academic freedom.

Now, academic freedom is absolutely vital to the intellectual life of a college or university. Professors must have the right to pursue, teach, and publish the truth as they see it. But academic freedom is not equivalent to moral anarchy. And morality imposes limitations on personal pleasure. When one accepts an Aristotelian, Kantian, or utilitarian approach to ethics, the essence of morality remains the same: to be a moral person one must be sensitive and responsive to others. To act morally is to act not only out of concern for oneself but also out of concern for others.

Not many professors act in just this way, deeply concerned with the ways in which their actions affect their students and their colleagues. There are faculty members who act conscientiously, who prepare their classes with care, who grade scrupulously, who offer students extra help, who work with colleagues on departmental matters, and who can be counted on to participate constructively in a variety of faculty activities. In short, these are the professors who care about others.

But what about those who do not, those who are excessively concerned with seeking their own advantage or well-being without regard to the welfare of others? Such individuals typically reveal their true character in a variety of ways. They support curricula that reflect faculty interests rather than student needs; they organize their courses to cover whatever material they enjoy rather than material their students need to learn; their office hours are as short as possible, and not at times convenient to those who wish to visit; they

have on their desks unread manuscripts sent to them for review months before; they never seem to attend a committee meeting—every proposed time is inconvenient.

Unfortunately, one comes across evidence of such selfish behavior all too frequently. Consider, for instance, this excerpt from an article that appeared some time ago in *The New York Times* with the headline "Seminars Aid Princeton Freshman." (I'll substitute the name Smith for the one in the press.)

Professor Smith used to worry that most Princeton University freshman saw full professors, if at all, at the head of long crowded lecture halls.

So Professor smith, a history instructor, helped start a seminar program that put him at the head of the table.

This fall, Professor Smith is teaching one of four new courses that . . . allow small groups of freshmen to work closely with full professors. . . .

Professor Smith said the seminars offer professors a chance to teach unorthodox or innovative materials that normally would not survive scrutiny by faculty and students committees.

"You can teach courses that fairly follow your interest," he added. His seminar concerns magic in Europe from 1350 to 1630, a subject he has written about extensively. Professor Smith said, freshmen are just the intelligent audience of nonexperts on whom to test his latest ideas about magic. . . .

A freshmen said Professor Smith and the students in his magic seminar often continued debating long after the class period ends. "It's a real free exchange between the professor and the students," she said. She added that she does not mind the course's heavy reading load because it includes such works as translated 15th century documents on how to recognize a witch."

Now such freshman seminars are popular with professors and too often for the very reasons

Professor Smith provides. Those who teach them can follow their own interests and try out their research ideas on students. It's much more enjoyable to discuss one's own research with a small group than to give lectures to a large group on subjects one may not be so interested in. In fact, the headline in the newspaper should not have read: "Seminars Aid Princeton Freshman." It should have read: "Seminars Aid Princeton Professors."

A freshman may have read little or nothing of Plato, Dante, Hume, or George Elliot; may not know the difference between the Renaissance and the Reformation, may not know Raphael from Rembrandt or Beethoven from Bartok. Is it really Professor Smith's judgment that what freshman need most is to study fifteenth-century documents on how to recognize a witch?

Well, perhaps he believed so and perhaps his course is worthwhile. But I would have more confidence in the whole enterprise if he didn't defend it in terms of how well it served the advancement of his own scholarly career.

I happen to favor small classes rather than large lectures for freshmen, but the classes should focus on what students need to learn, not on what faculty members may happen to want to teach. At my alma mater, Columbia College, all freshmen take a year long humanities course, taught in sections of twenty, where an instructor leads students in a discussion of great works of literature from Homer through Dostoyevsky. As sophomores, all students meet in small sections to take a semester's course in the history of art and another semester's course in the history of music.

None of these courses is designed to maximize the professor's pleasure. Indeed, the courses are hard to teach because they force professors to stretch themselves beyond their special fields of interest.

These courses have been taught for fifty years, and students have generally enjoyed them. But that is not the basic argument for them. They are not only enjoyable; they are, I believe, the most valuable and richest materials that could be presented to those who are beginning their collegiate careers. It is for this

reason that faculty members over the years have been willing to make the effort to teach these courses.

I say "make an effort" and that is a key concept, for morality requires one to make an effort, to go beyond what is easiest for oneself and try to do what is helpful to others.

Professors are given the privilege of pursuing their own research interests and shaping the minds of future generations. What they should provide in return is attention to duty: a willingness to acknowledge their obligations and sacrifice some degree of personal comfort for the good of their students, their colleagues, their school, and ultimately their society.

The welfare of a democratic community depends on the quality of the education it offers. What is going on in the classrooms on our nation's campuses is not merely of concern to professors and students but affects the future welfare of our nation. That is why colleges and universities deserve generous financial support, but it is also why what professors do makes such a difference for good or ill.

All of us at one time or another have benefited from the kindness of a teacher. All of us have suffered from a teacher's meanness. I like to think the acts of generosity outnumber the acts of selfishness. But I would have greater confidence in this supposition if more often I heard professors say things like: "It's inconvenient for me to come, but I'll be there anyway to help out," or "I know which course I'd like to teach but the students need a different course, so I'll teach that one." Show me a school where professors talk like that, and I'll show you a good school.

During the late 1960s and early 1970s, institutions of higher education witnessed a variety of what were then termed "innovations." These were typically defended as better for students, improvements in the quality of their academic lives. But it is intriguing to note how many of these innovations turned out to be better for the faculty, improvements in the quality of their academic lives. When required courses were eliminated, it was easier for the faculty members who didn't have to teach them. When examinations were eliminated, it was easier for the faculty who didn't have to construct and grade them. When grades were eliminated, it was easier for the faculty who didn't have to argue with students about them.

Let me relate to you a story that highlights my essential point about selfishness. This is the tale of one professor I know who, despite being a tough grader, is extremely popular with the students at his college. He teaches core materials in captivating fashion and spends many hours in his office conferring with the students and advising them how to improve their performance. As one would expect, his classes are in great demand; many students wish to enroll in them. But his department has passed a rule that no more than twenty-five students can be registered in any department course. Although the classes this man teaches are typically not advanced seminars but lower-level survey courses, the strict limit remains. Meanwhile, students are desperate to enroll; a black market in registration cards has even developed. But the faculty will not relent; they refuse to open the course up to more students, even though the professor wants very much to do so. Instead, students who have paid in excess of $15,000 a year to study at the college cannot get admitted into a course they wish to take with an instructor who wishes to teach them.

Why has the department been so unwilling to allow any additional registration? Is it because twenty-five rather than thirty-two or forty-one is the ideal number for a class? If the instructor does not agree, why not give him a chance to teach the larger number and then see whether it works? Or why not have colleagues visit the class and see for themselves whether instruction with a somewhat larger group is still effective. But no, the department is adamant. Twenty-five is all it will be. And never mind the students who are demanding to be let in. It's their hard luck. So at the first day of class, numerous students appear and the instructor is forced to tell them that although he would like to teach them and although the classroom has plenty of room, most of them must, by departmental decree, leave the room.

But why is such an anti-educational policy in force? The answer is simple. The other professors are selfish. Their classes are not nearly as popular and they want to ensure that their own classrooms are not empty. So they limit enrollment in their colleague's course in the hope that students will choose other departmental offerings. I should add that, by and large, the students opt to take classes with outstanding teachers in other departments and continue to stay away from the courses they didn't want to take in the first place.

I confess that each time I tell the story of this department I become outraged all over again, for I can think of few actions more inimical to the mission of a college than to lock students out of a classroom to which they have come seeking the opportunity to learn.

You may wonder whether this school's administration is aware of this situation. As it happens, on one occasion the instructor informed the college's president about the matter. He listened sympathetically and then replied, "Wait a few years until you have more seniority in the department. Then maybe you can change things." Obviously, administrators can be as irresponsible as faculty members.

While I have stressed cases of academic malfeasance, let me not suggest that they are the rule rather than the exception. Indeed, to underline the point, let me tell you the story of a most impressive person whom I met years ago. She was fresh out of graduate school and arrived at my college campus to begin her teaching career. I have never known anyone more committed to fulfilling all her responsibilities in the most conscientious manner. She went to the head of the department before classes began to show him her syllabi and get his suggestions about them. Then, when the semester began she found out that one of her classes was not responding well to her teaching, and so she asked the departmental head to visit her class, watch her teach, and make suggestions. After a few visits by the head and several hours of subsequent discussion with him, the situation very much improved. She always prepared for classes with the greatest care. She held office hours for students most afternoons, and the students, sensing her concern for them, used to come by in great numbers.

While working hard to perfect her teaching, she read papers at national conventions and submitted articles to professional journals. At first the articles were rejected because her style was quite dense. But eventually, after she revised her work with the help of her colleagues, her style improved, and her papers began to be accepted by prestigious journals. She was an active participant in departmental activities and could be counted on to volunteer whenever help was needed.

On one occasion the provost of the university called her department head and angrily charged that the department had acted improperly in some manner. The provost demanded that the head appear in less than an a hour accompanied by another member of the department to explain what the department had done. This professor was relaxing at home, tending to some personal business, when she was alerted to the situation. She immediately volunteered for this hazardous assignment, rushed over to school, went in with the department head to the provost, faced the provost's ire, and succeeded in persuading him that he was in the wrong and that the department had acted properly.

Never did she let any student or colleague down, and when she became a veteran teacher, she did for junior colleagues what others had done for her, helping them with their teaching and assisting them in preparing their work for publication. Today she is a senior member of the profession nationally renowned for her scholarship and celebrated on her campus as an inspiring teacher.

Many professors have had the pleasure of working with such a colleague, for to know a faculty member of this sort reminds one how noble the life of a professor can be. After all, what activity could be more worthwhile than acquiring knowledge and guiding others in acquiring it?

I shall never forget the late 1960s, when faculty members would say in private that they ought to vote one way on some issue, and then in public they would buckle under pressure and vote the other way. But it is not easy to stand up and be counted. Indeed, anyone who has chosen academic life in the hope of avoiding tough decisions has selected the wrong profession. Professors are constantly faced with the challenge of maintaining standards of excellence: in classrooms, in departmental meetings, in faculty meetings, whenever their advice is sought, whenever their recommendations are requested, whenever their evaluations are needed. In all these circumstances, a professor's academic integrity is on the line.

I should like to close by relating one final anecdote, this about a professor, call him Jones, whose conscientiousness and rectitude were legendary at his university. Once, at a meeting of his school's Phi Beta Kappa chapter, a question arose as to whether the list of students being proposed for new membership by the nominations committee reflected prejudice on the part of the committee members. Angry charges began to be hurled about the room, and things began to get out of hand. But then someone interrupted the proceedings and said with a sense of finality, "Look, there's nothing to argue about. This list must be right. It was approved by Professor Jones." Immediately, the debate stopped and without any further comment from anyone, the list of names was approved. For if Professor Jones had certified the list as fair, it was inconceivable to colleagues that the list could be unfair.

Few can attain such an unquestionable reputation for probity, but all professors are obligated to try.

ENDNOTES

1. This article was originally written as a speech April 11,1991.
2. Plato. *Protagoras.* In the *Collected Dialogues.* Edited by Edith Hamilton and Huntington Cairns, pp. 309–313. (Princeton, N.J.: Princeton Univ. Press) 1973.
3. Montaigne, Michel Eyquem de. *The Essays.* Translated by Jacob Zeitlin, 3 vols. New York, 1934–1936.

Closing Questions

1. What penalty, in your view, should be imposed on students who plagiarize other students' work?

   _____

   _____

   _____

   _____

2. How much say, if any, should students have in determining course content?

   _____

   _____

   _____

   _____

3. What should a professor do if threatened by a student to award an undeserved grade?

   _____

   _____

   _____

   _____

4. What is the distinction between education and indoctrination? Is it indoctrination if a professor espouses a position on an issue, say abortion, which he or she is convinced is correct?

   _____

   _____

   _____

   _____

5. Some professors receive prominent appointments at universities but never teach a course even though their names are listed next to a section. In this case, teaching assistants have responsibility for the course. What reasons support such a practice? What reasons argue against it?

_____

_____

_____

_____

6. How would you evaluate a professor who propositioned a student by promising her an A if she slept with him, but who insisted that he would assign her the grade she deserved if she did not?

_____

_____

_____

_____

7. Should the grading system be abolished? Argue pro or con.

_____

_____

_____

_____

8. How should a university respond to a professor who typically makes sexist, racist, or anti-Semitic remarks in class? How should a professor respond to students who make such comments in class? To what extent should a black professor kowtow to an overtly racist student?

_____

_____

_____

_____

9. Several years ago, I had a student to whom I had assigned a grade of "incomplete." About three years later, she sought to hand in her missing work at which time I refused to accept it. Arguing that she was entitled to hand in the work inasmuch as I never explicitly indicated a due date (verbally or on the syllabus), I countered her argument with the claim that a reasonable period of time was nonetheless implied. On appeal to the Academic Standing Committee, the student won and I was compelled to accept her paper. Do you agree with this decision? Argue pro or con.

_____

_____

_____

_____

10. Several years ago, I had a student who turned in a research paper replete with quotations but lacking any references. I refused to accept the paper, claiming it was plagiarized. In yet another challenge before the Academic Standing Committee (see Question 9), I was informed that in order to prove plagiarism, I would have to locate the exact sources the student used in his paper and prove that he intentionally misappropriated them. Not knowing from where the student took his quotations, I was unable to do so and lost the appeal. Since the student's paper was an excellent one, I was also obliged to give him an A. Was the decision of Academic Standing sound? How should a professor handle plagiarized papers? If other students in your course are plagiarizing, how should you? If you are caught, having plagiarized, should you be expelled? Given the chance to rewrite the assignment?

_____

_____

_____

_____

For Further Readings

Atherton, M., S. Morgenbesser, and R. Schwartz. "On Tenure." *Philosophical Forum* 10 (1979): 341–352.

Cahn, Steven M. *Saints and Scamps: Ethics in Academia.* Savage, Md.: Rowman & Littlefield, 1986.

————, ed. *Morality, Responsibility and the University: Studies in Academic Ethics.* Philadelphia, Temple University Press, 1990.

Hook, Sidney. *In Defense of Academic Freedom.* New York: Pegasus, 1971.

Hook, Sidney, Paul Kurtz, and Miro Todorovich, eds. *The Ethics of Teaching and Scientific Research.* Buffalo: Prometheus, 1977.

Jaggar, Alison. "Tenure, Academic Freedom, and Professional Competence." *Philosophical Forum* 10 (1979): 360–370.

Markie, Peter J. *Professor's Duties: Ethics Issues in College Teaching.* Savage, Md.: Rowman & Littlefield, 1994.

Robinson, George M., and Janice Moulton. *Ethical Problems in Higher Education.* Englewood Cliffs, N.J.: Prentice Hall, 1985.

Schneewind, Jerome. "On 'On Tenure.'" *Philosophical Forum* 10 (1979): 353–359.

Shils, Edward. *The Academic Ethics.* Chicago: University of Chicago Press, 1983.

Chapter 17

Moral Education of Children

Passages for Reflection

"Who knows the thoughts of a child?"
—*Nora Perry*

"No one has yet fully realized the wealth of sympathy, kindness and generosity hidden in the soul of a child. The effort of every true education should be to unlock that treasure."
—*Emma Goldman*

"Children are natural mythologists: they beg to be told tales, and love not only to invent but to enact falsehoods."
—*George Santanyana*

Opening Questions

1. Can virtue be taught?
2. Do men and women develop morally in different ways?
3. What is the difference between moral education and indoctrination?

In his dialogue *Meno* (87c–99e), Plato has Socrates consider whether virtue can be taught. While we never get an explicit answer, Socrates suggests that if virtue could be taught, we would know both teachers and students of virtue. Since Socrates was convinced that even the most exemplary Athenians had children who were not virtuous, he concluded that virtue cannot be taught and that it is instead a gift from the gods.

While few of us today might think that virtue is a gift from the gods, the question Plato asked more than two millennia ago still challenges us. Most of us are challenged by the problem of deciding what and how to teach virtue, or moral behavior, even assuming that it is possible to teach it.

We can identify several reasons for this. One is that many of us lack confidence in our knowledge of right and wrong. Call this the "problem of skepticism." Given a climate in which tolerance of diversity is revered as the most important moral virtue, many of us believe that what counts as true is culturally determined. Many of us believe that the values we hold dear are not held dear in other cultures, that absolute values cannot be found that we can confidently pass down from generation to generation. This being so, moral education strikes many of us as arbitrary.

It also seems presumptuous. If we cannot be sure whether our values are "correct" or, for that matter, that any competing values are "correct," then we are presumptuous in trying to pass off one moral code as definitive. Here is a second reason why we are challenged about how and what to teach our children. Call this the "problem of indoctrination." Aware of the thought control and social manipulation that characterized fascist governments in recent times (for example, the former USSR), we are wary that by imparting to our children our own moral code, we will be indoctrinating them no less than did the totalitarian states of times gone by. Read Aldous Huxley's *Brave New World* or George Orwell's *1984* to see the dangers posed by this kind of mind control.

A challenge is posed by the "problem of autonomy." This challenge comes to us by way of psychologist Lawrence Kohlberg, who has argued that passing on to children moral precepts and prohibitions, a list of dos and don'ts, invariably compromises a child's autonomy. It interferes with the child's ability to appreciate for herself what her duty is as a rational moral agent.

Compare our present misgivings about moral education with classical Aristotelianism. Aristotle had no compunctions about teaching children moral conduct. He thought that proper upbringing was needed for people to take pleasure, as adults, in acting according to what virtue requires and to suffer pain when practicing vice. By rewarding good behavior and punishing bad, Aristotle was convinced that the child's character would be molded into what it ought to become.

Aristotle was not confronted as much by the challenges of skepticism, relativism, and indoctrination. He identified with only one state—the city-state of Athens—and the ethic of that era was firmly rooted in what the Greeks were convinced was an essential human nature. Since human beings, in this view, are rational animals, the good life turned out to be a life wherein a person's animality is governed by reason. A successful moral education, then, habituates the person to live an animal life guided by reason.

But how, we might ask, do we respect this fact? How, exactly, do we become virtuous? We become virtuous, said Aristotle, by performing virtuous acts habitually until such time when virtue has become second nature. We acquire the virtue of courage, for example, by being exposed to dangerous situations and acting appropriately—which for Aristotle meant acting in moderation—and by having such conduct reinforced and rewarded. In this way, we grow up having the disposition to exhibit the right amount of courage when faced with dangerous situations. Moral education, then, is like physical education. Just as we become fit by doing things that require strength, we become good by behaving virtuously. Furthermore, just as our becoming fit in large part depends on a coach or trainer to lead us along, so, too, our ability to acquire virtue depends on a role model to lead us along. This, for Aristotle, was to take the form of a person who had a reputation in the community as a person of good moral character.

If, then, a person is blessed with a good upbringing and is fortunate enough to have had a training wherein virtue has become internalized, then the person is in a position as an adult to understand the reasons his actions are virtuous and to choose those actions simply for himself. On the other hand, not having had such an upbringing, not having had the discipline with which to confront the appreciation of the various virtues, moral philosophy would have little value. (Hitler would not have been a good ethics student, whereas Socrates was.) Such an understanding is the task of moral philosophy as conceived by Aristotle. Its purpose is to teach the reasons behind virtuous conduct. Equipped with this understanding, Aristotle is able to escape the problem of autonomy leveled at critics of moral education. For Aristotle, acting morally is acting with reason after a good moral start.

Notice how, for Aristotle, moral education is not a matter of haranguing our children with moral sermons, although this may be one means of instilling in them a virtuous character. Instead, the desired effect of moral education is to habituate children to feel displeased by what is wrong and delighted by what is right. Later, when children develop their ability to reason and acquire an understanding of the social and political world of adults, they can analyze what they learned as children. Until then, we habituate children by being role models.

We also habituate children by teaching them stories that set moral examples. By reading Aesop's "The Goose that Laid the Golden Egg," for example, we teach our children what happens when we are overcome with greed; by reading Margaret Williams's "The Velveteen Rabbit," we teach the value of friendship; by reading Aesop's "The Boy Who Cried Wolf," we teach the virtue of honesty. And if we are to believe William J. Bennett, whose book *The Book of Virtues* has become a best seller, the Aristotelian method of teaching the virtues also provides our children with moral literacy to make sense of what they see in life. It gives children reference points to make sense of their experiences, it helps anchor them in American culture, and it introduces them to a world of shared ideals.[1]

But we cannot move easily from Aristotle to Bennett. Whereas Aristotle's Athens had little concern for other peoples' ways of life since everyone shared the same ideals, in contemporary American society, pluralism and diversity are a fact of life. We cannot gloss over the diversity of American culture and speak of educating our young on "American culture" and exposing them to a "world of shared ideals." Instead, as Lawrence Kohlberg has argued, the task that confronts us is to teach children how to be autonomous (self-determining) and how to create self-designed life plans while we do not fall prey to indoctrinating them.

In his book *The Philosophy of Moral Development*, Kohlberg's express aim is "to demonstrate that moral education can be free from the charge of cultural relativism and arbitrary indoctrination." Drawing on the work of Piaget, who claimed that children go through moral stages involving changes in their understanding of moral rules, Kohlberg aspires to understand the concepts and reasoning involved in moral judgment and how they change in an individual over the course of time. He interprets moral development as a progression through stages characterized by different ways of understanding the world. According to Kohlberg, all children begin with what he calls a preconventional first level in which morality is determined largely by expected punishment and reward. They then move on to a conventional second level where social norms and need for approval dominate. From there, they progress to a postconventional third level where they are self-motivated to address universal moral principles, which enables them to transcend their own self-centeredness. The task of moral education, then, becomes the task of assisting students to move from one stage to another. This

---

[1]William J. Bennett, *The Book of Virtues* (New York: Simon & Schuster, 1993).

is brought about primarily through discussion of problematic moral dilemmas such as Kohlberg's famous "Heinz dilemma." In this hypothetical case, students meet someone named Heinz who lacks money to buy a lifesaving drug but obtains it by robbing a druggist. In asking children whether Heinz did the right thing, we sharpen their moral sensibility and help them move from the preconventional to the postconventional level.

But how does this avoid the problem of indoctrination? Kohlberg's answer is that this sequence of stages is universal and applies to all individuals in all cultures even though different individuals in different cultures may fail to move beyond a certain stage. In this manner, Kohlberg is able to reject the Aristotelian approach favored by Bennett, while avoiding the charge of relativism and the challenges that go with it.

Like Piaget before him, and also like John Dewey whose theory of childhood education revolutionized how America educates its young, Kohlberg stresses social cooperation for stimulating development.[2] Dewey argued that the individual goes through three stages in moral development. (Three is a favorite number among child development theorists.) At first, nonmoral needs such as nourishment are what motivate the individual. Next, the individual uncritically accepts group customs and moral standards. Finally, the individual becomes self-governing and reasons for herself or himself what is good or right.

For Dewey, the development from one stage to another is a process through which the individual becomes increasingly rational, social, and moral. Through various forms of cooperation, the individual acquires an increased aptitude for social relations and develops a greater awareness of the interests of others. In what has become his most famous legacy, Dewey insisted that this process be incorporated into the educational curriculum and not isolated from the broader contexts of inquiry in which moral concerns characteristically appear. He was particularly critical of the rigid and formal approach to education that characterized American schools in the latter part of the nineteenth century. He believed that this approach was predicated on the belief that children were passive creatures ready to be molded by the information and knowledge imposed on them. Viewing children as active, curious, and exploring creatures, Dewey instead argued that education ought to be a continuous reconstruction of experience as immature experiences develop toward more sophisticated ones underwritten by the skills of intelligence. The way to accomplish this, he argued, was to create the right kind of environment. This, for Dewey, meant constructing a miniature society that was to be the school. The school, he argued, should represent the institutions of the society wherein the classroom becomes a community of inquirers in which students cooperatively solve problems.

---

[2]See John Dewey, *Experience and Education* (New York: Collier Books, 1971).

Like Dewey, Kohlberg regarded social activities, in which children have opportunities to respond to the needs of others, as essential to moral development. Such activities, for Kohlberg, provide the social experience and cognitive challenges for transitions from one stage of development to another.

Whatever the differences among Piaget, Dewey, and Kohlberg, all agree that the individual evolves through stages, and they consider the highest stage to be where the individual is autonomous and uses abstract principles to settle moral affairs. This view has recently come under attack by Carol Gilligan who, in her book *In a Different Voice*,[3] has attacked Kohlberg in particular for concentrating too heavily on male subjects. In concluding that the highest stage of moral development is the one where the individual uses abstract principles to settle moral issues, Kohlberg found that women typically failed to reach this stage and thus had an immature approach to moral problems. Gilligan, on the basis of several studies incorporating both males and females, concludes that males and females address moral problems differently, one not being any better or worse than the other.

Gilligan argues that women, unlike men, emphasize a "care perspective" rather than an impersonal "justice perspective." Utilizing the findings of Nancy Chodorow, who argued that women are more attuned to others and that their moral ideals are defined through emotional attachment rather than impersonal separation, Gilligan argues that an ethic that is sensitive to the ideals of responsibility and care would do more justice to women than would an ethic that had women fixed at an earlier stage of development.

For Gilligan, the two distinct moral orientations have their origin in early childhood experiences. Where, as in most places, women are the primary caretakers of young children, identity formation in girls rests on their attachment to their mothers. The identity of boys, in contrast, is formed through an experience of separation from the mother. Consequently, females tend to define themselves in terms of their relationships with others, while the male experience of separating from others is usually central to male identity formation. Gilligan's criticism of Kohlberg, then, arises from what she sees as a failure to take seriously the differences in moral development between males and females. If she is right, such differences must be accounted for in our approach to moral education.

Other theories of moral development exist. The most infamous of these is that of Freud and the psychoanalytic tradition. For Freud and his followers, the child is born with sexual and aggressive drives that become frustrated by parental constraint. Fearing punishment and loss of parental love, the child learns to internalize the standards of the parents. Guilt, by the age of five or six, comes to replace punishment in controlling the

---

[3]Carol Gilligan, *In a Different Voice* (Cambridge, Mass.: Harvard University Press, 1982).

child's behavior. In this model, the task of moral education becomes the task of getting the child to identify with the parents and internalize the parents' or society's standards.

A common thread running through the theories of Aristotle, Kohlberg, Piaget, and Freud is the idea that moral reasoning plays no role in early childhood moral education. For each of these theorists, the child is viewed as a highly egocentric creature lacking the cognitive ability for moral reflection. This model of the child is a pervasive one and is reflected in the way we often "talk down" to children and refuse to teach them philosophy. It is also reflected in philosophical thought. Speaking of infants at least, Jeremy Bentham contended that they "had not yet attained that state or disposition of mind" in which "the whispers of simple morality" will influence their future conduct. John Stuart Mill referred to children as creatures not "in the maturity of their faculties," and Kant emphasized children's lack of ability to make rational decisions and the ability to be autonomous.

But is this model appropriate? The answer to this question has implications for moral education. If, as Aristotle believed, the child is incapable of moral reflection, then moral education might well be a matter of teaching children to associate pleasure with what is right and pain with what is bad, as we hope that grown children will choose right actions for themselves. But if the children are not the intellectual simpletons that many suppose, then our approach to moral education should reflect that fact.

Matthew Lipman and Gareth Matthews are two philosophers who object to viewing children as intellectual simpletons. For them, children are far more able and eager to think abstractly than adults generally recognize, even if the experiences of children are limited. Convinced that children are natural philosophers, Lipman founded the highly successful Institute for the Advancement of Philosophy for Children in the 1970s when it dawned on educators that a major aim of education is to make children more reasonable and that the way to do this is to improve their thinking. They reasoned that if reading and writing are taught to children under the discipline of literature, then reasoning and judgment could be taught to children under the discipline of philosophy. As with reading and writing, which children learn how to do, so, too, they reasoned, critical thinking might be something children learn how to do. They can only "do" such thinking if they have the ability to do it and not, as Aristotle and others suggest, if they are unable to do it until later in their lives.

While Piaget and Kohlberg believed that children could not "think about thinking" to any degree until the age of ten or eleven, Lipman drew different conclusions. He found children to be highly developed in their cognitive abilities before the age of seven or eight. By introducing children to texts in the form of stories, Lipman found that they discover how to reason effectively and how to apply their reasoning to life situations. The students would deliberate among themselves, and this process of deliberation would be internalized.

In *Dialogues with Children*[4] and, to a lesser extent, *Philosophy and the Young Child*,[5] Gareth Matthews has documented children's abilities to engage in philosophical analysis. The following story, taken from *Dialogues*, illustrates children's ability to understand epistemology (theory of knowledge). It occurs after a class of kindergartners had planted lettuce seeds:

Eddie: . . . how do we know it's really lettuce?

Teacher: The label says "Bibb Lettuce."

Eddie: What if it's really tomatoes?

Teacher: Oh. Are you wondering about the picture of tomatoes with the lettuce on the packet? It's just an idea for salad, after the lettuce comes.

Warren: They might think they're lettuce seeds and they might not know.

Earl: Maybe the seed looks the same as something else.

Teacher: Do you think they could make such a mistake?

Lisa: Just bring it back to the store if it's wrong.

Deana: The store people didn't even make it.

Eddie: You have to take it back to the gardener.

Deana: Maybe they printed a word they wanted to spell the wrong way. Maybe they mixed it up.

Eddie: They could have meant to put different seeds in there and then they turned around and went to the wrong table.

Wally: The wrong part of the garden. The tomato part.

Warren: So in case it's not lettuce it could be tomatoes.[6]

What these children are doing, as students of epistemology would know, is nothing less than challenging the warrant for believing our claims to knowledge. It is only one of several stories in the book substantiating Matthews's claim that children are natural philosophers. This should hardly surprise us since children and philosophy both begin in wonder.

My experience has confirmed Lipman and Matthews's findings if only on an anecdotal level and then, too, with an extremely gifted child. After reading Lipman and Matthews, I decided to test out their theory on my son, Joshua, who at the time was six years old. The story I recall most vividly is when Joshua had difficulty articulating an incident that

---

[4]Gareth Matthews, *Dialogues with Children* (Cambridge, Mass: Harvard University Press, 1984.)

[5]Gareth Matthews, *Philosophy and the Young Child* (Cambridge, Mass: Harvard University Press, 1980.)

[6]From Vivian Gussin Paley, *Walley's Stories* (Cambridge, Mass: Harvard University Press, 1981), pp. 183–184. Cited in Matthews, *Dialogues with Children*, pp. 49–50.

occurred in school one day. Drawing upon the philosophy of Ludwig Wittgenstein—a practice neither Lipman nor Matthews would condone—I said to Joshua: "Whereof we cannot speak, thereof we must be silent." (That is, "we ought not to speak about what we cannot say anything.") I explained to him what Wittgenstein meant by this and left the matter at that, not quite sure if he grasped its significance. Only several months later did I learn for sure that Wittgenstein's idea was not lost on Joshua. Joshua was observing me filling out an insurance form and asked me to explain what I was doing. After having difficulty at making the concept of insurance clear to him, I remarked that I know what insurance is, I just can't explain it to him. "Papa," he said in a condescending tone, "whereof we cannot speak, thereof we must be silent." Since then, I eagerly discuss my philosophical thoughts with Joshua with some fruitful results. (See p. 574 where I thank Joshua who, at the age of eight, caught me in a serious philosophical error.)

I mention this incident because I do not believe that it is unusual given the findings of Matthews and Lipman. (I also mention it because I want to brag about Joshua.) The problem is that adults are disposed to stifle philosophical discussion and instead rely on a model of education that Dewey had argued against which sees children as passive creatures ready to be molded by ideas that adults in their "wisdom" impose on them. Such stifling of philosophical reflection comes by way of adults turning aside their children's queries with such irritated responses as, "Oh, you know what I mean," or, "Why? Because I say so!" As Matthews points out, parents and teachers who refuse to enter into dialogue with their children discourage the spirit of intellectual inquiry.[7]

If, however, children are natural philosophers inherently enthusiastic about philosophical inquiry, then encouraging them to think critically has many advantages. One is that this would be an ideal way of having children study values, since in philosophy conceptual analysis plays an important role, and values are important concepts. In this model, we can better instill in our children the intellectual apparatus needed to handle the daunting moral problems that await them as adults. That children are capable of imaginative and provocative moral thought is evinced by the following example, again taken from Matthews.

> Ian (six years) found to his chagrin that the three children of his parents' friends monopolized the television; they kept him from watching his favorite program. "Mother," he asked in frustration, "why is it better for three people to be selfish than for one?"[8]

---

[7]Matthews, *Philosophy and the Young Child*, p. 21.

[8]Matthews, *Philosophy and the Young Child*, p. 28. Discussed in Michael S. Pritchard, "Moral Education: From Aristotle to Harry Stottlemeier." In Ann Margaret Sharp and Ronald F. Reed, eds., *Studies in Philosophy for Children* (Philadelphia: Temple University Press, 1992), pp. 20–21.

Ian's response is a challenge to utilitarian thinking and even has remarkable affinities with the work of the utilitarian critic, John Taurek.[9] In the light of Lipman and Matthews's work, you have to wonder how it is that American educators have not seen fit to incorporate philosophy into the precollege classroom.

The findings of Lipman and Matthews are not just relevant for educating young children. Nick Dianuzzo, a student of Lipman, has successfully employed Lipman's methods in assisting adolescents with narcotics addiction, getting them to critically examine the costs and benefits of their errant ways and to confront their addiction in a more rational manner. In Europe, especially, but also in America, a movement exists to view philosophy as a form of therapy. In America, an American Society for Philosophy, Counseling, and Psychotherapy has recently been established. Viewing philosophy as a tool in this manner is an exciting if controversial endeavor, but it is likely to be taken seriously given Martha C. Nussbaum's recent study of Hellenistic ethics. In her intriguingly titled book, *The Therapy of Desire*, Nussbaum takes seriously the work of Epicureans, Skeptics, and Stoics who saw philosophy not as a detached intellectual discipline but as an art of grappling with issues of daily human significance.[10]

---

[9]See John Taurek, "Should the Numbers Count?" *Philosophy and Public Affairs*, 6, 4 (Summer 1977): 293–310. Reprinted in my *Doing and Being: Selected Readings in Moral Philosophy* (New York: Macmillan, 1993), pp. 51–60.

[10]Martha C. Nussbaum, *The Therapy of Desire: Theory and Practice in Hellenistic Ethics* (Princeton, N.J.: Princeton University Press, 1994).

Matthew Lipman is Professor of Philosophy at Montclair State University. Author of numerous books and articles, he is also the founder of the Institute for the Advancement of Philosophy for Children.

Nick Dianuzzo is a former student of Matthew Lipman. He presently teaches philosophy at Passaic Community College.

Video Presentation

Guests: Matthew Lipman, Montclair State University, Institute for the Advancement of Philosophy for Children

Nick Dianuzzo, Passaic Community College, Straight and Narrow Drug Rehabilitation Center

Student Panel: Lisi Mediavilla, Elizabeth Ardizone, Wendy Harknett

I begin our discussion by asking Lipman and Dianuzzo to tell us about the Institute for the Advancement of Philosophy for Children (IAPC) and Straight and Narrow Drug Rehabilitation Center. Lipman, who founded IAPC in 1974, tells us that the Institute develops materials whose purpose is to teach children the art of ethical inquiry as well as to train professors to teach teachers how to effectively use the materials. The materials, which are in use in schools largely in Europe but also in the United States, center around stories depicting children engaged in reasoning and concept formation which they deliberate about in a "community of inquiry." (The phrase is from John Dewey, whom Lipman later mentions as the philosopher who has most influenced him.) We are told that the stories for the younger children are "mild" and consist of such "plots" as a mother and daughter disagreeing on what clothes to buy. The point is that the children reading the stories are exposed to situations of conflict where the mother and the daughter give reasons for their respective choice of clothes. The instructor, acting as a facilitator, then prompts the children to analyze the reasons put forward. As a result, the children develop their ability to make ethical judgments.

Nick Dianuzzo tells us that he works for the Straight and Narrow Drug Rehabilitation Center of the Board of Education of Paterson, New Jersey. There he utilizes Lipman's methods to help juveniles work through their chemical dependencies. He also does this by establishing a community of inquirers who analyze and discuss various scenarios involving drug addiction.

At this point, I ask Lipman how much philosophizing we can expect from young children since so many children, when asked, for instance, why they should be given something they cannot have, respond with a childish: "Because, I want it!" (Dianuzzo chips in that so many of his students initially do no better than this when asked why they should be provided with illegal drugs!) Lipman's answer is that until the age of eleven or twelve, students will not be adept at reason-giving; they become more adept at moral reasoning when they discuss what count as good reasons in assorted situations. Echoing this point, Dianuzzo notes that in a period of nine months, his students' reasoning abilities evolve from "I want to" to "the majority rules" to the point where they become "critics of utilitarianism."

We shift our discussion to the success and failures of IAPC and to its reception by the teaching community. Lipman observes that despite its enormous success, some teachers resist it. Instead, they remain committed to a more traditional approach in which philosophy is left out of the curriculum. He thinks that part of this resistance is justified inasmuch as philosophers in the past have tended to concentrate more on the analysis of ethical terms (metaethics) than on solving practical ethical issues. Later in the show, Lipman remarks that the philosophical community is generally receptive of his program, although it has not shown great enthusiasm. I also ask Dianuzzo how his use of Lipman's methods differs from traditional psychotherapy and whether his employment of these methods is at all therapeutic. This occasions discussion of the differences between Dianuzzo's methods and psychotherapy, as well as Lipman's methods and the "values clarification" movement that was in vogue in this country several years ago.

Following the break, Wendy Harknett asks Lipman about the extent to which parents utilize IAPC's materials on their own. Elizabeth Ardizone asks Dianuzzo how he stays clear of indoctrinating his students. And Lisi

Mediavilla asks Lipman how successful his program is and whether he has encountered much opposition from parents who think that morality is best taught at home. In speaking of the program's success, Lipman points out that IAPC has been selected to illustrate moral education as part of the distinguished Education 2000 program and has also been named Meritorious Education Program by the U.S. Department of Education.

In this previously unpublished essay, Matthew Lipman argues for the need to introduce philosophy into the primary school curriculum as part of a general program for educational reform. Maintaining that children are acutely aware of the world around them, rather than being the innocent babies critics of his proposal sometimes suggest, Lipman argues that we do no justice to children by denying them the ability to approach their world with a critical eye. He argues that philosophy liberates children when it allows them to examine their ideas in a critical but sympathetic environment.

Philosophy in the Primary School Curriculum

Matthew Lipman

I suppose that it's no secret that many people are dissatisfied with public education, both at the university level and the secondary and primary levels. But since primary education comes first, it is extremely important because the students who are going to secondary school and into colleges later on have their minds already shaped by the primary education they received. And so, if we're going to reform university education, I don't think we can do so at all without reforming secondary and primary education, for the products of this education will become the students and teachers of the future. Therefore, primary education has got to be carefully but thoroughly restructured.

You can advocate reform very passionately. Nevertheless, you have to have some idea of what you are going to do. What are the goals? What are the criteria? What sort of educated person do you want? We must propose goals for a reflective education and devise means suitable to achieve these goals.

To be very brief about it, let's assume that the goal of education is to educate students so that they become reasonable people. In other words, let's assume that the goal of education is reasonableness. Why? Because you cannot preserve democracy if the students the schools are turning out are not reasonable people, but are uncritical, unreflective, and prejudiced.

Democracy, to be vital and efficient, requires reflective citizens. It requires a structured approach so the processes that lead up to democracy are shaped and established by thinking human beings, not just learned human beings. You know the expression in English: you can be a learned ignoramus. You can be learned, have a lot of knowledge, but still be foolish, impulsive, or gullible because you don't think, because you are not reflective.

We want our students to think. When I say we, I don't mean just school teachers and school administrators, but all educators and parents. I think that parents generally, when they send their kids to school, have the secret hope in their heart that the school will teach their kids how to think, especially if they themselves have failed to teach them to think. Teach them to think, make them think, parents insist. This is one reason why education for thinking has not distressed parents. It has encouraged them. It has given them something they've always wanted.

But there are some educators who wish to preserve the status quo in education. These educators have been unable to devise ways of making children think and don't want to change the way in which they have been working until now. But you're always going to have people who continue to believe in the same traditional ways things have always been done, even though these ways aren't working very well. So what do you do to make education, especially on the primary school level, productive of thinking?

One thing you could aim at is to teach for thinking across the curriculum. You could aim to get children thinking in every lesson, in every subject, in every area, and in every moment of school life, on the playground, at lunchtime, in arithmetic, in natural science, in biological science, in language arts, in every moment of their activity. But how do you do it? What do you do to stimulate them, guide them, and nurture them into thinking across the curriculum? There is a traditional answer. It goes so far back that maybe people will feel that it is archaic or obsolete. That answer is the discipline called philosophy. *Philosophy is the discipline that prepares people to think in the other disciplines.*

We already have philosophy in the university. What is the function of philosophy in the university? Can you imagine all the philosophy departments removed? Just by some stroke, by some strange turn of events, suppose that there is no more philosophy? What would happen?

I would say that the people in each discipline would become more buried in their disciplines than they were ever before. They would become more specialized, more narrow, more technical than ever before. Now, the answer to this will be very quick. Are you accusing us, us in the other disciplines, of narrowness, specialization, and technical language? You in philosophy who speak only in obscure and technical jargon?

Yes, philosophy is guilty of all those things. But it has taken seriously its role of being a kind of clearinghouse of ideas on the university campus. It has been the discipline where ideas come together and interpenetrate one another. Philosophy departments are made up of people who feel some competence in at least some other discipline and possibly in many other disciplines. As a result, you have these subdisciplines of philosophy: the philosophy of education, philosophy of art, philosophy of science, philosophy of literature, and philosophy of many other areas.

Philosophy is never comfortable just by itself. It is comfortable only when it spreads over its banks and overflows into the whole terrain around it. And therefore, by its very nature, philosophy is a discipline that seeks to penetrate into the other disciplines. When you learn philosophy you learn to become skilled in thinking in the other disciplines, not just in the discipline of philosophy. You learn to penetrate intellectually into the concepts of physics, literature, art, education, or whatever. So, philosophy as practiced on the graduate school level already has this kind of preparation for thinking, for thinking in the disciplines, in its nature.

The question that might now be asked is, "That's all very well in university and we promise not to eliminate the philosophy departments, but can you make it available to children?"

I think that if you perform a few fairly simple operations on philosophy you can make it available to children. You can get rid of the abstract, obscure terminology. You can put it in the form of stories that children would be interested not only in reading but in reading together. You can present philosophy in dialogue rather than in lecture form. That will make philosophy more interesting.

You can, moreover, try to reshape the teacher's role so that he or she is no longer an all-knowing authority figure but, rather, a co-enquirer. The teacher becomes someone who shares and animates intellectual inquiry that is going on in the classroom. There are also other things that can be done.

Well, you might say, yes, these things *can* be done—but maybe they *shouldn't* be done. Maybe children don't need philosophy. Maybe children don't want philosophy. Why impose it on them? It is going to violate their innocence, the innocence of childhood? You are going to load them down with all sorts of philosophical notions. It's going to make them very gloomy and miserable. Keep philosophy away from them.

But I do not think that this is the case. Children do not lead lives which are totally sheltered from reality and from meaningful thought. They are aware that there is death as well as life going on. They are aware that there are financial problems and family problems, that there are all sorts of problems people go through that require reflection and solving. Not to help children think about the things that trouble them only makes them more troubled.

Furthermore, it's not a benefit to children to protect them from philosophy. On the contrary, philosophy can be a source of comfort and of healing to children. At the very least, philosophy gives them the feeling that they are thinking about the problems that they are faced with rather than doing nothing about them.

More than that, I think children not only need philosophy, they want it. We have seen in various parts of the world that children respond very warmly, very cordially when they have an opportunity to discuss things openly, especially when there is no final answer that some text or teacher provides. Children are excited by the opportunity or the freedom to discuss things for themselves. Suddenly, they feel a sense of liberation.

Both a cognitive and affective liberation goes with doing philosophy. They have been shielded from the activity of learning and thinking together. Children feel liberated to have their opinions sought out, their views listened to, their perspectives discussed. They begin—because they now have this opportunity to think for themselves—to listen to others, to their peers, to their classmates. They learn from what their classmates are thinking.

In the traditional classroom, children don't question each other. The idea of a community of inquiry where everybody is capable of speaking openly is a real novelty in a school setting. It is exciting for children to discover what the others in their class are thinking. It is also important that they learn to respect one another, that they learn to understand one another and to form a kind of community.

The community of inquiry is an unusual community. It is not just a community where people feel warmly about each other; it is a community where there is a certain method of exploration going on. There is exploration of philosophical ideas, even at the kindergarten, first-grade, or second-grade levels. This methodology is one of self-correction. Whenever things don't seem to go well, or be right—an invalid inference or weak reasoning for a conclusion—somebody has to offer a challenge, and this involves the community in a self-correcting process.

As children learn to participate in the self-correction that is going on in the group, they are capable of internalizing it and adopting it for themselves. Such internalization enables them to become more reflective, to think before they speak and act. Thus, as they internalize the group's self-corrective methodology, they become individually more self-critical. That is one of the things we want to encourage in them.

We want children to take initiative, not just wait to be criticized by the teacher. We want children to be capable of being autonomous, intellectually and morally self-governing. We want them to be self-critical so they are less likely to be swayed by impulse and emotion, and less likely to act in some irresponsible way. In other words, the greater the self-critical tendencies of the child, the greater the capacity for self-control. The reflective process has moral implications because it engages children in moral reasoning, not just in reasoning in some abstract sense not connected to their conduct.

Now, in order to introduce a program like philosophy with the aim of producing more reasonable human beings, it is necessary to have philosophy organized in a sequence that will begin at the beginning of school and move through all the school years. Philosophy as taught at the university level is not sequenced except in terms of historical dates. It is not logically sequenced. You cannot do this with children. You cannot present children with an unsequenced curriculum of philosophical skills and concepts.

To teach children philosophy, you have to have a curriculum that has a rational and sequential order. Certain skills precede the more complex, multiple-step skills. Some concepts are helpful for the understanding of other concepts. Some terms are pertinent for understanding other terms. And therefore you need a sequence.

The sequence of skills and concepts has to move with a kind of logical necessity from one step to the next so that children feel that the next step is always intuitively apparent and almost required. Such a sequentially designed curriculum contrasts with the kind of curriculum we have in the schools nowadays, which is largely a hodgepodge that has come into being over thousands of years. It is a curriculum in which there are almost no connections between one subject and the other. The student moves from one classroom where there is science to another classroom where there is art and he or she is in a different world. It is as if there is no continuity between one subject and the other. The student moves from one grade to the next with little continuity from one step to the next. The curriculum doesn't build, doesn't continue, doesn't grow.

The themes are not rehearsed and developed in the way, for example, a good piece of music is. In a good piece of music, the theme is introduced, developed, and strengthened and it builds. No such building goes on in the traditional hodgepodge curriculum in our schools.

The traditional curriculum is rarely criticized. Even when it has been criticized, it has seldom been subjected to experimental testing to determine what is really needed and what is not. How do we know how much time to give to algebra, to history, to the other subjects? We don't know. What we give students is often the result of historical accident.

How do we know to give no time to philosophy in our curriculum? We don't know. It's just that we *haven't* given it any. Therefore, we presume that we *shouldn't* give it any. It's a tradition and therefore you keep to the tradition without thinking about it. But how do we know that it wouldn't be a good idea if everybody had philosophy and had less of some of the other subjects? Until we begin to experiment longitudinally with some of these problems and see what results in better citizens, better scholars, and better thinking individuals and what does not, we're going to just go on doing what we are doing.

Another problem with the traditional curriculum is its incoherence—its lack of continuity, sequence, logical structure, and rationale. The curriculum represents certain aspects of the amassed knowledge of humankind. The curriculum in the schools is what we think we have to give children to civilize them, to make them understand the world as we know it. If we present it to them incoherently, then they will know it incoherently. And if they are irrational later, whose fault is it but ours for giving them an irrational curriculum or an ineffectual one?

One problem with the incoherence of the curriculum we have is that we don't try to develop it sequentially and logically, from beginning to end, from kindergarten to grade 12. Another reason for its incoherence is that those who developed the curriculum operated on the assumption that each stage of the curriculum must correspond to a stage of human development in the child. So they break the growth of the child into a set of stages and then they build the curriculum in a set of stages and try to coordinate point by point, one to one, a curriculum stage with a stage of growth.

These stages of growth are very debatable. I think that these stages have no more reality than the artificial segments in calculus that we mark off in curves. We try to express a curve in calculus by breaking it down into segments. Those segments are purely theoretical and purely abstract. They are just of our own invention; they are not real parts of the curve.

Similarly, you can break philosophy down into segments, but don't delude yourselves that each segment necessarily corresponds to a reality. When people develop a curriculum stage by stage and step by step in this manner, they tend to lose the sequential logical nature of the curriculum. In other words, they will develop stages as to what goes on in grade 1 and what goes in grade 2 and then they will develop a grade 1 curriculum and a grade 2 curriculum and so on to conform to these alleged stages of development. While these stages may have a genetic connection, they don't necessarily have a logical connection. Consequently, these curriculum stages don't have a logical sequence.

What is worse, these stages of the child's growth are put together by descriptions of children who are not in conditions or situations that call for maximum intellectual performance. They are largely the result of observing children under casual conditions of play or sitting together when they are not stimulated, when there is no educational intervention or interaction going on. Consequently, this is usually the lowest level of intellectual behavior that children can display rather than the highest. It means that the curriculum is then geared to the lowest level of cognitive development rather than to the highest.

The curriculum that results from this type of developmental stage theory is aimed at maintaining the *status quo*. It is aimed at keeping children down intellectually and not accelerating their development. So what you get in consequence from this same curriculum is

that children in the early stages of primary education are said to be incapable of abstract thought. And therefore education for them should concentrate along the physical aspects of education: teach children textures, colors, shapes, and sizes. Make them use their small muscles and their large muscles. Don't worry about their brains; they can't think abstractly. Give them illustrations and tell them stories and get them dancing and get them doing all sorts of things. So what if they don't think? They can't think anyhow! As a result, we have children in these earlier grades who are abstraction-deprived.

Most children are abstraction-deprived because the emphasis is all on the concrete. The concrete is overemphasized and the abstract is underemphasized. The children are starved for abstraction. It is not as if they can do without it. Abstractions are necessary because they are the concepts with which we understand the thinking domain. You have concepts with which you understand physics, concepts for history, concepts for art, and so forth. You can't do without concepts. You can't do without theory. You can't do without generalizations. You don't really begin to understand this concrete thing, this *rose*, until you grasp the abstract concept, *flower*.

If you're going to function, even practically, you need concepts. Because even practically you need the relationships between the abstract and the concrete, between the theoretical and the practical. You can't condemn children to live in a world of fact with no abstractions. If you do so, you make them helpless. You give them a world of mindless empiricism. A world where children cannot wonder, be thoughtful, be intellectually fulfilled. So children do need thought.

Now you might say, although they need thought, there is nothing they can do with it because it is still beyond them. They can't function in a world of philosophy. The concepts of philosophy are much too difficult, too complex for them. It is true that traditional philosophy deals with concepts that are very technical, specialized, and different from the concepts of everyday discourse. The philosophical terminology is different from every-day life. Some of the philosophical terms are like this. But we don't need the technical philosophical jargon. We don't have to use such terms with children. Yet, you'll find that we are already using abstract words with children that are a year and a half old or two years old, words that are rich in philosophical significance; words that professional philosophers use all the time. For example, take a child who just learned to speak. You may hear that child say something and it strikes you that the child may not have expressed himself accurately. You may say, "Johnny, is that true?" Note, you are using the word *true*, right? And you expect him to understand. In fact, you will hold him accountable if he doesn't know these things. If he keeps on saying things that are not true, you might be very unhappy with him. But your way of pointing it out is to use the abstract and the philosophical word *true*. And the fact is that Johnny understands the word *true* just as he understands the word *table* or *chair*, although you can point to a chair, but you can't point to an object that is the word *true*.

Children learn and do manage to function with abstract words like *true* and *fair* and don't seem to be having problems with them. They are fascinated by such words. They want to talk more about them because obviously they are not too clear as to what they mean. But they do work with them.

So, this is a plea to begin to recognize philosophy for *all* children, not just the gifted. If anything, it is needed more by what we call "special education" children than by any other group.

We've seen more experimental work that shows the success of doing philosophy with children with hearing impairments, children with learning disabilities, with children with reading problems, children with emotional problems, children with neurological problems. We know now the benefits of doing philosophy with all types of children.

So what I'm suggesting in conclusion is to see philosophy as (1) a valuable addition to the existing curriculum for all members of the school population, (2) a discipline that prepares us to think in the other disciplines, (3) as we move into the future, a *core subject* for the educational process as a whole.

In this essay, written exclusively for this book, Nick Dianuzzo discusses his use of philosophy in the treatment of chemically dependent juveniles. A former student of Matthew Lipman and trained by the Institute for the Advancement of Philosophy for Children, Dianuzzo's primary concern in this essay is to distinguish a philosophical approach to drug rehabilitation from the more traditional psychological approach.

Philosophical Rehabilitation: Autonomy through Education

Nick Dianuzzo

Most innovations and inventions are derived from a need or a void. Applying philosophy to drug rehabilitation was no different. It was derived from a void I saw in my students. In spite of the many different kinds of therapy the students were receiving, they still appeared to be very frustrated. Many of the problems they had, I believed, could have been solved by the students themselves if they had a more developed ability to reason. This ability to reason separates us from other sentient beings and appears to be severely lacking in the chemically addicted individual.

Taking an eclectic approach, I incorporated philosophy into the existing system at the drug rehabilitation center where I was working. Although therapeutic communities based on the Minnesota Method and Narcotics Anonymous are somewhat successful, the success rate, in reality, is somewhere around eight percent. If we consider spending the rest of one's life free of drugs as the minimum standard for "success," then even eight percent is a lofty number. Without being overly critical, we still could say that there is much room for improvement within the system. This is why I chose to build on the already existing system. For a large percentage of people going through rehabilitation, there was something lacking in the program that prevented them from remaining drug free and regaining their autonomy.

A philosophical approach to drug rehabilitation differs from a psychological approach (Minnesota Method/NA, AA) in three different respects: (1) individuals are seen as healthy rather than sick; (2) education is the major vehicle rather than therapy for the individual; (3) emphasis is placed on the individual to become dependent on himself/herself rather than on the group.

Starting from the premise that everyone is healthy rather than sick might seem to be a moot point. However, in actuality, it is a radical departure from the existing medical model. It's a positive approach rather than a negative one. If one is seen as healthy, then all physiological desires are the results of one's own intentionality, rather than an illness. This then eliminates the delusion that what is debilitating is beyond one's own control. It also establishes moral responsibility for one's intentions. I am not denying that physical dependencies develop. I am, however, convinced that the initial problem was derived from a faulty reasoning process. If this is the case, then the main focal point shifts from overcoming an illness to developing higher-order thinking skills and reasoning abilities in the chemically dependent individual. This is done under the realm of education.

Shifting the emphasis from therapy to education does not imply that the chemically dependent should be sent to "school" to overcome their problems. It has nothing to do with formal education in the traditional sense of a physical place for completion of a certain group of courses. The concern is with developing higher-order thinking skills. It is very common to hear someone say that they were not thinking when they made a mistake; however, this is a misconception. Everyone thinks, but not everyone is reflective in his or her thinking. Not everyone uses higher-order thinking skills in making decisions in life. When time isn't taken to evaluate the situations one is in, that is generally when mistakes are made. When life becomes a series of actions void of reflective thought, it is easy to see how a person can get caught up in a life of indulgence that can lead to such things as chemical dependency.

Higher-order thinking skills refer to the aspects of thinking that are concerned with making judgments. Higher-order thinking (critical thinking) is defined by Matthew Lipman as "thinking which aims at judgment, is governed by criteria, is sensitive to context and is self-correcting."

It would be hard to argue that choosing to get high or drunk to the point of self-destruction was based on reflective judgment. Obviously, then, this aspect of deliberation aimed at judgment is lacking in someone taken to excess. You are not going to find a well-thought-out list of criteria to support the argument that a life of dependency is advantageous. Once people have reached the point where they hand the decisions of their lives over to their desires, it becomes almost impossible to try to find alternatives for their lives.

A life driven by desire and dependency does not alter the fact that, in the beginning, the individual made a choice to give up control. Aristotle mentions (*Nicomachean Ethics*) that a person is responsible for his actions while drunk because he is the cause of his ignorance. This ignorance is brought about by a lack of higher-order thinking in one's judgments. By establishing that there was a capacity to choose initially, we can assume that this ability lies inside the chemically addicted, although it is dormant. What is necessary, then, is to activate and develop these skills.

Higher-order thinking skills can only be developed through practice. Therefore, we provide a hypothetical situation in which the individual can develop these skills. A community of inquiry is formed to help the individual develop these skills in a nonthreatening environment. It is an arena in which mistakes can be made without having to pay the consequences. This encourages examination of different possibilities of situations that were formerly thought to have only one possible solution.

In its early stages, the community of inquiry comes together to read and discuss short narratives about people in similar situations with similar problems. Focusing on a story rather than someone's personal life has two advantages. First, it removes the need for the participants to be defensive. Since they are dealing with fictional characters and situations, no one has to feel that any one person is being singled out or being attacked. Second, it naturally places everyone in an objective position to evaluate the different situations of the story. This vantage point is not the only possible perspective from which to evaluate a given situation. It is, however, the best situation to begin the process of developing higher-order thinking skills. Within the community of inquiry, one need only be concerned with establishing criteria for and making judgments about the situation without living through the actual events.

The evolution of the reasoning process in the juveniles that were part of the experiment will best exemplify how higher-order thinking develops through working in the community of inquiry. When I first formed the community of inquiry, the students were somewhat apprehensive. However, as they became more accustomed to an environment where all ideas are tolerated, they become very receptive.

One of the first concepts we discussed was how rules should be formulated. I gave them an example similar to the storyline in *Lord of the Flies* and asked them to decide who should make the rules. Every one of the participants in the community stated firmly that the only possible solution to this situation was to find out who was the strongest and have that person rule. The role of devil's advocate was of little help at that point. Giving them other possible alternatives was quickly dismissed as being absurd. The concept of the strongest ruling appeared so obvious to them that they quickly dismissed all other proposals. At this point, they still had a limited understanding of how life could function outside the realm of violence.

As time progressed and different topics were introduced in which all didn't share the same beliefs, they began to support their arguments by stating that more than just one of them held a particular view. That is when the principles of utilitarianism started to be embraced. For quite a while, all decisions were finalized based solely on the concept of majority rule. However, as time went on and their reasoning and argumentative skills developed, some of the students who were outnumbered still wanted to hold on to ideas that they felt were valid and logical. The concepts of minority rights were then introduced into the community. Their ethical system, if we can call it that, somewhat mirrored Rawls' ethical theory in that they were concerned with letting the majority have their way provided it did not affect the minority negatively. Developing ethically based decision-making skills is crucial to making sound judgments in the future.

The philosophical perspective is geared to the future. We cannot change the past so there is little point in dwelling there. The future is about choice, the intentionality of the individual. Ask people why they get high or drunk, and we will hear many excuses for their excesses: I was abused as a child, the pressures at work are unbearable, and so on. Most, if not all, excuses for substance abuse are based on cause and effect: "Something caused me to do this; I did not have a choice." This is an unacceptable position because it reduces a person to an object and removes all accountability from the individual. Furthermore, it is an admission that the past controls the future. These beliefs run completely contrary to the concept of autonomy. As previously stated, the ability to reason is what separates us from the rest of the sentient beings. Making choices rather than reacting to a stimulus-response situation is what makes us truly human. Therefore, reasoning is the component that needs to be developed in the chemically dependent. Developing the ability to establish sound criteria and to make critical judgments increases the chances that one can live successfully in an unsheltered world.

The third and most important difference is that the emphasis is placed on the individual's taking responsibility for himself or herself rather than on a group. In group therapy (NA/AA, etc.), the individual is expected to become dependent on the group and the program. An artificial environment is created in which the participants are encouraged not to leave. In essence, they are transferred from one subculture based on a form of dependency to another subculture based on dependency. Granted, it is probably better that people live in a subculture that is drug-free, but for whom is it better? It is definitely better for society. However, I am not sure that it is better for the individual. The question is, has the chemically dependent individual regained autonomy? If that is the case, as most programs say, that one must continue to go to meetings to stay clean and sober, then the answer is NO. The chemically dependent individual has not arrived at the point where he or she can function independently. If an individual is not independent, has control of his or her life really been regained? I don't believe that to be the case.

The philosophical approach differs from therapy in that it is only temporary. One comes to the inquiry to formulate ideas, hear different perspectives, and most importantly, to develop higher-order thinking skills to help make sound judgments for the future. However, it is never assumed that, once people enter the community of inquiry, they are not supposed to leave. On the contrary, it is designed to help develop the skills needed to cope with the problems that confront us in everyday life. When we are confronted with conflicting desires and messages, it is necessary to have the ability to analyze the situation to make the best judgment possible. This does not guarantee that we will not make mistakes. However, it will increase the chances of making good decisions. It will also allow for the flexibility needed if the initial judgments need to be modified.

Questions for Discussion

1. In the ethics course you are presently taking, are you learning to be moral? If not, what are you learning?

   _____

   _____

   _____

2. Should ethics be part of the regular public school curriculum?

   _____

   _____

   _____

3. Aristotle emphasized role models for moral education. What role models can you identify and what virtues do they exhibit that we should teach our children to emulate? (What is the difference between a role model and a hero?)

   _____

   _____

   _____

4. Aristotle insists that we train children to be moral by habituating them to certain modes of conduct. Does Aristotle's program interfere with children's autonomy? Discuss.

   _____

   _____

   _____

5. Discuss the Freudian claim that the internalization of external threats, for example, fear and punishment, is a large part of morality.

   _____

   _____

   _____

6. The "values clarification movement," popular in this country several years ago, was a program in which college instructors would assist students in clarifying their values without implying that any one set of values was better than another. What are the benefits and liabilities of such a program?

_____

_____

_____

_____

7. Following Aristotle, William J. Bennett recommends a directive moral education. Discuss the plausibility of such an approach in a society that is pluralistic and multicultural.

_____

_____

_____

_____

8. Carol Gilligan maintains that boys and girls approach ethical dilemmas differently. Drawing on your personal experience, discuss whether or not this is true and, if you think it is, discuss how boys and girls characteristically handle moral disputes.

_____

_____

_____

_____

9. How would you devise a curriculum of moral education that reflected the insights of Aristotle, Kohlberg, or Gilligan?

_____

_____

_____

_____

10. The conservative philosopher Allan Bloom has argued that the popularity of ethical relativism (see pp. 12–13) has led to the downfall of current education, including moral education. How might ethical relativism be implicated in this charge?

_____

_____

_____

_____

For Further Reading

Aristotle. *Nicomachean Ethics*. Translated by Terence Irwin. Indianapolis, Ind.: Hackett, 1985, esp. pp. 33–40.

Bennett, William J., ed. *The Book of Virtues*. New York: Simon & Schuster, 1993.

Bloom, Allan. *The Closing of the American Mind*. New York: Simon and Schuster, 1987.

Dewey, John. *Experience and Education*. New York: Collier Books, 1971.

Gilligan, Carol. *In a Different Voice*. Cambridge, Mass.: Harvard University Press, 1982.

Kohlberg, Lawrence. *The Philosophy of Moral Development*, Vol. 1. New York: Harper & Row/Chicago: University of Chicago Press, 1971.

Matthews, Garreth B. *Dialogues with Children*. Cambridge, Mass.: Harvard University Press, 1984.

———. *Philosophy and the Young Child*. Cambridge, Mass.: Harvard University Press, 1980.

Sharp, Ann Margaret, and Ronald F. Reed, eds. *Studies in Philosophy for Children: Harry Stottlemeier's Discovery*. Philadelphia, Penn.: Temple University Press, 1992.

Sher, George, and William J. Bennett. "Moral Education and Indoctrination." *The Journal of Philosophy* (November 1982), 665–677.

Chapter 18

The Homeless

Passages for Reflection

"The strength of a nation is derived from the integrity of its homes."
—*Confucius*

"But everybody needs a home so at least you can have some place to leave which is where most other folks will say you must be coming from."
—*June Jordan*

"The homeless are simply surplus souls in a system firmly rooted in competition and self-interest in which only the "strongest" will survive."
—*Mitch Snyder*

"Home is where I hang my hat."
—*Unknown*

Opening Questions

1. Do the homeless have a right to adequate housing?
2. Do the homeless have a right to privacy on the streets?
3. Can living on the streets be rational?

Recent surveys indicate that approximately one-third of the American homeless population are mentally ill. Although the total number of homeless Americans is in dispute, ranging anywhere from 350,000 to 500,000, the number of homeless who have severe and persistent mental illness is easier to determine. The National Institute of Mental Health has estimated that 2.4 million Americans should be classified as chronically mentally ill and that approximately 1.5 million of these individuals live "in the community."[1] This broad category includes those who live in halfway houses, those who live with their families or by themselves in rooming houses or cheap hotels, those who have been referred for short-term stays in psychiatric wards of local hospitals, and those who live simply in the streets. In his book, *Rachel and Her Children: Homeless Families in America,*[2] Jonathan Kozel reports that in New York City alone, 28,000 homeless people live in emergency shelters, and an additional 40,000 are on the streets and in other public places. Of those that are sheltered, about 10,000 are individuals and 18,000 are parents and children. Recent studies found that between 500,000 and 600,000 people are homeless on any given night.

Given these alarming statistics, the question we must ask is what, if anything, should be done about the homeless? What obligations do we have to the dysfunctional homeless who, on account of their mental illness, are condemned to live wretched and miserable lives? The scope of this discussion is limited to the "mentally ill homeless." While there are surely some homeless individuals who are not mentally ill and "choose" to live on the streets, the number of such people is presumably small. It is estimated that 50 percent of the homeless population have a primary psychosis, 30 percent have a mood disturbance such as manic depressive illness, and 10 percent have personality disorders and abuse drugs.

This essay, with some modifications, was originally published as "The Freedom to Be Psychotic?" *Journal of Law and Health* 2 (1987–1988): 17–42. Reprinted in Bernard M. Dickens, ed., *The International Library of Essays in Law and Legal Theory,* Areas 20 *Medicine and the Law* (Aldershot, Hants: Dartmouth Publishing Co., 1993).

[1]Morgenthau and Agrest, "Abandoned," *Newsweek* (Jan. 6, 1986): 14.

[2]Kozel, Jonathan. *Rachel and her Children: Homeless Families in America* (New York: Ballantine Books, 1988).

Historically, America's solution has been to treat such people with or without their consent. This practice, however, has come under attack since it raises grave moral and legal questions. Does society have the right to deprive an individual of freedom because of persistent mental illness? If so, on what grounds? Because freedom is a fundamental value in Anglo-American society, the practice of coercively treating mentally ill patients has often been viewed with great distrust.

Part of the concern over involuntary commitment is that in the last quarter of the nineteenth century, mental hospitals had become vast warehouses for psychotic human beings. These institutions were typically located in rural settings far from the patients' communities of origin. They existed throughout America where almost 600,000 patients had been gathered by the mid-1950s. The patients were ruled over by superintendents who, while for the most part benevolent, possessed great authority over their patients' lives.

In recent years, owing largely to radical changes in the care and treatment of institutionalized patients, the pendulum has swung away from treating patients in sprawling and isolated state hospitals to treating them on an outpatient basis. Among the factors contributing to these changes have been the advent of antipsychotic medications, the growth of in-patient psychiatric wards in general hospitals, and an open-door policy. A revised understanding of the doctor-patient relationship has also contributed to these changes. While previously society had employed a paternalistic model according to which "doctor knows best," today's preferred model (preferred by patients, that is) is more autonomy-oriented with patients viewed as consumers of health care and physicians as suppliers of health-related services.

But even though we have moved away from the locked-ward policy of the past, large mental hospitals have never been eliminated and neither has the warehousing of the mentally ill. This became a major factor in the upsurge of activism during the late 1960s and early 1970s when civil libertarians championed the view that mental illness is a myth perpetrated by psychiatrists interested in keeping "undesirables" at bay. Activists made these hospitals a prime target and attacked them through class actions in the United States courts. What resulted was literally madness in the streets: a massive emptying of state hospitals that forced chronic seriously ill patients into the community to be supported by a network of community centers which then-president John F. Kennedy signed into legislation.

But if involuntary commitment was problematic because it deprived patients of their civil liberties, deinstitutionalization has never proved effective. One reason for this is that the nation reneged on its promise to provide the kind of community-based mental health care that chronic patients desperately need. While the situation has improved under the Clinton administration, it has not been remedied. *The 10th Annual Report on Hunger and Homelessness* by the U.S. Conference of Mayors, released December 19, 1994, warned that emergency food and homeless shelters in many cities may have to turn needy people away because of insufficient resources. Another reason is that psychiatrists have been forced to work within a framework of liberty that is misguided when the issue concerns people who suffer from severe and persistent mental illness. Or so I shall argue.

In the history of philosophical and social thought, *liberty* (or *freedom*) has been used in two distinct senses. In one sense, *liberty* refers to a condition characterized by the absence of coercion or constraint (*negative liberty*). In quite another sense, *liberty* refers to the possession of the means to achieve the objective we choose of our volition (*positive liberty*). People are free in the negative sense of liberty if they are not compelled to act as they would not choose to act by the will of another. People are free in the positive sense of liberty if, in addition to the absence of coercion, they possess the means or the power to achieve the objectives they desire. A few moments of reflection will show you that negative liberty is the concept glorified by European and American individualism and liberalism.

But whether we understand liberty in its negative or positive sense, it is a fundamental value, the infringement of which is a serious matter. This is not to say that we are never permitted to override it. Several grounds have been proposed as justifications for its infringement, including the "harm principle" and the "principle of paternalism."

The harm principle is the most widely accepted liberty-limiting principle. Under the terms of this principle, a person's liberty of action can be constrained in order to prevent harm to others. With the exception of anarchists, few will dispute that the law has authority to constrain people from performing acts that will seriously injure other people. Laws that threaten thieves, murderers, or rapists with punishment, for example, are usually perceived as a necessary part of any social order. Individual acts of coercion whose intent is to prevent people from harming others are therefore considered morally permissible.

The principle of paternalism is more controversial. Under the terms of this principle, a person's liberty of action can be constrained in order to keep that person from harming himself or herself, or in order to confer a benefit on that person. Paternalistic interferences are undeniably sometimes justified, such as when a parent forbids a child to play with fire. The problem is whether such interference is justified beyond such obvious cases. Is interference justified, for example, when the person constrained is a mature adult? If so, under what conditions?

These are not the only principles that have been proposed to justify the limitation of liberty. The limitation of liberty has been argued to be justified: (1) to prevent behavior that causes shame, embarrassment, and discomfort to onlookers (the offense principle); (2) to benefit others, such as using people as research subjects if the research project promises some potentially great benefit to other members of society (the social welfare principle); and (3) to prevent the impairment of institutional practices that are in the public interest (the public harm principle).[3] But the harm principle and the principle of paternalism have been most often employed to justify the legal practice of involuntary commitment. Many of these other principles have been considered too controversial to serve as bases for legal practices.

Broadly speaking, involuntary commitment of the mentally ill is justified on the following grounds. First, the individual must be in some way mentally disabled. This disability is variously described as "illness," "disease," "disorder," and so on depending on the wording of the relevant statute. Beyond that, one or more incapacitating conditions must exist resulting from the mental disability. The five general categories of incapacitating conditions are: (1) impaired judgment, (2) the need for hospitalization, (3) the need for care or treatment, (4) disablement, and (5) dangerousness to self or others. Since an increasing number of jurisdictions require that the person in question is shown to be either dangerous to himself or herself or others (the fifth condition), it is this condition that needs to be examined further.

The requirement that a person be dangerous to himself or others on account of mental illness rests on the principle of paternalism. Legally, the principle is expressed in terms of the state's function as *parens patriae* (literally, "parent of the country"), the power of the state to act as sovereign and guardian of persons under legal disability. The dangerousness to self criterion is applied to two types of cases: potential suicides and people who expose themselves to harm.

Committing a person because he is dangerous to himself raises grave questions about the state's power to protect people from themselves. The psychiatrist Thomas Szasz has contended that a person has "an unqualified right to be dangerous to himself—whether it be to take up smoking, have an abortion, or commit suicide."[4] His claim is that mental illness is a myth, implying that those who contemplate suicide or who otherwise expose themselves to harm do so out of "problems of living." Against this view, mainstream psychiatrists argue that mental illness is a disease that necessitates treatment when the patients pose some kind of danger.

But whether mental illness is a disease depends on a satisfactory analysis of the concept of *disease*—an analysis of interest to both physicians and philosophers. Construed narrowly, *disease* means *disease of the body*. From the libertarian's perspective, any broader interpretation introduces a value judgment suggesting that psychiatry is a form of social

---

[3]See Joel Feinberg, *Social Philosophy* (Englewood Cliffs, N.J.: Prentice Hall, 1973), p. 20.

[4]Cited in Slovenko, "Civil Commitment in Perspective," *Journal Pub. L.* 20, 3 (1971): 23–26.

control. The history of medical views on masturbation is a case in point. In the eighteenth and nineteenth centuries, when sexual activity was thought to be bad for the soul, masturbation was thought to be a dangerous disease. However, while not denying that *disease* means disease of the body, mainstream psychiatrists see mental illness as a disease which, affecting the brain, manifests itself in aberrant thought and behavior. Like a diseased pancreas which manifests itself in diabetes since it is the pancreas's job to secrete insulin, a diseased brain manifests itself in aberrant behavior since the brain's job is to regulate conduct. From the psychiatrist's point of view, psychiatry is no more value-laden than endocrinology. Since Szasz's position is out of the mainstream of psychiatry, we may safely assume that some homeless exist who are dangerous to themselves precisely because of their mental illness.

The requirement that a person must be dangerous to others because of mental illness rests on the harm principle. Legally, the principle is expressed in terms of the police power of the state. The harm principle is the least problematic of the liberty-limiting principles, and so commitment on this standard appears least problematic. But appearances are deceiving. Compare civil with criminal confinement. In both cases, the state decides that society will benefit from the deprivation of the person's liberty. But criminal imprisonment, unlike civil commitment, is imposed only *after* the defendant has committed or attempted a dangerous act, while civil commitment is imposed before.

One explanation for treating mentally ill patients differently than the criminal population is the assumption that hospitalization is likely to benefit them.[5] But if this is so, then the harm principle is not being utilized but the principle of paternalism which is more difficult to justify. And even if we assume that the harm principle is invoked, the legislature must still choose a standard of dangerousness for deciding whether a person should remain at liberty. This is no easy task. At a minimum, it calls for a determination both of what acts are dangerous and how probable it is that such acts will occur. Traditionally, legislatures have factored in four different elements in determining dangerousness: (1) magnitude of harm, (2) probability of harm, (3) frequency of harm, and (4) imminence of harm. Add to this the types of harm that may occur, say, to the person, property, or public morals, and the task is further exacerbated.

As a matter of practice, opponents of civil commitment rarely contest the legitimacy of commitment when the patient in question is acutely psychotic. The widespread consensus is that patients who are acutely ill and dangerous may be committed and treated without their consent. The real issue concerns the patient who, while not presently dangerous to

---

[5]See Note, "Civil Commitment of the Mentally Ill: Theories and Procedures," 79 *Harvard Law Review* 77, 1288 (1966): 1289–1291.

herself or others, is *potentially* dangerous. The typical scenario involves the patient who is involuntarily treated while acutely ill, responds to therapy, and threatens to again become dangerous when released onto the streets. The question is what to do with these patients when, given their past history, they are noncompliant outside the hospital setting. On the one hand, the Fifth Amendment of the U.S. Constitution protects them from being committed against their will if they are in no imminent danger to themselves or others. On the other hand, without constant policing, they typically become dangerous and a threat to society.

Libertarians who object to commitment on paternalistic grounds are fond of enlisting the support of liberal philosopher John Stuart Mill. In Mill's famous book, *On Liberty,* he states his antipaternalism in this oft-quoted passage:

> The sole end for which mankind are warranted, individually or collectively, in interfering with the liberty of action of any member, is self-protection. That the only purpose for which power can be rightfully exercised over any member of a civilized community, against his will, is to prevent harm to others. His own good either physical or moral, is not sufficient warrant.[6]

Underlying Mill's antipaternalism was his belief that the search for truth and happiness required an unfettered competition among different ideas and lifestyles. He thus argued that so long as people do not interfere with the liberty of others, they should be allowed the right to be idiosyncratic and to live as they choose. It is in Mill's name that civil libertarians voice their objections and defend the right of the mentally ill homeless to be psychotic.

Beyond the moral and legal problems surrounding involuntary commitment, practical problems center on the inadequacy of mental health facilities. For these reasons, the reform known as *deinstitutionalization* has become an alternative way of handling America's mentally ill homeless.

Deinstitutionalization refers to the hopeful goal of releasing most chronic mentally ill patients from state-run asylums and returning them to the community. This idea, which began in 1963 when John F. Kennedy signed into legislation a network of community centers to support deinstitutionalized patients nationwide, has the virtue of leaving patients at liberty while at the same time providing needed care. The program was largely predicated on the therapeutic power of psychopharmacology (the managing of medications that successfully treat mental illness). It was believed that even chronic schizophrenics could be released into the community if they took their regular doses of tranquilizers or neuroleptics (antipsychotic medications).

---

[6]John Stuart Mill, *On Liberty* (Indianapolis, Ind.: Hackett, 1978 [1859], p. 9).

While the goal was laudable—and still is—the program has never succeeded. The government has never provided the kind of community-based mental health care that chronic patients desperately need. In the heyday of deinstitutionalization, spending by state governments was more than adequate. In the 1980s, spending totaled $6.2 billion. But the dollars never followed the patients. Even when 63 percent of the nation's chronic mentally ill were at large in the community, two-thirds of all state and local mental health funding went to mental institutions that housed a fraction of their former patient population. The result was a staff-to-patient ratio that exceeded 1.5 to 1 in public and private hospitals nationwide. In New York State, for instance, from a high of 93,000 resident mental patients in 1955, the hospital population dropped to 20,000; yet not a single mental hospital closed, and two-thirds of $1.5 billion budget (approximately $990 million) was spent on the sparsely inhabited hospitals at which most of New York's mentally ill were unwelcome. What was missing was effective community care. The result was that many of the chronic mentally ill went into the community getting minimal treatment, if any at all.[7] In the mid-1990s, the situation has worsened. Driven by budgetary concerns, government has become increasingly concerned with closing down mental hospitals and downsizing those that stay open.

The main reason why deinstitutionalization has failed is the law's bias in favor of the rights of the mentally ill. Because of legal barriers to involuntary commitment, psychiatric treatment has been difficult to administer. While deinstitutionalized patients are referred for outpatient treatment, they get minimal support from mental health agencies. They eventually become ill again, lose touch with their caseworkers, and get into trouble with the law. This accounts for the so-called revolving-door syndrome which mental health professionals often lament.

Another reason the system has failed is the law's obsession with the rights of the mentally ill. Given the presumption of (negative) liberty and the difficulty of applying liberty-limiting principles, psychiatrists are forced to work within a libertarian framework in which the rights of the mentally ill homeless are protected to their detriment. As Donald Treffert so eloquently put it, mentally ill patients are "dying with their rights on."[8]

One suggested proposal to solve the homeless situation is mandatory outpatient treatment. The purpose of this proposal is to extend the state's civil commitment powers to compel patients to take their medications and continue contact with their therapists upon discharge. The proposal has the virtue of short-circuiting the revolving-door syndrome

---

[7]Morgenthau and Agrest, p. 14.

[8]Donald Treffert, "Dying with Their Rights On." *American Journal of Psychiatry* 130 (1973): 1041.

while being attractive to civil libertarians who see it as the least restrictive alternative to inpatient hospitalization.

Many states now have statutory provisions that appear to allow for mandatory outpatient treatment. Surveys suggest, however, that these provisions are infrequently employed. Perhaps the main reason for this is that statutes often use identical criteria to identify patients who are appropriate for inpatient commitment and those who can receive outpatient care. If those that can be committed on an outpatient basis are also those that can be committed on an inpatient one, committing on an outpatient basis will rarely be used for fear of legal liability. Another reason is enforcement. The specter of mental heath police patrolling the homeless is not an inviting one.

However we evaluate the several proposals designed to treat the mentally ill homeless, the medical perspective, with its imperative to treat, is in opposition to the civil libertarian one, with its imperative to protect civil liberty rights. Construed this way, the battle lines are drawn around those who would treat patients involuntarily and those who would defend liberty rights to the medical detriment of the right-holder.

The issue need not be construed this way. A different construction is grounded in an alternative understanding of *rights*. Although no clear consensus exists as to what rights are, we can construe them as claims yielded by justified rules and principles. In most views, rights are construed to be correlative with obligations. To say, for example, that "Smith has a right to X" means that others have an obligation to treat Smith in a certain way. In precisely what way others are obligated to treat Smith depends on the right in question and how we understand the concept. Sometimes, to say that "Smith has a right to X" means that others are obligated not to interfere with that to which Smith has a right. Construed this way, rights are *warnings against interference*. This, for example, is how we understand what it means for Smith to have the right to her personal possessions. Other times, saying that "Smith has a right to X" means that others are obligated to provide Smith with the means to acquire or use X. This is how we understand "the right to health care" when that term is used by health-care reformers. Construed this way, rights are *entitlements*. It follows that to say someone has a right to something leaves open the question of how we should construe that right. If rights are construed as warnings against interference, then others are obligated not to interfere with the right-holder. If rights are construed as entitlements, then others are obligated to furnish the right-holder with the means to effectuate the right. These interpretations are not exclusive of each other. Sometimes we respect people's rights by leaving them alone; at other times, we respect people's rights when we enable them to realize their goals.

The question we must ask, then, is how should we construe the right of the homeless to roam the streets and live in the gutters? From a legal perspective, the right to be free is a warning against interference. That a person has the legal right to liberty means that others, for example, the state and its agencies, are obligated not to interfere with that person's actions so long as the actions are not illegal (fall within the scope of the liberty-limiting principles). What the right does not mean is that the state is obligated to provide the right-holder with the means needed to make liberty meaningful, such as food, clothing, education, and *shelter*. In a word, no legally recognized entitlements exist in the American system of justice. The question is whether construing rights in this fashion does justice to the right to be free. Do we respect the liberty rights of the mentally ill homeless by leaving them free on the streets to their medical detriment?

Consider once again that champion of liberalism, John Stuart Mill, whom civil libertarians are so fond of quoting. While Mill did construe the right to be free as a warning against interference, he did so out of fear of the "tyranny of the majority" which he saw rampant in his day. Mill's belief was that truth and happiness require an unrestricted competition among conflicting ideas and lifestyles. He thought that these would come about only if people remained free to experiment with different lifestyles and live as they deemed fit. However, when Mill spoke about the right to be free, he conceded, in an important if overlooked passage:

> This . . . is meant to apply only to human beings in the maturity of their faculties. We are not speaking of children, or of young persons below the age which the law may fix as that of manhood or womanhood. *Those who are still in a state to require being taken care of by others must be protected against their own actions as well as against external injury* [emphasis added].[9]

This last sentence presumably includes the mentally ill homeless.

If this is Mill's position, then a profound irony can be found in civil libertarians citing Mill to prevent the state from treating the mentally ill homeless against their will. For so understood, Mill is construing the right to be free as a warning against interference presupposing that, when free, people's rational though idiosyncratic lifestyles will work to the betterment of society. Where this presupposition is false, then Mill concedes that society has a legitimate right to provide for those who cannot provide for themselves. The upshot is this: freedom from interference (negative freedom) makes sense only when people are free to live according to a self-designed plan. If people are not free to live a life according to such a plan, then to construe this right as a warning against interference is absurd.

---

[9]Mill, *On Liberty,* p. 9.

For obvious reasons, the mentally ill homeless are not free to live a self-designed and rational life precisely because of their mental illness. This being so, we respect their freedom not by leaving them alone, but by providing them with the wherewithal to live meaningful lives. This includes, at a minimum, providing them with medical treatment followed by adequate housing.

Treating the mentally ill homeless is no mean feat. Over the last decade, research has documented the difficulty of engaging this population in traditional mental health services. Among the factors that have contributed to their rejection of services include a distrust and frustration with a mental health system that is fragmented, difficult to negotiate, and composed of programs based on expectations that leave little room for individual choice. The silver lining in this cloud is that studies suggest those who are willing to accept such services perceive them to be important and meaningful. In a study conducted by the New York State Office of Mental Health, the New York City Health and Hospitals Corporation, and the Center for Psychiatric Rehabilitation at Boston University between 1991 and 1994, it was found that the mentally ill homeless can be successfully engaged, served, and housed by a highly individualized, rehabilitation-oriented supported housing approach in which the goals and aspirations of people helped mold the array of services and supports that were offered.[10]

---

[10]See *Evaluations Bulletin* 2:5 (November 1994).

Lina Levit Haber, M.D., is a practicing psychiatrist in Rockland County, New York, and an attending psychiatrist on the Project Help homeless unit of Rockland Psychiatric Center. Born in Moscow, she is a former Mead-Johnson Fellow in Community Psychiatry. She is married to Joram Graf Haber.

William David Perry, R.N., is the treatment team leader on the Project Help homeless unit of Rockland Psychiatric Center, Rockland County, New York.

Video Presentation

Guests: Lina Levit Haber, M.D., Rockland Psychiatric Center

David Perry, R.N., Rockland Psychiatric Center

Student Panel: Rigo Ramos, Susan Stovall, Vicky Panos

Since Dr. Haber and Mr. Perry both work for Project Help in New York, I begin by asking them to discuss what the project is about. We learn that the project is an outreach program dedicated to assisting homeless individuals who are in dire need of psychiatric care. Perry tells us that the short-term goal is to treat the most severely disabled homeless patients with the more long-term goal of keeping illness under control while finding them adequate housing. We learn that Dr. Haber's role is to assess the mental status of the patients she treats, administer and monitor medications, and educate her patients about mental illness so that they do not neglect their treatment upon release from the hospital. When I ask Dr. Haber about the extent of insight her patients have into their medical condition, she responds that they have little or no insight and frequently become noncompliant upon release from the hospital, only to return to Project Help in the future.

I next ask Perry whether "the homeless," as people refer to them, constitute a monolithic group. He answers yes and no, pointing out that while the homeless people he sees are not the agitated individuals admitted to Project Help at Bellevue Hospital in New York City, they are nevertheless suffering from some form of mental illness. I then ask for a profile of a typical mentally ill homeless person, which Dr. Haber provides by describing a disorganized individual, often HIV positive and tuberculosis positive, who is psychotic, in dire need of medical care, and can frequently be found rummaging through garbage and talking to himself or herself. She points out, however, that they will be taken to Bellevue only if they are dangerous to themselves or others or are so disorganized as to be unable to care for themselves. This leads me to ask whether any danger exists of the non-mentally-ill homeless being caught in Project Help's net. Both Perry and Haber deny that such danger exists and argue that greater danger lies in not picking up those who need to be treated. Perry points out how Project Help is scrupulously careful in determining who does and does not need to be treated, while Haber contends that picking out those who stand in need of treatment is easy. She also points out the manner in which the legal system looks out for the rights of the mentally ill.

Having discussed the way in which the legal system safeguards the rights of the mentally ill homeless, we turn to issues of aftercare. I ask what happens to these patients after they are discharged from the hospital. Usually, says Perry, they go to a shelter and rarely do they go back to the streets. He points out that, in his experience, patients are usually willing to work with the caseworkers who stay on the cases following discharge. Dr. Haber adds that the question of what to do after discharge is a sticky one. On the one hand, health care managers are reluctant to keep these patients in the hospital inasmuch as it costs the state at least $105,000 per patient. On the other hand, many patients, upon release, return to their troubled ways. From Dr. Haber's perspective, this fact argues for keeping patients for longer rather than shorter stays, while Perry prefers a more aggressive outreach program.

Following the break, Susan Stovall asks Perry about the status of Larry Hogue, a mentally ill homeless individual featured on the television program *60 Minutes* who is notorious for establishing a pattern of harassing his "neighbors," getting committed and treated, and being discharged only to harass people again. Perry, who has worked with Larry Hogue, points out the difficulties with Larry Hogue-type problems. Rigo Ramos asks Dr. Haber how successful Project Help is, and Vicky Panos asks Haber how the law and psychiatry get along. Dr. Haber, who has treated the notorious Billy Boggs against her will, discusses (along with Perry) how the mental health system usually prevails once the decision is made to legally keep a patient in a hospital for treatment.

In this article, written exclusively for this book, John Abbarno addresses the problem of homelessness within the context of privacy and the right thereto. After exploring the nature and value of privacy, Abbarno concludes that privacy is essential both for selfhood and self-respect. In the absence of privacy, which is the condition of the homeless, the homeless lack the liberties that are necessary conditions for moral personhood. Thus, Abbarno shows how homelessness reframes the conflict between privacy and liberty in a way not frequently understood or appreciated. John Abbarno is editor of The Ethics of Homelessness Value Inquiry Book Series. Amsterdam and Atlanta: Rodopi, in press.

Homeless Exposure: Moral Aspects of Life without Privacy

John M. Abbarno

Privacy is a relatively new concept to undergo philosophical scrutiny. Over the past twenty-five years, a number of definitions have been proposed that attempt a coherent meaning among the various contexts. The most innovative were made by James Rachels, Jeffrey Reiman, Charles Fried, and more recently, Julie Inness. They focus on the bodily and moral psychological dimensions. I rely on these as groundwork for the characterization of privacy among the homeless presented in this essay. The aim is to underscore the right of privacy that will clarify our moral obligation to the homeless.

We value privacy as a domain in which we edit our life plans, recognize degree of intensity of emotions, and modify vices for public activities. It is a dimension of restricted access by means of others. Privacy is a veiled inner sanctum which, if exposed, threatens what we choose. For some people, it would obscure trust in personal relationships and social institutions. As citizens in a democratic society, we would accept these characterizations as minimal conditions to be free and dignified persons. In *Griswold v. Connecticut*, the Supreme Court recognized the extended protection of individuals' privacy in several key areas formulated in the First, Fourth, and Fifth Amendments. The result is the emergence of a constitutional right of privacy which covers expressed protection from intrusion as stated in the Fourth Amendment: "This amendment explicitly affirms the right of the people to be secure in their persons, houses, papers, and effects, against unreasonable searches and seizures."[1]

What occurs, however, with those people for whom a "retreat into a private place" is not a possibility, namely the homeless? What relationship is there between an individual's internal self-worth and external conditions?

This essay focuses on aspects of noninformational privacy and its moral implications. Intrusions against others by electronic surveillance, phone tapping, and tampering with personal mail are less an issue among the homeless. This doesn't minimize the moral concerns of informational privacy. It is not, however, an invaded area the homeless customarily face.

I shall argue that intrusions of privacy have

existential ramifications and are not as blatantly prohibitive among the homeless population. This type of intrusiveness overcomes their personal space and undermines their dignity and self-worth. It has the potential of irreparably changing their status as the "new underclass"[2] of society since they lack the modicum of cohesion found among African-Americans and Native Americans. Over an extended period of time, this displacement may eliminate the homeless from any active role in the moral community. We are dangerously close to that threshold since the homeless who are powerless have no means of persuasion.

Two values contribute to the altered moral status among this population: liberty as it is expressed in social policies and privacy. In so-called normal moral circumstances, each of us can identify how both of these values enhance each other. However, among the homeless these values not only are conflicting, but in many instances, privacy is meaningless. If liberty is valued, it is in part for what it protects us from so that our choices are honored; this assumes a modicum of capability. This capability is psychological as well as physical aptitude to be safely left alone to succeed or fail in our choices. Negative liberty implies a power individuals have to procure their own ends unimpeded.

Unclear lines exist between other cases. For example, a neighbor employs a community health nurse as an aide to be with her ailing mother during the days so that she can work. This nurse is an old acquaintance whom you know has a drinking problem. Is it invasive to offer this background that may also indicate a lack of your neighbor's good judgment in hiring people? Or you may be asked to accommodate the college's lack of space by sharing your single office with a colleague. This may curtail office hours, a style of advising students, eating habits, or even a quick ten-minute nap! Is this invasiveness or meeting the common good? We experiment, in part, with adjustments to our private selves for the infractions on us and their duration, to say nothing of what emotional concern they may incur on our liberty.

Isaiah Berlin reminds us, in his "Two Concepts of Liberty," that where the line is drawn is a matter of debate. "Men are largely interdependent, and no man's activity is so completely private as never to obstruct the lives of others in any way."[3] As shown by the examples, the obstruction admits of degrees. Nonetheless, one can find imaginative alternatives to reconcile such conflicts. Among the homeless, the conflict between liberty and privacy is not reconciled. It becomes a way of life. Since social policies are written for efficiency, they have a tendency to treat groups homogeneously. Differences are shadowed by the common need to be sheltered, thereby presuming that privacy is superfluous. The McKinney Homeless Assistance Act[4] of 1987 reflected this notion. It introduced matching funds for the homeless that provided shelters and transitional housing. These well-intended measures failed. The homeless felt vulnerable to physical harm in shelters, and the housing left them without hope of stability since the occupants had nowhere to "transition to" due to unemployment. The McKinney Act did not allow for family accommodations and placed the burden of housing on the communities that were in need of relief. Many communities simply declined to seek the assistance.

The spaces that social policies provided were makeshift at best. Any exercise of plans for self-improvement, encouraging a child to have hope, or simply to fully feel the range of emotions requires a space, a place of one's own. Prohibiting this level of privacy is a denial of more than a space: it imposes on a place in which one reevaluates choices; a place that makes one feel secure or insecure in one's relations with others; a place where one can discern strengths, weaknesses, and fill out the ideal of oneself assessing values essential for human flourishing. It is a private space reserved for oneself, apart from others, to explore liberties of one's mental and physical powers, which can only be enhanced by privacy. "Privacy is a condition about which claims may be made as to an individual's freedom from unwanted intrusions upon or disclosures of their affairs as well as their freedom to limit and define for themselves their engagements with others."[5] It is the context wherein one intimates respect and develops friendships and trust in oneself and others. Privacy is necessary for moral development. Just think of how misplaced anger, jealousies, mistrusts, and self-betrayals shadowbox in this space. As Charles Fried supportively writes, "To respect, love, trust, and feel affection for others and to regard ourselves as persons among persons, then privacy is the necessary atmosphere for these attitudes and actions, as oxygen is for combustion."[6]

Fried's analogy expresses the essential role of privacy in moral life, namely, the necessary condition for constitutive values of character. Privacy accommodates the inner tension wherein one sustains and monitors feelings for their cogent extensions of oneself. For instance, we may say hurtful things to a friend, lover, spouse, or colleague. The intensity of the expression, "its taking aim," may be for the freedom one feels to be cathartic among these relations and without fear of abandonment. Such intimacies may have a wider range of alternatives for adjusting to these feelings, transforming them into a fuller understanding of the conflict.

The phenomenon of homelessness reframes the conflict between privacy and liberty within greater constraints. In the United States there are an estimated 750,000 to 1 million homeless persons for whom privacy is compromised by expressed liberty itself—the liberty of "being left alone." Their choices are reduced to finding a manner of survival on the streets. This includes intermittent shelter stays. Some find abandoned warehouses and tenement buildings where privacy is reduced to a cubicle space that is rat-infested and short-lived. The fear of invasions by other homeless or by construction crews preparing to raze the building keep the homeless migratory. In the absence of sustained privacy, the homeless are without liberties that enhance moral selfhood.

Although figures are difficult to firm up based on social work studies, the average length of homelessness is usually six months to four years. The longer one is without an inviolate moral space, the less likely one is to function with self-esteem since one no longer has control over denying access to one's way of life. Eventually, the homeless person acquiesces to the condition. Hubert Humphrey once wrote, "We act differently if we think we are being observed. If we can never be sure whether or not we are being watched and listened to, all our actions will be altered and our very character will change."[7] During a walk down sidewalks in major cities such as Chicago, Washington, New York and Atlanta (to name a few), you can observe people wrapped in blankets for the night, or pitching you for donations so they can find food or a bed for the night. Others take to the parks for a bench. These people remind us that the bonding agent, the thread of personhood in us, is a fragile one; they have adapted to a way of being far removed from what they initially would have accepted. Many, for instance, become shameless for bathing and urinating in public, a practice many homeless feel is part of the environment of street life.

Over the past fifteen years, our social institutions have developed policies and programs to save their humanity. There have also been vociferous urges to simply "take them" from public view. Some were prompted by cries of disgust from people using subway and bus terminals. Humanitarian pleas came from the National Office for Homelessness in Washington, D.C. Nonetheless, the motives resulted in the involuntary removal of the homeless to shelters and, in some cities, to jail. In these cities, ordinances were enacted that made their low levels of raw comfort "illegal." Conduct such as panhandling, sleeping on park benches, and bathing and urinating in public were judged as violations of the law and arrests were made. It is difficult to avoid bathing in public if one is homeless! These ordinances were indictments against a condition of a group of people whose freedom to do otherwise was severely limited, both by a physical condition and a diminished sense of self-worth.

Sweeping the homeless from subways and terminals into jails should be prohibited by the Eighth Amendment as cruel and unusual punishment. The involuntary status of homelessness is not a condition the law can deter by punishment. Instead, it exacerbates the felt denigration and profound loss of moral respect. It is simply indecent for there to be a social restriction against an involuntary condition. We do not, for example, punish victims of Turrets syndrome for verbally assaulting people on the street, nor epileptics for any inadvertent damage caused to merchandise while having a seizure. The homeless, then, are paradoxically free in this negative sense. They are left to choose their means of survival so long as it doesn't offend the public. The meaning of *offense* is more widely defined as tolerance wears thin. Yet, by eliminating their privacy, this becomes an offense felt by the public, however inadvertent.

By being placed in shelters, the homeless are not offered privacy but a different set of fearful conditions. In short, the homeless are unwelcome in the community—a community of people who want to be protected from a homeless person's disclosed life. One can argue that this resistance is based on the privacy of the "onlooker"; that is, not to have the private living habits of unknown others involuntarily imposed on one's way of life is a right left unmet. However, the strength of this claim rests on whether the onlooker has more alternatives to avoiding this alleged rights infringement, other than being a witness to this condition, than the homeless person has in being in and disclosing his or her condition. The argument could add some other social cases to suggest a systematic trend to hide our "broken" citizenry. This is a concern best developed at another time.

Without a private space, the homeless make a strong effort to control what domain they can, as a semblance of freedom in their lives. They find, however, that this control is illusive without a right to a private space. This is underscored by what Lon Fuller terms a tragic dilemma of liberty:

Freedom can be thought as a capacity to choose from a large number of possibil-

ities. However, if the number is bewildering or without priority, or the possibilities are beyond reach, the condition becomes chaos. A psychological manifestation of this phenomenon is schizophrenia. Acute schizophrenics must be helped to systematize some of the smallest tasks; *or* freedom can be regarded as order and regularity, the freedom that comes from functioning within known limits or internalized structure.[8]

This latter functioning is most difficult "to balance" without the existential kind of privacy discussed earlier: a place for readjustments on one's ever-developing sense of self.

An internalized structure is a form of maintaining control amidst open external conditions. Persistence in maintaining one's autonomy in this manner has deleterious effects since this does not alter the environment one lives in. It narrows choices and imposes an unyielding view on the world as it is. "This kind of freedom can lead to rigidity, confinement, and a loss of autonomy."[9]

A right to privacy entitles one to be selective regarding whom one will disclose feelings, ideas, or possessions. "People have the right to have the world be what it appears to be precisely in those cases in which they regard privacy as essential to the diminution of their own vulnerability."[10]

Assuming that rights and duties are correlative and stabilizing components of a moral community, there are unsatisfied claims the homeless make on society. Since the homeless cannot honor society's claim upon them, they become unequally regarded in contrast with those who can. It becomes a vicious circle, without a "home" (place). Their capacity to meet social obligations is perceived as altered: policies are developed to meet their perceived needs which mitigates their autonomy rather than enhancing it. Consequently, the private space they need as moral selves is further removed. The hope of reinstatement of rights against society appear less likely. Among these foiled rights is the privacy that sustains their moral status in the community.

There is a sense in which the meaning of privacy is interactive and communal insofar as members acknowledge each other's "private" domain as a way of demarcating it. Since privacy flourishes when there is a mutual regard for one's ability to be trusted to hold another's confidence, it is best sustained in the context of an autonomy that is relational; this I shall call *conventional autonomy*. I believe this sense offers an empathetic perspective on homelessness and privacy that more clearly shows that one's self-respect, freedom, and dignity are central to being a person; that these are not possible without the interdependence of individuals in the community. More specifically, conventional autonomy functions from the following characteristics:

1. It recognizes that a person's self-worth is gained through discovery among the members of society.
2. Any one individual or group's attained goods are realized by cooperative effort among people of different needs and abilities.
3. The common good sought for is open to alterations based on what is reasoned to be most valued for the collective without demeaning the life of any one individual or group of individuals.

According to this view of autonomy, what I direct my life toward, what order I construct, is not independent of consideration (positive or negative, direct or indirect) of others. The interdependence assumes that people have varied degrees of capability, and cooperative means optimize these relations. These relations are varried; one's efforts are more completely exercised with one person rather than another (for example revealing fears to a friend may win encouragement; if revealed to another, they may cause distrust). Conventional autonomy is formed in a matrix and is not absolute, independent of human context. It is nurtured in community, and within this membership a person also intuitively selects what and with whom to disclose aspects of his or her life that are endearing as well as those that are invio-late—sacred to who he or she is—for example how he or she sees himself or herself reflected among others in the community. This self-image develops as circles of influence evolve from our choices and discoveries.

The value of conventional autonomy (in these examples) permits a sliding emphasis that is determined by the context of community and on conditions of human actions being performed at certain times, toward appropriate parties, and relevant to the common good. Privacy is exercised through conventional autonomy. Concealment of oneself is altered by consent. It is the cooperative functioning of these values that disposes one to conceal certain information from some people and not others, and to choose some roles and reject others that may be either too restrictive or too liberal for one's self-concept.

Consider an exposure of a "private condition" at an inopportune moment. What, for instance, would occur if a faculty member whose driver's license was revoked for DWI is requested by the department head to drive a guest speaker to the airport after his or her lecture. Should such honest disclosure of a rather complicated response best be concealed until another time? A decision to conceal such a habit that would affect one's role in one's community is contingent upon one's willingness to be responsible for those affected. In such circumstances, this involves a contingent privacy. *Contingent privacy* is the effort to conceal information, aspects of one's character, from parties who have a right to know. The difficulty may be the occasion upon which one *must* choose to conceal or not. In this case, this could not have been foreseen. What makes these contingent is one's efforts to avoid or engage relationships, roles, and living conditions that may eventually impose a direct personal choice to disclose or not to disclose.

To the extent one's own self-worth and dignity are grounded in conventional autonomy, denigrating other members denigrates oneself, whether explicitly or implicitly. The communal obligation toward one another is grounded in conventional autonomy. This can flourish, or it can be diminished by making choices that are less than how we view ourselves in private. Continuing with the faculty member, what prompts a disclosure for the general good is the avoidance of the potential offense and harm to the guest speaker. In addition, there is the imminent embarrassment that would ensue upon the college. The contingent right to privacy is trumped by the more stringent result of jeopardizing the common fabric of trust and integrity in social roles and offices. These are roles that are regarded as trustworthy in large part due to the character of the agents occupying them, in whom privacy is intact. We can imagine circumstances when the honor of such privacy becomes a *prima facie* duty, trumped by the individual for the good of the community. A recent example is the government worker who revealed the private records of the toxic ingredients in cigarette production. Or surgical nurses who witness surgeons operating under the influence of alcohol or any other impairment to performing their role. Contingent privacy in these cases is negotiated by the obligation to avoid harm to the community. At a different level, one may ask, What ground is there for the contingent privacy to select the more stringent of the conflicting values? This I distinguish as the "reservoir of privacy itself"—the self that discerns and agonizes over what value choice is cogent with other respects of himself or herself.

I shall refer to this concept of privacy as substantive. *Substantive privacy* is the depth of one's relationships, those relatively few in which one feels a sense of unity and vulnerability. Within these relationships are expressions of trust, love, faith, friendship, and honor that are manifest in how one values social roles. Without substantive privacy, contingent privacy is thwarted. Privacy at this level is so closely bound with one's identity that, one could argue, when it is deprived, so is one's specific humanity. Sartre's phenomenology of "the look" so aptly demonstrates the nakedness one feels when observed—in his words—as an object. The unabashed shame of being caught transforms the subject into an object by "the look." At this moment the person is diminished by having an intention disclosed so one is left to compare oneself in relation to the other. One is caught and profoundly modified from the outside.

Similar accounts of this erosion of inner self appear in Erving Goffman's "On Characteristics of Total Institutions."[11] Goffman graphically writes of the mortified selves as part of the conditions of prisons and psychiatric hospitals. Such humiliating displays are also recounted in Victor Frankel's writings and the recent Rodopi publication of James Watson's *Between Auschwitz and Tradition*. The views poignantly show how social institutions deprive people of being persons. With invasions of this depth, a sense or privacy is likely to be irrevocably lost.

In our society, the substantive privacy of the homeless cannot be satisfied by shelters. The lives of the homeless are continually manipulated—to streets, to shelters, to jails, but not to a place, as one person expressed to me, "that he could open with his own key." Theirs is a stationless existence. Social policies maneuver them as "problems" since they are emptied of roles. (I would speculate that this may be the reason intolerance is increasing.) The solution is to find out-of-sight roles for them, and even these are incomplete for the population.

The McKinney Act for the Homeless does not provide accommodations for homeless families. More recently, HUD secretary Henry Cisneros announced that unusable military bases will be available to house these people. However helpful at some political level these efforts appear, they systematically deny the essential privacy—the substantive privacy—of homeless people. These are facile social efforts that disregard society's moral obligation to view these lives as conditions. The longer they go morally unfulfilled, the more the conditions will disintegrate their moral self-hood. The current policies leave the homeless vulnerable to their own liberties without the privacy that will enhance their self-respect. Unless we satisfy their right to a substantive privacy, they will lose their autonomy and community membership.

ENDNOTES

1. David M. O'Brien, *Privacy, Law, and Public Policy*. New York: Praeger Publishers, 1979, p. 178.
2. *Underclass* is used as an antonym for *middle class* for those whose lack of education, income, and employment do not follow "middle-class values." According to Christopher Jencks, it conjures up the chronically jobless high school dropout with children who has little or no money to support them and probably has a record crammed with welfare dependence. See Christopher Jencks, *Rethinking Social Policy*. Cambridge: Harvard University Press, 1992, pp. 199–201.
3. Robert M. Stewart, ed., *Readings in Social and Political Philosophy*. New York: Oxford University Press, 1986, p. 93.
4. The McKinney Homeless Assistance Act was the first official intervention by Congress to support housing for the homeless. It has undergone revisions after criticisms. Congress continues to address ways the Act could be more of an assistance than an obstacle to communities.
5. O'Brien, *Privacy, Law, and Public Policy*, p. 16.
6. Ferdinand Schoeman, ed., *Philosophical Dimensions of Privacy*. New York: Cambridge University Press, 1984, p. 205.
7. Ibid., p. 241.
8. Lon Fuller, cited in Edmund V. Ludwig, "The Mentally Ill Homeless: Evolving Involuntary Commitment Issues." *Villanova Law Review*, 36 (1991): 1095.
9. Ibid., p. 1095.
10. Wasserstrom, Richard. In Ferdinand Schoeman, ed., *Philosophical Dimensions of Privacy*. New York: Cambridge University Piers, 1984, p. 323.
11. Erving Goffman, *Asylums*. Chicago: Aldine, 1962, p. 118.

Closing Questions

1. Do people have a right to food and shelter? Does society have a duty to house those who cannot house themselves?

   _____

   _____

   _____

   _____

2. The following is taken from *Matter of Seltzer v. Hogue* (187 AD2d 23) (1994) and concerns the homeless Person Larry Hogue who gained national fame by repeatedly menacing passersby in New York City upon his numerous releases from psychiatric facilities:

   > The main question to be resolved on these appeals is whether the appellant, the Chief Executive Officer of Creedmore Psychiatric Center, met her burden of demonstrating, by clear and convincing evidence, that the respondent Larry Hogue is mentally-ill and in need of continued care and treatment, and that he poses a substantial threat of physical harm to himself or others, thereby justifying his retention at Creedmore Psychiatric Center. . . . The respondent, Larry Hogue, was admitted to Creedmore Psychiatric Center pursuant to Mental Hygiene Law Section 9.27, upon the application of the Commissioner of the New York City Department of Mental Health. . . . Hogue had been at Bellevue Hospital pursuant to court order for an evaluation of his competency to stand trial on a misdemeanor charge arising out of an incident in Manhattan in which Hogue allegedly scraped paint from a car. In their examining certificates, doctors Robert H. Berger and Henry C. Weinstein from Bellevue concurred that Hogue was suffering from an organic brain disorder which was the result of a head injury he had sustained in the military. Dr. Berger noted that significant frontal lobe damage was present. Both doctors concurred that Hogue was suffering from schizophrenia, residual type, and chronic substance abuse. The doctors noted that Hogue denied any mental illness or substance abuse, lacked insight into his illness or the impact of substance abuse on his behavior, thinking, and impulse control, and did not feel the need for any treatment. Dr. Berger further noted that Hogue had a history of prior psychiatric hospitalizations as well as a history of several criminal arrests involving threatening and destructive behavior. Dr. Weinstein observed that Hogue's past history indicated that he immediately stopped compliance with any treatment recommendations and began substance abuse upon his release from psychiatric hospitals. Finally, both doctors were of the opinion that Hogue would immediately deteriorate after his discharge and that, if discharged, he would be a danger to others. On January 21, 1993, . . . Hogue, through his counsel, re-

quested a court hearing . . . to contest his need for involuntary care and treatment.

How would you decide this case?

_____

_____

_____

_____

3. In response to an increasing number of complaints, New York City officials have erected barriers closing off areas frequented by the homeless. One must now have a ticket to stay inside a bus station, and it is a crime to sleep in the parks. Advocates for the homeless say these measures force them to either live on the streets, which is difficult in cold weather, or go to city shelters, which many regard as dangerous. In your judgment, do the homeless have a right to stay in public places? If not, on what grounds?

_____

_____

_____

_____

4. In the early years of Bill Clinton's presidency, his administration sought an unprecedented $1.7 billion to "break the cycle of homelessness and prevent future homelessness." The amount was more than four times the funds that were at the time available to heavily impacted areas. Would you support your tax dollars going to such an effort?

_____

_____

_____

_____

5. Between 1980 and 1988, a fourfold increase has occurred in the homeless population. This increase has been attributed to several factors: deinstitutionalization of the mentally ill, the crack epidemic of the 1980s, changes in the housing market, rent control, joblessness, and divorce. Which factors do you see as playing a key role? What other factors might have contributed to this phenomenon?

_____

_____

_____

_____

6. A correlation has been established between mental illness and homelessness. In your judgment, does mental illness cause homelessness or does homelessness cause mental illness? Answer the same question regarding the correlation between homelessness and alcohol or drug abuse.

_____

_____

_____

_____

7. Homelessness has been said to be a consequence of "family breakdown," and "married couples hardly ever become homeless as long as they stick together." To what extent does this make sense?

_____

_____

_____

_____

8. Will building more "cubicle hotels" solve the problem of homelessness?

_____

_____

_____

_____

9. Are the homeless passive victims of circumstance?

_____

_____

_____

_____

10. At present, a person can be involuntarily committed who is dangerous to himself or others. Should patients be institutionalized who, like "Billy Boggs" and Larry Hogue, are not presently dangerous but have a documented history of becoming dangerous?

_____

_____

_____

_____

11. If you were to become homeless, how should society treat you? What rights would you assert? What needs would you have?

_____

_____

_____

_____

12. Can choosing to be homeless ever be rational if a person can afford adequate housing?

_____

_____

_____

_____

For Further Reading

Abbarno, John, ed. *The Ethics of Homelessness.* Value Inquiry Book Series. Amsterdam and Atlanta: Rodopi, in press.

Bloch, Sidney, and Paul Chodoff. *Psychiatric Ethics.* New York: Oxford University Press, 1981.

Brooks, Alexander C. *Law, Psychiatry and the Mental Health System.* Boston: Little, Brown, 1974.

Fuller, Lon. "The Mentally-Ill Homeless: Evolving Involuntary Commitment Issues." *Villanova Law Review* 36 (1991).

Haber, Joram Graf. "The Freedom to Be Psychotic?" *Journal of Law and Health* 2: 157–171. Reprinted in Bernard M. Dickens, ed., *The International Library of Essays in Law and Legal Theory: Medicine and the Law.* Aldershot, Hants: Dartmouth Publishing Co., 1993.

Haber, Joram, and Lina Haber. "Law and Psychiatry." *The Encyclopedia of the Philosophy of Law* Garland, forthcoming.

Isaac, Rael Jean, and Virginia C. Armat. *Madness in the Streets: How Psychiatry and the Law Abandoned the Mentally-Ill.* Chicago, Ill.: Free Press, 1990.

Jacob, Joseph. "The Right of the Mental Patient to His Psychosis." *The Modern Law Review* 39: 17–42. Reprinted in Bernard M. Dickens, ed., *The International Library of Essays in Law & Legal Theory: Medicine and the Law.* Aldershot, Hants: Dartmouth Publishing Co., 1993.

Jencks, Christopher. *The Homeless.* Cambridge, Mass.: Harvard University Press, 1994.

Chapter 19

Environmental Ethics and Future Generations

Passages for Reflection

"Never does nature say one thing and wisdom another."

—*Juvenal*

"What the 21st century will be like depends on whether we learn the lessons of the 20th century and avoid repeating its worst mistakes . . . . For example, it would be disastrous if we began to renew our entire system of social relations by acting like a bull in a china shop."

—*Mikhail Gorbachev*

"Wilderness is the raw material out of which man has hammered the artifact called civilization."

—*Aldo Leopold*

"Man has lost the capacity to foresee and to forestall. He will end by destroying the Earth."

—*Albert Schweitzer*

Opening Questions

1. Are we morally obligated to respect the environment?
2. What obligations, if any, do we have to future generations?
3. Is the wilderness valuable in and of itself?

In recent years, environmental concern has focused on a host of problems ranging from the depletion of the ozone layer and the destruction of the rain forests to the pollution of rivers and streams. Many of these problems are a direct result of human activities. Thus, the amount of carbon dioxide in the atmosphere has increased dramatically since the Industrial Revolution and this has resulted in global warming. But even prior to the Industrial Revolution, the conversion of forests to agricultural fields, especially in North America, released large amounts of carbon dioxide into the air as trees were destroyed or left to decay. Since little was then known about trace gasses in the atmosphere, people of that era hardly considered the impact of their activities on future generations. The same cannot be said for people today. Knowing the adverse effects of our activities both for the present and future generations, we cannot afford to hide our heads in the sand. The question we must ask is what, if anything, should we do about today's environmental problems?

At first glance, it is strange to ask what, *if anything*, we should do about these problems, since many of us are convinced that something must be done. For many of us, to endure activities that will lead to the ruination of our natural environment is intolerable. If we continue to dump toxic waste into rivers, cut down forests, and strip-mine land, we will make the world inhabitable. But even if we agree that something must be done, what it is that we must do is not quite clear. Consider the considerable conveniences and economic benefits associated with activities that pollute the environment. How many of us would be willing to sacrifice such benefits in the name of a healthier environment? Would you and I be willing to give up the conveniences of the automobile (the single most significant polluter of our air) in exchange for cleaner and safer air? Would people be willing to forego the pleasures of living in luxurious condominiums or using disposable diapers if it meant not leveling a redwood grove?

Many of us *would* be willing to forego the benefits of industry and technology if we were convinced that our health were truly in jeopardy. Many of us are unwilling to give up such pleasures only because we underestimate their harms or because the harms associated with them are too remote to concern us. But a utilitarian analysis, properly undertaken, would reveal that maximizing pleasure if doing so means the ruination of our lives is truly unprofitable. Utilitarians would remind us that in assessing the consequences of our actions, we need to do so from a point of view that considers the interests of those affected in the long run as well as in the immediate future. This would include the interests not only of the present but of future generations.

But can we talk of the "interests of future generations?" Some philosophers think not. They think it incoherent to talk of the interests of people who do not yet exist.[1] How, for instance, can individuals who do not now exist have claims on people who do in fact exist? The issue is a thorny one especially if obligations derive from rights, as many philosophers commonly assert. The law of estates embraces this view in many jurisdictions. It prohibits us from bequeathing our possessions to our potential relatives. I cannot, for instance, leave my personal belongings to a son I hope to have, although I can to leave it to a son I actually have. If nonexistent people cannot have claims on existing ones, then why should we be obliged to respect our (distant) progeny?[2]

The issue has no obvious solution. Some philosophers take the position that just as the dead have rights even though they no longer exist (for example, the right to rest in peace), then potential people can have rights even though they don't exist.[3] But do dead people have rights? Suppose you are obligated not to interfere with the "rest" of a dead person or are obligated to carry out the deceased person's last wishes. That these obligations arise from that person's present rights is not clear. More probably, the obligations arise indirectly out of the interests of other people. Even if we agree that future people have rights, which people in the future we are talking about remains unclear. Are we talking about our remote descendants or just those who may be harmed or benefited by our conduct?

Even if we could resolve the question of whether future people have rights, we would still have to determine how to balance these rights against the rights of actual people.[4] May we, for instance, exterminate a single actual person if doing so meant saving a generation of distant people? In a *Star Trek* episode that raised this question, the crew of the *Enterprise* traveled back in time and landed on Earth prior to World War II. There they encountered the activities of a pacifist, played by Joan Collins, whose antiwar sentiments would have delayed America's discovery of the Atomic Bomb. This, in turn, would have resulted in a despot com-

---

[1]See, e.g., Richard T. DeGeorge, "Do We Owe the Future Anything?" *Law and the Ecological Challenge* (1978): 180–190. Reprinted in James Sterba, ed., *Morality in Practice*, 3rd ed. (Belmont, Calif.: Wadsworth, 1991).

[2]But see Thomas Magnell, "Present Concerns and Future Interests," pp. 589–593.

[3]See Sterba, *Morality in Practice*, p. 76.

[4]For a valuable discussion about how to weigh and balance the interests of actual people versus the interests of future people, see Josef Popper-Lynkeus, *The Individual and the Value of Human Life*, translated by Andrew Karl Kelley with Joram Graf Haber (Savage, Md.: Rowman and Littlefield, 1995).

ing into power and causing greater misery than that caused by World War II. The crew was faced, then, with either killing the pacifist and preventing the despot from taking power, or not killing her and allowing the suffering of those who would be under the despot's control. Complicating this dilemma was the fact that the character played by Joan Collins existed then and there, whereas those under the despot's control only potentially existed. (It didn't help that Captain Kirk fell in love with the pacifist!) The episode ended with the pacifist being hit by a truck and with Dr. McCoy preventing Kirk from coming to her rescue.

Some philosophers argue that all this talk of actual versus potential people is irrelevant since the future is too uncertain and unforeseeable to worry ourselves about. If we stay true to form, we will always have the technology to solve whatever problems we are likely to encounter. For example, we are now reversing the degeneration of the ozone layer. As Jan Narveson is fond of pointing out, our most valuable resources are in unlimited supply. Resources, he says, do not consist of pieces of raw material, but of how much we can do with that material. How much we can do with that material depends on how ingenious we are. Hence, the most valuable resource we possess is *sand*, the virtually unlimited material out of which silicon is made, from which we make computer chips on which we depend for our technical know-how.[5] Thus, the main reason why we have so far not invested heavily in environmentally friendly actions has been economics. But just as we switched from coal to natural gas, which is cleaner and in greater abundance, we could undoubtedly tap other environmentally friendly sources (say, the sun) if we needed to. We could also develop an efficient electric car, find storehouses for toxic wastes (the moon?), and so forth.

Admittedly, this talk about actual versus potential people also sounds odd. I am reminded of Ludwig Wittgenstein's comment that philosophers are ever trying to show the fly the way out of the bottle even while suggesting that it is the philosopher who puts the fly there.[6]

Our discussion of whether we should respect the environment for the benefit of people (real or potential) presupposes that human benefit is the relevant criterion in determining our obligations in regard to the rest of the environment. Some philosophers, however, resent this "anthropocentric" bias. For them, the environment would be valuable even if people did not value it. They claim that something is morally objectionable about the destruction of nature beyond the adverse effects it has on people. To prove this point, Peter Wenz[7] asks us to imagine that we

---

[5]Jan Narveson, *Moral Matters* (Peterborough, Ontario: Broadview Press, 1993), p. 160.

[6]Wittgenstien also thought that philosophy *should* show the fly the way out of the bottle.

[7]This example is taken from Peter S. Wenz, "Ecology and Morality." In Harlan B. Miller and William H. Williams, eds., *Ethics and Animals* (Clifton, N.J.: Humana Press, 1983), pp. 185–191.

are piloting a bomber over the ocean when we notice that we are dangerously low on fuel. In an effort to reduce the weight of the plane, we are forced to unload some bombs either in the middle of the ocean or on a cluster of islands not inhabited by anything other than viable ecosystems (rivers, sandbars, meadow mice, flowers, etc.). If we unload the bombs in the ocean, the bombs will deactivate harmlessly, whereas if we unload them on the islands, we would destroy their ecosystem. All things being equal, most of us would feel obligated to drop the bombs in the ocean. The question is: Why? What basis exists for having obligations to the environment other than human welfare?

Several attempts have been made to develop an environmental ethic that is free of an anthropocentric bias. The most interesting of these have been influenced by the environmentalist Aldo Leopold (1887–1948), who argued against the view that the wilderness has value only insofar as it is valuable to people. Instead, Leopold advocated expanding the boundary of the moral community to include animals, plants, and the soil. This *land ethic*, as it is called after Leopold's essay by that name, is "holistic" or "biocentric" in nature: it regards human beings as part of an interdependent system or community. Since a *community* is a collection of individuals engaging in cooperative behavior, and *ethics* is a code of conduct ensuring cooperation among its members, what results is an ethic regarding nature as inherently valuable over and above its utility value. Leopold writes:

> The land ethic simply enlarges the boundaries of the community to include soils, waters, plants, animals, or collectively the land. . . . In short, a land ethic changes the role of homo sapiens from conqueror of the land community to plain member and citizen of it. It implies respect for his fellow-members, and also respect for the community as such. . . . A thing is right when it tends to preserve the integrity, stability, and beauty of the biotic community. It is wrong when it tends otherwise.[8]

To appreciate what drives the biocentric approach, it may be helpful to remember that human beings are part of nature like nature's other many members. We are composed of elements (oxygen, hydrogen, and carbon) like other natural bodies even if our arrangement and proportions are exceedingly unique. In this view, humankind is not placed on the planet by an outside agent such as God but developed from the earth and is the earth. As one philosopher has poetically put it, humankind is the earth reflecting upon itself.[9]

---

[8]Aldo Leopold, "The Land Ethic." In *A Sand County Almanac* (New York: Oxford University Press, 1966), pp., 219, 220, 240.

[9]I believe it was Tom Berry who said this under the influence of Pierre Teilhard De Chardin. See Teilhard's *The Phenomenon of Man* (New York: Harper & Row, 1959). (The song, "We Are the World," is reminiscent of this idea.)

We are tempted to say that we have an anthropocentric ethic that argues against respecting nature since it is only human welfare that is morally relevant, while we have a nonanthropocentric ethic that argues for respecting the environment for its own sake. But this would be a false dichotomy. We can derive a rich environmental ethic from anthropocentric premises where the benefits of conservation far exceed its costs.[10] We can even derive an environmental ethic from the "sentientist" claim that the interests of all sentient beings (not just human beings) determine moral obligations. In this view, we might have a moral obligation to preserve the environment if its destruction would harm some nonhuman animals.[11] Even so, defenders of a land ethic would insist that deriving an environmental ethic from anthropocentric or sentientist concerns leads to doing the right thing (conserving nature) for the wrong reasons (human or animal welfare). Instead of respecting nature for nature's sake, we would be respecting nature for our sake or the sake of nonhuman animals. The person who respects nature for those reasons would be no different from the student who does not cheat on exams because he or she is afraid of getting caught rather than because it is wrong to cheat on exams.

Having refined this distinction, we are still in the position of deciding whether the biocentric approach is intellectually compelling. We still need to ask whether an environmental system can serve as the locus of moral value. Let us return to Peter Wenz's case where he asks us to choose between dropping a cargo of bombs harmlessly in the ocean or on a cluster of islands containing viable ecosystems. Assuming that we would drop the bombs harmlessly in the ocean, Wenz infers that we have a *prima facie* obligation to respect nature beyond anthropocentric concerns. Aside from the fact that intuitions vary and are notoriously unreliable, Wenz's case proves very little.

Suppose we were given the choice between dropping our bombs not harmlessly in the ocean or on the cluster of islands that Wenz describes (call these Wenz's Islands), but between Wenz's Islands and, say, Gilligan's Island—that is, an island populated with human beings. Let us also suppose, to forestall objections, that Gilligan's Island is void of any viable ecosystems.[12] Presumably, even Wenz would say that we should drop the bombs on his cluster of islands. The reason for this would have something to do with the relative value of human beings vis-à-vis the environment. But if this is so, then even if the environment has inherent value, its

---

[10]See, for example, William Godfrey-Smith, "The Value of Wilderness." *Environmental Ethics* 1 (Winter 1979): 309–319 and John Passmore, *Man's Responsibility for Nature* (New York: Charles Scribner's Sons, 1974).

[11]See, for example, Bernard Rollin, "Environmental Ethics" in Steven Luper-Foy, ed., *Problems of International Justice* (Boulder, Col.: Westview Press, 1988), pp. 125–131.

[12]I owe this caveat to Joshua Levit Haber.

value pales next to the value of people. If that is so, then why should we respect the environment unless it is in our interest to do so? Why *not* develop nature if doing so benefits human beings?

Let us suppose, then, that the value of nature pales next to the value of human beings and for that reason fails to fortify the claims of holistic environmentalists (or "deep ecologists" as they are sometimes called). Still, we cannot deny that such a view is inspirational inasmuch as, in their view, the earth is a much more comforting place to live than, say, in a Cartesian view which sees human beings and the external world at odds with each other.[13] But poetry aside, is there any reason to believe that the deep ecologist has shown we have a *moral* obligation to the environment as such? We may need to distinguish moral value from value as such. While not denying the value of ecosystems, environments, forests, and biospheres, we might be fairer to say that while these have value, their value is aesthetic rather than moral, like a great work of art has aesthetic rather than moral value. And just as we should not wantonly destroy great works of art because of their unique beauty, complexity, and history, so, too, we ought not to wantonly destroy the environment. Perhaps, finally, we should reserve the term *ethics* for codes of conduct governing what people (or sentient beings) should and should not do.

Other efforts have been made at establishing an environmental ethic other than the biocentric one characteristic of deep ecologists. A more individualistic approach might appeal to the rights or interests, say, of trees and plants. In this view, the problem with, say, strip-mining is that it fails to give weight to the survival and health of the plants it destroys. But while we admittedly talk about what is "good" for plants, and while some of us believe that if we talk to plants they will respond favorably, we take a huge step when we go from there to talking about plants (or trees) having rights, for the simple reason that they lack consciousness.

Yet another effort at establishing an environmental ethic that is nonanthropocentric is by appealing to religious beliefs. (Tom Berry takes this approach.) The claim is made that God has entrusted us with the care of the environment and we should respect it for that reason, or also that God is immanent in nature, giving it a special value. The problem with this tack is that it requires a premise at least as controversial as the conclusion it tries to establish.

A more promising tack is taken by Thomas E. Hill, Jr.,[14] who asks whether, utilities aside, we can explain the uneasiness we feel at some-

---

[13]See Descartes, *Meditations on First Philosophy*, where in Meditation II a distinction is drawn between conscious minds and mechanically arranged substances.

[14]See Thomas E. Hill, Jr., "Ideals of Human Excellence and Preserving Natural Environments." *Environmental Ethics* 5 (1983): 211–224. Reprinted in Joram Graf Haber, ed., *Doing and Being: Selected Readings in Moral Philosophy* (Englewood Cliffs, N.J.: Prentice Hall, 1993), pp. 428–441.

one who would, say, pave a garden of wild flowers with asphalt or strip-mine a large section of the Appalachians. Having rejected efforts at establishing an independent environmental ethic, Hill concludes that our uneasiness derives not from these actions but from the agents who perform them. What kind of person, asks Hill, would view Yellowstone Park as a potential site for a condominium complex, or a three-thousand-year-old sequoia as a profitable museum item? A person, says Hill, who suffers from a lack of humility.

According to Hill, only someone extraordinarily arrogant would view the natural world as so much utility for humanity to use and abuse. A more proper attitude is to appreciate that human beings are only on the planet for a short time relative to a universe that transcends them in grandeur. We should, then, be humbled when contemplating the starry skies in August on a clear New England night, the magnificence of a red-wood forest, or the splendor of Niagara Falls. Failure to do so, says Hill, bespeaks a lack of humility which, as a vice, is a trait that we ought not to cultivate.

Hill's argument is noteworthy inasmuch as he does not appeal to quasi-metaphysical entities as loci of moral value while at the same time accounting for our uneasiness toward those who would wreck the environment with impunity. Instead, he aims to explain our uneasiness by employing a virtue-based approach which looks not at actions and how they are right or wrong, but at agents and how they are good or bad. Hill's argument gives rise to the problem that it could be turned around and used against him. Rather than minimizing the uniqueness of human beings against a universe that transcends them, we could easily stress their uniqueness and assert their arrogance. In other words, reflecting on our apparently unique ability to understand the world can be a ground of arrogance just as much as it can be a ground of humility. Kant said that he was moved by the starry stars at night just as much as the moral law within.

To conclude, environmental ethics represents one of several attempts to expand ethics beyond distinctly human interests. Other efforts include, most notably, the animal rights movement (see Chapter 3) which has affinities with environmental ethics but differences as well. We can safely say that philosophical attempts to expand the moral community are the most pervasive characteristic of applied ethics in the 1990s, as ethicists have reacted to what they perceive to be the narrow position that people alone are morally considerable.

While I don't deny that something is to be said against anthropocentrism, I find it unclear what that something is. People surely ascribe value to people and deny it to nonpeople, as the "in" crowd in high school ascribes value to "in" people and denies it to others. But being suspicious of anthropomorphism is not enough to establish an expansionist ethic, particularly one that is environmentalist. More argumentation is required. The field is young and the work just begun.

Eric Katz is Professor of Philosophy at New Jersey Institute of Technology. He was the first student in the United States to write a doctoral dissertation on environmental ethics and is today the author of several articles in that field.

Video Presentation

Guest: Eric Katz, Professor of Philosophy, New Jersey Institute of Technology

Student Panel: Sucila Fernandez, Mary Lou Casagrande, Jackie Enfield

By way of introduction, I ask Katz to provide an overview of environmental ethics, to which he responds that what I refer to as "environmental ethics" covers various and sundry movements in the field. For some, environmental ethics is about taking conventional moral categories and applying them to issues that concern the environment; for others, including Katz, it is about taking a revolutionary approach to ethics by asking, "What kind of entities are morally considerable?" and answering with "nature" rather than "human beings." As Katz eloquently puts it, his concern is not so much with "the ethics of nature" as it is with "the nature of ethics."

Not content with this distinction, I press Katz to differentiate between the approach that utilizes conventional categories to solve environmental problems and the more radical approach to which Katz refers. Katz explains his position by saying that nature has value in and of itself, making it wrong for us to destroy nature even if doing so would benefit people. If, say, we were able to destroy the ozone layer and later replace it with an artificial shield, this would be wrong even though people might benefit from the shield. The reason for this is that we would be deprived of the value that is inherent in the original ozone layer. In this regard, says Katz, environmental ethics parallels conventional ethics: conventional ethics argues that even if the whole human race would benefit by enslaving a minority of people, to do so would be wrong since the enslaved minority has inherent value.

We next discuss how environmental ethics is part of a larger concern to extend the moral community beyond the interests of the human one.

I ask Katz to explain how environmental ethics differs from the animal rights movement. After citing Mark Sagoff's paper addressing this very same question, Katz answers that environmental ethics is more radical in that it takes whole systems and natural objects as loci of moral value as opposed to individual sentient beings such as human beings and animals.

The conversation turns to a discussion of Katz's controversial paper, "The Big Lie: Human Restoration of Nature" (pp. 579–586). I ask him to explain the *big lie*. He says it is a term used by Robert Elliot in a paper of his called "Faking Nature." There, Elliot attacks "the restoration thesis" according to which a restored nature, if such a thing were possible, could not possibly be "as good as new." Drawing an analogy with objects of art, Katz agues that even if we had the technology to restore a decimated environment to a state that would be indistinguishable from the original, it is a big lie to think that the restored nature would be just as valuable just as it is a big lie to think a duplicated work of art is as valuable as its original. The reason for this is that the copy lacks the "historical genesis" of the original. Furthermore, inasmuch as the artifact is, by definition, constructed for the sake of human beings, it is fundamentally anthropocentric and consequently less valuable than its natural archetype. Thus, though good reasons may be found for having a replica when we cannot have the original (for example, restored beaches that have been eroded by a storm), the original is never as good as new and for that reason alone we should respect nature.

Following the break, members of Bergen Community College's environmental club throw some questions Katz's way. The president of the club, Sucila Fernandez, asks Katz to comment on recent attempts to develop Walden Woods. Mary Lou Casagrande asks Katz about the rain forests of Brazil. And vice-president Jackie Enfield asks Katz about preservation and ethical responsibility. The show concludes with a brief discussion about the relationship between environmental ethics and virtue theory.

In this essay, Eric Katz questions the environmentalists' concern for the restoration of nature and argues against the view that humanity has the ability and obligation to restore nature where it has been damaged. In Katz's view, even if we were able to flawlessly replace a decimated environment, the replaced version would be an artifact and thus would not be as valuable as the original. To think that the replicated version would be as good as the original feeds an anthropocentric ethic that Katz thinks we are better off abandoning.

The Big Lie: Human Restoration of Nature

Eric Katz

> The trail of the human serpent is thus over everything.
> —*William James,* Pragmatism

I

I begin with an empirical point, based on my own random observations: the idea that humanity can restore or repair the natural environment has begun to play an important part in decisions regarding environmental policy. We are urged to plant trees to reverse the "greenhouse effect." Real estate developers are obligated to restore previously damaged acreage in exchange for building permits.[1] The U.S. National Park Service spends $33 million to "rehabilitate" 39,000 acres of the Redwood Creek watershed.[2] And the U.S. Forest Service is criticized for its "plantation" mentality: it is harvesting trees from old-growth forests rather than "redesigning" forests according to the sustainable principles of nature. "Restoration forestry is the only true forestry," claims an environmentally-conscious former employee of the Bureau of Land Management.[3]

These policies present the message that humanity should repair the damage that human intervention has caused the natural environment. The message is an optimistic one, for it implies that we recognize the harm we have caused in the natural environment and that we possess the means and will to correct these harms. These policies also make us feel good; the prospect of restoration relieves the guilt that we feel about the destruction of nature. The wounds we have inflicted on the natural world are not permanent; nature can be made "whole" again. Our natural resource base and foundation for survival can be saved by the appropriate policies of restoration, regeneration, and redesign.

It is also apparent that these ideas are not restricted to policymakers, environmentalists, or the general public—they have begun to pervade the normative principles of philosophers concerned with developing an adequate environmental ethic. Paul Taylor uses a concept of "restitutive justice" both as one of the basic rules of duty in his biocentric ethic and as a "priority principle" to resolve competing claims.[4] The basic idea of this rule is that human violaters of nature will in some way repair or compensate injured natural entities and systems. Peter Wenz also endorses a principle of restitution as being essential to an adequate theory of environmental ethics; he then attacks Taylor's theory for not presenting a coherent principle.[5] The idea that humanity is morally responsible for reconstructing natural areas and entities—species, communities, ecosystems—thus becomes a central concern of an applied environmental ethic.

In this paper I question the environmentalists' concern for the restoration of nature and argue against the optimistic view that humanity has the obligation and ability to repair or reconstruct damaged natural systems. This conception of environmental policy and envi-

Eric Katz, "The Big Lie: Human Restoration of Nature", *Research in Philosophy and Technology*, Vol. 12, 231–241. © 1992 JAI Press, Inc.

ronmental ethics is based on a misperception of natural reality and a misguided understanding of the human place in the natural environment. On a simple level, it is the same kind of "technological fix" that has engendered the environmental crisis. Human science and technology will fix, repair, and improve natural processes. On a deeper level, it is an expression of an anthropocentric world view, in which human interests shape and redesign a comfortable natural reality. A "restored" nature is an artifact created to meet human satisfactions and interests. Thus, on the most fundamental level, it is an unrecognized manifestation of the insidious dream of the human domination of nature. Once and for all, humanity will demonstrate its mastery of nature by "restoring" and repairing the degraded ecosystems of the biosphere. Cloaked in an environmental consciousness, human power will reign supreme.

II

It has been eight years since Robert Elliot published his sharp and accurate criticism of "the restoration thesis."[6] In an article entitled "Faking Nature," Elliot examined the moral objections to the practical environmental policy of restoring damaged natural systems, locations, landscapes. For the sake of argument, Elliot assumed that the restoration of a damaged area could be recreated perfectly, so that the area would appear in its original condition after the restoration was completed. He then argued that the perfect copy of the natural area would be of less value than the original, for the newly restored natural area would be analogous to an art forgery. Two points seem crucial to Elliot's argument. First, the value of objects can be explained "in terms of their origins, in terms of the kinds of processes that brought them into being."[7] We value an art work in part because of the fact that a particular artist, a human individual, created the work at a precise moment in historical time. Similarly, we value a natural area because of its "special kind of continuity with the past." But to understand the art work or the natural area in their historical contexts we require a special kind of insight or knowledge. Thus, the second crucial point of Elliot's argument is the co-existence of "understanding and evaluation." The art expert brings to the analysis and evaluation of a work of art a full range of information about the artist, the period, the intentions of the work, and so on. In a similar way, the evaluation of a natural area is informed by a detailed knowledge of ecological processes, a knowledge that can be learned as easily as the history of art.[8] To value the restored landscape as much as the original is thus a kind of ignorance; we are being fooled by the superficial similarities to the natural area, just as the ignorant art "appreciator" is fooled by the appearance of the art forgery.

Although Elliot's argument has had a profound effect on my own thinking about environmental issues, I believed that the problem he uses as a starting point is purely theoretical, almost fanciful.[9] After all, who would possibly believe that a land developer or a strip mining company would actually restore a natural area to its original state? Elliot himself claims that "the restoration thesis" is generally used "as a way of undermining the arguments of conservationists."[10] Thus it is with concern that I discover that serious environmentalist thinkers, as noted above, have argued for a position similar to Elliot's "restoration thesis." The restoration of a damaged nature is seen not only as a practical option for environmental policy but also as a moral obligation for right-thinking environmentalists. If we are to continue human projects which (unfortunately) impinge on the natural environment (it is claimed), then we must repair the damage. In a few short years a "sea-change" has occurred: what Elliot attacked as both a physical impossibility and a moral mistake is now advocated as proper environmental policy. Am I alone in thinking that something has gone wrong here?

Perhaps not enough people have read Elliot's arguments; neither Taylor nor Wenz, the principal advocates of restitutive environmental justice, list this article in their notes or bibliographies. Perhaps we need to re-examine the idea of recreating a natural landscape; in what sense is this action analogous to an art forgery? Perhaps we need to push beyond Elliot's analysis, to use his arguments as a starting point for a deeper investigation into the fundamental errors of restoration policy.

III

My initial reaction to the possibility of restoration policy is almost entirely visceral: I am outraged by the idea that a technologically created "nature" will be passed off as reality. The human presumption that we are capable of this technological fix demonstrates (once again) the arrogance with which humanity surveys the natural world. Whatever the problem may be, there will be a technological, mechanical, or scientific solution. Human engineering will modify the secrets of natural processes and effect a satisfactory result. Chemical fertilizers will increase food production; pesticides will control disease-carrying insects; hydroelectric dams will harness the power of our rivers. The familiar list goes on and on.

The relationship between this technological mind-set and the environmental crisis has been amply demonstrated, and need not concern us here.[11] My interest is narrower. I want to focus on the creation of artifacts, for that is what technology does. The recreated natural environment that is the end result of a restoration project is nothing more than an artifact created for human use. The problem for an applied environmental ethic is the determination of the moral value of this artifact.

Recently, Michael Losonsky has pointed out how little we know about the nature, structure, and meaning of artifacts. "[C]ompared to the scientific study of nature, the scientific study of artifacts is in its infancy."[12] What is clear, of course, is that an artifact is not equivalent to a natural object; but the precise difference, or set of differences, is not readily apparent. Indeed, when we consider objects such as beaver dams, we are unsure if we are dealing with natural objects or artifacts. Fortunately, however, these kinds of

animal-created artifacts can be safely ignored in the present investigation. Nature restoration projects are obviously human. A human built dam is clearly artifactual.

The concepts of function and purpose are central to an understanding of artifacts. Losonsky rejects the Aristotelian view that artifacts (as distinguished from natural objects) have no inner nature or hidden essence that can be discovered. Artifacts have a "nature" that is partially comprised of three features: "internal structure, purpose, and manner of use." This nature, in turn, explains why artifacts "have predictable lifespans during which they undergo regular and predictable changes."[13] The structure, function, and use of the artifacts determine to some extent the changes which they undergo. Clocks would not develop in a manner which prevented the measurement of time.

Natural objects lack the kind of purpose and function found in artifacts. As Andrew Brennan has argued, natural entities have no "intrinsic functions," as he calls them, for they were not the result of design. They were not created for a particular purpose; they have no set manner of use. Although we often speak as if natural individuals (for example, predators) have roles to play in ecosystemic well-being (the maintenance of optimum population levels), this kind of talk is either metaphorical or fallacious. No one created or designed the mountain lion as a regulator of the deer population.[14]

This is the key point. Natural individuals were not designed for a purpose. They lack intrinsic functions, making them different from human-created artifacts. Artifacts, I claim are essentially anthropocentric. They are created for human use, human purpose—they serve a function for human life. Their existence is centered on human life. It would be impossible to imagine an artifact not designed to meet a human purpose. Without a foreseen use the object would not be created. This is completely different from the way natural entities and species evolve to fill ecological niches in the biosphere.

The doctrine of anthropocentrism is thus

an essential element in understanding the meaning of artifacts. This conceptual relationship is not generally problematic, for most artifacts are human creations designed for use in human social and cultural contexts. But once we begin to redesign natural systems and processes, once we begin to create restored natural environments, we impose our anthropocentric purposes on areas that exist outside human society. We will construct so-called natural objects on the model of human desires, interests, and satisfactions. Depending on the adequacy of our technology, these restored and redesigned natural areas will appear more or less natural, but they will never be natural—they will be anthropocentrically designed human artifacts.

A disturbing example of this conceptual problem applied to environmental policy can be found in Chris Maser's *The Redesigned Forest*. Maser is a former research scientist for the United States Department of Interior Bureau of Land Management. His book attests to his deeply felt commitment to the policy of "sustainable" forestry, as opposed to the short term expediency of present day forestry practices. Maser argues for a forestry policy that "restores" the forest as it harvests it; we must be true foresters and not "plantation" managers.

Nonetheless, Maser's plans for "redesigning" forests reveal several problems about the concepts and values implicit in restoration policy. First, Maser consistently compares the human design of forests with Nature's design. The entire first chapter is a series of short sections comparing the two "designs." In the "Introduction," he writes, "[W]e are redesigning our forests from Nature's blueprint to humanity's blueprint."[15] But Nature, of course, does not have a blueprint, nor a design. As a zoologist, Maser knows this; but his metaphorical talk is dangerous. It implies that we can discover the plan, the methods, the processes of nature, and mold them to our purposes.

Maser himself often writes as if he accepts that implication. The second problem with his argument is the comparison of nature to a mechanism that we do not fully understand. The crucial error we make in simplifying forest ecology—turning forests into plantations—is that we are assuming our design for the forest mechanism is better than nature's. "Forests are not automobiles in which we can tailor artificially substituted parts for original parts."[16] How true. But Maser's argument against this substitution is empirical: "A forest cannot be 'rebuilt' and remain the same forest, but we could probably rebuild a forest similar to the original if we knew how. No one has ever done it. . . . [W]e do not have a parts catalog, or a maintenance manual. . . ."[17] The implication is that if we did have a catalog and manual, if nature were known as well as artifactual machines, then the restoration of forests would be morally and practically acceptable. This conclusion serves as Maser's chief argument for the preservation of old-growth and other unmanaged forests: "We have to maintain some original, unmanaged old-growth forest, mature forest, and young-growth forest as parts catalog, maintenance manual, and service department from which to learn to practice restoration forestry."[18] Is the forest-as-parts-catalogue a better guiding metaphor than the forest-as-plantation?

This mechanistic conception of nature underlies, or explains, the third problem with Maser's argument. His goal for restoration forestry, his purpose in criticizing the short-term plantation mentality, is irredeemably anthropocentric. The problem with present-day forestry practices is that they are "exclusive of all other human values except production of fast-growth wood fiber."[19] It is the elimination of other human values and interests that concerns Maser. "We need to learn to see the forest as the factory that produces raw materials. . . ." to meet our "common goal[:] . . . a sustainable forest for a sustainable industry for a sustainable environment for a sustainable human population."[20] Restoration forestry is necessary because it is the best method for achieving the human goods which we extract from nature. Our goal is to build a better "factory-forest," using the complex knowledge of forest ecology.

What is disturbing about Maser's position is that it comes from an environmentalist. Unlike

Elliot's theoretical opponents of conservation, who wished to subvert the environmentalist position with the "restoration thesis," Maser advocates the human design of forests as a method of environmental protection and conservation for human use. His conclusion shows us the danger of using anthropocentric and mechanistic models of thought in the formulation of environmental policy. These models leave us with forests that are "factories" for the production of human commodities, spare-parts catalogs for the maintenance of the machine.

I began this section with a report of my visceral reaction to the technological re-creation of natural environments. This reaction has now been explained and analyzed. Nature restoration projects are the creations of human technologies, and as such, are artifacts. But artifacts are essentially the constructs of an anthropocentric world view. They are designed by humans for humans to satisfy human interests and needs. Artifactual restored nature is thus fundamentally different from natural objects and systems which exist without human design. It is not surprising, then, that we view restored nature with a value different from the original.

IV

To this point, my analysis has supported the argument and conclusions of Elliot's criticism of "the restoration thesis." But further reflection on the nature of artifacts, and the comparison of forests to well run machines, makes me doubt the central analogy which serves as the foundation of his case. Can we compare an undisturbed natural environment to a work of art? Should we?

As noted in Section II, Elliot uses the art/nature analogy to make two fundamental points about the process of evaluation: (1) the importance of a continuous causal history; and (2) the use of knowledge about this causal history to make appropriate judgments. A work of art or a natural entity which lacks a continuous causal history, as understood by the expert in the field, would be judged infe-

rior. If the object is "passed off" as an original, with its causal history intact, then we would judge it to be a forgery or an instance of "faked" nature.

I do not deny that this is a powerful analogy. It demonstrates the crucial importance of causal history in the analysis of value. But the analogy should not be pushed too far, for the comparison suggests that we possess an understanding of art forgery that is now simply being applied to natural objects. I doubt that our understanding of art forgery involves basic ontological questions about the meaning of art. Cebik claims that it is mistake to focus exclusively on questions of value when analyzing art forgeries, for the practice of forgery raises fundamental issues about the status of art itself.[21]

According to Cebik, an analysis of forgeries demonstrates that our understanding of art is dominated by a limiting paradigm—"production by individuals." We focus almost exclusively on the individual identity of the artist as the determining factor in assessing authenticity. "Nowhere . . . is there room for paradigmatic art being fluid, unfinished, evolving, and continuous in its creation." Cebik has in mind a dynamic, communally based art, an ever-changing neighborhood mural or music passed on for generations.[22] Another example would be classical ballet, a performance of which is a unique dynamic movement, different from every other performance of the same ballet.

These suggestions about a different paradigm of art show clearly, I think, what is wrong with the art/nature analogy as a useful analytical tool. Natural entities and systems are much more akin to the fluid evolving art of Cebik's alternative model than they are to the static, finished, individual artworks of the dominant paradigm. It is thus an error to use criteria of forgery and authenticity that derive from an individualistic, static conception of art for an evaluation of natural entities and systems. Natural entities and systems are nothing like static, finished objects of art. They are fluid, evolving systems which completely transcend the category of artist or creator. The perceived disvalue in restored natural objects does not derive from a misunderstanding over the identity of the creator of the objects. It derives instead from the misplaced category of "creator"—for natural objects do not have creators or designers as human artworks do. Once we realize that the natural entity we are viewing has been "restored" by a human artisan it ceases to be a natural object. It is not a forgery; it is an artifact.

We thus return to artifacts, and their essential anthropocentric nature. We cannot (and should not) think of natural objects as artifacts, for this imposes a human purpose or design on their very essence. As artifacts, they are evaluated by their success in meeting human interests and needs, not by their own intrinsic being. Using the art/nature analogy of forgery reinforces the impression that natural objects are similar to artifacts—artworks—and that they can be evaluated using the same anthropocentric criteria. Natural entities have to be evaluated on their own terms, not as artworks, machines, factories, or any other human-created artifact.

V

But what are the terms appropriate for the evaluation of natural objects? What criteria should be used? To answer this question we need to do more than differentiate natural objects from artifacts; we need to examine the essence or nature of natural objects. What does it mean to say that an entity is natural (and hence, not an artifact)? Is there a distinguishing mark or characteristic that determines the descriptive judgment? What makes an object natural, and why is the standard not met through the restoration process?

The simple answer to this question—a response I basically support—is that the natural is defined as being independent of the actions of humanity. Thus, Taylor advocates a principle of non-interference as a primary moral duty in his ethic of respect for nature. "[W]e put aside our personal likes and our human interests. . . . Our respect for nature means that we acknowledge the sufficiency of the

natural world to sustain its own proper order throughout the whole domain of life."[23] The processes of the natural world that are free of human interference are the most natural.

There are two obvious problems with this first simple answer. First, there is the empirical point that the human affect on the environment is, by now, fairly pervasive. No part of the natural world lies untouched by our pollution and technology. In a sense, then, nothing natural truly exists (anymore). Second, there is the logical point that humans themselves are naturally evolved beings, and so all human actions would be "natural," regardless of the amount of technology used or the interference on nonhuman nature. The creation of artifacts is a natural human activity, and thus the distinction between artifact and natural object begins to blur.

These problems in the relationship of humanity to nature are not new. Mill raised similar objections to the idea of "nature" as a moral norm over a hundred years ago, and I need not review his arguments.[24] The answer to these problems is twofold. First, we admit that the concepts of "natural" and "artifactual" are not absolutes; they exist along a spectrum, where various gradations of both concepts can be discerned. The human effect on the natural world is pervasive, but there are differences in human actions that make a descriptive difference. A toxic waste dump is different from a compost heap of organic material. To claim that both are equally non-natural would obscure important distinctions.

A second response is presented by Brennan.[25] Although a broad definition of "natural" denotes independence from human management or interference, a more useful notion (because it has implications for value theory and ethics) can be derived from the consideration of evolutionary adaptations. Our natural diet is the one we are adapted for, that is "in keeping with our nature." All human activity is not unnatural, only that activity which goes beyond our biological and evolutionary capacities. As an example, Brennan cites the procedure of "natural childbirth," that is, childbirth free of technological medical interventions. "Childbirth is an especially striking example of the wildness within us . . . where we can appreciate the natural at first hand. . . ." It is natural, free, and wild not because it is a nonhuman activity—after all, it is human childbirth—but because it is independent of a certain type of human activity, actions designed to control or to manipulate natural processes.

The "natural" then is a term we use to designate objects and processes that exist as far as possible from human manipulation and control. Natural entities are autonomous in ways that human-created artifacts are not; as Taylor writes, "to be free to pursue the realization of one's good according to the laws of one's nature."[26] When we thus judge natural objects, and evaluate them more highly than artifacts, we are focusing on the extent of their independence from human domination. In this sense, then, human actions can also be judged to be natural—these are the human actions that exist as evolutionary adaptations, free of the control and alteration of technological processes.

If these reflections on the meaning of "natural" are plausible, then it should be clear why the restoration process fails to meet the criteria of naturalness. The attempt to redesign, recreate, and restore natural areas and objects is a radical intervention in natural processes. Although there is an obvious spectrum of possible restoration and redesign projects which differ in their value—Maser's redesigned sustainable forest is better than a tree plantation—all of these projects involve the manipulation and domination of natural areas. All of these projects involve the creation of artifactual natural realities, the imposition of anthropocentric interests on the processes and objects of nature. Nature is not permitted to be free, to pursue its own independent course of development.

The fundamental error is thus domination, the denial of freedom and autonomy. Anthropocentrism, the major concern of most environmental philosophers, is only one species of the more basic attack on the preeminent value of self-realization. From within the perspective of anthropocentrism, humanity believes it is justified in dominating and molding the non-human world to its own human purposes. But a policy of domination transcends the anthropocentric subversion of natural processes. A policy of domination subverts both nature and human existence; it denies both the cultural and natural realization of individual good, human and non-human. Liberation from all forms of domination is thus the chief goal of any ethical or political system.

It is difficult to awaken from the dream of domination. We are all impressed by the power and breadth of human technological achievements. Why is it not possible to extend this power further, until we control, manipulate, and dominate the entire natural universe? This is the illusion that the restoration of nature presents to us. But it is only an illusion. Once we dominate nature, once we restore and redesign nature for our own purposes, then we have destroyed nature—we have created an artifactual reality, in a sense, a false reality, which merely provides us the pleasant illusory appearance of the natural environment.

VI

As a concluding note, let me leave the realm of philosophical speculation and return to the world of practical environmental policy. Nothing I have said in this essay should be taken as an endorsement of actions that develop, exploit, or injure areas of the natural environment and leave them in a damaged state. I believe, for example, that Exxon should attempt to clean up and restore the Alaskan waterways and land that was harmed by its corporate negligence. The point of my argument here is that we must not misunderstand what we humans are doing when we attempt to restore or repair natural areas. We are not restoring nature; we are not making it whole and healthy again. Nature restoration is a compromise; it should not be a basic policy goal. It is a policy that makes the best of a bad situation; it cleans up our mess. We are putting a piece of furniture over the stain in the carpet, for it provides a better appearance. As a matter of policy, however, it would be much more significant to prevent the causes of the stains.

NOTES

1. In Islip Town, New York, real-estate developers have cited the New York State Department of Environmental Conservation policy of "no-net loss" in proposing the restoration of parts of their property to a natural state, in exchange for permission to develop. A report in *Newsday* discusses a controversial case: "In hopes of gaining town-board approval, Blankman has promised to return a three-quarter-mile dirt road on his property to its natural habitat. . . ." Katti Gray, "Wetlands in the Eye of a Storm," Islip Special, *Newsday*, April 22, 1990, pp. 1, 5.

2. *Garbage: The Practical Journal for the Environment,* May/June 1990, rear cover.

3. Chris Maser, *The Redesigned Forest* (San Pedro: R. & E. Miles, 1988), p. 173. It is also interesting to note that there now exists a dissident group within the U.S. Forest Service, called the Association of Forest Service Employees for Environmental Ethics (AFSEEE). They advocate a return to sustainable forestry.

4. Paul Taylor, *Respect for Nature: A Theory of Environmental Ethics* (Princeton: Princeton University Press, 1986), pp. 186–92, 304–06, and Chapters Four and Six generally.

5. Peter S. Wenz, *Environmental Justice* (Albany: State University of New York Press, 1988), pp. 287–91.

6. Robert Elliot, "Faking Nature," *Inquiry* 25: 81–93 (1982); reprinted in Donald VanDeVeer and Christine Pierce, eds., *People, Penguins, and Plastic Trees: Basic Issues in Environmental Ethics* (Belmont: Wadsworth, 1986), pp. 142–150.

7. Ibid., p. 86 (VanDeVeer and Pierce, p. 145).

8. Ibid., p. 91 (VanDeVeer and Pierce, p. 149).

9. Eric Katz, "Organism, Community, and the 'Substitution Problem,'" *Environmental Ethics* 7(1985): 253–55.

10. Elliot, p. 81 (VanDeVeer and Pierce, p. 142).

11. See, for example, Barry Commoner, *The Closing Circle* (New York: Knopf, 1971) and Arnold Pacy, *The Culture of Technology* (Cambridge: MIT Press, 1983).

12. Michael Losonsky, "The Nature of Artifacts," *Philosophy* 65: 88 (1990).

13. Ibid., p. 84.

14. Andrew Brennan, "The Moral Standing of Natural Objects," *Environmental Ethics* 6: 41–44 (1984).

15. Maser, *The Redesigned Forest*, p. xvii.

16. Ibid., pp. 176–77.

17. Ibid., pp. 88–89.

18. Ibid., p. 174.

19. Ibid., p. 94.

20. Ibid., pp. 148–49.

21. L. B. Cebik, "Forging Issues from Forged Art," *Southern Journal of Philosophy* 27: 331–46 (1989).

22. Ibid., p. 342.

23. Taylor, p. 177. The rule of noninterference is discussed on pp. 173–179.

24. J. S. Mill, "Nature," in *Three Essays on Religion* (London: 1874).

25. Andrew Brennan, *Thinking About Nature: An Investigation of Nature, Value, and Ecology* (Athens, GA: University of Georgia Press, 1988), pp. 88–91.

26. Taylor, p. 174.

Thomas Magnell is Professor of Philosophy at Drew University. Formerly a student of A. J. Ayer, he is the editor of Ayer's *Metaphysics and Common Sense* (Boston, Mass.: Jones and Bartlett, 1994), the editor of the *Journal of Value Inquiry,* and the author of several articles on contemporary philosophical concerns.

Video Presentation

Guest: Thomas Magnell, Professor of Philosophy, Drew University

Student Panel: Marc Gussen, Michelle Harknett, Wolfe Lewis

Since this is the final episode, I begin by reminiscing about previous shows that addressed a variety of contemporary issues. This is a lead-in for discussing what might be the ethical issues beyond the 1990s. Knowing that Magnell had written on this theme, mentioning what he calls *temporal bigotry,* I ask him to explain what he means by this term. After quipping that *temporal bigotry* is an "idea whose time has come," he says that it is a species of bigotry that results when we favor the interests of individuals in one span of time over the interests of those in another. As an example, he mentions Gilbert and Sullivan's *The Mikado* in which the Lord High Executioner Ko-Ko reserves a special place on his list for "those who praise with enthusiastic tone all centuries but this and every country but his own." Like the people on Ko-Ko's list, says Magnell, we show concern for ourselves and those in our immediate future but little concern for those in the distant future. To the extent that this is true, we are, he says, temporal bigots.

Having defined *temporal bigotry* (or *diachronic discrimination,* as he also calls it), I ask Magnell how he manages the objection that the people we're not concerned with do not now exist and for all we know might never exist. His first answer is that their nonexistence does not mean that we're any less bigots. Bigotry, he points out, is an "intentional concept"— it is a belief state that can be had regardless of whether what the belief refers to exists. To illustrate, suppose a white person were to dislike a person falsely believed to be black, as the sheriff takes Gaylord Ravenal to be in the musical *Showboat.* That the person is mistaken about the true color of the disliked person does not make the person any less of a racist. Analogously, even if we are mistaken in thinking people will exist in the distant future, our present discounting of their interests betrays a type of bigotry.

Magnell's second answer is this: suppose we didn't have to take into consideration the interests of potential as well as actual people. If this were so, then, say, had the Nazis been successful in eliminating the entire Jewish people, they would have had an excuse against the charge of temporal bigotry inasmuch as they could not have been accused of failing to consider the interests of future Jews. But far from serving as an excuse against bigotry, Nazism is a prototype of bigotry.

I next comment on how Magnell's thesis is part of the general tendency of moral philosophers to widen the moral community by considering interests other than those of actual human beings. He agrees and says that it is incumbent upon us to consider the interests of the distant future. Although we cannot be certain whether a future generation will exist if one does exist, they will want those things that are the preconditions of any civilization. This includes, among other things, nonrenewable environmental resources.

After the break, Marc Gussen asks Magnell about the role of the imagination in envisioning what future generations may or may not want. Michelle Harknett asks him about the truth of environmentalist predictions and what this entails for our present responsibilities. And Wolfe Lewis asks Magnell about the extent to which his thesis impacts on the abortion controversy. (Gussen perceptively suggests that you can criticize abortion on grounds of temporal bigotry.)

In this essay, Thomas Magnell introduces the concept of temporal bigotry, *which is bigotry against those of a time span other than the present. He puts forward the concept in an effort to show that we are obligated to respect the interests of our distant progeny and that failure to do so reveals a form of discrimination no less pernicious than racial and sexual discrimination.*

Present Concerns and Future Interests

Thomas Magnell

It would be hard to find anyone who views the worldly future with complete indifference. Wrapped in visions and forebodings, the future fascinates. It is a nexus of emotion. We may long for or regret what has been. But it is towards what may be that we direct our hopes and fears:

> Hope springs eternal in the human breast:
> Man never is, but always to be blest.
> —Pope

> Ah, my Beloved, fill the Cup that clears
> Today of past Regrets and future Fears.
> —FitzGerald

Yet when it comes to moral thought and practice, the future is not given its due. Though not surprising, this is nonetheless dismaying. We are all too ready to compromise future interests for those we perceive to be our own. We give short shrift to future interests because we do not attend to them as we should. Indeed, we hardly attend to some important future interests at all. In this we show failings of imagination, sympathy and reason, all of which need to be addressed.

MARKING OUT THE FUTURE

When we talk about the future, we commonly cut it up in ways that leave it all of a piece. We do this when we contrast the near term with the far, or the short run with the long. The near term eventually merges into the far, the short run gradually advances into the long, as we project the course of time's arrow. The dif-

Thomas Magnell, "Present Concerns and Future Interests" *Dialogue and Humanism*, No. 4, 1993.

ferences that set them apart are largely matters of degree. But the future can also be divided into spans that mark out periods which significantly differ in kind. Future interests are best thought of as falling into two such periods: the politically enfranchised future and the politically unenfranchised future.

The politically enfranchised future encompasses a period in which future interests are given serious political consideration in the present. Its length will depend on the kind of future interests that do in fact exert some influence on present political decisions. This may vary from society to society. One might be excused for thinking that in contemporary America the period can cover only a few years at most, our political representatives being what they are. It is especially hard to resist this thought in the heat of an election year. Nevertheless, when we reflect on the actions of our representatives in the cooler climate between elections, some grounds can usually be found to be more temperate. To be sure, there are plenty of reasons to think that the common denominator of all politicians is a self-serving interest to attain and retain power, usually by winning the next election. But where the electorate shows concern for interests that go beyond the next election, even the most opportunistic politician will pay heed to these interests and do something to take them into account. As it is, most people today are willing to give some attention to their own future interests, to the future interests of those they love, their spouses, children, friends and relations, and perhaps to the future interests of those they expect to love, their future children and grandchildren.

These future interests are similar in nature. They are all self-regarding, or very nearly so.

Giving consideration to one's own future interests is clearly a matter of prudence. And giving consideration to the interests of those one loves and may expect to love is largely a matter of prudence as well. If this is right, then in our society, the length of the politically enfranchised future is set by the self-regarding and nearly self-regarding future interests that enter into broadly prudential assessments that may be made today.

I shall not specify the length of the politically enfranchised future with precision. It would be futile, I think, to try to do so, in part because of the difficulties in determining the limits of what constitutes serious political consideration. But evidence suggests that we do recognize a politically enfranchised future spanning perhaps as much as one-hundred years and probably no less than fifty. Worries over the size of the national debt and the funding requirements of the Social Security System show a concern for interests several decades ahead. Urban planning and resource management may try to take into account some more distant interests. Ecological concerns may seem to range much further than a century. But when serious consideration is separated from mere rhetoric, I think it will be found only to go the limit. In any case, there is no need to regard my estimate of the length of the politically enfranchised future as anything more than a working hypothesis. Whether it is too liberal or too conservative is less important than its basis: the actual limits of recognized self-regarding and nearly self-regarding interests.

The politically unenfranchised future is an open-ended period in which future interests are given no serious political consideration in the present. It begins where the politically enfranchised future leaves off and goes on indefinitely. On the working hypothesis I have advanced, the start of the politically unenfranchised future can be placed 50 to 100 years hence. By and large, we fail to identify interests this far ahead with our own. Removed from self-regarding considerations, these more distant future interests do not enter into our prudential assessments. This is

why the period is markedly different. Whereas the politically enfranchised future is so clearly a future that belongs to us that it can almost be thought of as an extended present, the politically unenfranchised future is a foreign world beyond our reach. The future interests of that world are for us other-regarding interests, or so at first it must seem. To begin with, then, they may enter into our moral rather than our prudential assessments and concern for the interests of the politically unenfranchised future may be typically moral.

TEMPORAL BIGOTRY

The history of moral reform has been punctuated with calls to recognize, combat and end bigotry. Racism, sexism, age discrimination, religious and nationalistic prejudice are among its best known forms. To these may be added speciesism, though it has been slow to gain recognition outside of philosophical circles and truly widespread awareness of it does not seem to be in the offing. Bigotry is evil because it is unjust; unjust because it is unfair; and unfair because it favors one class of individuals at the expense of another. At its worst, bigotry displays an utter disregard for the interests of the class not favored.

We ought to show the same moral concern for every individual or class of individuals whose interests we may affect by our actions. Ideally, that concern ought to represent nothing less than a full consideration of all morally relevant interests. I shall say nothing here about the theoretical status of this action-guiding principle, since that would take us too far afield. As a practical matter, I doubt much hangs in the balance anyway. Whether we take it to be a meta-ethical principle acting as a precondition of moral thought, or a basic normative principle acting as a dictate of justice, its structures will be practically the same.

It may be objected that where the needs of one individual or class of individuals are greater than those of another, we ought to show more concern for the one with the greater needs; we ought to show favoritism when the needs are disparate and apportion our concern accordingly. But though likely to be well motivated, the objection is misplaced. It is not that we ought to show more concern for the needy than for the well-off, but that we ought to *do* more for the needy than for the well-off, and that we have to do this simply to show the same concern for both. The interests of the blind deserve no more consideration than the interests of the sighted. But they deserve no less. This alone is reason to do more for the blind than for the sighted. It goes without saying that we not only do not do enough for the blind and the needy in general, we do not show anywhere near enough concern for them. But this just underscores the fact that we have a long way to go before we show the same concern for all.

I want to draw attention to another form of bigotry, one which I believe is no less significant than those which are well known. I shall call it temporal bigotry. Those who like the sound of technical jargon may prefer to refer to it as diachronic discrimination. By whatever name, temporal bigotry is a matter of showing more concern for the interests of individuals in one span of time than for those in another. It favors interests and thereby weighs benefits and harms on mere temporal grounds. But a benefit is a benefit, a harm a harm, whether it occurs in the distant future or the present. The location of its occurrence in time is in itself no more relevant to its worth than its location in space.

It is possible to show excessive concern for past or future interests over present interests. Ancestor worship may represent a type of temporal bigotry, as may romanticism of the past or the future. W. S. Gilbert had Ko-Ko, the Lord High Executioner, reserve a place on his little list for:

The idiot who praises, with enthusiastic
   tone,
All centuries but this, and every country
   but his own.

There is no need to linger over these types of bigotry. Some flamboyant Victorians were guilty of these excesses which contributed to the tenor of the age. Gilbert's barbs invariably had a sting. We, however, by and large, are not. On the contrary, we fail all too plainly to show enough concern for times other than the present. While there is every reason to suppose that we ought to have a greater concern for past and future interests in general, it is the interests of the politically unenfranchised future that I wish to speak to.

It can hardly be denied that we seldom act with the interests of the politically unenfranchised at heart. It does not follow from this alone that we are temporal bigots. But this should make us sensitive to a charge of temporal bigotry. If our lack of action does not reflect lack of concern, there is a good deal of explaining away to do. As it is, most people feel no need to try to do even this. That by itself strongly suggests an entrenched bigotry.

There are two factors which may be appealed to in an attempt to explain away our lack of action directed towards the interests of individuals in the politically unenfranchised future. The first is that while some actions have long-term consequences, others are more localized and, like ripples on a pond, soon leave no mark. It is reasonable to suppose that most of our actions fall into this latter category, even if we cannot say for sure which of our actions these are. In that case, most of our actions may not range into the politically unenfranchised future, their effects having dissipated before then, For these, there is no call to give any consideration to the interests of individuals in this period. All this is true, but it still leaves a sizable class of actions that do range into the politically unenfranchised future.

The second factor that may be appealed to is the widely recognized need to discount the future. In one sense, it is a sound practice, indeed a requirement of moral and prudential practical reasoning, to discount the future. We must predict the consequences of our actions in order to determine their effects on future interests. Accurate predictions are hard to come by. And difficulties in prediction often increase in direct proportion to the time they span. One reason for this, in addition to the more obvious ones, is that wants are mutable and change in ways that are hard to foresee over long periods of time. Predictive problems raise epistemic barriers against our ability to foresee the consequences of our actions on the politically unenfranchised future. Where these are not insurmountable, we must still make difficult assessments reflecting determinations of subjective probability in order to gauge the prospects of the consequences of our actions. In general, we cannot help but be less confident of the consequences of our actions on the politically unenfranchised future than on less distant times. Discounting the future in this sense is a matter of discounting future consequences for reasons of uncertainty and is entirely legitimate. It is just well-tempered consequentialism.

But there is another sense in which the future may be discounted. Future interests may be allowed to count for less the further removed they are from our own, with interests of the politically unenfranchised so distant as to count for next to naught. This, however, cannot be justified on epistemic grounds, or on any other. It favors one set of interests over another for its location in time. It shows less concern for the interests of the politically unenfranchised future than for the interests of the politically enfranchised future or the present. Discounting future interests is never warranted. It is nothing more than temporal bigotry.

The two factors combined, discounting the future in the legitimate sense of discounting future consequences for the subset of our actions that may have a bearing on the interests of the politically unenfranchised future, are important. But they do not completely account for our lack of purposeful action with respect to these interests. It is not even plausible to think that they do. The actions we take or fail to take in a concerted way with regard to the management of non-renewable resources, the protection of the environment, the control of population growth, the elimination of extreme poverty, and the reduction of nationalistic passions that fan the flames of war clearly have a bearing on the interests of the politically unenfranchised future. If we cannot foresee the effects of alternative policies with precision, it is clear enough that if we do not address such basic issues in earnest, the prospects of a continuing civilization are dimmed. These have become or are fast becoming preconditions of civilization. What we do or leave off doing to brighten or dim the prospects of maintaining the preconditions of civilization can surely be counted to bear on the interests of the politically unenfranchised future.

An ideological principle might yet be called on to fend off a charge of temporal bigotry. It might be suggested that the little we purposefully do for individuals in the politically unenfranchised future does not reflect a lack of concern for their interests, but displays an altogether appropriate policy of libertarian laissez-faire. But whatever the merits of libertarianism, this suggestion is not really tenable. It would be disingenuous to construe our lack of action as ultimately being, in fact, a matter of benign neglect rather than tacit, near indifference. Doctrinaire non-interventionism is not widespread and not likely to become so. Perhaps we ought to be more circumspect in our readiness to interfere in the affairs of others, as non-interventionists affirm. Yet even if we were never justified in imposing our own desires, values and cultural attitudes on others, and only the most skeptically inclined of extreme moral or cultural relativists would go this far, it would not be wrong to act to meet what others would avow as their self-regarding interests. We may not always be able to tell what others would want us to do for them; others may be mistaken in what they avow, at any rate superficially; and of course in some cases, we ought not to do as others wish. But I think it is safe to say that few individuals in the future would object to our undertaking to maintain the preconditions of civilization. And in this case, it is hard to see how anyone could seriously maintain that their wishes are not to be trusted or respected.

There is no reason to doubt, then, that we do not show the same concern for the politically unenfranchised future as we do for the politically enfranchised future or the present. We are, in other words, temporally bigoted.

Indeed, my classifications of the future themselves give some indication of the nature and extent of our temporal bigotry. For unless I have gerrymandered the future, we show a willingness to enfranchise the interests of just a small part of the future, the part that may be likened to an extended present on the basis of self-regarding or nearly self-regarding interests. There is, however, no moral justification for limiting the reach of serious political consideration to the few generations whose interests we are disposed to identify with our own.

Temporal bigotry is insidious. Intellectual work, artistic or scientific, is treated with disdain if it offers little prospect of immediate benefits. Research and development is largely tied to present interests. Even pure research is expected to pay off in the politically enfranchised future, if it is to receive substantial support. It is not surprising that when philosophical work is held up to this parochial, pragmatic standard, it comes up short. But this is a false standard. It is the standard of a temporal bigot. The history of intellectual work done without the expectation of securing near-term benefits is unambiguous. The ultimate benefits of such work is cost-effective, to say the least.

Still it may be urged that there are moral grounds for limiting our concern for future interests. Is it not bad faith to show concern for a distant future when not enough concern is shown for the acute problems of today? "Attend to the present", it will be said, "the future can take care of itself!" This last point which is calculated to appeal to our limited sympathies, is a case of special pleading. It draws on a fear of divided concern over competing interests.

But a recognition of temporal bigotry does not call for a lessening of present concern for present interests, any more than a recognition of racism calls for a lessening of concern for the favored race. And as a rule, recognizing bigotry for what it is raises the general level of concern. This is not all that surprising, inasmuch as bigots are not noted for being overly generous in their concern for the class they favor. Klansmen do not stand out for their superabundant consideration of the interests of whites. Then as well, where present needs are great, we should already do more to meet those needs than to meet lesser needs in the politically unenfranchised future merely to show the same concern for both sets of interests. As legitimate discounting of future consequences can only lower our assessments of future needs, the fear of divided concern is groundless. Finally, while the interests of the politically unenfranchised future might compete with our own in a limited way, at a basic level, there is a predictable harmony of interests. For it is in the interests of all future individuals that we pay heed to our acute problems, since these are also problems of maintaining the preconditions of civilization. At this level, concern for future interests can only reinforce concerns for the present.

Questions for Discussion

1. Imagine what life would have been like had we been environmentally conscious during the Industrial Revolution. Would you prefer that the Revolution had not taken place and that we had inherited an environmentally better world instead of the one we presently possess?

    _____

    _____

    _____

2. Make a list of the costs and benefits of those practices that are polluting the environment. To what extent would you be willing to give up the benefits of these practices?

    _____

    _____

    _____

3. Is human benefit the only morally relevant criterion in determining our obligations to the rest of the world?

    _____

    _____

    _____

4. Can a person do wrong on a desert island if the person is the only animal on that island? Can a person do right? To what extent can we act ethically at all on such an island?

    _____

    _____

    _____

5. Keeping in mind the correlativity thesis of rights and obligations, according to which obligations derive from rights, would anyone do wrong if everyone decided not to have children and let the human race become extinct?

    _____

    _____

    _____

6. Why might people say that anthropocentric ethics has a decidedly Western flavor?

_____

_____

_____

7. Do potential people have rights? What about species and ecosystems? What problems do you see with ascribing rights to such entities?

_____

_____

_____

8. The snail darter is thought to exist in only one part of one river. Suppose this stretch of river would be destroyed by the building of a dam which was needed for the economic development and well-being of that area. Is the value of the snail darter sufficient to outweigh the economic hardship that would be alleviated by the building of the dam?

_____

_____

_____

9. Eric Katz ("The Big Lie") believes that a replicated environment would not be as valuable as the original any more than a replicated piece of art would be as valuable as its original. Do you agree? Is his analogy a good one?

_____

_____

_____

10. Suppose that we are obligated to protect the environment. What would this mean in those cases where we could save a valued wilderness but only by bringing pain and suffering upon some human beings?

_____

_____

_____

_____

For Further Reading

Feinberg, Joel. "The Rights of Animals and Unborn Generations." In William T. Blackstone, ed., *Philosophy and the Environmental Crisis,* Athens, Ga.: University of Georgia Press, 1974.

Hill, Thomas E., Jr. "Ideals of Human Excellence and Preserving Natural Environments." *Environmental Ethics* 5 (1983): 211–224.

Leopold, Aldo. *A Sand County Almanac.* New York: Ballantine Books, 1970.

Medina, Vicente. "The Nature of Environmental Values." In John Gilroy, ed., *Environmental Risks: Environmental Values and Political Choices* Boulder, Co.: Westview Press, 1995.

Naess, Arne. *Ecology, Community and Lifestyle,* translated and ed. David Rothenberg. Cambridge, England: Cambridge University Press, 1989.

Passmore, John. *Man's Responsibility for Nature: Ecological Problems and Western Traditions.* New York: Scribner's, 1974.

Pojman, Louis, ed. *Environmental Ethics: Theory and Applications.* Portola Valley, Ca: Jones and Bartlett, 1997.

Regan, Tom, ed. *Earthbound: New Introductory Essays in Environmental Ethics.* New York: Random House, 1984.

Sterba, James P. "The Welfare Rights of Distant Peoples and Future Generations: Moral Side-Constraints on Social Policy." *Social Theory and Practice* (1981): 99–119.

Taylor, Paul W. *Respect for Nature: A Theory of Environmental Ethics.* Princeton, N.J.: Princeton University Press, 1986.

VanDeVeer, Donald, and Christine Pierce, eds. *People, Penguins, and Plastic Trees.* Belmont, Calif.: Wadsworth, 1986.

Videophilosophy®

Ethics in the '90s

a 26-part video series with Joram Graf Haber

Each 30-minute video will broaden classroom discussions of current issues. The range of topics in the series provides versatility for use with any syllabi. The series is a unique customized companion to the text, *Ethics for Today and Tomorrow*. The viewer is afforded the advantage of both watching the guests interact with Professor Haber, and reading their contributed essays that expand their individual viewpoints on vital issues. The series can be used effectively as an autonomous telecommunications course. Tapes are available separately or as a complete set.

1. *Introduction to Ethics in the '90s*—ISBN 0–7637–0002–9
2. *Ethics and Religion*—ISBN 0–7637–0003–7
3. *Crime in the Suburbs*—ISBN 0–7637–0004–5
4. *Physician-Assisted Suicide*—ISBN 0–7637–0005–3
5. *Living Wills*—ISBN 0–7637–0006–1
6. *Ethics in Sports I*—ISBN 0–7637–0007–X
7. *Ethics in Sports II*—ISBN 0–7637–0008–8
8. *Terrorism*—ISBN 0–7637–0009–6
9. *Date Rape*—ISBN 0–7637–0010–X
10. *Animal Rights*—ISBN 0–7637–0011–8
11. *Racism/Anti-Semitism I*—ISBN 0–7637–0012–6
12. *Racism/Anti-Semitism II*—ISBN 0–7637–0013–4
13. *Philosophical Ethics*—ISBN 0–7637–0014–2
14. *Ethics in Advertising*—ISBN 0–7637–0015–0
15. *Ethics in Academia*—ISBN 0–7637–0016–9
16. *Ethics in Journalism*—ISBN 0–7637–0017–7
17. *Moral Education*—ISBN 0–7637–0018–5
18. *Feminist Ethics*—ISBN 0–7637–0019–3
19. *Environmental Ethics*—ISBN 0–7637–0020–7
20. *Capital Punishment*—ISBN 0–7637–0021–5
21. *Ethics and Literature*—ISBN 0–7637–0022–3
22. *Legal Ethics*—ISBN 0–7637–0023–1
23. *Ethics in War*—ISBN 0–7637–0024–X
24. *Ethics and Science*—ISBN 0–7637–0025–8
25. *The Homeless*—ISBN 0–7637–0026–6
26. *Ethics Beyond the '90s*—ISBN 0–7637–0027–4

for further details about the series and ordering information, please contact

Jones and Bartlett Publishers, Inc.
Videophilosophy®
40 Tall Pine Drive
Sudbury, MA 01776
1–800–832–0034 • (508) 443–5000
or fax your request to (508) 443–8000

Index